I0882169

ROUTLEDGE HANDBOOK OF CONSTITUTIONAL LAW IN GREATER CHINA

The *Handbook of Constitutional Law in Greater China* surveys important issues of constitutional law in Mainland China, Hong Kong, Macau, and Taiwan. It synthesizes existing scholarship, debates, and views on important constitutional issues in the four jurisdictions. Written by a range of scholars, it contributes to both national and comparative scholarship on constitutional law in these jurisdictions. The book includes four parts:

- **Part I:** History. This part explores the constitutional movement of the Qing dynasty; constitutional projects in modern China; and aspects of the drafting and implementation history of the Hong Kong and Macau Basic Laws.
- **Part II:** Structure. This part discusses the relationship between the party-state and the Chinese constitutional order; Chinese constitutionalism; constitutional aspects of city development under the SAR concept; constitutional review in Mainland China; a history of Taiwan's 'Council of Grand Justices'; and judicial review in both Hong Kong and Macau.
- **Part III:** Rights, Society, and Economy. This part deals with Hong Kong's National Security Law and its impact on the 'one country, two systems model'; social movements and constitutionalism; LGBT rights advocacy; the integration of capitalist regions within socialist China; the constitutional relevance of labour reforms in Mainland China; healthcare rights in both the Mainland and the SARS; and foreign investment under Art. 18 of the PRC Constitution.
- **Part IV**: Transnational Engagement. This part surveys comparative writings on China's constitution; the influence of international human rights treaties on China's constitutional order; the international dimension of Hong Kong's constitutional order; and the changing role of the 'overseas judges' in Hong Kong.

Exploring both historical and cutting-edge constitutional issues, this reference book is an important reading for law researchers, lawyers, graduate students, undergraduates, and practitioners in the field of constitutional law and politics in Mainland China, Taiwan, Hong Kong, and Macau.

Ngoc Son Bui: Professor of Asian Laws, Faculty of Law, University of Oxford.

Stuart Hargreaves: Associate Professor, Faculty of Law, The Chinese University of Hong Kong.

Ryan Mitchell: Assistant Professor, Faculty of Law, The Chinese University of Hong Kong.

ROUTLEDGE HANDBOOK OF CONSTITUTIONAL LAW IN GREATER CHINA

Edited by

Ngoc Son Bui, Stuart Hargreaves, and Ryan Mitchell

Routledge
Taylor & Francis Group
LONDON AND NEW YORK

Designed cover image: Getty Images

First published 2023
by Routledge
4 Park Square, Milton Park, Abingdon, Oxon OX14 4RN

and by Routledge
605 Third Avenue, New York, NY 10158

Routledge is an imprint of the Taylor & Francis Group, an Informa business

British Library Cataloguing-in-Publication Data
A catalogue record for this book is available from the British Library

ISBN: 978-0-367-65185-5 (hbk)
ISBN: 978-0-367-65186-2 (pbk)
ISBN: 978-1-003-12824-3 (ebk)

DOI: 10.4324/9781003128243

Typeset in Times New Roman
by KnowledgeWorks Global Ltd.

CONTENTS

List of Contributors viii

PART I
History **1**

1 The Late Qing Constitutional Movement in the Global Constitutional Moment of the 1900s 3
Egas Moniz Bandeira

2 Constitutional Projects in Modern Chinese History 18
Ryan Martínez Mitchell

3 The History of the Drafting and Implementation of the Basic Law of the Hong Kong Special Administrative Region 34
Albert H.Y. Chen

4 Reconstituting China's Periphery: Orchestrating Political Convergence via the Hong Kong and Macau Basic Laws 49
Jason Buhi

PART II
Structure **65**

5 "The Flower of Democracy Blooms Brilliantly in China [中国的民主之花绚丽绽放]": The Chinese Communist Party and the Chinese Constitutional Order 67
Larry Catá Backer

6 Constitutionalism with Chinese Characteristics?: Which Constitutionalism? 85
Peng Chengyi

7 The Debate on Constitutional Standing and Greater Autonomy for Cities: Lessons from (and for) the Special Administrative Regions of Hong Kong and Macao 98
Amal Sethi

8 Constitutional Review "With Chinese Characteristics": Law, Institutions and Recent Developments 113
Guobin Zhu

9 One Council Two Constitutional Courts: A Holistic View of the Council of Grand Justices (1948–2021) 135
Zhaoxin Jiang

10 Judicial Review in Hong Kong 151
Rehan Abeyratne

11 Judicial Review and Standards of Review in Macao: A Study Based on the TUI Decisions 169
Shiling Xiao

PART III
Rights, Society, and Economy **185**

12 National Security Law in Hong Kong: Transforming 'One Country, Two Systems' as a Model of Regional Autonomy 187
Carole J. Petersen

13 Rights Movements, Civil Disobedience, and Civil Unrest: Social Movements and Constitutionalism in Mainland China, Hong Kong, and Taiwan 204
Han Zhu

14 'Runaway Legitimation' and Its Limits: LGBTQ Rights in China 221
Darius Longarino

15 Involving and Integrating 'Capitalist' Special Administrative Regions in 'Socialist' National Development of China: Squaring the Circle of 'Two Systems' in 'One Country' 236
Pui-yin LO

16 Market Mentality or Social Solidarity?: The Constitutional Relevance of Labour Reforms in Contemporary China 251
Su Bian

17 Assessing Healthcare Rights and Responsibilities Under the Constitutional Orders of Mainland China and the Special Administrative Regions 266
Barry Solaiman

18 The Protection of Foreign Investment in China Constitutional Law: An Evolving Constant 286
Ma Ji and Dini Sejko

PART IV
Transnational Engagement **301**

19 China's Comparative Constitution 303
Ngoc Son Bui

20 International Human Rights Treaties in the People's Republic of China Constitutional Order 325
Jizeng Fan

21 The International Dimension of the Hong Kong Constitutional Order 342
Michael Ramsden

22 Hong Kong's Overseas Judges Under the National Security Law 356
Stuart Hargreaves

Index 371

CONTRIBUTORS

Rehan Abeyratne: Associate Professor, and Executive Director, Centre for Comparative and Transnational Law, Faculty of Law, The Chinese University of Hong Kong

Larry Catá Backer: W. Richard and Mary Eshelman Faculty Scholar, Professor of Law and International Affairs, Penn State Law, The Pennsylvania State University

Egas Moniz Bandeira: Researcher, the Max Planck Institute for Legal History and Legal Theory

Su Bian: Lecturer, School of Liberal Arts and Law, Jiangsu Ocean University

Jason Buhi: Associate Professor, Andreas School of Law, Barry University

Ngoc Son Bui: Professor of Asian Laws, Faculty of Law, University of Oxford

Albert H.Y. Chen: Cheng Chan Lan Yue Professor and Chair of Constitutional Law, Faculty of Law, The University of Hong Kong

Peng Chengyi: Associate Professor, School of Government, University of Chinese Academy of Social Sciences; Associate Research Fellow, Institute of World Economics and Politics, Chinese Academy of Social Sciences

Jizeng Fan: Associate Professor of Law, Law School, Shandong University of Business and Technology; Associated Researcher, Law School, Sichuan University

Stuart Hargreaves: Associate Professor, Faculty of Law, The Chinese University of Hong Kong

Ma Ji: C.V. Starr Lecturer of Law, Peking University School of Transnational Law

Zhaoxin Jiang: Associate Professor, Law School, Shandong University

Pui-yin Lo: Barrister-at-law (England and Wales and Hong Kong); Part-time Lecturer, Department of Law, The University of Hong Kong, and Visiting Fellow, Centre for Chinese Law, Faculty of Law, The University of Hong Kong

Darius Longarino: Research Scholar in Law, and Senior Fellow, Paul Tsai China Center, Yale Law School

Ryan Mitchell: Assistant Professor, Faculty of Law, The Chinese University of Hong Kong

Carole J. Petersen: Professor of Law, William S. Richardson School of Law; the University of Hawaii at Manoa

Michael Ramsden: Associate Professor, Faculty of Law, The Chinese University of Hong Kong

Dini Sejko: Research Associate, Centre for Comparative and Transnational Law, Faculty of Law, The Chinese University of Hong Kong

Amal Sethi: Senior Fellow, Faculty of Law, University of Hamburg

Barry Solaiman: Assistant Professor, Hamad Bin Khalifa University

Shiling Xiao: PhD candidate, Faculty of Law, The University of Hong Kong

Guobin Zhu: Professor of Law, School of Law, City University of Hong Kong

Han Zhu: Assistant Research Professor, Faculty of Law, The University of Hong Kong

PART I

History

1

THE LATE QING CONSTITUTIONAL MOVEMENT IN THE GLOBAL CONSTITUTIONAL MOMENT OF THE 1900s

Egas Moniz Bandeira

Introduction

The constitutional history of the late Qing Empire is mostly understood as a history of reception, i.e., of how Chinese political and intellectual actors adapted the Japanese model set by the Meiji Constitution of 1889,[1] which in turn was based on various European models, mainly, although not exclusively, of German origin.[2] Accordingly, the official policy of 'constitutional preparation' (*yubei lixian* 預備立憲) instituted in 1906 is interpreted as a belated response to the challenges of Western modernity,[3] which by its conservative nature was at odds with the 'tide of the time' (*shidai chaoliu* 時代潮流).[4]

But what was really the 'tide of the time' in which the late Qing constitutional movement took place? The late Qing constitutional effort—marked by the government's declaration of intent of September 1906 and the promulgation of the Outline of a Constitution by Imperial Decree (*Qinding Xianfa Dagang* 欽定憲法大綱) in August 1908—took place roughly at the same time as a series of states throughout Eurasia and Northern Africa adopted, readopted, or at least planned to adopt written constitutions, most notably, Russia (May 1906), Persia (December 1906), and the Ottoman Empire (July 1908). Indeed, as Peter Zarrow has remarked, 'this was an era of international constitution-making, as modernising elites from Iran, Portugal and Mexico to the Ottoman and Russian Empires sought to provide clear foundations for the political order.'[5]

Since Vladimir Lenin (1870–1924) drew a line between the Russian Revolution of 1905 and those of Persia (1906), the Ottoman Empire (1908), and China (1911), which supposedly lead to the progress of 'hundreds of millions of people,'[6] research has been plentiful in identifying revolutionary movements on a global level.[7] In contrast, there is still a tendency to write constitutional history under separate national or at best regional lenses, obfuscating a veritable 'constitutional fever'[8] which was closely related, but not identical, to the revolutionary wave. Whereas the study of constitutions has traditionally focused on their function of 'controlling the state,'[9] more recent studies stress that constitutions can fulfil a wide array of diverse, even contradictory, functions, including

DOI: 10.4324/9781003128243-2

illiberal ones,[10] a versatility which ultimately made the concept so popular. By undertaking a contextual analysis of the Qing Empire's constitutional reforms, the present chapter contributes to the historical underpinning of constitutional studies by showing how the Qing 'constitutional preparation' was an important part of the 'tide of the time,' and how in turn China contributed to establishing constitutions as a ubiquitous element of modern statehood.

Background: A Century of Constitutional Transformations

The long 19th century was a century of constitutions. Throughout the world, traditional modes of legitimation came to be replaced by written constitutional documents which defined the organisation of states and determined the form and content of state action.[11] Typically being the results of power struggles, constitutions—and particularly the notion of 'constitutionalism'—often refer to more than just the document as such but connote certain material institutions like some kind of separation of powers, a degree of popular representation, and fundamental rights.[12] Yet, constitutions were far more than instruments to limit the government's power. In fact, England, often deemed to be the 'birthplace of modern constitutionalism,'[13] to this day remains one of the few states never to have promulgated a coherent constitutional charter. Rather, formal constitutions were as often instruments of reaction as of revolution; they were intimately connected to state power, imperialism, and militarism as much as they were means of anti-imperialist resistance.[14] They were useful to organise ethnic, religious, linguistic, and other diversities, as well as symbols of newly gained statehood. In short, in the long 19th century, 'to have a formal Constitution well-nigh became a universal fashion, a symbol of modernism.'[15]

While in most—but not all—independent states of Western Europe and the Americas, modern constitutions were instituted before the half of the 19th century, this development took more time to happen in other parts of the world. In some of the largest and most populous empires of Eurasia, governments did not take up or resisted the idea, and the large disruptions which would engender thorough reconfigurations of statehood and warrant the adoption of formal constitutions would only take place later, in the first decade of the 20th century. The Czar of Russia and, concomitantly, King of Poland, Alexander I (1777–1825), granted a constitution to Poland in 1815 and, at the opening of the Polish *Sejm* in 1818, announced that he would grant a constitution to the Russian Empire as well. However, he stipulated that the people must first 'reach the appropriate maturity' for such a system of government.[16] Not only did the Czar never deem the condition to have been fulfilled, but his successor, Nicholas I (1796–1856), also dropped the idea altogether and instead promoted two large codifications of Russian law in contrast to the supposedly 'foreign' idea of a constitution.[17] It is remarkable that by setting the prerequisite of 'maturity,' Alexander I expressed a trope which would also become a hotly debated point of contention in the Ottoman, Japanese, and Qing constitutional debates, and beyond.

Centralisation of power was the main theme of legal and political reforms in the Ottoman Empire.[18] Beginning from Sultan Selim III (r. 1789–1808), and in particular in the period known as *Tanzimât* ('reordering,' 1839–1876), successive rulers introduced reforms aimed at introducing legal-rational norms and centralising the empire. In a similar fashion to the reform projects in Japan and China, Ottoman 'reformers aimed to strengthen the state internally and improve its world standing' 'through selective borrowing from more successful rivals.'[19] Eventually, the Ottoman Empire came to promulgate a constitution in 1876. While the constitution was introduced at a time of severe external crisis and pressure, it was also the culmination of several decades of internal reform negotiated within various transcultural and transnational networks.[20] Yet, the first iteration of the 1876 constitution was short-lived. Ill-received abroad, it also lacked the support of the Sultan, Abdülhamid II (1842–1918), and of the government itself. Following a disastrous military defeat against Russia, the Sultan prorogued the parliament in 1878 and returned to the pre-constitutional system, although he did not formally revoke the constitution.

Yet, the 1876 constitution remained a reference for the entirety of the Ottoman Empire's constitutional history.[21] Externally, Ottoman constitutional thought had a profound impact throughout the Islamic world, being a reference not only in Persia,[22] but as far as Afghanistan[23] and Malaya.[24] In Persia, the second half of the 19th and first decade of the 20th century saw a vigorous debate on constitutions and related concepts.[25] There too, constitutionalism was associated with a strong, legal-rational state, at the same time as it was derived from vernacular notions of statehood, namely Islamic law. However, the implementation of the idea was not immediate in Persia, either. It was only due to the Eurasia-wide upheavals of the mid-1900s that the country adopted a constitution.

Late Qing Constitutionalism and China's Standing in the World

In China, it was in the last quarter of the 19th century that Chinese intellectuals began leading a vigorous debate about reforming the structure of the Qing Empire. Beginning from the 1870s, articles in newspapers advocated for measures such as the convocation of a parliament as a means to improve the communication between the government and the population.[26] Literati took the debate to their books in the 1880s and expanded it to the notion of a constitution in the 1890s.[27] Japan's adoption of a constitution in 1889 proved to be a pivotal event in global constitutional history,[28] and Japan's military victory over China in 1895 intensified the existing reformist discourse within China. By the turn of the century, Chinese intellectuals were generally aware not only of the constitutions of Japan, the United States, and Western Europe,[29] but also of the constitutionalising trend of the wider world. Their own polity, the Qing Empire, thus emerged together with the Russian and the Ottoman Empires as one of the few states which had not yet adopted a constitutional form of government. Moreover, intellectuals tended to perceive a strong correlation between the existence of a constitutional government and the country's political and economic strength, which they increasingly came to understand as a causal relationship.

One example for this are the writings of Zheng Guanying 鄭觀應 (1842–1922), who had advocated parliamentarianism in newspaper articles since the 1870s and became one of the first to advocate the adoption of a constitution in the 1890s. Zheng classified the powers of Europe into different tiers, the first tier of seven imperialist powers being comparable to the seven Warring States of ancient China (475–221 BC),[30] a type of identification which had been common in East Asia since the early 19th century.[31] For Zheng, world politics was a life-and-death struggle between imperialist powers. Although he counted Russia as a first-tier power akin to ancient Qin, which went on to unify China in 221 BC, he saw its non-constitutional condition was an anomaly.[32] Rather, Zheng saw the Ottoman Empire, Persia, and China as victims of imperialism and went into considerable detail describing the Ottoman Empire's alleged woes, ranging from rampant corruption to widespread drug consumption.[33] In order to overcome such a condition, Zheng concluded, the only possible remedy was the adoption of a constitutional system as the core of national 'self-strengthening.'[34]

Other observers were perceptive about Russia's fundamental problems beneath its grandiose façade and were ready to connect them to the lack of a constitution. Whereas earlier Chinese analysts of Russia analysts had stressed the feats of Czars like Peter the Great (1672–1725),[35] the country's situation by the turn of the century hardly allowed for such enthusiastic evaluations.[36] In 1902, Liang Qichao 梁啟超 (1873–1929), the central figure of late Qing constitutional thought, expressed utter elation about the prospect that the country's political system could soon collapse:

> Bang! A Russian revolution! Shazam! Russia cannot avoid revolution after all! Yeah! It is hardly possible that there will not be a revolution in Russia![37]

Liang Qichao's personal views on Russia shifted considerably, as did his general political stance. By 1903, he came to 'dream of Russia' and favour an 'enlightened autocracy' (*kaiming zhuanzhi* 開明專制), and when the Revolution of 1905 really happened, he stopped talking much about Russia.[38] At any rate, his perception of Russia's weakness reflected the general analysis of the time that the adoption of a constitution was the ineluctable pathway to modernity, and that, although China was late in adopting a constitution, she was actually in the same boat as the other large Eurasian empires. Thus, the preface to an important compendium of constitutional texts analysed in 1902:

> If I look around at all the countries in the world, the countries which use autocracy to exert their uncivilised barbarian *ancien régime* are so scarce that they can be counted on the fingers of one hand, like Turkey and Russia. They are rare like stars in the morning sky. What could one still say about Turkey? Or take Russia: Although at the surface she seems to be looking proudly at the world, I heard the comments of specialists in surveying countries, and her internal situation is precarious like a pile of eggs. It is, again, clear that she will not be able to conserve her autocratic form of government.[39]

The Russo-Japanese War and Its Global Effects

The Russo-Japanese War of 1904/05, in which a large non-constitutional European power was defeated by a much smaller, but upcoming and constitutionalised Asian country, is often treated as a turning point in China's constitutional history. In fact, it was less of a surprise than a confirmation of the preceding intellectual debates. Apprehensive Chinese observers followed the war as a real-life test for their hypothesis of the superiority of constitutionalism over autocracy. As soon as the war ended, the hypothesis was confirmed, leading Chinese publications to brim with assertions that 'this was not a war between Japan and Russia, but a war between the two systems of constitutionalism and autocracy.'[40]

The war had a wide-reaching impact not only in the affected regions, but throughout Eurasia and even globally.[41] Russia's defeat in the war fuelled widespread social and political unrest. In October 1905, Russian Czar Nicolas II issued a manifesto which granted some basic civil liberties and foresaw the creation of an advisory and legislative body elected by universal male suffrage, the State Duma. On 6 May 1906

(23 April Old-Style Calendar), the Czar promulgated the Fundamental Laws of the Russian Empire.[42] In Persia, protests against governmental tariff hikes broke out in late 1905, setting off what would become known as the Persian Constitutional Revolution. On 5th August, the Persian Shah Mozaffar ad-Din (1853–1907, r. 1896–1907) ceded to the pressure and announced the adoption of a constitution as well as the convening of a national assembly, the *Madjlis*. A constitution partially modelled on the Belgian charter was passed on 31 December 1906.

It was not only the war itself which had an impact on the Chinese constitutional process. Chinese actors were highly interested in what was happening in those empires which Chinese observers had long identified as being in the same boat as themselves. The interest in Russia as one of the world's foremost imperial players was further strengthened by direct diplomatic relations as well as cross-border personal contacts. Chinese interest in Persia was strong, too.[43] Although the events in Persia were noticed somewhat less often than those in Russia, two factors at times made the country perhaps even more relatable to the Chinese public: Chinese publications liked to stress the antiquity of Persia's civilisation, as well as its decay into contemporary weakness, making the country another victim of imperialist pressures, a problem to which the constitution, if implemented correctly, was deemed to be the solution.[44]

Russia, Persia, and China's 'Constitutional Preparation'

The impact of Russia's and Persia's constitutions in the Qing Empire was complex and ultimately exacerbated the internal contradictions within the political spectrum, accelerating the downfall of the empire. We may distinguish three main effects. First, they served as an exhortation for the adoption of a constitution in China; secondly, as a call for caution and gradualism; and thirdly, as a warning against 'sham constitutionalism' and as an element in revolutionary propaganda. Additionally, anti-constitutionalists and anarchists debated the current global constitutional wave within their transnational intellectual networks.[45]

The first effect was essentially a prolongation of the lesson drawn from the Russo-Japanese War: If Russia and Persia were now introducing constitutions, China became even more isolated as a non-constitutional country. The exhortative lesson can be represented by the conclusion of a comparison between China and Russia published in the journal *Tongxue bao* 通學報:

> Alas! The Russians have demanded the adoption of a constitution, and now they have achieved success. There is only us left as an autocratic polity! If we work with fervent determination to be a great power, how could we not be as powerful as the Han [Empire]?[46]

However, the situations of Russia and Persia did not improve after the respective adoption of constitutions. Violence and unrest persisted to shake both countries, leading Chinese observers to question what was going wrong, and deriving the second lesson for Chinese constitutionalism. The answer, often, was not that the constitutional transformation of the monarchy was wrong as such, but that it was happening too hastily without the necessary preconditions for a constitutional system being fulfilled.

This was the position taken by the Chinese government itself. In November 1905, the Committee of Ministers (*Zhengwuchu* 政務處) sent a circular telegram to the governors-general and provincial governors making clear that Russia, where the October Manifesto had just been issued, fundamentally differed from China.[47] The Qing government, stressed the telegram, did not want to hastily react to protests but remain in charge of its own reform process. Therefore, the government was 'examining the old established schemes of antiquity and investigating the recent best laws of the West' to adapt them to the current Chinese situation. Indeed, a much-publicised delegation of five high-ranking politicians, accompanied by a large entourage, had been just dispatched to visit and investigate the political and legal systems of 14 countries.[48] While the group placed an emphasis on Japan, Great Britain, Germany, the United States, and France, their sojourn in Russia was also highly instructive.[49] After all, it was the only country toured that did not have an established constitutional government but was in the process of establishing one.

In principle, the constitutional commissioners agreed that constitutionalism was inevitable in Russia, too.[50] What they saw there, however, was worrying. In May 1906, when the commission was in Saint Petersburg, the first Duma was in session, but repression was mounting again. The commissioners' reports, in particular that of Duanfang 端方 (1861–1911), write of a tense situation with ongoing strikes and conflicts between government and parliament. After an audience with Sergei Witte (1849–1915), the mastermind behind the Russian constitution who had just been sacked from his post as Prime Minister to make place for a more conservative successor, Duanfang recorded his interlocutor to have been deeply pessimistic about the situation:

> 'Although this country has been preparing for constitutionalism for over a hundred years, the people is still not fully equipped with knowledge, and it is very hard to adjust it at once. Probably, with the present declaration, the current government cannot but succumb to public opinion, but it will definitely not be able to satisfy its wishes.' He [Witte] is deeply worried that convulsion will be hard to be dispersed. This is the real state of Russia's current preparation for constitutionalism.[51]

What were the lessons for the Qing Empire? The Qing government should stay in charge and not wait to be cornered by popular demands as Russia's. But while many intellectuals were impatient to adopt a constitution, the government argued that first a foundation would need to be built in an extensive process of 'constitutional preparation,' which would thoroughly reconfigure all aspects of the Chinese state—including the establishment of modern institutions, the drafting of codes, and the development of a modern educational system. Indeed, a gradualist approach and the belief that a constitution had to conform to the national conditions were common across the world.[52] In the late Qing Empire, the Russian and Persian constitutional experiences provided for a vivid real-life case-in-point. As constitutional commissioner Dai Hongci 戴鴻慈 (1853–1910) argued,

> But if you establish a constitution with empty words, wherein the citizens do not have general knowledge nor legal thinking, then there is no one to deliberate on the laws nor to observe them. The evils of such an approach are about the same as not having a constitution at all.[53]

It might seem that this position was merely a governmental one, but it was not. Similar arguments could also be seen in otherwise reform-oriented, pro-constitutional media.

Commentaries on the Russian troubles deduced a need for 'constitutional preparation' in China, often putting a strong emphasis on the aspect of education.[54] Commentaries on Persia recognised the country's difficulties and vowed that China must not repeat that country's experience of humiliation. One article, for example, manifested clear disappointment about the Persian constitution's failure to alter the country's international situation:

> Look at Poland, which had established a constitution before vanishing. By now, venerable Persia has also established a constitution, but the competition for spheres of influence between England and Russia is not much different from the past, and Germany's power is even poised to increase in response to the constitution.[55]

Considering such circumstances, the Qing government decided to pursue its path of cautious gradualism. On 1 September 1906, it decided that it would 'prepare the foundations of constitutionalism' within 'several years' (*shunian* 數年), a formula which seems to have been the result of intense debates within the government.[56] In this process, the public service would be restructured, laws codified, the educational system, finances as well as the military and police forces would be reformed. The decision was greeted with great fanfare within the country and even abroad: Young Turk intellectuals enthusiastically hailed the Chinese declaration. Identifying China with their own imperilled nation, they predicted that a constitutional China would thenceforth be able to withstand foreign encroachment.[57]

Although in 1906 the Qing government still had more support for its constitutional plan than the Russian government at the same time, the enthusiasm did not last long. The Qing court's approach of caving to constitutionalist demands yet insisting on a long and gradual 'preparation' seemed half-hearted and alienated both conservative and reformist sectors.[58] In 1906 and 1907, constitutional preparation produced a number of lacklustre reforms which, essentially, represented unsatisfactory compromises. As the central government's position had been factually weak, but theoretically absolute, attempts to consolidate power came to be denounced as despotism. The vagueness of the government's declaration added to a sense that the government was not earnest in its commitment to constitutionalism.

Hence, the Qing court became the object of the same criticism as the Russian government. Since the Russian parliament (the *Duma*) was subordinated to the State Council as a partly appointed upper chamber and could not control the cabinet, the new constitutional system was termed 'sham constitutionalism.'[59] According to Max Weber (1864–1920), 'in the same manner as "hypocrisy is the homage vice pays to virtue," the express codification of such a deeply insincere sham constitutionalism (*Scheinkonstitutionalismus*) is likewise a deeply humiliating homage the "idea" of autocracy pays to the constitutional principle.'[60] Not long after, Weber's notion of a façade which purportedly codified constitutionalism, but in reality was an instrument of 'bureaucratic rationalisation of autocracy,'[61] was adapted in East Asia. The very term 'sham constitutionalism' (*jia lixian* 假立憲) became a catchword used by revolutionaries and increasingly discontented reformers to decry the Qing government's 'constitutional preparation.'[62] This accusation was more than a mere parallel development; rather, Chinese revolutionaries directly pointed towards the Russian constitutional experience as a chilling negative example for China, making it the third effect of the contemporary global constitutional wave on Chinese discourse. The most explicit example for this can be seen in one of the two frontispieces of the August 1908 edition of the magazine *Minbao* 民報, the organ of the Revolutionary Alliance (*Tongmenghui* 同盟會) led by Sun Yat-Sen 孫逸仙 (1866–1925). The photo showed horrifying atrocities committed by Russian soldiers. Its caption read: 'This is the woeful scene of slain corpses laid out to the public after Russia established a constitution. You who are hoping for a constitutional government, why do you not take this as a warning?'[63]

The Ottoman Empire and a Constitutional 'Outline'

Under the backdrop of the government's cautious policies, pressure for more decisive constitutional reforms mounted significantly. From 1907 on, large-scale petition movements called for the 'speedy introduction of a parliament,' increasingly cornering the government. In 1908, another international event increased the pressure. Under the leadership of the Committee for Union and Progress (*İttihad ve Terakki Cemiyeti*), Abdülhamid II was forced to reinstate the constitution he had himself effectively prorogated in 1878, in an event known as the Young Turk Revolution. The event produced a similar constitutional enthusiasm as, two years before, the Qing government's declaration of intent. Hence, as the *North China Herald* remarked, the rapidity of Turkey's transformation could 'hardly fail to give fresh stimulus to the cause of constitutional government that' was 'finding so many new adherents in different parts of the world.'[64]

The North China Herald's assessment proved to be generally correct, but not exclusively. Certainly, apprehensive, sceptical, or even critical interpretations of the Turkish constitution could be found across the political spectrum. One aspect which was particularly salient about the Ottoman constitution was the ethnic and religious diversity which it responded to. While the revolutionary Zhang Zhongduan 張鍾端 (1879–1911) expressed marvelled admiration about what he perceived to be the Ottoman revolution ethnic and religious fairness,[65] others used the relationship between Turks and Greeks in their propaganda against the Manchus, who ruled the Qing Empire.[66]

Frequently, however, monarchists and revolutionaries alike drew positive conclusions from the Ottoman events for their own political agendas. It is indeed debatable whether the Ottoman upheaval was really a 'revolution,' since it left the Sultan on the throne.[67] Accordingly, it could be appropriated by both Chinese monarchists and revolutionaries. For the former, the Ottoman Empire was now a constitutional monarchy, substantially increasing the pressure on China as the last large Eurasian empire which was not constitutional. The *Shenbao* not only went so far as to express fear about an imperialist Ottoman Empire possibly exerting imperialist pressure on Xinjiang 新疆[68] but also became all dreamy about the possibility that, if China followed suit to the recent constitutional developments in Persia, Turkey, Egypt, and Morocco, the country could become a mighty military power just like Japan.[69] The revolutionaries, on the other hand, praised that the Young Turks had been successful in carrying out a popular revolution. As Zhang Zhongduan summarised this ambiguity,

> Observers across the globe think that this [the positive results of the political turnover in the Ottoman Empire] is the glory of the monarch, the glory of the officials. But I think that it is in fact the glory of the people![70]

Responding to the various pressures for a constitution, Empress Dowager Cixi 慈禧 (1835–1908) issued an edict on 22 July 1908, decreeing that an 'outline of a monarchic constitution' based on the 'best regulations found in different countries' be 'quickly' drafted.[71] Just little over a month later, on 27 August 1908, the government hastily promulgated the Outline of a Constitution by Imperial Decree, a parliamentary law, an electoral law, and a detailed roadmap of 'constitutional preparation' foreseeing the adoption of the final constitution and the convening of the national assembly for 1916.[72]

In the following three years, the government's helpless groping for constitutional policies increasingly rendered its position precarious. Several factors further increased the impression that the government was carrying out 'sham constitutionalism.' The Constitutional Outline, which was closely modelled after the Japanese constitution of 1889 but also contained some significant deviations from it, put a strong focus on securing the Emperor's position.[73] In 1910, the government further ceded to the massive pressures by shortening the plan to a total of five years, foreseeing the constitution for 1913. According to the revised plan, the government appointed a cabinet half a year later, in May 1911. However, the institution was mainly composed of Manchus, particularly imperial relatives, and came to be known as the 'imperial kinsmen's cabinet' (*huangzu neige* 皇族内閣).[74]

At the same time, 'constitutional preparation' actually weakened the central government by empowering local elites and ambitious political actors, who seized the opportunity of emerging constitutional government to further their own interests. Conforming to the plan of building parliamentary institutions from the bottom up, elections for provincial assemblies were carried out in 1909.[75] Given the very strict voting requirements, only 0.39% of the population had voting rights, gearing the election towards the educated gentry.[76] The next year, a parliamentary assembly was convoked at the central level, the Political Advisory Council (*Zizhengyuan* 資政院), which consisted of delegates from the regional assemblies as well as imperially appointed members. Local elites made extensive use of the new venue as well as the new means of communication with the Qing court, severely pressuring the government. In late 1911, a number of provinces entered into open revolt, successively declaring 'independence' from the Qing.[77] On 1 January 1912, they proclaimed the Republic of China, and less than two months later, the Qing Emperor abdicated. Rather than in the global constitutional wave of the 1900s, China was now participating in the global revolutionary wave mentioned by Lenin. Although the negotiated transition between Qing and Republic led to considerable continuities between the two, the Qing Empire did not survive its own 'constitutional preparation.'

Conclusion

The Late Qing Empire's constitutional experience was closely embedded in a Eurasia-wide wave of 'constitutional fever.' 'Constitution' was the dominant term of political debates in the last years of the Qing, as Chinese intellectuals and officials largely perceived constitutions to be the key legal and political instrument of mighty and developed powers. Yet, they did not only look to Japanese and Western models. Rather, they were keenly aware of a wider constitutionalising trend, in which several polities in Eurasia and Northern Africa were undergoing similar transformations and enacting or reenacting constitutional documents.

The Eurasian 'constitutional fever' was by no means a well-defined uniform programme for political action. In its core, 'constitutionalism' referred to little more than some type of division of work between various branches of the state as stipulated by a legal framework of elevated normativity. Although this usually presupposed the presence of a popular representation, the liberal interpretation of constitutions as an instrument to limit the ruler's power often faded into the background. Japanese and Chinese governmental interpretations, not without internal contradictions, tended to describe the separation of powers as a merely functional division of work under the unlimited supremacy of the emperor.[78] While its detractors lambasted this version of constitutionalism as a 'sham,' most of its proponents genuinely believed that it was the key to solve the various political problems of the time. Hence, as Avi Rubin writes about the Ottoman Empire, 'there is little sense in limiting constitutionalism to a single narrative about the development of any certain ideology.'[79] Rather, it can be seen as a discourse revolving around a comparatively narrow conceptual nucleus, which took widely different forms according to the respective local historical and political circumstances.[80]

Why did this constitutional discourse become so dominant, and why did Chinese actors turn to various constitutional sources? Across Eurasia, traditional modes of legitimation had been embattled and were losing their efficacy. Constitutions were a way to replace these, but at the same time also a vessel to save these into a new era. In Europe, the divine right of kings gave way to rationalist notions of legal and constitutional codifications, all the while new constitutions also were used to secure the position of religion.[81] In the case of China at the turn of the 20th century, Hawkling Lugine Yen (Yan Haoling 嚴鶴齡, 1879–1937) argued in his doctoral thesis presented in 1911 at Columbia University that the 'Confucian Classics' were the traditional Chinese equivalent of the Magna Carta in England and the Constitution in the United States. Yen wrote that the Confucian Classics 'hold on the minds of the people has been shaken, their venerableness derided, and they have been again and again charged with responsibility for the present degeneration and decay of China.'[82] Yet, he hoped that the 'Classics will survive this rude treatment, and in time, after having discarded their dilapidated garment will come out triumphant in the winning garb of "new learning."'[83] In other words, the new constitution came to be imagined as the country's new 'fundamental charter immutable for ten thousand generations.'[84] For Yen as for the Qing government, it was a new garb for the Classics, whereas others attached different meanings to it according to their respective circumstances and agendas. The flexibility of constitutionalism as a vessel which could fit a wide array of diverging ideologies and political goals, accompanied by the allure of the 'magic virtue of words'[85] contained in constitutional documents, made it a supremely useful tool for intellectuals and political actors.

Scholarship has pointed to a number of mechanisms which have played a role in the globalisation of constitutional law. [86] Several of these are also applicable in the case of the late Qing Empire. Pressures from the outside often expect countries to conform to certain global norms.[87] In a process of constitutional learning, 'countries copy legal and constitutional innovations from their most successful rivals in the hope of achieving similar success.'[88] In their seminal paper on the evolution of global constitutionalism, David Law and Mila Versteeg cite Japan as an example for the first mechanism, since the Meiji Constitution was in part motivated by the desire to receive a 'treatment as a full and equal peer in the society of nation-states.'[89] To an extent, this was also the case in China, where some officials expressed their hope that the constitution would give their country a modern shape. Yet, while there was considerable pressure for reforms of the judicial system, foreign observers and governments were much less enthusiastic about the constitution itself, often deeming that the Chinese were too enthusiastic in their constitutional endeavours, and advising for a slower pace.[90] Chinese intellectuals and officials themselves tended to place emphasis on how constitutions would strengthen the country politically, economically, socially, and militarily, and how the Qing Empire would be able to leverage this constitutional strength internationally.

The mechanism of constitutional learning from the successful was a strong stimulus for the Qing government to use the Japanese model as its main, albeit not exclusive, blueprint. However, by late Qing times, Chinese elites were acutely aware that they shared a 'world stage' not only with the West and Japan, but also with the wider world.[91] They were aware that a number of other empires were facing similar challenges and undergoing similar transformations as the Qing Empire, and in particular that they were trying to use constitutions to overcome their challenges. Hence, they not only copied innovations from their most successful rivals but also sought to learn from the experiences of their peers, or to employ the experiences of their peers in their own discourses according to their respective political agendas. Many saw that the new constitutions in Russia and Persia were not visibly contributing to these countries' revitalisation. Hence, they came to the conclusion that China must proceed in a gradual way, placing the constitution as the finishing stone rather than as the basis for the reform programme. Others came to accuse the Qing court of the same 'sham constitutionalism' just as in Russia, and at the same time as the Ottoman constitution was a motivation for reformist monarchists, revolutionaries praised its 'revolutionary' character. However, as complex as the effect of the global constitutional wave on China was, they show that simple diffusionist models do not suffice to explain the emergence of the Qing constitution. Rather, 'constitutions' emerged as a fundamental category of the Chinese state as an important part of a global—and not just Western—movement co-producing the basic legal and political instruments of modern nation-states.

Notes

1 Takahashi Kazuyuki 高橋和之 (ed), *Nitchū ni okeru Seiō rikkenshugi no keiju to henyō* 日中における西欧立憲主義の継受と変容 [The reception and adaptation of Western constitutionalism in Japan and China] (Iwanami Shoten, 2014).

2 See Takii Kazuhiro, *The Meiji Constitution: The Japanese Experience of the West and the Shaping of the Modern State* (transl David Noble, International House of Japan, 2007); Ando Junko. *Die Entstehung der Meiji-Verfassung: Zur Rolle des deutschen Konstitutionalismus im modernen japanischen Staatswesen* [The emergence of the Meiji Constitution: On the role of German constitutionalism in the modern Japanese state] (Iudicium, 2000).

3 Ssu-Yu Teng and John King Fairbank (eds), *China's Response to the West: A Documentary Survey 1839–1923* (7th edn, Harvard University Press, 1979).

4 Cui Xuesen 崔學森, 'Qingting zhixian yu Mingzhi Riben' 清廷制憲與明治日本 [The Qing Court's constitution-making and Meiji Japan] (PhD diss., Peking University 2015) I.

5 Peter Zarrow, 'Constitutionalism and the Imagination of the State: Official Views of Political Reform in the Late Qing,' in Peter Zarrow (ed), *Creating Chinese Modernity: Knowledge and Everyday Life, 1900–1940* (Peter Lang, 2006), 78; See also Meribeth E. Cameron, *The Reform Movement in China: 1898–1912* (Octagon Books, 1963), 101.

6 Vladimir Il'ich Lenin, 'Demokratiia i narodichestvo v Kitae' [Democracy and populism in China], in Institut Marksizma-Leninizma pri TSK KPSS (ed), *Polnoe sobranie sochinenii* (5th edn, Politizdat, 1966–1981), vol. 21, 400–406.

7 Most recently Erik Zürcher, 'The Young Turk Revolution: Comparisons and Connections' (2019) 55 Middle Eastern Studies 481. See also Rebecca Karl, *Staging the World: Chinese Nationalism at the Turn of the Twentieth Century* (Duke University Press, 2007); Don C. Price, *Russia and the Roots of the Chinese Revolution, 1896–1911* (Harvard University Press, 1974).

8 'Ejiputo no kenpōnetsu' 埃及の憲法熱 [Egypt's constitutional fever] *Kokumin shimbun* 國民新聞 (Tokyo, 22 August 1908).

9 Scott Gordon, *Controlling the State: Constitutionalism from Ancient Athens to Today* (Harvard University Press, 1999).
10 Tom Ginsburg and Alberto Simpser (eds.) *Constitutions in Authoritarian Regimes* (Cambridge University Press, 2014).
11 For the definition of 'constitution' see Hermann Heller, *Staatslehre* [Theory of the State] (ed Gerhart Niemeyer, 6th edn, J. C. B. Mohr, 1983), 273, 281–315.
12 Heller, *Staatslehre*, 305–315.
13 Markus Prutsch, *Making Sense of Constitutional Monarchism in Post-Napoleonic France and Germany* (Palgrave, 2013), 179.
14 Kelly Grotke and Markus Prutsch (eds). *Constitutionalism, Legitimacy, and Power: Nineteenth-Century Experiences* (OUP, 2014).
15 Benjamin Akzin, 'The Place of the Constitution in the Modern State' (1967) 2 Israel Law Review 1, 1.
16 'Izvestiia vnutrenniia' [Internal news] *Severnaia Pochta ili Novaia Sanktpeterburgskaia Gazeta* (Saint Petersburg, 30 March 1818, Julian calendar), 1.
17 Tatiana Borisova, 'Russian National Legal Tradition: Svod versus Ulozhenie in Nineteenth-century Russia' (2008) 33 Review of Central and East European Law 295.
18 See Nader Sohrabi, *Revolution and Constitutionalism in the Ottoman Empire and Iran* (CUP 2011), 34–71; Avi Rubin, *Ottoman Nizamiye Courts: Law and Modernity* (Palgrave, 2011).
19 Sohrabi, *Revolution and Constitutionalism in the Ottoman Empire and Iran*, 34.
20 Aylin Koçunyan, *Negotiating the Ottoman Constitution 1839–1876* (Peeters, 2018); Robert Devereux, *The First Ottoman Constitutional Period: A Study of the Midhat Constitution and Parliament* (Johns Hopkins Press, 1963), 251.
21 See Erik J. Zürcher, *The Young Turk Legacy and Nation Building: From the Ottoman Empire to Atatürk's Turkey* (I.B. Tauris, 2010).
22 Sohrabi, *Revolution and Constitutionalism in the Ottoman Empire and Iran.*
23 Said Amir Arjomand, 'Constitutional Developments in Afghanistan: A Comparative and Historical Perspective' (2005) 53 Drake Law Review 943.
24 See Iza Hussin, 'Circulations of Law: Cosmopolitan Elites, Global Repertoires, Local Vernaculars' (2014) 32 Law and History Review 773; Hanif Md Lateh, Izziah Suryani Mat Resad, and Ahmad Faathin Mohd Fadzil. 'Penilaian Kanun I Esasi 1876 sebagai Sumber Pembentukan Perlembagaan Johor 1895' [The Assessment of Kanun I Esasi 1876 as the Source for the Formation of the Johore Constitution 1895] (2016) 38 Islāmiyyāt 103.
25 Sohrabi, *Revolution and Constitutionalism in the Ottoman Empire and Iran*, 299.
26 Rudolf G. Wagner, 'The Free Flow of Communication between High and Low: The Shenbao as Platform for Yangwu Discussions on Political Reform 1872–1895.' (2018) 104 T'oung Pao 116.
27 Onogawa Hidemi 小野川秀美, *Shinmatsu seiji shisō kenkyū* 清末政治思想研究 [Research on political thought in the late Qing] (Misuzu shobō, 1984), 52–85; and Lloyd Eastman, 'Political Reformism in China before the Sino-Japanese War' (1968) 27 Journal of Asian Studies 695.
28 Linda Colley, *The Gun, the Ship, and the Pen: Warfare, Constitutions, and the Making of the Modern World* (Norton 2021), 384–400.
29 Zarrow, 'Constitutionalism and the Imagination of the State,' 54.
30 Zheng Guanying 鄭觀應, *Zheng Guanying ji* 鄭觀應集 [Works of Zheng Guanying] (Xia Dongyuan 夏東元 ed, 2 vols, Renmin chubanshe, 1988), 66–67, 822.
31 David Mervart identifies the use of 'Warring States' as a descriptor for Western powers since Yamamura Saisuke's 山村才助 (1770–1807) *Miscellanea from the western seas* (*Seiyō zakki* 西洋雜記, 1801). David Mervart, 'Reading European Universal Histories in Japan, 1790s–1840' (2021) 64 Historical Journal, 43. In China, the use is attested since 1861. Yen-p'ing Hao and Erh-min Wang, 'Changing Chinese Views of Western Relations, 1840–95,' in John K. Fairbank and Kwang-Ching Liu (eds), *The Cambridge History of China: Volume 11: Late Ch'ing, 1890–1911, Part 2* (Cambridge University Press, 1980), 189. On the relationship to international law, see Rune Svarverud, *International Law as World Order in Late Imperial China: Translation, Reception and Discourse, 1847–1911* (Brill, 2007), 153–161.
32 Zheng, *Zheng Guanying ji*, 338–339.
33 Ibid 403–404.
34 Ibid 338–339.

35 For example, Kang Youwei 康有爲. *Riben bianzheng kao; E Bide bianzheng ji* 日本變政考；俄彼得變政記 [Study of the Japanese reforms; Account of the reforms of Peter the Great of Russia] (Jiang Guilin 蔣貴麟 ed, Hongye shuju, 1987).
36 Alison Adcock Kaufman, 'One Nation Among Many: Foreign Models in the Constitutional Thought of Liang Qichao' (PhD diss, University of California, 2007), 199.
37 Liang Qichao 梁啓超, 'Geming! Eluosi geming!' 革命！俄羅斯革命！ [Revolution! Revolution in Russia!] (1902) 9 Xinmin congbao 新民叢報 72. The Chinese original carries additional emphasis marks beneath the text.
38 Kaufman, 'One Nation Among Many,' 193–195; Tang Xiaobing, *Global Space and the Nationalist Discourse of Modernity: The Historical Thinking of Liang Qichao* (Stanford University Press, 1996), 140–141.
39 Zhou Kui 周逵 (tr), *Wanguo xianfa zhi* 萬國憲法志 [Account of the constitutions of the world] (Guangzhi shuju, 1902), 1a. The preface was penned by Zhao Bizhen 趙必振 (1872–1956).
40 'Lixian jiwen (Dongfang zazhi linshi zengkan xianzheng chugang)' 立憲紀聞 (東方雜志臨時增刊憲政初綱) [Records of constitutionalism (Special edition of the Eastern Miscellany: a first outline of constitutional government)], in Zhongguo shixuehui 中國史學會 (ed), *Xinhai geming* 辛亥革命 [The Xinhai Revolution] (Shanghai renmin chubanshe, 1957), vol. 4, 12.
41 John W. Steinberg and David Wolff (eds), *The Russo-Japanese War in Global Perspective: World War Zero* (Brill, 2007).
42 See Ivan Sablin, 'Russia in the Global Parliamentary Moment, 1905–1918: Between a Subaltern Empire and an Empire of Subalterns' in Holger Weiss (ed), *Locating the Global Spaces, Networks and Interactions from the Seventeenth to the Twentieth Century* (DeGruyter, 2020).
43 William A. Figueroa, 'China and the Iranian Left: Transnational Networks of Social, Cultural, and Ideological Exchange, 1905–1979' (PhD diss.: University of Pennsylvania, 2020), 53–63.
44 Egas Moniz Bandeira, 'China and the Globalisation of Constitutions: Constitutional Thought in the Qing Empire (1838–1911)' (PhD diss.: University of Heidelberg/Tohoku University, 2019), 278–284.
45 This aspect of the Chinese constitutional movement shall not be discussed in this chapter; on late Qing anarchism see Gotelind Müller-Saini, *China, Kropotkin und der Anarchismus: Eine Kulturbewegung im China des frühen 20. Jahrhunderts unter dem Einfluß des Westens und japanischer Vorbilder* [China, Kropotkin, and anarchism: A cultural movement in early 20th-century China under the influence of the West and of Japanese models] (Harrassowitz, 2001). See further Egas Moniz Bandeira, 'China and the Political Upheavals in Russia, the Ottoman Empire, and Persia: Non-Western Influences on Constitutional Thinking in Late Imperial China, 1893–1911' (2017) 8 Journal of Transcultural Studies 2, 40, 64–69.
46 'Lun woguo yu Eguo lixian zhi bijiao' 論我國與俄國立憲之比較 [On a comparison between our country's and Russia's adoption of a constitution] (1906) 1 Tongxue bao 通學報 53, 54. The main article, ending with this excerpt, has been extracted from another unnamed paper.
47 'Zhengwuchu zhi ge dufu dian' 政務處致各督撫電 [Telegram by the Council of Ministers to all governors-general and provincial governors] *Shibao* 時報 (Shanghai, 18 November 1905), apud Pan Chong 潘崇, 'Qingmo wudachen chuyang kaocha yanjiu' 清末五大臣出洋考察研究 [Research on the overseas investigation of the five commissioners] (PhD diss., Nankai University, 2010), 114.
48 On the mission, see Richard S. Horowitz, 'Breaking the Bonds of Precedent: The 1905–6 Government Reform Commission and the Remaking of the Qing Central State' (2003) 37 Modern Asian Studies 4, 775; E-tu Zen Sun, 'The Chinese Constitutional Missions of 1905–1906' (1952) 24 Journal of Modern History 3, 251.
49 See Moniz Bandeira, 'China and the Political Upheavals in Russia, the Ottoman Empire, and Persia,' 57–62, and Nikolai A. Samoilov, Rossiia i Kitai v XVII–nachale XX veka: Tendentsii, formy i stadii sotsiokul'turnogo vzaimodeistviia [Russia and China from the 17th to the beginning of the 20th century: Tendencies, forms and stages of socio-cultural interactions] (Izdatelnyi dom Sankt-Peterburgskogo Gosudarstvennogo Universiteta, 2014), 112.
50 Duanfang 端方, *Duan Zhongmin Gong zougao* 端忠敏公奏稿 [Drafts of memorials by Mr. Duan Zhongmin] (3 vols, Wenhai chubanshe, 1967) 694–695.
51 Ibid 679.
52 For a famous debate on Japan, see Herbert Spencer, *The Life and Letters of Herbert Spencer* (ed David Duncan, Methuen & Co., 1908), 319–323.

53 Cai Erkang 蔡爾康, Dai Hongci 戴鴻慈, and Zaize 載澤, *Li Hongzhang lipin Oumei ji; Chushi jiu guo riji; Kaocha zhengzhi riji* 李鴻章歷聘歐美記; 出使九國日記; 考察政治日記 [Record of Li Hongzhang's visit to Europe and the United States; Diary of a mission to nine countries; Diary of the investigation of politics and administration] (eds Zhang Xuanhao 張玄浩 et al., Yuelu shushe, 1985), 485–486.

54 Moniz Bandeira, 'China and the Globalisation of Constitutions' (n *47*), 284–295.

55 Wang Deyuan 汪德淵, 'Jiuwang juelun er' 救亡決論二 [On what determines survival or death, 2] (1907) 6 Zhengyi tongbao 政藝通報, 3a.

56 Gugong Bowuyuan Ming-Qing dang'anbu 故宮博物院明清檔案部 (ed), *Qingmo choubei lixian dang'an shiliao* 清末籌備立憲檔案史料 [Archival material concerning constitutional preparation in the late Qing] (Zhonghua shuju, 1979), vol. 1, 43–4. See further 'Lixian jiwen,' in Zhongguo shixuehui (ed), Xinhai geming, vol. 4, 13–17; Norbert Meienberger, *The Emergence of Constitutional Government in China (1905–1908): The Concept Sanctioned by the Empress Dowager Tz'u-hsi* (P. Lang, 1980), 39–42.

57 Nader Sohrabi, 'Global Waves, Local Actors: What the Young Turks Knew about Other Revolutions and Why It Mattered' (2002) 44 *Comparative Studies in Society and History* 45, 55–56.

58 See also Douglas Reynolds, *China, 1898–1912: The Xinzheng Revolution and Japan* (Harvard University Press, 1993), 191–192; Murata Yūjirō (transl Joshua A. Fogel), 'Dynasty, State, and Society. The Case of Modern China,' in Joshua A. Fogel and Peter G. Zarrow (eds), *Imagining the People: Chinese Intellectuals, and the Concept of Citizenship, 1890–1920* (first published 1997; Routledge, 2015).

59 See Ivan Sablin, Egas Moniz Bandeira, Jargal Badagarov, Martin Dorn, and Irina Sodnomova, 'Duma, yuan, and beyond: Conceptualizing parliaments and parliamentarism in and after the Russian and Qing Empires,' in Ivan Sablin and Egas Moniz Bandeira (eds), *Planting Parliaments in Eurasia, 1850–1950: Concepts, Practices, and Mythologies* (Routledge, 2021).

60 Max Weber, 'Rußlands Übergang zum Scheinkonstitutionalismus' [1906] 23 ArchSozWiss 165, 249.

61 Ibid 228.

62 This assessment remained the standard interpretation of the movement in Chinese historiography until recently. See, e.g., Gao Fang 高放, Qingmo lixian shi 清末立憲史 [Constitutional history of the late Qing] (Huawen chubanshe, 2012).

63 'Lixianguo pushi tu' 立憲國暴屍圖 [Image of corpses laid out in a constitutional state] (1908) 23 Minbao 民報, (iv).

64 'Constitutional Government,' *North China Herald* (Shanghai, 8 August 1908), 333.

65 Hong Fei 鴻飛 [Zhang Zhongduan 張鍾瑞], 'Tu'erji lixian shuo' 土耳基立憲說 [Commentary on Turkey's adoption of a constitution] (1908) 7 *Henan* 河南.

66 On this type of analogies, see Egas Moniz Bandeira, 'Between Chaos and Liberty: Chinese Uses of the French Revolution of 1789,' in Ying-kit Chan and Chen Fei (eds), *Alternative Representations of the Past. The Politics of History in Modern China* (De Gruyter, 2020), 130.

67 Banu Turnaoğlu, *The Formation of Turkish Republicanism* (Princeton University Press, 2017), 119–120.

68 'Lun Tuerqi lixian yu Zhongguo zhi guanxi' 論土耳其立憲與中國之關繫 [On the relationship between Turkey's adoption of a constitution and China] *Shenbao* 申報 (Shanghai, 2 August 1908) 3–4. See Egas Moniz Bandeira, 'Late Qing Parliamentarism and the Borderlands of the Qing Empire—Mongolia, Tibet, and Xinjiang (1906–1911)' (2020) 11 Journal of Eurasian Studies 15, 21–22.

69 'Jinnian zhu wu lixianguo' 今年之五立憲國 [This year's five constitutional states], *Shenbao* (Shanghai, 24 September 1908) 2–3.

70 Hong Fei, 'Tu'erji lixian shuo,' 25.

71 In Gugong Bowuyuan Ming-Qing dang'anbu (ed), *Qingmo choubei lixian dang'an shiliao* vol. 2, 683–684.

72 Ibid vol. 1, 53–67.

73 Cui Xuesen, 'Qingting zhixian yu Mingzhi Riben,' 109–115.

74 Edward J. M. Rhoads, *Manchus & Han: Ethnic Relations and Political Power in Late Qing and Early Republican China, 1861–1928* (University of Washington Press, 2000), 166–170.

75 See Joshua Hill, *Voting as a Rite: A History of Elections in Modern China* (Harvard University Asia Centre, 2019), 74–105.

76 Chang P'eng-Yüan 張朋園, *Zhongguo minzhu zhengzhi de kunjing: Wanqing yilai lijie yihui xuanju shulun* 中國民主政治的困境, 1909–1949: 晚清以來歷屆議會選舉述論 [The difficulties of democratic politics in China, 1909–1949: An exposition of the elections for the various parliaments since the late Qing] (Linking, 2007), 55.
77 See Chen Fei. 'Disassembling Empire: Revolutionary Chinese Students in Japan and Discourses on Provincial Independence and Local Self-Government' (2017) 51 Journal of Asian History 2017, 283.
78 See, e.g., Richard H. Minear, *Japanese Tradition and Western Law: Emperor, State, and Law in the Thought of Hozumi Yatsuka* (Harvard University Press, 1970).
79 Avi Rubin, *Ottoman Rule of Law and the Modern Political Trial: The Yildiz Case* (Syracuse University Press, 2018), 77–78.
80 Ibid 78.
81 Michel Rosenfeld, 'Constitution and secularism: a Western account' in Susanna Mancini (ed), *Constitutions and Religion* (Edward Elgar, 2020).
82 Hawkling Lugine Yen [Yan Haoling 嚴鶴齡], *A Survey of Constitutional Development in China* (Columbia University, 1911), 14.
83 Ibid 14.
84 On the idea of the constitution as the transfiguration of traditional Chinese modes of governance, see Egas Moniz Bandeira, 'From dynastic cycle to eternal dynasty: The Japanese notion of unbroken lineage in Chinese and Korean constitutionalist debates, 1890–1911' (2022) 7 GIH 517; see in particular p. 527.
85 J. O. P. Bland, *Recent Events and Present Policies in China* (first published 1912, Hyperion Press, 1973), 222.
86 See, e.g., David S. Law and Mila Versteeg, 'The Evolution and Ideology of Global Constitutionalism,' (2011) 99 California Law Review 1163.
87 Ibid 1177–1183.
88 Ibid 1173.
89 Ibid 1179.
90 Egas Moniz Bandeira, 'Political Reforms in a Global Context: Some Foreign Perspectives on Constitutional Thought in Late Imperial China.' (2017) 3 CCPS 139.
91 Rebecca Karl, *Staging the World: Chinese Nationalism at the Turn of the Twentieth Century* (n 7).

Bibliography

Colley L. *The Gun, the Ship, and the Pen: Warfare, Constitutions, and the Making of the Modern World* (W. W. Norton, 2021).

Fogel JA and Zarrow PG (eds), *Imagining the People: Chinese Intellectuals, and the Concept of Citizenship, 1890–1920* (first published 1997; Routledge, 2015).

Hill J. *Voting as a Rite: A History of Elections in Modern China* (Harvard University Asia Centre, 2019).

Karl RE. *Staging the World: Chinese Nationalism at the Turn of the Twentieth Century* (Duke University Press, 2007).

Kurzman C. *Democracy Denied, 1905–1915: Intellectuals and the Fate of Democracy* (Harvard University Press, 2008).

Price DC. *Russia and the Roots of the Chinese Revolution, 1896–1911* (Harvard University Press, 1974).

Rhoads EJM. *Manchus & Han: Ethnic Relations and Political Power in Late Qing and Early Republican China, 1861-1928* (University of Washington Press, 2000).

Tang X. *Global Space and the Nationalist Discourse of Modernity: The Historical Thinking of Liang Qichao* (Stanford University Press, 1996).

Wagner R. 'The Free Flow of Communication between High and Low: The Shenbao as Platform for Yangwu Discussions on Political Reform 1872–1895' (2018) 104 *T'oung Pao*, 116.

Zarrow P. 'Constitutionalism and the Imagination of the State: Official Views of Political Reform in the Late Qing,' in Peter Zarrow (ed), *Creating Chinese Modernity: Knowledge and Everyday Life, 1900–1940* (Peter Lang, 2006).

2
CONSTITUTIONAL PROJECTS IN MODERN CHINESE HISTORY

Ryan Martínez Mitchell

Introduction

As is well known, the Constitution of the People's Republic of China has not been converted into a judiciable source of law that serves as an external check upon legislative or executive authority. It has, nonetheless, taken on great significance as a source of norms for coordinating political behavior, and its successive revisions have often encoded major new political developments.

Great changes and new periods in political life have often been associated with changes to (or wholesale replacement of) the then-current Constitution. Similarly, the relationship between constitutional texts and one-party rule under the rubric of the "people's democratic dictatorship" has generally been not so much a site of tension as one of conditional, instrumental engagement. In short, despite China's modern history of party-based rule before and after 1949, the appeal of "constitution-based" governance and the symbolic power of constitutional texts have never waned.

Building upon recent strains of constitutional scholarship concerning the epistemic and ideological dimensions of constitution-making, I will argue that constitutional discourse in modern China has functioned as a key milieu for articulating essentially historical claims about the collective will of the populace, the legitimate aims of the state, and the norms to be applied in pursuit of these aims.

The first section below will examine the relationship between constitutions and historical narrative, both as a general and comparative phenomenon, as well as in specific relation to the case of China. It will present the argument that written constitutions have invariably served as texts that both lie *within* historical understandings and *produce* such understandings—the latter at times explicitly. The second section will look in more detail at the specific relationship between the phenomena of Communist Party historical-narrative production and corresponding constitutional transitions, with a focus on how this relationship was consolidated over the course of the 1945–54 period. The third section will then discuss in broad strokes the relationship between subsequent constitutional developments and official Party verdicts on history, from the contestations of Cultural Revolution-era factions to the productions of the Reform Era Party leadership under Deng Xiaoping, and more recently of Xi Jinping's "New Era of Socialism with Chinese Characteristics."

 DOI: 10.4324/9781003128243-3

Constitutions and Historical Narratives

Situating the Will in Modern Constitution-Making

The notion that the public law framework of a polity is an artificial product of legislation that can be revised in pursuit of certain goals is a modern political belief.[1] The same is true of the related idea that such legislation can and should embody the will of "the people" as *pouvoir constituant*.[2] In the realm of legal theory, these notions have been associated with the rise of the positivist view on the nature and function of legal authority, though positivism per se has been given varying elucidations and applications by its interpreters. Despite such variations, constitutional rule as an intentional norm-legislating practice, per se, is indeed largely a product of Enlightenment thought.

Paul Kahn has recently situated the Constitution of the United States in respect to these intellectual origins, arguing that its implementation in the American form of popular government marked a shift in the direction of a "project" epistemic framework for articulating and applying public law.[3] He illustrates the key elements of such an episteme by reference to one of the key passages in the case of *Marbury v. Madison*:

> That the people have an original right to establish for their future government such principles as, in their opinion, shall most conduce to their own happiness is the basis on which the whole American fabric has been erected. The exercise of this original right is a very great exertion; nor can it nor ought it to be frequently repeated. The principles, therefore, so established are deemed fundamental. And as the authority from which they proceed, is supreme, and can seldom act, they are designed to be permanent. [...] Certainly all those who have framed written Constitutions contemplate them as forming the fundamental and paramount law of the nation, and consequently the theory of every such government must be that an act of the Legislature repugnant to the Constitution is void.[4]

In Kahn's analysis, this one passage from *Marbury* illustrates "all of the elements of a project of constitutional governance" typical of the Enlightenment turn toward public law legislation. It features three moving parts: the legislative actor ("the people"), the set of "abstract norms" ("such principles") that the actor legislates, and, importantly, the end-product of this activity ("the 'American fabric' of institutions and laws").[5] Without any of these three elements, it would not be possible to speak of the US Constitution as a "project," for it would lack either an agent to carry out that project, an intellectual content differentiating the project from disorganized social activity, or a concrete result in terms of lasting institutions and policies seen as outcomes of that project.

As should already be clear, this way of viewing constitutional law is closely related to the more obvious transition from the unwritten, political constitutionalism of English history to the form of written constitutionalism and judicial review that has been globalized in part via US influence. There is little doubt that the US model of constitutional supremacy and of the courts' role as interpreters of constitutional meaning has played an increasingly dominant role in global constitutional discourse, particularly from the early 20th century through the present.[6] Of course, other models have also played a major role in the global spread of constitutional ideas, including Britain's unwritten constitution and the statist models of Wilhelmine Germany and Meiji Japan.[7]

The "project" model of constitutionalism—the argument that the text and its rules are direct expressions of the popular will—is a more difficult fit for these models. In many cases, they lack either a clear legislative actor (as in English "custom of the realm from time immemorial") or impose other limitations not present to the same degree in US-style constitutionalism. The norms and institutions of a Prussian or Meiji-style constitution, for instance, were not explicitly the creations of the legislator but were often conceived as preexisting elements of an underlying social order that is merely *reflected* by the constitution, though not created by it. The question as to whether they are, then, fully open to revision and amendment has historically been a fraught one.[8]

Kahn suggests that, in addition to the "project" framework, there is available an alternative conceptual premise that plays a countervailing role in shaping modern constitutional practice: that of the "system."[9] Natural law, classical economics, and behavioral psychology, for example, all conceptualize human action as consisting mostly of byproducts of unwilled causes or incentives. To the extent that constitutional orders are viewed as collections of norms with disparate origins and effects, some intended and others emergent, they are systems rather than projects. Such views are at work whenever legislative *will* as such is displaced from its central role in legal interpretation.

Historically, *both* conservative and Marxian political traditions have embraced just such a "system" perspective, despite opposing accounts of system effects and opposed normative commitments.[10] Interpretations of constitutions that focus on either the absolute character of "natural" rights, the "essential" features of the underlying society, or, alternatively, on the constitution's function as mere reflections of "class interests" may represent completely incompatible political ideologies: however, they are actually united in respect of their refusal to see in a constitutional text an expression of the "will of the People." While still asserting a very close relationship between constitutions and history, such views connect the former with, e.g., the "organic" growth of a concrete society or the operation of "laws" of historical irrespective of subjective human volition.[11]

With these distinctions in mind, it is possible to examine how Chinese constitutional law and politics have over time dealt with the issues of historical subjectivity and will. As will be argued, recurring claims based on the view of constitutional law as a subjective "project" of the people has often accompanied major political shifts, and in particular those connected with Executive power as well as claims to "living constitutionalism" and the exercise of *pouvoir constituant*.[12]

Chinese Constitutionalism through 1946

Some key premises of constitutional discourse in the People's Republic of China have major antecedents before 1949. Traditionally, imperial China had many important expressions of normative authority influencing the use of state power, but these took forms rather different from the post-Enlightenment written constitutions of the West. Both (criminally focused) legal codes and the "inherited commands" of former emperors exerted significant roles in regulating state policy, as did critical commentary on state policy by scholar-officials.

However, as is the case in the West, the epistemic frame of constitutional order as a collective, intentional project of "the people" is a modern phenomenon in Chinese thought. Its first major expressions took place during the 1890s movement for constitutional reform and state modernization that accompanied the Qing Dynasty's defeat. In the period leading up to and during the short-lived "Hundred Days' Reform" movement of 1898 under the Guangxu Emperor, a growing group of notable Chinese scholars and intellectuals called for emulation of foreign constitutional governance, with some advocating Anglo-American models but rather more seeing in Meiji Japan's Prussian-derived approach an ideal balance of tradition and modernity.[13]

These constitutional reform efforts, while extremely significant from an intellectual history perspective, were rapidly quashed by conservative elements in government. As a result, intellectuals committed to constitutional rule split into two broad camps, one of which continued to advocate constitutional monarchy via peaceful reform and the other of which instead pursued the aim of a revolutionary overthrow of the Qing dynasty and its replacement with a republic. During the period between 1898 and 1912, when the latter cause succeeded, there were extensive debates among the newly emerging cadre of young intellectuals who had received political and legal training in the West and Japan.

In these early debates over constitutionalism, many figures on both sides portrayed *xianzheng*, or constitutional governance, as an end to be pursued in and of itself. Important reformist writings like those of Liang Qichao had, since the 1890s, already drawn historically significant connections between constitutional rule and civic or political consciousness. The problem of the extent to which China's constitution should serve as a transformative implement for the reconstruction of state power as well as social relations, versus the extent to which it should instead serve to describe and reaffirm an existing pre-legal social and political status quo, remained unresolved over a protracted period of decades. Among the most important figures in the course of those issues, eventual resolution was Zhang Junmai, who supplemented his early studies at Waseda University in Tokyo with subsequent graduate study of law, politics, and philosophy in Berlin. Although he was a skeptic of revolution, Zhang embraced the 1912 Constitution of the Republic of China (ROC), including its Article 2, which held that "the sovereignty of the Republic of China belongs to the people."[14] However, the nature of that sovereignty's legal significance and reflection in the state's public law architecture—or its relationship with the notion of "sovereignty" as applied in diplomatic contexts—was quite ambiguous. For Sun Yat-sen's movement, popular sovereignty meant some form of democratic oversight; for the former Qing Viceroy Yuan Shikai, who emerged as President from the political dealings that established the new Republic and quickly displaced his allies of convenience, there was no such implication.

The constrained Executive position created for Yuan was notoriously insufficient to contain his ambitions, and in 1916, he arranged his own installation as Emperor of a new dynasty, under the reign name *Hongxian* or "Great Constitution."[15] This much-maligned imperial restoration lasted only briefly, but it did definitively mark the failure of the ROC in its first incarnation; Yuan's death was followed by the rise of the warlord era, during which various military cliques vied for power throughout much of China, repeatedly occupying Beijing and issuing short-lived new constitutional documents and plans, until the Guomindang (KMT)-led reunification of China in 1928.[16]

In this situation of chaos and conflict, Sun's KMT shifted toward a Leninist model of governance. As expressed in Sun's *Outline for the Founding of the National Government*, issued the year before his death in 1925, this entailed *inter alia* the plan that "constitutional rule" was to come only after preceding periods of "military rule" and then "tutelary (i.e. Party-based) rule" intended to correct China's historically backward social conditions.[17] Under Sun's successor Chiang Kai-shek, the KMT accordingly issued a constitution in 1931, the *Provisional Constitution for the Political Tutelage Period*, which established a *de facto* party-state in which the party monopolized powers of legislation as well as of constitutional interpretation.[18]

Subsequently, in 1936, a Draft Constitution was developed that was intended to establish a more permanent system with clearly defined separation of powers (albeit one still heavily favoring Chiang's own Executive authority, in a state rather than Party role).[19] The adoption of this Draft Constitution was delayed by Japan's full-scale invasion in 1937, and it was not until 1946 that a heavily revised version would be adopted not only following the Chinese People's Political Consultative Conference (*Zhongguo Renmin Zhengzhi Xieshang Huiyi*) (CPPCC) held under KMT auspices but also, unprecedentedly, involving compromises with another political actor struggling with it for hegemony over the Chinese state and society: the Communist Party.[20] It was with the Constitution of 1946 that, effectively for the first time, China's competing political parties came together to agree upon a text that they hoped would be accepted as expressing a "will of the People" capable of producing consensus across ideological and factional lines. Though it was to be ill-fated, the "compromise" Constitution of 1946 was a major conceptual turning point.

Defining the Chinese Historical Subject and Its Constitutional Projects

Failed Compromise

Between August 1945 and April 1946, the Communist Party and KMT were engaged in negotiations aimed at determining the possibility and terms of a unity government. In the "double-tenth agreement" of October 1945, both sides agreed to recognition of each other's legal status and committed to pursuing constitutional governance. The next phase of negotiations came with the convening of the Political Consultative Conference (PCC), involving both parties and also, in key roles, members of third parties and other prominent individuals. Meeting in Chongqing between January 15 and February 1, 1946, the PCC produced a so-called Joint Program for Political Administration that reiterated in greater detail the shared commitment to constitutional government, democratization on a multi-party basis, and a range of other specific provisions on matters ranging from military issues to economic policies. These were paired with a number of other fundamental policies, including on public ownership of utilities and natural resources, that could be used as a foundation for cooperation across the various parties' vast ideological gulfs.[21]

From the end of January through April, the various basic policies agreed to by the PCC were then incorporated into a draft Constitution. The Berlin-trained legal scholar/political theorist Zhang Junmai played an especially important role in guiding this drafting process both due to his acknowledged academic expertise and, in particular, his unique political profile at the head of the independent Democratic Socialist Party. Zhang's politics emphasizing both civil and political rights and socialist economic policies, combined with his record of criticism against both the Communists and KMT (which had led to harassment and imprisonment by the latter in the interwar years), now (briefly) made him a sort of ideal totem of compromise.[22]

The draft Constitution produced by April, and agreed to in principle by all parties, was both qualitatively and quantitatively different from previous Chinese constitutional documents. It was considerably longer and more detailed than previous draft constitutions, and it also emphasized principles of the separation of powers, judicial independence, and individual rights protections more than its main predecessors.[23] Moreover, despite the great influence of the US Constitution (which was also exerted in postwar constitutions drawn up elsewhere), the draft also contained significant elements drawn from other sources, such as the Weimar Constitution that had impressed Zhang during his studies in Germany, as well as France's new 1946 Constitution. Accordingly, the 1946 constitutional draft also included "the right of existence [and] the right to work," alongside civil and political rights, and also a commitment to "equitable distribution of land ownership and control of capital in order to obtain a well-balanced development of public economy and private livelihood," commitments to providing work opportunities and welfare benefits, and other such provisions meant to reflect progressive socialist ideals.[24]

Ultimately, however, increasing tensions between the Communist Party and KMT, worsened by distrust and military build-up in Manchuria, soon led to a collapse of the planned convention. Ultra-conservatives in the KMT had greatly contributed to the breakdown in talks by taking a hardline stance on outstanding issues regarding party representation and regional autonomy during a party conference in March. By November, relations between the parties had worsened beyond repair and the all-out conflict was again in full swing. It was only due to the need for third party support, and in particular the lobbying and insistence of Zhang Junmai, that it was the early 1946 joint draft that went up for a vote at the year's end, instead of one more geared toward KMT dominance.[25] Despite the deteriorating situation, the Constitution adopted by the KMT-dominated Assembly did include the provisions on "fundamental national policies." China at last had a full, written constitution. Moreover, against all the odds, it had one that embodied independent intellectuals' longstanding project for the articulation of a state that could tolerate individual freedom while also committing to widely shared collective goals, including more equal economic development, preservation of national territory, and upgrading China's global status.

Despite this major step in the direction of an Anglo-American style judicialized constitutionalism, the actual effectiveness of the 1946 Constitution was immediately mitigated by the KMT government's issuance of a set of "Temporary Provisions Effective During the Period of Communist Rebellion" endowing Chiang and the KMT with emergency powers beyond those stipulated in the constitutional text.[26] These "temporary provisions" were only lifted by the ROC government on Taiwan in 1991, and Taiwan's current status as a bastion of judicial constitutionalism in Asia dates to the liberalization of the regime that occurred after this point.[27]

The Communist Party's Turn to History

The resumption of civil war ended in Nationalist defeat and the establishment of the People's Republic of China in October 1949, which was preceded by a revised iteration of the CPPCC, now under Communist Party domination as extensive (or more so) as the Nationalist control had been in 1946. The Common Program that emerged from this conference is often regarded as the ur-constitutional text that established the original legitimacy of the PRC state, and which has served as the basis for the subsequent empowerment of the National People's Congress (NPC) as the legislative embodiment of the Chinese people's *pouvoir constituant*, including in the form of subsequently enacted constitutions.

Meanwhile, both the brief phase of cooperation with the KMT in 1945–46 and the later decision to pursue its own version of the CPPCC/Common Program format for the creation of a new Chinese state were based upon major ideological shifts in the Communist Party itself. These shifts were also closely tied to both Mao Zedong's personal status within the Party as well as the official account of its history that he promoted as a basis for his own authority and policy platform. Although Mao had been close to a *de facto* Party leader since the Zunyi Conference of 1935 and had effectively entrenched this role with the Yan'an "Rectification Movement" beginning in 1942, his status was not officially cemented until 1945 with the promulgation of the "Resolution on Certain Historical Questions." As the Resolution itself phrased it, in the words of Mao's secretary Hu Qiaomu: "the Party has produced its leader, Mao Zedong, during its process of struggle."[28]

Mao's close associates and theoretical advisors-cum-secretaries Hu Qiaomu, Tian Jiaying, and Chen Boda were each involved in the historical and ideological initiatives of the Yan'an period.[29] Hu, in particular, played a major role in drafting the 1945 resolution on history and Chen composed a longer official history of the Party that same year.[30] All three had been raised up within the Party ranks based on Mao's personal influence and were strong supporters of his ideological line. Ultimately, the 1945 historical resolution presented an account of the recent past of the Chinese Communist Party and its relationship with Chinese society that focused on Mao's "correct" advocacy of "winning the masses," pursuit of a policy of "New Democracy" (i.e. cooperating in coalition government with other forces across ideological lines) rather than immediate total revolution, and opposition to the "mistakes" taken by Party center during the 1931–35 period. While these "mistakes" covered a range of different topics, the most important consisted in an overly doctrinaire "leftist" interpretation of Marxism, a failure to pursue a policy of cooperation with domestic foes in resistance against the Japanese invasion, and a failure to recognize the primacy of peasant mobilization and rural land reform rather than urban proletarian revolution. Seizing upon Stalin's characterization of China as a "semi-feudal and semi-colonized" society, the Resolution justified Mao's "New Democracy" platform as the most realistic path to socialism.

All of these historical premises were reflected in the willingness of the Party under Mao in 1945–46 to embrace the general premises of the 1946 PCC's Joint Program as well as the framework of coalition government and agreed-upon "fundamental national policies" in the 1946 Constitution. However, they were more directly embodied in the framework of the 1949 Common Program. Like its predecessor, this ur-constitutional text established agreements about the basic structure of government that would later be established by specific pieces of constituent legislation and also stipulated a set of core national policies depicted as consensus positions across all political groups. These were framed in such a way as to speak to China's historical experience of foreign imperialism and "semi-colonial" status, with an emphasis on policies such as national autonomy, promoting economic development without immediate radical redistribution, cooperation among "labor and capital" (albeit now with a greater emphasis upon the interests of the former), maintaining territorial cohesion and "cooperation" among the Han majority and minorities, etc.

These and other major "consensus" policies were presented in the Common Program as the basis for political unity and the further articulation of features of the new state's constitutional system. It was, in fact, considered possible at the time that no subsequent "full constitution" would be adopted, but rather only specific pieces of organic legislation to define various features of the government.[31] This view would not be decisively rejected until the mid-1950s.

Constitutions and History-Making in the People's Republic of China

Pouvoir Constituant *in the Mao Era*

During the early 1950s, debates unfolded over whether the People's Republic of China should maintain its "Common Program" of 1949 as the *de facto* constitutional text for the new state, or whether it should instead adopt a full written Constitution. The Party center was, in fact, in favor of the former position as late as 1952, as the CPPCC was scheduled to hold its second tri-annual session after the inaugural session of 1949. As per the Communist Party's own official position, in other words, the Chinese people's *pouvoir constituant* was due to be reactivated once again. Based on the Common Program, one of the core functions of the CPPCC was to prepare for the establishment of a NPC, to replace it as a standing legislature.[32]

The function of the Common Program of 1949 as a compromise between different sectors of Chinese society based on shared aims and historical experiences was the key consideration during the debates over what further steps should be taken in the construction of the PRC state. This was on display, for example, in October 20, 1952, letter from Liu Shaoqi to Stalin, in which he represented the Chinese Communist Party center to ask the latter's advice about this question. As Liu summarized, the Common Program had already established a working basis for the core policies of the PRC state, the major branches of government had already been created by organic legislation, effective cooperative relations among classes and the continued "transitional" policies that allowed the existence of capitalist enterprise were all in place, and major features of the existing arrangement could not practically be changed until China had made more progress toward "the stage of socialism," as per Marxist theory. It might, then, be most appropriate to continue using the Common Program as the basis for China's loose constitutional framework.[33]

Stalin, however, disagreed with this assessment and instead strongly suggested that China should indeed draft a full Constitution in the near term, thus following the example of other Communist bloc states, such as Albania and Poland, as well as reinforcing domestic and global perceptions of the new regime's legality.[34] This was, in fact, the third occasion on which Stalin had suggested that China adopt a written constitution, the first having been in June 1949, also to Liu Shaoqi, and the second to Mao Zedong during the latter's 1950 visit to Moscow.[35] In each case, the gist of Stalin's comments was to emphasize that, although China was still only in a transitional phase toward socialism, a written Constitution would serve a positive role in that process of transition.

Stalin's third intervention proved dispositive, and soon after the Party leadership began the process of preparing for the drafting of a new Constitution. On January 20, 1953, the 20th meeting of the Central People's Government Commission adopted the decision to move forward in drafting a state Constitution as well as replacing the CPPCC with the NPC, which still had to be designed.[36] At the end of the year, a Constitutional Drafting Committee was appointed, with Mao Zedong as the chairman, and members including fellow Party leaders Deng Xiaoping, Peng Zhen, Dong Biwu, Li Weihan, and Zhang Jichun, as well as Mao's close associates Hu Qiaomu, Tian Jiaying, and Chen Boda.[37] Since 1949, these three Marxist historian/theorists/secretaries had served as experts on theoretical issues for the Party Secretariat. Based on extant accounts, the initial drafting process was largely directed by Mao and this coterie while staying at Hangzhou's scenic West Lake from December 24, 1953 through the beginning of the following year. Although this involved extensive consultation of foreign examples, the constitutional models that proved to be by far the most relevant, and which Mao strongly emphasized, were those of the Soviet Union.[38]

Two prominent legal scholars acting as consultants for the drafting group, Zhou Gengsheng and Qian Duansheng, were intimately familiar with Western constitutional law and theory. Nonetheless, their practical influence appears to have been quite limited. Indeed, based on Chen Boda's later statements, the Hangzhou drafting process actually worked initially from a draft that he himself had "spent the latter half of 1953 composing."[39] The draft produced under the direction of Mao and his Marxist theorist/historian secretarial crew during this stay in Hangzhou was completed in March 1954 and subsequently discussed in plenary meetings of the Party Politburo and the full constitutional drafting committee through September of that year. In many respects, the 1954 Constitution draft reproduced the key features of the Soviet system, including with the design of the NPC and its designation as the highest organ of state power, as well as in other branches of government including the judicial system and executive organs.

Some limited but significant departures from the Soviet model included clear designation of the NPC's Standing Committee as the holder of the NPC's supreme authority whenever the latter was not in session (the Presidium of the Supreme Soviet, though holding a similar role, was not explicitly designated as such in the Soviet Constitution), the establishment of China's distinct autonomous region system for ethnic minorities, and, perhaps most notably, the creation of an office of State Chairman or "President" (*guojia zhuxi*). The latter role, which during the drafting process it was always understood would go to Mao himself were it to be established, involved both symbolic functions as head of state as well as a measure of significant practical authority: the State Chairman was to be formally in command of the nation's armed forces and also empowered to convene a "Supreme State Conference," which could serve as an irregular policymaking body that would submit proposals to the NPC, State Council, or other government organs for "consideration."

Officially approved histories of the drafting process record Mao as opposing the designation of the State Chairman as head of state, usually on the basis of his own "modesty."[40] Some proponents of the provision, meanwhile, argued that "the affection of hundreds of millions of people cannot be erased," and that Mao's modesty on this issue was another sign of his "greatness."[41] Although the political maneuverings behind this topic remain murky, available records seem to indicate that Mao's main concern may have been with ensuring substantive rather than only symbolic power. Mao's own comments on his new State Chairman position at times emphasized a practical policy role, e.g., as a "buffer between the State Council and the NPC Standing Committee."[42] Meanwhile, the constitutional drafting and adoption process in mid-1954 moved into a phase of national "discussion" and "critique" that in various respects presaged later political movements.[43] The connection of constitutional discourse with verdicts on (recent) history was thus reinforced.

In practice, Mao's new position helped to facilitate his continued direct involvement in policymaking. Between 1954 and 1959, when Liu Shaoqi took up the position of State Chairman, Mao made 15 uses of the power to convene the Supreme State Conference[44]; in doing so, he continued to push for more thorough reorganizations of China's society on the basis of his own interpretation of Marxism and the Chinese people's current progress toward establishing socialism. Thus, the state Executive position that had been appended to the Constitution to create a role for Mao combined with his position as

Chairman of the Communist Party to maintain his outsized role in governance and claim to represent the popular will, via exceptional exertions of authority.

Reform, History, and Will

The constitutional order of 1954 remained formally in place for just over 15 years, however only a few years into that span it had already been severely compromised by exceptional exertions of authority via Party policies and movements, mostly directly spearheaded by Mao himself. The Anti-Rightist Campaign of 1957–59, the Great Leap Forward, and other top-down political mobilization initiatives operated almost entirely beyond the constraint of the normal state organs.[45]

Mao's claim to operate as an embodiment of the *pouvoir constituant* was to have even more dramatic repercussions from 1966, with the launching of the Cultural Revolution movement which subverted not only the organs of government, but also existing hierarchies of intra-Party authority. During this process, Mao's thought "combining Marxist theory with the practical historical experience of the Chinese revolution" was used as the basis for a radical reorganization of the state. The complex machinations of elite political struggle during the period, which would last until Mao's death in 1976, were, once again, manifested in initiatives to change China's constitution.

The first such attempt occurred in 1970, as several of the leading figures in the Cultural Revolution, including Lin Biao, Kang Sheng, and Chen Boda, organized a constitutional drafting process to replace the 1954 Constitution with one more aligned with Mao's new, more radical line. Aside from the total sidelining of the NPC and other state organs since 1966, the position of State Chairman was vacant, Liu Shaoqi having died in 1969 while held captive by Maoist Red Guards. Other aspects of the 1954 Constitution, including the lack of provisions for direct exercise of authority by the Party and the subordination of the armed forces to the state, would also be changed.

One of the most contentious aspects of the 1970 constitutional revision initiative by Mao's supporters concerned the issue of the State Chairman position. Indeed, it was largely over this issue that the draft constitution of 1970 failed to be adopted. Mao at this point favored elimination of the State Chairman position, while Lin Biao, who in the course of the Cultural Revolution had been designated as Mao's heir apparent, favored its retention—he was subsequently accused of trying to maneuver himself into the role as a way to preemptively circumvent Mao's authority.[46] Chen Boda and others who had played an active role in the first part of the Cultural Revolution were caught up in the ensuing political conflict, which saw the elimination of Lin and his faction and the rise to prominence of the so-called Gang of Four centered on Mao's wife Jiang Qing.[47]

The 1970 draft constitution was not adopted, but many of the innovations it introduced in the attempt to reorganize the state around Maoist thought—and specifically the explicit entrusting of all political authority to the Communist Party as an embodiment of *pouvoir constituant*—were subsequently revived in the 1975 Constitution drafted and adopted under the Gang of Four.[48] Like the 1970 draft, the 1975 Constitution was in essence a crystallization in legal text of a new state system in which regular organs of government and the legal system would be permanently subordinated to the Party on the level of both policymaking and everyday execution. The State Chairman position, however, was now removed, in line with Mao's wishes. After Mao's death in 1976, Hua Guofeng was installed as Party Chairman and overthrew the Gang of Four in an internal coup backed by various Party and military leaders seeking a return to more moderate policies.[49]

Hua issued his own new constitution in 1978 as part of the broader transition away from Cultural Revolution-era policies, and toward a return to a mode of governance oriented around state rather than exclusively Party institutions. Though reviving many features of the 1954 Constitution, the position of State Chairman remained absent. This to change, however, with Deng Xiaoping's subsequent rise to authority. Deng reproduced aspects Mao's playbook of 1945 in his assertion of intra-Party authority, first articulating an ideological agenda—in his case, calling for more far-reaching "Reform and Opening-Up" than was being pursued under Hua—and subsequently cementing the authority of this agenda with a resolution on history, which was issued in mid-1981. Hu Qiaomu, who had drafted Mao's resolution in 1945, also led the drafting of Deng's in 1981; at the same time, he was charged to direct drafting a new state constitution to replace Hua's of 1978.[50]

As had been the case in 1945–54, the political shifts of 1981–82 involved first the assertion of a new intra-Party orthodox consensus on the nation's and the Party's own history, its progress toward the achievement of socialism, the "mistakes" of the previous generation of leaders, and the guidelines for future progress. The revised state constitutional order was then established on the basis of this intra-Party consensus; in its Deng-era form, emphasizing the need for "seeking truth from facts" and avoiding the errors of "the personality cult" that Mao had established. Ironically, one of the primary means by which Deng's Party center sought to shift away from these "mistakes" of the Mao era was via the reintroduction of the State Chairman position, albeit now as an almost entirely ceremonial and symbolic role with no clearly delineated practical authority.[51] One of Deng's key initiatives at this point, central to the shift toward collective governance, was the new arrangement whereby the positions of Party leader and State Chairman would be clearly separated and held by different officials. This arrangement would, however, last only through the 1990s, when under Jiang Zemin these positions, as well as that of Chairman of the Central Military Commission, were once again united in the hands of a single official.

Conclusion

Arguably, the notions of collective governance and dispersal of policymaking authority that Deng introduced early in the Reform Era as a way of correcting the historical "errors" of the preceding period were already under considerable strain by the turn of the millennium. They have subsequently been reversed to a substantial degree under Xi Jinping, as many aspects of state authority have again been united under his direct control as head of both Party and government. While the principle of democratic centralism is apparently still fully in place in terms of broad policy decisions, Xi's position as an exceptional embodiment of the "will of the people" has been reiterated in various contexts, including in the assertion of his "Thought" as the ultimate guideline for Party ideology and state policy, as well as, notably, in his emulation of Mao's and Deng's mode of consolidating their desired reorderings of the state. Like both predecessors, Xi has also overseen both a new Party resolution on history and significant changes to the constitutional text.[52] In addition, the beginning of his administration was associated with a controlled national "debate" on constitutionalism that seemingly intentionally called back to similar moments in 1954 and 1982.[53]

While the Xi era resolution on history did not clearly identify "errors" of preceding leaders as did Mao's and Deng's, it did note significant "problems" that had emerged during the previous decades. Above all, these centered on issues of corruption, mismanagement, and unstable or uneven growth. Xi's intra-Party authority has turned in part on the claim to bring a new level of strict supervision to the Party's own governance and implementation of policies.[54] Meanwhile, in terms of state organization, by far the most widely noted and commented-upon aspect of his rule has been the removal of term limits for the positions of State Chairman and Vice-Chairman. Given the recent history of these positions being held by the Party's General Secretary, and the lack of specific provisions for term limits for that position (though two terms each had been served by his two most recent predecessors), this move has been seen as a striking reassertion of Executive authority.

These and other changes have been associated with a number of other major initiatives connected with both history and notions of the popular will. Xi's broader policy agenda, for example, has been closely linked with "Two Centennial Goals" of the Communist Party and the PRC state.[55] Having passed the former in 2021 and looking now toward the latter, due to be achieved in 2049, it is clear that historical narratives, claims about popular will, and reorganization of state power in part via changes to the constitutional text remain intimately tied together in Chinese political life.

Notes

1 See Martin Loughlin, *Foundations of Public Law* (Oxford University Press, 2010), 303, 321.
2 Cf. Reinhart Koselleck, et al., "Staat und Souveränität." In Otto Brunner, Werner Conze, and Reinhart Koselleck, eds., *Geschichtliche Grundbegriffe: Historisches Lexicon zur Politisch-Sozialen Sprache in Deutschland,* vol. 6, (Stuttgart: Klett-Cotta, 1972–1990), 1–54.
3 Paul Kahn, *Origins of Order: Project and System in the American Legal Imagination* (New Haven: Yale University Press, 2019).
4 *Marbury v. Madison*, 5 U.S. 137 (1803).
5 Ibid., 99.
6 See David S. Law and Mila Versteeg, "The Evolution and Ideology of Global Constitutionalism," *California Law Review* 99 (2011): 1163–1258.
7 Cf. Linda Colley, *The Gun, the Ship, and the Pen: Warfare, Constitutions, and the Making of the Modern World* (New York, NY: Liveright Publishing, 2021).
8 Michael Stolleis, *Public Law in Germany, 1800–1914* (New York, NY: Berghahn Books, 2001); Girish Bhat, "Recovering the Historical Rechtsstaat," *Review of Central and East European Law* 32, no. 1 (2007): 65–98.
9 See, e.g. Kahn, *Origins of Order*, 65, 91.
10 Cf. Adrian Vermeule, *The System of the Constitution* (Oxford: Oxford University Press, 2011); Marco Goldoni and Michael A. Wilkinson, "The Material Constitution," *The Modern Law Review* 81, no. 4 (2018): 567–597.
11 The traditional Soviet view of law as a direct expression of class relations, as in the work of Evgeny Pashukanis, is emblematic of this form of interpretation. See Evgeny Pashukanis, *The General Theory of Law and Marxism* (London: Routledge, 2017).
12 He Xin, "The Party's Leadership as a Living Constitution in China," *Hong Kong Law Journal* 42 (2012): 73–94.
13 See Peter Zarrow, *After Empire: The Conceptual Transformation of the Chinese State, 1885–1924* (Stanford, CA: Stanford University Press, 2012).
14 Provisional Constitution of the Republic of China. *World Constitutions Illustrated*, HeinOnline. Available at: https://heinonline.org/HOL/P?h=hein.journals/chinsoc5&i=182. Article 2.
15 *See* Stephen R. MacKinnon, *Power and Politics in Late Imperial China: Yuan Shi-kai in Beijing and Tianjin, 1901–1908* (Berkeley, CA: University of California Press, 1980).
16 Ibid.

17 Sun Zhongshan, "Guomin Zhengfu Jianguo Dagang," April 12, 1924. Available at: http://www.sunyat-sen.org/index.php?m=content&c=index&a=show&catid=46&id=6693

18 Provisional Constitution for the Political Tutelage Period, *World Constitutions Illustrated*, HeinOnline. Available at: https://heinonline.org/HOL/P?h=hein.cow/zzcn0071&i=3. Article 85; Article 30 ("During the period of political tutelage, the National Congress of Kuomintang delegates ... shall exercise the governing powers on behalf of the National People's Congress ... During the recess of the National Congress of Kuomintang delegates, the Central Executive Committee of the Kuomintang shall exercise the said powers.").

19 Yao Baoxian, "*Xianzheng Gongzuo yu Zhanshi Shishi Xianzheng Wenti* [Constitutional Work and the Problem of Implementing the Constitution during Wartime]," *Xin Zhengzhi* 3, no. 3 (1940): 58–61.

20 Li Cuiyan, "*1939–1940 Nian Zhishijie Guanyu 'Xianzheng yu Kangzhan' de Taolun jiqi Jiazhi Tixian* [Intellectuals' Debates on "Constitutionalism and the War of Resistance" during 1939–1940 and Their Manifestation of Values]," *Kangri Zhanzheng Yanjiu* 4 (2006): 84–103.

21 "Heping Jianguo Gangling [Joint Program for Political Administration]," *Minguo Ribao*, February 2, 1946. In the same section of the Joint Programme, the parties also committed to "maintaining friendly relations with the USA, Soviet Union, UK, and France as well as other democratic states, adhering to treaties with good faith, and making efforts at economic and cultural cooperation, in order to collectively plan for world prosperity and progress," pursuing trade agreements on a basis of "equality and mutual benefit," and other provisions including "improving the status of members of the Chinese diaspora."

22 See, e.g. Roger B. Jeans, *Democracy and Socialism in Republican China: The Politics of Zhang Junmai (Carsun Chang), 1906–1941* (Lanham, MD: Rowman & Littlefield, 1997); Li Hongxi, *Zhang Junmai Xiansheng de Minzhu Xianfa Sixiang* [The Democratic and Constitutional Thought of Dr. Zhang Junmai] (Jinian Zhang Junmai Xiansheng Bai Ling Ming Dan Xueshu Yantaohui, 1986).

23 Cf. Zhang Zhenguo, "*Cong 'Wu Wu Xiancao' Dao 'Zhonghua Minguo Xianfa* [From the "5.5 Draft Constitution" to the "Constitution of the Republic of China"]," in He Qinhua, ed., *20 Shiji Xifang Xianzheng de Fazhan ji qi Biange* [The Development and Transformation of Constitutionalism in the 20th Century] (Beijing: Falü Chubanshe, 2005).

24 Anonymous, "Zhang Junmai Yanjiang Weilai Xianfa Wenti [Address of Zhang Junmai on the Issue of the Future Constitution]," *Da Gong Bao*, June 28, 1946; cf. Li Fupeng, "Weima Xianfa Shehuiquan de Zhongguo Zhuanhua [The Chinese Adaptation of the Weimar Constitution's Social Rights]," *Huanqiu Falü Pinglun* 42, no. 3 (2020): 133–146.

25 Anonymous, "Zhang Junmai Shang Shu Jiang Zhuxi Dui Shiju Ti Si Xiang Jianyi [Zhang Junmai Submits a Petition to Chairman Jiang, Making Four Suggestions on the Current Situation]," *Yi Shi Bao* (Tianjin), November 18, 1946.

26 Discussed in Yeh Jiunn-Rong, "*Constitutional Reform and Democratization in Taiwan: 1945–2000*," in Peter C. Y. Chow, ed., *Taiwan's Modernization in Global Perspective*, 47–77 (Westport, CT: Greenwood Publishing Group, 2002).

27 Ibid.

28 Central Committee of the Communist Party of China, "Guanyu Ruogan Lishi Wenti de Jueyi [Resolution on Certain Historical Issues]," April 20, 1945. Available at: http://www.people.com.cn/item/20years/newfiles/b1040.html

29 See, e.g. Hu Qiaomu Zhuan Bianxie Zu, *Hu Qiaomu Zhuan* [*Biography of Hu Qiaomu*] (Beijing: Dangdai Zhongguo Chubanshe, 2015): 79–85.

30 Ibid.

31 See Han Dayuan, "Waiguo Xianfa Dui 1954 Nian Xianfa Zhiding Guocheng De Yingxiang [The Influence on Foreign Constitutions on the Drafting of the 1954 Constitution]," *Bijiaofa Yanjiu* 4 (2014): 51–64.

32 Ibid., 55.

33 Ibid. Cf. Tong Yawen, *Lun Liu Shaoqi Dui 1954 Nian Xianfa De Yingxiang* [Liu Shaoqi's Influence upon the 1954 Constitution], MA Thesis, Central South University (2011).

34 Zhang Haixia and Zhang Zhifen, "Mao Zedong Yu 1954 Nian Xianfa De Zhiding [Mao Zedong and the Drafting of the 1954 Constitution]," *Fujian Dangshi Yuekan* 6 (2010): 8–10.

35 Ibid., 8.

36 Ibid.

37 See Zhejiang Sheng Dang'an Guan, "Mao Zedong Zhuxi Zai Hangzhou Qicao Xin Zhongguo Di Yi Bu Xianfa [Mao Zedong Drafts New China's First Constitution at Hangzhou]," *Zhejiang Jiyi* 12 (2011): 42–45.
38 See Han, "Waiguo Xianfa Dui 1954 Nian Xianfa Zhiding Guocheng De Yingxiang," 55–61.
39 Chen Xiaonong (ed.), *Chen Boda Zui Hou Koushu Huiyi* [Chen Boda's Final Oral Recollections] (Hong Kong: Yangguang Huanqiu Chubanshe, 2005): 117.
40 Li Fengtao, "Jiemi Xin Zhongguo Di Yi Bu Xianfa Dansheng Beihou: Mao Zhuxi We He Shandiao 'Guojia Yuanshou' Tiaowen [Uncovering New China's First Constitution: Why Chairman Mao Deleted the 'Head of State' Clause]," *Renmin Wang: Zhonguo Jingji Zhoukan*, December 5, 2009.
41 Ibid.
42 "San Wei Lingxiu Yu 1954 Nian Xianfa [Three Leaders and the 1954 Constitution]," *tuanjiewang.cn*, February 27, 2018. Available at: http://www.tuanjiewang.cn/2018-02/27/content_133404.htm
43 Diamant, Neil J. and Xiaocai Feng, "The PRC's First National Critique: The 1954 Campaign to 'Discuss the Draft Constitution'," *The China Journal* 73 (January 2015): 1–37.
44 See, e.g. "'Da Duzhe' He Xinhua She De Guoji Cankao Baodao ['Great Readers' and the Xinhua Agency's International Reference Reports]," *Dang Shi Bolan* 4 (2008): 4–10.
45 Cf. Stanley Lubman, *Bird in a Cage: Legal Reform in China after Mao* (Stanford: Stanford University Press, 1999); Jianfu Chen, *Chinese Law: Context and Transformation* (Leiden: Martinus Nijhoff Publishers, 2008).
46 Yu Ruxin, "1970 Nian Xianfa Xiugai Cao'an Jiedu [Explaining the 1970 Constitutional Revision Draft]," *Mingde Gongfa Wang*, July 11, 2012. Available at: http://www.calaw.cn/article/default.asp?id=7312
47 See Chen Xiaonong (ed.), *Chen Boda Zui Hou Koushu Huiyi*, 372–375.
48 Constitution of the People's Republic of China (1975). *World Constitutions Illustrated*, HeinOnline. Available at: https://heinonline.org/HOL/P?h=hein.cow/cprechfj0001&i=1
49 Yang Rong and Jiang Guohua, "Lishi De Guaidian: Xie Zai 'Qi Ba Xianfa' Banbu Shishi 30 Zhounian [A Historical Turning Point: Written on the 30th Anniversary of the Promulgation of the "78 Constitution"]," *Changsha Ligong Daxue Xuebao (Shehui Kexue Ban)* 24, no. 1 (2009): 32–37.
50 See, e.g. Cheng Zhongyuan, "Hu Qiaomu Dui Yi Jiu Ba Er Nian Xianfa Xiugai De Gongxian [Hu Qiaomu's Contribution to the Revision of the 1982 Constitution]," *Zhongong Dangshi Yanjiu* 8 (2011): 40–46.
51 Xu Chongde. "Xianxing Xianfa De Chansheng [The Birth of Our Current Constitution]," in *Xu Chongde Zixuanji* [*Xu Chongde's Selected Works*] (Beijing: Zhongguo Renmin Daxue Chubanshe, 2007).
52 See, e.g. Sheng Yang and Cao Siqi, "19th CPC central committee kicks off sixth plenary session, to table landmark resolution," *Global Times*, November 8, 2021. Available at: https://www.globaltimes.cn/page/202111/1238387.shtml
53 Zheng Yongnian, "Zhongguo de Xianzheng Zhi Zheng Shuoming le Shenme? [What Does China's 'Constitutional Governance' Debate Mean?]," *Ai Sixiang*, June 18, 2013. http://www.aisixiang.com/data/64914.html
54 "Xi Jinping Fazhi Sixiang Shi Makesizhuyi Zhongguohua Zui Xin Chengguo [Xi Jinping Thought on the Rule of Law Is the Latest Achievement of the Sinicization of Marxism]," *Renmin Ribao* [People's Daily], 30 December 2020. Available at: http://politics.people.com.cn/n1/2020/1230/c1001-31983343.html
55 Kou Jie, "14th Five-Year Plan: Institutional advantages herald promising future for China's centennial goal," *Qiushi*, October 27, 2020. Available at: http://en.qstheory.cn/2020-10/27/c_554507.htm

Bibliography

Bhat, Girish. "Recovering the Historical Rechtsstaat," *Review of Central and East European Law* 32, no. 1 (2007): 65–98.

Central Committee of the Communist Party of China. "Guanyu Ruogan Lishi Wenti de Jueyi [Resolution on Certain Historical Issues]," April 20, 1945. Available at: http://www.people.com.cn/item/20years/newfiles/b1040.html

Chen, Jianfu. *Chinese Law: Context and Transformation*. Leiden: Martinus Nijhoff Publishers, 2008.
Chen, Xiaonong (ed.). *Chen Boda Zui Hou Koushu Huiyi [Chen Boda's Final Oral Recollections]*. Hong Kong: Yangguang Huanqiu Chubanshe, 2005.
Cheng, Zhongyuan. "Hu Qiaomu Dui Yi Jiu Ba Er Nian Xianfa Xiugai De Gongxian [Hu Qiaomu's Contribution to the Revision of the 1982 Constitution]," *Zhongong Dangshi Yanjiu* 8 (2011): 40–46.
Colley, Linda. *The Gun, the Ship, and the Pen: Warfare, Constitutions, and the Making of the Modern World*. New York, NY: Liveright Publishing, 2021.
Dayuan, Han. "Waiguo Xianfa Dui 1954 Nian Xianfa Zhiding Guocheng De Yingxiang [The Influence on Foreign Constitutions on the Drafting of the 1954 Constitution]," *Bijiaofa Yanjiu* 4 (2014): 51–64.
Diamant, Neil J. and Xiaocai Feng. "The PRC's First National Critique: The 1954 Campaign to 'Discuss the Draft Constitution'," *The China Journal* 73 (January 2015): 1–37.
Foucault, Michel. *The Order of Things: An Archaeology of the Human Sciences*. New York, NY: Routledge, 2005.
Goldoni, Marco and Michael A. Wilkinson, "The Material Constitution," *The Modern Law Review* 81, no. 4 (2018): 567–597.
He, Xin. "The Party's Leadership as a Living Constitution in China," *Hong Kong Law Journal* 42 (2012): 73–94.
Hu Qiaomu Zhuan Bianxie Zu. *Hu Qiaomu Zhuan [Biography of Hu Qiaomu]*. Beijing: Dangdai Zhongguo Chubanshe, 2015.
Jeans, Roger B. *Democracy and Socialism in Republican China: The Politics of Zhang Junmai (Carsun Chang), 1906–1941*. Lanham, MD: Rowman & Littlefield, 1997.
Kahn, Paul W. *Origins of Order*. New Haven, CT: Yale University Press, 2019.
Koselleck, Reinhart. "Staat und Souveränität." In Otto Brunner, Werner Conze, and Reinhart Koselleck, eds., *Geschichtliche Grundbegriffe: Historisches Lexicon zur Politisch-Sozialen Sprache in Deutschland*, vol. 6. Stuttgart: Klett-Cotta, 1972–1990: 1–54.
Law, David S. and Mila Versteeg. "The Evolution and Ideology of Global Constitutionalism," *California Law Review* 99 (2011): 1163–1258.
Li, Cuiyan. "1939-1940 Nian Zhishijie Guanyu "Xianzheng yu Kangzhan" de Taolun jiqi Jiazhi Tixian [Intellectuals' Debates on "Constitutionalism and the War of Resistance" during 1939–1940 and their Manifestation of Values]," *Kangri Zhanzheng Yanjiu* 4 (2006): 84–103.
Li, Fengtao. "Jiemi Xin Zhongguo Di Yi Bu Xianfa Dansheng Beihou: Mao Zhuxi We He Shandiao 'Guojia Yuanshou' Tiaowen [Uncovering New China's First Constitution: Why Chairman Mao Deleted the 'Head of State' Clause]," *Renmin Wang: Zhonguo Jingji Zhoukan*, December 5, 2009.
Li, Fupeng. "Weima Xianfa Shehuiquan de Zhongguo Zhuanhua [The Chinese Adaptation of the Weimar Constitution's Social Rights]," *Huanqiu Falü Pinglun* 42, no. 3 (2020): 133–146.
Loughlin, Martin. *Foundations of Public Law*. Oxford: Oxford University Press, 2010.
Lubman, Stanley. *Bird in a Cage: Legal Reform in China after Mao*. Stanford, CA: Stanford University Press, 1999.
MacKinnon, Stephen R. *Power and Politics in Late Imperial China: Yuan Shi-kai in Beijing and Tianjin, 1901–1908*. Berkeley, CA: University of California Press, 1980.
Pashukanis, Evgeny. *The General Theory of Law and Marxism*. Milton Park: Routledge, 2017.
Stolleis, Michael. *Public Law in Germany, 1800–1914*. New York: Berghahn Books, 2001: 56–75.
Sun, Zhongshan. "Guomin Zhengfu Jianguo Dagang," April 12, 1924. Available at: http://www.sunyat-sen.org/index.php?m=content&c=index&a=show&catid=46&id=6693
Tong, Yawen. *Lun Liu Shaoqi Dui 1954 Nian Xianfa De Yingxiang* [Liu Shaoqi's Influence upon the 1954 Constitution], MA Thesis, Central South University (2011).
Vermeule, Adrian. *The System of the Constitution*. Oxford: Oxford University Press, 2011.
"Xi Jinping Fazhi Sixiang Shi Makesizhuyi Zhongguohua Zui Xin Chengguo [Xi Jinping Thought on the Rule of Law Is the Latest Achievement of the Sinicization of Marxism]," *Renmin Ribao* [People's Daily], December 30, 2020. Available at: http://politics.people.com.cn/n1/2020/1230/c1001-31983343.html
Xu, Chongde. "Xianxing Xianfa De Chansheng [The Birth of Our Current Constitution]." In *Xu Chongde Zixuanji [Xu Chongde's Selected Works]*. Beijing: Zhongguo Renmin Daxue Chubanshe, 2007.

Yang, Rong and Jiang Guohua. "Lishi De Guaidian: Xie Zai 'Qi Ba Xianfa' Banbu Shishi 30 Zhounian [A Historical Turning Point: Written on the 30th Anniversary of the Promulgation of the "78 Constitution"]," *Changsha Ligong Daxue Xuebao (Shehui Kexue Ban)* 24, no. 1 (2009): 32–37.

Yao, Baoxian. "*Xianzheng Jiben Gongzuo yu Zhanshi Shishi Xianzheng Wenti* [Constitutional Work and the Problem of Implementing the Constitution during Wartime]," *Xin Zhengzhi* 3, no. 3 (1940): 58–61.

Yeh, Jiunn-Rong. Constitutional Reform and Democratization in Taiwan: 1945–2000. In Peter C. Y. Chow, ed., *Taiwan's Modernization in Global Perspective*. Westport, CT: Greenwood Publishing Group, 2002: 47–77.

Yu, Ruxin. "1970 Nian Xianfa Xiugai Cao'an Jiedu [Explaining the 1970 Constitutional Revision Draft]," Mingde Gongfa Wang, July 11, 2012. Available at: http://www.calaw.cn/article/default.asp?id=7312

Zarrow, Peter. *After Empire: The Conceptual Transformation of the Chinese State, 1885–1924*. Stanford, CA: Stanford University Press, 2012.

Zhang, Haixia and Zhang Zhifen. "Mao Zedong Yu 1954 Nian Xianfa De Zhiding [Mao Zedong and the Drafting of the 1954 Constitution]," *Fujian Dangshi Yuekan* 6 (2010): 8–10.

Zhang, Zhenguo. "Cong 'Wu Wu Xiancao' Dao 'Zhonghua Minguo Xianfa' [From the '5.5 Draft Constitution' to the 'Constitution of the Republic of China']." In He Qinhua, ed., *20 Shiji Xifang Xianzheng de Fazhan ji qi Biange [The Development and Transformation of Constitutionalism in the 20th Century]*. Beijing: Falü Chubanshe, 2005.

Zhejiang Sheng Dang'an Guan. "Mao Zedong Zhuxi Zai Hangzhou Qicao Xin Zhongguo Di Yi Bu Xianfa [Mao Zedong Drafts New China's First Constitution at Hangzhou]," *Zhejiang Jiyi* 12 (2011): 42–45.

Zheng, Yongnian. "Zhongguo de Xianzheng Zhi Zheng Shuoming le Shenme? [What Does China's 'Constitutional Governance' Debate Mean?]," *Ai Sixiang*, June 18, 2013. Available at: http://www.aisixiang.com/data/64914.html

3

THE HISTORY OF THE DRAFTING AND IMPLEMENTATION OF THE BASIC LAW OF THE HONG KONG SPECIAL ADMINISTRATIVE REGION

Albert H.Y. Chen

The Hong Kong Special Administrative Region (HKSAR) of the People's Republic of China (PRC) was established in 1997 upon the termination of British colonial rule in Hong Kong. The Basic Law of the HKSAR is the constitutional instrument of post-colonial Hong Kong. It defines the political and legal systems of the HKSAR and regulates its relationship with the Chinese central government. Since its enactment by China's National People's Congress (NPC) in 1990, it has shaped and steered developments in Hong Kong in political, legal, social, economic and other domains.

This chapter discusses the history of the drafting and implementation of the Basic Law. It traces the origins of the Basic Law to the Sino-British negotiation on Hong Kong's future in 1982–1984 and the Joint Declaration (JD) signed in 1984, in which the concept of "One Country, Two Systems" (OCTS) was codified. It examines the process of the drafting of the Basic Law in 1985–1990.

Even though the Basic Law only came into effect in Hong Kong in 1997, it had the effect of shaping Hong Kong's transition from 1990 to 1997 and gave rise to constitutional controversies in this transition period. After reviewing developments in this period, the chapter then recounts the history of the implementation of the Basic Law from 1997 to 2021. It demonstrates that the tensions and conflicts inherent in OCTS have plagued the process of the implementation of the Basic Law. In retrospect, some of the major difficulties and controversies in this process can at least partly be traced back to the Basic Law itself.

The Drafting of the Basic Law

The Basic Law does not stand alone. It originated from the JD, which expressly stipulated that the policies set out in the JD regarding post-1997 Hong Kong would be provided for in a "Basic Law". The text of the JD (including its three annexes) itself

 DOI: 10.4324/9781003128243-4

was a joint product of the two governments and was only concluded after two years of strenuous negotiations.[1] Approximately half of the provisions of the Basic Law were largely reproduced from the JD.

After the JD was concluded, China began to engage in the task of drafting the Basic Law. The official policy was to welcome the participation and input of Hong Kong people in the drafting process. In mid-1985, a 59-member Basic Law Drafting Committee (BLDC) was appointed; 23 of its members were from Hong Kong, mainly from the business and professional elite, but also including a few individuals from the labour and religious sectors. Nine of the Hong Kong members were serving or former members of the Executive Council or Legislative Council (LegCo) of colonial Hong Kong. In late 1985, a 180-member Basic Law Consultative Committee (BLCC) was established in Hong Kong, consisting entirely of Hong Kong people from different walks of life, largely nominated by business, professional and social bodies.[2]

The Chinese government never recognised publicly that the British or the colonial Hong Kong government had any role to play in the drafting of the Basic Law. The Chinese government considered the making of the Basic Law a purely domestic affair of the PRC. However, both British and Chinese sources published subsequently reveal that the British did provide significant inputs during the drafting process via behind-the-scene diplomacy.[3]

The BLDC held its inaugural meeting in Beijing in July 1985. The meeting decided on the timetable for the drafting of the Basic Law. The first draft of the Basic Law would be completed and released for public consultation in early 1988. After the consultation exercise, a second draft would be prepared and submitted to the NPC Standing Committee (NPCSC) in early 1989. There would be a second round of consultation. The final version of the Basic Law would be submitted to the NPC for enactment in early 1990. This timetable was strictly followed in practice.[4]

The inaugural meeting of the BLDC also decided that research work in preparation for the drafting of the Basic Law would commence immediately. The plan was that at the second plenary session of the BLDC to be held in the first half of 1986, the topics to be covered in the Basic Law would be decided upon, and the drafting work would then begin. It was also decided that a BLCC would be established in Hong Kong to collect the views of Hong Kong people and provide input to the BLDC. In December 1985, the BLCC held its inaugural meeting.

In April 1986, the second plenary session of the BLDC was held in Beijing. The structural outline of the Basic Law was adopted. The meeting decided to set up five sub-groups of the BLDC specialising in different topics to be dealt with in the Basic Law. Initial drafts of various chapters of the Basic Law were to be prepared by the relevant sub-groups for consideration by the BLDC at its plenary sessions.

During the period of Basic Law drafting which concluded in early 1990, the BLDC held a total of nine plenary sessions, and its five sub-groups held a total of 73 meetings in Beijing and other Chinese cities. Each sub-group was led by two co-conveners, one from mainland and one from Hong Kong. There was a fairly high degree of transparency of the meetings of the BLDC and its sub-groups. The usual practice was that journalists from Hong Kong were notified about these meetings, and representatives of the BLDC or its sub-group met with journalists after the meeting was held. As regards the BLCC, it initially formed eight sub-groups, which were reorganised into six in 1987. The BLCC held a total of eight plenary meetings and produced a huge volume of research papers and consultation reports.

The discussion and debates in the Hong Kong community and among politicians, political groups, social activists, civil society organisations and business and professional elites began with the consultative activities launched by the BLCC in 1986 and further developed during the consultation on the Hong Kong government's Green Paper on the "1987 review of developments in representative government".

In 1985, the colonial government had introduced elections (by "functional constituencies" and "electoral college") to a portion of LegCo seats for the first time in Hong Kong's history.[5] The "1987 review" was for the purpose of deciding whether "direct election" (by universal suffrage) to a portion of LegCo seats should be introduced in 1988. In Sino-British diplomacy following the conclusion of the JD, the Chinese government had opposed the introduction of such direct election in 1988 on the ground that constitutional change in colonial Hong Kong should "converge" with the model of the HKSAR's political system as prescribed by the Basic Law, and that before the Basic Law was finalised, no significant constitutional change should be introduced unilaterally by the British in Hong Kong. By late 1985, the British had come to accept in principle this concept of "convergence". The White Paper published on the basis of the "1987 review" decided against the introduction of direct election in 1988 but promised that such election to a portion of LegCo seats would be introduced in 1991.

The political elite and public opinion in Hong Kong had divided views on certain fundamental issues arising from the drafting of the Basic Law, particularly as regards the degree of Hong Kong's democratisation that should be codified in the Basic Law. The conservative political forces were led by the "Business and Professional Group" (BPG or "Group of 89 persons") of the BLCC. The establishment of the BPG in August 1986 was followed by the formation in October 1986 of a pro-democracy alliance of 91 civil society organisations and more than 300 individuals (including 19 BLCC members) known as the "Joint Committee on the Promotion of Democratic Government" (JCPDG), which stood at the other end of the political spectrum. The JCPDG represented Hong Kong's nascent democracy movement and advocated the introduction of Western-style liberal democracy in Hong Kong.[6] Within the BLDC, only two Hong Kong members advocated this position; they were Szeto Wah and Martin Lee, who had been elected into LegCo in 1985 by the functional constituencies of teachers and lawyers, respectively.

In 1986–1987, initial or tentative drafts of various chapters of the Basic Law were produced and discussed at meetings of the relevant BLDC sub-groups, followed by discussion at plenary sessions of the BLDC itself. At the seventh plenary session of the BLDC in April 1988, the first consultative draft of the Basic Law was adopted. It was then published for public consultation. There was a five-month consultation period ending on September 30, 1988. In this period, the discussion and debates in the Hong Kong community on issues arising from the draft Basic Law reached a new climax.[7]

During the consultation period, the first draft of the Basic Law was discussed in considerable detail in LegCo and in the British Parliament. LegCo's debate on the draft Basic Law took place on 13–14 July 1988. The British House of Lords' debate on the subject took place even earlier, on June 10, 1988, followed by the House of Commons' debate on the draft Basic Law on July 15, 1988.

After the end of the consultation period, sub-groups of the BLDC held several meetings to consider revisions to the first draft of the Basic Law. For example, the subgroup on the political system met twice in Guangzhou in November and December 1988 and adopted a controversial electoral plan for the HKSAR known as the "Cha-Cha model" (named after Louis Cha Leung-yung and Cha Chi-ming, two influential Hong

Kong members of the BLDC). The revisions proposed by the sub-groups were finalised and voted upon at the eighth plenary session of the BLDC in January 1989; the procedure required each article of the draft to be endorsed by a two-thirds majority vote. This second draft of the Basic Law was submitted to the NPCSC in February 1989 and then published for a second round of public consultation. The improvements (particularly from Hong Kong's perspective) to the first draft evidenced by the second draft were substantial,[8] although the provisions on the electoral model and the pace of democratisation were still controversial.

The following are key examples of significant improvements in the second draft as compared to the first draft. Firstly, as regards the application of mainland Chinese law to the HKSAR, article 17 of the first draft had provided that the State Council may issue a directive to the HKSAR government to apply in Hong Kong any specified mainland law that relates to defence, foreign affairs or other matters of national unity and territorial integrity that are not within the HKSAR's autonomy. But under article 18 of the second draft (which is the equivalent of article 17 of the first draft), mainland laws that are applicable in the HKSAR shall be listed in Annex III to the Basic Law and are limited to matters of defence, foreign affairs and other matters not within the SAR's autonomy.

Secondly, as regards the power of the Central Authorities to veto laws made by the HKSAR legislature, article 16 of the first draft had provided that this veto power is applicable to any law that is considered inconsistent with the Basic Law or legal procedures. However, under article 17 of the second draft, the exercise of the veto power is limited to circumstances in which the Hong Kong law is considered to be inconsistent with Basic Law provisions relating to matters within the jurisdiction of the Central Authorities or the relationship between the Central Authorities and the HKSAR.

Thirdly, as regards the scope of the jurisdiction of the HKSAR courts, article 18 of the first draft had provided that Hong Kong courts should have no jurisdiction over cases concerning matters of defence and foreign affairs, or concerning "executive acts" of the Central People's Government. Under article 19 of the second draft, the exclusion of the courts' jurisdiction is limited to cases concerning "acts of state". This was considered an improvement, as the concept of "act of state" already existed in English common law and was well understood by judges and lawyers in Hong Kong.

Fourthly, as regards the enactment of legislation in the HKSAR to safeguard national security, article 22 of the first draft had provided that the HKSAR should prohibit by law any act that harms national unity or subverts the Central People's Government. The wording of the prohibited acts was changed in article 23 of the second draft to treason, splitting up the country (secession), sedition and theft of state secrets.

Less than two months after the publication of the second draft of the Basic Law, the student movement sparked off by the mourning of the death of Hu Yaobang, former liberal-minded Chinese Communist Party (CCP) General Secretary, began to engulf Beijing, culminating in the infamous "June 4th incident" at Tiananmen Square. Hong Kong saw the largest demonstrations in its history, in which hundreds of thousands of people marched in support of the student movement and in protest against the crackdown. The actions taken by the Chinese authorities to quell the student movement precipitated an unprecedented crisis of confidence in Hong Kong.

For a while, all activities of the BLCC were suspended. Szeto Wah and Martin Lee – two members of the BLDC who had led the Hong Kong protests and formed the "Hong Kong Alliance in Support of Patriotic Democratic Movements in China" – were expelled from the BLDC. Two other members – Louis Cha and Bishop Peter Kwong Kong-kit – resigned from it of their own accord.

Generally speaking, the demand in the Hong Kong community for more rapid democratisation grew stronger than ever before.[9] Even some leading members of the BPG now joined forces with the "moderates" and some of the "democrats" to propose a new model of the political system known as the "4-4-2 model". Compared to the BPG's previous proposals, the new "4-4-2 model" incorporated more directly elected elements and allowed a faster pace of democratisation. At the same time, Unofficial Members of the Executive and Legislative Councils jointly promoted a model with even more democratic components. The British government proposed further revisions to the draft Basic Law on a large number of issues, including speedier democratisation in Hong Kong. Sino-British diplomacy behind the scene finally led to a "compromise" regarding an increased number of directly elected LegCo members in 1991 and an arrangement on the "through train" transition of the last colonial LegCo elected in 1995 to become the first LegCo in 1997.[10]

The ninth and last plenary session of the BLDC was held in Beijing in February 1990. Revisions to the second draft of the Basic Law were finalised and voted on. The final version of the draft was presented to the NPC on March 28, 1990, and adopted by it on April 4, 1990. The process of the drafting of the Basic Law, which took four years and eight months, was finally concluded.

Comparing the finally enacted version of the Basic Law with the second draft published in 1989, the most significant new provisions in the final version are those on the electoral arrangements for the Chief Executive (CE) and LegCo. On other matters, the difference between the final version and the second draft is considerably less than that between the first and the second drafts.

It is noteworthy that in the final version, the provisions regarding the qualifications for the CE, principal officials, Executive Council members and the majority of LegCo members were tightened to exclude those with a right of abode in foreign countries. In previous drafts, the qualifications related to Chinese nationality and Hong Kong permanent resident status but did not expressly include the absence of a right of abode overseas. As regards article 23 of the Basic Law, the final version reinstated the concept of subversion in the first draft, adding it to the other prohibited acts in article 23 of the second draft. Also added to article 23 was a prohibition on foreign political bodies from engaging in political activities in the HKSAR, and a prohibition on Hong Kong political bodies from establishing ties with foreign political bodies.

Developments in the Period of Transition 1990–1997

In 1991, 18 of the seats in LegCo were opened to direct election by universal suffrage for the first time. The "pro-democracy" politicians, who had led the massive demonstrations in Hong Kong in support of the student movement in Beijing in 1989, won a landslide victory.[11]

In 1992, the newly arrived Governor of Hong Kong, Christopher Patten, announced an ambitious plan for electoral reform in Hong Kong which involved a radical broadening of the franchise of functional constituencies (increasing the number of eligible voters in these constituencies from less than 100,000 to over two million).[12] The Chinese Government condemned the plan as being inconsistent with the Basic Law and the agreement reached in 1990 between the Chinese and British Governments. In

1993, 17 rounds of negotiation were held between the two governments but no settlement was reached. Governor Patten then unilaterally put the bill for the reform to LegCo, which passed it by a narrow majority. The 1995 LegCo election was thus conducted in accordance with the new electoral scheme.[13] The Chinese Government responded by "establishing another stove", rescinding its previous consent to the LegCo elected in 1995 continuing as the first LegCo of the HKSAR in 1997. Arrangements were made for the establishment of a Provisional Legislative Council in 1997 to take charge of Hong Kong legislative matters before the first LegCo could be elected in accordance with the Basic Law.[14]

The last major development in the colonial legal system was the enactment of the Hong Kong Bill of Rights Ordinance in 1991.[15] This legislative measure was part of the British Hong Kong Government's response to the crisis of confidence in Hong Kong arising from the 4 June incident. The Hong Kong Bill of Rights Ordinance translated into domestic law the provisions of the International Covenant on Civil and Political Rights (ICCPR) which Britain had already applied to Hong Kong in 1976. Corresponding amendments were made to the Letters Patent – Hong Kong's constitutional instrument.[16] Under the new constitutional regime, Hong Kong courts were empowered to review and to strike down laws and administrative actions that the courts determined to be inconsistent with the human rights guarantees in the Hong Kong Bill of Rights or the ICCPR. Since 1991, a body of case law has developed in which Hong Kong courts exercised this power of constitutional review and applied principles of "proportionality" to check whether a restriction on a relevant right is constitutional.[17]

The Implementation of the Basic Law, 1997–2021

The Exercise of Powers by the Central Authorities

Under the Basic Law, the major powers which the central government has over the HKSAR include those provided for in articles 17 (invalidation of Hong Kong legislation), 18 (application of national laws to Hong Kong), 158 (interpretation of the Basic Law) and 159 (amendment of the Basic Law) of the Basic Law. Some but not all of these powers have been exercised since the Basic Law came into in 1997.

The NPCSC has not exercised its power under article 17 to nullify a SAR law that exceeds the scope of the SAR's autonomy. Under article 18, national laws (as listed in Annex III to the Basic Law) may be applied to the SAR. There are currently 14 national laws listed in Annex III, including the Nationality Law, National Flag Law, Law on the Territorial Sea, Law on the Garrisoning of the HKSAR, Regulations on Diplomatic Privileges and Immunities and the HKSAR National Security Law.[18] The NPC has not exercised its power under article 159 to amend the Basic Law, although in 2021 it authorised the NPCSC to amend Annexes I and II to the Basic Law, which govern the electoral system in the HKSAR. The amendments were introduced in March 2021.

Under article 158 of the Basic Law, the NPCSC may issue an interpretation of the Basic Law. Five interpretations have been issued so far. The first interpretation was promulgated in 1999 on articles 22 and 24 of the Basic Law relating to the right of abode in the SAR of children born in the mainland of Hong Kong permanent residents. This interpretation was issued because the SAR government submitted to the central government a request for interpretation after the Court of Final Appeal (CFA) rendered its decisions in early 1999 in the cases of *Ng Ka Ling*[19] and *Chan Kam Nga*.[20] The

Government had estimated that the CFA's interpretation of the relevant Basic Law provisions (with which it disagreed) would result in 1.67 million mainland residents being entitled to migrate to Hong Kong in the next ten years. Responding to the CE's request for interpretation, the NPCSC issued its interpretation in June 1999, overruling the CFA's interpretation.[21] In *Lau Kong Yung*,[22] the CFA considered the effect of the NPCSC interpretation. The court recognised its binding force and retroactive effect (in the sense that it stated the true legal position at the time the Basic Law came into force), as well as the "free-standing" power of the NPCSC to promulgate an interpretation of any Basic Law provision at any time.

After 1999, the NPCSC has exercised the power of Basic Law interpretation on four other occasions. In 2004, acting on its own initiative (instead of at the request of the CE of the HKSAR), the NPCSC issued an interpretation of the Basic Law provisions relating to the procedure of electoral reform. In 2005, upon the request of the Acting CE of the HKSAR, the NPCSC issued an interpretation to clarify the term of office of a CE who succeeds one who resigns before completing his term of office. In 2011, the CFA in the *Congo* case[23] used for the first time the reference procedure in article 158(3) of the Basic Law to refer certain Basic Law provisions relating to foreign affairs and "acts of state" to the NPCSC for interpretation. This *Congo* case concerned whether the applicable law of foreign sovereign immunity in the HKSAR was the same as that in the mainland. In November 2016, the NPCSC, acting on its own initiative, issued an interpretation of article 104 of the Basic Law, which relates to the oath-taking requirements applicable to officials, judges and members of the Legislative and Executive Councils. This interpretation was particularly controversial, as it was issued three days after Hong Kong's High Court heard a case on oath-taking and before the court delivered judgement in that case. In this case,[24] the government argued that two pro-"Hong Kong independence" Legislative Councillors had been disqualified by reason of their failure to comply with the oath-taking requirements stipulated in article 104 of the Basic Law and other Hong Kong legislation.

In addition to interpretations, the NPCSC has also promulgated three decisions on electoral reform in Hong Kong[25], two decisions on "co-location" of mainland and Hong Kong immigration checkpoints in the Shenzhen Bay Port and the West Kowloon Express Rail Station, respectively,[26] and two decisions in 2020 on the extension of the term of office of the sixth-term Legislative Council (2016–2020) and the qualifications of LegCo members, respectively.[27]

The Development of the Political System

Shortly after the handover, the colonial system of "three-tier" government (LegCo; Urban and Regional Councils; District Boards) was reformed to become a "two-tier" one. This took place in 2000, when the Government introduced a new framework for the administration of municipal affairs[28] under which the Urban Council and the Regional Council were abolished. Their existing functions were partly transferred to the LegCo and partly to the Government itself. At the same time, the existing District Boards were reformed and reconstituted District Councils, of which there are 18. These district bodies consisted of a majority of elected members and a minority of appointed members, until appointed seats were phased out in 2015.[29]

Since direct elections to portions of LegCo seats were introduced in Hong Kong in the 1990s, a distinctive mode of political polarisation came into existence in Hong

Kong, which continued to shape Hong Kong politics after 1997 until the electoral reform of 2021.[30] This was the division of Hong Kong's political forces between pro-China forces (also known after 1997 as "pro-Establishment" forces) and pro-democracy forces (the "pan-democrats" and subsequently also the "localists").[31] The pro-China camp supports the policies of the PRC government towards Hong Kong, including its cautious and gradualist approach to Hong Kong's democratisation. This camp also supports, or recognises the legitimacy of, the CCP-led regime in mainland China and generally refrains from criticising its human rights record. On the other hand, the pan-democrats advocate Western-style liberal democracy for Hong Kong. They are critical of authoritarian one-party rule in China and its human rights record. Since geographical constituency-based direct election by universal suffrage to a portion of LegCo seats was introduced in Hong Kong in 1991, the pro-democracy politicians consistently succeeded in capturing approximately 55–60% of the popular votes for that portion of LegCo seats elected by universal suffrage. The pattern remained unchanged after 1997 and continued up to 2016 (the year of the last LegCo election before the electoral reform of 2021).[32]

Since the establishment of the HKSAR, the effectiveness of governance in Hong Kong has depended on a loose coalition of pro-China political parties and independent legislators, who collectively occupied the majority of seats in LegCo.[33] But there has never been any ruling party in the HKSAR. No single political party has ever occupied the majority of, or any number close to half of the seats in LegCo. As provided for in the Basic Law, the CE is elected by an Election Committee (EC). Most of the members of this Committee did not belong to any political party, but the majority of the Committee's members have generally been considered "pro-China" rather than supportive of the pan-democrats. Members of the pro-China camp in LegCo are generally supportive of the CE and his or her administration, although such support cannot be guaranteed in every instance of policy, bill or item of financial expenditure, because these elected legislators have to be answerable to their own constituencies. In practice, the Liaison Office of the Central People's Government in Hong Kong has played a significant role – informal rather than constitutionally ordained – in promoting, coordinating and supporting this pro-China camp of politicians in Hong Kong. This is the strategy of the "patriotic United Front", a long-standing practice in the history of the CCP involving cultivation of, cooperation with and building a political alliance with, friends and supporters of the CCP for the purpose of achieving the CCP's objectives.[34]

A watershed event in the post-1997 history of Hong Kong was the HKSAR government's attempt to enact a national security law for the purpose of implementing article 23 of the Basic Law, which requires the HKSAR to enact laws on treason, secession, sedition, subversion and protection of state secrets. The legislative exercise was aborted after a march of an estimated half-million people on July 1, 2003, to protest against the bill.[35]

The pan-democrats, who led the social movement against the bill, then launched a movement to demand the speedy democratisation of the HKSAR.[36] Pro-democracy politicians found in the Basic Law a powerful source of legitimacy for their demands. The Basic Law allows changes to the existing system for the election of the third-term CE in 2007 and the fourth-term LegCo in 2008. Thus, the pan-democrats' slogan was "double universal suffrage": the introduction of universal suffrage for the election of the CE in 2007 and universal suffrage for the election of all legislators in 2008.

In early 2004, Beijing responded to the democracy movement in Hong Kong. On April 6, 2004, the NPCSC issued an interpretation of the Basic Law, which elaborates upon Annexes I and II to the Basic Law by stipulating a procedure for initiating changes to the relevant electoral methods. The procedure requires the CE to submit a report to the NPCSC on whether there is a need to introduce electoral reform, whereupon the NPCSC will decide on the matter. After this interpretation was promulgated, CE Tung Chee Hwa submitted a relevant report to the NPCSC on April 15, 2004. Another session of the NPCSC was immediately convened to consider the report, and on April 26, the NPCSC promulgated its Decision on the matter. The Decision ruled out the introduction of universal suffrage for the CE and all legislators in 2007 and 2008, respectively, but permitted political reforms in 2007 and 2008 within certain parameters.[37]

In October 2005, Donald Tsang, who had succeeded Tung Chee Hwa following the latter's resignation from the office of CE in spring 2005, introduced an electoral reform proposal for 2007–2008. On December 21, 2005, the proposal was rejected by 24 "pan-democrats" in LegCo voting against it, mainly on the grounds that it was not democratic enough and that the Government had failed to provide a timetable for the introduction of universal suffrage.[38]

In December 2007, Donald Tsang, who had been re-elected CE for another term, initiated again the procedure for electoral reform. On December 29, 2007, the NPCSC decided that neither the CE nor all legislators may be elected by universal suffrage in 2012, though the electoral arrangements for the CE and LegCo in 2012 may be reformed within certain parameters. The Decision also stated that "the election of the fifth CE of the HKSAR in the year 2017 may be implemented by the method of universal suffrage; that after the CE is selected by universal suffrage, the election of the LegCo of the HKSAR may be implemented by the method of electing all the members by universal suffrage".[39]

In April 2010, Tsang introduced an electoral reform proposal for the 2012 CE and LegCo elections. Again the pan-democrats opposed the proposal on the ground that it was not democratic enough. Ten days before the proposal was to be voted on by LegCo, the Government decided to grant a major concession to the pan-democrats by modifying the proposal substantially to adopt the Democratic Party's counter-proposal regarding five additional District Councils' seats in LegCo being elected by all voters in Hong Kong who did not already have the right to vote in any existing functional constituency. With the support of the Democratic Party, the Government secured the necessary two-thirds majority in LegCo for the electoral reform to be passed on June 24–25, 2010.[40]

As the NPCSC in its 2007 Decision had set 2017 as the target date for the implementation of universal suffrage for the election of the CE, pro-democracy activists in Hong Kong began in 2013 to focus their attention on the precise model for such election. Benny Tai, associate professor of law at the University of Hong Kong, proposed the idea of an "Occupy Central" campaign to put pressure on Beijing and the HKSAR government to introduce a model for universal suffrage that is consistent with international standards of democratic elections.[41]

On July 15, 2014, CE C.Y. Leung initiated the procedure for electoral reform and submitted a report to the NPCSC. On August 31, 2014, the NPCSC rendered its Decision on electoral reform in the HKSAR. It stated that the "broadly representative nominating committee" that would nominate candidates for election of the CE by universal suffrage in accordance with article 45 of the Basic Law should be modelled on the existing EC. "The nominating committee shall nominate two to three candidates .... Each candidate must have the endorsement of more than half of all the members of the nominating committee". The Decision explained that "the principle that the Chief Executive has to be a person who loves the country and loves Hong Kong must be upheld. ... The method for selecting the Chief Executive by universal suffrage must provide corresponding institutional safeguards for this purpose".

Pro-democracy forces in Hong Kong condemned the electoral model as "fake universal suffrage": given the proposed composition of the nominating committee, only pro-China political figures and no pan-democrats were likely to gain majority support from the nominating committee and thus become candidates in the election of the CE by universal suffrage.[42] In protest, students and other democracy activists launched the "Occupy Central Movement", also known as the "Umbrella Movement", which started in late September and continued until mid-December 2014.[43] On June 18, 2015, LegCo rejected the bill to introduce universal suffrage for the election of the CE; with the pan-democrats voting against it, it failed to secure the requisite two-thirds majority for the amendment of Annex I to the Basic Law.

Developments in 2016–2021

After the failure of political reform in 2015, the new generation of political activists who came on the scene[44] distanced themselves from the traditional pan-democrats, who since the 1980s had struggled to realise democracy in Hong Kong within the constitutional framework of "One Country, Two Systems". These younger activists believed that the authoritarian PRC regime would not tolerate the existence in the HKSAR of a genuine democracy. Thus, they went one step further to question the premise that Hong Kong should remain part of the PRC. Political activists who held such views became known as the "localists". Some of the "localists" advocated self-determination or even independence for Hong Kong.[45]

In the LegCo election of September 2016, some "localists" were barred from being candidates in the election, on the ground that their political views were inconsistent with the declarations they had signed (as required by the electoral law) that they would uphold the Basic Law and owe allegiance to the HKSAR.[46] Despite this move, a total of six "localists" were elected into LegCo in this election, collectively capturing 19% of the popular votes.[47] The success of the "localists" proved to be short-lived, as some of them were subsequently stripped of their LegCo seats by the court on the ground of their failure to comply with the oath-taking requirement in the Basic Law and local legislation.[48] These "disqualification" cases were particularly controversial as the NPCSC intervened in the course of the judicial proceedings in the first "disqualification" case by issuing an interpretation of article 104 of the Basic Law (which concerns the oath-taking requirement). In the by-elections held to fill the vacancies arising from the disqualification of these legislators, some "localists" were again barred from participation.[49]

The escalating tension between opposition politicians and the government reached a climax in 2019 during the social movement against a proposed extradition law, which gave rise to massive protests, riots, and half a year of civil unrest unprecedented in the history of the HKSAR. A murder committed in Taiwan by a Hong Kong resident prompted the HKSAR government to introduce in March 2019 the Fugitive Offenders and Mutual Legal Assistance in Criminal Matters Legislation (Amendment) Bill, which provided for *ad hoc* extradition on a case-by-case basis between Hong Kong and any other jurisdiction, including Taiwan, Macau and mainland China. The bill was considered necessary because although Hong Kong's existing law provided for extradition pursuant to treaties between Hong Kong and foreign states, it did not allow rendition between Hong

Kong and another part of China, and under HKSAR law, Taiwan is part of China. Opponents of the bill perceived it as putting innocent Hongkongers at risk of being extradited to mainland China, where (it was feared that) they might not receive a fair trial. Massive protests resulted in the bill being shelved on June 15; on September 4, the CE announced that the bill would be formally withdrawn when the new LegCo session opened in October.[50]

Nonetheless, protests continued for several months, with protesters expressing dissatisfaction that the government had only accepted one of the "five principal demands" of the movement.[51] The "five demands" had included the withdrawal of the bill, independent investigation of alleged police brutalities during the social movement, official acknowledgement that the protest against the bill was not a "riot", non-prosecution of protesters and introduction of universal suffrage for the election of the CE and all legislators. The "five demands" enjoyed popular support, as evidenced by the fact that pan-democrats and other opposition activists who voiced these demands in their election campaign secured an unprecedented victory in the District Council election on November 24, 2019.[52] In spring 2020, the social movement subsided with the onset of COVID-19.

In a surprise move in May 2020, the NPC rendered a decision to plug what it considered a legislative gap made obvious by the anti-extradition movement. Given that the HKSAR had – for 23 years after the Basic Law came into effect – failed to discharge its constitutional duty of implementing article 23 of the Basic Law, the central government now asserted that it could legitimately intervene to fill the void. Pursuant to the NPC's authorisation, the NPCSC at the end of June 2020 enacted the Law on Safeguarding National Security in the HKSAR (NSL) and invoked article 18 of the Basic Law in adding the law to Annex III to the Basic Law for the purpose of application in Hong Kong. The NSL creates four types of offences relating to secession, subversion, terrorism and collusion with foreign forces to endanger national security. Although the NSL empowers Hong Kong's law enforcement authorities and courts to investigate, prosecute and try cases arising from the NSL, it also establishes a national security office in Hong Kong that is directly under the central government and confers on it powers of investigation and transfer of suspects to the mainland for trial in certain exceptional circumstances.[53]

The NSL was highly controversial and attracted international attention. Some countries imposed sanctions against Hong Kong and the PRC or their officials on the ground that the NSL threatens civil liberties and infringes upon Hong Kong's autonomy. The full effect of the implementation of the NSL remains to be seen.[54]

The NSL was the first of two measures forming a single package introduced by Beijing to restore the practice of "One Country, Two Systems" to what Beijing considered to be the correct path after the deviations and disturbances that began with the Occupy Central movement and culminated in the anti-extradition movement. The second measure was an overhaul of Hong Kong's electoral system introduced by the NPC Decision on Improving the Electoral System of the HKSAR (dated March 11, 2021), in pursuance of which the NPCSC amended Annexes I and II to the Basic Law.[55] The amendments significantly changed the existing electoral system.

The declared purpose of the reform was to provide institutional safeguards for the implementation of the principles of "patriots ruling Hong Kong" and "executive-led government" and to restore effective governance in the HKSAR.[56] In practical terms, the general orientation of the electoral reform is to significantly reduce the number of seats which the "pan-democrats" or other opposition politicians could hope to win in the EC and in LegCo. This is achieved by, for example, reducing the number of LegCo seats that are elected by universal suffrage from 35 to 20, abolishing the five District Councils' seats created by the 2010 political reform, creating 40 new LegCo seats elected by the EC, reconstituting the EC and replacing voting by individuals with corporate voting in sub-sectors of the EC that previously practised voting by individuals.[57] As a result, the EC elected in September 2021 was entirely dominated by pro-Establishment forces. In the LegCo election on December 19, 2021, pro-Establishment forces won 89 of the 90 LegCo seats.

Conclusion

Political tensions and conflicts between the "pro-China" and "pro-democracy" camps have plagued the process of the implementation of the Basic Law. Political instability in post-1997 Hong Kong can be attributed to the inherent contradiction between the "two systems" within "One Country, Two Systems" (the authoritarian party-led system in the mainland and a semi-democratic system with some elements of liberal constitutionalism in Hong Kong). In retrospect, it seems that some of the major difficulties and controversies can actually be traced back to the history of the drafting of the Basic Law itself in the late 1980s.

For example, in retrospect, the requirement in article 23 of the Basic Law that the HKSAR should on its own legislate to safeguard national security was based on an over-optimistic assessment of the determination of the HKSAR government and the willingness of the populace in Hong Kong to implement article 23. Moreover, the commitment in the Basic Law to the eventual realisation of democracy as universal suffrage (in the election of the CE and all legislators) resulted in "an inherently unstable regime, because [the regime] will be taken to task to deliver" with regard to the constitutional promise of universal suffrage.[58] Thus, the political system of the HKSAR – which could not be changed without the consent of both the central government and (before the Basic Law amendment in 2021) a two-thirds majority in the HKSAR legislature – was unstable and lacked sufficient legitimacy. In affirming the ultimate goals of universal suffrage, the Basic Law legitimises the struggle for such universal suffrage and, in a sense, de-legitimises the existing political system that falls short of the ideal of universal suffrage.

After the failure of "Occupy Central", some democracy activists in Hong Kong gave up the hope of achieving democratisation within the framework of "One Country, Two Systems" and became advocates of Hong Kong's self-determination or independence. They participated actively in the "anti-extradition bill" movement of 2019. Thus, dissatisfaction with an existing system of autonomy may ultimately lead to demands for secession. The case of Hong Kong illustrates this logic at work. In response, the PRC authorities enacted the NSL in 2020 and introduced the electoral reforms of 2021. These developments may be interpreted as being designed to assert the absolute priority of the "One Country" principle over the "Two Systems" principle in OCTS, and to crush secessionist demands once and for all.

Notes

1 For the history of the negotiation of the Joint Declaration, see Steve Tsang, *Hong Kong: An Appointment with China* (I.B. Tauris 1997); Chung Sze-yuen, *Hong Kong's Journey to Reunification* (Chinese University Press 2001); Percy Cradock, *Experiences of China* (John Murray 1994).

2 See generally Emily Lau, 'The Early History of the Drafting Process', in Peter Wesley-Smith and Albert Chen (eds), *The Basic Law and Hong Kong's Future* (Butterworths 1988) ch 6 (90–104).

3 See generally Albert H.Y. Chen and Michael Ng, 'The Making of the Constitutional Order of the Hong Kong SAR: The Role of Sino-British Diplomacy (1982-90)', in Kevin Tan and Michael Ng (eds), *Constitutional Foundings in Northeast Asia* (Hart 2021) ch 3.

4 On the history of the drafting of the Basic Law, see the following sources on which the following account is largely based: Ming K. Chan and David J. Clark (eds), *The Hong Kong Basic Law* (Hong Kong University Press 1991); Wang Shuwen (ed), *Introduction to the Basic Law of the Hong Kong Special Administrative Region* (Beijing, Law Press 2000); Wen Wei Po (ed), *Jibenfa de dansheng* (*The Birth of the Basic Law*) (Hong Kong, Xianggang wenhui chubanshe 1990); Zhang Jiefeng, Yang Jianxing, Lu Yongxiong and Chen Luqian, *Bubian wushinian? Zhong Ying Gang jueli Jibenfa* (*No Change, For Fifty Years? China, Britain and Hong Kong Struggle Over the Basic Law*) (Hong Kong, Langchao chubanshe 1991).

5 See generally Albert H.Y. Chen, 'Development of Representative Government' in Johannes Chan and C.L. Lim (eds), *Law of the Hong Kong Constitution* (3rd edn, Sweet & Maxwell 2021) ch 8.

6 See generally Ming Sing, *Hong Kong's Tortuous Democratization* (RoutledgeCurzon 2004); Alvin Y. So, *Hong Kong's Embattled Democracy* (John Hopkins University Press 1999); Zhang Jiefeng et al. (n 4 above).

7 See generally William McGurn (ed), *Basic Law, Basic Questions* (Hong Kong, Review Publishing Co. 1988).

8 In internal communications within the British government, its Foreign and Commonwealth Office expressed the view that 'all the provisions of the Joint Declaration [were] reflected in the [second] draft Basic Law': see Chen and Ng (n 3 above), note 120 and the accompanying text.

9 Sing (n 6 above) 114–122; So (n 6 above) 155–182.

10 Chen and Ng (n 3 above).

11 See Lau Siu-kai and Louie Kin-sheun (eds), *Hong Kong Tried Democracy: The 1991 Elections in Hong Kong* (Hong Kong Institute of Asia-Pacific Studies, Chinese University of Hong Kong 1993).

12 See So (n 6 above), ch 7.

13 See Kuan Hsin-chi et al. (eds), *The 1995 Legislative Council Elections in Hong Kong* (Hong Kong Institute of Asia-Pacific Studies, Chinese University of Hong Kong 1996).

14 See Kuan Hsin-chi et al. (eds), *Power Transfer and Electoral Politics: The First Legislative Election in the Hong Kong Special Administrative Region* (Chinese University Press 1999).

15 See Johannes Chan and Yash Ghai (eds), *The Hong Kong Bill of Rights: A Comparative Approach* (Butterworths Asia 1993).

16 These amendments sought to ensure that the laws of Hong Kong would be consistent with the human rights standards set out in the ICCPR. See Andrew Byrnes and Johannes Chan (eds), *Public Law and Human Rights: A Hong Kong Sourcebook* (Butterworths 1993).

17 *See* Albert H.Y. Chen, "The Interpretation of the Basic Law – Common Law and Mainland Chinese Perspectives" (2000) 30 Hong Kong Law Journal 380, 418–420. The operative force of the Hong Kong Bill of Rights and Hong Kong courts' power of judicial review of legislation on human rights grounds and related principles of proportionality have survived the handover: see, e.g., *Ng Kung Siu* (1999) 2 HKCFAR 442; *Leung Kwok Hung* (2005) 8 HKCFAR 229.

18 Annex III has been amended four times after 1997, resulting in four national laws being added: Law on the Exclusive Economic Zone and the Continental Shelf (added in 1998); Law on Judicial Immunity from Compulsory Measures Concerning the Property of Foreign Central Banks (2005); National Anthem Law (2017); Law on Safeguarding National Security in the HKSAR (2020).

19 (1999) 2 HKCFAR 4.

20 (1999) 2 HKCFAR 82.

21 Under article 158 of the Basic Law, the NPCSC's interpretation did not have the effect of reversing the CFA's judgements and orders concerning the litigants in the *Ng* and *Chan* cases; it only meant that Hong Kong courts in future cases must follow the NPCSC's interpretation instead of the CFA's interpretation of the relevant Basic Law provisions.

22 (1999) 2 HKCFAR 300.

23 (2011) 14 HKCFAR 95, 395.
24 See n 48 below.
25 These decisions were promulgated in 2004, 2007 and 2014, respectively, in accordance with the procedure established by the 2004 Interpretation of the NPCSC.
26 For litigation relating to the NPCSC decision on December 27, 2017 on co-location in the West Kowloon express rail station, see *Leung Chung Hang v. President of Legislative Council* [2018] HKCFI 2657, [2021] HKCA 871 (co-location scheme upheld by the courts).
27 The first decision was made in August 2020 after the HKSAR Government decided, in view of the pandemic, to postpone the LegCo election originally scheduled for September 2020. The second decision, made in November 2020, had the effect of disqualifying four members of the sixth-term LegCo from continuing to serve during its extended term, as they had been disqualified by returning officers from being candidates in the LegCo election originally scheduled for September 2020.
28 See the Provision of Municipal Services (Reorganisation) Ordinance.
29 See the amendment enacted in 2013 to the District Councils Ordinance.
30 The following discussion draws on my chapter, 'The Autonomy of Hong Kokng under "One Country, Two Systems"', in Tai-lok Lui, Stephen Chiu and Ray Yep (eds), *Routledge Handbook of Contemporary Hong Kong* (Routledge 2019) 33–51 at 42–44.
31 Ngok Ma, "The Rise of "Anti-China" Sentiments in Hong Kong and the 2012 Legislative Council Elections" (2015) 15 China Review 39; Jinhyeok Jang, "Competing Political Visions in the Legislative Council of Hong Kong" (2016) 21 Journal of Chinese Political Science 89.
32 Ngok Ma, *Political Development in Hong Kong* (Hong Kong University Press, Hong Kong, 2007) 154, 223; Ma (n 31) 58, 62; This was the case in LegCo elections. The pro-China forces usually performed better in elections to District Councils, which do not have lawmaking power and are only concerned with district affairs. However, under the influence of the social movement against the extradition bill in 2019, pro-democracy politicians secured an unprecedented victory in the District Council election on November 24, 2019, in which they won 57% of the popular vote and 85% of the seats. See *Ming Pao* (Chinese newspaper), November 26, 2019.
33 Percy LT Lui, 'The Legislature', in Wai-man Lam et al. (eds), *Contemporary Hong Kong Government and Politics* (2nd edn, Hong Kong University Press 2012) 45–65.
34 See generally Sonny SH Lo, SCF Hung and JHC Loo, *China's New United Front Work in Hong Kong: Penetrative Politics and Its Implications* (Palgrave Macmillan 2019); Eliza Lee, "United Front, Clientelism, and Indirect Rule: Theorizing the Role of the Liaison Office in Hong Kong" (2020) 29 Journal of Contemporary China 763 <https://doi.org/10.1080/10670564.2019.1704996>.
35 See generally Hualing Fu et al. (eds), *National Security and Fundamental Freedoms: Hong Kong's Article 23 Under Scrutiny* (Hong Kong University Press 2005); Ngok Ma, "Civil Society in Self-defence: The Struggle against National Security Legislation in Hong Kong" (2005) 14 Journal of Contemporary China 465–482.
36 See generally Ming Sing, "Public Support for Democracy in Hong Kong" (2005) 12 Democratization 244–261. The following discussion draws on my chapter, "The Development of Representative Government" (n 5 above).
37 See generally Albert H.Y. Chen, "The Constitutional Controversy of Spring 2004" (2004) 34 Hong Kong Law Journal 215.
38 See generally Albert H.Y. Chen, "The Fate of the Constitutional Reform Proposal of October 2005" (2005) 35 Hong Kong Law Journal 537.
39 See Albert H.Y. Chen, "A New Era in Hong Kong's Constitutional History" (2008) 38 Hong Kong Law Journal 1.
40 See generally Albert H.Y. Chen, "An Unexpected Breakthrough in Hong Kong's Constitutional Reform" (2010) 40 Hong Kong Law Journal 259.
41 See generally Alvin Y. Cheung, "Road to Nowhere: Hong Kong's Democratization and China's Obligations Under Public International Law" (2014) 40 Brooklyn Journal of International Law 465, 494–498; Michael C. Davis, "The Basic Law, Universal Suffrage and Rule of Law in Hong Kong" (2015) 38 Hastings International and Comparative Law Review 275, 289.
42 See Albert H.Y. Chen, "The Law and Politics of the Struggle for Universal Suffrage in Hong Kong, 2013-15" (2016) 3 Asian Journal of Law and Society 189; Cora Chan, "Legalizing Politics:

An Evaluation of Hong Kong's Recent Attempt at Democratization" (2017) 16 Election Law Journal 296.

43 See generally Yongshun Cai, *The Occupy Movement in Hong Kong* (Routledge 2017); Ching Kwan Lee and Ming Sing (eds), *Take Back Our Future: An Eventful Sociology of the Hong Kong Umbrella Movement* (Ithaca, ILR Press 2019); Ngok Ma and Edmond W Cheng (eds), *The Umbrella Movement: Civil Resistance and Contentious Space in Hong Kong* (Amsterdam University Press 2019).

44 See generally Sonny S.H. Lo, "Ideologies and Factionalism in Beijing-Hong Kong Relations" (2018) 58 Asian Survey 392.

45 For the "localist" turn in Hong Kong politics since the 2012 LegCo election, see Ngok Ma, "The Rise of 'Anti-China' Sentiments in Hong Kong and the 2012 Legislative Council Elections" (2015) 15 China Review 39; Joseph Y.S. Cheng (ed), *New Trends of Political Participation in Hong Kong* (City University of Hong Kong Press 2014); Iam-chong Ip, *Hong Kong's New Identity Politics* (Routledge 2020).

46 Chan Ho Tin, one of the disqualified candidates, subsequently brought an election petition to challenge the returning officer's decision not to allow him to be a candidate, but failed before the Court of First Instance: *Chan Ho Tin v Lo Ying Ki Alan* [2018] HKCFI 345. The case was not appealed to a higher court.

47 "Localists and self-determination activists capture 6 seats, LegCo divided into 3 factions" and "Localist self-determination politicians capture 400,000 votes", Ming Pao, 6 September 2016 (in Chinese); C.K. Choy and J.M. Chan, "A preliminary analysis of the outcome of the LegCo election", Ming Pao, 6 September 2016 (in Chinese).

48 The first "disqualification" case related to Leung Chung Hang and Yau Wai Ching: *Chief Executive of the HKSAR v President of the Legislative Council and Leung Chung Hang Sixtus*, HCAL 185/2016 (CFI), [2017] 1 HKLRD 460 (CA), (2017) 20 HKCFAR 390 (leave to appeal refused by CFA). Four other Legislative Councillors were subsequently also disqualified on the ground of failure to take their oaths properly: *Nathan Law Kwun Chung* [2017] 4 HKLRD 115 (CFI), *Leung Kwok Hung* [2019] HKCA 173 (CA). For an analysis, see Han Zhu and A.H.Y. Chen, "The Oath-taking Cases and the NPCSC Interpretation of 2016" (2019) 49 Hong Kong Law Journal 381.

49 See, e.g., *Chow Ting v Teng Yu Yan* [2019] HKCFI 2135; *Au Nok Hin v Teng Yu Yan Anne* [2019] HKCFA 50; *Lau Wing Hong v Chan Yuen Man* [2019] HKCFI 2287.

50 The bill was formally withdrawn in LegCo on October 23, 2020. See generally Albert H.Y. Chen, "A Perfect Storm: Hong Kong-China rendition of fugitive offenders, 2019" (2019) 49 Hong Kong Law Journal 419.

51 For the anti-extradition bill movement, see generally Sonny Shiu-hing Lo, Steven Hung and Jeff Loo, *The Dynamics of Peaceful and Violent Protests in Hong Kong: The Anti-extradition Movement* (Palgrave Macmillan 2021); Z. Ibrahim and J. Lam (eds), *Rebel City: Hong Kong's Year of Water and Fire* (Singapore, World Scientific 2020).

52 See n 32 above.

53 See generally Hualing Fu and Michael Hor (eds), *The National Security Law of Hong Kong: Restoration and Transformation* (Hong Kong University Press, 2022).

54 The major judicial decisions in the first and a half year of the NSL's implementation include *HKSAR v. Lai Chee Ying* [2021] HKCFA 3; *Tong Ying Kit v. Secretary for Justice* [2021] HKCA 912; *HKSAR v. Tong Ying Kit* [2021] HKCFI 2200, [2021] HKCFI 2239; *HKSAR v. Ma Chun Man* [2021] HKDC 1325, [2021] HKDC 1406; *HKSAR v. Chung Hon Lam* [2021] HKDC 1484.

55 See Simon N.M. Young, 'The Decision of the National People's Congress on Improving the Electoral System of the Hong Kong Special Administrative Region', [2021] 60 International Legal Materials 1163.

56 See the papers of the LegCo Subcommittee on Decision of the NPC on Improving the Electoral System of the HKSAR, at <https://www.legco.gov.hk/yr20-21/english/hc/sub_com/hs102/agenda/hs10220210401.htm>.

57 See Simon Young, *'Political System Transformation in Hong Kong', VerfBlog,* 13 April 2021, <https://verfassungsblog.de/political-system-transformation-in-hong-kong/>, DOI: 10.17176/20210413-174446-0.

58 H.C. Kuan, "Escape from Politics: Hong Kong's Predicament of Political Development" (1998) 21 International Journal of Public Administration 1423 at 1444.

4

RECONSTITUTING CHINA'S PERIPHERY

Orchestrating Political Convergence via the Hong Kong and Macau Basic Laws

Jason Buhi

Introduction

There has always been a symbiosis between Macau and Hong Kong, two neighboring territories along China's southern coast. Both began their modern history as outposts of European empires, administered by Portugal and Great Britain, respectively. Their proximity to each other and the great terrestrial empires of China ultimately resulted in similar repertoires of governance. Whereas that trend occurred in an ad hoc manner for most of the European colonial period, however, it has been consciously expedited since the consolidation of these territories under a single sovereign.

Macau and Hong Kong were reconstituted as Special Administrative Regions (SARs) of the People's Republic of China (PRC) upon their respective handovers in the late 1990s. Both are now governed under the PRC's "One Country, Two Systems" (OCTS) policy, the doctrinal framework of which rests upon legal foundations codified in similar international treaties and constitutional charters. In the case of Hong Kong, those governing documents are the *Sino-British Joint Declaration* (SBJD) and the *Hong Kong Basic Law* (HKBL)[1]; for Macau, the *Sino-Portuguese Joint Declaration* (SPJD) and the *Macau Basic Law* (MBL).[2] All four documents contain Beijing's promise to honor 50 years of "a high degree of autonomy" for each territory upon its handover to exclusive PRC jurisdiction.[3]

Nonetheless, the future remains uncertain as recent developments are leveling local idiosyncrasies and challenging whether any meaningful degree of political autonomy will be tolerated by the ruling Chinese Communist Party (CCP). Beijing expressed a common vision for Macau and Hong Kong during the handover negotiations, and the recent extension of the PRC's national security apparatus has shifted the OCTS gravity decisively toward the center, expediting what now appears to be an orchestrated convergence of major differences. The question is whether this process will lead to a total or near-total amalgamation of the two ancient autonomies, as current PRC policies suggest.

This chapter traces the historic process of convergence between the two SARs by focusing on major incidents of congruence. Following this introduction, The "European Colonial Era" section begins with a brief review of developments during the pre-handover

DOI: 10.4324/9781003128243-5

period, outlining watershed moments in the otherwise slow, incidental trends of coalescence under separate European administrations. The "Planning the Transition to Chinese Sovereignty" section discusses the shift in gravitational poles from horizontal to vertical as the PRC prepared to resume exclusive control. The processes of negotiating and drafting the Joint Declarations and Basic Laws are analyzed, with codified differences in governing repertoires highlighted. The "Implementation" section examines the implementation of the Basic Laws to date, exploring key moments of top-down-driven convergence between the SARs under PRC administration. Finally, The "Conclusion" section provides concluding observations.

European Colonial Era

Macau and Hong Kong occupy small isthmuses and outlying islands along the sprawling coastline of China's Guangdong Province. Both were sparsely populated villages before the arrival of European empires transformed them into bustling centers of international trade. Portuguese-governed Macau was the capital of intercourse between Europe and Asia for nearly 300 years, until the United Kingdom supplanted it by colonizing Hong Kong in 1841.

Indeed, the deployment of a contemporary model of colonial governance in Hong Kong disrupted the centuries-old status quo of Macau. Prior to the British arrival, Macau was a uniquely autonomous establishment under the shared jurisdiction of both the Chinese and Portuguese empires.[4] Too distant to be managed by Lisbon and too useful to be assimilated by Beijing, the territory enjoyed centuries of *de facto* autonomy through the governance of a locally elected Senate.[5] Its status as a Sino-Portuguese joint venture was suspended in 1846, when Lisbon dispatched a military governor to transform the city into an "executive-led" colony in the frame of Hong Kong – a coup made possible by the proximity of the British Royal Navy.[6] Macau was also forced to follow Hong Kong's example and transform itself into a free port to maintain economic relevancy, ending the practice of financing local government and charitable services from trade duties imposed on foreign commerce.[7]

The two cities' governance diverged again in the 20th century, when Portuguese Macau reintroduced a legislative assembly – albeit one characterized by the indirect election of special interest groups.[8] Those so-called "functional constituencies" were the hallmark of elections under Portugal's fascist *Estado Novo* regime.[9] Portugal's dictator, Antonio Salazar, drew upon contemporary Catholic social thought to implement a form of indirect representation based upon the Medieval European guild system.[10] Rather than vote as individuals, the franchise was shunted through artificial functional constituencies that classified people based on their professions. Given their dependency upon government for privileges (including licenses, permits, and grants), their corporate votes skewed pro-establishment.[11] The model was exported to serve as the legislature in all of Portugal's colonies.[12] Macau's Legislative Assembly underwent several tweaks in the decades that followed, including the addition of some directly elected seats and the appointment of Chinese representatives, but never lost its predominately corporate character.[13]

Functional representation was abruptly discarded across the Portuguese empire as soon as the *Estado Novo* was overthrown in 1974,[14] with one exception: Macau's system was retained at the behest of local establishmentarians.[15] Indeed, a remarkable thing occurred when British Hong Kong finally decided to create a legislature in 1985: although functional constituencies had no prior role in British tradition, they made their way across the Pearl River Delta to become a fixture of Hong Kong's Legislative Council.[16] It is doubtful that proliferation could have occurred without PRC approval.[17] Indeed, by that time, the handovers of Hong Kong and Macau had already been promised.

Planning the Transition to Chinese Sovereignty

The PRC began to take a more active role in pursuing the handovers of Macau and Hong Kong in the 1970s, binding the fates of the territories together. In 1972, the PRC successfully requested that the UN Special Committee on Colonialism reclassify them so that they "not be included in the list of colonial territories covered by the declaration of the granting of independence to colonial countries and people."[18]

Beijing also rebuffed a Portuguese offer to exit Macau in 1974, citing its desire to settle the returns of Macau and Hong Kong at a later date.[19] In reality, the PRC was still then locked in the throes of the Cultural Revolution, and botching the return of Macau may have had catastrophic consequences for the desired acquisitions of Hong Kong and Taiwan. Landmark changes needed to be made to create a solid foundation for any future receipts.

With the rise of Deng Xiaoping and the return of administrative rationality to Beijing in the late 1970s, the CCP set about the formalities prerequisite to reclaiming its coveted irredenta. Two of the PRC's first special economic zones were established in adjacent Shenzhen and Zhuhai in 1980. Then, Deng announced the imminent recovery of both Hong Kong and Macau in June 1982.[20] The current PRC Constitution was promulgated later that year, Article 31 of which establishing that the PRC's National People's Congress (NPC) could create SARs.[21] The PRC simultaneously began its diplomatic push to secure the handovers.

Joint Declarations

In fact, the PRC had already assumed *de facto* control of Macau's Chinese population in the 1960s,[22] and Portugal agreed to a handover in a secret memorandum signed in 1979.[23] Deng decided that securing and detailing Hong Kong's return would take precedence, however, and the negotiations between London and Beijing that resulted in the SBJD treaty lasted from September 1982 to September 1984. Thereafter, the PRC turned its attention back to Macau. The PRC renewed its diplomatic outreach to Portugal in late 1984 and negotiations were set to begin in 1986.

The PRC made its intentions known in the interim. Beijing would attempt to acquire the same handover date for both Hong Kong and Macau, with a state-run newspaper even proposing to integrate both territories into a singular SAR.[24] Libson was incensed by these suggestions and threatened to leave Macau post haste, a maneuver that won the Portuguese significant negotiating leverage.[25]

Whereas the SBJD negotiations took two years, the SPJD took only six months. The process was expedited by the carryover of the PRC negotiating team and its proffering of the SBJD as a template.[26] As such, a comparative review of the documents yields the points of dissent that the Portuguese negotiators were able to secure – not the least of which, of course, was the existence of a separate SAR with its own Basic Law.

The treaty provisions outlining central-local relations are materially identical. SBJD Article 3 and SPJD Article 2 are the most substantive provisions, containing 12 "basic policies" that the PRC promised to pursue regarding its new SARs. Hong Kong and

Macau were each to be constituted under the direct authority of the Central People's Government (CPG) and endowed with "executive, legislative and independent judicial power, including that of final adjudication."[27] Each was further pledged to be a free port, to have its own currency and independent finances, and to enjoy "a high degree of autonomy, except in foreign and defense affairs" to last for 50 years.[28]

Reflections of different colonial-era governing practices remained. For example, Hong Kong and Macau's legacies as common law and civil law legal jurisdictions were acknowledged.[29] This not only recognized the jurisprudential differences but also continued the practice that Macau's governor enjoyed a unique ability to quasi-legislate via executive decree. The composition of the future legislatures emphasized the Macau executive's preeminence as well. Whereas Macau's legislature was promised that "the majority of its members shall be elected," Hong Kong's "shall be constituted by elections."[30] Macau's phrasing continues the late Portuguese-era practice of reserving legislative seats for executive appointment. Nonetheless, it has also ironically, it has also preserved for Macau a higher proportion of directly elected seats than Hong Kong in post-handover practice.

The greatest deviation from Portuguese colonial practice are the provisions on judicial structure. Macau would receive a local court of final adjudication with judges appointed by its Chief Executive (CE) following a recommendation from an "independent commission composed of local judges, lawyers and noted public figures."[31] Never before 1991 had Macau hosted a local court of appeal.[32] This new judicial structure was based upon Hong Kong's, with Macau benefiting from the SBJD template in this regard.[33]

Along with securing a separate handover date, the most seriously contested matter during the SPJD negotiations was the issue of nationality for Macau citizens. The Portuguese sought dual nationality, but PRC law does not recognize dual citizenship. The resolution was annexed to the SPJD.[34] Whereas the British granted "British Dependent Territories" residency status to Hongkongers via its British National Overseas passport, they did not extend an actual right to abode in the United Kingdom. Portugal, meanwhile, was successful in offering what essentially amounts to a passport with the right to abode in Portugal to any applicant born in Macau before 1981.[35]

Annex I of each treaty set the course of things to come, declaring that the NPC would promulgate basic laws for future governance under Communist rule.[36] Thus, the contents of these treaties would go on to influence the constitutional charters of the SARs themselves.

Basic Laws

PRC leaders undertook to prepare for the administration of its new SARs by drafting constitutional charters known as the HKBL and MBL.[37] These documents would elaborate and implement the contents of the Joint Declarations as well as Beijing's own desires for the future SARs. Just as with the treaties, the HKBL was negotiated first, meaning that a comparative analysis focused on the differences contained in the MBL can yield an identification of Macau's local characteristics as perceived by the drafters.

Beijing constituted drafting committees to manage the framing process. The membership of each committee was selected by the National People's Congress Standing Committee (NPCSC) in Beijing and, unlike the treaty negotiation process, included elite local residents. Hong Kong's drafting committee had 59 members, 23 of whom were from Hong Kong.[38] Macau's was composed of 48 members, 19 of whom were based in Macau.[39] Indeed, the mainland delegation was composed of almost entirely the same personnel, including all of the same lawyers, in both negotiations. Not surprisingly, they were influenced by the approach and method adopted for Hong Kong.[40]

Regarding their negotiating philosophy, Lu Ping, the Secretary-General of the MBL Drafting Committee and Director of the Hong Kong and Macau Affairs Office, stated:

> Because the State's basic principles and policies towards Hong Kong and Macau are identical, in drafting the Basic Law of Macau Special Administrative Region, we took care to make it essentially identical to the Basic Law of the Hong Kong Special Administrative Region regarding the general structure and major principles.[41]

Both the committee secretariats were located in Beijing, and Beijing dictated the pace of both negotiations.[42] Each of the Drafting Committees was divided into the same five working groups assigned to prepare a corresponding chapter of the respective basic law.[43] Both broadened their bases somewhat by establishing a small consultative council, yet never yielded the core's commanding role.[44] The HKBL was submitted to the NPC in 1990 and the MBL in 1993.

A side-by-side comparison of the two Basic Laws thus yields both a general framing of SAR governance under the PRC, on the one hand, and a short catalog of differences that identifies what the drafters understood the "Macau characteristics" to be, on the other.[45] This section highlights both by surveying significant points of negotiation that occurred during the MBL drafting process. In turn, Section "Implementation" will discuss whether those differences are being honored.

Preamble

The HKBL begins by declaring "Hong Kong [...] was occupied by Britain after the Opium War in 1840," while the MBL states "Macau [...] was gradually occupied by Portugal after the mid-16th century." Controversy surrounded the word "occupation" during the MBL drafting process. The Macau Drafting Committee's Central-Local Relations Group unanimously recognized that the historical experiences of Macau and Hong Kong were unique, as the original Portuguese presence at Macau was agreed to by the Ming and Qing Dynasties. Nevertheless, its members could not agree on how to represent that fact.[46] Although some proposed replacing the word "occupation" with "settlement," a majority insisted upon binding Macau with Hong Kong into a reductive narrative,[47] perhaps justifying the approach that central authorities have since taken to both on key matters.

General Provisions

Chapter I of the Basic Laws provides general provisions that transform several of the treaty commitments into domestic law, thereby codifying the PRC's basic policies toward the SARs. For example, Article 5 of each Basic Law echoes the treaties by promising that "[t]he socialist system and policies shall not be practiced in the [SARs], and the previous capitalist system and way of life shall remain unchanged for 50 years." Also reflecting those treaties, however, MBL Article 8 differs in stipulating that, "[t]he original laws, decrees, administrative regulations and other regulatory documents of Macau shall be retained" while HKBL Article 8 speaks of the common law, rules of equity, and customary law. Thus, the Basic Laws codified the Macau executive's authority to issue decrees *sua sponte*, a privilege that the late-colonial era British governor lacked.[48] Whether this remains a material difference given recent reforms is discussed later.

Central-Local Relationship

Chapter II describes the relationships between the CPG and the SARs. There appears to have been no major debate on several important articles during the MBL drafting process, including the appointment and removal of the CE (Article 15) and the application of national laws to Macau (Article 18), as these issues were decisively settled during the HKBL drafting process. Nevertheless, significant debates regarded: (i) the military garrison; (ii) selection of deputies to the NPC; and (iii) national security legislation.

Unlike Hong Kong, there is no specific text about a military garrison in Macau's governing documents.[49] As debate within the Central-Local Working Group yielded no consensus, the language of MBL Article 14 states only that the CPG is responsible for Macau's "defense." Thus, the NPCSC subsequently passed the "Law on the Garrison of the Macau" in 1999.[50] This law states clearly what the HKBL does but the MBL does not: that a local garrison shall be led by the PRC Central Military Commission; its expenses shall be borne by the CPG; and it shall not interfere in local affairs except upon request by the local government in maintaining public order or disaster relief.[51]

MBL Article 21 regards the selection of Macau deputies to the NPC. Despite numerous requests for universal suffrage of NPC deputies during the public consultation, the Central-Local Working Group held firm that the selection be consistent with the processes used throughout the PRC,[52] meaning an indirect selection process controlled by the NPC itself.[53]

MBL Article 23 requires Macau to "enact laws, on its own, to prohibit any act of treason, secession, sedition, subversion" against the CPG. Although the provision mirrors the HKBL, different opinions were expressed during the drafting process with reference to the Portuguese Criminal Code's definition of treason.[54] The issue was left to Macau authorities to resolve via local legislation, which would be done in 2009 and is discussed later.

Basic Rights and Obligations of Residents

Chapter III regards the rights and obligations of residents. While a great deal of debate is evinced throughout, major debates surrounded (i) local permanent residency and nationality; (ii) the protection of fundamental rights; and (iii) the application of international human rights accords.

Despite the Portuguese success in resolution of the nationality issue during the treaty drafting process, the PRC was adamant that Chinese persons living in Macau and Hong Kong receive "residency" rather than "nationality" status as the SARs were not to be treated as independent entities.[55] Article 24 defines "permanent residency" and the conditions for obtaining such status. The most serious question confronting the Macau Residents' Rights and Obligations Group regarded defining under what conditions children born outside of the SAR to parents who later became SAR residents could become local permanent residents. Whereas this question escaped preliminary consideration in Hong Kong, a majority of the MBL drafters agreed that so long as one of the parents is a Chinese citizen who becomes a permanent resident of Macau, their child should automatically receive permanent residency as well.[56] Thus, the Macau group added the phrase "and children of Chinese nationality born outside Macau after they became permanent residents" to Article 24(2) – a clause fatefully absent from the HKBL.

The fundamental rights of SAR residents are described for the remainder of Chapter III. Much popular opinion expressed during the public consultations sought to elaborate on the freedoms contained in this article. However, the committees concluded that the definition of all freedoms should be regulated by the laws of the SAR.[57] The laws were long applied in a more clinical fashion in Macau, as Macau's civil law tradition lacks experience with the common law concept of judicial review.[58] Even if otherwise, the courts' power of constitutional review was made subject to final interpretation by the NPCSC.[59]

MBL Article 40, like HKBL Article 39, weaves the *International Covenant on Civil and Political Rights* (ICCPR) and international labor conventions as applied to Macau into the constitutional fabric. Oddly, the Portuguese side simply overlooked this detail while negotiating the SPJD, so that document does not require their inclusion as the SBJD does. The PRC agreed to their inclusion after Portugal raised the issue in a Joint Liaison Group following Tiananmen Square,[60] though it insists that the rights contained in these conventions are non-self executing and must be implemented through local law.[61]

Political Structure

Chapter IV is lengthy and describes the SAR political systems. Most strikingly, the MBL does not contain the aspirations toward election of the CE and Legislative Assembly contained in Articles 45 and 62 of the HKBL, respectively. Instead, MBL Article 47 states simply that the CE "shall be elected or negotiated locally and appointed by the [CPG]."

The Political System Group stated that it was not necessary to include an aspiration to universal suffrage because the language of the SPJD, stipulating selection through either election or consultation, did not rule out its possibility in the future.[62] In the meantime, Annexes I stipulate that the CEs "shall be elected by a broadly representative election committee in accordance with this law and appointed by the [CPG]."[63] Those election committees once again incorporate the corporatist form of the colonial Portuguese functional constituency system,[64] and although tweaked over the years, they remain in place to this day.

Other

The remainder of the Basic Laws addresses various topics, including the economy, cultural and social matters, external affairs, and the interpretation and amendment of the texts. While the economic, cultural, and social provisions differ in reflecting the different endowments of the territories, the core provisions reflecting central-local relations remain the same.[65]

From a textualist standpoint, this section presented an important catalog of differences. Identifying and maintaining them depends upon a knowledge and willingness of scholars and jurists in the region, as well as the restraint of PRC authorities. Indeed, the question remains whether any of these unique characteristics will be preserved under a sole sovereign.

Implementation

The HKBL and MBL came into effect upon the respective handover of each jurisdiction. After 156 years of British administration, Hong Kong was yielded to the PRC on 1 July 1997. And after 446 years of Portuguese joint administration, Macau was released to the exclusive jurisdiction of the PRC on 20 December 1999.

The handovers have reshaped the territories in every way. Both are among the most densely populated regions of the world,[66] and both have become increasingly reliant upon the Chinese mainland for economic stability, especially since the introduction of the Individual Visit Scheme in 2003.[67] Macau – with its protected monopolistic gambling economy – is now among the world's richest places per capita.[68] Although tremendous disparities of opportunity persist,[69] and local culture is threatened by overdevelopment,[70] Macau must thus far be considered a success by most macroeconomic measures.

Beijing also likes to showcase Macau as a political success. Although it is difficult to determine public sentiment in Macau, appearances suggest that implementation of OCTS has thus far gone more smoothly there than in neighboring Hong Kong – though it really began there under vastly different conditions in the 1960s. The most common recent episodes of unrest in Macau are small-scale labor strikes, not large pro-democracy demonstrations.[71] Macau's protected economy would make political agitation self-defeating even if the will existed, and the PRC's leaders have more than once praised the pliant city for conformance.[72]

While the MBL has not yet been directly interpreted by the NPCSC, the frequent interpretations of parallel provisions in the HKBL likely apply to Macau with equal force. Any doubt about that is mitigated by the Macau Government's voluntarily adopting legislation to bring the city into compliance with the NPCSC's decisions for Hong Kong,[73] further expediting political convergence. The section that follows illustrates several key moments.

The formal OCTS framework faced its first major test in 1999, when the issue of permanent residency in Hong Kong resulted in the first NPCSC interpretation of a basic law. As stated, the definition of residency in Article 24 of each Basic Law is similar, with one major distinction: the HKBL made no statement regarding the right of abode for children born in mainland China to at least one parent who later acquired Hong Kong permanent residency. Presented with a case, the Hong Kong Court of Final Appeal (CFA) sought to resolve the issue by awarding the right of abode to such children.[74] The Hong Kong Government opposed that judgment and petitioned the NPCSC to override the CFA's interpretation, which it did.[75] While the final outcome reinforced a textual difference between the Basic Laws, there is little doubt that the NPCSC's definitive statement on central-local relations and the right of final interpretation of the Basic Law applies equally to both jurisdictions.

Indeed, the Macau CFA refused to acknowledge the practice of judicial review of legislative acts until 2006.[76] While there have since been nascent displays of constitutional review in Macau,[77] any judicial push-back to government initiatives has thus far been rare and perfunctory. Perhaps the most notable legal case touching on Macau's political structure in the first two decades of the MBL was a 2006 decision of Macau's Court of Second Instance holding that the CE's administrative decrees must be made pursuant to existing enabling legislation passed by Legislative Assembly.[78] Given that a majority of Macau's legislature was composed of indirectly selected and CE-appointed persons, however, this decision was a matter of procedure over substance.

Meanwhile, Beijing designs overarching policies for both cities in tandem.[79] The CPG's Hong Kong and Macau Affairs Office manages the macro-affairs of both territories, and the State Council made little distinction between the SARs when it declared in 2014 that "[a]s a unitary state, China's central government has comprehensive jurisdiction over all local administrative regions, including the HKSAR. The high degree of autonomy [...] is not an inherent power, but one that comes solely from the authorization by the central leadership."[80]

This pronouncement by the new Xi administration redefined the original understanding of OCTS, at least from the perspective of many in Hong Kong. Whereas much of the Hong Kong polity attempted to resist a series of encroachments upon local autonomy, however, Macau has often worked quietly to comply. For example, Macau's Government voluntarily brought its electoral law regime into compliance with the NPCSC's November 2016 interpretation of the HKBL.[81] There, the NPCSC intervened in an active case before the Hong Kong courts to secure its desired outcome, disqualifying two legislators elected upon a pro-independence platform ostensibly for befouling their oaths of office. The decree was ultimately used by the local government to disqualify a total of six legislators, depriving the pan-democratic camp from exercising a legislative veto.[82] Although Macau had no independence movement, the local government still voluntarily changed its laws to enhance the candidate screening powers of Macau's Electoral Affairs Committee – a body whose membership is entirely appointed by the CE.[83]

Indeed, the Macau SAR Government has undertaken to move itself into closer alignment with the CPG's wishes on other occasions. In 2009, it smoothly adopted Article 23 national security legislation originally intended for and rejected by Hong Kong after a mass protest in 2003.[84] The demonstrators feared that that law would pose a threat to civil liberties, including speech and procession. Although Macau's Article 23 legislation has never been officially invoked, its spirit has long been felt in the application of local restrictions on political activity,[85] academic freedom,[86] and assembly.[87]

The pace of political convergence has expedited in the past two years. Macau's Article 23 legislation has since been eclipsed by Beijing's proclamation of a controversial National Security Law (NSL) for Hong Kong in July 2020.[88] That NSL has had a chilling effect upon the millions of Hongkongers who took to the streets in the summer of 2019 to register their anxiety over the Hong Kong Government's then-proposed bill to allow for extradition of local persons to mainland China for trial. It introduced and criminalized the vaguely defined offenses of secession, subversion, terrorism, and collusion with foreign forces.[89] While there are some significant differences between Macau's Article 23 legislation and the new NSL,[90] the NSL declares a global extraterritorial scope, thereby enveloping Macau.[91] As usual, rather than speak in favor of local autonomy, Macau's authorities praised these developments.[92]

With protest subdued, Beijing next moved to eliminate all dissenting voices. To further consolidate its stranglehold over organized politics in Hong Kong, the NPCSC adopted another decision in November 2020 that enabled Hong Kong's administrative authorities to disqualify anyone considered "unpatriotic" from serving in the local legislature.[93] Specific offenses triggering disqualification include ever speaking in favor of independence, questioning Beijing's sovereignty over Hong Kong, seeking foreign assistance, or committing "other acts that endanger national security."[94] The Hong Kong Government disqualified four opposition lawmakers minutes after the law was announced, and 15 others resigned the next day.[95] Many have subsequently been jailed for their participation in an unofficial primary election.[96]

Then, in March 2021, the NPC passed a law altering Hong Kong's electoral system in two major ways.[97] First, it transforms Hong Kong's bipartite, 70-seat Legislative Council (35 directly elected and 35 functional constituency seats) into a tripartite, 90-seat configuration (20 directly elected, 30 functional constituency, and now 40 selected by a committee).[98] This tripartite configuration more closely resembles Macau's late-colonial/post-handover Legislative Assembly, whose present configuration is 14 directly elected seats, 12 functional constituency seats, and 7 seats appointed by the city's CE. Indeed, Macau's legislature now has a higher percentage of directly elected seats than Hong Kong's.[99] Second, the electoral reform law creates a candidate qualification review committee to ensure that only those who are sufficiently patriotic run for the directly elected seats.[100] In both ways, Hong Kong is reshaped in Macau's image.

The impact of the NSL regime on Hong Kong's political system was so sudden that Macau briefly appeared liberal in comparison. That was until 9 July 2021, when Macau's Electoral Affairs Committee (CAEAL) invoked the 2016 amendments to Macau's election law to disqualify 21 prospective candidates.[101] The Macau Court of Final Appeal upheld the disqualifications before the end of the month.[102]

The CFA reasoned that as no fundamental right is absolute under the MBL – including the right of permanent residents' to vote and be elected (Article 26) – all can be regulated "in accordance with the law."[103] Paying only cursory attention to principles of proportionality, it relied on provisions of the Legislative Council Election Law and NSLs to conclude that the applicants were guilty of having organized Macau's June 4th vigil, publicly mourning human rights activist Liu Xiaobo, and giving political speeches in Taiwan.[104] Furthermore, in reviewing the CAEAL's procedures, the Court demonstrated maximum deference to political forces by solemnifying its observation that "the legislature did not require that the relevant facts be verified by court trial."[105]

Interestingly, the CFA relied on the 1982 PRC Constitution to complete its reasoning, even though direct reliance upon the PRC Constitution of law has been rebuked within the mainland itself.[106] Nevertheless, the CFA opined "[t]he above content is obviously provocative and slanderous. It is clearly contrary to the resolution and characterization of the June 4th incident made by the central government. It damages the credibility and prestige of the central government and challenges the long-term actual leadership of the Communist Party of China" as declared through the 2018 amendment of Article 1 of the PRC Constitution.[107]

Thus, by late 2021, the polities of both cities were brought to heel; their always disadvantaged democratic segments deprived of voice. The remaining differences between the two SARs political systems are relatively modest: idiosyncratic differences in the offices of local public administration[108]; slightly different legislative seating arrangements; Macau's CE officially wielding the power of decree (now little more than a formality given Hong Kong's captured legislature); consultations with Macau's civil society shunted through "patriotic associations" rather than Hong Kong's elite co-optation model; and Macau's candidates for direct elections still being presented via an uninspiring party slate system. If the convergence is to continue to completion, one should expect to witness further diminishment of differences between the two political orders in the years ahead.

Conclusion

A great leveling is occurring between Macau and Hong Kong – one that not only irons out differences between the two local governments but also has placed them solidly under Beijing's streamlined command and control. Always symbiotic, coincidental colonial era trends have given way to a planned convergence that is expediting in both its political and economic dimensions. Recent events include the adoption of comprehensive national security legislation and the disqualification of any organized political opposition to chill present and future dissent. While Macau continues to enjoy a lucrative national monopoly on gaming, closer regional economic integration is advertised and expected. The construction of a Macau-Hong Kong-Guangdong bridge symbolizes and manifests Beijing's policy of integrating the Greater Pearl River Delta region, perhaps even foreshadowing an eventual legal and territorial integration.[109]

Neither Macau nor Hong Kong's future has never been certain. Political circumstances decided far beyond their boundaries often demanded comprehensive local reform. Yet, the situation has changed fundamentally. Whereas pre-handover parallels were often adopted voluntarily or coincidentally, post-handover change is now being driven by an activist central government. The OCTS policy could be interpreted and managed in a laissez-faire manner that protects the rich cultural diversity of Hong Kong and Macau,[110] but the present administration has subordinated that to its pursuit of expanding the reach of its omnipresent national security apparatus.

The practices developed over the next generation will determine whether the sun will set on Macau and Hong Kong's historic identities or, on the contrary, if the OCTS model will provide an opportunity for genuine autonomy to be realized within Chinese borders – one that appreciates and preserves the values of diversity and popular consent. Ultimately, the success or failure of the PRC's OCTS model might be finally judged in 2049: the year that represents the *de jure* end of Macau's promised 50 years of autonomy as well as the 100th anniversary of the foundation of the PRC.[111] Thus, the successes and failures of the SARs will reflect the successes and failures of the PRC itself, and it remains to be seen if the dialectic will end in extension, convergence, or assimilation. Although it is unclear what the future holds, this much is certain: the Basic Laws will not be the final constitutions of Hong Kong and Macau.

Notes

1 *Joint Declaration of the Government of the United Kingdom of Great Britain and Northern Ireland and the Government of the People's Republic of China on the Question of Hong Kong*, signed at Beijing 19 Dec 1984; *Basic Law of the Hong Kong Special Administrative Region of the People's Republic of China*, National People's Congress [Beijing], adopted 4 Apr 1990, effective 1 Jul 1997 (hereinafter "HKBL").

2 *Joint Declaration of the Government of the People's Republic of China and the Government of the Republic of Portugal on the Question of Macau*, [Beijing] March 1987 (hereinafter "SPJD"); *Basic Law of the Macau Special Administrative Region of the People's Republic of China*, National People's Congress [Beijing], adopted 31 Mar 1993, effective 20 Dec 1999 (hereinafter "MBL").

3 SBJD at Art. III(12); HKBL at Art. 5; SPJD at Art. II(12); MBL at Art 5.

4 Several authors refer to this era of historic Macau's governance as "shared sovereignty." *See* Hao Zhidong, *Macau: History and Society* (Hong Kong: HKUP, 2011), 37; Wu Zhiliang, 澳门政治制度史 (*History of Macau's Political Institutions*) (Guangzhou: Guangdong Renmin Chubanshe, 2009), 101 (referring to "mixed jurisdiction").

5 Charles Boxer, *O Senado da Câmara de Macau* (*The Municipal Council of Macau*) (Macau: Tipografia Macau Hung Heng Lda, 1997).

6 Jason Buhi, *The Constitutional History of Macau* (New York: Routledge, 2021), at *Chapter III: The Era of Imperial Consolidation.*

7 Unfortunately, that shift prompted Portuguese Macau to turn to alternative sources of finance, including gambling, opium, and the export of cheap "coolie" labor. Id. at 30–32, 68–69, 82.

8 *Decreto-lei No. 23:228 de 15 de Novembro 1933, Promulga a Carta Organica do Imperio Colonial Portugues* (Decree-law No. 23:228 of 15 Nov 1933, Promulgating an Organic Charter of the Portuguese Colonial Empire) [Lisbon: Ministry of the Colonies] at Art. 52.

9 Nuno Estevão Ferreira, *Da Câmara Corporativa do Estado Novo: Composição, Funcionamento e Influência* (The Corporate Chamber of the New State: Composition, Function, and Influence), Doctoral Thesis, University of Lisbon Institute of Social Sciences (2009).

10 Jason Buhi, "*A History of the Dictatorial Origins of Hong Kong's Opaque and Unrepresentative Legislature*," Hong Kong Free Press, 14 July 2019, *available at* https://hongkongfp.com/2019/07/14/history-dictatorial-origins-hong-kongs-opaque-unrepresentative-legislature/.

11 And they still do. Note for example that Macau "reformed" its functional constituency system in 2008 by imposing stricter registration and regulation requirements for kaifong associations. The impact was especially felt by labor-oriented kaifong, which had been proliferating in the early post-handover years. Following the amendment, new registrations dropped precipitously, while financial support to existing labor associations from the Macau Foundation (often seen as a slush fund for the CE) increased tenfold. *See* Lio Chi Fai and Meng U Ieong, "Labor Protests in Macau (2000–2017)," in Meng U Ieong (Ed.) *Macau 20 Years after the Handover: Changes and Challenges under One Country, Two Systems* (New York: Routledge, 2020), 82–83.

12 1933 Organic Charter, *supra* note 9.

13 Buhi, *Constitutional History*, (New York: Routledge), *supra* note 6, at 127–128 (describing the 1953 Organic Law of the Portuguese Overseas), 134–135 (describing the 1963 Political-Administrative Statute of Macau Province).

14 *Lei no. 2/74 de 14 de Maio de 1974* (Law 2/74 of 14 May 1974) [Lisbon] permanently dissolving functional representation at Lisbon; *Decreto 360/74 de 17 Agosto de 1974* (Decree 360/74 of 17 August 1974) dissolving the Overseas Ministry and all overseas legislative assemblies and advisory boards whose methods of creation were "repugnant" to the democratic revolution.

15 Buhi, *Constitutional History*, *supra* note 6, at 150–155, citing Jose Eduardo Leandro, *Macau nos Anos de Revolução Portuguesa* 1974–1979 (Macau During the Years of the Portuguese Revolution, 1974–1979) (Lisbon: Gravida, 2011), 87–88.

16 *See generally* Christine Lou (Ed.) *Functional Constituencies: A Unique Feature of the Hong Kong Legislative Council* (Hong Kong: Civic Exchange Guides, 2006).

17 "[S]ince the 1974 Revolution [the Portuguese] have never implemented any political reform in Macau without the tacit or overt endorsement of PRC officials." Sonny Lo Shun Hing, *Political Development in Macau* (Hong Kong: Chinese UP, 1995), 248.

18 *Other Questions Relating Non-Self-Governing Territories*, 1972 U.N.Y.B. (United Nations Juridical Yearbook) 625, U.N. Sales No. E.74.I.1; *see also* UN Resolutions 2908 (XXVII) of 2 Nov 1972 and 2918 (XXVII) of 14 Nov 1972, reflecting the change.

19 Carmen Mendes, *Portugal, China and the Macau Negotiations, 1986–1999* (Hong Kong: HKUP, 2013), 24.

20 *Id.* at 37, *citing* Moises Silva Fernandes, *Sinopse de Macau nas Relacoes Luso-Chinesas, 1945–1995* (*Synopsis of Macau in Luso-Chinese Relations*) (Lisbon: Orient Foundation, 2000), 381–385.

21 *Constitution of the People's Republic of China, 1982*, National People's Congress [Beijing] adopted 4 Dec 1982.

22 Buhi, *Constitutional History*, 143–154; Francisco Gonçalves Pereira, *Accommodating Diversity: The People's Republic of China and the "Question of Macau" (1949–1999)* (Macau: Scientific and Cultural Center of Macau, 2013), 104–107.

23 *Act of Conversations upon the Question of Macau Conducted by the Portuguese Ambassador in Paris*, also known as the "Secret Act," dated 8 Feb 1979, published in *Diario de Noticias*, 9 Jan 1987.
24 Mendes, *supra* note 20, at 50, citing text of *Guangjiaojing* newspaper (Hong Kong) 16 Mar 1985.
25 *Id.* at 47.
26 These treaty provisions were derivative of Beijing's "Nine-Point Proposal" intended to reunify the mainland and Taiwan. *See* "Chairman Ye Jianying's Elaborations on Policy Concerning Return of Taiwan to the Motherland and Peaceful Reunification," 30 Sep 1981, *available at* https://en.wikisource.org/wiki/Nine-PointProposal.
27 SBJD at 3(3); SPJD at Art. 2(12).
28 SBJD at Arts. 3(2) and 3(12); SPJD at Arts. 2(2) and 2(12).
29 SBJD at Annex I.2; SPJD at Annex I.3.
30 SBJD at Annex I.1; SPJD at Annex I.3.
31 *Id.* at Annex I(1).
32 Law No. 112/91, *The Law of the Bases for the Judicial Organization of Macau* (Lisbon, Assembly of the Republic) 20 Aug 1991.
33 *See* SBJD at Annex I(3).
34 SPJD, Memorandums 1 & 2 at Annex.
35 SPJD at Memorandums 1 & 2; *see also* Yash Ghai, "The Basic Law of the Special Administrative Region of Macau: Some Reflections," *The International and Comparative Law Quarterly*, Vol. *49*(1): 191–193 (Jan 2000).
36 SBJD and SPJD at Annex I(1).
37 HKBL and MBL, *supra* note 1.
38 *See* "The Basic Law: Enactment of the One Country, Two Systems Concept," Hong Kong Government, *available at* https://www.basiclaw.gov.hk/filemanager/content/en/files/anniversary-reunification15/anniversary-reunification15-ch1-3.pdf.
39 *See* "*Breve Introdução sobre a Lei Basica de Macau*" ("Brief Introduction to the Basic Law of Macau") *available at* http://www.basiclaw.org.mo/index.php?p=17_0.
40 Ghai, *supra* note 35, at 184.
41 *Id., citing* Paul Fifoot, "One Country, Two Systems—Mark II: From Hong Kong to Macau." *International Relations,* Vol. 12, 25–28 (1994).
42 The PRC-based members initiated the negotiations by visiting Hong Kong and Macau in turn. Indeed, the PRC expelled Martin Lee and Szeto Wah, the most vocal advocates of democratization on the Hong Kong committee, following Tiananmen Square.
43 In both cases, these were (i) The Special Group on the Relationship between the Central and Local Government; (ii) The Residents' Rights and Obligations Group; (iii) The Political System Special Group; (iv) The Economic Special Group; and (v) Cultural and Social Affairs Special Group.
44 The Hong Kong consultative committee had 180 members; Macau's had 90.
45 For a complete list of textual differences, *see* Buhi, *Constitutional History*, (New York: Routledge), *supra* note 6, at 191–196.
46 Luo Wenjian et al., 澳门特别行政区基本法解析：立法背景和立法原意的探究/骆伟建 (*An Analysis of the Basic Law of the Macao Special Administrative Region: A Probe into the Legislative Background and Legislative Intent*) (Beijing: Social Sciences Literature Publishing House, 2020), 37–38, citing the work report submitted to the Fifth Plenary Session of the Central and Special Administrative Region Relations Group in December 1990.
47 *Id.*
48 Also described in MBL Article 50 and Macau Law No. 13/2009 "*Legal System Concerning the Establishment of Internal Regulations.*"
49 HKBL Art 14; SBJD Annex I(12).
50 Adopted by the 10th Meeting of the NPCSC on 28 June 1999. The Macau Legislative Assembly has since enacted Law No. 6/2005 "The Chinese People's Liberation Army Garrison in Macau Assists in Maintaining Public Security and Relieving Disasters," and Law No. 23/2009 "Rights and Immunities of the Chinese People's Liberation Army Garrison in Macau for Performing Defense Duties."
51 *Id.* at Arts. 2 and 3.

52 Luo, *Analysis, supra* note 46, at 105–109.
53 Fu Hualing and D.W. Choy, "Of Iron or Rubber: People's Deputies of Hong Kong to the National People's Congress," in Fu Hualing et al., (Eds.) *Interpreting Hong Kong's Basic Law: The Struggle for Coherence* (New York: Palgrave MacMillan, 2008), at 201–228.
54 Luo, *supra* note 46, at 113–117.
55 *Id.* at 120–126; Mendes, *Negotiations*, at 39, 57–58.
56 Luo, Analysis, (Beijing: Social Sciences Literature Publishing House), *supra* note 46, at 122, *citing* "Compilation of Documents of the Basic Law Drafting Committee of the Macau Special Administrative Region of the People's Republic of China," (hereinafter "Compilation") edited by the Office of the Macau Basic Law Committee of the NPCSC, at 196.
57 *Id., citing* Compilation at 264 regarding the notes of the ninth plenary meeting of the Residents' Rights and Obligations Group.
58 Jorge Godinho & Paulo Cardinal, "Macau's Court of Final Appeal," in Simon Young & Yash Ghai (Eds.) *Hong Kong's Court of Final Appeal: Justice and the Development of the Law in China's Hong Kong* (Cambridge: Cambridge University Press, 2013); Judith Krebs, "One Country, Three Systems? Judicial Review in Macau after Ng Ka Ling," *Washington International Law Journal*, Vol. 10, at 111–146 (Dec 2000).
59 MBL Art. 143; HKBL Art. 158.
60 Mendes, *Negotiations*, *supra* note 20, at 85–87.
61 Luo, *Analysis*, *supra* note 46, at 160.
62 *Id.* at 175, citing minutes of 14th meeting of Political System Group.
63 SPJD Annex I at Art. 2.
64 Annex I of both Basic Laws stipulate a scheme of selection by a committee divided proportionally between industrial, cultural, social, and *ex officio* interests.
65 For instance, while the SARs are granted a separate legal personality in international for a (HKBL 116/MBL 112), its foreign affairs are commanded by the CPG (HKBL & MBL 13). Furthermore, while the local Courts of Final Appeal possess the power of final adjudication, the power of final interpretation resides in the NPCSC (HKBL 158/MBL 143).
66 Macau with over 600,000 residents packed into 30 km^2 of land, and Hong Kong with 7.4 million in 1,104 km^2.
67 The Individual Visit Scheme allows mainlanders to visit the SARs without the need for business visa or tour groups.
68 Macau boasting a per capita income of 58,000 USD in 2021. Macau, *CIA World Factbook*, *available at* https://www.cia.gov/the-world-factbook/countries/macau/#economy.
69 Jason Buhi, "Corporate Social Responsibility, Casino Capitalism, and the Constitution of Macau," *UCLA Pacific Basin Law Journal,* Vol. 37(1) (2020); Macau's gaming revenue peaked at seven times that of Las Vegas in 2014. Charles Riley, "Macau's Gambling Industry Dwarfs Vegas," *CNN*, 6 Jan 2014, *available at* http://money.cnn.com/2014/01/06/news/macau-casino-gambling/index.html.
70 *See* Lei Chin Pang, "Spatial Politics in an Eastern Casinopolis: Urban Space, Power and Resistance in Macau," in Ieong Meng U (Ed.) *Changes*, *supra* note 11, at Chapter II, at 19–35.
71 Lio and Ieong, *supra* note 11, at 74, citing 554 labor protests between 2000 and 2017.
72 *See, for example*, Holmes Chan, "China Leader Xi Jinping Praises Macau for Promoting Patriotism and 'Choosing Unity Over Infighting," *Hong Kong Free Press*, 20 Dec 2019, *available at* https://hongkongfp.com/2019/12/20/china-leader-xi-jinping-praises-macau-promoting-patriotism-choosing-unity-infighting/.
73 The NPCSC has issued five official interpretations the HKBL: in 1999, 2004, 2005, 2011 and 2016.
74 *Ng Ka Ling v. Director of Immigration* supra note 64; HKBL Interpretation by Tenth Standing Committee Session of Ninth NPC, (Beijing) 26 June 1999.
75 *See* Johannes Chan et al., *Hong Kong's Constitutional Debate: Conflict Over Interpretation* (Hong Kong: HKU Press, 2000). The CFA confirmed the NPCSC interpretation's local effect in *Lau Kong Yung v. Director of Immigration*, [(1999) 3 HKLRD 778].
76 Macau Court of Final Appeal, Cases 1/2000 and 2/2000 (initially denying judicial review of legislative acts; ultimately reversed later in cases 9/2006 and 28/2006).
77 *See* Jorge Godinho & Paulo Cardinal, "Macau's Court of Final Appeal," (Cambridge: Cambridge University Press), *supra* note 58; Shiling Xiao, Judicial Review and Standards of Review in Macao: A Study Based on the TUI Decisions, *infra*.

78 Macau Court of Second Instance TSI-A-233-2005-VP 27 April 2006, Proc 223/2005.
79 The CPG utilizes the same offices and personnel to manage the affairs of both territories, i.e., the Hong Kong and Macau Affairs Office of the State Council.
80 "*White Paper on 'One Country, Two Systems' Policy in Hong Kong,*" PRC State Council (Beijing) 10 Jun 2014.
81 "Interpretation of Article 104 of the Basic Law of the Hong Kong Special Administrative Region of the People's Republic of China by the Standing Committee of the National People's Congress" (Beijing) (7 Nov 2016).
82 Han Zhu and Albert Chen, "The Oath-Taking Cases and the NPCSC Interpretation of 2016: Interface of Common Law and Chinese Law," *Hong Kong Law Journal,* Vol. *49*(1): 381–415 (2019).
83 Jason Buhi, "Macau's Response to the November 2016 Interpretation of Hong Kong's Basic Law," *HKU Scholarship Blog,* 21 December 2016, *available at* http://researchblog.law.hku.hk/2016/12/macaus-response-to-november-2016.html, citing Article 9 of the 2016 amendment to Law 3/2001.
84 Macau Special Administrative Region National Security Law, Macau Law no. 2/2009, promulgated 26 Feb 2009, English translation *available at* https://www.cecc.gov/resources/legal-provisions/macau-special-administrative-region-national-security-law-chinese-and; Fu Hualing et al., *National Security and Fundamental Freedoms: Hong Kong's Article 23 Under Scrutiny* (Hong Kong: HKU Press, 2005).
85 *See, for example,* Jason Chao, "Review of the 2014 Civil Referendum on Chief Executive Election of Macau," *Medium, available at* https://medium.com/jason-chaos-depository/review-of-the-2014-civil-referendum-on-chief-executive-election-of-macau-93709e75a6ce.
86 *See, for example,* Raquel Carvalho, "Macau Academic Sacked for 'Imposing His Political Beliefs on Students," *SCMP,* 18 Aug 2014, *available at* https://www.scmp.com/news/china/article/1575637/macau-activist-bill-chou-lose-academic-job-after-suspension.
87 *See, for example,* Jorge Menezes, "Something Is Wrong When Macau Bars Mention of Tiananmen Square Massacre," *Hong Kong Free Press,* 4 Jun 2020, *available at* https://hongkongfp.com/2020/06/04/something-is-wrong-when-macau-bars-mention-of-tiananmen-square-massacre/, referring to Macau CFA decision No. 58/2020.
88 Law of the People's Republic of China on Safeguarding National Security in the Hong Kong Special Administrative Region (hereinafter NSL), NPCSC (Beijing), 20 June 2020.
89 *Id.* at Arts. 20–30.
90 For example, whereas Macau's is enforced by local officials, the NSL is overseen by a new mainland agency established in Hong Kong (*Id.* at Arts. 12; 48–60); and whereas Macau's courts have enforcement authority, the NSL allows for mainland authorities to assume the case under certain circumstances (*Id.* at Arts. 55–59).
91 *Id.* at Art. 38.
92 Renato Marques, "Implementation of Hong Kong National Security Law a Reference for Macau," *Macau Daily Times,* 19 July 2021, *available at* https://macaudailytimes.com.mo/implementation-of-national-security-law-in-hk-reference-for-macau-security-chief.html
93 "Decision of the Standing Committee of the National People's Congress on the Qualifications of Members of the Legislative Council of the Hong Kong Special Administrative Region," *NPCSC* (Beijing) 11 Nov 2020.
94 *Id.* at Art. 1.
95 Lily Kuo and Helen Davidson, "Hong Kong Opposition Lawmakers All Quit after Four Ousted," *Guardian,* 11 Nov 2020, *available at* https://www.theguardian.com/world/2020/nov/11/china-pro-democracy-hong-kong-lawmakers-opposition-oust (last visited 29 Aug 2021).
96 Maggie Shum, "In Hong Kong, Dozens of Arrests for Pro-democracy Activities will Have a Chilling Effect," *Washington Post,* 12 Jan 2021, *available at* https://www.washingtonpost.com/politics/2021/01/12/hong-kong-dozens-arrests-pro-democracy-activities-will-have-chilling-effect/.
97 "Decision of the National People's Congress on Improving the Electoral System of the Hong Kong Special Administrative Region," *NPCSC* (Beijing) 11 Mar 2021.
98 *Id.* at Art. IV.
99 SPJD Art I.1 and MBL Art. 68 require that a majority of seats in Macau's legislature be elected, though this author disagrees that functional constituency seats should be considered elected.

100 *Id.* at Art. V.
101 Danny Mok, "In First for Macau, Election Chiefs Disqualify 21 Opposition Members from Running in September Legislative Elections," *SCMP*, 10 Jul 2021, *available at* https://www.scmp.com/news/article/3140585/first-macau-election-chiefs-disqualify-21-opposition-members-running-september.
102 Association of New Progress Macau et al. v. Macau Electoral Affairs Committee, Case No. 113/2021, *Macau Court of Final Appeals*, 31 Jul 2021, *available at* https://www.court.gov.mo/sentence/zh-82dd686a58b1d3bf.pdf.
103 *Id.* at 2.
104 *Id.* at 20; citing Articles 6(8) and 10(1)(12) of the Macau SAR Legislative Council Election Law, and Law No. 5/2006 as amended by Law No. 14/2020 on national security.
105 *Id.* at 51–54.
106 See *Qi Yuling v. Chen Xiaoqi* (2001), where the Supreme People's Court (SPC) [Beijing] relied on Article 46 of the PRC Constitution granting specific educational rights. The interpretation was unceremoniously withdrawn by the SPC on 18 Dec 2008, with the deciding judge, Huang Songyu, jailed for life on charges of corruption.
107 *Id.* at 53. That 2018 amendment introduced CCP leadership into the main text of the 1982 PRC Constitution for the first time.
108 Hong Kong's administration will always be larger to serve a larger population. However, Macau still retains some legacy positions as a result of its civil law heritage, such as the Office of the Procurator, and the bifurcation between Judiciary Police (tasked with investigations) and Public Security Police (charged with public order, customs, and immigration). Even then, reforms in Macau have increased coordination between the police forces.
109 *See for example* Sonny Lo, "Central Planning on Macau-Hengqin and Hong Kong-Qianhai Integration: Implications for 2049, 2047 and Taiwan," *Macau Business*, 18 Sep 2021, *available at* https://www.macaubusiness.com/opinion-central-planning-on-macau-hengqin-and-hong-kong-qianhai-integration-implications-for-2049-2047-and-taiwan.
110 Jason Buhi, *The Perpetual Dance: Interpreting 'One Country, Two Systems' through the Lens of Tongbian Dialectics, Hong Kong Law Journal*, Vol. 44: 865 (2014).
111 SPJD, *supra* note 2, at Article 2(12). Hong Kong's pledge extends from its handover in 1997 through 2047.

PART II

Structure

5

"THE FLOWER OF DEMOCRACY BLOOMS BRILLIANTLY IN CHINA [中国的民主之花绚丽绽放]"

The Chinese Communist Party and the Chinese Constitutional Order

Larry Catá Backer

Introduction

Chinese Marxist Leninist constitutional theory is modernity's nightmare.[1] The development of a constitutional order from out of a revolutionary movement[2] has produced a constitutionalist framework that is quite consciously distinct from that common to the West and its baseline liberal democratic constitutional orders. From liberal democratic baseline constitutional perspective, it is "the other" of constitutional theory[3] – adjudged only as a function of the ideal[4] – which for the greater portion of the established constitutional jurisprudence elite is, by their definition, some variation of late 20th century classical liberal democratic constitutionalism.[5] At best then, and grudgingly, this constitutional "other" is given space within the constitutional discourse as "authoritarian" constitutionalism, and in this way conflating Marxist-Leninist constitutional systems with more traditional ordered or bureaucratized dictatorship.[6] The pejorative is deliberate. It is meant to marginalize in a precise way, one that is centered on the deviation (negative) of principles of Marxist-Leninist constitutionalism from that cluster of principles and values that expressed as and are memorialized in the constitutional orders of liberal constitutionalism. Today that difference continues to be grounded in geographic hubs,[7] with the ancient seat of liberal constitutionalism in Western European and North American states after 1788, and that of post-Soviet Marxist-Leninism in China. It is also the yardstick against which liberal democratic constitutional theorists in the West judge what for them are fundamentally illegitimate deviations within their own constitutional orders.[8]

The constitutionalism of liberal democratic orders starts from the premise that all sovereign power is vested in a government whose authority is ordered and constrained by a constitutional document[9] and vested in a government suitable for the times but loyal to its core premises.[10] Beyond that, and certainly in the United States, the operationalization of this core set of premises is open ended and marked by enormous disagreement, even from the start of the Republic,[11] and substantial changes over time

DOI: 10.4324/9781003128243-7

in the popular taste for government and the self-reflexive understanding of the sovereign societal order it is meant to manifest.[12] It is from these premises, and these sometimes great contests among key political elements, that the concept of constitutionalism has been given form.[13] These are the premises from which it is possible to construct those limits within which legitimate expression of the constitutionalism principle, within (or without) a written constitution, is embedded first in the social consciousness and then into the law and norms of international bodies.[14]

This long introductory exposition is made necessary because the power to affect global judgments about distinctions between legitimate and illegitimate constitutional orders, and even to identify a system as legitimately constitutionalist, has been a central element in Western liberal democratic approaches to the study and classification of the constitutional system of China.[15] And it is meant to underscore the challenges of the way that protective and reactive discursive tropes craft each (from the others' perspective) as defective. Indeed, it also has become an important element of Chinese constitutional discourse through the beginning of China's constitutional "New Era."[16] More importantly, perhaps, it has been instrumental in the way in which the study of such systems is prejudged as not merely a constitutional deviation, but a deviation for inconsistent with the core political principles of liberal democracy that such systems might not be understood as legitimately constitutional.[17] The object of Chinese constitutional theory, then, is sometimes reduced to a project of alignment with what is perceived to be the core expectations drawn from liberal democratic orders,[18] or as described at the start of this contribution, as its reconstruction as something that mimics but cannot be constitutional, taking as its starting point the 3 core tenets of liberal democratic constitutionalism.[19]

Chinese constitutional theory quite consciously[20] starts from a very different place, though it shares many of the values of liberal democratic constitutionalism investing them with a meaning derived in large measure from its own theoretical starting points.[21] It is based on the certainty that "The Flower of Democracy Blooms Brilliantly in China" [中国的民主之花绚丽绽放],[22] only that it comes from a very different conceptual space. At its core is the premise of the delegation of sovereign authority from the people to its leading forces constituted as a vanguard party. Administrative authority is then vested in the organs of state which accept the leadership of the Party and its guidance in the governance of the nation. While Chinese constitutional discourse before the New Era debated the relationship between the constitution of the vanguard and the constitutionalization of the state apparatus, the role of the vanguard itself as a decisive and representative element within the Chinese constitutional order could not be avoided.[23] That left open only two significant terrains for debate. The first was one that looked to the nature of the scope and exercise of political authority by the CPC, the other looked to the forms that discretionary exercises of authority were either organized or constrained by the CPC's own rules, political line, or by the fundamental strictures of its objectives as a communist vanguard.

This contribution examines the Chinese constitutional system within the parameters of its own formal political assumptions.[24] China asserts with greater confidence that it has moved toward a legitimately constitutionalist governance system in which power is divided between a vanguard party, which serves as the repository of political power, and the administrative organs of government. But in the process it has embraced a set of core political and human values quite distinct from that at the core of liberal democratic constitutional theory. The distinctions start with the delegation of sovereign authority from the masses to its vanguard and lead to the constitution of state power in ways that reject liberal democratic principles of separation of powers and (judicial) review. In Chinese Leninist constitutionalism, the CPC stands at the center of the political order. The CPC serves an institutional role within Chinese constitutionalism and also represents the political power of the Chinese polity directly in the political ordering of the government. The CPC, in turn, is constrained by the normative basis on which Chinese constitutionalism is ordered – Marxist Leninism and Mao Zedong Thought, Deng Xiaoping Theory, the important Thought of Three Represents, the Scientific Outlook on Development, and Xi Jinping Thought on Socialism with Chinese Characteristics in the New Era Theory.[25] And that precisely is both the essence of Chinese Marxist-Leninist Constitutionalism and its reconstruction of political power within the Leninist vanguard and through them to the apparatus of the state built to operationalize its political "line" (its policies and objective). As Stanley Lubman wrote, "although they have continued to emphasize the importance of the role of law, at the same time they also insist on maintaining the dominant role of the CPC in Chinese society, and cannot resolve the contradiction between these two policies."[26] And yet, the essential problem of constitutionalism remains the same – the protection of systems of authority and government "against arbitrary will."[27]

These premises serve as the ideological basis for the Chinese political model and a constraint on the exercise of authority within both the Leninist vanguard Communist Party of China (CPC) and state organs constituted under law for the purpose of exercising the popular will under the leadership of the CPC.[28] Thus framed, the Chinese constitutional system can be understood as both distinctly and legitimately constitutionalist.[29]

The contribution embeds the substantive political theory of Leninist constitutionalism on which the political order is organized with its expression in the organization of the state. It starts with a consideration of the Chinese state constitution (Xianfa). It then turns to a consideration of the constitution of the political order institutionalized within the Constitution of the CPC. It then examines the relationship between the administrative organs of state and the organs of CPC governance. Lastly, it situates both constitutions within the hierarchies of Chinese constitutional authority, one in which the state constitution provides the cage of regulation that embodies the CPC core Basic Line.[30] This last contributes to the accountability mechanisms built into the system of Chinese constitutionalism grounded on the operating premise that the CPC is at the center, the navigator and helmsman of the nation one that is consonant with the core anti-arbitrary assertion of power principle at the center of constitutionalism.[31] Simultaneously, it rationalizes the forms of dynamism in normative Chinese constitutionalism built around authoritative responses to the core contradictions[32] that challenge, of which is reflected in the approach to the application of constitutional norms in each historical era of development. The recent quite significant movement from the normative framework of Reform and Opening Up to that of New Era ideology was framed both through the lens of the shift of contradiction, and its effect of the interpretation of constitutional norms.[33] A caveat: the discussion that follows is focused on the formal constitution of the Chinese political order manifested in its core institutions; to that end, the analysis will focus on the documents authoritatively constituting both the state apparatus and the nation's political vanguard.[34]

The Political Theory of Leninist Constitutionalism: State and Party Autonomous and Entwined

When one approaches Chinese constitutional theory, and the role of the CPC within it, from the outside, one starts with the current state constitution.[35] One does not do this necessarily because it is the apex memorialization of the political order within Chinese Marxist-Leninist constitutional theory; it is not. Instead such a starting point is useful because, like the anthropologist and their subjects,[36] that tends to be the reference point for liberal democratic constitutionalism which serves as the prism through which non-liberal democratic constitutional orders may be grasped.[37] It also, in this case, provides in written form the description of the political system itself and the special relationship between the vanguard, as the holder of political authority, the masses with respect to which the vanguard has precise responsibilities, and the state apparatus (the government) as the mechanisms through which rule-based systems of operationalization may be realized.[38]

The preamble provides a historical context for the function of Xianfa he document that sets out, in the form of law, the political and ideological basis for the legitimate establishment and functioning of state organs (in accordance with law including the law of the state constitution) but only within the now legalized core principles of the people's democratic dictatorship, and democratic centralism, and the socialist system the defining feature of which is the leadership of the CPC. The last paragraph of the preamble to the state constitution[39] provides the interpretive context for situating the constitutional document. It also describes its essence within the system of Chinese constitutionalism not as the supreme manifestation of popular authority vested in and delegated through a state apparatus, but as something quite distinct. Note the language:

> This Constitution affirms, in legal form, the achievements of the struggles of the Chinese people of all ethnic groups and stipulates the fundamental system and task of the state. It is the fundamental law of the state and has supreme legal force. The people of all ethnic groups, all state organs and armed forces, all political parties and social organizations, and all enterprises and public institutions in the country must treat the Constitution as the fundamental standard of conduct; they have a duty to uphold the sanctity of the Constitution and ensure its compliance.[40]

The State constitution is an affirming rather than a constituting document. The constituting occurs elsewhere. That affirmation also takes on a special character that is inherently limited by its terms – it is confined to a legal form, to the rules that reflect the superior political determination of political will exercised by those who have the responsibility for the exercise of sovereign political authority. With that comes the corollary that this exercise of political authority is itself constrained elsewhere. The state constitution is binding, in legal form, only because a superior political force has consented to be bound by its terms, and to bind the people to it in the management of their government and its operation through systems of rules, responsibilities, punishments, and privileges expressed as and through law. It is, in this sense, the manifestation, in legal form, of the concrete expression of the political will of those exercising political authority and to that extent binding on that authority as well, but it provide no limit on the power of that superior political authority to change this legal expression. That normative constraint on the exercise of sovereign authority is necessarily located elsewhere.

The preamble of Xianfa also points its readers to where those constraints are located, identifies the holder of political authority, and expresses the foundational political premise of a people's democratic dictatorship under which the state constitution acquires legitimacy.

> We the Chinese people of all ethnic groups will continue, under the leadership of the Communist Party of China and the guidance of Marxism-Leninism, Mao Zedong Thought, Deng Xiaoping Theory, the Theory of Three Represents, the Scientific Outlook on Development and Xi Jinping Thought on Socialism with Chinese Characteristics for a New Era, to uphold the people's democratic dictatorship, ... develop the socialist market economy and socialist democracy, improve socialist rule of law, ..., in order to build China into a great modern socialist country that is prosperous, strong, democratic, culturally advanced, harmonious and beautiful, and realize the great rejuvenation of the Chinese nation.[41]

First, the ultimate normative constraints on the exercise of authority, and in the interpretation of the state constitution are found in the basic principles of Chinese Marxist Leninism identified in the preamble.[42] Second, the responsibility for advancing social progress through the application of those normative constraints within the contemporary context falls to the CPC which asserts a role of leadership. That role of leadership, in turn, is exercised through the operationalization of the principle of people's democratic dictatorship, now reconstituted as a legal-constitutional principle.[43] Within these constraints, a number of fundamental objectives are identified, including, from the excerpt above, the key objectives of socialist markets and rule of law which serve as the basis for the development of a specific vision of Chinese progress.

The fundamental role of the principle of "people's democratic dictatorship" then finds its way into the very first article of the state constitution,[44] also with the affirmation of the fundamental socialist character of the economic system,[45] and the leadership of the CPC.[46] It is legally impermissible to damage the socialist system (and therefore by definition its defining feature – the leadership of the CPC).[47] While "all power in the People's Republic of China belongs to the people,"[48] that power is to be exercised under the leadership of and through the organs of the CPC.[49] Consider the express meaning of the provision: the state constitution and its legal order are meant to express, in legal form, an important element of the socialist system, an essential feature of which is the leadership of the CPC: Xianfa, then, is an expression of and must be read against and guided by the socialist system that stands both apart and above the state constitution. At the same time, as the expression of the socialist system, it must be respected as an element of that system and is in that sense the supreme legal expression of the socialist system that itself stands at the apex of the constitutional order of the Chinese political-constitutional order. In that form, the state constitution structures the legal forms within which the socialist system, under the leadership of the CPC, operates to give legal effect to its principles and to ensure that those principles may appropriately be enjoyed by the people for whose welfare the structures of the socialist state are established, maintained, and modified to suit the times under the leadership of the CPC.

With political authority assigned to the CPC as the defining feature of socialism in China and its functioning as a people's democratic dictatorship, the state constitution then notes that the power allocated to the state in the form already described may be exercised through the National People's Congress system.[50] These state organs are to "practice the principle of democratic centralism."[51] Democratic centralism expresses both a style of decision-making and the reinforcement of a core principle of leadership ultimately sourced in the leadership of the CPC and its highest collective organs under a (sometimes singular) leadership core.[52] Its essence derived from a contemporary engagement with the rectifications of 1942 and its justification as a matter of the principles of then emerging of the forms of CPC leadership and its working style.[53] This in turn provides the basis for the structures of what I have elsewhere called China's endogenous democratic system.[54] The elaborate system of consultation is nicely described in the SC White Paper 2021.[55]

It is within that expression, in legal form, of the normative and political basis for the legitimate exercise of sovereign authority within and for the nation that the issue of the relationship of the legal forms of the state constitution to the constituent political and social collectives of the nation are then ordered. That ordering, set out in Xianfa Article 5, has generated substantial discussion among elite academic, CPC, and policy circles within China[56] but might be read in its simplest and most direct form from its own text on the practice of law-based governance and socialist rule of law. First it establishes the principle that the state "shall practice law-based governance and build a socialist state under the rule of law."[57] Recall here that "building a socialist state" must, according to Article 1, be understood as a function of the leadership of the CPC as its key feature, a feature that, like any other aspect of the socialist system (including socialist law and rule of law), may not be damaged by any organization or individual.[58]

At its broadest, of course, this responsibility to build a socialist state under the rule of law also suggests that no individual or organization, including the CPC itself, may damage the socialist system or its rule-of-law-based processes without betraying its own essential leadership responsibilities recognized (though not created) under the state constitution. This is emphasized in the provisions of Article 5 that then follow. First, the state (and its organs) is charged with safeguarding "the unity and sanctity of the socialist system."[59] This necessarily includes safeguarding the paramount leadership role of the CPC as the essential feature of socialism with Chinese characteristics. Second, no exercise of authority by or through the state organs "shall be in conflict with the Constitution."[60] Clearly that encompasses the usual supremacy provisions of constitutional documents generally, establishing the necessary hierarchy of law within a state constitutional order. But in this case, it appears to do more than that, for that legal supremacy itself acknowledges its own obligation to avoid damaging the socialist system, a key element of which is the leadership of the CPC. Third, Article 5 establishes the principle that all state organs and other collective organizations (including the CPC itself) are bound by the state constitution and its legitimately enacted laws.[61] This is supplemented by an additional provision that prohibits extending any "privilege beyond the Constitution or the law" to any individual or organization, including presumably the CPC itself.[62]

Taken together, and certainly from a Western perspective, the aggregate principles of Article 5 suggest that all political organizations are subject to and subordinate in authority to the law of the Constitution. That is an argument that has been made by influential commentators both within and beyond China. The argument has also been made that Xianfa is itself irrelevant with respect to the CPC on the principle that any such constraint would have to fail as an effort that damages the socialist system by inhibiting the leadership of the CPC. Both arguments provide insight but miss the precise meaning with which these provisions were drafted to establish the core principles of the State-Party System. First, as the legalists would suggest, as drafted Xianfa clearly provides that the CPC is and must be subject to its provisions. But the state constitution also acknowledges that this subordination is not a function of the legal power represented by the state constitution itself, but by the determination by the CPC itself that the socialist system itself and the expression of its leadership of the masses (directly and through the state organs) be exercised through law. It is the CPC that binds itself, it is not bound. To that extent, the anti-legalists have a strong point. But it is a point they take too far. Indeed, to suggest that the CPC falls outside the reach of the state constitution is to suggest that the CPC is itself incapable of developing and abiding by its own rule system in its leadership role. That this vanguard are the masters of Xianfa is clear enough from the terms of Articles 11-3 and 5. But to challenge the CPC's authority to exercise its leadership of the socialist system itself by suggesting it incapable of binding itself to its own rules would appear to produce a substantial damage to the socialism itself.

Instead, whet emerges from these provisions is the affirmation, in legal form, of the supremacy of socialism, and the socialist path, all under the leadership of the CPC. Socialism and the socialist path collectively express, the form of the expression of supreme sovereign authority in China, the realization of is vested in the CPC exercising leadership authority for the nation. That authority is then expressed through the constitution and operation of the organs of state power operating the law of the State Constitution, binding all national and political organs, the exercise of which must be undertaken inconformity with the core principles of state socialism with Chinese characteristics, the authority over the legitimate expression of which is in the CPC. Yet that is a major constitutional concession that expresses the essence of constitutionalism in China – that the sovereign authority and its normative framework are themselves bound by their own rules.[63] More importantly, perhaps, is the equally core principle that the CPC is itself the expression of the socialist system (and its normative principles) to which it is bound beyond its legal expression in the state constitution. To understand the nature and scope of that relationship between the sovereign political authority (the COC leadership within the socialist system) and its normative constrains (the core principles of socialism with Chinese characteristics) it is necessary to look elsewhere. That elsewhere is in the constitution of the CPC itself,[64] to which this contribution next considers.

The Constitution of Sovereign Political Authority: The Communist Party of China and Political Constitution of the Nation

If the highest political authority in China is vested in or proceeds from the socialist system, one which may be affirmed (but not contained) in legal form,[65] one must look elsewhere for the articulation of those vessels within which it is either contained, held, or expressed. That is, it is necessary to determine the manner in which this socialist system is incarnated, made manifest, and to identify the institutional organs through which it is realized. In the process of that incarnation and identification between system and its legitimate (institutional) holder, one can determine the constraints (expressed as a function of fidelity to and the core principles) around which the system distinguishes itself from other systems.[66] To understand the Chinese socialist system,[67] then, it is necessary to understand the principles under which it is constituted as unique,[68] and to identify the collective whose legitimacy is dependent on the exercise of (political) authority subject to and in furtherance of the elaboration and protection of those principles.

It is in this sense that 依法治国 (yifa zhiguo; governing the nation in accordance with law) is not merely something that can be dismissed as an ideological and strategic message about power relations,[69] but it is rather the expression of the fundamental constitutional ordering in which law itself is meant to express and rationalize the socialist system operating under the constraints of its principles and guided by its vanguard. It is in this sense as well that one may constrain and contextualize the fundamental character of the vanguard as representative – it is not itself, but rather the incarnation of actors, systems, and principles that define and limit the extent of its discretionary choices.[70]

The socialist system, the affirmance of the legal form of which is found in the state constitution, must be memorialized somewhere;[71] and a good starting point is in the Constitution of the CPC.[72] Its General Program attempts a more or less comprehensive exposition of the constitution of the vanguard, its character, its representative function, and the constraints under which it operates, and the principles' fidelity to which mark the outer boundaries of legitimate exercise of representative leadership authority within the Chinese socialist system. The General Program starts with an exposition of the essence of the role of the CPCV as a vanguard force within the Chinese socialist system (the legal form of which assumes the position of paramount foundation for authority in the state organs). That role is comprehensively representative.

> The Communist Party of China is the vanguard of the Chinese working class, the Chinese people, and the Chinese nation. It is the leadership core for the cause of socialism with Chinese characteristics and represents the developmental demands of China's advanced productive forces, the orientation for China's advanced culture, and the fundamental interests of the greatest possible majority of the Chinese people. The Party's highest ideal and ultimate goal is the realization of communism.[73]

The CPC, then, is the ultimate fiduciary, the receptacle in which sovereign authority is vested for a very specific purpose beyond which it is not within the power of the CPC to venture. The elaboration of the constraints and expectations of this leadership responsibility is then elaborated in the 33 paragraphs that follow. These elaborations might effectively be understood as the operational principles which are affirmed in legal form in Xianfa Article 1– effectively the elaboration of the principles and characteristics of the Chinese socialist system and of the CPC's leadership role within it. It is to that extent, at least, that the CPC Constitution acquires a constitutional dimension as the written expression of both the character of sovereign authority and the manner of its legitimate exercise.

First, the CPC's leadership authority takes as its guide to action the fundamental principles of Marxist Leninism as elaborated within the national context of China.[74] The essence of that elaboration in the thought of Mao Zedong, the theory of Deng Xiaoping, and the principles of Sange Daibiao and Scientific outlook on Development and Xi Jinping New Era Thought are then elaborated and their connection with the organic growth of the theoretical and practical basis of the Chinese socialist system explained. The object is to perfect the socialist system with Chinese characteristics through the work of the CPC.[75] The leadership role of the vanguard is then to move the development and implementation of the Chinese socialist system from its contemporary stage of development (described in the General Program for many years as "in the primary stage of socialism")[76] to the establishment of a Chinese communist society. To that end, the role of the CPC as the driver of the "basic economic system" is justified but only consonant with this core aims, with respect to which economic development "is the Party's top priority."[77] The correct exercise of CPC leadership within the socialist system is marked by its ability to point to progress in the movement to the establishment of a communist society.[78]

Also to that end, and within the guiding principles of its theoretical foundations, the CPC must develop a *basic line*, the affirmance of which in legal form is the charge of and undertaken through the state constitution.[79] But that Basic Line must itself be made accountable to the basic tenets of the socialist system itself and the fundamental driving purpose of the vanguard, one that legitimates the delegation of leadership authority to it, and the system must distinguish itself from others, especially liberal democratic systems. Here one encounters the constitutionalization of the "Four Cardinal Principles" in the General Program.[80] The precise nature of CPC leadership is then elaborated. These comprise the responsibility for leading "the people in developing the socialist market economy ... in developing socialist democracy... in developing an advanced socialist culture... in building a harmonious socialist society... [and in] in building a socialist ecological civilization."[81] The relationship between CPC leadership and the military, ethnic groups, the unaffiliated masses and patriotic forces, and foreigners and foreign powers are then elaborated.[82]

The object of these elaborations is to set the boundaries and trajectories for the exercise of leadership to move the Chinese nation from the present to the next stage of historical development, that is, from the "new era" of development to the next era of development. That, in turn, is based on the principles of the realization of "the Chinese Dream of national rejuvenation" for which the emphasis on following the basic line (an affirmation of the context of the Chinese socialist system in political form) is underlined.[83] That ultimately requires an emphasis of the CPC at the center of both socialism and of tits elaboration as culture, politics, economics, and law. It follows that a central element of CPC leadership is self-perfection – perfecting the vanguard is a necessary step in the perfection of the nation that then follows. That, in turn, is a function of adherence to the CPC basic line, of applying the principle of emancipating the mind and seeking truth from facts, of the fundamental representative obligation of serving the people, of the application of principles of democratic centralism (here as a political rather than legal construct), and in self-accountability and self-discipline of party members and party organs. And thus, the foundation of Chinese political constitutionalism:

> Leadership of the Communist Party of China is the most essential attribute of socialism with Chinese characteristics, and the greatest strength of this system. The Party exercises overall leadership over all areas of endeavor in every part of the country.[84]

The constitutionalism that creates the boundaries for the legitimate exercise of that leadership that constrains the abuse of discretionary authority of the CPC in its vanguard role is found in its political constitution. The legal form of that leadership is expressed in the state constitution which within the constellation of Chinese constitutionalism is understood as binding on the CPC precisely because it is an expression in legal form of the basic line of the CPC and thus a core element of the expression of its leadership. The implications are clear; while the state constitution provides the structure and rules for the operation of the state, the leadership of the CPC is paramount in guiding discretionary decision-making by officials, and its basic line and leadership decisive for the interpretation and performance of the legislative, judicial, and executive functions delegated to the administrative apparatus. But the leadership of the CPC is itself constrained by its own normative systems and its representative character. The policing of those limits, though, are consigned to the CPC itself. And it is here that one finds fertile ground for substantial development of Chinese constitutionalism on its own terms.[85]

These principles and structural characteristics were well on display in the period after 2013, when the government, under the leadership of the CPC, began a multi-year project of transitioning from the era of Reform and Opening Up established under the leadership of Deng Xiaoping to the "New Era" under the leadership of Xi Jinping. The change was undertaken within the parameters of the Chinese constitutional order, and yet it also reflected substantial development of the policies and forms of interpretive within the overall normative framework of Chinese constitutionalism. The initial consolidation of this constitutional movement was announced in Xi Jinping's Report to the 19th CPC Congress in 2017 in which the constitutionally significant progress into a "New Era" was officially described.[86]

> The importance of the New Era announcement was largely lost to the West; just another ideological bauble with no real meaning, other than perhaps relating to the personal power of specific leaders.... First the New Era signaled that China was entering a different historical stage that opened both the premises and operating conditions of the past to reform. Principal among these were the great pillars of the prior Deng Xiaoping Era: socialist modernization, socialist democracy, the relationship of the CPC to the state and the masses, and the understanding and role of law in the relationship between the state and political organs. Principal among the changes from the Deng Xiaoping Era was a movement away from the key focus of socialist modernization—the development of productive forces—to a new focus on the distributive effects of wealth creation. This marked a long journey from the principal contradiction of the first, Mao Zedong Era, which focused on class struggle in the construction of Party and polity in the wake of the establishment of the "New" China in 1949, through the focus on development, to a new focus on distribution.[87]

New Era theory, then, reconstituted the forms of expression of constitutional principle rather than revising those principles themselves.[88] The focus has been on the development of Chinese and socialist principles of democracy,[89] of rule of law,[90] and a distinctive socialist path toward the realization of development and democratic political principles centered on and from the political vanguard.[91] The amendment of the Chinese state constitution to remove presidential term limits nicely illustrates the way that movement from one historical era to another can substantially affect practice in fidelity to core normative principles of the Chinese constitutional model. One of the great innovations of the move from the era of class struggle under Mao Zedong to the era of Reform and Opening Up (and its focus on the development of productive forces) was the determination that it was important to limit the role of leading cadres at the core of leadership of the CPC.[92] New Era theory, however, with its returning the CPC at the center suggested that the state constitution aligns with the structures and practices of the political constitution of the CPC. Because there were no corresponding limits to leadership of senior cadres in the CPC, such limits in the state constitution appeared incompatible with political expectations. In either case, the principles of political constitutionalism remain unchanged; its interpretation and application, however, change with the times and the collective interpretation of the approach to meeting the challenges of the principal contradiction. In this case, that meant to give effect to the notion that the threat of left error that supported the policy choice to apply term limits in 1981 no longer applied in 2017, when the threat of right error appeared more important.[93] Thus, when Chinese officials defended the change by suggesting the change "benefits protecting the authority of the party center and collective leadership with Comrade Xi Jinping at its core, and benefits the strengthening and perfecting of the national leadership system,"[94] it could be understood to mean that the change was compatible with the normative basis of socialism with Chinese characteristics and aligned with the policy priorities of the new historical era and deeply embedded in the crafting of an evolving manifestation of consultative democracy.[95] More precisely, it served as a concrete manifestation of the order of superiority at the apex of which was the CPC constitution. At the same time, it suggested that the great task of the vanguard political body, its constitutional responsibility, would itself be centered on self-discipline as a function of its normative values as expressed in each historical era. Matching power with responsibility will pose the greatest secondary contradiction of this new era.[96]

Conclusion

This contribution has considered the constitution of the Party-State system as the constitutionalization of Chinese socialism as both a legal and a political construction. Both are interlinked through the mechanism of Leninist vanguardism – interposing an organ representing the leading social forces of the nations constituted as a communist party, as the leading organ both representative and responsible for the legitimate advancement of the core principles of Chinese socialism and the movement of Chinese socialism toward its eventual end – the establishment of a communist society in China. That long term project requires the constitution of both a political organ bound by the principles and objectives of socialism itself and an apparatus that constitutes the rule-based expression of these responsibilities and the legitimate form of its manifestation. From these insights, it is possible to develop a theory of Chinese Marxist-Leninist political constitutionalism. Liberal democratic systems invest all political authority in a government that is then divided usually along functional lines (executive, legislative, judicial, and sometimes administrative). Chinese Marxist-Leninist constitutional systems vest all political authority to a vanguard party, which holds responsibility for leading and guiding the nation, the administration of which is then organized in a government also functionally organized. The objectively articulated normative framework of liberal democratic constitutions is built into its constitutional structures, in its text, application, and interpretation. That of Chinese Marxist-Leninist constitutionalism is built into the dual instruments of the CPC's political constitution, and the administrative constitution of the state. Both are guided by and built on the core normative structures of Marxism and Leninism and applied in a dynamic as a function of historically contingent contradictions the overcoming of which serves as the path through socialism to the establishment of a communist society. It is within this framework that the leadership of the Party molds its policies and assesses their fidelity to the system – and it is through this that the concepts of socialist democracy,[97] socialist rule of law and legality,[98] and socialist culture[99] are elaborated.

Notes

1 Günter Frankenberg, "Authoritarian Constitutionalism: Coming to Terms with Modernity's Nightmare," in Helena Alviar Garcia and Günter Frankenberg (eds.), *Authoritarian Constitutionalism: Comparative Analysis and Critique* (Edward Elgar 2019).
2 See Randall Peerenboom, China's Long March Toward Rule of Law (Cambridge 2009).
3 Baogang He & Mark E. Warren, "Authoritarian Deliberation: The Deliberative Turn in Chinese Political Development," (2011) Perspectives on Politics 9:269.
4 Robert A. Dahl, *On Democracy* (Yale University Press 1998), pp. 35–83.
5 Mark V. Tushnet, "Authoritarian Constitutionalism," (2015) Cornell Law Review 100:391.
6 See, e.g., Alexei Trochev & Peter H. Solomon Jr., "Authoritarian Constitutionalism in Putin's Russia: A Pragmatic Constitutional Court in a Dual State," (2018) Communist and Post-Communist Studies 51:201–214; Melissa Crouch, "Pre-Emptive Constitution-Making: Authoritarian Constitutionalism and the Military in Myanmar," (2020) Law & Society Review 54(2):487–515.
7 Roberto Niembro, "Conceptualizing Authoritarian Constitutionalism. A Latin American View," Völkerrechtsblog, 17 July 2017, doi: 10.17176/20170717-082012 ("it is a concept that refers to a very sophisticated way in which ruling elites with an authoritarian mentality exercise power in not fully democratic states … the regime's liberal democratic constitution, instead of limiting the power of the state and empowering those who would otherwise be powerless, is used for practical and authoritarian ideological functions.")
8 Alexander Somek, "Authoritarian Constitutionalism: Austrian Constitutional Doctrine 1933 to 1938 and Its Legacy," in Christian Joerges & Navraj Singh Ghaleigh (eds.), *Darker Legacies of Law in Europe: The Shadow of National Socialism and Fascism over Europe and its Legal Traditions* (Hart 2003).
9 See, Edward S. Corwin, The 'Higher Law' (Background of American Constitutional Law Cornell University Press 1955).
10 For a variation developed during the crisis of government between 1919 and 1945, see Arthur N. Holcombe, *Government in a Planned Democracy* (WW Norton 1935) (looking to a rationalized system that was applied eventually only for a short time as democratic socialism in European and other liberal democratic states and that served to support the legitimation of a form of liberal democratic administrative-bureaucratic constitutionalism).
11 See, e.g., Thomas Paine, "The Rights of Man," in Howard Fast (ed.), *The Selected Work of Tom Paine*, pp. 93–279; John C. Calhoun, "A Discourse on the Constitution and Government of the United States," in Ross W.E. Lence (ed), *Union and Liberty: The Political Philosophy of John C. Calhoun* (first published 1850, Liberty Fund 1992); James Fenimore Cooper, *The American Democrat* (first published 1838, Liberty Fund reprint of 1931 edition).
12 Both key early modern thinkers essential to the development of western constitutionalism tended to tie the political premises of the organization of human collectives in its ideal form to the nature and character of the humans it is meant to incarnate and serve. See, e.g., Thomas Hobbs, *Leviathan: Or the Matter, Forme and Power of a Commonwealth, Ecclesiasticall and Civil* (First published 1651, Project Gutenberg eBook #3207 edition 2002); John Locke, Two Treatises on Government (first printed 1690, reprinted from The Works of John Locke (ten volumes) London: Thomas Tegg 1823).
13 Louis Henkin, "A New Birth of Constitutionalism: Genetic Influences and Genetic Defects," (1993) Cardozo Law Review 14:533, 535–536.
14 Larry Catá Backer, "From Constitution to Constitutionalism: A Global Framework for Legitimate Public Power Systems," (2009) Penn State Law Review 113(3):671. See generally Giovanni Sartori, "Constitutionalism: A Preliminary Discussion," (1962) American Political Science Review 56:853, 853–862.
15 See, e.g., Ding Xiaodong, "Law According to the Chinese Communist Party: Constitutionalism and Socialist Rule of Law," (2017) Modern China 43(3):322–352; Qin Qianhong and Ye Haibo, Socialist Constitutionalism (City University of Hong Kong Press 2017); Fu Hauling and Zhai Xiaobo, "What Makes the Chinese Constitution Socialist?" (2018) I-CON 16:655–663 (distinguishing between normative constitutionalists and political constitutionalists; ibid, 656–659).
16 Xi Jinping, Secure a Decisive Victory in Building a Moderately Prosperous Society in All Respects and Strive for the Great Success of Socialism with Chinese Characteristics for a

New Era, Speech delivered at the 19th National Congress of the Communist Party of China (October 18, 2017) <http://www.xinhuanet.com/english/download/Xi_Jinping's_report_at_19th_CPC_National_Congress.pdf> accessed 31 October 2921.

17 For this type of effort, see, e.g., Tom Ginsburg and Alberto Simpser (eds) *Constitutions in Authoritarian Regimes* (CUP 2014).

18 See, e.g., Yan Lin and Tom Ginsberg, "Constitutional Interpretation in Lawmaking: China's Invisible Constitutional Enforcement Mechanism," (2015) The American Journal of Comparative Law 63(2):467–492.

19 Larry Catá Backer, "Party, People, Government and State: On Constitutional Values and the Legitimacy of the Chinese State-Party Rule of Law System," (2012) Boston University International Law Journal 30:331.

20 China, State Council White Paper, China: Democracy that Works (Beijing 4 December 2021) (hereafter SC White Paper 2021). In the original 中国的民主 (2021 年 12 月) 中华人民共和国 国务院新闻办公室; available <http://www.gov.cn/zhengce/2021-12/04/content_5655823.htm>(hereafter 中国的民主).

21 Jiang Shigong, "Written and Unwritten Constitutions: A New Approach to the Study of Constitutional Government in China," (2010) Modern China 36(1):12. Larry Catá Backer, "Party, People, Government and State," supra, pp. 336–337 ("These judgments have formed the basis for analysis of Chinese constitutionalism. The pre-Deng Chinese state governance architecture could be dismissed as anti-constitutional, rather than criticized for failures to appropriately incorporate constitutional principles …. After Deng, China was judged from a constitutional perspective – and it was judged increasingly harshly, or simply dismissed as a capitalist but totalitarian state.").

22 中国的民主, supra 前言 [Preface].

23 For what at one time was a position more sympathetic to liberal democratic constitutionalist sensibilities, see Albert Chen, "The Discourse of Political Constitutionalism in Contemporary China: Gao Quanxi's Studies on China's Political Constitution," (2014) China Review 14(2):183.

24 These assumptions are expressed most authoritatively in its constitutive documents, the state constitution (Xianfa), and the Constitution of the Communist Party of China; but it is also authoritatively popularized and projected outward to foreigners in publications like the SC White Paper 2021, supra.

25 Constitution of the Communist Party of China <> accessed 31 October 2021.

26 Stanley Lubman, "Bird in a Cage: Chinese Law Reform after Twenty Years," (2000) Northwestern Journal of International Law and Business 20:383 399. See also John Gardner, Chinese Politics and the Succession to Mao (Palgrave 1982) ("But as good Leninists, China's leaders intended that the Party should remain in full control, that the extension of freedoms should be gradual, and that there should be no decline into 'anarchism.'" Ibid., 141).

27 Charles Howard McIlwain, Constitutionalism Ancient and Modern (Cornell University Press 1947), p. 140. See also Larry Catá Backer, "Reifying Law–Government, Law and the Rule of Law in Governance Systems," (2007) Penn State International Law Review 26:521.

28 Cf., Jiang Shigong, "Chinese style constitutionalism: On Backer's Chinese Party-State Constitutionalism," (2013) Modern China 40(2):133–167.

29 Andrew Peng, "Sinicized Marxist Constitutionalism: Its Emergence, Contents, and Implications," (2011) Global Discourse 2:83–107; see also Terrell Carver, "Varieties of Constitutionalism: A Response to 'Sinicized Marxist Constitutionalism' by Chengyi (Andrew) Peng," (2011) Global Discourse 2(1):109–114.

30 Xingzhong Yu, "Legal Pragmatism in the People's Republic of China," (1989) Journal of Chinese Law 3:29. Yu speaks of such cages of regulation in Peng Zhen's explanation of the legitimacy of law as a function of *shiji* (actualities) as determined by the CPC Ibid., p. 42–43. The concept extends to the content of the state constitution – as a memorialization of the actualities of the current era of historical development of China under the guidance of the CPC and reflecting its line (ibid., pp. 44–45).

31 See, Larry Catá Backer, "From Constitution to Constitutionalism," supra (describing the essential characteristics of trans systemic constitutionalism as a system for the implementation of core political principle that avoids abuses of power.

32 Mao Zedong, "On Contradiction" (August 1937), reprinted from the *Selected Works of Mao Tse-tung* in <https://www.marxists.org/reference/archive/mao/selected-works/volume-1/mswv1_17.htm> accessed 28 February 2022, The foundational role of the theory of

contradiction in Chinese constitutionalism cannot be understated as both a normative guide and as a discursively disciplinary concept within a system that is inherently dynamic and moving forward through the trigger that each contradiction represents in history. See, Larry Catá Backer, The Genetics of China's New Era: Red Genes and Inter-Generational Leninism–Considering "用好红色资源, 传承好红色基因 把红色江山世世代代传下去 习近平 [Make good use of red resources, inherit the red gene, and pass on the red country from generation to generation, Xi Jinping], Emancipating the Mind in the New Era: Bulletin of the Coalition for Peace & Ethics 16(1):71, 72, 75–77 (2021). As a consequence, there is a relational and dynamic element between the core normative values of Chinese constitutionalism and its specific application rationalized through the framework of the core contradiction and articulated in the core project of each core of leadership. See, e.g., Larry Catá Backer, "The Rule of Law: The Chinese Communist Party, and Ideological Campaigns: Sange Daibiao (The 'Three Represents'), Socialist Rule of Law, and Modern Chinese Constitutionalism," (2006) Journal of Transitional Law and Contemporary Problems 16(1):101–174.

33 Larry Catá Backer, "Toward New Era Thought: Reflections on Xi Jinping, Speech at the Meeting Celebrating the 40th Anniversary of Reform and Opening Up," (2020) Emancipating the Mind in the New Era: Bulletin of the Coalition for Peace & Ethics 15(1):121–144.

34 Discussion of the success or failures of the constitutional system to live up to its theory or to work toward its idealized form is beyond the scope of this contribution. Cf., Zheng Shiping, Party vs. State in Post 1949 China (New York: Cambridge University Press 1997).

35 On the history of constitution making and its relation to the CPC, see, Hungdah Chiu, "The 1982 Chinese Constitution and the Rule of Law," (1985) Review of Socialist Law 11(2):143–160.

36 Johannes Fabian, Time and the Other: How Anthropology Makes Its Object (Columbia University Press 2014). Cf., Donald C. Clarke, "New Approaches to the Study of Political Order in China," (2010) Modern China 36:87–99.

37 Janet Maybin, "Language, Struggle and Voice: The Bakhtin/Volosinov Writings," in Margaret Wetherell, Stephanie Taylor, and Simeon J. Yates (eds.) Discourse Theory and Practice: A Reader (Sage 2003), 64 et seq.

38 Cf., Qianfan Zhang, "A Constitution without Constitutionalism? The Paths of Constitutional Development in China," (2010) International Journal of Constitutional Law 8(4):950–976.

39 Constitution of the People's Republic of China adopted 5th Session of the 5th National Peoples' Congress and promulgated 4 December 1982, as amended 1988, 1993, 1999, 2004 and 2018 (hereafter the "state constitution" or "Xianfa").

40 Xianfa, supra, preamble.

41 Xianfa, supra, preamble.

42 For a simple explanation of the structures for the normative development of contemporary Chinese Marxist Leninism, see, Josephine Ma, Explainer: From Mao Zedong to Xi Jinping: how China's Communist Party leaders have shaped its ideology," South China Morning Post (30 June 2021) <https://www.scmp.com/news/china/politics/article/3139347/mao-xi-how-chinas-communist-party-leaders-have-shaped-its> accessed 29 October 2021.

43 The notion of the people's democratic dictatorship has undergone some development but its origins can be traced back to the development of the thought of Mao Zedong. See Mao Zedong, "In the People's Democratic Dictatorship," Remarks delivered in commemoration of the 28th Anniversary of the Communist Party of China (30 June 1949) <https://www.marxists.org/reference/archive/mao/selected-works/volume-4/mswv4_65.htm> accessed 30 October 2021. In relevant part Mao suggests provides the essence of the concept:

> "You are dictatorial." My dear sirs, you are right, that is just what we are. All the experience the Chinese people have accumulated through several decades teaches us to enforce the people's democratic dictatorship, that is, to deprive the reactionaries of the right to speak and let the people alone have that right.. . Who are the people? At the present stage in China, they are the working class, the peasantry, the urban petty bourgeoisie and the national bourgeoisie. These classes, led by the working class and the Communist Party, unite to form their own state and elect their own government .... Why must things be done this way? The reason is quite clear to everybody. If things were not done this way, the revolution would fail, the people would suffer, the country would be conquered. "Don't you want to abolish state power?"

> Yes, we do, but not right now; we cannot do it yet .... The people's state protects the people. Only when the people have such a state can they educate and remould themselves by democratic methods on a country-wide scale, with everyone taking part, and shake off the influence of domestic and foreign reactionaries (which is still very strong, will survive for a long time and cannot be quickly destroyed), rid themselves of the bad habits and ideas acquired in the old society, not allow themselves to be led astray by the reactionaries, and continue to advance – to advance towards a socialist and communist society.

See also N. Knight, "On Contradiction and on New Democracy: Contrasting Perspectives on Causation and Change in the Thought of Mao Zedong," (1990) Bulletin of Concerned Asian Scholars 22:18–34.

44 Xianfa, supra, Art. 1 "The People's Republic of China is a socialist state governed by a people's democratic dictatorship that is led by the working class and based on an alliance of workers and peasants."

45 Ibid. ("The socialist system is the fundamental system of the People's Republic of China.").

46 Ibid. ("Leadership by the Communist Party of China is the defining feature of socialism with Chinese characteristics.").

47 Ibid.

48 Ibid., Art. 2.

49 Ibid., preamble ("Through the long process of revolution, development and reform, a broad patriotic united front has formed under the leadership of the Communist Party of China, with the participation of other political parties and people's organizations and including all socialist working people, people involved in building socialism, patriots who support socialism, and patriots who support China's reunification and are dedicated to the rejuvenation of the Chinese nation.").

50 Ibid. Art. 2 ("The organs through which the people exercise state power are the National People's Congress and the local people's congresses at all levels. The people shall, in accordance with the provisions of law, manage state affairs, economic and cultural undertakings, and social affairs through various channels and in various ways.").

51 Ibid., art. 3.

52 The Chinese media has provided a nice summary explanation that has been widely distributed for western audiences. See Robert L. Kuhn, "How does 'democratic centralism' work?, CGTN (20 October 2017) <https://news.cgtn.com/news/77417a4d31597a6333566d54/index.html> accessed 26 October 2021.

53 Mao Zedong, "Rectify the Party's Working Style," Address at the opening of the Party School of the Central Committee of the Communist Party of China (1 February 1942) <https://www.marxists.org/reference/archive/mao/selected-works/volume-3/mswv3_06.htm> ("they do not realize that the Communist Party not only needs democracy but needs centralization even more. They forget the system of democratic centralism in which the minority is subordinate to the majority, the lower level to the higher level, the part to the whole and the entire membership to the Central Committee"). This ordering concept with its apex in the leadership of the CPC now acquires a legal form. See generally Douglas Howard, "Democratic Centralism in Revolutionary China: Tensions within a People's Democratic Dictatorship," (2017) Open Journal of Philosophy 7(4):448–466. For its European and Soviet origins, see, Klaus von Beyme, "A Comparative View of Democratic Centralism," (1975) Government and Opposition 10(3):259–277.

54 Larry Catá Backer, "Popular Consultation and Referendum in the Making of Contemporary Cuban Socialist Democracy Practice and Constitutional Theory," (2019) University of Miami International & Comparative Law Review 27:37–130.

55 SC White Paper 2021, supra. at II.3.

56 Among the most subtle and interesting in that respect is Tong Zhiwei, *Right, Power, and Faquanism: A Practical Legal Theory From Contemporary China* (Xu Ping (trans) Brill, 2018).

57 Xianfa, supra, Art. 5.

58 Ibid., Art. 1.

59 Ibid., Art. 5.

60 Ibid.

61 Ibid. ("All state organs and armed forces, all political parties and social organizations, and all enterprises and public institutions must abide by the Constitution and the law. Accountability must be enforced for all acts that violate the Constitution or laws.").
62 Ibid.
63 Larry Catá Backer, "The Rule of Law, the Chinese Communist Party, and Ideological Campaigns: Sange Daibiao (The Three Represents), Socialist Rule of Law, and Modern Chinese Constitutionalism," (2006) Transnational Law & Contemporary Problems 16:29; Chongyi Feng, "China's Socialist Rule of Law," in John Garrick and Yan Chang Bennett (eds.), China's Socialist Rule of Law Reforms Under Xi Jinping (Taylor & Francis, 2016).
64 Cf., Zheng Yongnian and Chen Gang, "The Chinese Communist Party: An Institutional Perspective," in David S.G. Goodman (ed.), *Handbook of the Politics of China* (Edward Elgar 2015).
65 Xianfa, supra., art. 1 and discussion supa.
66 Cf. Niklas Luhmann, Social Systems, in John Bednarz and Dirk Baecker (trans.) (Stanford University Press 1984), esp. 437–477.
67 And to contrast it to that of the now defunct European Soviet version, see Solomon Schwartz, "The Communist Party and the Soviet State," (1953) Problems of Communism 2:8.
68 This turns on its head the traditional western analysis that "the legitimacy-inducing potential of performance factors has become depleted, the CCP has resorted to new methods of legitimacy-building and new sources of legitimation." Aleksandra Kubat, "Morality as Legitimacy under Xi Jinping: The Political Functionality of Traditional Culture for the Chinese Communist Party," (2018) Journal of Current Chinese Affairs 47(3):47–86, 49.
69 See, e.g., Susan Trevaskes, "A Law Unto Itself: Chinese Communist Party Leadership and Yifa zhiguo in the Xi Era," (2018) Modern China 44(4):347–373.
70 "We must observe the Party's fundamental purpose of wholeheartedly serving the people, and put into practice the Party's mass line in all aspects of governance. We must regard as our goal the people's aspirations to live a better life, and rely on the people to move history forward." Xi Jinping, Secure a Decisive Victory in Building a Moderately Prosperous Society, supra n. 13.
71 But Jiang Shigong argues that it may exist in written and unwritten form, a point that is well taken. See Larry Catá Backer, "Jiang Shigong 强世功 on "Written and Unwritten Constitutions" and Their Relevance to Chinese Constitutionalism," (2'14) Modern China 40(2):119–132.
72 Communist Party of China, The Constitution of the Communist Party of China (Revised and adopted at the 19th National Congress of the Communist Party of China on October 24, 2017) <http://www.xinhuanet.com//english/download/Constitution_of_the_Communist_Party_of_China.pdf > accessed 31 October 2021 (Hereafter the CPC Constitution). The Constitution of the CPC has undergone a long period of evolution that in some respects mirrors the evolution of the state constitution. See, e.g., Constitution of the Communist Party of China adopted by the 9th National CPC Congress 4 April 1969 < https://www.marxists.org/subject/china/documents/cpc/ninth_congress2.htm > accessed 20 October 2021, though one that also tended to be elaborated in writing with constitutive effect.
73 Ibid., General Program.
74 Ibid.("The Communist Party of China uses Marxism-Leninism, Mao Zedong Thought, Deng Xiaoping Theory, the Theory of Three Represents, the Scientific Outlook on Development, and Xi Jinping Thought on Socialism with Chinese Characteristics for a New Era as its guides to action.").
75 Ibid. ("All Party members must cherish deeply, uphold long term, and continue to develop this path, this theoretical system, this socialist system, and this culture, which the Party has developed through great hardship.").
76 Ibid.
77 Ibid.
78 Ibid. ("In this new era in the new century, the strategic objectives of economic and social development are to finish building a moderately prosperous society in all respects by the time the Party marks its centenary and to build China into a great modern socialist country in every dimension by the time the People's Republic celebrates its centenary.").
79 Ibid. ("The basic line of the Communist Party of China in the primary stage of socialism is to lead all the people of China together in a self-reliant and pioneering effort, making economic

development the central task, upholding the Four Cardinal Principles, and remaining committed to reform and opening up, so as to see China becomes a great modern socialist country that is prosperous, strong, democratic, culturally advanced, harmonious, and beautiful.").

80 CPC Constitution, General Program. For a contemporary interpretation that seeks to embed itself in the contemporary expression of CPC working styles, see Huiming Guo, "Adhere to the Four Cardinal Principles and Socialism with Chinese Characteristics," (2020) Learning and Education 9(3):72–75 < https://pdfs.semanticscholar.org/ddf2/7a1e5b1328bc6376bb11dd94921e127661fb.pdf > accessed 21 October 2021.

81 CPC Constitution, supra, General Program.

82 Ibid.

83 Ibid. (the CPC "must follow its basic line; exercise self-supervision and strengthen self-governance in every respect; strengthen its long-term governance capacity, its advanced nature, and its purity; and, in the spirit of reform and innovation, make comprehensive moves to press ahead with the great new project of Party building.").

84 Ibid.

85 Ding Xiaodong, "Law According to the Chinese Communist Party: Constitutionalism and Socialist Rule of Law," (2017) Modern China 43(3):322–352; Lance LP Gore, "Rebuilding the Leninist Party Rule: Chinese Communist Party under Xi Jinping's Stewardship," (2016) East Asian Policy 8(1):5–15.

86 Xi Jinping, Secure a Decisive Victory, supra n16.

87 See, Larry Catá Backer, '"The Emerging Trajectories of Chinese Constitutionalism in the 'New Era'": Text of Remarks Delivered at Event, "China's Changing Constitution," Trinity College Oxford ("Extended Play" Version)' (Law at the End of the Day, 21 November 2018) < https://lcbackerblog.blogspot.com/2018/11/the-emerging-trajectories-of-chinese.html#more > accessed February 28, 2022.

88 See, e.g., 十个明确: 习近平新时代中国特色社会主义思想的核心内容的进一步概括 ("Ten clarifications: a further summary of the core content of Xi Jinping Thought on Socialism with Chinese Characteristics for a New Era") < http://www.qstheory.cn/laigao/ycjx/2021-11/16/c_1128070643.htm> accessed 28 February 2022.

89 See, 中国新型政党制度 (China's New Political Party System) <http://www.xinhuanet.com/politics/2021-06/25/c_1127596748.htm> accessed 27 February 2022.

90 See, e.g., Lu Xu, "The Changing Perspectives of Chinese Law: Socialist Rule of Law, Emerging Case Law and the Belt and Road Initiative," (2019) The Chinese Journal of Global Governance 5:153–175.

91 See, 中共建黨百年 | 習近平七一講話全文 (Xi Jinping, Speech at a Ceremony Marking the Centenary of the Communist Party of China (July 1, 2021)) <http://www.xinhuanet.com/english/special/2021-07/01/c_1310038244.htm> accessed 20 February 2022.

92 See, Resolution on certain questions in the history of our party since the founding of the People's Republic of China.
(Adopted by the Sixth Plenary Session of the Eleventh Central Committee of the Communist Party of China on June 27, 1981) <https://china.usc.edu/chinese-communist-party-central-committee-%e2%80%9cresolution-certain-questions-history-our-party-founding> accessed 1 March 2022.

93 See, e.g., Lea Shih, "Debunking three myths about the end of presidential term limits in China," (Merics, 6 April 2018) <https://merics.org/en/analysis/debunking-three-myths-about-end-presidential-term-limits-china> accessed 27 February 2022.

94 "China says lifting term limits is about protecting authority of party," Reuters (4 March 2018) <https://www.reuters.com/article/us-china-parliament-politics/china-says-lifting-term-limits-is-about-protecting-authority-of-party-idUSKBN1GG0CR> accessed 26 February 2022 (quoting Zhang Yesui, a vice foreign minister and spokesman for the NPC).

95 See, Larry Catá Backer, Deliberative Democracy (协商民主) in Context; Considering the Revisions to Democratic Centralism in the Chinese Communist Party Constitution in the Shadow of Suggested Changes to Leadership Term Limits (Law at the End of the Day, 4 March 2018) <https://lcbackerblog.blogspot.com/2018/03/deliberative-democracy-in-context.html> accessed 1 March 2022.

96 The genesis can be traced back to the revolutionary period. See, Mao Zedong, "On Practice: On the Relation Between Knowledge and Practice, Between Knowing and Doing" (July 1937);

reprinted from the *Selected Works of Mao Tse-tung* in <https://www.marxists.org/reference/archive/mao/selected-works/volume-1/mswv1_16.htm> accessed 1 March 2022. That project continues to be focused at both elite and grass roots cadres. See, e.g., 学习画报; 习近平: 筑牢理想信念根基树立践行正确政绩观 在新时代新征程上留下无悔的奋斗足迹 来源; 中央纪委国家监委网站 2022-03-01 <https://www.ccdi.gov.cn/toutun/202203/t20220301_174990_m.html> (Learning Pictorial; Xi Jinping: "Build a solid foundation of ideals and beliefs, set up and practice the correct view of political achievements, and leave a regretless struggle in the new era and new journey" Source Website of the Central Commission for Discipline Inspection and State Supervision Commission I March 2022).

97 A constitutional principle built out of the fundamental insight of the constitutional political principle of democratic centralism and its core binary: core-collective, arranged in a strict hierarchy from the greatest to the fewest. See, New Regulations for the Central Committee: Codifying Xi Era Democratic Centralism (China Law Translate, 1 December 2020) <https://www.chinalawtranslate.com/new-regulations-for-the-central-committee-codifying-xi-era-democratic-centralism/> accessed 1 March 2022. For the foundational discussion, see discussion in Larry Catá Backer, Crafting a Theory of Socialist Democracy For China in the 21st Century: Considering Hu Angang's (胡鞍胡鞍胡鞍胡鞍钢钢钢钢) Theory of Collective Presidency in the Context of the Emerging Chinese Constitutional State," (2014) Asian-Pacific Law & Policy Journal 16(1):29–82.

98 See, e.g., Xu Wei, "Key Role of Socialist Rule of Law Stressed," China Daily (8 December 2021) https://www.chinadaily.com.cn/a/202112/08/WS61afebbfa310cdd39bc79f2a.html accessed 25 February 2022. For a perspective from the liberal democratic side, see, Moritz Rudolf, "Xi Jinping Thought on the Rule of Law: New Substance in the Conflict of Systems with China," SWP Comment No. 28 (April 2021) <https://www.swp-berlin.org/publications/products/comments/2021C28_Jinping_RuleOfLaw.pdf> accessed 26 February 2022.

99 See, John Garrick and Yan Chang Bennett, ""Xi Jinping Thought": Realisation of the Chinese Dream of National Rejuvenation?," China Perspectives 2018/1-2:99–105 <https://journals.openedition.org/chinaperspectives/7872> accessed 27 February 2022.

6

CONSTITUTIONALISM WITH CHINESE CHARACTERISTICS?

Which Constitutionalism?

Peng Chengyi

As the title of the chapter suggests, it seeks to pluralize the conception of constitutionalism. This is not hard to understand if we took Rousseau's famous comment on constitution seriously:

> It [constitution] is not engraved on marble or bronze, but in the hearts of citizens. It is the true constitution of the state. Everyday it takes on new forces. When other laws grow old and die away, it revives and replaces them, preserves a people in the spirit of its institution and imperceptibly substitutes the force of habit for that of authority. I am speaking of mores, customs, and especially of opinion, a part of the law unknown to our political theorists but one on which depends the success of all the others; a part with which the great legislator secretly occupies himself, though he seems to confine himself to the particular regulations that are merely the arching of the vault, whereas mores, slower to arise, form in the end its immovable keystone.[1]

However, it is questionable how many constitutional scholars could or would take the above quote seriously. Rousseau's insight may well go beyond their capability of comprehension given legal positivism has been so influential that it is now deeply entrenched in today's legal scholars' mind, and most of the latter's tasks have been "puzzle-solving" in Thomas Kuhn's sense as uncovered in his famous book *The Structure of Scientific Revolutions*. Nevertheless, it is still worth endeavoring to enlarge our conceptual frameworks toward constitutionalism, so that we may attain a more cosmopolitan and less parochial or partial view. Besides this major aim, this chapter would also seek to provide a picture of China's increasingly complicated ideological landscape as well as shed light on the emerging constitutionalisms' implications.

Pluralization of Constitutionalism

As we all know, with over four decades of rapid economic growth, China has emerged as a great power on the world stage with rising impact throughout the world. A crucial question that has attracted the concerns of many outsiders and insiders alike is the

DOI: 10.4324/9781003128243-8

political path the Chinese leadership would steer China toward. Perhaps many could agree that the Chinese leadership has no realistic choice other than constitutionalism, but the question is which constitutionalism since there are more than one constitutionalism discourse in China, such as liberal constitutionalism, Confucian constitutionalism, and sinicized Marxist constitutionalism?

In fact, the pluralization of constitutionalism discourse in the academia has appeared well in the first decade of the 21st century. Three land-marking relevant conferences are worth mentioning here. The first is "The 100th Anniversary of Constitution Setting-up in China and the Future of Chinese Constitutionalism (中国立宪 100 周年及中国宪政的未來)," held at City University of Hong Kong in October 2008.[2] The majority of the attendees are within the liberal paradigm, but Larry C. Backer from the US is an exception, as he introduces an interesting and path-breaking theorization of Chinese constitutional development since Deng Xiaoping's Reform and Opening Up. In contrast to the mainstream contempt of the Chinese constitution as a sham, Backer develops a legitimate framework for understanding the construction of Chinese constitutionalism. While his theory is not the mainstream, nor supported by the authority of China, it nevertheless provides a new perspective for China's constitutional development in the future and attained some influences. For example, Shigong Jiang, a professor based in Beijing University of China, has written two English articles engaging with Backer's party-state model of Chinese constitutionalism.[3]

Talking about Confucian constitutionalism, a group of devout Confucian practitioners held a conference entitled "The Unfolding of Reform and China's Future - Principles, Values, Motivations of Confucianism, and Contemporary Explorations (改革开放与中国前途 – 儒家的义理, 价值, 动力及当代探索)" at Confucius's hometown – Qufu, Shandong in April 2009. Jiang Qing, the leading figure of the so-called mainland Neo-Confucians, gave the keynote address at this conference titled "Reflections on 'Confucian Religious Constitutionalism' (关于"儒教宪政"的思考)," in which he shared his latest thoughts on the issue of constitutionalism for China. Even though some "mainland new Confucians" such as Chen Ming immediately expressed doubts about Jiang Qing's specific constitutional framework, Jiang Qing's call for and justification of developing a form of constitutionalism based on China's own cultural tradition did find resonance among members of the audience.

The third conference worth mentioning is the conference titled "The Theory and Practice of Socialist Constitutionalism with Chinese Characteristics" held at Changsha, Hunan Province in May of 2010. It was co-hosted by the law schools of Hunan University and Jilin University and attended by some influential retired political figures such as Luo Haocai, previously vice-chairman of the National Committee of the Chinese People's Political Consultative Conference, as well as some famous authoritative persons in the legal studies such as Guo Daohui and Li Buyun. Even though the theme of the conference is about socialist constitutionalism, however, the majority of the attendees are influenced by the liberal paradigm of constitutionalism, despite there are a few who are indeed exploring native version of constitutionalism with Chinese characteristics.

In the ideological realm, the debate about constitutionalism is even more vehement. As a matter of fact, the aspiration of constitutionalism as an ideology date back to about 100 years ago, when the Chinese intellectuals were aspiring and trying to help China recover from the chaos inflicted by colonialism, imperialism, and civil war and transform it into a stable and strong state. At that time, they were facing the same choices of western liberal path, traditional Confucian path, and sinicized Marxism path. The ideological chaos was regarded as unprecedented in the long Chinese history. The ideological battle ends up with the victory of the sinicized Marxism in the mainland China. After four decades of opening up and reform, the ideological realm in China, however, has been jumbled again. While China has doubtlessly succeeded in finding a way for rejuvenating its national strength, the aspirations for constitutionalism have persisted among the liberals, who seek to build a constitutional government based on Western models. Some of them have issued the Charter 08 (零八宪章) in 2008 in China and generated some impact both domestically and overseas. To some, the latter proposals of the hard-core liberal camp have not gone beyond the tenets of the Charter.

The vehement debate about constitutionalism in the ideological realm has continued into the post-2012 era. Not long after the new political leadership of China was elected in the 18th National Congress of the Chinese Communist Party (CCP) in November 2012, the 2013 *Southern Weekly* incident occurred. The incident led to a threat of strikes by the newsroom staff of the Southern Weekly as well as actual demonstrations outside the newspaper's headquarter in Guangzhou, China. The Southern Weekly is also referred to as Southern Weekend, one of the most influential media outlets in China based in Guangzhou, China. Although it is a part of the Nanfang Media Group, a provincial government-owned media corporation, it is well known for its outspokenness as well as pro-liberal views and stances. On surface, it is about press freedom, since it is a conflict between the Propaganda Department of Guangdong Province and the Southern Weekly, in which the original New Year's special editorial of the latter was changed under the pressure from the propaganda officers. On a deeper level, however, it is an ideological competition related to constitutionalism, since the special new year editorial is trying to graft the hot notion of "Chinese Dream" made popular by the new General Secretary Xi Jinping with the heavily value-laden Western political terminology of constitutionalism. As a result, the title of the editorial has been changed from "Chinese Dream, Constitutionalism Dream" to "We are Closer to the Dream than Any Other Times."

The reason for the incident to emerge is the liberals' partly wishful and partly strategic optimism about Xi's political reform prospect as inspired from his open-minded remarks in a speech delivered on the 30th anniversary of the 1982 Constitution in December 2012. Xi's remarks that "No organization or individual has the privilege to overstep the Constitution and the law, and any violation of the Constitution and the law must be investigated," as well as "the life of the Constitution lies in its implementation" excited the liberal reformists who read the speech as a sign of his determination to undertake a liberal overhaul of the political system. This triggered an open letter with constitutional reform demands signed by 72 liberal intellectuals, (《改革共识倡议书》), as well as the above Southern Weekly incident. They urged the CCP to uphold constitutional government, ensure the rights enshrined in the Chinese Constitution, and set up checks and balances on the power of the Party-state.

In response, a loose coalition of conservatives, including party ideologues and leftist intellectuals, responded by unleashing a spate of ferocious counterattacks in a number of key Party publications. Adopting an ideological stance, they argued that constitutional government is a by-product of Western capitalism, incompatible with China's own practice of socialism, and that China's political system must reflect the country's social and cultural conditions. They argued that the campaign for constitutional government was part of a malicious Western plot to subvert the CCP, just as Gorbachev's constitutional reform brought about the dissolution of the Soviet Union. And given the wide spread of the liberal constitutional paradigm among Chinese intellectuals, which is so deep and profound that it is fair to say the notion of "constitutionalism" has become the pronoun of the liberal constitutionalism in mainland China. This has induced the "established," a translation of the term "tizhinei (体制内)" in Chinese, political scholars in China to call for a banning of "constitutionalism" as a basic political terminology in China. Besides the official reactions, the two constitutionalism discourses also emerge in this background, which are worth a careful look into their respective contents.

Contents of Each Constitutionalism

Liberal Constitutionalism

Since the Western idea of constitutionalism first entered China about one and half centuries ago, it has generated significant impacts on the history of China. We can divide the spreading history into two main periods. The first is from the late Qing to early Republican period, and the second is since PRC's Reform and Opening Up about four decades ago. There have been a lot of works written on it, so there is no need to go into details here. But it is worth pointing out the similarities and differences between the two periods. Just as a legal scholar in China, Zhang Qianfan points out, the journey of liberal constitutionalism in China as shown in the first wave takes three steps: first, the ideas of liberal constitutionalism are introduced and accepted by intellectuals; second, those intellectuals start to influence the officials and the populace's perceptions of these ideas; third, some "enlightened" officials push for institutional reform in light of the new ideas with the aid of the reform-oriented intellectuals as well as the populace; the end result depends upon the interactions between reform-oriented forces and conservative forces that have a vested interest in the status-quo.[4] While the Qing constitutional reform largely failed because of the strong opposition of the conservative forces in the court as well as the failure of liberal constitutionalism to take root among the populace, the three-step spreading road-map seems to apply to the second period as well with similar result.

Nevertheless, there are some important differences due to the very different settings and timings. First of all, the institutional dimension of the second period is not as prominent as the first period, as during the first period, there were quite a number of constitutional setting up trials. Second, the rational to advocate liberal constitutionalism has changed dramatically between the two periods. During the late Qing and early Republican period, liberal constitutionalism was largely taken up with very pragmatic purposes: to strengthen the state and save China from various problems, not least the external threat; at that time the liberal constitutionalism available for imitation is also not as liberal as today's. During the reform period, however, advocates of liberal constitutionalism want to endorse certain liberal principles to increase individual freedom. Third, the social and intellectual contexts have also changed dramatically. In today's China, the means of spreading liberal constitutionalism tenets have become much more diversified and complicated, but at the same time, the liberal intellectuals' influence has also decreased due to the changing circumstances, especially that brought by the rapid marketization process in the 1990s.

In terms of the contents, the Charter 08 provides a manifesto synopsis. It is published on December 10, 2008, the 60th anniversary of the Universal Declaration of Human Rights, by some liberal intellectuals and human rights activists in China. It imitates the anti-Soviet Charter 77 issued by dissidents in Czechoslovakia in both form and content. Since its release, it has reportedly gathered many signatures from people both inside and outside of China endorsing it. One of the main authors of Charter 08, Liu Xiaobo, was not only sentenced to 11 years' prison for the charge of "inciting subversion of state power" but was also awarded the Nobel Peace Prize for the year of 2010 for largely the same acts. The Charter basically summarizes all the core claims of liberal constitutionalism in China and calls for 19 specific reforms of current Chinese political regime to endorse the "universal values (普世价值)" of "mainstream civilization" as manifested in the Western world. The core tenets included in the Charter are six vague declarative values: freedom, human rights, equality, republicanism, democracy, and constitutionalism. The specific reform proposals are: constitutional revision in accord with the previous core tenets, separation of powers and checks and balances, legislative democracy in the sense that legislatures at all levels are directly elected by the people, judicial independence, public use of public instruments in the sense that all armed forces and civil servants should be politically neutral and loyal to the state only, human rights protection, election of public officials with the principle of "one person, one vote," urban-rural equality through abolition of the current urban-rural two-tier household registration system, freedom of association, assembly, expression, and religion, replacement of civic education for the current political education that has a strong ideological and partisan nature, private property protection, fiscal reform to democratize public finances and guarantee taxpayers' rights, social security, environmental protection, a federal republic, and transitional justice by restoring the reputation of and giving compensation to individuals and families that previously have suffered.

Given its nature as a manifesto, the Charter only briefly explains the proposals and does not offer an account of the theoretical rationale behind them; nevertheless, the liberal camp in China seems to have taken the claims of the Charter for granted and their intellectual findings have offered theoretical support to these claims. Take Li Buyun as example. He provides a four-element explication of liberal constitutionalism. He defines constitutionalism as "a political system which regards the realization of a series of democratic principles and system as its main content, rule of law as its basic guarantee, and the fulfillment of the most extensive set of human rights as its goal," and "supremacy of the constitution (宪法至上)" as its required external form.[5] The four elements refer to democracy, rule of law, human right, and supremacy of constitution. As those are quite familiar to us, there is no need to review the detailed explication here. It is just worth mentioning other interpretations of constitutionalism in China. For example, some scholars take a narrower vision by equating constitutionalism with rule of constitution and laws; some use it to denote limited government; while some others have regarded the essence of constitutionalism as residing in polyarchy as opposed to the concentration of powers, for without a dispersion of power the agreed "entrenched" rules could be annulled by dominant actors at their will. Nevertheless, Li's explication is comprehensive and also quite representative. It also demonstrates that most constitutional scholars in China have not developed as sophisticated an understanding of the philosophical foundations of constitutionalism as Western scholars do.

Confucian Constitutionalism

For a relatively long period of time, it has been widely thought that Confucianism and constitutionalism are incompatible, even antithetic. For example, Confucianism is usually associated with authoritarianism, rule of man instead of rule of law, collectivism, hierarchical role-based order, over-emphasis on obligation, and so on; while constitutionalism is founded on the rule of law, individual rights, equality, and so on. This view is a prominent feature of Chinese thought from the New Cultural Movement of the early 20th century to the "Asian Values" debates of recent decades. Even today it still holds some currency among many intellectuals both in and outside China. However, in recent years, some intellectuals are breaking off the yoke of this dominant view by exploring the constitutional resources within Confucianism and challenging previous conceptual frameworks. As we shall see, we can identify three main approaches on the issue of Confucian constitutionalism in contemporary academia, namely, the institutional approach, the ritualistic approach, and the religious approach.[6]

The first is the institutional approach in the narrow sense, because in a broad sense, Confucian Li (礼) and Confucianism as a state religion are also institutions. By institutional approach, it means to center on the checks and balances of power exercised by some substantive power-holding entities. This approach does not challenge the conceptual framework of the liberal constitutional paradigm and instead seeks to demonstrate that the institutions of a Confucian polity actually have mechanisms of checks and balances, which are the core of constitutionalism according to these authors. There are two main dimensions to this approach, with one focusing on the checks and balances along the horizontal line, in other words, among largely equal power-holding entities, and the other along the vertical line, which is between the monarch and his subordinate. For the first horizontal dimension, it is well explored by Jongryn Mo's case study of the Censorate of the Chosŏn Dynasty (朝鲜王朝) in Korean history, in which he shows that Confucianism is actually quite rich in ideas and practices promoting horizontal accountability, many of which meet the criteria of modern accountability theory.[7] While Mo mainly uses the term "accountability," he treats it as largely equivalent to the notion of "checks and balances" and also occasionally uses the latter in his article.

There is no need to go into details of Mo's analysis, but worth mentioning that the horizontal "checks and balances" within the Confucian polity unearthed by Mo is well supported by the vast literature devoted to this theme within contemporary Chinese academia. So while Mo's discoveries may be fresh to some in the West, the horizontal checks and balances within the Confucian polity have been well explored and to some extent even taken for granted in China.

The vertical dimension largely pertains to the power relationships along the vertical line of the Confucian hierarchy. Correcting the stereotype of absolutism running throughout Chinese history, some scholars contended that there is a certain degree of "checks and balances" even between the king and his subordinates. One good representative work on this is Jaeyoon Song's (2009) article on the complementary yet countervailing relationships between the Sovereign and his Ministers. In his article, Song analyzes the Southern Song commentaries on the *Zhou Li* (周礼) and argues that their elaborations of good government in fact have developed into "a systematic theory of constrained government, an indigenous articulation of 'constitutionalism' in the Chinese tradition."[8]

Song unearths a kind of mutual checks and balances between the King and the Grand Steward in the Confucian polity. On one hand, the supreme power of the Grand Steward over the bureaucracy is constrained by the King with the aid of the Royal Secretary; on the other hand, the emphasis of the authority of the Grand Steward, especially within its autonomous realms, also serves as an effective means for restraining the power of the

King. Even within the realms where the King could legitimately intervene in the state affairs of the Grand Steward, the presence of the Royal Secretary reduces the chances of the King making arbitrary decisions. This tension and balance between the Grand Steward and the King might provide resources even for contemporary politics, for on the one hand, "the Grand Steward represents the ideals of meritocracy, bureaucratic standardization, the rule of law, and limits to monarchical autocracy. In contrast, the king represents the ideals of responsive rulership, circumstantial justice, the rule of man, and a check against ministerial tyranny."[9]

The second is the ritualistic approach, which goes a step further by locating the core of Confucian constitutionalism in the Li (礼), a unique Confucian concept usually translated as "ritual," "propriety," "rites," "manners," "ceremony," "etiquette," "courtesy," "rules of proper conducts," etc. This approach does not focus so much on the internal "checks and balances," but more on the power-restraining or constitutional characteristics of the Confucian Li (礼), which has attracted much attention in the academic community.

This approach is perhaps the most fully explored among the three approaches and here we will mainly review the arguments defending the Confucian Li's constitutional nature as well as its advantages. Regarding the constitutional nature of the Confucian Li, they usually point out that the Confucian Li is a system of fundamental rules and norms established to maintain social order, cultivate virtuous characters, guide people to constrain their desires, and attune people's social life with the "Heavenly Way (天道)," and there are three features of the Li that qualify it as a constitution: the highest norms of a state, containing certain core founding principles, the stability and durability of its core elements.[10] Some have explored in depth the regime-legitimating and restraining functions of the Confucian Li, and the similarities between the ritual controversies occurred in the Chosŏn Korea and modern constitutional crises.[11]

Regarding the unique advantages of a ritualistic constitutionalism, they tend to point to the education function of the Li. For example, Chaihark points out that the Confucian Li serves such a role of promoting "Confucian civic virtue," because it "lies at the intersection of politics and education" and is "a marvelous combination of education, self-cultivation, training, discipline, restraint, authority, and legitimacy."[12] According to Chaihark, the process of "ritualization" is also the process of "humanization" and authority-gaining.[13] Chaihark also draws upon Foucault's insights about discipline to support his arguments. This is in fact further affirmed and elaborated in Hahm Chaibong's article "Confucian Rituals and the Technology of the Self: A Foucaultian Interpretation."[14] In this article, Chaibong argues that "by mistaking all technologies of the self - such as Confucian rituals - as states of domination that leave no room for freedom and individual initiative, modern theorists have left no room for the possibility of moral education in modern society," and it is particularly in this regard that Confucianism is not only suitable for democracy but "also fills an important lacuna in modern democratic theory."[15] Similarly emphasizing the educational function of the Li, Jin-Ha Kim introduces the other key Confucian dimension of "Music (乐)" into Confucian ritualistic constitutionalism and provides perhaps the most charitable account of the advantages of the Confucian constitutionalism so far.[16] It is beyond the scope here to review the specific analyses, but it is worth pointing out that for Kim, empowerment requires attunement and "the connatural resonance within/without the self as an acting participant in this ritual community reaches eventual politico-musical self-orchestration" which is "the ultimate state of tuning at the zenith of embodied constitutionalism."[17]

The third is the religious approach. It is mainly advocated and elaborated by Jiang Qing, regarded by some as a key figure of the "mainland new Confucians." Following his work on political Confucianism, Jiang Qing was keen in exploring and contemplating constitutionalism with Chinese native characteristics. He made it clear that this move is mainly a response to the "Fukuyama thesis" contending there are no alternatives to liberal democracy as the legitimate political form in the future of human history.

The two fundamental founding principles of Confucian religious constitutionalism are its religious nature and the "three-dimensional legitimacy" theory of political Confucianism. The religious nature is made explicit in the title of "Confucian religious constitutionalism," which is intentionally chosen by him because he regards Confucianism as a great religion embedded in Chinese civilization that is comparable to Buddhism, Islam, and Christianity. For Jiang, the Confucian religion has been the state religion for most of Chinese history and has performed well several functions, such as its provision of political legitimacy for the government, its provision of ethical norms for the regulation of social conduct, and its provision of religious faith for the people.

Besides the state religion definition of Confucianism, another reason for the religious nature in Jiang Qing's view is that the ultimate sovereignty of the regime lies with Heaven, which determines the transcendental, sacred, and religious nature of the Confucian religious constitutionalism. For Jiang, Heaven is the original source of the polity's legitimacy, as well as its "higher law" or "transcendental value." This is on the metaphysical level; on the mundane level, Heaven is diversified into Heaven, Earth, and People (天地人), respectively. Accordingly, sovereignty is manifested through the "kingly way of politics (王道政治)," which bridges the three diverse expressions noted above (王道通三). Institutionally, sovereignty is manifested through the "tri-cameral legislature," which embodies the three levels of legitimacy (三重合法性). This then relates to the second main feature of the Confucian religious constitutionalism, which we will review below.

The three-dimensional legitimacy of political power is a core argument of Jiang Qing's political Confucianism. According to Jiang, the legitimacy of the "kingly way of politics" has three dimensions. The first is the dimension of legitimacy from Heaven, which refers to the legitimacy that derives from sacred sources. More specifically, the political power must be sanctioned by the holy, transcendental Heaven which passes the Dao to the Confucian Classics with the orthodox Confucians as the exclusive interpreters. The second is the dimension of legitimacy from Earth, which refers to the legitimacy that derives from historical continuity. In other words, the political power must not deviate from the mainstream cultural and historical heritage of the nation. The third is the dimension of legitimacy from people, which refers to the legitimacy that derives from people's endorsement or consent. For Jiang, this last dimension would sound most familiar to Western ears, for it is the same as the legitimacy adopted in democratic regimes. However, Jiang Qing vehemently criticizes democratic regimes for the dominance of the last dimension of legitimacy, which consequently has led to many problems. Jiang Qing also has elaborations on the institutional arrangements, but there is no need to go into details here.

Sinicized Marxist Constitutionalism

The liberal perspective historically views the constitution of a Marxist-Leninist state as a "sham" that serves as "an artifice of propaganda designed to impress and mislead foreigners," or a "useless" document to rein in the government.[18] Consequently scholars influenced by this paradigm look contemptuously at the current Chinese constitution, which for them needs to be abolished, significantly revised, or judicialized. However, in recent years, in light of the significant progress of the constitutional framework of China, including its values and practices regarding the rule of law, this dominant liberal perspective has been challenged. Stephanie Balme and Michael Dowdle (2009), for example, have devoted their latest book *Building Constitutionalism in China* to exploring the empirical impacts of the emerging constitutionalism on many aspects of Chinese society, including its juridical, political, and social realms. A US constitutional scholar, Larry C. Backer, has also sought to establish a party-state model to grant legitimacy to China's current constitutional development in the international community. This effort has been echoed by the separate articulations of several scholars as well. Below will briefly review the context, the main contents of this constitutionalism paradigm.

The progress of rule of law in both theoretical and practical dimensions over the past 40 years in China surely plays the foundational role for the surging interests among scholars on the issue of constitutionalism in China. Meanwhile, the deep penetration and domination of Western Liberal Constitutionalism have induced two reactions from scholars outside of the legal realm, namely the articulation of the "constitutionalism abolition thesis" as well as some cultural conservatives' proposal of developing constitutionalism that is based on and also loyal to China's indigenous tradition. Within the legal realm, it has pushed some to rethink the preconceptions of the Western liberal constitutional paradigm both in and outside China and catalyzed their articulation of the sinicized Marxist constitutionalism paradigm. The fad of advocating the "Chinese Model" within Chinese academia and popular trend of shaking off the yoke of current dominant paradigms from the West, especially since the Western financial crisis, may have offered an amiable and supporting environment for the emergence of sinicized Marxist constitutionalism as well.

In terms of the contents, there are three main approaches toward Chinese constitutionalism that are under the canopy of sinicized Marxist constitutionalism. The first one takes into consideration the Communist Party of China as well as its ideologies but still emphasizes the core tenets of western liberal constitutionalism as the defining feature of constitutionalism, so focuses on rule of law, human rights, power check and balances, etc. For the emphasis on human rights and power check and balances, one could refer to Qianhong Qin and Haibo Ye's works.[19] But as this approach is landmarked by Backer's pioneering exploration, below will seek to have a closer look at his elaborations.

According to Backer, to understand this model with Chinese characteristics, one needs to first understand that "the Chinese constitution exists as a combination of polity and governing ideology, on the one hand, and the state apparatus, on the other hand."[20] A key component in this constitutional arrangement is the Communist Party, not as a political party or private actor in the Western sense, but as the institutionalization of the polity and the source of its substantive values. In other words, the Communist party as an autonomous community serves as the gatekeeper of political citizenship and the provider of the value framework for the state. As a result, Backer concludes four major features of the party-state model of the Chinese constitutionalism: (1) the division of citizenship between social and economic citizenship held by all, and political citizenship exercised through the Communist Party of China; (2) the subordination of state power and institutions to political authority; (3) institutionalization of political authority within a collective space (the Communist Party of China) beyond the control of any individuals that serves as the source and conduit of constitutional values to be implemented by the state apparatus; and (4) reliance on state and party self-discipline for the elaboration of rule of law values.[21]

While this approach is quite distinctive from previous approaches in that it brings the Communist Party of China as well as its ideologies into the constitutional structure, it still emphasizes rule of law as the defining feature of constitutionalism. That is why Backer argues that the Communist Party of China "retains its constitutionalist character to the extent that in its internal operations it observes the same rule of law framework as that imposed externally on the state apparatus." It is also why he regards pre-Deng Chinese state governance architecture as anti-constitutionalist. This approach, represented by Backer's model, is also shared by some famous scholars both in China and abroad.

The second approach within the Marxist constitutionalism paradigm is the party-state approach pillared on orthodox ideology. If Backer's approach is largely preoccupied with constraining governmental power through the rule of law mainly due to the deep influence of the liberal constitutional paradigm, this approach concentrates its attention on the constitutional order of Chinese politics as it is and takes its ideological dimension as the distinctive feature of Chinese constitutionalism. First of all, this approach sees a consistent constitutional developmental trajectory in China since its founding to today, and there are many works written on this. For them, during Maoist times, the fundamental categorical system of the Chinese socialist constitutionalism, including constituents such as the Constitution, the National Polity (guoti 国体), the state/government (zhengti 政体), the people, citizenship, democratic centralism, people's congress system, the fundamental rights and obligations, legislative power, judicial power, administrative power, chief of state, autonomous governance, and so on, and the actual working mechanisms of the constitutional order were all formed. The constitutional structure and thought was further developed by later administrations. For example, during Deng's time, he not only established the "Four Cardinal Principles" for China's reform and opening up and set up the goal of institutionalizing and legalizing the peoples' democracy but also developed the ideology of "Socialist Theory with Chinese Characteristics (中国特色社会主义理论)." This constitutional trajectory is further developed by later leaderships, as shown in the incorporation of "the rule of law," "human rights," "Three Represents," and "new era Xi Jinping thought" clauses into the Constitution.

The defining feature of this approach is its emphasis on the orthodox ideology. For example, tracing the constitutional development of China from the Common Program of 1949 to the current 1982 Constitution, Kam Wong (2006) points out that the Chinese "constitutions were not there to limit the government's power but to promote the ideology of the state and advance the cause of the Communist Party, that is to contribute to building a Communist State under Mao (the 1954 PRC Constitution) or to facilitate the social and economic reforms under Deng (the 1982 PRC Constitution)."[22] In other words, Wong further explains, "Traditional 'constitutionalism' in the West is built upon an individualistic foundation, adversarial processes and a zero-sum gain calculus," but Chinese "constitutionalism" is "premised more upon a collective mentality, centred more on a cooperative spirit and on a mutually beneficial understanding [that] Power need not be held in check but must be guided and directed to achieve collective goods."[23] Consistent with this approach within the canopy of sinicized Marxist constitutionalism, some have also resorted to Marxist and socialist legal philosophy to support it.

The third approach is the party-state approach pillared on an organic eclectic ideology that serves as a combination of the rule of law and orthodox ideology. It may mark the latest turn in constitutional thought among the leadership as well as some leading established intellectuals in China, even though they are using different terminologies. As mentioned above, given the dense liberal flavor of the notion of "constitutionalism," it has induced the "constitutionalism abolition thesis," so the government has used other notions with similar meanings, such as "rule of Constitution (依宪治国)," "socialist democratic politics (社会主义民主政治)," "Chinese style democracy (中国式民主)," and "socialist political civilization (社会主义政治文明)." While these different notions emerged in different contexts and differ to some extent in terms of their respective intensions and extensions, they all share an essential core, namely the organic unity of "the leadership of the Party, the position of the people as masters of the country, and the rule of law (党的领导, 人民当家做主, 依法治国)." An enormous literature has been devoted to this constitutional trinity as well. The three parts are held to be organically united since the leadership of the party is the guarantee of the latter two, while the people as masters are the essential requirement of socialist democratic politics and rule of law is the fundamental strategy of the Communist Party of China to lead the people to govern state affairs.

This approach combines certain core ideas from both liberal constitutionalism and Marxist ideological constitutionalism as reviewed earlier. It also could be regarded as the result of the interactions and dialogs between the latter two. The eclectic nature of this approach is also well illustrated in the new discursive terminologies of the current ideology. Shying away from the slogans of the Maoist period yet without embracing Western values in a whole-sale manner, party leaders and established intellectuals have sought to develop a "theoretical system of Socialism with Chinese Characteristics (中国特色社会主义理论体系)" that incorporates those newly coined ideas such as the "Three Represents," "Scientific Outlook on Development," "People-centeredness," "Harmonious Society," "Socialist Political Civilization," "Socialist Legal Ideas," "Chinese Dream," and "New Era Xi Jinping Thought." This discursive turn of Chinese ideology has been well captured by China scholars in Western academia as well. For example, through an application of discourse theory to an analysis of the newly emerging ideology, some argues that the Chinese party leaders and established intellectuals have "boiled socialism down to abstract values, independent of and autonomous from the economic base, marking a retreat from class and class struggle."[24] What is remarkable about this collection of terminology is that both the left and the right could interpret and utilize them in ways consistent with their respective core tenets, while the "Party rhetoric defines the opportunity structures for debate."[25] A related issue worth pointing out is the emergence of corresponding legal theory in the name of "Socialist Legal Ideas (社会主义法治理念)" for Sinicized Marxist Constitutionalism. It is a summation and theorization of China's legal reforms both in its practical and theoretical dimensions over the past four decades, and an inherent part of the grand theory of "Socialism with Chinese Characteristics" dealing with the juridical aspect; it is also a direct result of the adaptation and innovation of Marxist jurisprudence in the contemporary Chinese context.

Implications

China serves as a fascinating case for the study of the consequential effects of globalization in the ideological aspect, and the review above clearly demonstrates how the emergence of three constitutionalism discourses for the future of China is a direct result of the various interactions under the influence of globalization. We have touched on themes such as the internationalization of western liberal constitutionalism, the attempt to harmonize the western legal tradition into the sinicized Marxist political infrastructure by the Chinese government and established scholars, and the reactions of some cultural conservatives within the Chinese society toward the spread of Western norms and institutions. Nevertheless, China certainly is not a passive receptor of influence from the outside world only, but also a potential active exporter of ideas and concepts. Indeed, this dimension has attracted much attention and exploration by Chinese policymakers and scholars alike. They have actually undertaken many initiatives to push China's views and discourses to spread abroad. But most importantly, with China's overall national strength continuing to grow, its influence in the world will be greater even if China does not undertake any intentional campaigns. For example, there are works seeking to bridge the Chinese notion of Community of Common Destiny for Mankind and its position on global constitutionalism as well as its implications for the future of international law.[26] Thus, conceivably the constitutionalism discourse, once driven from developed Western states to other parts of the world may now also see some positive engagement from places like China. That may have a potentially important effect on the quality and shape of the future of constitutionalism as ideology and legitimating measure of governments worldwide. Here will just mention some of the possible implications of China's rising constitutionalism.

Depending on the viewer's perspective and horizon, the implications could be at discursive, theoretical and practical levels, with each level going one step further than the previous one. On the surface is the discursive level, where one may take the rising Chinese constitutionalism discourse as a sign of constitutionalism's discursive diversification in the world, breaking the yoke of liberal monopoly of the concept of constitutionalism. The three constitutionalism discourses in China may also remind us the similar and parallel constitutionalism discourses at the global level, namely the Islamic constitutionalism, the Marxist constitutionalism, and the liberal constitutionalism, despite the Islamic constitutionalism and Marxist constitutionalism are seldom mentioned in the mainstream academia of the West. One step further is the theoretical level, where the advantages of traditional Confucian constitutionalism and sinicized Marxist constitutionalism, as well as the vices of the western liberal constitutionalism could provoke reconsiderations of our mainstream political theories, especially regarding notions of freedom, authority, tyranny of majority, etc. With China's constitutionalism growing ripe both in practice and in theory, it may well bring a revolution to the field of normative political science. If the viewer's horizon is bigger with keener insight, he or she may well sense the practical implications of the rising Chinese constitutionalism, especially regarding its efficiency in coping with the rising populism worldwide than the alternatives as well as its prospect for the world peace order.

Notes

1 Jean-Jacques Rousseau, *The Basic Political Writings* (Donald A. Cress tr, Hackett Publishing Company, 1987) 172.

2 It is worth noticing that the university-affiliated press has a series on constitutionalism in China that has published eight books in Chinese.

3 See Shigong Jiang, 'How to explore the Chinese path to constitutionalism? A response to Larry Catá Backer' (2014) 40,2, Modern China 196–213; Shigong Qiang, 'Chinese-style constitutionalism: On Backer's Chinese party-state constitutionalism' (2014) 40,2, Modern China 133–167.

4 Qianfan Zhang, 'Reflection on China's one hundred years' constitutional journey and its prospects (中国百年宪政历程的反思与展望) ' (2008), Legal Studies 4.
5 Buyun Li, *Constitutionalism and China* (Law Press, 2006) 3.
6 Another scholar Zhongqiu Yao has also written on Confucian constitutionalism and published quite some works, but it seems that he does not have a clear definition of terms used, instead he equates Confucian constitutionalism with Chinese constitutionalism, which in essence is about the mode of governance running through the long Chinese history (Zhongqiu Yao, *On Confucian Constitutionalism* [City University of Hong Kong Press, 2016] 4); in other places, he seems to take constitutionalism as political institutions that cannot be separated from traditional civilizations (Zhongqiu Yao, *Daotong and the Constitutional Order* [Central Compilation & Translation Press, 2017] 3–4).
7 Jongryn Mo, 'The challenge of accountability: Implications of the censorate,' in D. A. Bell, & H. Chaibong (eds.), *Confucianism for the Modern World* (CUP, 2003).
8 Jaeyoon Song, 'The Zhouli《周禮》and constitutionalism: A Southern Song political theory' (2009) 36, Journal of Chinese Philosophy 424.
9 Ibid, 435.
10 Qianfan Zhang, 'Tradition and modern: On the constitutional nature of Li (传统与现代:论"礼"的宪法学定性)' (2001) 1, Journal of Jinling Law (金陵法律评论) 119.
11 Hahm Chaihark, 'Ritual and constitutionalism: Disputing the ruler's legitimacy in a Confucian polity' (2009) 57, American Journal of Comparative Law 135.
12 Hahm Chaihark, 'Constitutionalism, Confucian civic virtue, and ritual propriety,' in D. A. Bell, & H. Chaibong (eds.), *Confucianism for the Modern World* (CUP, 2003) 43.
13 Ibid, 44,49.
14 Hahm Chaibong, 'Confucian rituals and the technology of the self: A Foucaultian interpretation' (2001) 51, Philosophy East and West 315.
15 Ibid, 315, 322.
16 JIn-Ha Kim, 'Tuning: Constitutional emplotment under the Confucian rule of ritual,' in *The 65th Annual Conference of the Midwest Political Science Association*, Chicago, 2007.
17 Ibid, 4.
18 Kam Wong, 'Human rights and limitation of state power: The discovery of constitutionalism in the people's republic of China' (2006) 7, Asia-Pacific Journal on Human Rights & the Law 1, 1.
19 Qianhong Qin & Haibo Ye, *The Study of Socialist Constitutionalism* (City University of Hong Kong Press, 2017).
20 Larry Backer, 'The party as polity, the communist party, and the Chinese constitutional state: A theory of state-party constitutionalism' (2009) 16, Journal of Chinese and Comparative Law 101, 110.
21 Ibid, 102.
22 Kam Wong (n 15), 37.
23 Ibid.
24 Guoxin Xing, 'Hu jintao's political thinking and legitimacy building: A post-marxist perspective' (2009) 36, Asian Affairs: An American Review 213, 213.
25 Gilley, B., & Holbig, H., 'The debate on party legitimacy in China: A mixed quantitative/qualitative analysis' (2009) 18, Journal of Contemporary China 339, 342.
26 Björn Ahl, 'Chinese Positions on Global Constitutionalism, Community of Common Destiny for Mankind and the Future of International Law' (2021) 9, The Chinese Journal of Comparative Law 304–327.

7

THE DEBATE ON CONSTITUTIONAL STANDING AND GREATER AUTONOMY FOR CITIES*

Lessons from (and for) the Special Administrative Regions of Hong Kong and Macao

Amal Sethi

Introduction

The last few decades have seen a global boom in urban agglomeration due to improved economic opportunities. In the early 1900s, only 10% of the world's population lived in cities,[1] compared to approximately 55% today.[2] It is estimated that this will increase to 70% by 2050.[3]

Despite being major population hubs and dominant economic players, cities are noticeably absent from national constitutions.[4] They are typically creatures of the federal or provincial government and depend on these political units for their continued functioning and existence. This has been criticised on several grounds. First, constitutionalism may become irrelevant to a large share of a country's population if the needs of cities are left unaddressed.[5] Second, cities are unable to address issues such as income inequality, housing, immigration, refugee rights, and environmental problems on their own.[6] Third, it makes cities susceptible to corporate capture.[7] Fourth, since cities are typically more progressive and diverse than the rest of the country, national politics are often indifferent to city residents' values and priorities.[8] Fifth, it results in federal and provincial politicians meddling in city affairs.[9]

In recent years, a commonly proposed response has been to overhaul the existing statist framework by emancipating cities and providing them with constitutional standing and greater autonomy.[10] These suggestions have not only been limited to academic circles but have also been the focus of political and social discussions in both Global South and Global North countries.[11]

* The author would like to thank Jisha Garg, Sumit Chatterjee, and Anshul Dalmia for their assistance with this chapter.

DOI: 10.4324/9781003128243-9

While this may seem like a straightforward fix, very few examples exist to assist us in envisioning this alternative reality. Even in cases where some cities have constitutional standing and/or considerable autonomy, this was typically granted by federal or provincial governments to further specific economic-political agendas or for administrative ease.[12] In these cases, the federal or provincial government dictates the terms, not the constitution. None of these examples are centred on the constitutional recognition of cities as an autonomous or distinct government order.[13] Thus, the statist system is still intact.

Constitutionalism in Greater China is seen as a niche subfield by traditional constitutionalists and rarely enters broader global discussions. However, Greater China's experience with its autonomous cities has a lot to add to the debate on greater autonomy and constitutional standing for cities. Although the four direct-administrated municipalities of Beijing, Chongqing, Shanghai, and Tianjin can most certainly contribute to the debate in meaningful ways, they are less than perfect examples precisely because the People's Republic of China's (PRC) government granted them their autonomy to forward economic-political agendas and for administrative ease. Rather, the case studies from Greater China that arguably have more to contribute to the emerging debate of cities' constitutional autonomy than any other potential case study around the globe are the Special Administrative Regions (SARs) of the PRC – Hong Kong SAR (HKSAR) and Macao SAR (MSAR) – and the 'one country, two systems' principle defining their governance structure.

The two existing SARs, while a part of the PRC, have significant autonomy and are recognised as distinct autonomous entities according to the 'one country, two systems' principle defining their governance. Moreover, while they do not have constitutional standing *per se*, their autonomy is guaranteed under the international bilateral treaties that created them (coupled with domestic legislation codifying those treaties).[14] This guarantee of autonomy might arguably accord protection comparable to, if not higher than, the constitutional entrenchment of autonomy. Therefore, the SARs are comparable real-life examples of cities with constitutional standing and greater city autonomy. In addition, HKSAR, with an area of 2,754 km^2 and a population of 7,500,700, and MSAR, with an area of 115.2 km^2 and a population of 682,800, are large and mid-sized cities with entrenched autonomy, thereby providing varying contexts. Hence, the SARs are vital cases to help illuminate the debate on constitutional standing and greater autonomy for cities. At the same time, studying the SARs critically from the lens of greater autonomy and constitutional standing simultaneously adds to questions regarding the autonomy of the SARs (something that has gained significant importance since the HKSAR protests of 2019 and 2020).

Consequently, this chapter will examine the debate on constitutional standing and greater autonomy for cities using the cases of HKSAR and MSAR with a view to drawing lessons from them (and for framing future discussions on the SARs autonomy as well). The rest of this chapter proceeds as follows. The subsequent section provides a *tour d'horizon* of the existing SARs and their history to lay the groundwork for the following discussions. This chapter then discusses how, on close observation, the SARs provide reasons for scepticism regarding the possibility of constitutional standing and greater autonomy translating into actually achieving the policy goals pursued by its proponents. Furthermore, if these scepticisms are not grave enough, this chapter goes on to explore whether the SARs' 'one country, two systems' model is a suitable way to envision cities with constitutional standing and greater autonomy. Answering in the negative, the chapter highlights certain practical, legal, and political challenges that would make creating constitutionally autonomous cities using the 'one country, two systems' model very unlikely. In fact, these challenges make any type of city with constitutional standing and greater autonomy a nearly unattainable ideal. The penultimate section of this chapter provides direction for the future of the debate on constitutional standing and greater autonomy – both generally and with regard to the SARs. It suggests (1) reasons to stick with the statist framework and (2) reforms within existing statist structures that would help realise the same goals that constitutional standing and greater autonomy seek to achieve. It then builds on this analysis and draws lessons for the SARs' own future. More specifically, it polemically makes a case for how future discussions regarding the status of the SARs could benefit from seeing the potential advantages of a statist framework and carving out a solution within a statist framework that mutually advantages both the SARs and the mainland. The last section concludes.

HKSAR and MSAR – An Annotated History

To understand the history behind the SARs, we need to go back in time. In the mid-1500s, Portuguese people and businesses began settling in Macao to carry out trade.[15] In the following centuries, they continued doing so without exercising sovereignty or using military force.[16] After the Chinese government lost the Opium War in 1840, the Portuguese government saw its window of opportunity and invaded Macao.[17] In 1887, Portugal forced China to sign the Protocol of Lisbon and the Treaty of Peking, allowing Portugal to administer Macao permanently.[18]

Britain first took over Hong Kong Island in 1842 after defeating China in the First Opium War.[19] After the Second Opium War in 1860, Beijing was also forced to cede Kowloon, the area on the mainland opposite Hong Kong Island.[20] In 1898, to strengthen its control in the Asia-Pacific region due to facing a threat from other colonial powers, Britain obtained a 99-year lease of additional land known as the New Territories.[21] The New Territories make up 86.2% of Hong Kong's territory and now house approximately half its current population.[22] Due to the scarcity of land on Hong Kong Island and Kowloon, substantial infrastructure investments were made in the New Territories during the 1970s, some of which would only break even financially after the end of the lease in 1997.[23] Their respective colonialists administered Hong Kong and Macao as capitalist societies with minimal governmental intervention.

In 1971, when the PRC obtained its seat in the United Nations (UN), it began to use the international fora to reclaim its lost sovereignty in the Greater China region.[24] With colonisation frowned upon internationally, the PRC managed concessions at the UN, and the UN General Assembly passed a resolution delisting Hong Kong and Macao from its list of non-self-governing territories awaiting self-determination.[25]

On 25 April 1974, army rebels conducted a military coup and overthrew Portugal's authoritarian Estado Novo regime.[26] Shortly after the coup, Portugal began its democratisation process and was keen to shrug off its colonial past.[27] This included proposing Macao's handover to the PRC in 1978.[28] The PRC government rejected this proposal,[29] which resulted mainly from two factors. First, the PRC judged the timing inappropriate, as it feared that it would marginalise the British in the region and jeopardise Hong Kong's economic future.[30] Second, the PRC believed that the early transfer of Macao would impact its plans concerning Taiwan, which was considered a higher priority at the time.[31]

With the New Territories lease ending in 1997, and without a clear official position from the PRC government on Hong Kong, future development in Hong Kong became difficult, as banks were unwilling to give loans in light of the uncertainty.[32] The situation could not be left to resolve itself; otherwise, there would be severe economic consequences.[33] As a result, the PRC and Britain commenced negotiations over Hong Kong's future status in the early 1980s.

The British considered it unfeasible to split the ceded territories and restore only the New Territories to the PRC. Initially, the British governor of Hong Kong, Murray MacLehose, proposed that Britain should continue administering the whole of Hong Kong after 1997, though without holding sovereignty.[34] This plan was unacceptable to the PRC. A newer British plan proposed maintaining the British presence in the territory with the PRC's consent and making the entire territory a special economic zone under Chinese sovereignty.[35] The PRC rejected this plan and, furthermore, refused to recognise the 'unfair and unequal treaties' under which Hong Kong Island and Kowloon were ceded to Britain in perpetuity.[36] This frustrated the British, who felt that the PRC was bound by its international commitments.[37]

After lengthy, intense negotiations, Britain found itself with no other option but to concede to the PRC's demands.[38] This saga ended with the signing of the Sino-British Joint Declaration in 1985, which provided that Britain would restore Hong Kong to the PRC and that the PRC would exercise sovereignty over Hong Kong Island, Kowloon, and the New Territories from 1 July 1997 onwards. The British government did obtain some concessions, however. Hong Kong would be governed as a Special Administrative Region under the 'one country, two systems' principle. Per this principle, PRC's socialist system would not be practised in Hong Kong. Hong Kong would retain its capitalist system with open borders and low tariffs, as well as its social and political institutions, including its laws, currency, immigration system, police forces, executive branch, legislature, and independent judiciary. The PRC would only be responsible for HKSAR's defence and foreign affairs.[39] Otherwise, the PRC would be obliged not to interfere in these internal matters of HKSAR for 50 years. This way, Britain and other Western countries could recover the investments they had already made in Hong Kong.

On 4 April 1990, the National People's Congress promulgated the Basic Law, which was to function as HKSAR's constitution. It mirrored many of the basic principles underlined in the Sino-British Joint Declaration. It also addressed issues such as fundamental rights, explicitly defining Hong Kong's political structure, and specified that the Standing Committee of the National People's Congress (SCNPC) had the final authority to interpret the Basic Law.[40]

With the Hong Kong issue resolved and prospects on the Taiwan reunification front looking unlikely, the PRC moved to settle the question of Macao. In 1986, talks started between the PRC and Portugal. In April 1987, the two governments formally signed the Joint Declaration on the Question of Macao in Beijing. The Declaration provided that the PRC would resume the exercise of sovereignty over Macao effective 20 December 1999 and would establish MSAR under the same model used in Hong Kong's reunification and for the same period of 50 years.[41]

The Autonomous City – Will It Provide a Better Reality?

Despite some apprehension regarding the full attainment of the promise of the 'one country, two systems' principle, there is a lot to admire about HKSAR and MSAR, at least on the economic front. HKSAR has the 19th and 23rd highest per-capita GDP (PPP) and GDP (nominal), respectively. MSAR has the 7th and 8th highest per-capita

GDP (PPP) and GDP (nominal). When it comes to economic freedoms, Hong Kong has often taken the top spot over the last five years in the Heritage Foundation's Economic Freedom Index, and Macao has been ranked between 32 and 37, with scores in the same range as Germany, the United States, Sweden, and Japan.

This economic success is mainly because the SARs are port islands with strategic locations in the Asia-Pacific region and close to mainland China. HKSAR and MSAR serve as hubs connected with virtually the whole globe. From the 1600s to the early 1900s, Macao was the West's entrepôt in East Asia.[42] Following the British lease of the New Territories, Hong Kong's port, with its deeper waters, took over this role.[43] Nevertheless, for reasons beyond this chapter's scope, Hong Kong and Macao developed economies largely dependent on their status as port cities until the late 1950s.[44] From 1950 to 1980, during which the UN-imposed a trade embargo on China, Hong Kong focused on industrialisation, developing export industries, such as textiles and plastics, that benefited from its port.[45] This led to an economic boom. Between 1970 and 1990, Macao became a massive manufacturing hub for textiles and garments and used its water links with Hong Kong to export goods worldwide.[46] Industries in Hong Kong and Macao were aided by the lack of trade controls and the low taxes from their respective colonial powers, as well as proximity to the mainland, which became a source of cheap labour.[47]

Due to manufacturing moving to the PRC and rising competition from other countries, neither HKSAR nor MSAR relies on manufacturing as their primary source of income post-reunification. Using the capital it gained in the manufacturing business, HKSAR developed into a financial, technological, tourism, and transportation hub.[48] It also provides PRC companies with an entry into international markets.[49] Macao's economy depends mainly on a thriving gaming and tourism sector, and moderately on its status as an offshore financial centre and tax haven.[50] As a microeconomy (which most cities, if given constitutional standing and autonomy, would become), MSAR's economic growth is highly volatile.[51] This has reduced its capacity to respond to challenges and risks and delivers weaker growth momentum.[52] As a result, MSAR hopes to further diversify its economy by creating a service platform for commerce and trade cooperation between the PRC and Portuguese-speaking countries.[53] Both SARs' current economies are massively assisted by their free-market economies, low taxation rates, access to the world-class Hong Kong Port, strategic locations in the Asia-Pacific region, proximity to the mainland, and a symbiotic relationship with each other and the mainland. Yet this economic success and its underlying drivers are among the leading reasons for scepticism regarding whether constitutional standing and greater autonomy translate into addressing the goals they hope to achieve.

A caveat should be offered immediately. The scepticisms described below in no way imply that HKSAR and MSAR are failed or undesirable entities. Neither do they imply that HKSAR and MSAR have failed nor undesirable economic and/or political systems. From more than one perspective, the two SARs have achieved significant success across different fronts. However, this section argues through the examples of HKSAR and MSAR that constitutional standing and greater autonomy for cities might not be an answer to the challenges raised by its proponents.

Given HKSAR and MSAR's unique geographical advantages and the benefits of their booming economies to the PRC, it is questionable whether their economic success can be replicated in non-major port cities, especially when the state has no incentive to retain certain cities as dominant financial players. Many cities that are economic hubs are only so because the state desires them to be. A significant reason for HKSAR and MSAR's economic status – both past and present – is that the mainland benefits from them and has consequently encouraged their growth to the extent that it does not compromise national interests.[54] It is not necessary for the state to continue to focus on certain cities in a new regime in which powers are transferred from the state to those cities.[55] States might develop new economic centres and would have the land and natural resources to do so. They might even impose policies that could thwart certain autonomous cities' economic growth.

This is just one point of scepticism. HKSAR and MSAR have pursued aggressive neoliberal policies in the pursuit of investment and economic growth. This has worsened situations in most[56] policy areas that proponents of constitutional standing and greater autonomy for cities believe would be progressively addressed. Inequalities are incredibly high in the SARs and far worse than on the mainland, which has a highly regulated socialist economy.[57] The SARs have managed to attract investors and compete in international markets by keeping wages artificially low.[58] Their neoliberal policies are such that income inequalities will only continue increasing.[59] Moreover, these policies have resulted in terrible living and employment conditions for many people.[60] Social welfare programmes and social security spending are also far below those of countries with similar GDPs.[61] Public housing is one area where HKSAR and MSAR perform *prima facie* better than many developed countries, but even there, the demand is nowhere close to being met.[62] On the contrary, high real estate rates as a consequence of neoliberal policies in the SARs have been a cause of major social unrest.[63] These trends arise because officials believe that providing social welfare programmes, public housing, social security, etc. requires raising more taxes from the rich, potentially discouraging investment and stifling economic growth.[64] The SAR governments have also taken minimal concrete steps to address environmental challenges, fearing economic losses.[65]

Attempts to change laws to address the issues described above have been very slow, and the governments often yield to business lobbies.[66] This has only made the SARs more susceptible to corporate capture. Officials have stated on the record that the aforementioned policy decisions are necessary to grow economically.[67] Interestingly, less-perfect examples of cities with high autonomy and constitutional standing, such as Dubai and Singapore, exhibit the same circumstances – as important port cities in strategic locations and economies with highly neoliberal policies – where several goals that their proponents seek to achieve are compromised.[68]

It might be argued that HKSAR and MSAR are outlier cases and that there are more reasons for optimism than scepticism, especially in Western democracies that espouse progressive values. This is likely not the case. Contemporary cities often lack the land and natural resources to develop manufacturing industries or carry out agricultural activities. Thus, even where they have ports in strategic locations, they need to build a predominantly service-based economy (even if the service is provided via ports or by the aid of their strategic locations). Moreover, there is always a possibility that the strategic worth of ports might decrease under different or reorganised regimes. HKSAR's port has been losing business in recent years as China develops its mainland ports to become self-reliant.[69] Other states might do the same, to the point of bankrupting major ports, if they do not see value from the cities, they are based in. To be competitive and build a diversified, sustainable economy, cities will need to attract investments that are primarily only possible with low taxes and free-market policies. Hence, it is likely that the entire factual matrix seen above will be reproduced in most cases.

The Autonomous City – An Almost Unattainable Ideal

Let us assume that the SARs are indeed outliers, and advocates who demand constitutional standing and greater autonomy for cities are correct. Alternatively, advocates might consider the scepticisms raised not significant enough. They could even consider constitutional standing and greater autonomy for cities as causes still worth pursuing because of other goals; for example, making constitutionalism more relevant to the majority of the population, preventing federal and provincial politicians from meddling in city affairs, and ensuring that city residents' values, concerns, and priorities are addressed. In such a case, the SARs and their 'one country, two systems' governance model might be an excellent way to go about granting constitutional standing and greater autonomy for cities. After all, the 'one county, two systems' model provides cities with enough autonomy to address almost every concern independently, and the cities are recognised as distinct units of governance. Nevertheless, certain practical, legal, and political challenges make it nearly impossible to create constitutionally autonomous cities using the 'one country, two systems' model (or any other type of model).

At the top of the list of these challenges is how cities could possibly achieve their 'one country, two systems' status. There have been calls for constitutional standing and greater autonomy in individual cities across the globe.[70] These movements have not been vociferous, but if they were, every time a city desires more autonomy and constitutional standing, there cannot be a movement for the same. This approach would be both inefficient and impractical. One way around this challenge is to reorganise a polity's governance structures to replicate the SAR model. Countries with unitary systems could reorganise their governance structures to adopt the 'one country, two systems' model, wherein cities become the second system. On the other hand, federal countries might consider scrapping their existing distribution of powers between federal and provincial governments. They could even retain provinces for administrative reasons and create a 'one state, three systems' model, where the federal government, state government, and cities have different constitutionally entrenched powers.

A fundamental concern with either of these approaches is that, unlike Macao and Hong Kong, most cities cannot simply proceed with 'business as usual' in a reorganised regime. Hong Kong and Macao retained their existing governance structures (albeit with specific tweaks) and laws, and their citizens were not given a say in the PRC's governance. The PRC was granted control over the SARs' foreign relations and defence, which the respective colonial masters previously handled. In the ordinary course of politics, the PRC would, by law, neither provide the SARs with any funds or public goods nor take any away from them. The PRC and the SARs already had, dating back to colonial times, self-contained economies and commercial deals in place for the supply of public goods.

In almost all cases, administrative questions around a city's mode of governance, taxation, income distribution, power distribution, representation in federal/provincial governments, and supply of public goods would need to be addressed. How would cities determine what their individual political and economic systems would be? Would any powers be allotted to higher levels beyond defence and foreign affairs? Would higher levels of government only administer rural areas? Would cities levy and collect their own taxes, or would taxes be collected at one point and allocated to cities later? What share of provincial and federal government income would cities be entitled to (if any)? What would the formula for this allocation be? How would cities be represented in provisional and federal legislatures? Would cities be entitled to any public goods from the federal/provincial governments, or would they have to make their own arrangements from scratch? These questions are (1) not easy, (2) lack objectively correct answers, (3) would take years to answer, (4) would cause ample political disagreement, and (5) can cause across-the-board vacuums if not answered before an overhaul of the statist regime.[71]

Beyond the above, some other specific issues also require consideration. These other issues are harder to overcome, making replicating the 'one country, two systems' model (or a comparable model) very improbable. To start with, cities are very diverse in size and circumstances. Many cities may be unable to exercise the kind of autonomy the SARs have because they are too small and lack the capacity. For all its economic successes, the mid-sized MSAR has a highly volatile economy and is susceptible to panics.[72] As a response to this, proponents of constitutional standing and greater autonomy could argue that at least megacities the size of Hong Kong should be recognised as distinct units of governance and given SARs-like autonomy.[73]

There are four issues with such a possible suggestion. First, this option has the potential to exclude a large portion of the population from the new constitutional regime. This throws the entire premise of the case for greater autonomy and constitutional standing for cities into question.[74] Second, as Ming-Sung Kuo has written, if the constitution itself lists which specific cities would be recognised as distinct units of governance, it 'would turn a constitution into an unwieldy toponymic text.'[75] Third, if we want to avoid the previous problem and let federal or provincial governments decide which cities merit what type of constitutional standing and greater autonomy, we would again leave cities' fates in the hands of their provincial and federal masters. A new neutral institution could also be created to deal with these issues, but as will be discussed later in this section, that would be a herculean task due to constitutional rigidity and a general lack of political will. Fourth, even if the constitution lists a fixed formula specifying when cities are eligible for constitutional status and greater autonomy, determining this formula raises methodological questions. These are not unanswerable questions, but it is still another practical problem that would create logistical issues and cause ample political disagreement. Moreover, due to rapid changes in demographics, these formulas would require constant updating, which might ultimately raise the same issues as the third point above. All these problems (or at least the last three) rear their heads if it is suggested that instead of providing SAR-like autonomy only to megacities, different degrees of autonomy be provided within a single country.[76]

There is yet another practical consideration: disputes and legal questions are bound to arise. They even do in the SARs. No matter how well-defined the division of power is, overlaps and disagreements are unavoidable and must be addressed to avoid political crisis or stalemate. Using existing 'Federal Courts' or 'Provincial Courts' to resolve such disputes raises questions of impartiality since the respective governments appoint judges. In Greater China, where questions of interpretation regarding the Basic Laws of HKSAR and MSAR are in the hands of the SCNPC, their interpretation has been highly contentious.[77] It might be necessary to create entirely new courts with unique appointment procedures to guarantee impartial adjudication of issues. Even if solutions are sought within the existing judicial system, some supplementary matters would need to be addressed. A regime in which the city is a distinct entity could increase courts' workloads. To address this, depending on how courts are structured in a given country (i.e., whether the apex court in the country is the court of the first instance for constitutional issues), it might be required to allocate more powers to some courts, increase the apex court's docket size, or create more courts. Some smaller developed countries might not need any change on this front other than adding a specific set of disputes to their apex court's jurisdictional scope, which would still require a constitutional amendment in most places. This would be a more complex challenge in larger countries and require procedural and administrative transformations of the legal system. Many, if not all, changes in this area would require some degree of constitutional change.

Constitutional change brings us to the last point that makes constitutional standing and greater autonomy for cities an unattainable ideal. Pretty much any issues discussed above require large constitutional amendment packages or, debatably, redrafting constitutions entirely – especially if we are to rethink our entire existing constitutional frameworks. This would require the agreement of existing powerholders; yet in most cases, there is a complete lack of political will and incentives to do so.[78] Politicians tend to oppose giving away their powers to other levels of government and instead seek more powers.[79] HKSAR itself illustrates how the PRC has repeatedly tried to erode its autonomy and refused to grant more autonomy.[80] Additionally, in many countries – particularly in the Global North – constitutional structures are very rigid, and amendments are extremely difficult to pass.[81] Creating the SARs was relatively easy because the PRC had political incentives and the will to reintegrate the ceded territories into the mainland, the SAR model was the most suitable way to do so, and minimal reforms were needed on the mainland or in Hong Kong and Macao. Envisioning something that requires radical rethinking of constitutional frameworks will be a more formidable challenge due to rigid constitutional structures and a lack of political will, and this cannot be overlooked. As a result, it could be stated that replicating the SAR model (or even an alternate model that provides constitutional standing and greater autonomy for cities) is an unattainable proposal.

What's Next – Both Globally and In the SAR's

While some have argued the existing statist framework has not been favourable to cities, it is not all black and white. As Oran Doyle mentions, the present statist order came about as a tool to alleviate the ambiguity that stemmed from grouping the globe into geographically separate legal systems.[82] If cities develop as alternative points of constitutional authority, with several 'one country, two systems' or 'one country, three systems' states emerging, undesirable uncertainties might re-emerge across the board.[83] Doyle also contends that it may be inappropriate to treat cities as unitary actors existing in opposition to their provinces or country.[84] Cities are not unitary actors that exist in isolation, relying on adjoining rural areas for their food, water, labour, natural resources, etc. (in fact, the SARs are heavily reliant on the mainland for the same). If cities were pitted against rural areas or the rest of the province or country, intra-regional problems might arise, or national unity and cohesion could be negatively impacted.[85] Additionally, while city dwellers argue that state policies are unresponsive to their progressive values, rural dwellers have similar complaints and claim that the state is not entirely responsive to conservative values either.[86] Neither end of the spectrum might be altogether desirable.[87] The existing statist framework provides an arguably desirable moderating effect because all different opinions need to be taken into account (or at least considered) to some extent. Finally, although exceptions always exist, the state's redistributive capacities and ability to provide welfare services generally diminish with decentralisation.[88] Most of the worst affected states during the COVID-19 pandemic (and many that were criticised for their responses) were states with high decentralisation.[89] Scholars have recognised this concern if too much autonomy is ceded to the local levels as well.[90]

Nevertheless, one would be hard pressed to argue that all of the challenges that proponents of constitutional standing raise are not real. Therefore, in light of the perceived benefits of a statist framework and the impossibility of overhauling it, a pragmatic next step might be to consider reforms within the existing statist framework to help tackle cities' challenges. Challenges that are highlighted by proponents of constitutional spaces and greater autonomy for cities primarily result from two factors.[91] First, most countries have a significant democratic deficit, and votes in cities count less than votes in rural areas.[92] This happens at both provincial and federal levels and for reasons rooted in apportionment systems and/or the apportionment process not keeping up to date with demographic changes. Working towards remedying these defects and having more representatives from urban areas in provincial and federal legislatures could help cities deal with policy problems and ensure that national/provincial policies are more responsive to their concerns and views. It might also discourage interference in city affairs or attempts to diminish cities' power, as cities would matter more politically. Above all, it will help make constitutionalism more relevant to city dwellers, as their voices would be more represented in constitutional bodies. Taxation and finances are other issues that could be tackled more easily at the provincial and federal levels. The problem with most cities is not that they are powerless (although they might require more power over specific issues), but that they lack sufficient funds to implement policies and provide services effectively.[93] The solution is twofold: first, cities could be provided with enhanced taxation powers (or other ways to raise funds), and second, provincial and federal funding could be allocated more equitably to cities.

Addressing the two abovementioned issues would go a long way towards resolving several predicaments faced by cities, as most other problems are related to them in some way or the other. Likewise, tackling cities' problems in the above manner allows them to retain all the benefits that the statist regime provides them. Although these reforms would also not be easy, they are more feasible than completely overhauling governance structures.

The above analysis regarding the benefits of the statist framework and ways to address the challenges of cities also has implications for HKSAR and MSAR's own future, especially as their existing autonomous status lapses in the coming decades. This provides an opportunity to rethink the status of the SARs in a way that provides a win-win solution for all parties involved.

An important point the above discussions highlight is that HKSAR and MSAR are heavily dependent on the mainland. It can be argued that their existence would be impossible without the mainland's cooperation. As was earlier discussed, if the mainland does not see a benefit from the SARs, it can very easily diminish their significance, like was the case with the HKSAR port. In a worst case scenario, the mainland could even potentially cripple the SARs, considering their serious dependence on the mainland for food, water, labour, electricity, etc. Beyond this, as was seen earlier, there are several areas of policy where the SARs can do much better.

Discussions on the future of the SARs can be framed in terms where both the mainland and the SARs mutually benefit. Complete separation from the mainland might not help the SARs in the long term. The SARs might gain from the advantages of operating within a statist framework and not as completely independent entities. In fact, as the SARs tackle problems of inequality and everyday sustenance, they could themselves benefit from tweaking the current 'one country, two systems' model and ceding some autonomy to the mainland in exchange for assistance on various fronts. At the same time, the SARs would most certainly not want to be stuck with the same issues faced by 'powerless' cities worldwide. Hence, they could potentially convince the mainland that providing them with a meaningful say in their affairs and high levels of governance and fiscal autonomy is also in the mainland's best interest. The aforesaid will facilitate a scenario that promotes investor and market confidence in the SARs. In turn, such a regime enables the relatively closed and regulated mainland to retain the SARs as its door to international markets and as offshore financial hubs.

Since the SARs will be at an unequal footing compared to the mainland when questions regarding their eventual status are decided, such a way of thinking about the future of SARs can potentially result in the best outcome for the SARs. The SARs will also have an easier path than others to becoming cities with fiscal capabilities and an optimal democratic say, considering the PRC will be forced to think about the status of the SARs one way or the other in the coming years. This will avoid several hurdles that cities across would otherwise face in even moderately changing the *status quo*.

Conclusion

HKSAR and MSAR are examples of cities that have managed to outperform all expectations. Yet, at the same time, as this chapter described, their histories do not leave us optimistic about overhauling statist regimes and giving cities constitutional standing and greater autonomy. Even if this was not the case, implementing a world order where cities have constitutional standing and greater autonomy will be extremely challenging (if not impossible), and it is doubtful that the SAR model (or any other model) can be replicated on a large scale. In light of these realities and of the advantages that existing statist regimes provide, this chapter has attempted to suggest a more realistic way of addressing some of the problems scholars ascribe to cities' lack of constitutional standing and greater autonomy. Specifically, it advocates reducing the democratic deficit for urban voters and making more funds available to city governments or expanding their ability to raise finances. Based on the discussions contained therein, this chapter has also suggested how future discussions regarding the status of the SARs could also benefit from seeing the potential advantages of a statist framework and carving out a solution within a statist framework that mutually advantages both the SARs and the mainland.

Notes

1 Reference to the city is to the standard English meaning of the word in the Oxford English Dictionary, i.e., 'The built-up and densely inhabited part of a region as distinguished from the countryside or urban areas'.

2 See *World Urbanization Prospects: The 2018 Revision* (UN DESA, 2019) 1.

3 ibid.

4 Ran Hirschl, *City, State: Constitutionalism and the Megacity* (OUP, 2020) 11–15.

5 ibid 11–15; See also Richard Schragger, 'The Attack on American Cities' (2018) 96 Texas Law Review 1163, 1233.

6 See ibid; See also Erika Arban, 'Constitutional Law, Federalism and the City as a Unique Socio-economic and Political Space' in Ballin Hirsch and others, (eds), *European Yearbook of Constitutional Law: Volume 2* (TMC Asher, 2020) 324; See also Schragger (n 6) 1233; See also Toni Massaro and Shefali Milczarek-Desai, 'Constitutional Cities: Sanctuary Jurisdictions,

Local Voice, And Individual Liberty' (2018) 50:1 Columbia Human Rights Law Review 115, 3–108; See also Gerald Frug & David Barron, *City Bound: How States Stifle Urban Innovation* (Cornell University Press, 2008).

7 Hirschl, *City, State* (n 4) 11–15.

8 See Hirschl, *City, State* (n 4) 11–15; See also Schragger (n 5) 1233; See also Massaro and Milczarek-Desai (n 6) 3–108; See also Erika Arban, 'Metropolitan Cities, Federalism and Socio-economic Challenges' (2018) 1 Rivista di Diritti Comparati Special 226, 237–239.

9 See Jennifer Pagliaro, 'Could Charter City Status Protect Toronto from Provincial Meddling?' (*The Star*, 18 June 2019) <https://www.thestar.com/news/city_hall/2019/06/18/could-charter-city-status-protect-toronto-from-provincial-meddling.html> accessed 15 September 2021; See also Kristin Good and others, *Charting A New Path: Does Toronto Need More Autonomy?* (Institute on Municipal Finance and Governance, 2020) 5.

10 Different nuances in these arguments exist. Nonetheless, for some of the arguments on this point See Arban, 'Constitutional Law, Federalism and the City' (n 6), 338–343; See also Hirschl, *City, State* (n 4) 11–15; See also Good and others (n 9) 1–12; See also Alok Kumar, 'The City in the Constitution' (2019) 3 EPW 11, 11–12; See also Schragger (n 5) 1233; See also Massaro and Milczarek-Desai (n 6) 97–107; See also Barbara Norman, 'Are Autonomous Cities Our Urban Future?' (2018) 9 National Communication 2111.

11 See Stephanie Flanders, 'Should Britain Let Go of London?' (*BBC News*, 26 March 2013) <https://www.bbc.com/news/business-21934564> accessed 15 September 2021; See also Pagliaro (n 9); See also Harriet Bulkeley and others, 'Enhancing Urban Autonomy: Towards A New Political Project For Cities' (2018) 55(4) Urban Studies 702–719.

12 Arban, 'Metropolitan Cities' (n 8) 237–239.

13 Ran Hirschl, 'Urbanization, Megacities, Constitutional Silence' in Hirsch and others (n 6) 310.

14 See text body accompanying footnotes 15–41 for the history and explanation behind the same.

15 Ming Chan, 'Different Roads to Home: The Retrocession of Hong Kong and Macau to Chinese Sovereignty' (2003) 12 Journal of Contemporary China 493, 495.

16 ibid.

17 ibid 497.

18 ibid.

19 'Hong Kong's Handover: How the UK Returned It to China' (*BBC News*, 29 June 2017) <https://www.bbc.com/news/world-asia-china-40426827> accessed 15 September 2021.

20 ibid.

21 Steve Tsang, *Modern History of Hong Kong* (HKU Press, 2003) 35–37.

22 'New Territories (Region, Hong Kong, China)' (*Britannica Encyclopaedia*) <https://www.britannica.com/place/New-Territories> accessed 15 September 2021.

23 David Akers-Jones, *Feeling the Stones: Reminiscences by David Akers-Jones* (HKU Press, 2004) 108–109.

24 James Crawford, *The Creation of States in International Law* (OUP, 2006) 249.

25 ibid.

26 '1974: Rebels Seize Control of Portugal' (*BBC*, 25 April 1974) <http://news.bbc.co.uk/onthisday/hi/dates/stories/april/25/newsid_4754000/4754581.stm> accessed 15 September 2021.

27 Norrie MacQueen, 'Portugal: Decolonization without Agency' in Martin Thomas and Andrew Thompson (eds), *The Oxford Handbook of the Ends of Empire* (OUP, 2017) 174–176.

28 Jim Mann, 'Portugal Agrees to Return Macao to China in 1999' (*Los Angeles Times*, 24 March 1987) <https://www.latimes.com/archives/la-xpm-1987-03-24-mn-245-story.html> accessed 15 September 2021.

29 ibid.

30 Chan (n 15) 499.

31 ibid.

32 Akers-Jones (n 23) 108–109.

33 ibid.

34 'Lord MacLehose' (*The Guardian*, 2 June 2000) <https://www.theguardian.com/news/2000/jun/02/guardianobituaries1> accessed 15 September 2021.

35 Wei-Bin Zhang, *Hong Kong: The Pearl Made of British Mastery and Chinese Docile-Diligence* (Nova Publishers 2006) 62.

36 Chan (n 15) 499.
37 ibid.
38 For a detailed explanation of the negotiation; See Roger Buckley, *Hong Kong: The Road to 1997* (CUP, 1997) and Mark Roberti, *The Fall of Hong Kong* (Wiley, 1996).
39 The SARs do have some powers, however, to enter into treaties with other countries and international organisations. See Eric Ip, 'Comparative Constitutional Politics in the Chinese Special Administrative Regions of Hong Kong and Macau' in Hirsch and others (n 6) 103.
40 ibid 101–127.
41 ibid 106–127.
42 Victor Sit, 'Evolution of Macau's Economy and Its Export-Oriented Industries' (1991) 6 The Copenhagen Journal of Asian Studies 63, 65–66.
43 ibid.
44 See Sit (n 42), 63–88; See also Tsang (n 21) 161–175.
45 See generally Suzanne Berger and Richard Lester, *Made by Hong Kong* (OUP, 1997).
46 Sit (n 42), 70–71.
47 ibid 63–88; See also Tsang (n 21) 161–175.
48 Samantha Yim, 'Economic and Trade Information on Hong Kong (HKTDC Research, 29 September 2020) <https://research.hktdc.com/en/article/MzIwNjkzNTY5> accessed 15 September 2021.
49 Clare Baldwin and others, 'The Mainland's Colonization of the Hong Kong Economy' (*Reuters*, 31 December 2014) <https://www.reuters.com/article/us-hongkong-china-economy-specialreport-idUSKBN0K901320141231> accessed 15 September 2021.
50 'Macau – The World Factbook' (Central Intelligence Agency 2021) <https://www.cia.gov/the-world-factbook/countries/macau/> accessed 15 September 2021.
51 ibid.
52 Jiang Sheng, 'How Macau Is Developing Diversified Industries for Sustainable Economic Development' (*World Finance*, 27 July 2020) <https://www.worldfinance.com/banking/how-macau-is-developing-diversified-industries-for-sustainable-economic-development> accessed 15 September 2021.
53 ibid.
54 See Sheng (n 52); See also Noah Sin, 'Explainer: How Important Is Hong Kong to China as a Free Finance Hub?' (*Reuters*, 29 May 2020) <https://www.reuters.com/article/us-hongkong-protests-finance-explainer-idUSKBN2350VO> accessed 15 September 2021.
55 Some evidence from the American experience with constitutional home rule shows that state governments lose their incentive to address urban and metropolitan policy. For this point, See Good and others (n 9) 4.
56 One policy area where city autonomy has addressed city needs is immigration. HKSAR and MSAR have been able to allow as many foreigners as they need into their cities. However, the immigration is only based on market forces. Both SARs barely consider human rights in their immigration policies. They take in no refugees, and most migrant workers suffer from low wages and poor living conditions. See Maggie Lau and others, 'Poverty in Hong Kong' (2015) 15 China Review 23, 23; See also Simon Zhao and Li Zhang, 'Economic Growth and Income Inequality in Hong Kong: Trends and Explanations' (2005) 3(1) China: An International Journal 74, 90–96; See also Zhidong Hao, 'Social Problems in Macau' (2005) 62 China Perspectives 1, 5.
57 See Zhao and Zhang (n 56) 103; See also Hao (n 56) 5; See also Hon-Kwong Lui, *Income Inequality and Economic Development* (HKU Press, 1997).
58 See Mingjie Sheng and Chaolin Gu, 'Economic Growth and Development in Macau (1999–2016): The Role of the Booming Gaming Industry' (2018) 75 Cities 72, 75–76; See also Zhao and Zhang (n 56) 87–93.
59 Zhao and Zhang (n 56) 102; See also Yufan Hao and others, *Political Economy of Macao since 1999: The Dilemma of Success* (Springer 2017) 7–8.
60 See Hao (n 56) 1–18; See also Maggie Lau and others (n 56) 23.
61 See Dicky Lai and Ernest Chui, 'A Tale of Two Cities: A Comparative Study on the Welfare Regimes of Hong Kong and Macao' (2014) 13 Social Policy and Society 263.
62 See Zhao and Zhang (n 56) 95–96; Hao (n 58) 6.
63 See Hao and others (n 59) 7–8; See also Alexandra Stevenson and Jin Wu, 'Tiny Apartments and Punishing Work Hours: The Economic Roots of Hong Kong's Protests' (*The New York*

Times, 22 July 2019) <https://www.nytimes.com/interactive/2019/07/22/world/asia/hong-kong-housing-inequality.html> accessed 15 September 2021.

64 Zhao and Zhang (n 56) 97.

65 Hao (n 56) 7; Joyce Woo, 'Hong Kong Air Pollution Blamed on Political System' (*PHYS*, 26 June 2010) <https://phys.org/news/2010-06-hong-kong-air-pollution-blamed.html> accessed 1 October 2021.

66 See Zhao and Zhang (n 56); See also Hao (n 56) 6.

67 Quinn Slobodian, 'Democracy Doesn't Matter to The Defenders of Economic Freedom' (*Guardian*, 11 November 2019) <https://www.theguardian.com/commentisfree/2019/nov/11/democracy-defenders-economic-freedom-neoliberalism> accessed 15 September 2021.

68 Amal Sethi, 'City, State: Constitutionalism and the Megacity, by Ran Hirschl' (2021) 51 Publius: The Journal of Federalism e14.

69 Zihua Liu, and others, 'A Competitive Analysis of Port of Hong Kong: From External to Internal' (2020) 5 (7) Journal of Shipping and Trade 1, 1–3.

70 See Flanders (n 11); See also Pagliaro (n 9).

71 An example of this could be that if cities start figuring out arrangements with higher levels of governments (or other countries) for their most basic needs only after are accorded constitutional standing and autonomy, there could be an absolute breakdown of the public distribution system in cities.

72 Sheng (n 52).

73 Scholars have in fact argued for megacities to be recognised as distinct units that exercise greater autonomy without explicitly defining what greater autonomy would entail. See Richard Schragger, 'Federalism, Metropolitanism, And the Problem of States' (2019) 105 Virginia Law Review 1537; See also Arban 'Metropolitan Cities' (n 8); See also Hirschl (n 4), *City, State*.

74 Ming-Sung Kuo, "Making Constitutionalism Progressive Again: A Primer on City Constitutionalism and State (Re)Formation in a New Constitutional Geography" (Forthcoming) MLR, Early View available at <https://onlinelibrary.wiley.com/doi/10.1111/1468-2230.12692> accessed on 21 September 2021.

75 ibid.

76 Such a suggestion could take the form of a practical application of the principle of subsidiarity where cities might have one of four tiers of autonomy (high, medium, low, or none), depending on their capabilities. Only cities with the highest capabilities would have SAR-level autonomy; others could benefit from lesser autonomy, in line with their capacities. In fact, such an option also suffers from the additional predicament of not having any well-defined principles to demarcate such tiers of autonomy. For this point, See Richard Schragger, 'Cities as Constitutional Actors: The Case of Same-Sex Marriage' (2005) 22 Journal of Law and Politics 147, 178; See also Frug and Barron (n 8) 43.

77 See Albert Chen, 'Constitutional Adjudication in Post-1997 Hong Kong' (2006) 15(3) Pacific Rim Law and Policy Journal 627, 627–682.

78 Hirschl, *City, State* (n 4), 51–102.

79 Kumar (n 11) 12.

80 Maya Wang, 'China's Fast Train to Erode Hong Kong's Autonomy' (*Human Rights Watch*, 17 June 2018) <https://www.hrw.org/news/2018/06/17/chinas-fast-train-erode-hong-kongs-autonomy> accessed 15 September 2021.

81 Hirschl, *City, State* (n 4), 51–102.

82 Oran Doyle, "Spatial statism: Afterword to the Foreword by Ran Hirschl and Ayelet Shachar" (2020) 18(1) International Journal of Constitutional Law 29, 34.

83 ibid.

84 ibid.

85 See Henry Olsen, 'The Urban-Rural Divide Is Defining Politics Worldwide. Canada's Election Is Proof.' (*Washington Post*, 22 October 2019) <https://www.washingtonpost.com/opinions/2019/10/22/urban-rural-divide-is-defining-politics-worldwide-canadas-election-is-proof/> accessed 15 September 2021.

86 See generally Glenn Harlan Reynolds, 'Splitsylvania: State Secession and What to Do About It' (2019) 94 Notre Dame Law Review Online 90, 90–99.

87 See generally J.M Berger, *Extremism* (MIT Press, 2018).

88 See Markus Crepaz, 'Veto Players, Globalization, and the Redistributive Capacity of the State: A Panel Study of 15 OECD Countries' (2001) 21(1) Journal of Public Policy 1, 1–22.
89 See e.g., on why this is the case Jamison Chung, 'How Federalism Has Harmed Public Health' (*The Reg Review*, 23 December 2020) <https://www.theregreview.org/2020/12/23/chung-federalism-harmed-public-health/> accessed 15 September 2021.
90 Yishai Blank, 'The City and the World' (2005–2006) 44 Columbia Journal of Transnational Law 875, 934; Yishai Blank, 'Localism in the New Global Legal Order' (2006) 47 Harvard International Law Journal 263, 271.
91 For a detailed explanation of this point, see Amal Sethi, Towards Reimagining the Autonomous City (2022) <https://ssrn.com/abstract=3851586> accessed 1 March 2021.
92 See Jon Emont, 'Why Geography Is Undermining Democracy Around the World' (*The Atlantic*, 4 January 2017) <https://www.theatlantic.com/international/archive/2017/01/electoral-college-trump-argentina-malaysia-japan-clinton/512153/> accessed 15 September 2021.
93 Enid Slack, *How Much Local Fiscal Autonomy Do Cities Have? A Comparison of Eight Cities around the World* (IMFG, 2017).

Bibliography

1. Arban E, 'Constitutional Law, Federalism and the City as a Unique Socio-economic and Political Space' in Ballin Hirsch et al., (eds), *European Yearbook of Constitutional Law: Volume 2* (TMC Asher, 2020).
2. Blank Y, 'The City and the World' (2005–2006) 44 Columbia Journal of Transnational Law 875.
3. Doyle O, 'Spatial statism: Afterword to the Foreword by Ran Hirschl and Ayelet Shachar' (2020) 18(1) *International Journal of Constitutional Law* 29.
4. Frug G and Barron D, *City Bound: How States Stifle Urban Innovation* (Cornell University Press, 2008).
5. Hao Y and others, *Political Economy of Macao since 1999: The Dilemma of Success* (Springer, 2017).
6. Hirschl R, *City, State: Constitutionalism and the Megacity* (OUP, 2020).
7. Ip E, 'Comparative Constitutional Politics in the Chinese Special Administrative Regions of Hong Kong and Macau' in Ballin Hirsch et al., (eds), *European Yearbook of Constitutional Law: Volume 2* (TMC Asher, 2020).
8. Kuo M, 'Making Constitutionalism Progressive Again: A Primer on City Constitutionalism and State (Re)Formation in a New Constitutional Geography' (2022) 85(3) Modern Law Review 801.
9. Schragger R, 'The Attack on American Cities' (2018) 96 Texas Law Review 1163.
10. Zhao S and Zhang L, 'Economic Growth and Income Inequality in Hong Kong: Trends and Explanations' (2005) 3(1) China: An International Journal 74.

8

CONSTITUTIONAL REVIEW "WITH CHINESE CHARACTERISTICS"*

Law, Institutions and Recent Developments

Guobin Zhu

A general perception among Chinese constitutional law scholars exists that constitutional review as institution and mechanism is an integral part of the constitutional arrangement under the current Constitution (1982).[1] The view is somewhat mistaken but is not completely wrong. The aim of this Chapter is to examine that while substantial constitutional change has not yet taken place, or to say, will not take place in a foreseeable future, it is arguable that a unique Chinese brand of constitutional review system has taken root and is still evolving.

A classical understanding of the concept of judicial review constitutes "a court's power to review the actions of other branches or levels of government; esp., the courts' power to invalidate legislative and executive actions as being unconstitutional"[2]. The understanding is largely based on the doctrine and practice of the separation of powers and checks and balances. It has become an established part of contemporary constitutionalism in Western jurisprudence. Constitutional review, another expression of judicial review closely associated with the discussion of constitutional law, is the power of courts to examine whether legislation enacted by the parliament or acts of the executive authorities are consistent with written constitution and, within this query, to determine their validity. This system commands a primordial condition: courts have constitutional jurisdiction and exercise it on the basis of constitutionality. Needless to say, constitutional review is an innovation and construct derived from the American constitutional experience modelled after *Marbury v. Madison*[3] that now has become a norm or standard justifying and attesting democratic constitutional-making, and a reference for other countries to modernize their constitutional regime.

* This chapter is written partly based on my previous writing "Constitutional Review in China: An Unaccomplished Project or a Mirage?", first published in (2010) 43 SUFFOLK U. L. REV.625, pp. 625–653. However, for the purpose of this Handbook, the original text has received substantial revision, including deletion, and important updates to include new laws and reference materials.

DOI: 10.4324/9781003128243-10

If the above definition was literally applied to China, any constitutional scholar would have to conclude without any ambiguity that constitutional review does not exist in China. First, the current Constitution (1982) does not contain any such provisions for it. Second, Chinese courts are not granted, expressly or implicitly, the power to review the constitutionality of law and instead their task is merely to apply law, without the power of interpretation of law in adjudicating cases. Judicial review of constitutionality by courts is far from being an institutional fact, nor a mainstream idea in Chinese jurisprudence of constitutional law. That said, it is worth noting that China has tried judicial approach to constitutional review by way of *Qi Yuling* case; unfortunately, *Qi Yuling* had not lived for long in Chinese judicial history.[4]

A more holistic approach to constitutional review once appeared in 2000s in Chinese legal debate that contemplated contemporary public law in a way different from the classic approach. The differences lie in the understanding of the functions of constitutional review which, in my view, should be the assurance of compliance of constitutionality and dispute resolution. The assurance of compliance of constitutionality seems to be the first and original meaning of constitutional review. The second function of it, i.e., resolution of disputes among different branches of government, is being widely acknowledged as an equally important mechanism in both mature and emerging democracies. The role of "arbitrator" is in most, if not all, cases played by independent courts, but it may also be played by the national legislature and the bodies under it such as in the case of China as provided for by the Constitution.

In accordance with the current Constitution, the courts do not possess the power to assure the compliance of constitutionality in adjudicating cases. As regards the second element/function of constitutional review, we shall be able to assert that constitutional review of this nature exists in China and that the Constitution has established a system of constitutional review with the power of review vested in the legislature, instead of courts.

This chapter will first explore the constitutional provisions and theory regarding constitutional review of legislation and the rationale behind. Second, it will examine the theoretical and practical development in recent years of the establishment of the "System of Filing and Review" (*Bei'an Shencha Zhi*, F&R), a constitutional review system with Chinese characteristics and a system charged with the second function of constitutional review, and evaluate the efficiency of it. It ends up with some observation on the future of the system development.

Constitutional Review of Legislation as Framed by the Constitution and the Theory

The People's Congress System and Constitutionalism

The Chinese fundamental political system as framed by the Constitution is people's congress system. Based on the Constitution, this system has the following salient features: (i) "All power in the People's Republic of China belongs to the people"[5]; (ii) "The organs through which the people exercise state power are the National People's Congress and the local people's congresses at different levels"[6]; (iii) "All administrative, supervisory, adjudicatory and procuratorial organs of the state shall be created by the people's congresses and shall be responsible to them and subject to their oversight"[7]; (iv), "The state institutions of the People's Republic of China shall practice the principle of democratic centralism".[8]

Under the people's congress system, the National People's Congress ("the NPC") is "the highest organ of state power", whose permanent body is the Standing Committee of the National People's Congress ("the NPCSC"),[9] and in the meanwhile, the NPC and the NPCSC "exercise the legislative power of the state".[10] These provisions qualify the constitutional status of the NPC (and the NPCSC as "its permanent organ") and define it as both the sole highest organ of state power and the national legislature. This confirms that all state power is actually centralized in one body and no separation of powers is practiced as institutionalized under most democratic constitutions. This regime that centralizes a high degree of power under the constitutional principle of "democratic centralism" is believed to have been rooted in the previous practice of the government under the Communist Party of China ("the CPC") in the 1930s and 1940s.[11] It radically differs from the conventional Western conceptualization of the separation of powers. Though it looks like a parliamentary system considering that the NPC is also the highest legislature of China, the people's congress system is still substantively different from a Westminster system in light of the fact that the creation of the supervisory, judicial and procuratorial organs is completely subject to the decision of the NPC (with the CPC orchestrating behind the screen) and, probably the most importantly, the NPC is not constituted through democratic election.

The NPC, while generally acknowledged as a "rubber-stamp", does have a substantial role to play in decision-making and law-making process. Although Dowdle thinks that "it is no longer a secret that the National People's Congress has recently shed its "rubber-stamp" character and emerged as an independent and influential force in China's political arena",[12] the main role of the NPC is basically limited to the implementation of the policies and programmes made by the CPC by translating them into laws or regulations. The claim that the NPC has become an "independent" force is indeed questionable, in view of the recent constitutional amendment in 2018 which constitutionalizes the leadership of the country by the CPC by adding this sentence "The leadership of the Communist Party of China is the most essential feature of socialism with Chinese characteristics" to Art. 1[13] and creates the Commissions of Supervision at all levels, a brand new state institution under the NPC and parallel to people's courts and people's procuratorates,[14] all together further confirming the full leadership of the CPC across all state and political institutions and holistically institutionalizing the Party-State structure. The five constitutional amendments since 1988[15] have gradually confirmed this position. The dynamics of the relationship between the Party and the State can only be understood in this framework of "Party-State" structure. However, it is arguable that the NPC could realize a "soft-landing" for constitutionalism in China by reforming the people's congress system and transforming it into a full range and all-round legislative body.[16]

In theory, the NPC enjoys the total power of state and is a totalitarian type body. As the highest organ of state power, the NPC exercises a full range of powers which can be categorized into legislative power, decision-making power, power of appointment and removal, and power of supervision.[17] It is believed that "its power to legislate for China is preeminent among the multiple powers that it exercises".[18] As part of the power of supervision, the NPC and the NPCSC together exercise the power of constitutional review and ensure the compliance of law with the Constitution.

"Legislative Supervision" as Constitutional Review: Its Foundation and Rules

The supervisory power is a mandatory power of examination, investigation, overseeing, rectification and review to be exercised by the NPC and the people's congresses at all levels over the organs created by them, the purpose of which is to fully guarantee the implementation of national laws, prevent the executive and judicial branches of government from abusing power and protect people's fundamental rights and interests.[19] As the highest organ of state power as well as the highest legislature, the NPC exercises the power of supervision over legislative acts, law enforcement, executive actions, the judiciary, state personnel and military and foreign affairs.[20]

The NPC's supervisory power over laws and regulations is often called "legislative supervision" (*Lifa Jiandu*), which refers to the supervisory activities of "the people's congresses and their standing committees to examine whether laws, regulations and other normative instruments violate the Constitution, laws, and resolutions and decisions of the people's congresses", the purpose of which is "to ensure that general laws are consistent with the Constitution and basic laws, regulations consistent with laws, all normative instruments consistent with laws, resolutions and decisions made by the people's congresses, and to maintain the unity of the State legal system".[21]

The Constitution has provided for the foundation for legislative supervision, in other words, constitutional review of legislation, when it states that "no law or administrative or local rules and regulations shall contravene the Constitution".[22] Some have claimed that any review must be confined to "law", "administrative regulations" and "local regulations". This is not true. Based on the 2000 *Law on Legislation* (*Lifa Fa*, 2015 revised), "legislation" encompasses seven categories: (i) laws, (ii) administrative regulations, (iii) local regulations, (iv) autonomous regulations and specific regulations (of national autonomous regions), (v) regulations (made by special economic zones), (vi) rules (of departments of central government and local governments), and (vii) military regulations and rules.[23]

Scholars regard the above seven forms of law as "formal laws", which refer to "the normative legal instruments taking statutory forms, which are made by the specific institutions of the State in exercising legislative power, and in accordance with legal procedures".[24] Apart from "formal laws", in Chinese civil society, there exist many "substantive laws", which, in the broad sense of law, constitute parts of law system in China. They are: (i) resolutions and decisions adopted by the NPCSC and local people's congresses and their standing committees; (ii) decisions and decrees issued by the Central Military Commission, the State Council and local people's governments at all levels; and (iii) decisions, orders, directives made by departments of the State Council, departments of local people's governments at all levels.[25] The "substantive laws" also include resolutions, decisions, and directives adopted by the Central Committee of the CPC and functional departments of the CPC, some of which are jointly adopted by the Central Committee of the CPC and the State Council, i.e., the Central People's Government. Although the above forms of normative instruments are not officially recognized by *Law on Legislation* as "formal laws and regulations", they should be taken for parts of functional law, and real law in view of the fact that they are made by the specific institutions, applied to unspecified objects and repetitively, and have general legal effect. As such, these "substantive laws" should be included in the range of review by legislature.[26]

The practice of decentralization of law-making in China, which means the State Council and the local people's congresses and their standing committees can make administrative and local regulations and rules, contradicts the conventional theory of unitary state/unitarism that China practices and it mirrors a kind of de facto legislative federalism. Furthermore, the diversity of categories and forms of laws underlines the complexity of law system. This gives rise to the necessity of creating a system of review of legislation, being it "laws", "regulations" or "rules", the purpose of which is to "uphold the uniformity and dignity of the socialist legal system".[27]

The system of legislative review develops at two levels and for two purposes: (i) the review of law on the basis of constitutionality and (ii) the review of other forms of law on the basis of legality. The Constitution authorizes the NPCSC to exercise the power of constitutional review, i.e., the review of constitutionality of law by defining that: "The NPCSC exercises the following functions and powers: (i) interpreting the Constitution and overseeing its enforcement; ... (vii) revoking administrative regulations, decisions and orders formulated by the State Council that are in conflict with the Constitution or laws; (viii) revoking local regulations and resolutions formulated by the state organs of power in provinces, autonomous regions and cities directly under central government jurisdiction that are in conflict with the Constitution, laws, or administrative regulations".[28] The NPCSC's power to examine whether administrative regulations and local regulations actually contravene the Constitution is the power of constitutional review by nature.

Review of Constitutionality and Legality

Based on the above provisions, the NPCSC also exercises the power of review of both constitutionality and legality of other regulations and rules. As a matter of both law and fact, the Constitution and the *Law on Legislation* do not make a clear distinction between the review of constitutionality and the review of legality, and between the two procedures of review. In accordance with the hierarchy of law and the structure of authority of law- and regulation-making bodies, the *Law on Legislation* defines the system and process of legislative review as follows:[29]

> The power to modify or revoke laws, administrative regulations, local regulations, autonomous regulations, separate regulations, or rules shall be as follows:
>
> i. The NPC shall have the power to modify or revoke inappropriate laws enacted by its Standing Committee, and have the power to revoke autonomous regulations and separate regulations approved by its Standing Committee <u>which contravene the Constitution</u> or the provision of paragraph 2, Article 75 of this Law;[30] [Emphasis added]
> ii. The NPCSC shall have the power to revoke administrative regulations <u>which contravene the Constitution and laws</u>, have the power to revoke local regulations which contravene the Constitution, laws, and administrative regulations, and have the power to revoke autonomous regulations and separate regulations approved by the standing committee of the people's congress of a province, autonomous region, or municipality directly under the Central Government which contravene the Constitution or the provision of paragraph 2, Article 75 of this Law; [Emphasis added]

iii. The State Council shall have the power to modify or revoke inappropriate State Council departmental rules and the rules of local governments;
iv. The people's congress of a province, autonomous region, or municipality directly under the Central Government shall have the power to modify or revoke inappropriate local regulations made and approved by its standing committee;
v. The standing committee of a local people's congress shall have the power to revoke inappropriate rules made by the people's government at the same level;
vi. The people's government of a province or autonomous region shall have the power to modify or revoke inappropriate rules made by the people's governments at the next lower level;
vii. The empowering authority shall have the power to revoke regulations made by the empowered authority which transcend the scope of empowerment or contravene the purpose of empowerment, and when necessary, may revoke the empowerment.

The above definitions reveal that the review of constitutionality is conducted by the NPC and the NPCSC (see paragraphs (i) and (ii)), while the review of legality is conducted by the State Council (see (iii)), local people's congress and its standing committee (see (iv) and (v)) and local people's government (see (vi)). Interestingly, the arrangement of legislative review in the Constitution and laws displays a pyramidal structure of authority, mirroring the administrative division of the country and corresponding to the institutional establishment.

Being the highest organ of state power and the highest legislature of the country, the NPC and NPCSC's power of constitutional review corresponds to the theory of the people's congress. Under the polity of the people's congress, only the NPC and NPCSC can exercise this constitutional power. Qin Aolei (秦奥蕾) and Wang Kai conclude that the review of constitutionality by the NPC or NPCSC applies to the following categories of laws and regulations:[31] (i) law; (ii) administrative regulations made by the State Council under Art. 89 of the Constitution regarding the functions and powers of the State Council;[32] (iii) local governmental rules regarding "concrete local administrative matters" under Art. 107 of the Constitution; (iv) local regulations concerning "local affairs" which need to be regulated locally under Arts 99 and 104 of the Constitution; (v) local regulations concerning matters that have not been regulated by national laws or administrative regulations yet; (vi) autonomous regulations and specific regulations; and (vii) other "not yet formalized substantive laws". Qin and Wang actually expanded the scope of review by including category (iii) which should be subject to the review of legality by the State Council and/or the local people's congress concerned.

However, it is appropriate to include the category (vii) which includes resolutions, decisions, and directives jointly adopted by the Central Committee of the CPC and the State Council. This category of normative instruments has substantive authority of law and general legal effect. The review of them certainly constitutes a challenge to the current constitutional regime and poses serious problems of feasibility and applicability. The dilemma we are facing is how to understand the constitutional provisions in regard to the role and status of the ruling party: on the one hand, "... all political parties and public organizations ... in the country must take the Constitution as the basic norm of conduct, and they have the duty to uphold the dignity of the Constitution and ensure its implementation"; on the other hand, "the Chinese people of all nationalities will continue to adhere to the leadership of the CPC, ...",[33] and "Leadership by the Communist Party of China is the defining feature of socialism with Chinese characteristics".[34]. The question now is whether the CPC and its decisions and acts in the capacity of the ruling party are subject to constitutional scrutiny and review. The answer to it, which constitutes an interesting and meaningful academic subject matter, will obviously be no easy.

Hierarchy of Legal Authority as the Basis of Review

The people's congresses at different levels and the State Council have differentiated roles of law review to play and the review must observe a hierarchical and tiered system of legal authority or effect. The Constitution and the *Law on Legislation* actually have established a set of rules to guide the practice.

The system of legal authority or effect is structured as follows:[35] (i) The Constitution has the highest legal authority, and no national law, administrative regulations, local regulations, autonomous regulations and special regulations, or administrative or local rules shall contravene the Constitution; (ii) National laws (made by the NPC and the NPCSC) have higher legal authority than administrative regulations, local regulations and (departmental and local) rules; (iii) Administrative regulations (made by the State Council) have higher legal authority than local regulations and administrative or local rules; (iv) Local regulations (made by the people's congress and its standing committees at provincial level) have higher legal authority than local rules issued by governments at the same level and lower level; and (v) Local rules (enacted by the people's government of a province or autonomous region) have higher legal authority than local rules enacted by the people's government of a districted city or an autonomous prefecture within the administrative region of the province or autonomous region. In addition to the above, "the rules of different departments of the State Council shall have equal authority, as well as State Council departmental rules and the rules of local governments".[36]

Following the hierarchy of law and the order of legal effect, once a conflict of law matter arises, the NPC and the local people's congresses shall directly annul these conflicting laws, regulations and rules or demand the enacting authorities to annul or alter them on their own.

However, the above process of review of laws and regulations on the basis of constitutionality and legality is subject to two exceptions, the provisions of which are derived from the Constitution and the *Law on Legislation.* First, autonomous regulations and specific regulations made by the people's congresses of national autonomous areas can vary national law, administrative regulations and local regulations "in the light of the political, economic, and cultural characteristics of the nationality or nationalities in the areas concerned",[37] "provided that any such variance shall not violate the basic principles thereof, and no variance is allowed in respect of any provision of the Constitution or the *Law on Regional National Autonomy (Minzu Quyu Zizhi Fa)* and provisions of any other law or administrative regulations which are dedicated to matters concerning national autonomous areas".[38] Thus the inconsistency, if it exists, should not be regarded as contravention of constitutional and national law as long as the prescribed conditions are met.

Second, the revised *Law on Legislation* has made special arrangement as to the making of local regulations by the people's congress and its standing committee of a "districted city", also translated as "city divided into districts" (*Shequ de Shi*), as follows: "The people's congress and its standing committee of a districted city may, according to the city's specific circumstances and actual needs, enact local regulations on urban and rural development and administration, environmental protection, and preservation of history and culture, among others, provided that they do not contravene the Constitution, laws, administrative regulations, and the local regulations of the province or autonomous region where the city is located, unless provided otherwise for the enactment of local regulations by a districted city".[39] The inconsistency under this condition is permissible as the power of regulation-making for "districted city" derives directly from the delegation of power by the NPC under the 2018 Constitutional Amendment.[40]

Filing and Review: Non-judicial Review of Constitutionality

A Brief Retrospect of the Origin of F&R System

The review of constitutionality of legislation is conducted via the system of "Filing and Review" (*Bei'an Shencha*, hereafter abbreviated as F&R). Basically, F&R is first of all a long-time practice to implement the ambiguous intent of the Constitution which permits the creation of a review process within the people's congress system.

The filing system started in 1979 and first applied to local regulations and rules. Until the end of 1983, the filing work was mainly conducted by the Section of Politics and Law of the General Office of the NPCSC, the major objectives of which were to: (i) review the constitutionality and legality of regulations and rules; (ii) manage the register, and conduct statistics and filing; (iii) periodically report to the NPCSC on the situations of law-making by local people's congresses. The General Office did find a "small amount" of local regulations and rules inconsistent with national laws and policies and requested the NPCSC to refer these cases to the standing committees of provincial, regional and municipal people's congress concerned for resolution, as observed by Cai.[41]

From 1984 to 1988, the filing of laws and regulations became the responsibility of the Liaison Bureau of the NPCSC, and the actual work was reduced to the implementation of the technical work, including: registration, statistics and filing (which meant sorting out local regulations and rules and then put them into different folders). Since 1988, the NPCSC was requested to conduct the work of review of all regulations and rules submitted to it, but the review was basically carried out as a matter of routine.

The situation of no active review lasted for about 5 years until July 1993 when the Secretariat of the General Office of the NPCSC took up the responsibility of filing and review of regulations and rules submitted by local people's congresses, in accordance with *The Outline of Work for the 8th NPCSC (Bajie Quanguo Renda Changweihui Gongzuo Yaodian)*. Based on the "Outline", the whole process of filing and review consisted of six steps.

The effectiveness of the system depends mainly on the reaction of the local people's congresses, the regulations of which were under challenge. Cai's observation is rather critical when he said that: "As a matter of fact, only a few local standing committees rectified the regulations by virtue of the opinions adopted by the special commissions, many others chose to insist on their original opinions based on various reasons".[42]

Two subsequent events together have enhanced this non-judicial means of review of constitutionality. One was the establishment of the organ in May 2004 specially in charge of filing and review of laws and regulations within the NPCSC, i.e., the Division of Filing and Review of Regulations (*Fagui Bei'an Shencha Shi*), the mission of which was to shoulder the task of filing and review of regulations. The second was the adoption of *The Working Procedure Relative to Filing and Review of Administrative Regulations, Local Regulations, Autonomous Regulations and Specific Regulations, and Regulations of Special Economic Zones* (*Xingzheng Fagui, Difangxing Fagui, Zizhi Tiaoli he Danxing Tiaoli, Jingjitequ Fagui Bei'an Shench Gongzuo Chengxu*, hereafter referred to as "The Working Procedure") in 2000, and its subsequent revision in 2005, according to which active review of laws and regulations by the NPC and the NPCSC became possible. As we will see it later, this Working Procedure will be replaced by a newly revamped one, demonstrating a substantial progress of the system.

The Theoretical and Constitutional Basis for Review of Constitutionality

Institutionally, the NPC, and only the NPC, as we have seen it above, has the power to supervise and review the legislation adopted by the state organs created by it and under it. As a component of accountability, the state organs, including the State Council, the National Commission of Supervision, the Supreme People's Court and the Supreme People's Procuratorate, shall report their work to the NPC. This constitutional arrangement first mirrors the establishment of the people's congress system which is the fundamental political system of China, and it has made itself far different from typical Western system, be it parliamentary system, presidential system or the separation of powers system. The constitutional design is also responsive to the guiding principles of Chinese constitutional law: people's sovereignty[43] and democratic centralism.[44]

The system of review of constitutionality is primarily based on the principle of supremacy of constitution which has long been confirmed in the 1982 Constitution and it has survived the five amendments thereafter. In the Preamble of the Constitution, it is clearly stated that[45]:

> This Constitution, …; it is the fundamental law of the State and has supreme legal authority. The people of all nationalities, all State organs, the armed forces, all political parties and public organizations and all enterprises and institutions in the country must take the Constitution as the basic standard of conduct, and they have the duty to uphold the dignity of the Constitution and ensure its implementation. [Emphasis added]

Art 5 of the Constitution further adds that:

> The People's Republic of China governs the country according to law and makes it a socialist country under the rule of law.
>
> The State upholds the uniformity and dignity of the socialist legal system.
>
> No laws or administrative or local regulations shall contravene the Constitution. [Emphasis added]

The above constitutional provisions have been incorporated into the revised *Law on Legislation* in 2015, as follows[46]:

> The Constitution shall have the supreme legal effect, and no laws, administrative regulations, local regulations, autonomous regulations, separate regulations, or rules shall contravene the Constitution.

The constitutional intent of establishing a review system to examine the constitutionality and legality of laws and regulations had not been formalized and institutionalized until the 34th Chairman's Meeting of the NPCSC adopted the above-mentioned The Working Procedure on 16 October 2000. The adoption of it was the first and foremost step towards the institutionalization of constitutional review under the current constitutional framework in China. As a matter of fact, the Working Procedure, a product based on limited accumulated experience, did reflect the need to systematize the work of F&R. To some extent, the symbolic significance of it is farer than the actual one.

Starting from 2000, with the publication of the Working Procedure, F&R, as rightly observed by a scholar, has become "an oversight tool employed by China's top legislature, the Standing Committee of the National People's Congress (NPCSC), to ensure that sub-statutory legislation – ranked below national statutes as to legal force, such as local legislation – conforms to national statutes and policy".[47] More importantly, F&R has been given the mission to ensure "review of constitutionality" (*Hexianxing Shencha*) by the CPC at its 19th National Congress on 18 October 2017. In his report titled "Secure a Decisive Victory in Building a Moderately Prosperous Society in All Respects and Strive for the Great Success of Socialism with Chinese Characteristics for a New Era", Xi Jinping, the Secretary General of the CPC, declared that "We will strengthen oversight to ensure compliance with the Constitution, advance the review of constitutionality, and safeguard the authority of the Constitution".[48] [Emphasis added] Since this point of time, the term of "review of constitutionality" has been officially adopted and publicly entered into political discourse for the first time; it has gained the legitimacy in academic writings.

In the light of this development of high significance, the Working Procedure (2000), revised first the first time at the 40th Chairman's Meeting of the NPCSC on 19 December 2005, has been repealed and replaced by *The Working Measures for Filing and Review of Regulations and Judicial Interpretations (Fagui Sifa Jieshi Bei'an Shencha Gongzuo Banfa*, hereafter "The Working Measures"*)*, adopted at the 44th Chairman's Meeting of the NPCSC on 16 December 2019. The Working Measures have laid down the solid foundation of F&R in general and of constitutional review in particular. The Working Measures are highly regarded by professionals, legal scholars, as well as people working at the NPC. For example, the Division of Filing and Review of Regulations of the Legislative Affairs Commission under the NPCSC regards the adoption of the Working Measures as "a major achievement made by the NPCSC in strengthening the construction of F&R system".[49] Wang Kai believes that "after revision and improvement for many years, the current F&R system has become the major, or to say, the most efficient supervision system of constitution and laws in China".[50]

F&R as the Major Mechanism of Review

According to Chinese constitutional law, the system of F&R of administrative and local regulations is an integral part of legislative system. In practice, it serves as the basis as well as the major process of constitutional review. Under this system, *bei'an* means "filing", "filing for record" or "for the record" as often translated and used interchangeably in English, and *shencha* means examination, review and audit. The system is rooted and first instituted in the Constitution and *Organic Law of Local People's Congresses and Local People's Governments at Various Levels* (*Difang Geji Renmin Daibiao Dahui he Difang Geji Renmin Zhengfu Zuzhi Fa*; adopted in 1979, and revised in 1982, 1986, 1995, 2004, 2015, 2022), and then fully developed in the *Law on Legislation* (2000, and revised in 2015).

The Constitution first provides for the foundation for the system by promulgating that:[51]

> The people's congresses of provinces and cities directly under the Central Government jurisdiction and their standing committees may, provided there is no conflict with the Constitution, laws or administrative regulations, enact local regulations, which shall be reported to the National People's Congress Standing Committee <u>for the record</u>. [Emphasis added]

And it further institutes a system of filing and approval for regulations adopted by the people's congresses of national autonomous areas and the people's congresses of cities divided into districts and their standing committees by defining that:

> The people's congresses of national autonomous areas have the power to enact autonomous regulations and specific regulations in the light of the political, economic, and cultural characteristics of the nationality or nationalities in the areas concerned. The autonomous regulations and specific regulations of autonomous regions shall be submitted to the NPCSC <u>for approval</u> before they go into effect. Those of autonomous prefectures and counties shall be submitted to the standing committees of the people's congresses of provinces or autonomous regions for approval before they go into effect, and they shall be reported to the NPCSC <u>for the record</u>. [Emphasis added] [52]
>
> The people's congresses of cities divided into districts and their standing committees may, provided there is no conflict with the Constitution, laws or administrative regulations, or with the local regulations of their province or autonomous region, enact local regulations in accordance with the provisions of law, which shall be submitted to the standing committee of the people's congress of their province or autonomous region <u>for approval</u> before they go into effect. [Emphasis added.][53]

The *Organic Law of Local People's Congresses and Local People's Governments at Various Levels*, as amended in 2022, refined the above provisions and also identified the State Council as the institution receiving filing by articulating it as follows[54]:

> The people's congresses of provinces, autonomous regions, and municipalities directly under the Central Government may, in the light of the specific conditions and actual needs of their respective administrative areas, formulate and promulgate local regulations, which must not contravene the Constitution, the law, and the administrative regulations; they shall report such local regulations to the NPCSC and the State Council <u>for the record</u>.
>
> The people's congresses of cities divided into districts and autonomous prefecture may, in the light of the specific conditions and actual needs of their respective areas, formulate local regulations, which must not contravene the Constitution, the law, administrative regulations, and the local regulations of their respective provinces and autonomous regions; they shall report such local regulations to the standing committees of the people's congresses of the respective provinces and autonomous regions <u>for approval</u> before implementation, and submit them to the Standing Committee of the National People's

> Congress and the State Council <u>for the record</u> via the standing committees of the people's congresses of the respective provinces and autonomous regions. [Emphasis added]

The *Law on Legislation*, as amended in 2015, has fully developed a structured and layered system on the above basis and consolidated relevant provisions, for example, by stating that:[55]

> Administrative regulations, local regulations, autonomous regulations, separate regulations and rules shall, within 30 days from the date of promulgation, be reported to the organ concerned for the record in accordance with the following provisions:
>
> i. Administrative regulations shall be reported to the Standing Committee of the National People's Congress <u>for the record</u>;
> ii. Local regulations formulated by the people's congress of a province, autonomous region or municipality directly under the Central Government and the standing committee thereof shall be submitted to the Standing Committee of the NPC and the State Council <u>for the record</u>, while local regulations formulated by the people's congress of a city divided into districts or an autonomous prefecture and the standing committee thereof shall be submitted to the Standing Committee of the NPC and the State Council <u>for the record</u> via the standing committee of the people's congress of the province or autonomous region in which the said city or autonomous prefecture is located;
> iii. Autonomous regulations and special regulations formulated by the people's congress of an autonomous prefecture or autonomous county shall be submitted to the Standing Committee of the NPC and the State Council <u>for the record</u> via the standing committee of the people's congress of the province, autonomous region or municipality directly under the Central Government in which the autonomous prefecture or autonomous county is located. When autonomous regulations or special regulations are submitted for the record, information on the changes made to relevant laws, administrative regulations and local regulations shall be explained;
> iv. Department rules and local government rules shall be submitted to the State Council <u>for the record</u>, while local government rules shall be concurrently submitted to the standing committee of the people's congress at the same level <u>for the record</u>. Rules formulated by the people's government of a city divided into districts or an autonomous prefecture shall also be concurrently submitted to the standing committee of the people's congress and the people's government of the province or autonomous region in which the said city or autonomous prefecture is located <u>for the record</u>, and
> v. Regulations formulated upon authorization shall be submitted to the organ specified in the relevant authorization decision <u>for the record</u>. When regulations of a special economic zone are submitted for the record, information on the changes made to relevant laws, administrative regulations and local regulations shall be explained. [Above emphasis added]

F&R System: New Development

The adoption in 2019 of the above-mentioned *The Working Measures for Filing and Review of Regulations and Judicial Interpretations* does mark a new page of the F&R system development. There is a consensus among scholars and officials in charge of F&R work that the Working Measures represent "a major achievement" of the system.[56]

In Chapter Two of the Working Measures, "Filing", the detailed process and procedures are defined. Taking a few provisions for example:

> (i) A regulation or judicial interpretation shall be submitted to the NPCSC for filing within 30 days from the date when it is issued;[57] (ii) The paper versions of regulations and judicial interpretations shall be submitted for filing by the respective authorities, such as the State Council, provincial level people's congresses, etc.;[58] (iii) The General Office of the NPCSC shall conduct formal review of filed documents within 15 days from the date of receipt of such documents;[59] and (iv) Before the end of January each year, all submitting authorities shall summarize and submit to the General Office of the NPCSC the lists of regulations and judicial interpretations made, amended, repealed and approved in the previous year.[60]

Chapter Three, "Review", has defined the responsibilities and scope of review, the procedures of review and the criteria of review. Some new methods, procedures and improvements developed since 2000 have been and included, and normative criteria of review has been systemically formulated, together to ensure the smooth operation of the system of F&R. For example:

> (i) The review is presented in four forms: review ex officio, review upon request, review upon transfer, or special review;[61] (ii) Not only state organs, but also social organizations, enterprises, public institutions and citizens can make recommendation for review to the NPCSC according to the law and the recommendations shall be accepted and registered by the Legislative Affairs Commission;[62] (iii) Under certain circumstances and upon preliminary research, review process may not be initiated;[63] (iv) Regarding the criteria of review, the Working Measures presents more details as follows:[64] Where it is found during the review of or research on any regulation or judicial interpretation that the regulation or judicial interpretation violates the provisions of any law and falls under any of the following circumstances, relevant opinions shall be provided: (a) It makes provisions for any matter that shall only be governed by laws in violation of Article 8 of the Law on Legislation; (b) It, beyond the prescribed power, illegally sets the rights and obligations of citizens, legal persons, and other organizations, or illegally sets the powers and responsibilities of state organs; (c) It illegally sets administrative licensing, administrative punishment, or administrative compulsion, or adjusts or changes the administrative licensing, administrative punishment, or administrative compulsion set by law; (d) It is obviously inconsistent with legal provisions or contravenes the legislative purpose and principle of a law with a purpose of offsetting, changing or evading legal provisions; (e) It violates the empowerment decision or transcends the scope of empowerment; (f) It varies any matter that

shall not be varied according to the law, or the variating provisions violate the basic principles of the law; (g) It violates legal procedures; and (h) Other circumstances that violate the law; (v) About the handling of regulations and interpretations under review, the reviewing body shall communicate its opinion to the original enacting authority and require it to amend or repeal the regulation or judicial interpretation in a timely manner; if the communication fails, a written review or research opinion shall be provided to the enacting authority in accordance with Article 100 of the Law on Legislation to require it to feedback with a written handling opinion within two months;[65] (vi) "If an enacting authority fails to amend or repeal any regulation in a timely manner in accordance with the written review or research opinion, the specialized committee [under the NPC] and the Legislative Affairs Commission may legally submit a motion or recommendation for revocation of the regulation to the Chairmen's Meeting [of the NPCSC] which shall decide whether to submit the motion or recommendation to a session of the Standing Committee [of the NPC] for deliberation. If the enacting authority fails to amend or repeal any judicial interpretation in a timely manner based on the written review or research opinion, the specialized committee [under the NPC] or the Legislative Affairs Commission may legally submit a motion or recommendation requiring the Supreme People's Court or the Supreme People's Procuratorate to amend or repeal the judicial interpretation, or a motion or recommendation requiring the Standing Committee of the National People's Congress to make a legal interpretation, and the Chairmen's Meeting shall decide whether to submit the motion or recommendation to a session of the Standing Committee [of the NPC] for deliberation."[66]; and (vii) A specialized committee [under the NPC] and the Legislative Affairs Commission shall generally complete the review or research within three months after the review procedure starts, and submit a written review or research report.[67]

Out of all new provisions and arrangements regarding F&R, there are two particular articles in the Working Measures specifically dealing with the review of constitutionality in clarity that should attract our closer attention. It shows a special focus placed on constitutional review by the NPCSC, and it is presented as follows:

(i) The Constitution and Law Commission of the NPC[68] and the Legislative Affairs Commission under the NPCSC shall take initiative to review regulations and judicial interpretations should these documents involve constitutional issues; the reviewing organs shall produce a report in writing, and feedback the opinion to the regulations-making bodies;[69] and (ii) Where it is found during the review of or research on a regulation or judicial interpretation that that regulation or judicial interpretation violates the Constitution, the principles of the Constitution, or the spirit of the Constitution, relevant opinions shall be provided.[70]

According to above paragraph (ii), the review can be based not only on the provisions of the Constitution, but also on "the principles of the Constitution", or "the spirit of the Constitution". Although the Working Measures do not prescribe on how to extract the "spirit" of the Constitution, and how to proceed in the above situations, we may presume that the NPCSC has been given the power and discretion to handle constitutionality-related issues during review, and as required, it is under a duty to produce an opinion with binding effect to be feedbacked to the original document-making bodies. This is where the function and value of F&R system exist.

According to the Working Measures, the major authority of review, here referring to the Legislative Affairs Commission under the NPCSC, shall present its annual report to the NPCSC for deliberation and review. It is defined that:[71]

> The Legislative Affairs Commission shall submit to the Standing Committee of the National People's Congress an annual special report on the implementation of filing and review which shall be deliberated at a session of the Standing Committee.
>
> The report on the implementation of filing and review shall, after being amended based on the deliberation opinions of the members of the Standing Committee, be published in the Bulletin of the Standing Committee of the National People's Congress or on the website of the National People's Congress.

Interestingly, we discover that this practice of reporting on F&R by the Legislative Affairs Commission did start in 2017, which means it has already been implemented for two years before the official adoption of the Working Measures. Up to now, there are five reports on F&R submitted by the Commission to the NPCSC for deliberation, they are the Reports of 2017, 2018, 2019, 2020 and 2021. Zheng Lei describes this practice as "full coverage" F&R system. Actually, Zheng has just completed a thorough examination and analysis of the first four reports and produced a timely work on the operation of the F&R system.[72]

A Glimpse at Significant Work of F&R Completed by Reviewing Bodies

In the first Report on F&R submitted to the NPCSC by the Legislative Affairs Commission on 24 December 2017, the Chairman of the Commission presented some interesting and illustrative figures to demonstrate what the Commission had accomplished in 2017. Since 2013, the starting year of the 12th NPC, the Commission has completed review of a total of 4778 normative documents received by it, they included: 60 administrative regulations made by the State Council, 2543 local regulations submitted from provincial level people's congresses, 1647 local regulations from cities divided into districts, 15 autonomous regulations made by people's congresses of autonomous regions, 248 separate regulations made by people's congresses of autonomous regions, 137 local regulations from special economic zones and 128 judicial interpretations. Only in the year of 2017, the NPCSC received 889 normative documents for filing and review.

The table below with statistics which is prepared based on the five Reports can demonstrate the significant work completed by the reviewing bodies, and it is also able to provide for a general picture assisting us in better understanding of the actual work and achievements of F&R.[73] Starting from 2020 round of F&R, the NPCSC exercised its review power over the legislation from Hong Kong and Macau. In 2021 round of F&R, a new category of regulations, which is "supervision regulations" adopted by National Supervision Commission, is added.

Types of Normative Documents	2017	2018	2019	2020	2021
Administrative Regulations	18	40	53	25	16
Supervision Regulations					1
Provincial Local Regulations	358	640	516	500	779
Cities' Local Regulations	444	483	78	563	688
Autonomous Regulations and Separate Regulations	25	33	99	85	87
Local Regulations of Special Economic Zones	24	24	58	80	40
Judicial Interpretations	20	18	41	16	251
Ordinances of the Hong Kong Special Administrative Region[74]				20	42
Ordinances of the Macau Special Administrative Region[75]				21	17
Total	**889**	**1238**	**1485**	**1310**	**1921**

What is Next Step for Constitutional Review?

The mainstream scholars once agreed that there was no systematic practice of constitutional review in China, although the Constitution has provided for a review mechanism by the NPC and the NPCSC. As witnessed by Chen Yunsheng, "So far, the NPC or the NPCSC has never made a decision deeming unconstitutional a law, a regulation, an administrative action or a judicial act".[76] Hu Jingguang further pointed out that "there are situations in which normative documents violate the Constitution in actual social life and State activities in China, however the NPC and its Standing Committee have never used the Constitution and the *Law on Legislation* to start constitutional review".[77] The disparity between theory and practice still remains apparent and this situation seems to have seen some changes since recent years with effective implementation of F&R.

We may expect some sort of further breakthrough vis-à-vis the current constitutional regime, a radical change, however, will not be possible in the near future. Insofar as constitutional review is concerned, the first task is to truly apply the provisions of the Constitution regarding review of constitutionality of laws and regulations by the NPCSC, so that the authority of the Constitution as the fundamental law of the country can be gradually established. In the meantime, searching for a new constitutional solution with a workable mechanism, for example, judicial review of constitutionality, would require fundamental constitutional reform.

In the early years of twenty-first century, Chinese scholars have completed solid research as to which institution or mechanism would be suitable for Chinese system. Scholars discovered there existed five types of constitutional review in the world which are: (i) constitutional review by ordinary judicial institutions (the courts) (US model); (ii) constitutional review by constitutional court (German and Austria model); (iii) constitutional review by the legislature (British model); (iv) constitutional review by special political organ (French model); and (v) constitutional review by the supreme organ of state power (all ex-Socialist countries except ex-Yugoslavia, including China).[78]

As to the "right" way forward for China, constitutional scholars have put forward four major options/proposals for consideration: (i) Option I – Applying Judicial Review of Constitutionality. This is to follow the American model under which ordinary courts are granted the power to review the constitutionality of legislative and executive actions. In so doing, the SPC, not the NPC, should assume the responsibility of constitutional interpretation,[79] and the Constitution should be taken for basis of judgment;[80]

(ii) Option II – Establishing Constitutional Court, which refers to the continental European system, Kelsonian model, where a constitutional court is set to take charge of constitutional review; [81] (iii) Option III – Composite System of Review, a relatively new proposal basically applicable to China, which promotes a system of review combining the supreme organ of state power, i.e., the NPC and NPCSC, and judicial institutions; (iv) Option IV – Establishing Constitutional Council (*Xianfa Weiyuanhui*) or Constitutional Supervisory Committee (*Xianfa Jiandu Weiyuanhui*) under the NPC, the mainstream opinion, which has been debated for a long time and is believed to have solid basis for its realization. [In Chinese, "*weiyuanhui*" can be translated into "council", "committee" or "commission".]

The merit of Option IV lies in that the proposal does not contradict the current constitutional framework, respects the NPC as the supreme organ of state power and embodies the spirit of professionalism and procedure. It is believed that it carries with it fewer difficulties and greater feasibility and would encounter less political and professional resistance and would therefore be "the most possible choice so far".[82] Time has changed. Considering the full implementation of F&R system in China since recent years, Option IV would not be considered for now, although it seemed to be the most practical and feasible one, while other options would certainly not to be taken into account at all.

However, can constitutional review modelled after the American or Kelsonian model be an item on the political agenda of the political decision-makers in today's China? Taking into consideration all relevant factors, no such opportunity exists anymore, only F&R system remains available, and actually, we have witnessed, it has been endorsed by the CPC[83] and institutionalized under the NPC system. As regards the way forward in the coming future, scholars do not have much to say under the strong Party-State polity and ideological control today. Sadly, even the terminology of constitutionalism has become taboo in China. So far, we see no sign supportive of constitutional reform and "the prospects for a meaningful constitutional reform were limited", as rightly observed by Keith Hand and Thomas E. Kellogg years ago.[84] When we read Kellogg's following aspiration again: "Given the somewhat prohibitive environment for top-down reforms, it may be more fruitful for Chinese lawyers, academics, and activists to continue to pursue bottom-up strategies. In particular, lawyers and academics should continue to make rigorous, creative, and useful constitutional arguments to Chinese judges. Lawyers may also want to consider experimenting with greater use of international and comparative law",[85] we may feel dizzy. Like a world away today, because times have changed, the ever-expected environment favourable to political reform is no longer there in China.

Conclusion

Since the death of *Qi Yuling* in 2008,[86] constitutional review, constitutional litigation or judicialization of constitution has already ended in China. It looked like an ancient Greek tragedy and Qi was that forgotten hero. From the current point of view, judicial review of constitutionality would never be possible unless there was substantial political and constitutional reform, on the one hand.

On the other hand, the foundation of constitutional review by non-judicial institutions and avenue in the Constitution is present, but they need to be activated in such a way that unconstitutional legislative instruments (and executive acts) can be effectively corrected. To some extent, literally implementing the subsisting constitutional provisions and the

Law on Legislation is possible and therefore should be prioritized for the moment. It is noticeable that F&R system, with the creation of the Division of Filing and Review of Regulations under the NPCSC and the adoption of the Working Measures in 2019, is steadily progressing towards institution-building of (partial) constitutional review, although it is still far from our expectation in terms of its effectiveness.

In addition, what scholars and lawyers should continue to do is to promote and develop the theory that underlines the significance of a constitutional committee/council/commission to be established under the NPC. Such an organ can certainly make a sharper difference vis-à-vis the current somewhat marginal solution, and the creation of it would not challenge the current constitutional foundation and the authority of the CPC. At the same time and ideally, the courts can be given a somewhat active role to play in rectifying the unconstitutional executive acts, and in so doing, the courts can play a "checking" role and can balance the unlimited, but not always effective, jurisdiction of the NPC.[87] Whatever system or mechanism to be adopted in the near future, we should fully realise that there is a pressing need to establish a transparent and effective mechanism within the NPC system or to improve the legal and judicial process in order to effectively address citizens' constitutional claims.

Finally, the concept "to rule the country according to law and to build a Socialist country of the rule of law", as prescribed by the Constitution,[88] is the cornerstone supportive of moving constitutionalism forward, and corresponding action should be taken to realize it, including realistically instituting an effective mechanism of constitutional review. Otherwise, constitutionalism in China, though already at the "nascent" stage,[89] would remain a mirage forever.

Notes

1 The Constitution of the People's Republic of China ("the PRC") was promulgated in 1982 and has received five important amendments in 1988, 1993, 1999, 2004 and 2018, respectively. There exist four constitutions since the founding of the PRC which were promulgated in 1954, 1975, 1978 and 1982.

2 *Black's Law Dictionary* (8th ed., 2004) 864.

3 *Marbury v. Madison*, [1803] 5 U.S. (1 Cranch) 137, is a landmark case in constitutional history and the basis for the exercise of judicial review in the United States, under Article III of the United States Constitution.

4 *Qi Yuling* case has attracted much attention from both legal scholars and professionals in China as well as overseas Chinese law scholars. About the origin, and development and end of the case, Cf. Zhu Guobin, 'Constitutional Review in China: An Unaccomplished Project or a Mirage?', (2010) 43 *SUFFOLK U. L. REV.* 625, pp. 625–653; Tong Zhiwei, "A Comment on the Rise and Fall of the Supreme People's Court's Reply to Qi Yuling's Case", (2010) 43 *SUFFOLK U. L. REV.* 671, pp. 671–680; Shen Kui, "Is It the Beginning of the Era of the Rule of the Constitution – Reinterpreting China's First Constitutional Case", (2003) 12:1 *PAC RIM L & POL'Y J.* 199, pp. 199–232.

5 The Constitution, art. 2(1).

6 The Constitution, art. 2(2).

7 The Constitution, art. 3(3).

8 The Constitution, art. 3(1).

9 The Constitution, art. 57.

10 The Constitution, art. 58.

11 *Cf* Xu Chongde (ed.), *Xian Fa (Constitutional Law)* (Renmin University of China Press, 1999) 108–109.

12 Michael W. Dowdle, *The Constitutional Development and Operations of the National People's Congress*, (1997) 11 *COLUM. J. ASIAN L.* 1.

13 The Constitution, art. 1.
14 The Constitution. arts. 123–127.
15 *Supra note* 1.
16 *Cf* Sun Zhe, *A Study of the People's Congress System (Quanguo Renda Zhidu Yanjiu)* (Law Press, 2004) 29–30.
17 *Cf* Zhu Guobin, *Constitutional Law and Political Institutions of China (Zhongguo Xianfa yu Zhengzhi Zhidu)* (2nd ed., Law Press, 2006) 118–123.
Also *cf* Cai Dingjian, *The People's Congress System of China (Zhongguo Renmin Daibiao Dahui Zhidu)* (4th ed., Law Press, 2003) 259.
18 *Cf* Jiang Jinsong, *The National People's Congress of China* (Foreign Languages Press, 2002) 176.
19 The foundation of it derives from Art. 3(3) of the Constitution which reads:

> All administrative, supervisory, adjudicatory and procuratorial organs of the state shall be created by the people's congresses and shall be responsible to them and subject to their oversight.

20 *Cf* Can Dingjian, *supra note* 17, at 373–383.
21 Ibid., at 373.
22 The Constitution, art 5(3).
23 Law on Legislation, arts. 2, 103.
24 Qin Aolei & Wang Kai, "Constitutional Review in China" (Zhongguo Weixian Shencha), Hu Jingguang (ed.) *A Comparative Study of Constitutional Review (Weixian Shencha Bijiao Yanjiu)* (Renmin University of China Press, 2006) 326.
25 *Ibid.*, at 328.
26 *Ibid.*
27 The Constitution, art. 5(2).
28 The Constitution, art. 67.
29 Law on Legislation, art. 97.
30 Law on Legislation, art. 75(2) reads:

> An autonomous regulation or special regulation may vary the provisions of a law or administrative regulation, provided that any such variance shall not violate the basic principles thereof, and no variance is allowed in respect of any provision of the Constitution or the Law on Regional National Autonomy and provisions of any other law or administrative regulations which are dedicated to matters concerning national autonomous areas.

31 Qin Aolei & Wang Kai, *supra note* 24, at 329.
32 The Constitution, art. 89 defines that:
The State Council exercises the following functions and powers:

> 1. to adopt administrative measures, enact administrative rules and regulations, and issue decisions and orders in accordance with the Constitution and the statutes;
> ...
> 13. to alter or annul inappropriate orders, directives, and regulations issued by the ministries or commissions;
> 14. to alter or annul inappropriate decisions and orders issued by local organs of state administration at different levels; ...

33 The Constitution, "Preamble", para. 7.
34 The Constitution, art. 1; it is a newly added sentence under the 2018 Constitutional Amendment.
35 The Constitution, art. 5(3); Law on Legislation, arts. 87–89.
36 Law on Legislation, art. 91.
37 The Constitution, art. 116.
38 Law on Legislation, art. 75(2).

39 Law on Legislation, art. 72(2).
40 The Constitution, art. 100(2), states:

> The people's congresses of cities divided into districts and their standing committees may, provided there is no conflict with the Constitution, laws or administrative regulations, or with the local regulations of their province or autonomous region, formulate local regulations in accordance with the provisions of law, which shall go into force after submission to the standing committee of the people's congress of their province or autonomous region and the receipt of approval.

41 *Cf* Cai Dingjian, *supra note* 17, at 309–310.
42 *Ibid.*, at 301.
43 *Cf* The Constitution, art. 2, which reads:

> All power in the People's Republic of China belongs to the people.
> The National People's Congress and the local people's congresses at various levels are the organs through which the people exercise state power.
> The people administer State affairs and manage economic and cultural undertakings and social affairs through various channels and in various ways in accordance with the provisions of law.

44 *Cf* The Constitution, art. 3, which reads:

> The State organs of the People's Republic of China apply the principle of democratic centralism.
> The National People's Congress and the local people's congresses at various levels are constituted through democratic elections. They are responsible to the people and subject to their supervision.
> All administrative, supervisory, judicial and procuratorial organs of the State are created by the people's congresses to which they are responsible and by which they are supervised.

45 The Constitution, "Preamble", para. 13.
46 Law on Legislation, art. 87.
47 Wei Changhao, "Reining in Rogue Legislation: An Overview of China's Invigoration of the 'Recording and Review' Process", (2021) *Made in China Journal*, an open access quarterly on Chinese labour, civil society, and rights, posted on 19 September 2021; at https://madeinchinajournal.com/2021/09/19/reining-in-rogue-legislation/
48 An English version of the Report delivered by Xi Jinping, the Secretary General of the CPC, at the 19th National Congress of the CPC, has been translated by Xinhua News Agency and published at *China Daily* website: https://www.chinadaily.com.cn/china/19thcpcnationalcongress/2017-11/04/content_34115212.htm.
49 Division of Filing and Review of Regulations of the Legislative Affairs Commission under the NPCSC, *Introduction to "The Working Measures for Filing and Review of Regulations and Judicial Interpretations" (Fagui Sifa Jieshi Bei'an Shencha Banfa Daodu)* (China Democracy and Legal System Press, 2020) "Editors' Note" 1.
50 Wang Kai, "Chinese Practice of Review of Constitutionality" (Hexianxing Shencha de Zhongguo Shijian), (2020) *Leadership Science Tribune (Lingdao Kexue Luntan)* 11, 10.
51 The Constitution, art. 100 (1).
52 The Constitution, art. 116.
53 The Constitution, art. 100 (2).
54 The Organic Law of Local People's Congresses and Local People's Governments at Various Levels, art 10.
55 Law on Legislation, art. 98.
56 *Supra note* 47.
57 The Working Measures, art. 9.

58 The Working Measures, art. 10.
59 The Working Measures, art. 13.
60 The Working Measures, art. 16.
61 The Working Measures, art. 18.
62 The Working Measures, arts. 21–22.
63 The Working Measures, art. 23.
64 The Working Measures, art. 38.
65 The Working Measures, art. 41.
66 The Working Measures, art. 44.
67 The Working Measures, art. 36.
68 A newly created specialized commission under the NPC by the 2018 Constitutional Amendment; it is based on the former Law Commission.
69 The Working Measures, art. 20.
70 The Working Measures, art. 36.
71 The Working Measures, art. 52.
72 Zheng Lei, *Study of the Working Reports on Filing and Review (Bei'an Shencha Gongzuo Baogao Yanjiu)* (China Democracy and Law Press, 2021). Two chapters contained in the book written in English focus on the 2018 and 2019 reports, respectively.
73 The Five Reports on the work of filing and record prepared and submitted by the Legislative Affairs Commission to the NPCSC can be retrieved from the official website of the NPC: www.npc.gov.cn. They are at: http://www.npc.gov.cn/zgrdw/npc/xinwen/2017-12/27/content_2035723.htm; http://www.npc.gov.cn/npc/c12491/201812/afbfcb16af1d455b86dfb0cb4175ba2a.shtml; http://www.npc.gov.cn/npc/c30834/201912/24cac1938ec44552b285f0708f78c944.shtml; http://www.npc.gov.cn/npc/c30834/202101/239178b5d03944c7b453ddc6bdd7c087.shtml; and http://www.npc.gov.cn/npc/c30834/202112/2606f90a45b1406e9e57ff45b42ceb1c.shtml.
74 The review of Hong Kong ordinances is based on Art. 17(2)(3) of the Basic Law of the Hong Kong Special Administrative Region, which reads:

> Laws enacted by the legislature of the Hong Kong Special Administrative Region must be reported to the Standing Committee of the National People's Congress for the record. The reporting for record shall not affect the entry into force of such laws.
>
> If the Standing Committee of the National People's Congress, after consulting the Committee for the Basic Law of the Hong Kong Special Administrative Region under it, considers that any law enacted by the legislature of the Region is not in conformity with the provisions of this Law regarding affairs within the responsibility of the Central Authorities or regarding the relationship between the Central Authorities and the Region, the Standing Committee may return the law in question but shall not amend it. Any law returned by the Standing Committee of the National People's Congress shall immediately be invalidated. This invalidation shall not have retroactive effect, unless otherwise provided for in the laws of the Region.

75 The review of Macau ordinances is based on Art. 17(2)(3) of the Basic Law of the Macau Special Administrative Region which is similar to the above-cited Basic Law of Hong Kong.
76 Chen Yunsheng, *Judicialisation of Constitutional Supervision (Xianfa Jiandu Sifahua)* (Peking University Press, 2004) 452.
77 Hu Jingguang & Han Dayuan, *Chinese Constitution (Zhongguo Xianfa)* (Law Press, 2004) 162.
78 *Cf* Qin Aolei & Wang Kai, *supra note* 24, at 368–370.
79 *Cf* Wang Lei, "China's Institution for Constitutional Interpretation" (Zhongguo de Xianfa Jieshi Jigou), Xu Chongde (ed.), *Constitution and Democratic Politics (Xianfa yu Minzhu Zhengzhi)* (China's Procuratorate Press, 1994).
80 *Cf* Huang Songyou, "Constitutional Judicialization and its Significance – A Comment on Today's 'Response' by the SPC" (Xifa Sifahua Jiqi Yiyi – Cong Zuigao Renmin fayuan Jintian de Yige Pifu Tanqi), *People's Courts' Daily (Renmin Fayuan Bao)*, 13 Aug 2001.
81 *Cf* Huang Xuexian, "Discussion on the Way to Improve Constitutional Supervision Mechanism in China" (Wanshan Woguo Xianfa Jiandu Jizhi de Tantao), (2002) *Research on Constitution (Xianfa Yanjiu)* 342–355.

Also *cf* Chen Yunsheng, *Judicialisation of Constitutional Supervision (Xianfa Jiandu Sifahua)* (Peking University Press, 2004), at 501.

82 Qin Aolei & Wang Kai, *supra note* 24, at 370.

83 *Supra note* 48.

84 Thomas E. Kellogg, "The Death of Constitutional Litigation in China?", (2009) *China Brief* 7, at 6.

85 *Ibid.*, at 6–7.

86 *Ibid.*

For a better understanding of the case of Qi Yuling, also *cf.*: Zhu Guobin, "Constitutional Review in China: An Unaccomplished Project or a Mirage?", (2010) 43, No. 3 *Suffolk University Law Review*, pp. 625–653; Shen Kui, "Is it the Beginning of the Era of the Rule of the Constitution? Reinterpreting China's 'First Constitutional Case'", (2003) 12, No. 1 *Pacific Rim Law & Policy Journal*, pp. 199–232; and Tong Zhiwei, "A Comment on the Rise and Fall of the Supreme People's Court's Reply to Qi Yuling's Case," (2010) 43, No. 2 *Suffolk University Law Review*, pp. 671–680.

87 *Cf.* Zhu Guobin, "Weak Courts, Weak Rights – Assessing the Realization of Constitutional Rights in the PRC Courts", (2013) 43, Part 2 *HKLJ* at 713–743.

88 The Constitution, art. 5(1), which is an Amendment to the Constitution, adopted in 1999.

89 Thomas E. Kellogg & Keith Hand, "NPCSC: The Vanguard of China's Constitution?", (2008) 2 *China Brief* 4.

9

ONE COUNCIL TWO CONSTITUTIONAL COURTS

A Holistic View of the Council of Grand Justices (1948–2021)

Zhaoxin Jiang

In the current comparative constitutional law literature, significant deficit exists. As Ran Hirschl noted a couple of years ago, "contemporary discussions about comparative reference, and comparative constitutional law more generally, often proceed *as if there is no past, only present and future.*"[1] His disappointed observation has been echoed by Mark Tushnet's recent emphasis on the "importance of temporality": "there is much more to be said about judicial time."[2] This chapter is to reduce a deficit about the oldest post-WWII constitutional court, the Council of Grand Justices, and to revisit the Second Wave of Global Development of Judicial Powers[3] by fleshing out the Greater China's greater constitutional legacies. Between 1948 and 2021, the Council of Grand Justices made a total of 813 interpretations[4] starting in the city of Nanjing, then Taipei. A constitutional court has been formalized and inaugurated in 2022, replacing the Council, to signal further judicialization of the constitutional review in Taiwan. The closure of Council of Grand Justices, however, may serve as a caveat that the chunk of legacies created by the Council may be at the risk of disappearing.

This chapter proposes a holistic view of Council of Grand Justices (1948–2021) as comprising two constitutional courts: China's Constitutional Court and Taiwan's Constitutional Court. As is registered in the *Max Planck Encyclopedia of Comparative Constitutional Law*: "*Taiwan's Constitutional Court,* also known as the Council of Grand Justices, stands as one of *the oldest constitutional* courts in the world. *Established in 1948 under the Republic of China Constitution*...."[5] To borrow Tom Ginsburg's words, "the Council of Grand Justices in the Republic of China (ROC), formally constituted since the establishment of the ROC government on mainland China in the late 1940s was the first historical instance of the entrenchment of modern constitutionalism in a Chinese context. Because of the monopoly of mainland-born Chinese, they controlled the government for its first four decades of existence. The need to preserve the rhetorical 'face' of the one China paradigm was a constraining condition on constitutional reform and judicial politics."[6] In short, the same one Council comprises two constitutional courts over time.

Since a huge bulk of English literature has been written on Taiwan's constitutional Court, Tom Ginsburg as one leading example, this chapter shifts the narrative focus on the older era of the Council of Grand Justices: China's Constitutional Court (1948–1971). During the 24 years, the Council had considered a thousand more petitions and

DOI: 10.4324/9781003128243-11

produced a hundred more interpretations that announced the triumph of constitutionalism in the name of China.[7] Among others, the fact that a constitutional court had become embedded in the Chinese context during Chiang Kai-shek's regime invites us to reassess the current theses regarding the correlation between the courts and the constitutional politics. But how to explain this achievement? In his assessment of Taiwan's democratization, Tom Ginsburg improvised a benchmark "Confucian Constitutionalism" to measure the role of "the Grand Justices of the Republic of China."[8] Ginsburg rightly referenced the Confucian Constitutionalism but ironically left undiscussed the Justices themselves. This chapter is written to give voice to the longest serving President of Judicial Yuan in Taiwan, Xie Guansheng, and the longest serving Grand Justice, former President of Judicial Yuan Weng Yuesheng. They made the best leadership not just for the Council of Grand Justices but also in the global league of "towering judges."[9] For a short biography of them, see the table below:

Presidents of Judicial Yuan	*Education background*	*Incumbency*
Wang Chonghui	Doctor of Civil Law, Yale Law School (1906)	President (1948–1958)
Xie Guansheng	Doctor in Law, Paris University (1924)	Vice President (1950–1958) President (1958–1971)
Weng Yuesheng	Doctor in Law, Heidelberg University (1966)	Grand Justice (1972–2007), President (2003–2007)

This chapter comprises six sections. The "'House of Lords': A Brief History of China's Constitutional Court" section provides a brief institutional history of China's constitutional court. Emphasis is added to the increasingly empowered China's constitutional court under the leadership of Xie Guansheng, whose timely growth prevented the stateless constitutionalism from degrading into the lawlessness for the society in Taiwan. In the voices of the former two Presidents of Judicial Yuan, the following three sections summarize the greater constitutional legacies produced by China's constitutional court. The "The Standards for Constitutional Review" section highlights the standards of constitutional review, the fresh and proud products created by the active China's constitutional court in the mid-20th century. The "A Triumphant Constitutional Court in a Failed State" section provides a summary of the court-related writings from Xie Guansheng to reflect on the legacies of China's constitutional courts in grappling with the stateless constitutionalism dilemma. The "The Longest Second Wave of Judicial Development" section argues that the Council of Grand Justices in the five-power constitutional system survived reinvigorated as a fledging consequential court. The political transition of the 1970s in Taiwan started at least with a strong constitutional court, constantly guarded and empowered from the very beginning, smoothly leading up to the post-1989 new wave of court-centered constitutionalism. The "Framing Taiwan's Constitutional Court (1972–2021)" section provides a summary of the evolution of Taiwan's constitutional court by focusing on the leader of the movement, Weng Yuesheng, the longest serving Taiwanese Grand Justice and most revered former President of Judicial Yuan in Taiwan. Last section concludes with a major argument that during the era of expanding global cold war, the fact that the Council of Grand Justices became a stronger guardian of the constitution resulted in greater constitutional legacies for the Greater China's future constitutional development. The two decades' development of China's constitutional court has produced a unique pattern of constitutional interpretation and judicial review.

"House of Lords": A Brief History of China's Constitutional Court

On a later occasion in 1970 when Xie Guansheng, the longest serving President of Judicial Yuan (1958–1971) in Taiwan, reflected on the meaning of the constitutional interpretations, he came to a conclusion that Sun Yat-sen's constitutional government was eventually enforced regardless of the worsening political situations in Taiwan. In his view, two salient achievements had been accomplished since 1948 the Council of Grand Justices was founded. First, the continuity of Chinese legal tradition and the dignity of the Republic of China constitution were safeguarded successfully. Second, the five-power constitutionalism had been embedded into the Chinese society in Taiwan. Xie believed "the fundamental driving force for today's comprehensive success in Taiwan has been the Constitution of Republic of China. In the future after we have retaken the Mainland and reconstruct the nation, all will be dependent on the Constitution of the Republic of China."[10]

Above all, the Judicial Yuan had established itself as the leading voice of Sun Yat-senian constitutionalism after the decades of active constitutional interpretations. To echo with the prediction of Roscoe Pound in 1947: "the Judicial Yuan is at the head of the judicial system much as is the house of Lords in the Great Britain. I assume it will be composed both of lawyers and of statesmen. Thus it will be a highly appropriate body for the function of interpreting the constitution."[11] Pound had made an interesting point. That is, Judicial Yuan is closer to "the house of Lords in the Great Britain," rather than an American style of Supreme Court. As the apex court in the five-power constitutional system, the Judicial Yuan under the leadership of Wang Chonghui and Xie Guansheng had become a strong guardian of the Council of Grand Justices and its power to interpret the constitution. The Judicial Yuan, therefore, is worthy of the title "House of Lords." The success story of Judicial Yuan was pretty much linked to the persona on the top of the court.

After the WWII when Wang Chonghui came back to lead the Judicial Yuan in 1948, he did not wait to use the constitutional interpretation power to create an active constitutional court in the mid-20th century. Lacking political capital notwithstanding, Xie Guansheng took over the judicial leadership to continue the active cause of the constitutional court in Taipei. Above all, Xie at that time had become the unparalleled authority in the judicial system with three decades of working experience at the headquarter of the system, being the most trustworthy and most dependable man to the two former Presidents of Judicial Yuan, Ju Zheng(1932–1948) and Wang Chonghui (1948–1958). What is most important, Xie knew the visions his two predecessors had in common for the Judicial Yuan to carry on.

After Wang Chonghui (1958) had passed away, Xie Guansheng was appointed to the presidency of Judicial Yuan. Xie found himself in a much better position. Above all, through the past two decades, Xie had become the most powerful person in the Judicial System. Before Chiang Kai-shek government was evicted from the UN in late 1971, Xie Guansheng was already the voice of Chinese five-power constitutionalism and the leading authority of the judicial improvement.

In 1971, two Grand Justices had passed away, with one losing consciousness during an intensive long Council review panel meeting.[12] This anecdote was just one example of the Justices' full devotion and hard work in interpreting the constitution. At the pressure of the Taiwanese representatives, Chiang Kai-shek asked Xie to work out the list of candidates. On July 15, 1971, the Control Yuan confirmed the two.[13] That became the last time for the two to work together to nominate the Grand Justices. The next day, the American President Nixon announced that he would visit the mainland China in May 1972. Xie wrote to himself: "the news came out, shocked everyone."[14]

For the President of Judicial Yuan, it would be surprising otherwise. In September 1971, the UN decided to consider the China representation question in its agenda. A month later, the "Republic of China," carefully guarded by the constitutional court, disappeared from the UN. Gone with it, the legitimacy of the judicial leadership, the constitutional interpretations, the Council of the Grand Justices, and the power and structure of the former China's national apex court. No one would feel more disappointed than the President of Judicial Yuan Xie Guansheng. In December 1971, Xie passed away, away with the leading spirit of China's Constitutional Court.

The Standards for Constitutional Review

Over two decades since founded, the Council of the Grand Justices had built up enough experiences in making constitutional interpretations. The largest number of turnouts helped situate the Council of Grand Justices into a unique position in the post-WWII global development of court. For a quick view, please see the following Chart No. 1 on the annual number of the Council of Grand Justices' interpretations:

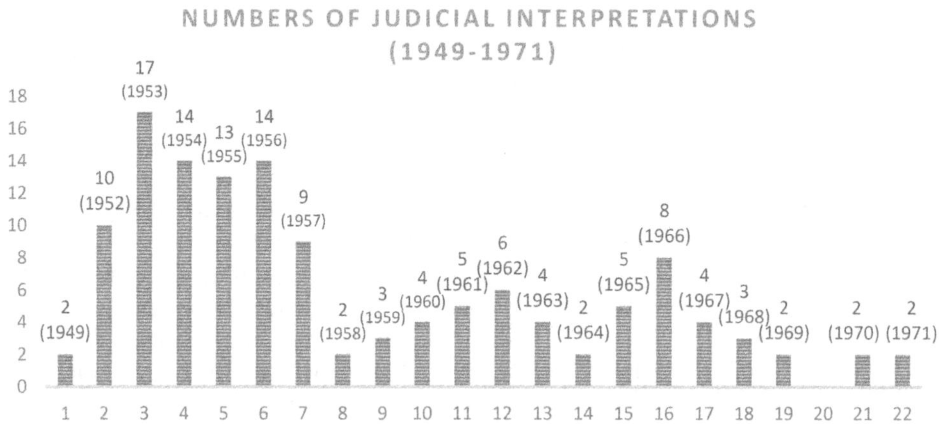

Chart No. 1 A Summary Number of the Judicial Interpretations (1949–1971)

As the President of Judicial Yuan, Xie Guansheng reflected in his report on the Judicial System for the past two decades, "since the government moved to Taiwan, there unavoidably arose a series of difficulties for the constitutional enforcement. Thanks to the nation-wide uniform support of the constitution, the whole constitution could be smoothly functioning over more than a decade. As a novel institution, the constitutional interpretations produced by the Council of the Grand Justices had played a substantive role in making the constitution functioning."[15] Up to the year of 1970, when Xie Guansheng summarized a new tradition created by the former China's apex court, he was generalizing a new legacy for the later global development of court—the unparalleled achievement after 20 years' guarding the China-centered liberal constitutionalism during the increasingly intensified cold war era. Judging it in any senses, the legacy should be valuable and cherished by all that are interested in the improvement of court-centered constitutionalism.

For Xie Guansheng, one legacy for China then and in the distant future, the largest number itself aside, was clearly the established standards of constitutional review, with which the Sun Yat-senian five-power constitutionalism had been guarded with extreme care and due diligence into the Chinese social and political context. Seeing through the President of Judicial Yuan's perspective, China's constitutional court was unrefutably the only qualified one that should take the pride and privilege in defining the standards of constitutional review based on its most consistent active practices for the past two decades. After all, when the experiences and the numbers both built up, it was a good time for standards of interpretation to be carved out. In the late 1960s, the President of Judicial Yuan Xie did not shy away from doing this honorable job. According to Xie, standards of interpretation established so far could be broken down into the following four[16]:

1. Standard one—The Fundamental Constitutional Theories and the Spirits of Constitution: For one example (Interpretation No. 3), as Xie explained, it was not clear in the constitution if the Control Yuan may propose statutory bills to the Legislative Yuan, but the Council of Grand Justices invoked the preamble of the constitution—"this constitution is created based upon the teachings bequeathed by Dr. Sun Yat-sen" and abided by the separate but equal principle of the five powers. The Council concluded that "it is consistent with the spirit of the Constitution that the Control Yuan may introduce statutory bills to the Legislative Yuan on matters within its authority." For another example, according to the separation of power principle, the Council declared "any member of the Legislative or Control Yuan should not concurrently be the representative of the National Assembly" (Interpretation No. 15), and the "National Assembly representative should not serve concurrently as in the provincial council" according to "the purpose of the Constitution which established different levels of local public opinion authority and endowed each level with different powers."
2. Standard two—The Legislative Intentions: According to the constitution, for example, the Control Yuan had the power to impeach public servants who had malpracticed or committed malfeasances. However, it was not clear if the representatives of public opinions were included in the definition of public servants. The Council of Grand Justices decided to exclude the representatives of public opinions from the reach of the Control Yuan's power after carefully searching for the legislative intentions during the legislation process (Interpretation Nos. 14, 33). Questions regarding the Control Yuan's inherent power to propose statutory bills (Interpretation No. 3) and the prohibition for the member of Control Yuan to act concurrently as the representative of the National Assembly(Interpretation No. 15) were all resolved in accordance with the legislative intentions originally guiding the process of constitution-making.
3. Standard three—General Constitutional Doctrines and Institutions: Before the implementation of the constitution, for example, the personnel of the political party had been lawfully regarded as public servants of the Republic of China. In the other constitutionalism state in general, on the contrast, political parties were civil associations whose members should not be deemed as public servants. Considering what had been interpreted was contextualized in a party state and one privileged

Kuomintang party, the Council of Grand Justices made very bold interpretations (Interpretation Nos. 5, 7) in line with the general constitutional doctrines such as this one observed in the western countries.

4. Standard four—The Practical Need of the State: For example, the Constitution provided members of the Legislative Yuan should serve a term of three years and members of the Control Yuan a term of six years. "Terms shall start from the date when those Members take office and expire at the end of the term as provided in the Constitution. However, our state has been undergoing a severe calamity, which makes re-election of the second term of both Yuans de facto impossible. It would contradict the purpose of the Five-Yuan system as established by the Constitution, if both the Legislative and Control Yuans ceased to exercise their respective powers." Therefore, according to Xie, the Council of Grand Justices made decision in response to the practical need of the state that "before the second-term Members are elected, convene and are convoked in accordance with the laws, all of the first-term Members of both the Legislative and Control Yuans shall continue to exercise their respective powers."[17] (Interpretation No. 31) For another example, the election of Vice/President and making constitutional amendments should abide by the law and take a standard overall number (3045 in this case) of the National Assembly for the votes to be calculated. In Taiwan, however, it was infeasible to hold the reelection of the National Assembly Delegates and extremely difficult to fill most vacancies with substitutes. Therefore, the Council of Grand Justices decided that the "total number of National Assembly Delegates" should be calculated based on the number of those delegates who were elected in accordance with the laws and were still able to convene at the location of the Central Government. (Interpretation No. 60) Because of the two interpretations, the five-power government system was sustained. The barricade for the National Assembly to fulfill its duty was so removed.

Clearly aware of the legacies the Council of the Grand Justices had created theretofore, the President of Judicial Yuan Xie Guansheng took pride to assert the role of China's constitutional court as the leader of judicial review at that time:

> Noting that the number of constitutional interpretation cases in Germany and Italy's constitutional courts was between few and nothing, which was far less than ours, the expectation of a rigid constitution to be smoothly enforced would substantially be hinged onto the job of interpretation. It was especially so during the special time. U.S. was the first to create the judicial review and vest the power in the courts to review the constitutionality of the legislative bills and the executive decisions and annul any declared unconstitutional. Some have called American government a 'Government by Judiciary', which might be overexaggerated; it however manifested the vital importance of the constitutional interpretations.[18]

Unquestionably, Xie Guansheng and his Grand Justices had done a wonderful job.

A Triumphant Constitutional Court in a Failed State

During the 1950s and 1960s, Xie became the undisputable authority of the five-power constitutional law and the judicial system. The combination of his book *A Brief Survey of the Chinese Constitution*[19] and the two landmark articles of "The Judicial Development for the Past Two Decades (1967)"[20] and "The Council of Grand Justices for Two Decades (1970)"[21] amounted to a declaration of the consummation of a peaceful constitutional revolution in the Chinese context. The success of Council of Grand Justices has become the symbol of this revolution, which had proved the Sun Yat-senian five-power constitutionalism,[22] the genius of the Chinese legal exceptionalism, could work out well and were working well in a complicated national and international political context.

As the key witness and crucial player in the process for two decades, Xie drew a conclusion that "two decades have passed away since the constitutionalism was phased into our country in 1948. Irrespective of the worsening situation, the government has been unrelentingly pursuing for the realization of constitutionalism. Our sincerity and determination in promotion of democracy and rule of law have been seen by all .... For us to protect the sovereignty, the human rights, the social stability and to build the base to retake and restore our country, there is nothing else to be dependent on but the Republic of China's legal tradition, the legal system and the ideas generated thereupon. The struggle against the communists should never be military war alone but also the political, economic and cultural wars. Legal tradition and legal system are equivalent to the guiding flag in the war. .... Therefore, *our war against the communists is a war between law and lawlessness.* We have to win this war."[23]

In May 1950, Chiang Kai-shek nominated Xie to be the Vice President of the Judicial Yuan. Xie took the office on June 1. Since at that time Wang Chonghui was about to visit Japan, Chiang started to directly consult Xie regarding the issues involving the Judicial Yuan and the constitutional issues.[24] In between 1951 and 1952, Xie became one member for both the constitutional sub-committee and judicial sub-committee of the Kuomintang Central Committee. Obviously, Xie's personal power and influence grew ever since. His interactions between Chiang Kai-shek turned to be more frequently. The Second Council of Grand Justices of 1952, for example, was anchored in by Xie's recommendation to Chiang Kai-shek personally.[25] The second (1958) and third (1967) Council of Grand Justices were similarly engineered by Xie.[26]

After two decades of leadership in the judicial system up to 1970, Xie had personally overseen and witnessed the judicial development in general and the development of the constitutional court in particular. When looking into the prospect by reflecting retrospectively, Xie had the legitimate reasons to be confident that "the new Chinese Constitution will prove stable enough to remain the supreme fundamental law of the Chinese people for endless generations to come."[27] Through the 1950s and 1960s, China's constitutional court under the leadership of Wang Chonghui and himself had been the most active constitutional court. Xie continued the tradition Wang created during the brief five years for an active constitutional court. It was especially so in light of the number of the constitutional interpretations, which was far ahead of its counterparts in Europe and beyond. According to Xie,

> From the appointment of the second Council of Grand Justices in September 1958 up to late June 1970, 480 comprehensive review conferences had been held and 286 plenary conferences .... The second Council (9/1958-8/1967) made 43 interpretations. As of the late June 1970, the third Council (started from September 1967) made 6 interpretations. To add them to all the previous interpretations, there are a total of 128 interpretations. Within it there are 34 constitutional interpretations and 94 unified interpretations. The ratio of constitutional cases is ¼ of the total number. Several years ago, two Grand Justices

> were sent to attend a conference in Europe who visited on their way the constitutional courts in Germany and Italy. *Their constitutional interpretation cases were extremely few, even nothing throughout a year.* The reasons for our exceptionally large number largely resulted from the special time period we have been through. The Grand Justices' constitutional interpretations, likely not satisfactory for all, have been done to the best of their wisdom and with their loyalty to the country.[28]

As we know, because of the increasingly worsened political situation in 1949, half of the newly appointed Grand Justices rejected the offer. By the time the Council convened again in 1952 in Taiwan, it comprised only nine grand justices. That most active era was created by the nine only. It seemed a highly efficient constitutional court. This has been achieved even though the interpretational rule of the Council had been overhauled and more strings attached to the interpretation making since 1957. However, there were problems. The newly enforced Law Governing the Council of Grand Justices (July 1957) required a minimum of 13 or 3/4 of the total number of Grand Justices to make the constitutional interpretation, an absolute majority (3/4) of the panel to agree on the interpretation (Article 13) When the second Council of Grand Justices was inaugurated in September 1958, 15 Grand Justices were appointed. The third Council of 1967 also had a total number of 15 Grand Justices. The reason for a Council of 15 Grand Justices rather than a full Council of 17 owed to the qualifications of the Grand Justices. According to the organic law of Judicial Yuan, the qualifications were only in favor of five categories of legal professionals, including (1) Supreme Court judges, (2) legislators, (3) law professors, (4) Judges of the International Court of Justices, or authors of authoritative books in public and comparative law, and (5) renowned scholars with affluent political experiences. As Xie explained, "the number of justices from each category should not exceed five. The qualified candidates in the category 1, 3, and 5 are easy to pick in Taiwan. Because of the limit of each category to five, therefore 15 rather than 17 Grand Justices were appointed to the second and third Council."[29]

Seemingly, the quorum of 15, plus the new addition to the publication of holding with the reasoning and dissenting opinions (Article 14), had fundamentally undermined the working efficiency of the Council of Grand Justices. In July 1968, for example, Xie chaired the Grand Justice's 346th Conference to continue the discussion of expiration of the valid time period issue in the criminal law. As Xie recorded in diary, "the review of this case started from the second Council of Grand Justices has taken up to a year by now. It went through three rounds of intense debates after it was brought for the Conference discussion. Today, eight out of the 14 present grand justices voted to pass the interpretation. Three grand justices wrote dissenting opinions adding up to thousands of words."[30] As a later President of Judicial Yuan complained,

> Since the Law Governing the Council of Grand Justices was enforced in July 1958, the scope and limits have been strictly restrained. As a result, the annual number of interpretations was a disappointing three. In sharp contrast, however, the annual number of the petitions has grown up to 60. There is a jarring gap for the interpretations to be considered and hammered out. This number is hardly compared to the annual number of 13 during the valid period of the Conference Rules of the Grand Justices (1948-1958). Apparently, it falls far short of the practical demand. In order to improve the interpretation's efficiency,

appropriate amendment should be applied to modify the limitations on the scope and procedure of the interpretation-making.[31]

Needless to say, the change of rule did play a role as argued by not a few scholars,[32] but definitely not the crucial one.

As Xie noted, for all the 34 constitutional interpretations, "there were recorded only two dissents (Interpretation nos. 86 and 120), with only one justice dissented in each case."[33] The constitutional interpretations had in most cases been made by a unanimous court in phase three (1958–1971). The increased time and labor were instead consumed by the Council's unified interpretation. To quote Xie here again, "the Council made 94 interpretations of other law and ordinances, with recorded dissents in 29 cases."[34] Apparently, the Council disunited on 1/3 of total occasions where unified interpretations were produced by a simple majority and where dissents generally could not generate a big problem at all. Judging on the numbers, therefore, the change of the law governing the Council should not have been the scapegoat for the Council's eclipsed efficiency in making the constitutional interpretations. The fundamental reason behind the change very likely was, in my view, linked to the emerging dilemma in the 1960s for a stateless constitutional court to guard a state-centered five-power constitutionalism.

The Longest Second Wave of Judicial Development

As the President of Judicial Yuan Xie Guansheng emphasized, the constitutional development during the 1960s was most difficult to achieve. After 1958, the rules changed more restrictive for the Council of Grand Justices to make the constitutional interpretations. The changed rule for constitutional interpretations constituted material impediments to the development of the constitutional court. However, as evidenced in the number of interpretations and in Xie's personal documents, it did not stop the court from making continued unanimous constitutional interpretations. Above all, the cold war grew intensified globally during the decade. Chiang's five-power constitutional government seemed to have smoothly functioned in Taiwan especially compared with the mainland central government, which first stuck with the great famine in the wake of the failed Great Leap Forward movement (1958–1962)[35] and then headed into the even more catastrophic cultural revolution stretching from the 1960s to most of the 1970s. For Chiang Kai-shek, a well-functioning constitutional court in place was a political success in the camp of liberal democracies. For the judicial leaders, it was indeed a triumph for the constitutional court overshadowing the slowing constitutional development at large. In general, there was a wide array of factors interplaying to impress their impact on China's constitutional court through the most crucial decade.

All in all, the political situation changed in the negative sense for the Council of the Grand Justices since late 1950s. First and foremost, the stateless constitutionalism was the typical result out of evolution of the political changes during the cold war era. Chiang Kai-shek's government's UN representation crisis was an overwhelming political disruption for the cold war constitutionalism spearheaded by the constitutional court. It was so ironical when the constitutional court had produced the biggest number of constitutional interpretations for the sake of China-centered constitutionalism; the court however lost the orbiting center it had been hinged on. Judging it in any sense, "stateless constitutionalism" could become a caveat of great meaning. In the case of China's constitutional court, it could manifest the most sensitive frailty of the constitutional court, whose dazzling triumph was contingent on its inherent demand for a triumphant state or a victorious ally. Without the triumph of the state or the triumphant ally, the constitutional court could hardly survive.

Second, there was another far-reaching political crisis for the constitutional court, which was Chiang Kai-shek's presidential crisis. When the political situation prompted unconventional responses from the court, the Council of Grand Justices under the leadership of Xie Guansheng opted for the non-constitutional amendment principle to tweak the provisional clause, rather than the constitution per se, to sit Chiang Kai-shek in the presidency for more terms (Interpretation No. 85). The court among the criticisms had thus saved both the constitution and Chiang's presidency. For this reason, China's constitutional court prevented a stateless constitutionalism from degrading into deeper constitutional crises. This in turn generated the political momentum in guarding the constitution and the constitutional court.

Third, there were the untoward Grand Justiceship crisis and the enduring paradigmatic crisis for the Judicial Yuan itself. For a good example, the shifted anger from the Legislative Yuan against other power-grabbing political branches like the Control Yuan onto the unprepared constitution-guarding Grand Justices could lead to the dead end of the constitutional court. Without the political savvy and the series of political bargaining from the President of Judicial Yuan, the survived constitutional court would look much different. It was not until the reputation of Judicial Yuan as the active guardian of constitution and constitutional court was established in Taiwan that the Council of Grand Justices could make the constitutional interpretation to empower and enhance itself (Interpretation No. 86), thus making the survival of the constitutional court more successful.

When Chiang Kai-shek's representation of China ended in UN, the era of Wang and Xie's judicial leadership also ended. Xie Guansheng passed away[36] in about two months after Chiang's government's eviction from the UN. As is manifested in Chiang's diary, "my son came to tell me that the President of Judicial Yuan Xie Guansheng fell fatally ill. Sigh! Another good man is passing away!"[37] From that year on, the Constitutional Court not just lost "China," but also the best of Chinese judicial leadership. After 1971, it changed in dramatic senses for the Council of Grand Justice. From 1972 up to today, the judicial leadership totally changed either because they did not have any experience with mainland Judicial System at all (such as the Presidents of Judicial Yuan Tian Jiongjin 12/1971–3/1977, Huang Shaogu 7/1979–4/1987), or they were Taiwanese having no mainland experiences at all (like the Presidents of Judicial Yuan Dai Yanhui 4/1977–6/1979, Lin Yanggang 5/1987–8/1994 and all others in later generations). In general, the ensuing era is a stateless era that prompted the rise of guarding the right movement in Taiwan, which was but called "liberal" democratic constitutionalism exactly in the same trope utilized during the era of state-centered liberal constitutionalism created by the Judicial Yuan from the mainland to the island. Viewed in the historical perspective, the year of 1971 was a landmark for the development of China's constitutional court—it announced the end of state-centered liberal constitutionalism for China on a whole and the start of right-centered liberal constitutionalism for the Taiwan province alone. In other words, the era of "the Taiwanese constitutional court"[38] did not start to phase in only until after 1971.

In a nutshell, China's constitutional court was vigorously growing when it lost China in the legal senses in late 1971. There was the loss for Chiang's government, but the gain for the constitutional court at Taipei. In retrospect, the Judicial Yuan in the five-power constitutional system survived reinvigorated as a fledging consequential court.

The political transition of 1970s in Taiwan started at least with a strong constitutional court, excellently guarded, and constantly empowered from the very beginning up to the post-1989 new wave of court-centered constitutionalism. With the later successful transition in Taiwan, China's constitutional court has crystalized a greater constitutional legacy for a greater China.

Framing Taiwan's Constitutional Court (1972–2021)

The longest serving Taiwanese Grand Justice (1972–1999, 2003–2007) and the former President of Judicial Yuan (1999–2007), Weng Yuesheng,[39] worked for 35 years in the Judicial Yuan and saw 500 interpretations (Interpretation Nos. 134–633) produced by the Council. Through the years, Weng "helped to instigate the constitutional change through interpretation … undoubtedly played a leading and important role"[40] for the continued development of constitutional court in Taiwan.

In January 1972, Professor Weng Yuesheng published an article on "Guardian of the Constitution"[41] as "the first one to advocate a shift in Taiwan from a Council of Justices to a Constitutional Court."[42] The rationale Weng provided for the Judicialization of the Council of Grand Justices was clear and simple: the constitution does not prevent the Grand Justices from interpreting the constitution by way of formulating an ad hoc court. Moreover, the image of court occupies a much higher moral ground in the hearts of the people than a council; and at the same time, it would be much easier for a court to realize the judicial functions and for the Grand Justices to be better safeguarded with the legitimacy of becoming the constitutional judges.[43]

A few months later, in July 1972, Weng, 40 years old, was appointed to be a Grand Justice in the Council, marking a new era of three Taiwanese pluralities in the Council and breaking the previous nationalism principle in constituting the council by a maximum of one grand justice per province. The complete dominance of Taiwanese Grand Justices was established in 1994, where there were 14 Taiwanese while only other 4 originated from the mainland.[44] The year 1972, therefore, not only signaled the fundamental policy shift in Taiwan after Chiang Kai-shek's government was driven out of the UN, but also the nuanced personal changes that pushed the Council transforming from a Chinese national constitutional court to a Taiwanese constitutional court.[45]

The moment came in 1992 when the political tide picked up speed amidst the global wave of democratization, the Republic of China constitution was amended to mandate the Council of Grand Justices to formulate ad hoc constitutional tribunal to try cases involving the dissolution of unconstitutionally organized political parties. The Legislative Yuan formalized the Grand Justices' Adjudication Act in 1993. Senior Justice Weng was delegated with the responsibility to chair the committee to design and institute the constitutional courtroom inside the Judicial Yuan's building. In December 1993, the Council heard its first case and made the Interpretation No. 334, setting the landmark case for the Council of Grand Justice to adjudicate a case before making interpretations.

During the province-wide Judicial Reform Conference in 1994, senior Justice Weng chaired the panel in discussion of the approach to replace the Council with a formal constitutional court, a clear step down the path toward judicialization of the constitutional interpretations. In 1999, the newly appointed President of Judicial Yuan Weng took the momentum to push forward the progress of transformation of the Council into the Constitutional court. By 1999, a firm consensus under Weng's leadership about the forthcoming institutionalization of constitutional court was reached among lawyers and laymen alike. Nonetheless, there was disagreement about the timetable and the format of change with the structure of the Judicial Yuan. In 2004, in the capacity of President of Judicial Yuan, Weng publicly called for the enactment of Constitutional Litigation Procedure Act, the complete and formal draft of which was submitted to the Legislative Yuan for consideration in 2006.[46] It was, however, not until 2019 the updated and expanded version of Constitutional Court Procedure Act (CCPA) was passed by the Legislative Yuan into law, which officially closed the Council of Grand Justices on January 4, 2022.

The new CCPA permanently "renames" the Council of Grand Justices to the "Constitutional Court" and endows it with expansive jurisdiction over (1) abstract review of the constitutionality of statutes and regulations, (2) constitutional complaint against the final court decisions, (3) disputes between constitutional organs, (4) impeachment against the President and/or the Vice President, (5) dissolution of unconstitutional political parties, (6) local self-governments, and (7) uniform interpretation of statutes and regulations. The CCPA also furnishes the constitutional court with the German model of chambers system (three justices per chamber), and the American model of separate court opinion writings, the admission of amici curiae, and the lowered simple majority threshold for decision-makings.[47]

With the conclusion of the Council of Grand Justices in Taiwan, it closed the dual history of the same "guardian of the constitution": 24 years as China's constitutional court (1948–1971) and 50 years as Taiwan's constitutional court.[48]

In his keynote speech during an academic conference in commemoration of Wang Chonghui, Weng fleshed out the legacies from his earliest predecessor: "the President Wang Chonghui's outstanding contribution to the developments of law, courts and politics in general has been awe-inspiring! .... At the very beginning, the institution of the Council of Grand Justices was more similar to the French Constitutional Council (Conseil constitutionnel) and later gradually coming closer to the German Constitutional Court. Today, the number of Grand Justices' published opinions has far outnumbered that from the Supreme Court of the United States."[49]

The above comment from the former President of the Judicial Yuan Weng about his predecessor Wang was but a fair judgment. Wang Chonghui constitutional court from mainland China to Taiwan is a trailblazer for the constitutional development in Taiwan through the means of constitutional interpretations. What made difference for the two was not just the difference between a French constitutional council and a German constitutional court on different stages. What matters more may be hinged on the roles the Grand Justices had played. As the longest serving Grand Justice, Weng explained in the public lecture in celebration of the 70th anniversary of the Council of Grand Justices in 2018 that "the Grand Justice shall be the guardian of the constitution. While unlike in Germany's case where the constitution is pretty much equivalent to the human rights per se, ... the role for the Grand Justices to play as the 'human right protector' should be irreplaceable."[50] Obviously, Weng's celebrating speech has well annotated the evolution of the constitutional court from mainland China to Taiwan: first as the guardian of the constitution, and then the right protector.[51] However, the driving force behind the evolution was nothing but the profoundly changing social and political contexts. After all, a constitutional court should be both the guardian of constitution and the right-protector at once. Nevertheless, only because a constitutional court at earlier stage had not played out the role of right protector does not invalidate it from being called a constitutional court.

Conclusion

In summary, this chapter argues for the two constitutional courts constituting the same one Council of Grand Justices, which add up to make much greater the Greater China's constitutional legacies. Above all, the globally hailed Taiwan's constitutional court's "peaceful constitutional revolution"[52] during the 1990s and early 2000s could not be either peaceful or a revolution at all without the legacies of China's constitutional court during the two critical decades around the mid-20th century. Second, China's constitutional court during the era of martial rule and the cold war not only actively did a lot but also spearheaded the longest second global wave of judicial review. This point becomes even clearer when compared with the cautious and uncertain beginning of the German constitution and Constitutional Court. To quote Bruce Ackerman, "when sixty-five West German politicians met in 1948 in a special parliamentary council to frame a constitution, they had no way of anticipating the economic boom of the 1950s and 1960s. All they saw around them was the ruin and misery of war. Looking past this wreckage, they confronted a history of failure."[53] During the same stretch of time, China's constitutional court has already become a confident constitution interpreter in the post-WWII and cold war context.

Third but not the least, it is about the Council of Grand Justices' interpretation approach and standards of constitutional review. With the petition and conference review approach, China's constitutional court over the two decades stood for an active guardian of the constitution and constitutionalism.[54] There had been no exception until 1993 in cases involving constitutional controversies of vital importance should the Council of Grand Justices directly formulate an ad hoc constitutional panel to hear the case.[55]

However, it starts to change in 2022 with the Constitutional Court Procedure Act enforced in Taiwan. The future is wide open into the promising unknown, yet the history of China's constitutional court, long in the penumbra, warrants the searching attention to the greater China's greater constitutional legacies.

Notes

1 See Ran Hirschl, 'Judicial Review and the Politics of Comparative Citations: Theory, Evidence and Methodological Challenges,' in Erin Delaney & Rosalind Dixon (eds.), *Comparative Judicial Review* (Edward Elgar Pub., 2018), 417–418.

2 See Mark Tushnet, 'After the Heroes Have Left the Scene,' in Christine Landfried (ed.), *Judicial Power: How Constitutional Courts Affect Political Transformations* (Cambridge University Press, 2019), 303–304.

3 The decades of constitutional development between 1945 and 1989 have been rounded up by Professor Tom Ginsburg as the second wave of judicial review, featuring the rise of post-fascism and post-colonialism constitutional courts. See Tom Ginsburg, *Judicial Review in New Democracies in Asian Cases* (Cambridge University Press, 2003), 96–99.

4 For a quick view of the interpretations, please see the "Leading Cases of the Taiwan Constitutional Court" in three volumes available at: https://cons.judicial.gov.tw/en/docdata.aspx?fid=5266.

5 See *Max Planck Encyclopedia of Comparative Constitutional Law* (online), available at: https://oxcon.ouplaw.com/view/10.1093/law-mpeccol/law-mpeccol-e538?rskey=l6eDme&result=1&prd=MPECCOL. Accessed 12 September 2021.

6 See Ginsburg, 'Confucian Constitutionalism? The Grand Justices of the Republic of China,' *supra note* 3, 106–108.

7 Within the first two terms (1948–1967), the Council had considered 1013 petitions and made 122 interpretations. Viewed in efficiency terms, the Council during the first two terms was most efficient constitutional court. See Ginsburg, *ibid.*, 124–125.

8 See Ginsburg's article 'Confucian Constitutionalism? The Grand Justices of the Republic of China,' (2003), available at: http://home.uchicago.edu/~tginsburg/pdf/articles/ConfucianConstitutionalism.pdf. For detailed discussion of "Confucian constitutionalism," see Bui Ngoc Bui, *Confucian Constitutionalism in East Asia* (Routledge, 2016).
9 See Rehan Abeyratne and Iddo Porat (eds.) *Towering Judges: A Comparative Study of Constitutional Judges* (Cambridge University Press, 2021).
10 See Xie Guansheng, 'The Council of Grand Justices for Two Decades,' (1970) 10(21) *Faling Yuekan* (*The Law Monthly*) 23.
11 See Roscoe Pound, 'The Chinese Constitution,' (April 1947) 22(2) *New York University Law Quarterly Review* 229; See also Roscoe Pound, 'On Five-Power Constitution,' (1946) 1(2) *Zheng Heng* (*Political Commentaries* 12.
12 See Xie Guansheng diaries on March 19, 1971.
13 See Xie Guansheng diaries on July 15, 1971.
14 See Xie Guansheng diaries on July 16, 1971.
15 See Xie Guansheng (1967), 'Xingxian Ershinian Lai De Sifa (The Judicial Development for the Past Two Decades),' in the Judicial Yuan ed., *Sifayuan Shishi Jiyao* (*A Brief History of Judicial Yuan: Volume 1)* (Self-published, 1982), 801.
16 See Xie Guansheng (1967), *ibid.*, 804–805.
17 English translations of the constitutional interpretations were all quoted from the official versions available at the Judicial Yuan's website.
18 See Xie Guansheng (1967), *supra note* 17, 805–806.
19 See Xie Guansheng, *A Brief Survey of the Chinese Constitution* (China Cultural Service, 1954/1970).
20 See Xie Guansheng (1967), *supra note* 17, 798–815.
21 See Xie Guansheng, *supra note* 9, 23–38.
22 In 1966, Xie discussed Sun Yat-sen's five-power constitutional theories with John Wu, the main author of the 1936 draft constitution over the dinner table. They agreed that 'Sun's five-power constitutional theories had not been invented by one time but brought out one after another over a stretch of four to five years, or even up to ten years, which seemed not finalized at all. Judging in this view, we can see our Founding Father's spirits in consistent hard-working and constant innovative thinking.' See Xie Guansheng diaries on May 25, 1966.
23 See Xie Guansheng (1967), *supra note* 17, 813–814.
24 See Xie Guansheng diaries on May 11, 23; June 1, 2, 1950.
25 See Xie Guansheng diaries on March 6, 17, 1952. Previously Chiang had consulted this with Wang Chonghui in January. See Chiang Kai-shek diaries on January 5, 1952.
26 See Xie Guansheng diaries on June 13, August 1, 1957; March 20, May 12, June 9, 14, September 13, 1958; August 12, December 21, 1967. For a quick history of the Council of Grand Jusitices making, please see Xie, *supra note* 9, 24.
27 See Xie, *supra note* 21, 52.
28 See Xie, *supra note* 9, 25.
29 See Xie Guansheng (1967), *supra note* 17, 803–804.
30 See Xie Guansheng diaries on July 10, 1968. Earlier in 1964, the number of Council of Grand Justices decreased to 13 after two passed away in 1964. Although the Council was still able to convene, it would run into difficulty whenever one or two Grand Justices were put on leave due to unexpected reasons. Xie recommended four candidates during the May. Chiang nominated two out of them, who were confirmed in September. See Xie Guansheng diaries on September 10, 1964.
31 See Tian Jiongjin, 'A Foreword,' *Collection of Council of Grand Justices Interpretations* (The Judicial Yuan, 1974). For a more detailed piece of academic reflections on the changing roles of the Council of Grand Justices, please see Jyh-pin Fa, 'Constitutional Developments in Taiwan: The Role of the Council of Grand Justices,' (1991) 40(1) *The International and Comparative Law Quarterly* 198–209.
32 For an example, see Jyh-pin Fa, 'Constitutional Developments in Taiwan: The Role of the Council of Grand Justices.'
33 See Xie Guansheng, *supra note* 9, 26.
34 See Xie Guansheng, *ibid.*

35 The great leap forward movement was one of the most disastrous political movement in China based on bad policies during the intensified cold war era. For a quick reference, please see Xin Meng et al., 'The Institutional Causes of China's Great Famine, 1959-1961,' (2015) 82 *Review of Economic Studies* 1568–1611.

36 The Vice President of Judicial Yuan, the best friend and associate of Xie, passed away a month earlier in the same year. In 1965, at the strong recommendation of Xie, Chiang Kai-shek nominated him to be the Vice President of the Judicial Yuan, who was appointed in June, 1966. See Xie Guansheng diaries on August 21, 1965; June 18, 1966; November 14, 1971.

37 See Chiang Kai-shek diaries on December 21, 1971. As a matter of fact, Chiang himself stopped writing diaries by 1972.

38 "The Taiwanese Constitutional Court (TCC)" seemed to have become a special term of emphatical value in the comparative hands. Tom Ginsburg is one typical example in emphasizing the role of TCC by ignoring and negating any role of China's constitutional court (CCC) in promoting the global development of the judicial reviewing courts. See Tom Ginsburg, 'Judicial Independence in East Asia: Lessons for China,' in Randall Peerenboom (ed.) *Judicial Independence in China: Lessons for Global Rule of Law Promotion* (Cambridge University Press, 2010), 254.

39 I have done up to 20 home interviews with Weng, the most revered Grand Justice in Taiwan from 2015 to 2019.

40 See Chien-Liang Lee, 'The Advocate and Practitioner of the Idea of Guardian of the Constitution ("HÜTER DER VERFASSUNG"): Prof. Yueh-Sheng Weng's Contributions to the Development of Democratic Constitutionalism in Taiwan,' (2011) 1(1) *European-Asian Journal of Law and Governance* 165.

41 See Weng Yuesheng, 'Guardians of the Constitution,' (1972) 17 *Constitutional Thought* 146–148; *NTU Law Review*, Vol. 1: 327–330.

42 See *supra note* 40, at 166.

43 See *supra note* 41, *NTU Law Review*, Vol. 1: 327, 330.

44 See Weng Yuesheng, *Yiwang Shuhuai: Wo De Sifa Rensheng* (*My Life in the Judicial Yuan: A Memoir*), (Li Jianliang (ed.), Yuan-Liou Publishing Co., Ltd., 2021), 351–353.

45 See *supra note* 42, at 171; also see *supra note* 45, at 341–344.

46 Weng Yuesheng, *Constitutional Interpretations and Judicial Reform in the Contemporary Rule-of-Law Sate: Professor Yuen-Sheng Weng's Collected Essays* (2020), 326–327.

47 For a good summary of the featuring changes, please see the news release by the Judicial Yuan on "The Taiwan Constitutional Court in a New Era," available at: https://www.judicial.gov.tw/en/cp-2083-358640-47e30-2.html.

48 For those interested, President Weng Yuesheng's newly published memoir (2021) provides the best and the most concise summary of the story of Taiwan's constitutional court.

49 See Wang Yuesheng's keynote speech (2016), Soochow University at Taipei, Taiwan. Italics were added later.

50 See Weng Yuesheng's Speech on 'The Irreplaceable Role of the Grand Justices as the Human Right Protector,' in the *United Daily News* (Taipei), September 17, 2018.

51 For more details about the transition in the roles of the Council of Grand Justices, please see Jiunn-rong Yeh and Wen-chen Chang, 'An Evolving Court with Changing Functions: The Constitutional Court and Judicial Review in Taiwan,' in Albert Chen; Andrew Harding (eds.), *Constitutional Courts in Asia: A Comparative Perspective* (Cambridge University Press, 2018), 110–140.

52 See Jiunn-rong Yeh, *The Constitution of Taiwan: A Contextual Analysis* (Hart Publishing, 2016), 8.

53 See Bruce Ackerman, *The Future of Liberal Revolution* (Yale University Press, 1992), 102–103.

54 Though, it has been acrimoniously criticized for not concurrently being a fundamental-right protector. Anyways, there is room for debate. In a jarring contrast, the American Chief Justice John Marshall's nearly utter ignorance of the fundamental rights, even worse in his intently suppression of bill of rights (for example, *Barron v. Baltimore*, 1833, negating the enforceability of the bill of rights in the states across the country), ironically never undermines his reputation as the father of the judicial review, upon which the notion of constitutional court rests. See the list of US Supreme Court Cases by the Marshall Court, available at: https://en.wikipedia.org/wiki/List_of_United_States_Supreme_Court_cases_by_the_Marshall_Court.

55 See Weng Yuesheng, *supra note* 44, 341–351.

Bibliography

B Ackerman, *The Future of Liberal Revolution* (Yale University Press, 1992).
A Chen & A Harding (eds.), *Constitutional Courts in Asia: A Comparative Perspective* (Cambridge University Press, 2018).
E Delaney & R Dixon (eds.), *Comparative Judicial Review* (Edward Elgar Pub., 2018).
T Ginsburg, *Judicial Review in New Democracies in Asian Cases* (Cambridge University Press, 2003).
C Landfried (ed.), *Judicial Power: How Constitutional Courts Affect Political Transformations* (Cambridge University Press, 2019).
R Peerenboom (ed.) *Judicial Independence in China: Lessons for Global Rule of Law Promotion* (Cambridge University Press, 2010).
The Judicial Yuan (ed.), *Sifayuan Shishi Jiyao (A Brief History of Judicial Yuan: Volume 1)* (Self-published, 1982).
Y Weng, *Yiwang Shuhuai: Wo De Sifa Rensheng (My Life in the Judicial Yuan: A Memoir)* (Yuan-Liou Publishing Co., Ltd., 2021).
G Xie, *A Brief Survey of the Chinese Constitution* (China Cultural Service, 1954/1970).
J Yeh, *The Constitution of Taiwan: A Contextual Analysis* (Hart Publishing, 2016).

10
JUDICIAL REVIEW IN HONG KONG*

Rehan Abeyratne

Introduction

This Chapter examines constitutional judicial review in the Hong Kong Special Administrative Region (HKSAR) from the 1990s to the present day.[1] Hong Kong occupies a unique position in Greater China as the only former British colony. It maintains a common law legal system, which forms the bedrock of a sui generis model of judicial review that incorporates liberal constitutional rights and aspects of socialist constitutionalism.

On 1 July 1997, sovereignty over Hong Kong transferred from the United Kingdom to the People's Republic of China (PRC). The Basic Law for the HKSAR also came into force that day.[2] The Basic Law is referred to and is treated as Hong Kong's 'mini-constitution' that governs the SAR within a 'One Country, Two Systems' (OCTS) framework.[3] The Basic Law, among other things, sets out Hong Kong's system of government, its relationship with Mainland China, and a range of judicially enforceable fundamental rights.[4] It further establishes constitutional supremacy over ordinary legislation, providing that 'No law enacted by the legislature of the Hong Kong Special Administrative Region shall contravene this Law.'[5] Thus, the Basic Law performs the traditional role of a constitution but operates in a subnational region, whose sovereignty lies with the PRC.

Despite its supremacy, the Basic Law is not the sole source of fundamental rights in the HKSAR. Fundamental rights are recognized in Part III of the Basic Law and in the Bill of Rights Ordinance (BORO).[6] The latter was enacted in 1991 to make the International Covenant on Civil and Political Rights (ICCPR) domestically enforceable in Hong Kong.[7] BORO served to assure the Hong Kong people and international investors that Hong Kong would continue to abide by international human rights standards following the handover of sovereignty from Britain to China.[8] It has a quasi-constitutional status through Article 39 of the Basic Law, which provides:

* This chapter draws from my previous work 'More Structure, More Deference: Proportionality in Hong Kong' in Po Jen Yap (ed), *Proportionality in Asia* (CUP 2020). I thank Stuart Hargreaves for helpful comments and Shun Yan Ip for excellent research assistance.

DOI: 10.4324/9781003128243-12

> The provisions of the International Covenant on Civil and Political Rights … as applied to Hong Kong shall remain in force *and* shall be implemented through *the laws* of the Hong Kong Special Administrative Region.[9]

Thus, constitutional judicial review in the HKSAR makes reference to three sources of rights: the Basic Law, BORO, and the ICCPR. To give effect to these fundamental rights, the Court of Final Appeal (CFA) has adopted the proportionality test, which was first introduced in Hong Kong by the Court of Appeal in the final years of British colonial rule.[10] Proportionality was initially developed in Germany before migrating across the world to become the most widely used test to adjudicate fundamental rights claims.[11] Proportionality is an intrusive form of judicial review. In contrast to earlier, more deferential standards such as *Wednesbury* unreasonableness, it requires the government to provide detailed evidence and reasons to justify restrictions on fundamental rights.[12]

The Basic Law and OCTS, in theory, require that the HKSAR exercises a 'high degree of autonomy' over its economic, political, and legal affairs.[13] In practice, however, Hong Kong's autonomy has been deeply contested from the outset and has been weakened in recent years, including in the judicial realm. The Basic Law guarantees the independence of the judiciary and created the CFA to replace the Judicial Committee of the Privy Council as the Special Administrative Region's (SAR's) court of final adjudication.[14] Moreover, the legal system (including the lower courts) and the laws previously in force in Hong Kong (including the common law) remain in place.[15] British colonial rule lasted from the mid-nineteenth century until 1997. As a result, British precedents and principles form the basis upon which Hong Kong courts exercise review over legislation. Judges follow the principle of *stare decisis* in which precedents of the higher courts are binding not only on Hong Kong residents and the other branches of government, but also on the courts themselves. Yet, despite this continuity and the fact that the CFA has final word on constitutional interpretation within Hong Kong, the National People's Congress Standing Committee (NPCSC) – a powerful, non-judicial body in Mainland China – has the ultimate power of interpretation over the Basic Law.[16]

This chapter consists of two main sections. The 'Judicial Review in the Shadow of the NPCSC' section examines judicial review on matters in which the NPCSC has been involved. The 'Proportionality and Fundamental Rights' section analyzes judicial review with respect to fundamental rights adjudicated that have thus far remained outside the NPCSC's purview. The chapter concludes with a discussion of how political developments in the HKSAR are likely to impinge upon judicial review going forward. In short, constitutional rights adjudication in Hong Kong is a balancing act between fundamental rights projection and the 'political sensitivities of the central government in Beijing,'[17] with the latter growing in scope and salience.

Judicial Review in the Shadow of the NPCSC

Hong Kong Courts' Approach to NPCSC Interpretations

In its very first constitutional judgment, the CFA boldly decided not only to resolve the case at hand, but also to opine on scope of its judicial review authority vis-à-vis the NPCSC. That case, *Ng Ka Ling v Director of Immigration* (1999) [*Ng Ka Ling No. 1*] concerned the right of abode under the Basic Law.[18] The applicants were children born in Mainland China to Hong Kong permanent residents. These children were denied permanent residency (right of abode) in Hong Kong by the Director of Immigration. Article 24(2) of the Basic Law confers permanent residency status, *inter alia*, on 'Persons of Chinese nationality born outside Hong Kong of [permanent residents].' However, Article 22(4) of the Basic Law states, 'For entry into the HKSAR, people from other parts of China must apply for approval' issued by Mainland authorities in consultation with the HKSAR government.

Pursuant to these constitutional provisions, the Immigration Ordinance in force at the time required individuals to have the following documents to establish permanent residency: (1) a valid travel document and certificate of entitlement; (2) a valid HKSAR passport; or (3) a valid permanent identity card.[19] The applicants in this case were physically in Hong Kong but lacked any of this documentation. The Direction of Immigration argued that, because they entered the HKSAR from Mainland China, Article 22(4) of the Basic Law and the Immigration Ordinance required them to produce a 'one-way permit' from the Mainland authorities along with a certificate of entitlement from the Director to claim the right of abode in Hong Kong.[20] The applicants, meanwhile, argued that they were entitled to the right of abode by virtue of Article 24(2) of the Basic Law and that the Immigration Ordinance was unconstitutional in restricting their rights therein.[21]

The case was significant not only for the many families that would be affected by the CFA's ruling, but also for the broader jurisdictional claims that the Court would make. As an initial matter, the CFA stated that the Basic Law is a 'living instrument intended to meet changing needs and circumstances.'[22] Hong Kong courts should adopt a 'purposive' approach to Basic Law interpretation and a 'generous' approach to fundamental rights and freedoms.[23] The CFA declared its authority to 'examine whether legislation enacted by the legislature of the Region or acts of executive authorities of the Region are consistent with the Basic Law and, if found to be inconsistent, to hold them to be invalid.'[24] This assertion of strong-form judicial review was uncontroversial given the constitutional status of the Basic Law and the preeminent role it conferred on the CFA.[25] The Court ruled in favor of the applicant children in this case, holding the ordinance unconstitutional to the extent it required children of permanent residents born in Mainland China to obtain permits and certificates of entitlement before they could claim their right of abode.[26]

The Court went on to declare (in obiter) that it had the jurisdiction 'and indeed the duty to declare invalidity if inconsistency is found' between 'legislative acts of the National People's Congress or its Standing Committee' and the Basic Law.[27] In claiming this broad jurisdiction, the Court made clear that acts of the National People's Congress (NPC) are 'acts of the sovereign' but noted that the Basic Law itself was enacted by the NPC pursuant to Article 31 of the PRC Constitution, which allows for the creation of SARs.[28] Having created the HKSAR and the Basic Law as the constitution for the region, the CFA noted that, as with any constitution, acts that are inconsistent with the Basic Law 'are of no effect and are invalid.'[29] It falls upon the courts of the region, which are endowed with 'independent judicial power' to adjudicate 'questions of inconsistency and invalidity when they arise.'[30] The CFA concluded, 'It is therefore for the courts of the Region to determine whether an act of the National People's Congress or its Standing Committee is inconsistent with the Basic Law, subject of course to the provisions of the Basic Law itself.'[31]

As it turned out, this obiter dicta would be the high watermark of the CFA's claim of jurisdiction over acts of the NPC and NPCSC in Hong Kong. Concerned about the potential influx of immigrants from the PRC that would result from the *Ng Ka Ling No. 1* ruling, the HKSAR government asked the CFA to clarify its judgment. The CFA responded with a terse second judgment [*Ng Ka Ling No. 2*] in which it conceded that the NPCSC had the authority to issue interpretations under Article 158 of the Basic Law that would bind the Hong Kong courts.[32] But it left open the possibility of holding such interpretations unconstitutional. It said:

> [T]he Court accepts that it cannot question, the authority of the National People's Congress or the Standing Committee to do any act which is in accordance with the provisions of the Basic Law and the procedure therein.[33]

This cleverly worded passage implies that if these institutions were to act contrary to the Basic Law, the Court could call those acts into question. However, the CFA has never effectuated this implicit power.

Following *Ng Ka Ling No. 2*, the NPCSC issued an Interpretation on the right of abode. The Interpretation effectively overruled the CFA, ruling that children born in the PRC to Hong Kong permanent residents required approval from the Mainland authorities before entering Hong Kong.[34] In other words, Article 22(4) takes precedence over Article 24(2), contrary to the CFA's judgment in *Ng Ka Ling No. 1*, which granted the right of abode under Article 24(2) to children lacking the relevant approvals under Article 22(4). The CFA dutifully followed the NPCSC Interpretation in subsequent right of abode cases. It held, among other things, that the NPCSC's power to interpret the Basic Law 'is in general and unqualified terms'[35] and that NPCSC Interpretations 'can clarify and supplement laws.'[36]

Hong Kong courts have shown even broader deference to NPCSC Interpretations in subsequent cases. Take, for instance, the legislative oath controversy in 2016. That year, Sixtus Leung and Yau Wai-Ching were elected to the Legislative Council.[37] Under Article 104 of the Basic Law and the Oaths and Declaration Ordinance, they were required to swear an oath of allegiance to the Basic Law and the HKSAR.[38] However, while taking the oath, Leung and Yau departed from the statutory language by referring to a 'Hong Kong nation' and using a derogatory term for China.[39] The oaths were, therefore, declared invalid. While the Legislative Council President was willing to allow them to retake their oaths, pro-establishment legislators staged a walked out to prevent that from happening. The Chief Executive and Secretary for Justice filed legal proceedings the same day to have Leung and Yau disqualified. While the case was pending before the Court of First Instance (CFI), the NPCSC issued an Interpretation of Article 104.[40]

The Interpretation made clear that 'anyone who fails to lawfully and validly take the oath' or 'who declines to take the oath' may not assume public office.[41] It further stated that the oath was to be taken 'sincerely and solemnly' and 'accurately, completely, and solemnly read out.'[42] If an oath was determined to be invalid, 'no arrangement shall be made for retaking the oath.'[43] The CFI subsequently ruled that Leung and Yau should be disqualified from Legislative Council office.[44]

On appeal, Leung and Yau raised several challenges. The most significant, for our purposes, were the claims they advanced on the scope and breadth of NPCSC jurisdiction. They argued that the NPCSC Interpretation should not be read to have retrospective effect and should therefore not affect this case.[45] They also contended that the

Interpretation effectively amended the Basic Law, which would be unconstitutional since the NPCSC did not follow the formal amendment procedures set forth in Article 159 of the Basic Law.[46]

The Court of Appeal, led by Chief Judge Andrew Cheung, rejected these arguments. On the question of retrospective application, the Court said the Interpretation 'sets out the true and proper meaning of art. 104 from day one. The question of whether it applies "retrospectively" to any given set of facts whether pending before the court or not therefore cannot and does not arise.'[47] This statement implies that NPCSC Interpretations can be applied to conduct that occurred prior to their publication, as was the case here with the lawmakers' improper oaths.

As to whether the Interpretation constituted a *de facto* amendment to the Basic Law, the Court stated, 'this argument does not even get off the evidential ground and must be rejected.'[48] The Court noted that the NPCSC is governed by the civil law system of Mainland China. Given the differences between that system and the common law system of Hong Kong, the Court said it had no basis on which to judge the 'proper scope of interpretation.'[49]

At the end of his principal opinion, Chief Judge Cheung discussed in obiter whether the Hong Kong courts ever had the power to review the constitutionality of NPCSC interpretations.[50] He said that apart from references to the *Ng Kg Ling* cases on the right of abode, petitioners' counsel had 'simply made no submission on this fundamental question of jurisdiction.'[51] He concluded by stating plainly, 'In my view, the Court has no jurisdiction to deal with the issue raised.'[52]

The CFA declined to grant leave to hear this case, but it provided reasons for that determination. Significantly, it reaffirmed one of its past judgments that held, 'The NPCSC's power to interpret the Basic Law is in general and unqualified terms.'[53] Further, in dismissing the petitioners' retrospectivity claim, it stated, '[The NPCSC] declares what the law is and has always been since the coming into effect of the Basic Law on 1 July 1997.'[54] The implication is that the NPCSC's Interpretations are beyond the scope of judicial review in Hong Kong courts and, as the Court of Appeal judgment suggested, courts will not prevent their retrospective application. As Cora Chan put it, 'The contrast with the bold position taken in 1999 [in *Ng Ka Ling No. 1*] … could not be starker.'[55]

Judicial Review of NPCSC Decisions

Andrew Cheung has since been elevated to the CFA and assumed the role of Chief Justice in early 2021. His deferential stance toward the NPCSC has become the prevailing view among the Hong Kong judiciary, even where the NPCSC operates outside the Basic Law framework.

Consider the 2018 judgment of the Court of First Instance regarding the constitutionality of the 'co-location' ordinance.[56] The ordinance set up a 'Mainland Port Area' within Hong Kong in which PRC laws would apply.[57] It was enacted as part of a 'co-location' agreement between Mainland China and the HKSAR to facilitate high-speed rail connections between the two jurisdictions. The 'Mainland Port Area' would be located within a new high-speed rail terminus in Hong Kong to permit passengers to clear Mainland immigration prior to boarding trains to the PRC. This agreement required the endorsement of the NPCSC before it could be enacted.[58] The NPCSC issued a 'Decision' approving the agreement, which was binding on the parties but did not constitute an 'Interpretation' of the Basic Law under Article 158.

The CFI considered several constitutional issues with respect to the co-location ordinance.[59] Two questions are especially relevant here: (1) to what extent should courts rely on NPCSC Decisions in determining the constitutionality of the ordinance under the Basic Law and (2) do Hong Kong courts have the authority to hold such a Decision unconstitutional if it is inconsistent with the Basic Law?

On the first question, the CFI was unwilling to determine the 'precise status' and 'legal effect' of NPCSC Decisions in Hong Kong.[60] As a lower court, it was reluctant make judgments on matters that may 'have far reaching implications but are not strictly necessary' to decide the case at hand.[61] The CFI went on to state that NPCSC Decisions at least count within the category of 'post-enactment materials' – that is, extrinsic interpretive aids published after the Basic Law was enacted – that the CFA had previously held were 'potentially admissible' in construing the meaning of ambiguous Basic Law provisions.[62] The CFA had made clear that courts should use these materials 'cautiously' and 'in conformity with common law principles' to ascertain their probative value in a particular case.[63] Here, the CFI concluded that the NPCSC Decision regarding the co-location agreement had 'high persuasive value in the particular circumstances of the present case.'[64] On the second question, the CFI simply declared, 'Hong Kong courts have no power … to determine whether the NPCSC Decision is invalid.'[65]

The Court of Appeal later affirmed this judgment, holding that the NPCSC Decision carried a 'highly persuasive weight' in the courts' construction of the Basic Law.[66] However, the appellate court diverged from the CFI in observing that the Decision was more consequential than 'ordinary post-enactment extrinsic materials' because of its crucial role in approving the co-location agreement.[67] While this judgment did not explicitly discuss whether Hong Kong courts could strike down an NPCSC Decision, its highly deferential tone suggests that it concurred with the CFI on this point.

Thus, while NPCSC Decisions are not formally accorded the same respect as Interpretations, they are, in practice, similarly beyond the scope of judicial review and treated with a comparable, if not identical, level of deference.

Judicial Review of the National Security Law

In 2020, the NPCSC took a more interventionist role in Hong Kong affairs. Frustrated by the HKSAR government's inability to pass a national security law following months of civil unrest, Mainland authorities took it upon themselves to draft and enact such legislation. On 22 May 2022, the NPC – the legislature and highest lawmaking authority in the PRC – adopted a decision authorizing the NPCSC to enact a national security law for Hong Kong.[68] The NPCSC drafted this law in secret – it was not subject to any public consultation nor was it released in draft form prior to its promulgation.[69] The National Security Law (NSL) was passed unanimously by the NPCSC and promulgated by Hong Kong's Chief Executive on the same day: 30 June 2020.[70]

Substantively, the NSL fundamentally altered Hong Kong's legal system and weakened judicial independence. It introduced four broad crimes: 'secession,' 'subversion of state power,' 'terrorist activities,' and 'collusion with foreign governments' that are punishable with sentences up to life imprisonment.[71] These offences apply not just in the HKSAR, but also extraterritorially, including to non-residents with no connection to Hong Kong.[72] Under the NSL, juries may be replaced by three-judge panels.[73] Moreover, only judges pre-selected by the Chief Executive (in consultation with the Chief Justice) are permitted to adjudicate national security cases.[74] The NSL, in another unprecedented provision, also permits criminal cases originating in Hong Kong to be moved to Mainland China and, hence, prosecuted and tried by PRC authorities and courts, respectively.[75]

Though the NSL ushered in sweeping changes, its status vis-à-vis the Basic Law and BORO was not clear from its text. On the one hand, the NPCSC inserted a provision granting the NSL a quasi-constitutional status. Article 62 of the NSL provides, 'This Law shall prevail where provisions of the local laws of the Hong Kong Special Administrative Region are inconsistent with this Law.'[76] On the other hand, Articles 4 and 5 provide, 'Human rights shall be respected and protected in safeguarding national security' and the 'principle of the rule of law shall be adhered to,' respectively.[77] As with NPCSC Interpretations and Decisions, then, Hong Kong courts would have to determine if the NSL was subject to judicial review and whether provisions therein could be held unconstitutional for inconsistency with the Basic Law or BORO.

The CFA addressed this issue in *HKSAR v Lai Chee Ying* (2021). Jimmy Lai, the founder of the pro-democracy Apple Daily tabloid newspaper, was arrested in December 2020 on the charge of 'collusion with a foreign country or with external elements to endanger national security' under Article 29(4) of the NSL.[78] He was initially denied bail by a magistrate based on NSL Article 42(2), which denies bail to defendants and criminal suspects 'unless the judge has sufficient grounds for believing that [they] ... will not continue to commit acts endangering national security.'[79] The District Court subsequently granted Lai's bail application,[80] leading the prosecution to appeal the decision to the CFA, which granted leave to determine the 'correct interpretation of Article 42(2) of the NSL.'[81]

The CFA rehearsed the events that led to the passage of the NSL, including the NPC Decision to authorize the NPCSC to formulate the law and the latter's listing of the NSL in Annex III of the Basic Law.[82] The CFA not only concluded that the NSL was passed in accordance with Article 18 of the Basic Law but also noted 'that safeguarding national security is a matter outside the limits of the HKSAR's autonomy and within the purview of the Central Authorities, the CPG having an overarching responsibility for national security affairs relating to the HKSAR.'[83]

It therefore follows, the Court held, that Hong Kong courts lack jurisdiction to review the constitutionality of the NSL.[84] It cited *Ng Ka Ling (No. 2)*, which had stated that the CFA could not question 'the authority of the National People's Congress or the Standing Committee to do any act which is in accordance with the provisions of the Basic Law and the procedure therein.'[85] This ambiguous formulation left open the possibility that the CFA could question NPC or NPCSC acts that do not accord with the Basic Law. Indeed, the defendant's counsel argued in *Lai Chee Ying* that even if the CFA were unable to hold the NSL unconstitutional, it could rely upon common law principles to conduct a weak form of review. Specifically, he asked the Court to invoke the principle of legality to 'read down' Article 42(2) to the extent it infringed upon the presumption of innocence and the right to liberty.[86] The CFA, however, rejected even this modest form of review and asserted unambiguously that it 'no power to hold any provision of the NSL to be unconstitutional or invalid as incompatible with the Basic Law and Bill of Rights.'[87]

All told, the NSL, like NPCSC Interpretations, is beyond the scope of constitutional judicial review in Hong Kong courts.[88] As a formal legal matter, the precise status and reviewability of NPCSC Decisions, such as the Decision approving the 'co-location' agreement, remain unresolved. In practice, though, it appears very unlikely that such

Decisions would be subject to judicial review, much less ruled unconstitutional for failing to comply with the Basic Law or BORO.

Proportionality and Fundamental Rights

This Part explores constitutional judicial review where Hong Kong courts adjudicate fundamental rights claims on their own without the NPCSC's intervention. While the specter of potential NPCSC involvement remains present, the fundamental rights cases considered herein were resolved with reference to the Basic Law and BORO, using common law interpretive methods and the proportionality test.

Civil and Political Rights

This section discusses the broad deference Hong Kong courts have displayed in applying the proportionality test, particularly where politically sensitive rights such as the freedom of expression and assembly as well as election-related rights are at issue.

Hong Kong courts initially adopted a relatively unstructured, three-pronged version of proportionality, which asks: (1) whether the government has legitimate aims for restricting fundamental rights; (2) whether the restrictions are rationally connected to those legitimate aims; and (3) whether the restrictions are proportionate (no more than necessary) to accomplish the legitimate aims.[89] Because BORO incorporates the ICCPR into Hong Kong law,[90] constitutional litigation on civil and political rights, such as the freedoms of expression and assembly, has often been framed in the Covenant's terms.

Consider *HKSAR v Ng Kung Siu* (1999).[91] This case concerned the freedom of expression in the context of flag desecration. During a public demonstration, two individuals defaced both the PRC national flag and the regional HKSAR flag. Both flags were cut or torn, and the Chinese character 'shame' was written on them. These individuals (respondents) were convicted for violating two ordinances that criminalized flag desecration.[92]

The respondents argued that these criminal provisions violated their rights to freedom of speech and expression. Article 27 of the Basic Law provides, 'Hong Kong residents shall have the freedom of speech, of the press, and of publication.'[93] Article 16 of BORO provides a more detailed – and limited – right to free expression, which reproduces Article 19 of the ICCPR. It provides, in relevant part, 'Everyone shall have the right to freedom of expression,' and that this right may be subject to restrictions that are provided by law and are necessary for, among other things, 'the protection of national security or of public order (ordre public).'[94]

As a preliminary matter, the CFA noted that the ICCPR had been incorporated into the Basic Law.[95] This meant that the permissible restrictions on the freedom of expression as expressly identified in the ICCPR and BORO would affect the Court's interpretation of Article 27 of the Basic Law. The Court then proceeded to examine whether the restriction was justified on the grounds of 'public order (ordre public)' – a permissible limitation under the ICCPR and BORO on which the government relied.[96]

Applying the proportionality test, the Court had to determine whether the government's legitimate aim of protecting the flag was encompassed by 'public order (ordre public).' The Court held that flag protection promoted general welfare and the interests of the collectivity as a whole because of their symbolic value in the context of the resumption of Chinese sovereignty over Hong Kong, and the OCTS arrangement.[97]

The Court then considered the question of necessity: whether the restrictions imposed on free speech by these statutes were no more than necessary to achieve the legitimate aim. The Court found that the expressive activity (flag desecration) proscribed by the relevant ordinances was a 'limited' restriction, banning only 'one mode' of expression, and leaving untouched a 'person's freedom to express the same message by other modes.'[98] Thus, it held, 'Having regard to what is only a limited restriction on the right to the freedom of expression, the test of necessity is satisfied. The limited restriction is proportionate to the aims sought to be achieved and does not go beyond what is proportionate.'[99]

At several points, the Court stressed the importance of the national and regional flags as 'unique symbol[s]' of national unity. This enabled a broad interpretation of 'public order (ordre public),' which is very deferential to the government and the legitimacy of its stated aims. *Ng Kung Siu* also made clear that Hong Kong courts must consider political context when adjudicating fundamental rights claims. At the end of the judgment, the Court noted the novel circumstances in which it was operating and reiterated the significance of the handover of sovereignty. It said, 'Hong Kong is at the early stage of the new order ... "one country, two systems" is a matter of fundamental importance, as is the reinforcement of national unity and territorial integrity.'[100]

In subsequent freedom of expression cases, the HKSAR government has continued to rely – successfully – on the public order (ordre public) justification, particularly on politically sensitive issues. Among other things, courts have upheld bans on candidates for elected office based on their political views, as well as restrictions on the right to free expression within the Legislative Council.[101]

A similar picture emerges on the freedom of assembly. In *Leung Kwok Hung v HKSAR* (2005),[102] protestors who were convicted of organizing and assisting in an unlawful assembly challenged the constitutionality of the Public Order Ordinance (Cap 245). They argued that it conferred excessive discretion on the Commissioner of Police to restrict the freedom of assembly, which is protected by Article 27 of the Basic Law and Article 17 of BORO. The ordinance permitted the Commissioner to restrict peaceful assemblies, *inter alia*, to uphold public order (ordre public).[103] The concept of public order (ordre public), as discussed, is found in the ICCPR and is reproduced in BORO. Both require that restrictions on the freedom of assembly must be 'in conformity with law' and necessary in a democratic society.[104]

The CFA noted that the phrasing 'in conformity with law' is equivalent to 'prescribed by law.'[105] Any laws restricting the freedom of assembly, therefore, must be 'adequately accessible' and 'formulated with sufficient precision' for citizens to regulate their conduct.[106] Once a law clears this hurdle, it is then subjected to the proportionality test to determine if it is 'necessary' in a democratic society.[107]

However, prior to applying proportionality, the CFA found that the scope of the Commissioner's discretion under the Public Order Ordinance was not sufficiently precise and, therefore, held that it failed to meet the 'prescribed by law' requirement.[108] The Court then severed the term 'public order,' meaning 'law and order' in the narrower sense, from its etymological cousin public order (ordre public), which is more broadly defined.[109] It held that the Commissioner's discretion to limit peaceful assemblies in order to uphold law and order was sufficiently precise and limited in scope to fulfill the 'prescribed by law' requirement.[110] The CFA went on to hold that this more limited discretion was rationally connected to the legitimate aim of maintaining public order and was no more than necessary to achieve it.[111] Thus, after severance, the Commissioner's statutory discretion was upheld.[112]

In more recent cases, Hong Kong courts have continued to tread carefully on freedom of assembly cases, showing broad deference to the government. The Court of Appeal, for instance, upheld restrictions on access to a public area outside the main government building complex, which had been fenced off following protests and subject to a stringent 'Permission Scheme' for entry.[113]

The CFA, meanwhile, reversed a lower court judgment that struck down regulations banning face coverings (including masks) not just in 'unlawful' or 'unauthorized' assemblies, but also in lawful public meetings and processions.[114] This judgment was also remarkable for its timing, as it was issued during the COVID-19 pandemic when masks were legally mandated in public. When faced with the argument that the impugned regulations contradicted COVID-related mask mandates and therefore were no longer justified under the proportionality test, the CFA simply dismissed these 'supervening events' as 'wholly irrelevant.'[115] The constitutionality of the regulations that prohibited face coverings, the Court said, had to be judged in the circumstances in October 2019 (prior to the pandemic) when they came into force even if 'subsequent events have changed the legal context.'[116] This extraordinary statement undermines the core of proportionality analysis, which is a fact-based, contextual inquiry that requires the government to justify the suitability and necessity of restrictions on fundamental rights.[117]

Proportionality's Fourth Step and 'Manifest' Unreasonableness

Over the past few years, proportionality analysis has become more structured, which has broadened judicial deference even in areas that are not apparently politically controversial or sensitive. In *Hysan Development Co Ltd v Town Planning Board* (2016), the CFA followed the Canadian and British jurisprudence to add a fourth step to the proportionality analysis.[118] The fourth step requires judges to engage in a broader balancing analysis, as it asks, 'whether a fair balance has been struck between the general interest and the individual rights intruded on.'[119] While this balancing requirement, in theory, should increase the scope of fundamental rights protection, it has proved inconsequential thus far.[120]

The more significant advent in *Hysan* was to formalize and expand a new standard of review. The CFA had previously held, in the context of socioeconomic rights, that government policies should be upheld unless they are 'manifestly beyond the spectrum of reasonableness (or manifestly without reasonable foundation).'[121] *Hysan* followed those judgments in linking this deferential standard to the margin of appreciation concept in the European Court of Human Rights (ECtHR) jurisprudence. The CFA in *Hysan* noted the difference in context between the Strasbourg Court and the CFA, as the former is a supranational court, and the margin afforded to member states is largely a function of this unique arrangement.[122] Thus, the concept as applied in Hong Kong is referred to as the 'margin of discretion' to avoid confusion.[123]

As to whether the concept should apply in a domestic context, the Court noted that UK courts, too, following the ECtHR, had adopted the 'manifest' standard of review in the socioeconomic policy realm, which signals a wide margin (or substantial deference) to the government.[124] The alternative standard is 'reasonable necessity' in which courts ask whether a restriction is 'no more than necessary' to advance the legitimate aim espoused by the government.[125] This was previously the default standard of review in proportionality analysis. However, *Hysan* extended the scope of the deferential 'manifest' standard beyond the socioeconomic rights context by listing factors courts should consider in choosing whether this standard or 'reasonable necessity' should apply in a particular case. The factors, drawn from ECtHR and British case law, are:

> (i) [T]he significance of and degree of interference with the right in question; and (ii) the identity of the decision-maker as well as the nature and features of the encroaching measure relevant to setting the margin of discretion.[126]

Thus, along with the additional structure that *Hysan* brought to proportionality analysis, it increased judicial discretion in terms of setting the standard of review. Judges have since applied the 'manifest' standard to defer to the government in cases that ordinarily would have been subject to more searching review.[127]

Progressive Rights Jurisprudence

This part (and the chapter) has thus far painted a bleak picture of judicial review in Hong Kong, with judges showing broad deference to the government on a range of fundamental rights claims. But it is important to note that Hong Kong courts do not merely serve as a rubber stamp. Courts have struck down restrictions on prisoner voting rights,[128] on eligibility requirements for indigenous village elections,[129] and for those convicted of minor offences seeking to stand for election.[130] They have given substance to social welfare rights,[131] and the right to travel.[132] In addition, they have recognized that the right against cruel, inhuman, or degrading treatment or punishment is a non-derogable and absolute right from which the government's immigration policies are not exempted.[133]

Perhaps most notably, Hong Kong courts have incrementally expanded the scope of lesbian, gay, bisexual, and transgender (LGBT) rights protection. In 2006, the Hong Kong Court of Appeal in *(William Roy) Leung v Secretary for Justice* had to determine whether a difference in the age of consent for homosexual and heterosexual sex under Section 118C of the Crimes Ordinance conflicted with the Basic Law and BORO.[134] The applicant challenged provisions in the Crimes Ordinance, which criminalized, among other things, 'buggery' under the age of 21.[135] As a gay man, he claimed that the ordinance violated his right to equality, as the ordinance set a higher age threshold for buggery (age 21) than heterosexual sex (age 16), and criminalized homosexual acts involving more than two people, but not similar heterosexual acts.[136]

The Court ruled in favor of the applicant, holding that the relevant provisions of the Crimes Ordinance constituted indirect discrimination based on sexual orientation, which violated the right to equality under Article 25 of the Basic Law and Article 22 of BORO.[137] The Court found that the impugned age differential 'significantly affects homosexual men in an adverse way compared with heterosexuals.'[138] Though the prohibition on 'buggery' under the age of 21 facially applied to everyone, in practice, it worked special harm on gay men. The Court, therefore, concluded that it constituted 'disguised discrimination' on the basis of sexual orientation, in violation of fundamental rights to equality and privacy.[139]

The Court also dismissed the government's contention, based on judgments from the ECtHR, that the legislature was owed a margin of appreciation in this case. It said, 'Where a there is a breach of rights based on race, sex or sexual orientation, the court will *scrutinise with intensity* the reasons said to constitute justification.'[140] This standard of 'intense scrutiny' would be applied in subsequent cases involving unconstitutional discrimination on the grounds of sex or sexual orientation to strike down other criminal prohibitions on same-sex conduct.[141]

Hong Kong courts have also been called upon to adjudicate status discrimination claims involving the LGBT community. These cases deal with, among other things, differential treatment in the marital rights and benefits of same-sex couples. As with the cases on sexual conduct, the courts have moved incrementally toward greater rights protection.

With respect to same-sex couples, Hong Kong courts have issued a series of judgments granting them greater, if not full, equality under the law. In *QT v Director of Immigration* (2018), the CFA granted leave to an appeal concerning a British national, whose spouse was employed in Hong Kong but was denied a dependent visa.[142] The couple entered into a valid same-sex civil partnership in England and met the relevant Immigration Department standards for a bona fide relationship that would ordinarily qualify QT for a dependent visa. QT challenged this decision on both administrative and constitutional law grounds. She argued that it was unreasonable in the *Wednesbury* sense and violated several of her constitutional rights, including the right to equality.[143]

The CFA, in applying proportionality analysis, accepted at step one that the Director's two policy aims were legitimate: (1) to encourage talented individuals to join the HKSAR workforce, with their families and (2) to maintain strict immigration controls. The government further stated – and QT did not contest – that it needed a bright-line rule to differentiate between those who do and do not qualify for dependent visas, as this would promote legal certainty and administrative convenience.[144]

At step two, the CFA held that the Director's exclusion of bona fide same-sex spouses was 'counter-productive and plainly not rationally connected' to its aim of recruiting talent to Hong Kong.[145] As for strict immigration controls, the Court acknowledged the convenience of bright-line rules but pointed out that QT and her partner 'are just as conveniently able to produce their civil partnership certificate. Excluding them on the basis of administrative convenience is irrational.'[146] The Court, therefore, ruled in favor of QT.

The following year, the CFA issued a landmark ruling in *Leung Chun Kwong v Secretary for the Civil Service* (2018).[147] In this case, a gay civil servant challenged two decisions – denying him civil service benefits and the ability to file joint taxes, respectively – that allegedly discriminated against him on the basis of sexual orientation.

The CFA reversed the Court of Appeal's judgment below, which relied, *inter alia*, on 'prevailing views of the community on marriage' to reject the applicant's claims.[148] The CFA held that such views are 'simply not relevant to a consideration of the justification exercise.'[149] When it applied the proportionality test, the first step was not at issue. All parties agreed that protecting the 'traditional family as constituted by heterosexual marriage' was a legitimate aim.[150] However, the CFA did not find a rational connection between this aim and the denial of benefits to same-sex married couples. As the Court put it:

> [W]e cannot agree with the Court of Appeal's analysis. Restricting these financial benefits to opposite-sex married couples on the ground that heterosexual marriage is the only form of marriage recognised in Hong Kong law is circular and therefore proceeds on the fallacious basis rejected by the Court in *QT* ... we are unable to accept the proposition that heterosexual marriage would be undermined by the extension of the employment and tax benefits to same-sex married couples.[151]

Having decided that the government's case failed at step two, it was not necessary for the CFA to explain its reasoning at steps three and four of the proportionality test.

This judgment has proved influential, leading to lower courts striking down other laws and policies that deny benefits to same-sex couples. In *Infinger v Hong Kong Housing Authority* (2020), the Court of First Instance struck down a Housing Authority policy that excluded same-sex couples from accessing public rental housing on the same terms as 'ordinary families.'[152] And in *Ng Hon Lam Edgar v Secretary for Justice* (2020), the CFI struck down provisions excluding same-sex spouses from entitlements and benefits under the Intestates' Estate Ordinance, Cap 73, and the Inheritance (Provision for Family and Dependents) Ordinance, Cap 481.[153]

However, courts have thus far declined to recognize a right to same-sex marriage within Hong Kong. In *MK v Government of the HKSAR* (2019), the Court of First Instance heard an application for judicial review on this issue.[154] The application was filed by a lesbian woman who claimed that the denial of her right to marry was unconstitutional as was the failure of the government to provide an alternative legal framework (such as civil unions) for same-sex couples.[155] Specifically, she claimed that the Marriage Ordinance and Matrimonial Causes Ordinance, which prohibited same-sex marriage, violated her rights to equality, freedom of conscience, and freedom of marriage.[156]

The Court's opinion focused on the right to marry in Article 37 of the Basic Law and Article 19 of BORO. It noted that when the Basic Law and BORO were adopted in the 1990s, no country recognized same-sex marriage.[157] Thus, 'marriage' in these instruments was intended to apply only to heterosexual couples.[158] The Court further noted, citing *QT* and *Leung Chung Kwong*, that Hong Kong courts have consistently interpreted 'marriage' as between a man and a woman.[159] Though the Court conceded that fundamental rights 'ought to be interpreted generously,' it concluded that the right to marry could not be read so broadly as to include same-sex couples.[160]

With respect to the claim that the Hong Kong government should provide an alternative legal framework in lieu of same-sex marriage, the applicant relied on the ECtHR's judgment in *Oliari v Italy*.[161] The European Court held that the Italian government violated Article 8 of the European Convention of Human Rights by failing to provide a legal framework to protect same-sex unions.[162] The Court in *MK* distinguished *Oliari* on the basis that 'prevailing legal, social, and political circumstances' in Italy and surrounding regions are fundamentally different to those in Hong Kong.[163]

After ruling against the applicant on both issues, the Court remarked in obiter dicta that the government should 'undertake a comprehensive review of this matter.'[164] The Court warned that in the absence of such a review, 'specific legislations, or policies or decisions of the Government' would be challenged in court on 'an *ad-hoc* basis, resulting in an incoherent state of the law at different times.'[165]

Conclusion

The *MK* judgment in the Court of First Instance is not the final word on same-sex marriage in Hong Kong.[166] However, it appears unlikely to be reversed in the current political climate. The enactment of the NSL, along with sweeping electoral changes that disqualify many opposition candidates and limit universal suffrage in the Legislative Council,[167] signals that the political foundations for constitutional judicial review have eroded, if not vanished altogether. In this increasingly constrained environment, it is unlikely that Hong Kong courts will become more assertive in reviewing the constitutionality of NPCSC interpretations, decisions, and laws, or of legislation and regulations enacted within the HKSAR. Rather, courts will probably continue to show broad deference to PRC and HKSAR lawmakers and may retrench their jurisdiction further to adapt to the new political and institutional equilibrium that characterizes the OCTS system in Hong Kong today.

Notes

1 HKSAR courts also exercise powers of administrative judicial review, which will not be discussed in this chapter.
2 The Basic Law was adopted at the Third Session of the Seventh National People's Congress in 1990 but only entered into force at the handover of sovereignty from Britain to China on 1 July 1997.
3 See CL Lim and Johannes Chan, 'Autonomy and Central-Local Relations' in Johannes Chan and CL Lim (eds), *Law of the Hong Kong Constitution* (3rd edn, Sweet & Maxwell 2021).
4 *See* Hong Kong Basic Law, ch I–IV.
5 ibid art 11.
6 Hong Kong Bill of Rights Ordinance, No 59 of 1991, Cap 383 (hereafter BORO).
7 For a detailed account of the origins and events leading to the passage of BORO, see Johannes Chan and Yash Ghai (eds), *The Hong Kong Bill of Rights: A Comparative Approach* (Butterworths 1993).
8 Richard Swede, 'One Territory–Three Systems? The Hong Kong Bill of Rights' (1995) 44 International and Comparative Law Quarterly 358, 359–360.
9 Hong Kong Basic Law, art 39 (emphasis added).
10 *R v Sin Yau Ming* [1992] 1 HKCLR 127.
11 Vicki C Jackson, 'Constitutional Law in an Age of Proportionality' (2015) 124 Yale LJ 3094–3096; Alec Stone Sweet and Jud Mathews, 'Proportionality and Rights Protection in Asia: Hong Kong, Malaysia, South Korea, Taiwan – Whither Singapore?' (2017) 29 Singapore Academy of Law Journal 774, 775.
12 Moshe Cohen-Eliya and Iddo Porat, *Proportionality and Constitutional Culture* (CUP 2013) 2 (noting two essential features of proportionality: 'it is standard-based rather than categorical, and it is results-oriented rather than being a formal and conceptual doctrine.').
13 Hong Kong Basic Law, art 2.
14 ibid arts 19, 82.
15 ibid arts 81, 8.
16 ibid art 158.
17 Po Jen Yap, *Courts and Democracies in Asia* (CUP 2017) 45.
18 (1999) 2 HKCFAR 4.
19 Immigration (Amendment) (No 3) Ordinance 1997 (No 124 of 1997), Schedule 1, para 2(c).
20 *Ng Ka Ling No. 1* (n 18) 23.
21 ibid 22, 24–25.
22 ibid 28.
23 ibid 28–29.
24 ibid 25.
25 Hong Kong Basic Law, arts 19(1), 80, 82.
26 *Ng Ka Ling No. 1* (n 18) 36.
27 ibid 26.
28 ibid; Constitution of the People's Republic of China (1982), art 31.
29 *Ng Ka Ling No. 1* (n 18) 26.
30 ibid.
31 ibid.
32 *Ng Ka Ling v Director of Immigration (No. 2)* [1999] 1 HKLRD 577.
33 ibid 578.
34 Interpretation by the Standing Committee of the National People's Congress Regarding Paragraph 4 in Article 22 and Category (3) of Paragraph 2 in Article 24 of the Basic Law of the Hong Kong Special Administrative Region of the People's Republic of China (26 June 1999).

35 *Lau Kong Yung v Director of Immigration* [1999] 3 HKLRD 778, 798.
36 *Director of Immigration v Chong Fong Yuen* [2001] HKLRD 533, 544.
37 *Chief Executive of the HKSAR v President of the Legislative Council* [2017] 1 HKLRD 460, 464.
38 ibid 464–465.
39 Po Jen Yap and Eric Chan, 'Legislative Oaths and Judicial Intervention in Hong Kong' (2017) 47 Hong Kong LJ 1, 3.
40 The NPCSC issued this interpretation on its own accord, without a referral from the CFA or the HKSAR government. See Johannes MM Chan, 'A Shrinking Space: A Dynamic Relationship between the Judiciary in a Liberal Society of Hong Kong and a Socialist-Leninist Sovereign State' (2019) 72 Current Legal Problems 85, 107.
41 Interpretation of Article 104 of the Basic Law of the Hong Kong Special Administrative Region of the People's Republic of China by the Standing Committee of the National People's Congress (7 November 2016) s 2(1).
42 ibid s 2(2).
43 ibid s 2(4).
44 *Chief Executive of the Hong Kong Special Administrative Region v President of the Legislative Council* [2016] 6 HKC 417, [47].
45 *Chief Executive of the HKSAR* (n 37) 469.
46 ibid.
47 ibid.
48 ibid.
49 ibid (adding that the perspective 'of a common law lawyer, untrained in the civil law system … is, with respect, quite simply irrelevant.').
50 ibid.
51 ibid 479–480.
52 ibid 480.
53 *Yau Wai Ching v CE of the HKSAR* (2017) 20 HKCFAR 390, [35] (citing *Lau Kong Yung* (n 35) 798).
54 ibid [35].
55 Cora Chan, 'Thirty Years from Tiananmen: China, Hong Kong, and the Ongoing Experiment to Preserve Liberal Values in an Authoritarian State' (2017) 17 International Journal of Constitutional Law 439, 448.
56 *Leung Chung Hang, Sixtus v President of Legislative Counsel and Secretary for Justice* [2018] HKCFI 2657.
57 ibid [9].
58 For an overview of the approval process, see *Government Announces Co-Location Agreement*, Government of the Hong Kong Special Administrative Region Press Releases, https://www.info.gov.hk/gia/general/201707/26/P2017072501134.htm.
59 For contrasting accounts on the constitutionality of the co-location ordinance, see Po Jen Yap and Jiang Zixin, 'Co-Location is Constitutional' (2018) 48 Hong Kong LJ 37; Stephen Thomson, 'The New Constitutional Disorder: The Unlawful Application of Mainland Chinese Law to Hong Kong' (2018) 54 Texas International LJ 115.
60 *Leung Chung Hang, Sixtus* (n 56) [61].
61 ibid.
62 ibid (citing *Chong Fong Yuen* [(n 36] 547).
63 *Chong Fong Yuen* (n 36) 547.
64 *Leung Chung Hang, Sixtus* (n 56) [74].
65 ibid [62].
66 *Kwok Cheuk Kin v Secretary for Justice* [2021] HKCA 871, [69].
67 ibid [71].
68 Decision of the National People's Congress on Establishing and Improving the Legal System and Enforcement Mechanisms for the Hong Kong Special Administrative Region to Safeguard National Security (Adopted at the Third Session of the Thirteenth National People's Congress on 28 May 2020), LN 135 of 2020.
69 Kent Roach, 'Echoes that Build to a Cacophony: Hong Kong's Security Law Compared to Illiberal Elements of the Security Laws of Liberal Democracies' Working Paper, 3 <https://ssrn.com/abstract=3763099> accessed 23 November 2021.

70 Decision of the Standing Committee of the National People's Congress on Adding a Law to the List of the National Laws in Annex III to the Basic Law of the Hong Kong Special Administrative Region of the People's Republic of China (Adopted at the Twentieth Session of the Standing Committee of the Thirteenth National People's Congress on June 30, 2020), Instrument A117; Promulgation of National Law 2020, Instrument A406.
71 Law of the People's Republic of China on Safeguarding National Security in the Hong Kong Special Administrative Region, GN (E) 72 of 2020 (hereafter NSL), arts 20–30.
72 ibid arts 37–38.
73 ibid art 46.
74 ibid art 44.
75 ibid arts 55–57.
76 ibid art 62.
77 ibid arts 4, 5.
78 *HKSAR v Lai Chee Ying* [2021] HKCFA 3, [2].
79 ibid [3]; NSL (n 71) art 42(2).
80 [2020] HKCFI 3161.
81 *Lai Chee Ying* (n 78) [7].
82 ibid [9–29]. Article 18 of the Basic Law provides that PRC laws listed in Annex III may be applied in Hong Kong by way of local legislation or, as was the case here, through promulgation by the Chief Executive.
83 ibid [32].
84 ibid [37].
85 ibid; *Ng Ka Ling No. 2* (n 32) 578.
86 *Lai Chee Ying* (n 78) [33].
87 ibid [42].
88 A lower court has stated that prosecutorial decisions under the NSL may be challenged via 'judicial review on the limited grounds of dishonesty, bad faith and exceptional circumstances.' *Tong Ying Kit v Secretary for Justice* [2021] HKCA 912, [71].
89 See *Leung Kwok Hung v HKSAR* [2005] 3 HKLRD 164.
90 Hong Kong Basic Law, art 39.
91 [1999] 3 HKLRD 907.
92 National Flag and National Emblem Ordinance, No 116 of 1997, s 7; Regional Flag and Regional Emblem Ordinance, No 117 of 1997, s 7.
93 Hong Kong Basic Law, art 27.
94 BORO, arts 16(2), 16(3).
95 *Ng Kung Siu* (n 91) 920.
96 ibid 922.
97 ibid 921–924.
98 ibid 921.
99 ibid 926.
100 ibid 926.
101 *See Chan Ho Tin v Lo Ying Ki Alan* [2018] 2 HKLRD 7; *HKSAR v Fong Kwok Shan Christine* (2017) 20 HKCFAR 425.
102 *Leung Kwok Hung* (n 89).
103 ibid [4]; Public Order Ordinance (Cap 245), s 14(1); BORO, art 17.
104 BORO, art 17.
105 *Leung Kwok Hung* (n 89) [18].
106 ibid [27].
107 ibid [36].
108 ibid [77].
109 ibid [82].
110 ibid [83].
111 ibid [90–93].
112 ibid [94].
113 *Cheung Tak Wing v Director of Administration* [2020] HKCA 124.
114 *Kwok Wing Hang v Chief Executive in Council* [2020] HKCFA 22, [6–18].
115 ibid [142–143].

116 ibid [143].
117 See Jamal Greene, 'Foreword: Rights as Trumps' (2018) 132 Harvard LR 30, 63 (noting that proportionality 'does not require extensive analysis of constitutional text, history, or precedent. Rather, it requires reliable access to social facts.'); Anne Peters, 'A Plea for Proportionality: A Reply to Yun-chien Chang and Xin Dai' (2021) 19(3) International Journal of Constitutional Law 1135, 1140 (noting that steps 2 and 3 of the proportionality test require that 'the restriction of the right must not be useless and it must be not more intense than needed in order to reach the public interest objective.').
118 *Hysan Development Co Limited v Town Planning Board* [2016] 19 HKCFAR 372.
119 ibid [77–78].
120 Alec Stone Sweet, 'The Necessity of Balancing: Hong Kong's Flawed Approach to Proportionality, and Why it Matters' (2020) 50 Hong Kong LJ 541 (arguing that *Hysan* 'fundamentally deformed' proportionality analysis by, among other things, 'virtually never reaching [step] ... 4 balancing.').
121 *See Fok Chun Wa v Hospital Authority*, (2012) 15 HKCFAR 409, [76].
122 *Hysan* (n 118) [89].
123 ibid [100].
124 ibid [96], [98–99]; *R (Carson) v Secretary of State for Work and Pensions* [2006] 1 AC 173.
125 *Hysan* (n 118) [83].
126 ibid [107].
127 See, for example, *Leung Kwok Hung (Long Hair) v Commissioner of Correctional Services* [2018] HKLRD 933 (applying the 'manifest' standard to a sex discrimination case); *Leung Kwok Hung (Long Hair) v Commissioner of Correctional Services* [2020] HKCFA 37, [56] (upholding the judgment on statutory grounds but noting that the 'outcome would not be different' under a constitutional analysis). In previous cases involving discrimination on suspect grounds such as race, sex, or sexual orientation, courts applied 'intense scrutiny' in examining the government's aims and justifications. See, for example, *(William Roy) Leung v Secretary for Justice* [2006] 4 HKLRD 211.
128 *Chan Kin Sum v Secretary for Justice* [2009] 2 HKLRD 166.
129 *Secretary for Justice v Chan Wah* (2000) 3 HKCFAR 459.
130 *Wong Hin Wai v Secretary for Justice* [2012] 4 HKLRD 70. See also Yap (n 17) 45 (noting a 'distinct contradiction' in the judicial outcomes between these cases and those involving 'major systemic electoral changes' or 'high-stakes' elections, where the courts have ruled in favor of the government).
131 *Kong Yunming v Director of Social Welfare* (2013) 16 HKCFAR 950.
132 *Gurung Kesh Bahadur v Director of Immigration* (2002) 5 HKCFAR 480.
133 *Ubamaka v Secretary for Security* (2012) 15 HKCFAR 743.
134 *Leung* (n 127) 217.
135 Crimes Ordinance, (1972) Cap 200, s 118C.
136 ibid s 118C, 118F (2) (a), 118H, 118J (2) (a).
137 *Leung* (n 127) 231, 238–240.
138 ibid 237.
139 ibid.
140 ibid (emphasis added).
141 See *Secretary for Justice v Yau Yuk Lung,* [2006] 4 HKLRD 196; *HKSAR v Yeung Ho Nam* [2019] HKCA 384.
142 [2018] HKCFA 28.
143 ibid [9]; *Associated Provincial Picture Houses Ltd v Wednesbury Corporation* [1948] 1 KB 223, 229–230 (holding that laws or government policies should be struck down only if 'so unreasonable that no reasonable authority could ever come to it.').
144 *QT* (n 142) [88].
145 ibid [90].
146 ibid [95–97].
147 [2019] HKCFA 19.
148 ibid [57]; *Leung Chun Kwong v Secretary for the Civil Service* [2018] 3 HKLRD 84, [124–126].
149 *Leung Chun Kwong* (n 147) [57].
150 ibid [58].

151 ibid [71–72].
152 [2020] HKCFI 329. The Housing Authority, however, has appealed this judgment and the case is currently pending before the Court of Appeal.
153 [2020] HKCFI 2412.
154 [2019] HKCFI 2518.
155 ibid [3–6].
156 ibid [6].
157 ibid [14].
158 ibid.
159 ibid [16].
160 ibid [20].
161 *Oliari v Italy* (2017) 65 EHRR 26.
162 ibid [186].
163 *MK* (n 154) [51].
164 ibid [57].
165 ibid.
166 The *MK* judgment is pending appeal and there are other cases on same-sex marriage working their way through the court system. See, for example, *Sham Tsz Kit v Secretary for Justice* [2020] HKCFI 2411 (rejecting an application for judicial review that sought a declaration that 'the laws of Hong Kong, in so far as they do not recognize foreign same-sex marriage, constitute a violation of Article 25 of the Basic Law of the HKSAR and Article 22 of the Hong Kong Bill of Rights.').
167 For a comprehensive overview of electoral changes in Hong Kong, see Eric Chan, 'The Legislative Council of Hong Kong' in Po Jen Yap and Rehan Abeyratne (eds), *Routledge Handbook of Asian Parliaments* (Routledge 2023, forthcoming).

11

JUDICIAL REVIEW AND STANDARDS OF REVIEW IN MACAO

A Study Based on the TUI Decisions

Shiling Xiao

Introduction

Macau and Hong Kong are two special administrative regions (SARs) of the People's Republic of China (PRC) established according to the idea of "One Country, Two Systems". Macau has a version of the Basic Law (MBL), of which the text is almost identical to Hong Kong's version of the Basic Law (HKBL). Macau's political and institutional model is the same as Hong Kong's.[1] The previous capital system, the way of life and the laws and legal system previously applied in Macau are retained, and the socialist system applied in China is not practised in Macau.[2] Macau exercises a high degree of autonomy and enjoys legislative, executive and judicial power, including the power of final adjudication.[3] The MBL guarantees Macau citizens a wide range of fundamental rights, which are even broader than those contained in the HKBL and the Constitution of the PRC.[4] The laws previously in force in Macau are preserved, except for those in contravention of the MBL and subject to amendment by the Legislative Assembly and other authorities of Macau.[5] On 1 October 1999, China adopted all laws, decrees, regulations and other rules previously applied in Macau, save for 33 which it found inconsistent with the MBL (which is equivalent to approximately 3.86 per cent of all laws reviewed).[6]

Professor Yash Ghai has asserted that the Basic Laws of the two SARs were legal instruments meant to keep the legal systems of the SARs separated from the Chinese one due to contents in relation to the high degree of autonomy and fundamental rights.[7] It appears true according to their text. But the crucial realities that the Basic Laws are Chinese pieces of legislation and that the infiltration of Chinese political-legal elements into the SARs are reshaping the legal system of SARs after the handovers.[8] This is particularly the case in Macau.[9]

This chapter examines the judicial review mechanisms of the Macau SAR and the judicial review practice of the Court of Final Appeal of Macau (Tribunal de Última Instância de Macau, TUI) in the last two decades after the handover (1999–2019). It especially focuses on these decisions relating to the court's power of judicial review, the use of proportionality and political-sensitive issues. It concludes that under "One

DOI: 10.4324/9781003128243-13

Country, Two Systems", the judicial review practice of the TUI is increasingly similar to that of Chinese courts. This chapter reveals the similarities between Macau's and Chinese judicial review practice from three aspects. First, although the TUI has affirmed that the courts in Macau have the power to review the constitutionality and legality of laws and regulations, it has been very reluctant to exercise this power, and even when it does, it declares that courts should play a passive role. Similarly, the Chinese courts have very limited power to review legal norms. They have no competence in constitutional review. It can only review administrative normative documents which are at the bottom of the hierarchy of the Chinese legal system and have the lowest legal force. Second, the TUI adopts a deferential attitude when employing the standard of proportionality in judicial review, which is the same as the Chinese courts. Third, like the Chinese courts, the TUI is conservative and self-restrained when facing political-sensitive cases. Cases concerning prohibition and restriction on freedom of assembly indicate this.

This chapter consists of a number of sections, apart from this Introduction. The "The Development of Judicial Review Mechanism in the Macau SAR" section explores the development of judicial review mechanisms in Macau after the handover. In this chapter, judicial review includes two categories: constitutional review and administrative review. Constitutional review is a proceeding that determines the compatibility of legislative or administrative actions with the constitution.[10] Administrative review is a proceeding that examines the conformity of administrative action with laws other than the constitution.[11] Third to fifth sections exhibit three groups of evidence proving the increasing convergence between Macau and China regarding their judicial review, application of proportionality and conservative attitude in sensitive cases. The "Conclusion: More Convergence of Macau Judicial Review towards China" section provides a conclusion and expectation of the development of judicial review in Macau.

The Development of Judicial Review Mechanism in the Macau SAR

Before detailing the development of Macau's judicial review mechanism after the handover, it is helpful to brief the distribution of governmental power in Macau. The Legislative Assembly is the sole legislature of Macau SAR and the statutes enacted by the Legislative Assembly is known as "laws".[12] The Chief Executive of Macau enjoys broad executive power. Besides the generic power of managing administrative affairs, it can also promulgate administrative regulations,[13] executive orders (*ordem executive*) and dispatch (*despacho*).[14] The TUI is the court of final appeal and at the apex of the judiciary system in Macau SAR. Article 143 of the MBL equips courts in Macau with the competence to interpret the MBL on their own in adjudicating cases.[15]

Constitutional Review in Macau SAR

An Unfortunate Kick-Off

In the era of colonial Macau, there were mechanisms of constitutional review. The courts could either appeal to the constitutional court in Lisbon or reject to apply the laws they consider unconstitutional and invalid.[16] Additionally, there was another remedy for constitutional rights violations – *amparo*, which was widely used by Spain and the Latin American States to uphold constitutional rights against legislative and executive acts.[17] However, as Paulo Cardinal asserted, the TUI delivered a "deadly blow" to constitutional appeal and *amparo* in the aftermath of the handover.[18] In its first two decisions, Case 1/2000 and Case 2/2000, the TUI stated that there was no route of litigation for reviewing the constitutionality of legislation in the legal system of Macau SAR. This statement proved itself as being detrimental to constitutional review in Macau.

In these cases, two applicants filed applications to the High Court of Justice for the leave of constitutional appeal to the constitutional court of Portugal. The High Court of Justice accepted their applications, but the leaves for constitutional appeal were not granted before 20 December 1999. The Fundamental Law on Judicial Organisation (Lei de Bases da Organização Judiciária), a new law on the judicial organisation of the Macau SAR, came into force on that day China resumed its sovereignty over Macau.[19] According to Article 70(2) of this law, the following pending proceedings must be terminated: appeals against a court's decision where (1) the court refuses to apply a rule on the ground of unconstitutionality or (2) the court has applied an unconstitutional rule. Article 70(4) provides that the courts in Macau cannot adjudicate issues pertaining to the violation of the Constitution of Portugal. Against this background, the applicants appealed to the TUI and raised two issues. Whether the two pending constitutional appeals have been terminated? If yes, whether the applicants have the right to file a new petition of constitutional review according to the MBL?

First, the TUI affirmed that the Fundamental Law on Judicial Organization had brought the two pending constitutional appeals to an end. Second, and more importantly, the TUI held that the legal system of the Macau SAR did not provide any route of litigation for addressing the issues of the constitutionality of a legislative provision.[20] In Case 9/2006, the TUI explained that the Code of Administrative Litigation Procedure (Código do Processo Administrativo Contencioso, CPAC) was enacted with an expectation that there would be a mechanism of constitutional review in the legal system of Macau SAR and the power of constitutional review would be conferred on the TUI.[21] This expectation, however, was frustrated because no law contains a route of litigation for reviewing the compatibility of a legislative provision with the MBL.[22] In contrast to the TUI's position, there is also no law specifically conferring constitutional review power on courts or providing constitutional review proceeding in Hong Kong, but the Hong Kong Court of Final Appeal (CFA) took the opportunity to confirm the court's power of constitutional review in its first major case.[23] In view of this comparison, the TUI's decisions were disappointing and unsatisfactory.

Moving to a Weak-Form Constitutional Review

However, changes occurred in 2006. In Case 9/2006, the TUI changed its opinion and admitted that the courts of Macau had the competence in interpreting the MBL and examining the compliance of a legislative provision with the MBL. It stated:

> When adjudicating cases, the courts can scrutinise whether or not a law violates the Basic Law. The courts should enforce Article 11 of the Basic Law and should not apply a law that contradicts the Basic Law and the principles thereof, without prejudice to Article 143 of the Basic Law. Since there is no specialised appeal procedure for reviewing whether a law is in compliance with the Basic

> Law in the legal system of Macau, the courts can review the conformity of laws with the Basic Law in the proceedings of individual cases.[24]

In Case 28/2006, the TUI further elaborated the necessity and constitutional foundation of constitutional review:

> The Basic Law does not stipulate any provision that expressly empowers the courts to review whether a legal norm in statutes, administrative regulations and other normative instruments that has a lower rank [than the Basic Law] contradicts the Basic Law.
>
> However, this power is derived from an integrated interpretation of various provisions of the Basic Law.
>
> In fact, in accordance with Article 19 (2) of the Basic Law, the courts have the power to adjudicate all cases in Macau, without prejudice to the restriction on the judicial power imposed by the legal system and principles previously in force in Macau.
>
> Article 11 of the Basic Law also states that no statute, decree, administrative regulation or normative instrument shall contravene with this Law.
>
> Nonetheless, the Basic Law does not establish any mechanisms, particularly political mechanisms, for settling the potential conflicts emerging in litigations between the Basic Law and legal norms in other laws in force. Therefore, the courts have to solve these conflicts in concrete adjudications.[25]

It concluded:

> If a court can interpret the Basic Law when adjudicating cases, the court for sure can conclude that certain legislative provisions or administrative regulations contravene the Basic Law. Under this circumstance, the court must enforce the provision of Article 11 of the Basic Law: therefore, it must not apply the law that is in contradiction with the provisions or general principles of the Basic Law, without prejudice to Article 143 of the Basic Law.[26]

Although the TUI confirmed that the courts in Macau were capable of constitutionally reviewing laws, it is a weak-form constitutional review. In Case 28/2006, the TUI stated that when the courts consider legislation or administrative regulations incompatible with the Basic Law, it should not apply them.[27] Disapplication does not affect the validity of the legislation and administrative regulations. It is incomparable to the declaration of unconstitutionality by the Taiwan Constitutional Court and the CFA, which has a general and binding force. In Case 8/2007, the TUI reiterated and emphasised:

> The finding that a provision violates a rule with a higher hierarchy is nothing more than an integral part of the court's reasoning. It is one step within the logical process that results in the final judgment but does not form a part of the determination. The court cannot use this as a basis to give a judgment that that provision is illegal with concrete and binding force. The finding is only valid in the case itself and does not yield any effect towards other cases or even other courts. The provision deemed illegal does not become invalid because of this particular determination.[28]

Abstract Review of Administrative Regulations

There are two approaches of reviewing administrative regulations in Macau. Besides the concrete review demonstrated above of the constitutionality and legality of administrative regulations, Articles 88–93 of the CPAC provide an abstract review procedure for scrutinising whether or not an administrative regulation is compatible with superior laws. Even though this proceeding applies to administrative regulations according to the text of the CPAC, the TUI interpreted it broadly to cover all administrative decisions that have the characteristic of generality and abstraction,[29] including administrative regulations, executive orders, despatches and policies, which can be repeatedly applied to a group of unspecific people.

The abstract review of administrative regulations is distinct from the concrete review in two aspects. Firstly, in a concrete review proceeding, the court scrutinises the constitutionality and validity of impugned regulations when solving particular civil, criminal or administrative controversies. The abstract review of administrative regulations is independent of concrete disputes. Secondly, and more importantly, the legal effect of a concrete review is to disapply an unconstitutional provision, while the decision of an abstract review has a generally binding force.[30] Once an administrative regulation is declared illegal in an abstract review proceeding, it becomes invalid to all cases and all courts according to Article 89(1) of the CPAC. The TUI emphasised that the abstract review of administrative regulations aimed to "remove an illegal administrative regulation provision from the legal system".[31]

Despite the fact that a decision of abstract review has more far-reaching effects than a concrete review, to institute an abstract review proceeding against administrative regulations is not easy, given two procedural restrictions. First, according to Article 88(2) of the CPAC, challenges against administrative regulations on the following grounds are precluded from the purview of abstract review: the impugned administrative regulation provision contradicts (1) the MBL, (2) the laws enacted by Beijing for Macau and (3) international treaties to which Macau is a member. The TUI stresses that if a person intends to challenge the constitutionality of administrative regulation, he cannot file a petition for an abstract review but raises the challenge in a concrete litigation case.[32] Second, people cannot file a petition for an abstract review unless an administrative regulation has been deemed unlawful on three occasions or unless the regulation has a direct adverse effect on their rights and interests without enforcement by the executive or judicial authorities (Article 90(1) of the CPAC). But the prosecutors are not restricted by those restrictions (Article 90(2) of the CPAC). They could institute an abstract review when considering an administrative regulation contrary to higher laws.

Administrative Review of Administrative Actions

Due to the influence of the Portuguese centralised model of administrative review, Macau established a specific administrative tribunal, the Administrative Tribunal (Tribunal Administrativo), which is specialised in litigation in relation to administrative, tax and customs duties matters. The Administrative Tribunal enjoys common and residual jurisdiction at first instance over administrative disputes.[33] Macau also enacted a specific law on administrative litigation procedure, the CPAC. But it adjusted the centralised model given its small size of territory and population.[34] It does not establish a high administrative court or a supreme administrative court. The Court of Second

Instance (Tribunal de Segunda Instância, TSI) is empowered with competence to adjudicate on the appeals from the Administrative Tribunal. The TUI is the competent court to hear appeals from the TSI.[35]

Besides hearing appeals, the TSI's and the TUI's jurisdiction of administrative litigation is not limited to appeals. According to the Basic Law of Judicial Organization, the TSI adjudicates cases at first instance against the actions of high officials of Macau, including the president and secretaries of the Legislative Assembly, members of the Executive Board and members of the Legislative Assembly, as well as judges and prosecutors (Article 36). The TUI decides cases against the actions of the Chief Executive at first instance (Article 44).

Reluctance to Review and Declare Legislative Provisions Unconstitutional or Illegal

As the section above exhibits, the courts in Macau have relatively broad judicial review jurisdiction over law, decrees, regulations and other normative documents, as well as administrative decisions, in both concrete and abstract reviews. But without examining the actual exercise of judicial review power, it hardly reflects the relative extent to which the courts influence the legislation-making and administrative decision-making. The extent to which the courts truly and effectively intervene in the legislative and executive actions ultimately depends on the actual exercise of the judicial review power on the ground.

Between 1999 and 2019, the TUI made 1258 decisions and 1068 judgements are accessible on its official website.[36] But the TUI scrutinised the constitutionality of laws and decrees in only 13 decisions[37] and scrutinised administrative regulations and other normative documents in two decisions.[38] In contrast to the big caseload, the number of cases involving judicial review of legislation and administrative regulations is very small. This indicates that the TUI was reluctant and timid to review legislation and administrative regulations.

Among these 15 cases above, the TUI only declared impugned legislative provisions unconstitutional or invalid in three cases. The TUI found that Article 5(2)(b) of Decree 21/87/M, which applied two different approaches to calculating service hours to the same class of civil servants, was in contravention of the MBL's guarantee of equality in Case 5/2010. In Case 7/2007, which concerns an abstract review of administrative resolution, the TUI declared the impugned administrative resolution invalid because it breached superior laws by reducing the salaries of deputy directors of the Monetary Authority of Macau. In Case 2/2017, the TUI held that Article 17 of the Internal Regulation of the Judicial Police was illegal and inapplicable because it imposed punishment on police which was not stipulated by superior laws.

In Case 2/2004 and Case 25/2011, the TUI found inconsistency between legal norms and the MBL, but it did not declare them unconstitutional or inapplicable. In Case 2/2004, Article 1(3) of the Civil Code provided that international conventions applicable to Macau should prevail over domestic laws. The TUI held that no norm could confer another norm a status superior to itself. Primary legislation is inferior to the constitution, and only the constitution could confer on international treaties a status superior to legislation.[39] Instead of declaring that provision unconstitutional, the TUI concluded that "In relation to the matters that are within the province of the constitution-maker, Article 1(3) of the Civil Code is an expression of goodwill of ordinary legislators. Therefore, for adjudicating this case, this provision is meaningless".[40]

In Case 25/2011, according to the text of Article 5(4) of Law 2/93/M, any notification of intention to organise assemblies and demonstrations must be signed by three organisers. The applicant submitted a notification with only one organiser's signature and this submission was rejected.[41] The applicant argued that Article 5(4) unconstitutionally restrained the right to assembly and demonstration.[42] The TUI admitted that the MBL did not contain a restriction on the minimum number of persons that could exercise this right. If reading Article 5(4) according to its text, this provision was inconsistent with the MBL and, therefore, inapplicable. However, the TUI adopted a remedial interpretation, to render it consistent with the MBL, that the maximum number of persons who sign a notification of intention to organise assemblies and demonstrations is three.[43]

The TUI's "passive" attitude towards judicial review and its self-constraint account for very few provisions having been declared unconstitutional and illegal. The TUI accorded significant deference to legislative and executive authorities in judicial review. It asserted that the courts should play the role of "passive supervision" in judicial review.[44] Judicial control of legislative provisions is based on the standard enshrined in the MBL. The judiciary should not go as far as acting like the legislature or substituting for the legislature to assess the rationality of laws on the grounds of "reasonable", "fair" or "ideal". Passive supervision is to remove a law that cannot be considered rational from all perspectives.[45] As demonstrated above, the TUI applied in Case 5/2010 the principle of equality enshrined in the MBL. It stated that if the situations were basically identical but treated unequally, then the principle of equality had been violated from the perspective of prohibition of arbitrariness.[46] In its opinion, the perspective or theory of prohibition of "arbitrariness" was a standard for determining the limits of judicial review. This substantively passive standard only condemns the unequal situations that are manifest and intolerable. Such situations could only occur where the different treatment prescribed by the legislator lacks justification, objectivity or rationality.[47]

The judicial review practice of the TUI is similar to its Chinese colleagues. The Chinese courts have no power to review the consistency of statutes, regulations and any other sources of law with the Constitution of the PRC. The power of constitutional review is conferred exclusively on the National People's Congress (NPC) and its Standing Committee (NPCSC) – the legislature of China. The courts cannot even cite the Constitution of the PRC as a source of law because the NPC and the NPCSC are the last authorities on the meaning of the constitution provisions.[48] The NPC and the NPCSC are entitled to amend, interpret and supervise the enforcement of the Constitution of the PRC.[49] Article 97 of the Law on Legislation expressly provides that they have the power to strike down unconstitutional statutes and regulations.[50]

Chinese Administrative Litigation Law (ALL) has long limited the Chinese courts' purview to specific administrative decisions. Until the 2014 amendment to the ALL, the NPC conferred power upon the Chinese courts of reviewing administrative normative documents.[51] But this empowerment is restricted. First, the court's judicial review jurisdiction does not cover statutes, regulations and rules. They can only scrutinise administrative normative documents, which have the lowest rank in the Chinese legal system. Second, a petition for reviewing an administrative normative document cannot be filed independently, but instead in a concrete dispute against administrative decisions. There must be a connection between the impugned administrative normative document and the administrative decisions. Lastly, the Chinese courts cannot declare an administrative normative document null and void. They can only refuse to apply it in a specific case.

To sum up, by an integrated interpretation of MBL, the TUI confirmed the courts in Macau had the power to review the constitutionality and legality of legislative provisions. However, the actual exercise of judicial review power by the TUI is akin to Chinese courts. In China, the courts have nearly no power to review legislative provisions. They can only scrutinise administrative normative documents of the lowest rank. The decisions of the TUI demonstrate that it is very reluctant to review legislative provisions and timid to declare a provision unconstitutional or invalid, which happened in only three cases in the last two decades.

Applying Proportionality Deferentially

Proportionality is a fundamental principle of Macau's administrative law. This principle is enshrined in Article 5 of the Code of Administrative Procedure (Código do Procedimento Administrativo), which requires that when an administrative decision conflicts with individual rights and interests that are protected by law, the impairment by the administrative decision of the individual rights and interests must be suitable and proportionate in respect to the purpose it pursues.

In practice, the TUI has never applied proportionality in judicial review of legal norms. In a recent decision, Case 112/2018, the TUI expressly rejected to employ proportionality to scrutinise legislative action. In this case, Article 14 of Law 10/2016 criminalised acts of unlawful cultivating, producing, manufacturing, extracting, preparing, acquiring and possessing narcotic drugs and psychotropic substances for exclusive personal consumption, of which the quantity was more than five times of daily reference intakes. People who violate this provision will be sentenced according to the provisions that punish the acts of manufacturing and trafficking narcotic drugs and psychotropic substances. Two applicants were charged with violating Article 14. They argued that this article was unconstitutional for encroaching their right to be presumed innocent.[52] They claimed that the amendment assumed people who possess drugs exceeding a certain amount to be drug manufacturers or drug traffickers and the assumption could not be disproved. The TUI dismissed their claims and gave the following reason:

> The impugned provision criminalises drug consumption only when possessing narcotic drugs and psychotropic substances exceeding a rather large amount. It is a choice of the legislature and it is not prohibited by the Basic Law. Courts should not judge this choice. The disproportionality of an executive authority's discretionary act is a ground for annulment by courts. But the disproportionality of legislative action is not [a ground for annulment by courts].[53]

Despite the refusal of the TUI to apply proportionality in judicial review of legislative action, it applied this principle in a few cases when reviewing administrative decisions. The TUI first elaborated proportionality and its subtests in Case 6/2000. The principle of proportionality comprises three subtests: suitability, necessity and balance, of which the content is not different from the standard model of proportionality.[54] This formula of proportionality has been applied in the next two decades.

However, the application of proportionality by the TUI is with significant deference accorded to the government. The TUI reiterated and emphasised that when considering whether the executive complied with proportionality, the court might intervene if an administrative decision violates this principle in an intolerable manner.[55] The court's role is to examine whether the exercise of discretionary power by the executive authorities is manifestly wrong or utterly unreasonable.[56] In the context of border control and immigration decisions, the TUI reiterated that the impugned decisions should not be struck down unless they manifestly violate proportionality.[57] In the context of disciplinary sanctions and administration of civil service, the TUI consistently claimed that the administrative decisions were generally not subject to judicial review, except in cases where there are obvious errors, manifest injustice and violation of the principle of proportionality.[58]

Take Case 69/2016 as an example. The applicant, a Hong Kong permanent resident, applied for a residential permit for a reunion with his wife, who is a permanent resident of Macau. His application was rejected by the Secretary of Security on the grounds that he would threaten the local public order and security. The facts on which the decision was made related to a minor offence occurred a decade ago and a penalty of a fine of 1000 HKD, and the associated criminal record was expunged.[59] The applicant argued that the decision made by the Secretary of Security was disproportionate and violated his right to family guaranteed by Article 38 of the MBL. The TUI made its attitude clear that it would intervene only when the impugned administrative decision intolerably violates proportionality.[60] It held that having regard to the overall interest of safeguarding the public order and security of Macau, the refusal of a residential permit was not unacceptable or intolerable.

The TUI's application of proportionality associated with low intensity of review is akin to the Supreme People's Court (SPC). In its comment on a case, *Wang Liping v. The Transportation Bureau of Zhongmou County*, the SPC stated:

> In administrative litigation, only when a concrete executive action seriously violates the principle of proportionality and causes severe damage to people's legitimate rights and interests, [the court] can apply the principle of proportionality to correct the executive action...Only if an executive act is manifestly unreasonable, constituting a fundamental breach of law, the court can intervene.[61]

To understand this deferential attitude associated with proportionality employed by the SPC when reviewing administrative decisions, it is essential to understand the dichotomy between "legality" and "reasonableness" in Chinese administrative law. By legality, the Chinese courts scrutinise the formal legality of executive actions: whether decision-makers act within the four corners of the power conferred on them, whether they correctly understand and apply the laws, whether the decision-making violates statutory procedures and whether the decision is based on sufficient evidence and correct facts.[62] By reasonableness, the courts are concerned with the discretionary decision-making and substantive merits of administrative decisions.

It has been the underlying principle of Chinese administrative litigation since the ALL of 1989 that courts are supposed to be concerned primarily with the formal legality of executive actions and not to substantively review the merits of executive acts.[63] Article 5 of the ALL of 1989 provides that "when people's courts hear administrative cases, they scrutinise the 'legality' of concrete executive actions".[64] This provision conveys the legislature's attitude, albeit implicitly, that the courts are supposed not to substantively review the reasonableness of executive acts. The interpretation of the SPC on several issues concerning the implementation of the ALL of 2000 expressly requires the courts to dismiss people's claims in the cases where the impugned concrete executive decisions are unreasonable but formally legal.[65] The ALL indeed provides several grounds of judicial review enabling the courts to review the substance and merits of administrative decisions, such as abuse of power and manifest impropriety. But the courts are timid and reluctant to use these grounds.[66] They stop themselves from intervening in executive decision-making and accord significant leeway to the executive authorities. In the comment of a case, *Chen Ning v. The Public Security Bureau of Zhuanghe Municipality,* the SPC emphasised:

> If courts strictly apply the principle of reasonableness to examine the discretionary executive acts, administrative efficiency will suffer from excessive constraints. The judiciary may be suspected of displacing the executive when they intervene in-depth in the fields of administration. Therefore, the review of executive discretion by applying the principle of reasonableness must be limited to a specially tailored level according to our domestic situations: the discretionary executive decision should be deemed lawful unless they are manifestly unreasonable.[67]

Proportionality is considered a highly protective standard of judicial review[68] to optimise constitutional rights to the "greatest extent possible given the legal and factual possibilities".[69] But in Macau and China, the application of proportionality associated with low intensity of review or a deferential attitude seriously inroads the role courts and proportionality play in safeguarding individual rights and interests from government's encroachment.

Conservative and Self-Constrained in Sensitive Cases

The Tiananmen Square protest of 1989 has a long-term political impact not only in China but also in Hong Kong and Macau. As a result of this event, China became much more cautious about the democratic ethos and concerned about national security and regime stability. Immediately after this event, China introduced Article 23, the national security clause, to the Basic Laws that mandated the SARs to enact laws on its own to "prohibit any act of treason, secession, sedition, subversion against the Central People's Government".[70] In Hong Kong, the concerns about massive human rights violations under the Chinese sovereign resulted in the Bill of Rights Ordinance being enacted in 1991.[71] Mass assemblies and demonstrations in memory of the Tiananmen Square crackdown were held annually before the outbreak of the pandemic in 2020 and the Hong Kong national security law of 2021.

Due to intense protests, subsequent to the Hong Kong government's trial to pass the Hong Kong extradition bill between 2019 and 2020, the NPCSC passed the national security law for Hong Kong. In Macau, the citizens are more receptive to a "Chinese" identity than Hong Kong people.[72] The society in Macau is more politically conservative.[73] The government enacted with little opposition from the legislators and citizens a national security law under Article 23 of the MBL in March 2009. Macau was praised by the central government for this enactment of legislation.[74] The courts also play a conservative role in cases that are politically sensitive. This chapter uses the TUI's decisions on restrictions on the right to assembly and demonstrations as evidence.

Between 1999 and 2019, The TUI received 22 appeals against the administrative decisions denying or restricting assemblies and demonstrations. Overall, the TUI awarded significant leeway to the executive when adjudicating these cases. In Case 75/2010, the applicant who was aggrieved by a decision of the Public Security Police Force appealed to the TUI. The TUI stated that "In principle, courts cannot judge whether the exercise of the discretionary power is appropriate in administrative litigation. It may only declare the illegality of an administrative decision and annul it in the circumstance where the exercise of discretionary power by the executive authorities is manifestly erroneous or totally unreasonable".[75] Due to the fact that the TUI is at the apex of Macau's judicial system and its decisions are final, once it supports decisions restricting people's right to assembly, the applicants cannot appeal to a higher court. The deferential and conservative attitude makes an inroad to the judicial protection of freedom of assembly.

In Case 34/2011 and Case 6/2011, the TUI supported the government's denial of assemblies that were close to the Office of the Chief Executive of Macau and the Central Liaison Office, respectively. Although the denied assemblies and demonstrations kept a reasonable distance from these buildings, the TUI still dismissed the appeals on the grounds that the event places were located in a high-density residential area, had intensive traffic or were close to schools and historical buildings.[76] In Case 95/2014 and Case 100/2014, the TUI supported the prohibition of public meetings on the theme of "Promoting Civic Referendum on the Election of Chief Executive of 2014" by redefining the term "assembly". The TUI stated that "an assembly (for the purposes of the freedom of assembly) means any gathering of people convened at some places for a common purpose of exchanging ideas, debating and forming an opinion collectively".[77] From the TUI's judgement, public meetings on the theme of "Promoting Civic Referendum on the Election of Chief Executive of 2014" were aimed to understand and survey Macau residents about their opinion regarding the possible change in the Chief Executive election. It was a survey, not an assembly prescribed and protected by laws because its purpose was not to exchange ideas, debate or form collective opinion. Therefore, the TUI denied its jurisdiction to the appeal.[78] The TUI's reasoning and decision were not logically persuasive. Public meetings that promoted civic referendum and universal suffrage assemblies were assemblies for residents to express their preference and to debate on the election of the Chief Executive by universal suffrage.

Case 94/2019 is even more controversial. The TUI rejected a series of public meetings supporting the anti-extradition bill amendment protests in Hong Kong. The organisers intended to hold public meetings, of which the purpose was to urge the Hong Kong police to strictly observe the Convention against Torture and not use force unlawfully.[79] The TUI prohibited the meetings on two grounds. First, no evidence certified by any authorities showed that the Hong Kong police used force unlawfully or tortured any protestors. There was plentiful evidence showing that protestors in Hong Kong were involved in crimes and the police had to maintain social order. The public meetings were seen to be unsubstantiated attacks against the Hong Kong police.[80] Second, the TUI stated that under "One Country, Two Systems", Hong Kong and Macau were independent regions and should not interfere with each other's domestic affairs. The Macau government cannot allow an assembly that might affect Hong Kong's local affairs.[81] But the TUI's reasoning was not convincing. As for the first reason, to urge the Hong Kong police to act by the requirements of international conventions is an expression of opinions and attitudes, which is the purpose of guaranteeing the right of assembly. As for the second ground, public meetings organised by civic society are not an act of government. The TUI regarded assemblies as interference with domestic affairs of other regions, which is not persuasive according to the international law or "One Country, Two Systems".

All of these decisions of TUI demonstrated that it did not want to provoke the Macau government and the central government. Its definition of assembly in Cases 95/2014 and 100/2014 narrowed down the scope of freedom of assembly. This is in sharp contrast to the Hong Kong court's approach to rights interpretation, that generous and purposive to the interpretation of those rights whilst restrictions to them are to be narrowly interpreted.[82] In Case 94/2019, the TUI for the first time used the principles enshrined in the Constitution of the PRC and the Basic Laws to restrict people's right to assembly and demonstration, saying that in contrast to Macau citizen's right to assembly and demonstration, upholding the basic constitutional principles of the SARs is undoubtedly more important legal interests.[83]

Conclusion: More Convergence of Macau Judicial Review towards China

This chapter has identified a high degree of similarity in judicial review practice between Macau and China in three aspects. First, Macau preserves its own legal system and retains judicial review mechanisms, hailing from the Portuguese legal systems and traditions, such as constitutional judicial review and abstract review of administrative regulations. But the judicial review practice by the TUI in the last two decades shows that these judicial review mechanisms were rarely used by the courts. Very few legislation and administrative regulations were reviewed by the TUI. Second, both in Macau and China, the application of proportionality is associated with significant deference accorded to the government. Proportionality does not play a role in judicial review as a strong individual rights protection tool. Third, the cases in relation to the right to assembly and demonstration reveal the TUI's conservative and self-restrained in adjudicating political-sensitive cases.

Ignazio Castellucci has observed that "Macau generally offers less resistance to the changes required by its reversion to the PRC. It offers a more homogeneous society with deep Chinese roots, smaller bargaining power, and greater legal flexibility vis-a-vis new governmental policies, whether introduced through legislation, administration, or the judiciary".[84] Some scholars have also noticed that the legal community of Macau is informed and characterised by Chinese legal elements through the judges, lawyers and government officials who are educated and trained with Chinese law in China.[85] For instance, from 2011 to 2019, Judge Sam Hou Fai, Judge Viriato Lima and Judge Song Man Lei were on the bench of the TUI. Both Judge Sam Hou Fai and Judge Song Man Lei started their legal education in China and received their LLB degrees from Peking University. When addressing important and controversial public law issues,[86] the TUI cited many Chinese sources, including the Constitution of the PRC, Chinese domestic laws and Chinese legal scholars' opinions.[87]

This chapter provides additional evidence of the convergence of Macau's judicial review towards China. There are increasing elements of "One Country" over "Two Systems" in Macau. This trend of convergence would probably continue and become increasingly obvious over the next two decades.

Notes

1 Eric C. Ip, *Hybrid Constitutionalism: The Politics of Constitutional Review in the Chinese Special Administrative Regions* (CUP 2019) 10.
2 Basic Law of Macau, arts 5 and 8.
3 MBL, art 2.
4 Eric C. Ip, 'The Evolution of Constitutional Adjudication in the Chinese Special Administrative Regions: Theory and Evidence' (2013) 61 *The American Journal of Comparative Law* 799, 826.
5 MBL, art 8.
6 The Yearbook of Macau 2020, p 121. available at https://yearbook.gcs.gov.mo/uploads/yearbook_pdf/2020/myb2020c.pdf.
7 Yash Ghai, 'The Intersection of Chinese Law and the Common Law in the Special Administrative Region of Hong Kong: Question of Technique or Politics?' (2007) *Hong Kong Law Journal* 363, 367.
8 Ignazio Castellucci, 'Legal Hybridity in Hong Kong and Macau' (2011) 57 *McGill Law Journal* 665, 694–695.
9 There are many excellent works that compare judicial review and human rights protection in Hong Kong and Macau. Most scholars contend that the Court of Final Appeal of Hong Kong is very active in reviewing legislative and administrative actions and its activism is regarded as a significant part of Hong Kong's constitutional landscape. In contrast, the Court of Final Appeal of Macau was "inactive", "timid" and deferential in judicial reviewing. But very few academic works notice the similarities between China and Macau in terms of judicial review practice. Ip, *Hybrid Constitutionalism* (n 1) 16; Albert H. Y. Chen and P. Y. Lo, 'The Constitutional Orders of "One Country, Two Systems": A Comparative Study of the Visible and Invisible Bases of Constitutional Review and Proportionality Analysis in the Chinese Special Administrative Regions of Hong Kong and Macau' in Rosalind Dixon and Adrienne Stone (eds), *The Invisible Constitution in Comparative Perspective* (CUP 2018) 260–261; Jorge Oliveira and Paulo Cardinal, 'Macau's Court of Final Appeal' in Simon N. M. Young and Yash Ghai (eds), *Hong Kong's Court of Final Appeal: The Development of the Law in China's Hong Kong* (CUP 2014) 618; Paul Cardinal, 'Fundamental rights in Macau: From Territory Under Portuguese Administration to Special Administrative Region of the PRC' in Jorge AF Godinho (ed), *Study on Macau Civil, Commercial, Constitutional and Criminal Law* (LexisNexis 2011) 28; Simon N. M. Young, 'Fundamental Rights and the Basic Laws of the Hong Kong and Macau Special Administrative Regions' in Jorge Oliveira and Paulo Cardinal (eds), *One Country Two Systems, Three Legal Orders – Perspectives of Evolution* (Springer 2009) 683.
10 Rainer Grote, 'Judicial Review', *Max Planck Encyclopaedia of Comparative Constitutional Law* (2018) para 1 <https://oxcon.ouplaw.com/view/10.1093/law-mpeccol/law-mpeccol-e334?rskey=LpB90t&result=1&prd=MPECCOL> accessed 12 October 2021.
11 *Ibid.*, para 22.
12 Under Portuguese colonial rule, the Legislative Assembly shared legislative power with the Governor of Macau. The decrees enacted by the Governor of Macau and the laws enacted by the Legislative Assembly have the same legal effect. Organic Statute of Macau, art 5; Yu Wang, 'The Discussion of source of law in Macau Special Administrative Region' (2014) 20 *Academic Journal of "One Country Two Systems"* 13, 17.
13 MBL, arts 50, 58, 64.
14 Before the Portuguese handover of Macau to China, the form was the *portaria* (訓令). Jorge AF Godinho, *Macau Business Law and Legal System* (LexisNexis 2007) 14.
15 HKBL, art 158; MBL, art 143.
16 Vitalino Canas, 'The General Regime of Fundamental Rights in the Basic Law and in the International Instruments' in Jorge Oliveira and Paulo Cardinal (eds), *One Country Two Systems, Three Legal Orders – Perspectives of Evolution* (Springer 2009) 673.
17 Paolo Cardinal, 'Revisiting the Macanese Amparo of Fundamental Rights: A Quest under the Searchlight of the Principle of Continuity with a Stopover in Comparative Law' (2009) 83 *Philippine Law Journal* 833, 836, 838–840.
18 Cardinal, 'Fundamental rights in Macau' (n 9) 29.

19 This law was amended by Law 9/2004 and Law 9/2009.
20 Case 1/2000, at 3; Case 2/2000, at 2.
21 Case 9/2006, at 8.
22 *Ibid.*, at 8.
23 Ip, *Hybrid Constitutionalism* (n 1) 121; Chen and Lo (n 9) 237.
24 Case 9/2006, at 3.
25 Case 28/2006, at 28–29.
26 *Ibid.*, at 31.
27 *Ibid.*
28 Case 8/2007, at 9.
29 Case 5/2005, at 9.
30 CPAC, art 88(1).
31 Case 28/2006, at 33.
32 Case 9/2006, at 7–8.
33 Basic Law of Judicial Organisation, art 30.
34 João Nuno Calvão da Silva, 'The Administrative Litigation of the MASAR' in Manual Trigo (ed), *Report on Macau Law* (LexisNexis 2014) 125.
35 CPAC, arts 8, 9.
36 The statistics are published on the website of the TUI. Available at http://www.court.gov.mo/zh/subpage/statisticstui (visited on 17 April 2020).
37 Cases 2/2004, 5/2010, 25/2011, 9/2012, 19/2012, 27/2012, 33/2012, 88/2018, 90/2018, 102/2018, 112/2018.
38 Cases 7/2007, 2/2017.
39 Case 2/2004, at 6.
40 *Ibid.*, at 7.
41 Case 25/2011, at 2.
42 *Ibid.*, at 2.
43 *Ibid.*, at 6.
44 Case 5/2010, at 34.
45 *Ibid.*, 34
46 Case 5/2010, at 32.
47 *Ibid.*, 35.
48 Alec Stone Sweet and Jud Mathews, *Proportionality Balancing and Constitutional Governance: A Comparative and Global Approach* (OUP 2019) 145–146.
49 Article 62 of the Constitution of the PRC provides that "The NPC exercises the following functions and powers: (1) to amend the Constitution; (2) to supervise the enforcement of the Constitution." Article 67 of the Constitution of the PRC provides that "The NPCSC exercises the following functions and powers: (1) to interpret the Constitution and supervise its enforcement."
50 The Law on Legislation was amended in 2015. The provisions of this law referred to in this chapter are the Law on Legislation of 2015.
51 Before the ALL of 2014, the Supreme People's Court implicitly and explicitly asserted that the Chinese courts could review rules (*guizhangs*) and administrative normative documents. In the Supreme People's Court Interpretation on the Administrative Litigation Law of 2000, Article 62(2) provided that when the people's courts hear administrative litigation cases, they can cite legitimate and valid rules and administrative normative documents in their judgements. In the Minutes of the Symposiums of the Supreme People's Court concerning Application of Laws in Adjudicating Administrative Cases, it explicitly affirmed that the courts could scrutinise *guizhangs* and administrative normative documents.
52 Case 112/2018, at 13.
53 *Ibid.*
54 Case 6/2000, at 11. "The normative core of the principle of proportionality is a prohibition of excess, which implies that there should be an appropriate relationship between means and purpose. This core meaning gives rise to the three elements of the principle of proportionality: suitability, necessity and balance. To achieve an aim, the measure to be taken should be suitable in relation to that aim. Amid all the suitable measures, the one that is least harmful to legitimate interests should be chosen. The conflicting interests should be balanced on a proportionate scale in light of the public interest at stake."

55 Cases 50/2010, 8/2012, 38/2012, 69/2012, 76/2012, 83/2012, 32/2013, 26/2014, 62/2015, 83/2016, 65/2018.
56 Cases 27/2003, 14/2005, 1/2006, 8/2006, 31/2006, 12/2011, 13/2011, 13/2012, 25/2012, 26/2014, 22/2017.
57 Case 36/2006.
58 Cases 27/2003, 26/2014, 104/2014, 101/2019.
59 Case 69/2016, at 9.
60 *Ibid.*, 17.
61 The Administrative Tribunal of the SPC, *Chinese Administrative Adjudication Cases Volume I* (China Legal Publishing House 2010) 92.
62 Dengfeng Yang, 'Reasonableness, Good Faith or Principle of Proportionality: Whither Legitimate Aim Test to Go' (2021) 4 *Peking University Law Journal* 943, 945.
63 The Administrative Tribunal of the SPC (n 61) 92, 98.
64 ALL of 2014, art. 6; ALL of 2017, art. 6.
65 Interpretation of the SPC on Several Issues concerning the Implementation of the ALL, 8 March 2000, art. 56.
66 Haibo He, 'On Obvious Improperness of Administrative Acts' (2016) *Chinese Journal of Law* 70, 72.
67 The Administrative Tribunal of thc SPC (n 61) 97–98.
68 Alec Stone Sweet and Jud Mathews, 'Proportionality and Rights Protection in Asia: Hong Kong, Malaysia, South Korea, Taiwan – Whither Singapore?' (2017) 29 *Singapore Academy of Law Journal* 774, 781.
69 Robert Alexy, *A Theory of Constitutional Rights*, 47 (Julian Rivers trans., OUP 2002).
70 Ip, 'The Evolution of Constitutional Adjudication in the Chinese Special Administrative Regions' (n 4) 819.
71 Chen and Lo (n 9), 238–239.
72 Ip, 'The Evolution of Constitutional Adjudication in the Chinese Special Administrative Regions' (n 4) 820.
73 Herbert Yee, *Macau in Transition: From Colony to Autonomous Region* (Palgrave 2001).
74 Castellucci (n 8) 701.
75 Case 75/2010, 6.
76 Case 34/2011, at 5; Case 6/2011, at 6–7.
77 Case 95/2014, at 6.
78 *Ibid.*, at 7–8.
79 Case 94/2019, at 2.
80 *Ibid.*, at 14–16.
81 *Ibid.*, at 16–18.
82 Ng Ka Ling and Others v Director of Immigration (1999) 2 HKCFAR 4, 34E-G; *HKSAR v Ng Kung Siu & Another* (1999) 2 HKCFAR 442, 455H-I; *Gurung Kesh Bahadur v Director of Immigration* (2002) 5 HKCFAR 480, [24].
83 Case 94/2019, at 18.
84 Castellucci (n 8) 699.
85 *Ibid.*, 703; Chen and Lo (n 9) 265.
86 Cases 28/2006, 100/2014.
87 Jorge Godinho and Paulo Cardinal, 'Macau's Court of Final Appeal' in Simon N. M. Young and Yash Ghai (eds), *Hong Kong's Court of Final Appeal: The Development of the Law in China's Hong Kong* (CUP 2014) 626; Dayuan Han, 'The Issue of the Effectiveness of the Constitution in Macau Special Administrative Region' (2016) 1 *Academic Journal of "One Country Two Systems"* 1.

Bibliography

Calvão da Silva JN, 'The Administrative Litigation of the MASAR' in Manual Trigo (ed), *Report on Macau Law* (LexisNexis 2014).

Cardinal P, 'Revisiting the Macanese Amparo of Fundamental Rights: A Quest under the Searchlight of the Principle of Continuity with a Stopover in Comparative Law' (2009) 83 *Philippine Law Journal* 833.

______ 'Fundamental rights in Macau: From Territory Under Portuguese Administration to Special Administrative Region of the PRC' in Jorge AF Godinho (ed), *Study on Macau Civil, Commercial, Constitutional and Criminal Law* (LexisNexis 2011).

Castellucci I, 'Legal Hybridity in Hong Kong and Macau' (2011) 57 *McGill Law Journal* 665.

Chen AHY and Lo PY, 'The Constitutional Orders of "One Country, Two Systems": A Comparative Study of the Visible and Invisible Bases of Constitutional Review and Proportionality Analysis in the Chinese Special Administrative Regions of Hong Kong and Macau' in Rosalind Dixon and Adrienne Stone (eds), *The Invisible Constitution in Comparative Perspective* (CUP 2018).

Ip EC, 'The Evolution of Constitutional Adjudication in the Chinese Special Administrative Regions: Theory and Evidence' (2013) 61 *The American Journal of Comparative Law* 799.

______ *Hybrid Constitutionalism: The Politics of Constitutional Review in the Chinese Special Administrative Regions* (CUP 2019).

Ieong MU and Wu X, 'A Securitized "One Country, Two Systems"?' (2021) 61 *Asian Survey* 663.

Krebs JR, 'One Country, Three Systems? Judicial Review in Macau after Ng Ka Ling' (2000) 10 *Washington International Law Journal* 111.

Oliveira J and Cardinal P (eds), *One Country Two Systems, Three Legal Orders – Perspectives of Evolution* (Springer 2009).

______ 'Macau's Court of Final Appeal' in Simon N. M. Young and Yash Ghai (eds), *Hong Kong's Court of Final Appeal: The Development of the Law in China's Hong Kong* (CUP 2014).

PART III

Rights, Society, and Economy

12

NATIONAL SECURITY LAW IN HONG KONG

Transforming 'One Country, Two Systems' as a Model of Regional Autonomy

Carole J. Petersen

Introduction

On 28 May 2020, the National People's Congress (NPC) of the People's Republic of China (PRC) adopted a Decision authorizing the NPC Standing Committee (NPCSC) to draft a law to protect national security in the Hong Kong Special Administrative Region.[1] Less than one month later, on 30 June 2020, the NPCSC adopted the Law of the People's Republic of China on Safeguarding National Security in Hong Kong (NSL).[2] The NSL was quickly added to Annex III of the Hong Kong Basic Law, which serves as Hong Kong's regional constitution,[3] and brought into force that same night.[4] The local police began arresting people for suspected violations the very next day.[5]

This chapter analyzes the impact of the NSL on 'One Country, Two Systems' as a model of regional autonomy. The second section begins by analyzing why the model described in the Sino-British Joint Declaration[6] and the Basic Law was originally viewed as promising an exceptionally high degree of autonomy, with the local government enjoying certain powers that are normally associated with an independent state. However, as demonstrated in the third section, the model also provided the Central Government with significant powers and inserted various connecting doors between the two legal systems. Article 23 – which obligated Hong Kong to enact legislation to protect what Beijing deems to be matters of national security – is one of those connecting doors. Although Hong Kong did have a number of relevant ordinances (including laws prohibiting treason, sedition, and theft of state secrets), it never fully implemented Article 23. Beijing used this gap in the local legislative framework – as well as the prolonged anti-government protests of 2019 – to justify its decision to impose the NSL on Hong Kong.[7]

However, as demonstrated in the fourth section of this chapter, the NSL has done much more than fill a perceived gap in Hong Kong's criminal law. Rather, the NSL has fundamentally altered the PRC's relationship with Hong Kong and greatly weakened the legal firewall that was supposed to separate the two legal systems. The NSL has established powerful new security institutions, which are now operating openly in the territory and under the direct control of Beijing. These institutions are robustly enforcing

DOI: 10.4324/9781003128243-15

the NSL and taking full advantage of their new powers. They have also helped to orchestrate a broad campaign to eliminate competitive politics in Hong Kong and ensure that only 'patriots' can serve in important sectors of society, including the public schools, the civil service, and the Legislative and District Councils.[8] Anyone who objects to these 'reforms' risks being accused of aiding the 'foreign forces' who were allegedly fomenting unrest in Hong Kong.[9]

The fifth section of the chapter then analyzes the sharpest end of the NSL – the new criminal offenses, which are being interpreted and applied in a manner that violates the International Covenant on Civil and Political Rights (ICCPR). The PRC is still not a state party to the ICCPR. Thus, the fact that the ICCPR continued to apply in Hong Kong after 1997 (and enjoyed constitutional status by virtue of Article 39 of the Basic Law) was considered a key indicator of Hong Kong's autonomy. Interestingly, the NSL states, in Articles 4 and 5, that the rights stated in the ICCPR and the Hong Kong Basic Law shall continue to be protected. Yet, thus far, it does not appear that the police or prosecutors are taking these provisions very seriously. Rather they are interpreting the vague language in the NSL as broadly as possible. As of this writing, there have only been a handful of convictions; but hundreds of residents have been arrested – primarily for non-violent speech acts or for political activities that were perfectly legal prior to the NSL.[10] Most will sit in jail for at least a year before trial, because the NSL reverses the normal presumption in favor of bail. The government has also begun prosecuting people under an old colonial law prohibiting 'sedition,' which had not been enforced for decades because of its conflicts with the freedom of expression.[11] In addition to individuals, the local authorities have also targeted the media, trade unions, political parties, and other civil society organizations.[12] The NSL purports to apply extra-territorially,[13] meaning that it can be used to threaten critics who live overseas.[14]

Eventually, we may see Hong Kong judges (particularly in the appellate courts) endeavor to interpret vague language in the NSL so as to better comply with the ICCPR. However, the NPCSC holds the overriding power of interpretation, of both the NSL and the Basic Law.[15] Thus, Hong Kong judgments that are deemed too liberal may only generate more intervention from Beijing, further damaging autonomy and the rule of law.

What Did 'One Country, Two Systems' Promise?

In order to understand the model of autonomy that was promised to Hong Kong, it is important to have some appreciation of the territory's history. From 1946 to 1971, Hong Kong was regarded as a 'colonized people' and listed by the United Nations (UN) as a non-self-governing territory under British administration. This created a legal presumption that the residents would, at the time of decolonization, exercise their right to self-determination and choose among three options: independence, association with an independent state, or integration with an independent state.[16] However, China had a competing territorial claim, partly because the New Territories portion of Hong Kong had only been leased to the United Kingdom for 99 years (whereas Hong Kong Island and Kowloon were ceded 'in perpetuity') and partly because China had long argued that all three treaties were 'unequal' and invalid.[17]

In 1972, the PRC formally requested that Hong Kong and Macau be deleted from the UN's list of non-self-governing territories, on the ground that they were not colonies but rather 'Chinese territory occupied by the British and Portuguese' authorities.[18] The United Kingdom did not object and the recommendation was adopted as part of a report to the UN General Assembly, without any discussion or public consultation. Although the UN continued to treat Hong Kong as a British colony well after 1972, the act of removing it from the list of non-self-governing territories meant that Hong Kong's future would be resolved through bilateral negotiations. The Joint Declaration was signed in 1984 and registered with the UN in 1985. At that point, Hong Kong entered the 'transition' period, during which time the Basic Law was drafted.[19]

If faithfully implemented, the high degree of autonomy promised in the Joint Declaration and the Basic Law might have provided a form of palliative *internal* self-determination, a way of resolving the conflict between China's territorial claim and the normal rights of a colonized people.[20] Indeed, on paper, 'One Country, Two Systems' provides Hong Kong with an extraordinary range of executive and legislative powers, including some that we would normally associate with an independent state.[21] For example, Hong Kong issues its own currency and travel documents and maintains its own border controls. It also maintains a separate customs regime and its own membership in the World Trade Organization. In addition to these specific powers, Hong Kong is vested with general executive and legislative powers, defined in exceedingly broad terms.[22]

Perhaps most importantly, the territory retained its separate common law legal system, with an independent judiciary and the power of final adjudication. There is no appeal beyond Hong Kong's Court of Final Appeal (CFA) and no mechanism by which a court in Mainland China can overturn a judgment in a specific case. The CFA is authorized to invite 'non-permanent judges' from other common-law jurisdictions and a number of distinguished judges from the United Kingdom, Australia, and New Zealand have served in that capacity.[23] These provisions were included to increase confidence in Hong Kong's ability to maintain rule of law and a high degree of civil liberties. Indeed, Hong Kong's judiciary has given meaning to the promise that the ICCPR would remain in force in Hong Kong. Since 1997, the CFA has repeatedly held that the Basic Law gives constitutional status to the ICCPR and that a local statute that purports to restrict ICCPR-protected rights is only valid if it constitutes a proportionate measure adopted in pursuit of one of the legitimate purposes specified in the ICCPR (which would include national security).[24] Prior to the enactment of the NSL, it was also common for Hong Kong judges to use the ICCPR and the Hong Kong Bill of Rights Ordinance as a guide when interpreting vague statutory language.

But 'One Country, Two Systems' was also plagued by inherent weaknesses, including the lack of a neutral dispute resolution mechanism, the uncertainty regarding 2047,[25] and the lack of detail in the Joint Declaration regarding local democracy. The treaty promised that the local government would be 'composed of local inhabitants' with a local legislature 'constituted by elections' and a Chief Executive who is 'selected by election or through consultations held locally' prior to being appointed by the Central Government.[26] A good faith interpretation of these provisions would support an expectation of local democracy. Indeed, Beijing and London both encouraged that expectation when the Joint Declaration was circulated for public consultation.[27] But Beijing later blocked democracy reforms in Hong Kong.[28] Lacking the legitimacy of an election victory, the appointed Chief Executive depends on Beijing for political support. This has created an informal system of 'patron-client politics' in which Beijing rewards those in Hong Kong who support the appointed Chief Executive.[29] However, Beijing also has numerous formal mechanisms by which it can intervene, which are addressed in the next section.

The Connecting Doors in 'One Country, Two Systems'

Despite the detailed provisions protecting Hong Kong's autonomy, Beijing was careful to install numerous 'connecting doors' in the Basic Law, enabling it to exercise influence over all three branches of government should it wish to do so. For example, Article 45 provides that Hong Kong's Chief Executive 'shall be selected by election or through consultations held locally and be appointed by the Central People's Government'. Beijing tightly controls the local selection process, ensuring that it can handpick the head of the executive branch. Beijing can also exercise legislative power over Hong Kong: the NPCSC can set aside a local law by determining that it is 'not in conformity' with the Basic Law (Article 17) or apply a national law to Hong Kong by adding it to Annex III of the Basic Law (Article 18).

Beijing also insisted, during the drafting of the Basic Law, that the NPCSC must retain the overriding power to interpret the Basic Law. In contrast, Hong Kong members of the Basic Law Drafting Committee argued that the power to interpret Hong Kong's constitutional instrument should rest with its own independent judiciary.[30] The result, stated in Article 158 of the Basic Law, is an awkward compromise between Hong Kong's common law system and China's socialist system. The local courts can and do interpret the Basic Law in the course of adjudicating cases. But the NPCSC (a political body controlled by the Chinese Communist Party) can issue a legislative interpretation at any time, which the Hong Kong courts are then obligated to follow. In theory, the NPCSC is supposed to consult the Basic Law Committee (which has representatives from Hong Kong) before exercising its powers under Articles 17, 18, or 158. But that process has been shrouded in secrecy, making it impossible to ascertain whether the Hong Kong members exercise any influence.[31] It was originally hoped that the NPCSC would use its power to interpret the Basic Law sparingly. However, as conflicts developed, Beijing began relying more often on NPCSC 'interpretations' and 'decisions' to influence legal and political outcomes in the territory. These documents are included on the Hong Kong government's published website for the Basic Law, where they are described as 'instruments' and treated as equivalent to the text of the Basic Law. In essence, the power of interpretation allows Beijing to amend and supplement Hong Kong's Basic Law, without having to go through the formal amendment process.[32] For example, in 2016, the NPCSC issued an interpretation of Article 104 of the Basic Law which was clearly intended to influence pending litigation. The case turned on the validity of the oaths of office taken by two elected Hong Kong legislators. As written, Article 104 of the Basic Law is very simple – it simply requires legislators, judges, and other officials to swear to uphold the Basic Law and to swear allegiance to the Hong Kong Special Administrative Region of the PRC. But before the Hong Kong judge could issue its judgment in the case, the NPCSC issued its own lengthy interpretation of Article 104, which added new requirements and stated that 'no arrangements shall be made for retaking' an oath that is determined to be invalid.[33] This was Beijing's way of signaling that it wanted the two elected legislators disqualified and to have no opportunity to retake their oaths of office.

Article 23 of the Basic Law is another example of a 'connecting door' between the two legal systems. Hong Kong residents were always concerned by Article 23 because similar criminal offenses have been used in the PRC to stifle free speech. But they were led to believe that the local legislature would define the relevant offenses. This is because Article 23 states:

> The Hong Kong Special Administrative Region shall enact laws on its own to prohibit any act of treason, secession, sedition, subversion against the Central People's Government, or theft of state secrets, to prohibit foreign political organizations or bodies from conducting political activities in the Region, and to prohibit political organizations or bodies of the Region from establishing ties with foreign political organizations or bodies.

Unfortunately, the Hong Kong government's only attempt to fully implement Article 23 was a dismal failure. The National Security (Legislative Provisions) Bill, which was introduced in Hong Kong's Legislative Council in 2003, was vastly superior to the NSL and, for the most part, complied with the ICCPR. But the local government made a number of mistakes, insisting on an accelerated timetable for legislative scrutiny and resisting many amendments proposed by legislators. This approach created significant public anxiety and more than 500,000 people joined a protest march on 1 July 2003. Although Chief Executive Tung Chee-Hwa subsequently offered some key amendments, it was too late to regain public confidence and even legislators who were traditionally pro-government were reluctant to support the Bill.[34] The government eventually withdrew the Bill and never attempted to reintroduce it. In retrospect, this was a grave mistake.

Despite this failure to fully implement Article 23, Hong Kong did have a significant body of local law that fell within its scope. For example, the Crimes Ordinance (Cap 200) prohibits both treason and sedition and the Official Secrets Ordinance (Cap 521) prohibits espionage and the disclosure of a wide range of government information.[35] The Societies Ordinance (Cap 151) gives the government broad powers to control the registration and operation of societies and it was amended, in 1997, to incorporate the final two clauses in Article 23.[36] Indeed, the local government used those powers, in 2018, to ban a tiny political party (with only two known members) that had peacefully advocated for independence.[37] Hong Kong also enacted, in 2002, the UN (Anti-Terrorism Measures) Ordinance (Cap 575).

Nonetheless, officials from Mainland China frequently complained that Hong Kong was 'the only place in the world' without laws protecting national security.[38] This complaint became especially common after the sustained period of anti-government protests in 2019. In January 2020, Luo Huining, the newly appointed Director of the Liaison Office of the Central Government in Hong Kong, proclaimed that the city was vulnerable to external forces, infiltration, and sabotage.[39] What he did not reveal was that Beijing had already decided to impose its own version of a national security law in Hong Kong. Ten days before it came into force, the NPCSC published a 'summary' of the law, which named the new offences (secession, subversion of state power, terrorist activities, and colluding with foreign forces) but did not define them. Local politicians who complained about this lack of transparency were accused of being unpatriotic.

When the NSL was published (on the night that it came into force), it became clear that it was designed to do far more than fill a perceived gap in local criminal laws. It also imported much of Mainland China's security apparatus into the territory and imposed a new set of criminal procedures for political offenses. The firewall that was supposed to separate the two criminal justice systems has largely disappeared for political offenses, causing foreign governments to question whether Hong Kong can still be treated as a separate legal system for trade and extradition agreements.[40] Moreover, while the ICCPR is formally still 'in force', it is now regularly violated. The extent of this transformation is illustrated in the next two sections.

New Security Institutions and a New Relationship with Beijing

The NSL has established powerful new security institutions, which are operating openly in Hong Kong, accountable to Beijing, and not subject to judicial oversight. The policy-making institution is the Committee for Safeguarding National Security, which is 'under the supervision of and accountable to' the Central Government (Article 12). Information relating to its work is 'not subject to disclosure' and its decisions 'shall not be amenable to judicial review' (Article 14). Hong Kong officials (including the Chief Executive) serve on this Committee but the key position is the National Security Advisor, who represents Beijing (Article 15). This gives Beijing a direct role in formulating policies to carry out the Hong Kong government's duties under the NSL, which extend well beyond enforcing new criminal offenses.

For example, education is one of the sectors that is targeted in the NSL, no doubt because university and secondary school students have played a leading role in Hong Kong's social movements. Article 9 obligates the Hong Kong government to strengthen its regulation of all matters concerning national security, including in schools, and Article 10 directs it to promote national security education. Soon after the NSL came into force, Hong Kong's Education Bureau directed local libraries to remove books that might violate the NSL.[41] Authorities have also disciplined more than 150 primary and secondary school teachers (and even deregistered some teachers for life) for involvement in the 2019 protests and other activities viewed as 'defaming the nation'.[42] In February 2021, the government issued 'guidelines and curriculum arrangements for safeguarding national security and national security education' and it has since introduced further guidance for the integration of national security education across several secondary school subjects.[43] Although Hong Kong's universities are still permitted to design their own curriculum, they have been instructed to develop compulsory national security courses.[44] Presumably, all of these policy decisions have been discussed and approved by the Committee for Safeguarding National Security, where Beijing's National Security Advisor has a seat at the table. This violates the Basic Law, which provides that Hong Kong's educational institutions 'of all kinds' may retain their autonomy and enjoy academic freedom.[45]

The NSL also establishes an operational institution, the Office for Safeguarding National Security of the Central People's Government.[46] It is staffed and funded by the Central Government and has broad powers. Its formal role is to collect and analyze intelligence information and to guide, coordinate, and generally supervise all of the relevant authorities in the Hong Kong Government. It also monitors 'organs of foreign countries and international organizations' and 'non-governmental organizations and news agencies' from outside Hong Kong and China.[47] Although its staff are supposed to abide by Hong Kong laws, there is no mechanism for holding them accountable for violations of those laws.[48] They are expressly exempted from the jurisdiction of the Hong Kong SAR for any acts performed in the course of their duty; their vehicles are also not subject to search, inspection, or detention by local law enforcement.[49]

The NSL also gives Beijing a role in local policing, something that would have been unthinkable under the original 'One Country, Two Systems' model of autonomy. Pursuant to Article 16 of the NSL, a new 'special branch' has been created in the Hong Kong Police Force to investigate NSL offences. It can recruit 'qualified professionals and technical personnel' directly from Mainland China.[50] It also has enormous new powers,[51] including the power to conduct warrantless searches of any 'premises, vehicles, vessels, aircraft and other relevant places and electronic devices that may contain evidence of an offence'.[52] The Committee for Safeguarding National Security quickly promulgated rules for such searches, as well as 'operating guidelines and principles' for covert surveillance without judicial approval.[53] Because the Committee's decisions are not 'amenable to judicial review', we can assume that these rules and guidelines cannot be challenged in court.[54]

The NSL also provides for a special prosecution division for NSL offences. Beijing has a direct role in determining who serves in this division and who shall lead it. The prosecutors are appointed by the Secretary for Justice but only after she has obtained consent from the Committee for Safeguarding National Security, which is supervised by the Central Government.[55] Thus far, the prosecutors in this special division appear to be enforcing the NSL with great energy. There is, however, no evidence that they are exercising prosecutorial discretion to avoid violating the ICCPR. The local authorities appear to be acting on the assumption that any restriction on civil liberties – no matter how draconian – is acceptable, so long as it is done in the name of national security. They are also taking full advantage of the procedural changes instituted by the NSL, including Article 46, which gives the Secretary for Justice the power to dispense with a jury trial,[56] and Article 42, which creates a legal presumption against bail, providing that bail shall not be granted unless there are 'sufficient grounds for believing that the criminal suspect or defendant will not continue to commit acts endangering national security'. The local government now routinely opposes bail applications, leaving many defendants in jail for more than a year while awaiting trial. Pretrial detention has thus become a convenient form of punishment, making a mockery of the presumption of innocence (although the NSL purports to protect it in Article 5).

Finally, the NSL has also created a special category of judges in Hong Kong. Pursuant to Article 44, the Chief Executive designates a list of judges from the Magistracies, District Courts, Court of First Instance (CFI), Court of Appeal, and the CFA who are authorized to 'handle cases' concerning offences that 'endanger national security'. Article 44 further provides that this list cannot include judges who have 'made any statement or behaved in any manner endangering national security'. Given the vagueness of this standard, it is possible that a judge who grants bail when the government opposes it or acquits a defendant may be removed from the list.

The NSL has thus created a new criminal justice system in Hong Kong, one that runs in tandem with its traditional common-law system but is reserved for political offenses. Beijing now has numerous mechanisms for influencing the investigation, detention, and prosecution of political opponents in the territory. But just in case this does not provide sufficient oversight, the NSL also contains a mechanism for removing a defendant to Mainland China. Article 55 states that the central authorities can exercise jurisdiction if (1) the case is 'complex' due to the involvement of a foreign country or external elements; (2) a 'serious situation occurs' and the Hong Kong Government is 'unable to effectively enforce' the law; or (3) a 'major and imminent threat' to national security has occurred. The procedures for shifting jurisdiction are remarkably simple: the Central Government only needs to approve a 'request' from Hong Kong's Chief Executive, which would certainly be made if Beijing suggested it. There appears to be no procedure by which an individual could judicially review the Chief Executive's decision to request that a case be transferred.

If the Central Government asserts jurisdiction then it will designate a prosecutor and the Supreme People's Court will designate a Mainland court to adjudicate the case. China's Criminal Procedure Law and all other relevant national laws will then apply, including those relating to investigations, interrogation, prosecution, trial, and penalties.[57] In essence, the NSL creates the possibility of extradition to Mainland China without even the formality of an extradition hearing (a supremely ironic result after the anti-extradition protests of 2019). This is why many foreign governments have suspended their extradition agreements with Hong Kong: they no longer trust that a fugitive will not be 're-extradited' to Mainland China.[58]

The next section examines the new criminal offenses, the limited number of NSL cases that have been resolved thus far, and the local government's decision to start enforcing the anti-sedition provisions of the Crimes Ordinance (which had been dormant for decades due to perceived conflicts with the ICCPR). It also considers whether the ICCPR can continue to play a meaningful role in Hong Kong's jurisprudence.

Vaguely Defined Criminal Offenses: Is There Still a Role for the ICCPR?

The one redeeming feature of the NSL is that Articles 4 and 5 expressly state that human rights, including those stated in the Hong Kong Basic Law and the ICCPR, shall continue to be 'protected in accordance with the law'. The question is: how can this be achieved in practice? The ICCPR does permit restrictions on the freedoms of expression, assembly, and association in the name of 'national security' but only to the extent that the restrictions are clearly defined and constitute necessary and proportionate measures.[59] The UN Human Rights Committee (the treaty-monitoring body for the ICCPR) has consistently reminded governments that they cannot simply invoke 'national security' as a broad justification.[60] Rather, any restriction must constitute a proportionate response to a tangible threat. Hong Kong's CFA has developed a similar proportionality test in its pre-NSL jurisprudence.[61] This is why some commentators have expressed hope that Hong Kong judges will endeavor to interpret and apply the NSL in a manner that complies with the ICCPR.[62] However, this will be exceedingly challenging as the new offenses are defined in broad language, some of which was borrowed from the Chinese Criminal Code.[63]

For example, the new offense of 'secession' (which carries a minimum sentence of ten years imprisonment and could lead to life imprisonment) is defined in Article 20 of the NSL:

> A person who organises, plans, commits or participates in any of the following acts, whether or not by force or threat of force, with a view to committing secession or undermining national unification shall be guilty of an offence:
>
> 1. separating the Hong Kong Special Administrative Region or any other part of the People's Republic of China from the People's Republic of China;
> 2. altering by unlawful means the legal status of the Hong Kong Special Administrative Region or of any other part of the People's Republic of China; or
> 3. surrendering the Hong Kong Special Administrative Region or any other part of the People's Republic of China to a foreign country.

This is a much broader definition of secession than proposed in the bill that was introduced in Hong Kong in 2003, in part because it does not include the use or threat of force as an element of the crime.[64] The *mens rea* element ('with a view to committing secession or undermining national unification') is also extremely broad.[65] The breath of the offense is compounded by Article 21, which criminalizes, *inter alia*, anyone who 'incites' the primary offense. The new special branch of the Hong Kong police has used Article 21 to arrest a large number of people for entirely peaceful speech acts, including the display of slogans that were common during the 2019 anti-extradition protests.[66]

Similarly, Article 22 (which defines the new offense of 'subversion') includes the vaguely defined act of 'seriously interfering in, disrupting, or undermining the performance of duties and functions in accordance with the law' by the Central or Hong Kong governments.[67] Although Article 22 does require proof that the defendant threatened or used force or 'other unlawful means' with the goal of 'subverting state power', the authorities are interpreting this language very broadly. This is clear from the decision to charge 47 Hong Kong residents (including lawyers and former legislators) with 'conspiracy to commit subversion' for their roles in an unofficial political primary for pro-democracy candidates for the Legislative Council. According to prosecutors, all 47 were part of a 'massive and well-organised scheme' to achieve a 'common criminal purpose' by gaining a majority in the Legislative Council and then using that power to undermine its proper functioning, paralyze the government, and compel the Chief Executive to resign.[68] Most of these defendants have been in custody since February 2021 because the prosecutors have relied on Article 42 of the NSL to oppose bail applications. When bail has been granted, it has been with exceedingly strict conditions, essentially requiring the defendant to retire from public life. For example, one candidate in the primary, Owen Chow, was granted bail over the objection of prosecutors so that he could complete his nursing degree while awaiting trial.[69] But his bail was revoked after he posted comments on social media, which prosecutors argued could 'incite hatred' against the government.[70] As of April 2022, only 14 of the 47 defendants were out on bail. The hardship for those in pretrial detention has been compounded by numerous adjournments, largely due to the enormous number of documents (some 10,000 pages) that need to be translated.[71] Of course, the complexity of the case is the direct result of the government's decision to prosecute such a large group of people and to allege that they were all part of the same criminal conspiracy.

The other offences created by the NSL were not even mentioned in Article 23 of the Basic Law and thus were not required to fill any 'gap' left by the failure to fully implement Article 23. Rather, it appears that Beijing decided to use the NSL as a vehicle to greatly increase the potential cost of expressing opposition to the local or central governments. For example, the NSL defines 'terrorist activities' so broadly that it could be used to prosecute individuals who damage the transit system during a political protest.[72] Of course, damage to public property was already punishable under pre-existing Hong Kong law. But defining such acts as 'terrorist' activity ensures heavier penalties (from ten years to life imprisonment if the act causes 'significant loss' of property). Equally important, the government can use all the special investigation powers and procedural rules (including the presumption against bail) that accompany the NSL.

Article 29, 'Collusion with a Foreign Country or With External Forces to Endanger National Security' is probably the broadest of the new offenses. It includes not only some uncontroversial language (such as a prohibition on waging war against the PRC) but also criminalizes the mere act of requesting sanctions against the PRC or China. This provision was the basis for the charges against Jimmy Lai and several employees of his former newspaper, the *Apple Daily*[73] (which was shut down after the police used their new powers to raid the newspaper and freeze the assets of its parent company[74]). Article 29 has also been used to threaten foreigners who lobby overseas for sanctions against Hong Kong or China.[75] Indeed, Article 29 is so broad (and has such a complex and awkward structure) that it is impossible to predict, with any certainty, how widely it may be applied.[76]

Commentators are watching to see whether the Hong Kong courts will use Articles 4 and 5 of the NSL as a guide to interpreting these broad offenses, so as to mitigate the conflicts with the ICCPR, particularly Articles 14 (right to fair trial), 19 (freedom of expression), and 21 and 22 (freedoms of assembly and association). In its first decision under the NSL, Hong Kong's CFA appeared to affirm the significance of Articles 4 and 5. The government had appealed the decision of a lower court to grant bail to Jimmy Lai, albeit with strict conditions. The CFA granted the government's appeal and held that the lower courts must enforce Article 42(2) as a specific exception to Hong Kong's ordinary bail regime.[77] However, it also stated that Articles 4 and 5 are 'centrally important to the interpretation of the NSL' and that 'those rights, freedoms and values are to be protected and adhered to' in applying the NSL.[78] In light of these comments, there was reason to hope that trial judges would try to interpret vague language in the NSL to comply with the ICCPR.

However, this did not occur in the first conviction under the NSL, that of Tong Ying Kit. Tong was arrested less than 24 hours after the NSL came in force. He had driven his motorcycle through the streets of Hong Kong flying a banner that stated: 'Liberate Hong Kong. Revolution of our Times'. He failed to stop at police check points and ultimately collided with a group of officers who were trying to stop him, injuring three (fortunately, not seriously). Had Tong taken this ill-advised motorcycle ride one day earlier, he probably would have been convicted of dangerous driving causing bodily harm and sentenced to, at most, three years in jail. Instead, he was charged with terrorist activities (Article 24) and incitement to secession (Article 21). Denied bail, he was detained for more than a year before trial. The Secretary for Justice also exercised her power, under Article 46 of the NSL, to set aside Tong's request for a jury trial. He was convicted of both offenses by a panel of three judges in the CFI and received a combined sentence of nine years.[79]

The court's analysis of 'terrorist activities' is worrying. Granted, the NSL defines the offense in broad terms but it does require the prosecution to prove that the defendant 'caused or intended to cause grave harm to the society' (Article 24) and there was no evidence that Tong deliberately collided with the police. Yet the court concluded that the element of 'grave harm' was satisfied because he mounted a 'blatant and serious challenge' to the authorities by failing to stop at police checkpoints and that this would 'certainly instill a sense of fear amongst the law-abiding members of the public'.[80] In fact, there was no evidence that the public felt anything close to the fear that one normally associates with acts of terrorism. By making such a large assumption regarding the public's perception of Tong's actions, the judges made the prosecution's job much easier, effectively 'defining terrorism downward'.[81]

Tong's conviction for incitement to secession is even more concerning because this charge has been used to arrest a significant number of people. Given that this offense clearly constitutes a restriction on freedom of expression, one would have expected the trial court to look to prior decisions by the CFA for guidance on how to interpret and apply such a statute. Indeed, there is a wealth of Hong Kong jurisprudence on this subject. For example, in *HKSAR v Chow Nok Hang*, the CFA interpreted a statute that prohibits acting 'in a disorderly manner' at a public gathering for the purposes of preventing the transaction of business.[82] Noting that the ICCPR has constitutional status in Hong Kong, the CFA held that the statutory provision must be narrowly construed because it restricts the freedoms of speech and assembly.[83]

In contrast, the judges who convicted Tong of incitement to secession never referred to the ICCPR or to any of the CFA's prior decisions on freedom of expression. Instead, they cited general case law on the offense of incitement and relied on cases that are all easily distinguishable, either because they predate the ICCPR or because they do not concern protected speech.[84] The trial judges also rejected a key argument from the defense – that the prosecution should be required to introduce at least some evidence as to how the 'incited act' of separating Hong Kong from China was to be carried out. In rejecting this submission, the court compared 'incitement to secession' to 'incitement to murder'. But that is a poor analogy. Murder is an achievable goal, something that an incited person could accomplish in a number of ways. In contrast, it was plainly impossible for the people who witnessed Tong's banner to separate Hong Kong from China. The fact that this made no difference to the judges indicates that they were not trying to interpret the offense of 'incitement to secession' in manner that would comply with the ICCPR. Doing so would have required an analysis of proportionality, including the question of whether it was necessary to suppress this type of speech in order to respond to a tangible threat to China's security and territorial integrity.

Instead, the court focused entirely on the meaning of the slogan: 'Liberate Hong Kong; Revolution of our Times', an issue that was contested and dominated the trial. The prosecution relied on an expert witness (a history professor) who testified that the slogan was used in 2016, by a candidate for the Legislative Council, to express a desire for independence. In contrast, expert witnesses for the defense (professors of political science and communication) testified that the slogan had evolved considerably over time. In their opinion (based on focus groups and other empirical data) the slogan had been recontextualized in 2019 during the anti-extradition protests and had taken on a wide range of new meanings. The defense thus argued that the slogan was too vague to be capable of inciting others to commit secession.

However, the testimony of the defendant's expert witnesses ultimately had no impact. The court decided that it did not have to resolve the dispute on the slogan's meaning because even the defense witnesses agreed that a desire for independence was *one* of the ideas that might be associated with it. This demonstrates just how broadly the offense of 'incitement to secession' is being applied in Hong Kong. Under the trial court's approach, the prosecution need only prove that a pro-independence message was one of the *possible* meanings of a slogan or statement.

Tong initially appealed his convictions and also the sentence of nine years. But then he mysteriously withdrew his appeal prior to the hearing. His barrister (who was informed by the court) told the press that he had 'no idea' why his young client would abandon his appeal.[85] This means that the judgment stands and it has already been cited, by the District Court, in the second conviction for incitement to secession.[86]

The *Tong Ying Kit* judgment was also cited in the case of *HKSAR v Tam Tak Chi*, in which a former radio host (known as 'Fast Beat') was convicted by the District Court for uttering seditious words and related charges under sections 9 and 10 of the Crimes Ordinance (Cap 200).[87] These offenses were dormant for decades as they were widely assumed to be unconstitutional after the ICCPR gained constitutional status in Hong Kong. Tam challenged the constitutionality of the prosecution, arguing, *inter alia*, that 'seditious intent' is defined in such broad and vague language that it fails to comply with Article 19 of the ICCPR. (The definition includes, for example, the intent 'to raise discontent or disaffection' among residents and to 'promote feelings of ill-will and enmity'.) However, the District Court did not seem to understand the requirements of the ICCPR and did not apply the traditional four-step proportionality analysis. The judgment has been rightly criticized[88] and hopefully will be appealed. There are also many other cases working their way through the system; according to media reports, 20 individuals and 4 media companies were charged with sedition between September 2020 and February 2022.[89] Because the sedition offenses are defined in a local ordinance, the Hong Kong judiciary has the power to declare them invalid if they are unconstitutional. But judges may be reluctant to do so, knowing that the NPCSC could issue its own interpretation of Article 39 of the Basic Law.

It should be noted that the UN Human Rights Committee has previously called upon Hong Kong to amend the sedition offenses to comply with the ICCPR and the local government gave assurances that it would do so.[90] Given that history, why has it instead resumed enforcing these old statutory provisions? Perhaps it just wants to be able to prosecute people for statements made before the NSL came into force. It may also hope to deflect some attention away from the NSL by relying on an old 'British colonial' statute. However, the NSL is affecting these cases because the CFA has held that the new presumption against bail applies even to non-NSL offenses, so long as they concern national security.[91] The CFA also held that the extraordinary investigation powers conferred by Article 43 of the NSL can be invoked for non-NSL offenses that concern national security. [92] This was surprising because there was no need to address this issue in an appeal relating to a bail application.

Conclusion

On paper, 'One Country, Two Systems' appeared to be a robust model of autonomy. Some commentators even analyzed it as a possible model for power-sharing in other territories.[93] But it was always flawed because the Joint Declaration – although binding as a matter of international law – lacked a dispute resolution clause and could not be effectively enforced. The United Kingdom has protested against breaches and adopted some countermeasures, including a special immigration route for Hong Kong residents who are eligible for British National (Overseas) passports and their dependents.[94] But most residents will not leave Hong Kong and there is little that the British government can do for them. It is also increasingly apparent that some of the key indicators of Hong Kong's autonomy – such as the incorporation of the ICCPR into the Basic Law and an independent judiciary – cannot prevent Beijing from imposing its own version of national security.[95]

This is not to suggest, however, that Hong Kong will become 'just another city' in China. Hong Kong's judiciary is still highly regarded by the international business community and it may be in Beijing's interest to allow it to function independently, at least in non-political criminal matters and civil litigation. Beijing may also be willing to allow the city to enjoy a somewhat higher degree of personal freedom than exists on the Mainland. For now, Hong Kong residents do continue to enjoy religious freedom, reasonable access to the internet, and a higher degree of academic and press freedom than exists in the Mainland. But those freedoms remain only because Beijing has chosen to tolerate them, perhaps hoping that the territory can still be marketed as a good place for international business and finance. After all, Hong Kong's legal system is still largely intact – as long as you have nothing to do with politics.

Notes

1 Decision of the National People's Congress on Establishing and Improving the Legal System and Enforcement Mechanisms for the Hong Kong Special Administrative Region to Safeguard National Security (adopted 28 May 2020) <https://www.elegislation.gov.hk/hk/A215> accessed 20 September 2021.

2 For an unofficial English translation of the NSL, published on 3 July 2020, see Hong Kong Government e-Gazette <https://www.gld.gov.hk/egazette/pdf/20202448e/egn2020244872.pdf> accessed 20 September 2021. For the first edited collection devoted to the new law, see Hualing Fu and Michael Hor (eds), *The National Security Law of Hong Kong: Restoration and Transformation* (Hong Kong University Press 2022).

3 Basic Law of the Hong Kong Special Administrative Region of the People's Republic of China (1990) <https://www.basiclaw.gov.hk/en/basiclaw/basiclaw.html> accessed 20 September 2021.

4 Hong Kong Government Gazette, LN 136 of 2020.

5 The Hong Kong Police reported that approximately 370 people were arrested on 1 July 2020, including nine arrested for suspected violations of the NSL; see Press Release of 1 July 2020, <https://www.police.gov.hk/ppp_en/03_police_message/pr/pr_archives.html?month=202007> accessed 15 March 2022.

6 Joint Declaration of the Government of the United Kingdom of Great Britain and Northern Ireland and the Government of the People's Republic of China on the Question of Hong Kong 1399 UNTS 33 (1984) (Joint Declaration).

7 For analysis of the anti-extradition movement of 2019 and the Central Government's decision to apply the NSL to Hong Kong, see Albert HY Chen, 'Constitutional Controversies in the Aftermath of the Anti-Extradition Movement of 2019' (2020) 50(2) Hong Kong Law Journal 610.

8 See, e.g., Hong Kong Government, 'Improve Electoral System: Ensure Patriots Administering Hong Kong' <https://www.cmab.gov.hk/improvement/en/home/index.html> accessed 10 October 2021; and Hong Kong Free Press, "Explainer: How Beijing Cracked Down on Hong Kong's Elections" (31 March 2021) <https://hongkongfp.com/2021/03/31/explainer-how-beijing-cracked-down-on-hong-kongs-elections/> accessed 11 October 2021.

9 The Hong Kong government regularly accuses foreign forces (and particularly the United States) of inciting anti-government protests in Hong Kong. See Hong Kong Special Administrative Region of the People's Republic of China, *Report on Hong Kong's Business Environment: A Place with Unique Advantages and Unlimited Opportunities* (2021), ch 1 <https://www.hkeconomy.gov.hk/en/pdf/Business_report_2021.pdf> accessed 15 October 2021.

10 For a list of individuals arrested, charged, and convicted (including some guilty pleas), see Lydia Wong and Thomas Kellogg, 'Individuals Arrested under the Hong Kong National Security Law or by the National Security Department' *China File* (19 January 2022) <https://www.chinafile.com/individuals-arrested-under-hong-kong-national-security-law-or-national-security-department> accessed 19 March 2022.

11 Crimes Ordinance (Cap 200), ss 9-11. For analysis, see Fu Hualing, 'Past and Future Offenses of Sedition in Hong Kong' in Fu Hualing, Carole J Petersen, and Simon NM Young (eds) *National Security and Fundamental Freedoms: Hong Kong's Article 23 Under Scrutiny* (Hong Kong University Press 2005).

12 See, e.g., Brian Wong, 'Hong Kong Prosecutors Slap 3 Apple Daily-Affiliated Firms with Colonial-Era Sedition Charge' *South China Morning Post* (Hong Kong, 10 February 2022); Austin Ramsy, 'As Hong Kong's Civil Society Buckles, One Group Tries to Hold On' *New York Times* (24 October 2021) <https://www.nytimes.com/2021/10/24/world/asia/hong-kong-civil-society.html> accessed 18 March 2022; and Lucas Niewenhuis, 'Citizen News Becomes Latest Hong Kong News Site to Shut Down' *SupChina*, <https://supchina.com/2022/01/03/citizen-news-becomes-latest-hong-kong-news-site-to-close-down/> accessed 18 March 2022.

13 NSL arts 36–39. For a critique, see Bing Ling, 'Extraterritorial Application of the Hong Kong National Security Law: A Legal Appraisal' in Hualing Fu and Michael Hor (eds), n 2 above.

14 See, e.g., NBC News, 'Hong Kong Issues Arrest Warrant for US Citizen Under New National Security Law' <https://www.nbcnews.com/news/world/hong-kong-issues-arrest-warrant-u-s-citizen-under-new-n1235574> accessed 20 March 2022.

15 NSL, art 65; Basic Law, art 158.

16 Carole J Petersen, 'Not an Internal Affair: Hong Kong's Right to Autonomy and Self-Determination Under International Law' (2019) 49 Hong Kong Law Journal 883–904. See also *Legal Consequences of the Separation of the Chagos Archipelago From Mauritius in 1965,* ICJ Advisory Opinion (25 February 2019) (recognizing that the right to self-determination was a crystalized norm of customary international law by 1960).

17 See generally, Peter Wesley-Smith, *Unequal Treaty 1898–1997: China, Great Britain, and Hong Kong's New Territories* (Revised Edition, Oxford University Press 1998). Beijing's claim that the treaties were invalid is dubious because the methods by which the United Kingdom acquired Hong Kong did not violate international law at the time. Roda Mushkat, 'Hong Kong as an International Legal Person' (1992) 6 Emory International Law Review 105, 114–115.

18 Nihal Jayawickrama, 'Public Law', in Raymond Wacks (ed), *The Law in Hong Kong, 1969–1989* (Oxford University Press, 2013) 50–51 (quoting from the Letter dated 10 March 1972, from Ambassador Huang Hua, Permanent Representative of the PRC to the UN, to the Chairman of the UN Special Committee).

19 For analysis of the drafting process and copies of the drafts that were distributed for public consultation, see Ming K Chan and David J Clark (eds), *The Hong Kong Basic Law: Blueprint for 'Stability and Prosperity' under Chinese Sovereignty?* (Hong Kong University Press 1991).

20 Jamie Trinidad, *Self-Determination in Disputed Colonial Territories* (Cambridge University Press 2018) 118; and Petersen, n 16 above.

21 Hurst Hannum, 'The Foreign Powers of Autonomous Regions' (1988) 57 Nordic Journal of International Law 273 (comparing Hong Kong to other regions); and Roda Mushkat, *One Country, Two International Legal Personalities: The Case of Hong Kong* (Hong Kong University Press 1997).

22 Basic Law, arts 8, 16–18, 43, and 48–79.

23 Basic Law, art 82. However, since the enactment of the NSL, a number of visiting foreign judges have resigned. See, e.g., Austin Ramsy, 'Two UK Judges Quit Hong Kong Court, Citing Lost Freedoms' *New York Times* (30 March 2022) <https://www.nytimes.com/2022/03/30/world/asia/hong-kong-british-judges.html> (accessed 30 March 2022).

24 *HKSAR v Chow Nok Hang* (2013) 16 HKCFAR 837, paras 28–36; and *HKSAR v. Fong Kwok Shan Christine* (2017) 20 HKCFAR 425 (CFA), paras 12–15.

25 Joint Declaration, para 3(12) (stating that the PRC's 'basic policies' would be stipulated in a Basic Law of Hong Kong and 'remain unchanged for 50 years'). However, people were encouraged to believe that 'One Country, Two Systems' could become permanent. *See* Danny Gittings, 'What Will Happen to Hong Kong After 2047?' (2011) 42 California Western International Law Journal, 37, 49–51 (summarizing statements by Deng Xiaoping).

26 Joint Declaration, para 3(4) and Annex I.

27 Gregory S Gordon, 'When "One Country, Two Systems" Meets "One Person, One Vote": The Law of Treaties and the Handover Narrative Through the Crucible of Hong Kong's Election Crisis' (2015) 16 Melbourne Journal of International Law 344, 368–377.

28 Alvin YH Cheung, 'Road to Nowhere: Hong Kong's Democratization and China's Obligations Under Public International Law' (2015) 40 Brooklyn Journal of International Law 465, 481–504.

29 Albert HY Chen, *The Changing Legal Orders in Hong Kong and Mainland China: Essays on "One Country, Two Systems"* (City University of Hong Kong Press 2021) 82.

30 Martin Lee, 'A Tale of Two Articles' in Peter Wesley-Smith and Albert HY Chen (eds), *The Basic Law and Hong Kong's Future* (Butterworths 1988).

31 Eric C Ip, 'Prototype Constitutional Supervision in China: The Lessons of the Hong Kong Basic Law Committee' (2016) 10 Asian Journal of Comparative Law 323.

32 See generally Johannes Chan, 'Reconciliation of the NPCSC's Power of Interpretation of the Basic Law with the Common Law in the HKSAR' (2020) 50 Hong Kong Law Journal 657.

33 Interpretation of Article 104 of the Basic Law of the Hong Kong Special Administrative Region of the People's Republic of China by the Standing Committee of the National People's Congress (Adopted by the Standing Committee of the Twelfth National People's Congress at its Twenty-fourth Session on 7 November 2016), unofficial English translation at <https://www.basiclaw.gov.hk/filemanager/content/en/files/basiclawtext/basiclawtext_doc27.pdf> (accessed 19 March 2022).

34 Carole J Petersen, 'Hong Kong's Spring of Discontent: The Rise and Fall of the National Security Bill in 2003' in Fu Hualing, Carole J Petersen, and Simon NM Young (eds) n 11 above.
35 The Official Secrets Ordinance was enacted in 1997 and largely modeled on the British Official Secrets Act 1989, which had previously been applied to Hong Kong.
36 Societies Ordinance (Cap 151), ss 5, 5A, 5D and 8.
37 Carole J Petersen, 'Prohibiting the Hong Kong National Party: Has Hong Kong Violated the International Covenant on Civil and Political Rights?' (2018) 48 Hong Kong Law Journal 789.
38 See, e.g., Tony Cheung, 'Hong Kong Is 'Only Place in the World Without National Security Law', Liaison Office Chief Says' *South China Morning Post* (Hong Kong, 15 April 2018).
39 Natalie Wong, 'Citing President Xi Jinping, Beijing's Hong Kong Envoy Luo Huining Says Lack of National Security Law Allows "Sabotage"' *South China Morning Post* (Hong Kong, 9 January 2020).
40 Carole J Petersen, 'The Disappearing Firewall: The International Consequences of Beijing's Decision to Impose a National Security Law and Operate National Security Institutions in Hong Kong' (2020) 50(2) Hong Kong Law Journal 633.
41 Chan Ho-him, 'National Security Law: Hong Kong Schools Told to Remove Books that Might Fall Foul of the Legislation' *South China Morning Post* (Hong Kong, 6 July 2020).
42 Ho-him Chan, 'Hong Kong Visual Arts Teacher Facing Disciplinary Action Over "Inappropriate" Political Cartoons Shared Online' *South China Morning Post* (Hong Kong 30 April 2021); and Ho-him Chan, 'Two More Hong Kong Teachers Deregistered for Life, One for 'Defaming the Nation' and the Other for a Protest-Related Crime' *South China Morning Post* (Hong Kong, 30 April 2021).
43 Hong Kong Government Press Release, 'EDB announces guidelines and curriculum arrangements for safeguarding national security and national security education' (4 February 2021) <https://www.info.gov.hk/gia/general/202102/04/P2021020400806.htm> accessed 18 October 2021.
44 For discussion of the compulsory courses and other changes in higher education, see Edward Vickers and Paul Morris, 'Accelerating Hong Kong's Reeducation: "Mainlandization", Securitization and the 2020 National Security Law' *Comparative Education* (published online: 13 March 2022) <https://www.tandfonline.com/doi/full/10.1080/03050068.2022.2046878?src=> accessed 19 March 2022.
45 Basic Law, art 137; see also Joint Declaration, Annex I(X). For analysis of the legal protections for academic freedom and the impact of the NSL, see Kelley Loper and Carole J Petersen, 'Academic Freedom in the Shadow of the National Security Law' in Hualing Fu and Michael Hor (eds), n 2 above.
46 NSL, arts 48–55.
47 NSL, art 54.
48 Ibid., art 50.
49 Ibid., art 60.
50 Ibid., art 43.
51 See Stuart Hargreaves, 'Past as Prologue: Intercept & Surveillance Rules Under Hong Kong's National Security Law' (2021) 20 Santa Clara Journal of International Law 48; and Simon NM Young, 'Police Powers Under the National Security Law' in Hualing Fu and Michael Hor (eds), n 2 above.
52 NSL, art 43.
53 For English translations see the Government's 'Safeguarding National Security' website <https://www.isd.gov.hk/nationalsecurity/eng/law.html> accessed 21 October 2021.
54 NSL, art 14. It should be noted, however, that Professor Albert Chen has argued that the Committee's decisions may be judicially reviewable. See Chris Lau, 'National Security Law: Decisions of New Committee in Hong Kong Not Above Judicial Review, Legal Expert Argues' *South China Morning Post* (Hong Kong, 11 July 2020).
55 NSL, art 18.
56 The government could also avoid a jury trial by prosecuting in the District Court (where there are no jury trials) but the District Court cannot sentence a defendant to longer than seven years. Article 46 of the NSL gives the Secretary for Justice the power to prevent a jury trial in the CFI, which can sentence defendants up to life in prison. For an unsuccessful challenge to a

decision by the Secretary for Justice to preclude a jury trial, see *Tong Ying Kit v. Secretary for Justice* [2021] HKCA 912.

57 NSL, art 57.

58 For further discussion of the international community's reactions, see Petersen, n 40 above.

59 ICCPR, art 19(3). See also UN Human Rights Committee, General Comment 34, Article 19, Freedoms of opinion and expression, 12 September 2011, CCPR/C/GC/34

60 Tae-Hoon Park v Republic of Korea, Communication 628/1995 (UN Human Rights Committee, 1998), para 10.3. For additional examples, see Carole J Petersen, 'Article 23 of the Hong Kong Basic Law: International Law and Institutions as Sources of Resilience' in Cora Chan and Fiona De Londras (eds), *China's National Security: Endangering Hong Kong's Rule of Law?* (Hart/ Bloomsbury, 2020) 231–249.

61 See, e.g., *HKSAR v Ng Kung Siu* (1999) 2 HKCFAR 442; and *HKSAR v Fong Kwok Shan Christine* (2017) 20 HKCFAR 425.

62 See, e.g., Po Jen Yap, 'Judging Hong Kong's National Security Law' in Hualing Fu and Michael Hor (eds), n 2 above; Kelley Loper and Carole J Petersen, 'Academic Freedom in the Shadow of the National Security Law' in Hualing Fu and Michael Hor (eds), n 2 above.

63 For examples, see Albert HY Chen, 'The National Security Law of the HKSAR: A Contextual and Legal Study', in Hualing Fu and Michael Hor (eds), n 2 above.

64 For analysis of the offense proposed in 2003, see Kelley Loper, 'A Secession Offense in Hong Kong and the "One Country, Two Systems" Dilemma' in Fu Hualing, Carole J Petersen, and Simon NM Young (eds), n 11 above.

65 NSL, art 20.

66 Lydia Wong and Thomas E Kellogg, *The National Security Law: A Human Rights and Rule of Law Analysis* (Center for Asian Law, Georgetown Law, 23 February 2021) Appendix C (listing arrestees and alleged offenses). See also Selina Cheng, 'Hong Kong Police Confirm 8 Arrested for Unlawful Assembly and "Inciting Secession" During Peaceful CUHK Campus Demo' *Hong Kong Free Press* (7 December 2020).

67 NSL, art 22.

68 See, e.g., *HKSAR v Mo Man Ching Claudia* [2021] HKCFI 1435 (summarizing the charges and denying the application for bail).

69 HKSAR v. Chow Ka Shing [2021] 4 HKLRD 109, [2021] HKCFI 2075.

70 Owen Chow Arrested for Violating Bail Conditions and Publishing Political Remarks' *The Standard* (12 January 2022) <https://www.thestandard.com.hk/breaking-news/section/4/185855/Owen-Chow-arrested-for-violating-bail-conditions-and-publishing-political-remarks> accessed 18 March 2022.

71 See Jessie Pang and James Pomfret, 'Trial of 47 Hong Kong Democracy Activists Charged with Conspiracy to Commit Subversion Adjourned till March' *Reuters* (29 November 2021) <https://www.reuters.com/world/china/trial-47-hong-kong-democracy-activists-charged-with-conspiracy-commit-subversion-2021-11-29/> accessed 18 March 2022.

72 NSL, art 24. For critique of the NSL's definition of 'terrorist activities' see, Mandates of the Special Rapporteur on the Promotion and Protection of Human Rights and Fundamental Freedoms while Countering Terrorism; the Working Group on Arbitrary Detention; the Special Rapporteur on Extrajudicial, Summary or Arbitrary Executions; the Special Rapporteur on the Promotion and Protection of the Right to Freedom of Opinion and Expression; the Special Rapporteur on the Rights to Freedom of Peaceful Assembly and of Association; the Special Rapporteur on the Situation of Human Rights Defenders; and the Special Rapporteur on Minority Issues, *Letter to the People's Republic of China*, OL/CHN 17/2020, 1 September 2020 <https://spcommreports.ohchr.org/TMResultsBase/DownLoadPublicCommunicationFile?gId=25487> (accessed 15 March 2022).

73 Clifford Lo and Jeffie Lam, 'Hong Kong National Security Law: 4 Former Apple Daily Staff Charged with Conspiracy to Collude with Foreign Forces' *South China Morning Post* (Hong Kong, 21 July 2021).

74 Apple Daily was the first of several media outlets to be shut down as a direct result of the NSL. See, e.g. Austin Ramsy, 'How Beijing Has Muted Hong Kong's Independent Media' *New York Times* (2 January 2022) <https://www.nytimes.com/article/hong-kong-media-muzzled.html> accessed 20 March 2022; and Timothy McLaughlin, 'I am Afraid that I Cannot Be a Journalist Anymore' *The Atlantic* (19 February 2022) <https://www.theatlantic.com/international/archive/2022/02/hong-kong-china-stand-news/622092/> accessed 17 March 2022.

75 See, e.g., Hong Kong Watch, 'Hong Kong Watch Co-Founder and CEO Benedict Rogers Threatened Under National Security Law' (14 March 2022) <https://www.hongkongwatch.org/all-posts/2022/3/14/hong-kong-watch-co-founder-and-ceo-benedict-rogers-threatened-under-national-security-law> (accessed 20 March 2022).

76 For analysis of the concerns of international banks, see Albert HY Chen and Simon NM Young, 'Liability for Imposing Sanctions under Hong Kong's National Security Law' (2020) 50(2) Hong Kong Law Journal 354 (arguing for an interpretation of Article 29 that would not capture financial institutions that are required by the laws of a foreign state to implement sanctions).

77 *HKSAR v. Lai Chee Ying* [2021] HKCFA 3, para 29 (citing Article 62 of the NSL) and para 70(b).

78 Ibid., paras 41–42.

79 *HKSAR v Tong Ying Kit* [2021] 16 HKCFI 2020.

80 Ibid., para 162.

81 Thomas E Kellogg and Eric Yan Ho-lai, *The Tong Ying-Kit NSL Verdict: An International and Comparative Law Analysis* (Center for Asian Law, Georgetown Law, 20 October 2021) 22–25.

82 *HKSAR v Chow Nok Hang* (2013) 16 HKCFAR 837, para 52 (citing section 17B of the Public Order Ordinance).

83 Ibid., paras 59–61 (setting aside the conviction under section 17B(1) of the Public Order Ordinance).

84 For example, the CFI cited (at paras 26–30) a British case that concerned a note that the defendant sent to a child to incite her to have sex with him.

85 Kelly Ho, 'First Hong Kong Activist Convicted under National Security Law Drops Appeal in Surprise Move' *Hong Kong Free Press* (13 January 2022) <https://hongkongfp.com/2022/01/13/first-hong-kong-activist-jailed-under-national-security-law-drops-appeal-in-surprise-move/> accessed 25 March 2022.

86 *HKSAR v. Ma Chun Man* [2021] HKDC 1325. The District Court sentenced the defendant to five years and nine months in prison. See Kelley Ho, 'Security Law: Nearly 6 Years Jail for Hongkonger Who "Incited Secession" with Pro-Independence Chants and Slogans' *Hong Kong Free Press* (11 November 2021) <https://hongkongfp.com/2021/11/11/breaking-hong-kong-man-jailed-for-5-years-9-months-for-inciting-secession-in-citys-2nd-security-law-sentencing/> accessed 18 March 2022.

87 [2022] HKDC 2008.

88 Angeline Chan, 'After Hong Kong Activist Tam Tak-chi's Conviction, We Still Don't Know What is Or Is Not Seditious' *Hong Kong Free Press* (6 March 2022) <https://hongkongfp.com/2022/03/06/after-hong-kong-activist-tam-tak-chis-conviction-we-still-dont-know-what-is-or-is-not-seditious/> accessed 28 March 2022.

89 Selina Cheng, 'Hong Kong Man Jailed for 8 Months in First Sedition Sentencing Since 1967 Riots' *Hong Kong Free Press* (2 February 2022) <https://hongkongfp.com/2022/02/01/hong-kong-man-jailed-for-8-months-in-first-sedition-sentencing-since-1967-leftist-riots> accessed 28 March 2022.

90 See, e.g., UN Human Rights Committee, Concluding Observations on the Third Periodic Report of Hong Kong, China, adopted by the Committee at its 107th session, UN Doc CCPR/C/CHN-HKG/CO/3 (29 April 2013), para 14.

91 *HKSAR v. Ng Hau Yi Sydney* [2021] HKCFA 42.

92 Thomas E Kellogg, 'How a Ruling by Hong Kong's Top Court Opens the Door to a More Intrusive Security Law' *Hong Kong Free Press* (17 December 2021) <https://hongkongfp.com/2021/12/17/how-a-ruling-by-hong-kongs-top-court-opens-the-door-to-a-more-intrusive-security-law/>.

93 See, e.g., Hurst Hannum, *Autonomy, Sovereignty, and Self-Determination: The Accommodation of Conflicting Rights* (Revised Edition 1996) ch 7.

94 GOV. UK, Guidance: British Nationals (Overseas) in Hong Kong (22 July 2020) <https://www.gov.uk/guidance/british-nationals-overseas-in-hong-kong> accessed 29 March 2022.

95 After this chapter was concluded, the United Nations Human Rights Committee (the treaty-monitoring body for the ICCPR) concluded its review of Hong Kong's fourth periodic report on its implementation of the ICCPR and expressed grave concerns regarding the impact of the NSL. See United Nations Human Rights Committee, Concluding Observations on the Fourth Periodic Report of Hong Kong, China, CCPR/CHN-HG/CO/4 (27 July 2022).

13

RIGHTS MOVEMENTS, CIVIL DISOBEDIENCE, AND CIVIL UNREST

Social Movements and Constitutionalism in Mainland China, Hong Kong, and Taiwan

Han Zhu

In recent years, the world has witnessed the emergence of social movements and constitutional change, in multiple waves and innovative forms, which have led to significant global constitutional challenges. Social movements in the Greater China area—mainland China,[1] Hong Kong, and Taiwan—have been part of this global trend, but they have taken different developmental trajectories and pushed constitutional development in various directions.

For the past three decades, social movements in China have been characterised by law-based rights movements. Although Chinese rights activists have struggled to go beyond legalistic rights advocacy, their efforts have ended in failure and an increasingly hostile legal environment since 2013. By contrast, democratic movements in Taiwan and Hong Kong reached a climax in 2014, marked by two unprecedented civil disobedience movements: the Sunflower and Occupy Central movements. The Sunflower movement has dramatically changed the political landscape in Taiwan, whereas Hong Kong's Occupy Central movement failed to achieve its political agenda and led to radicalisation of social mobilisation. Civil disobediences in Hong Kong ultimately escalated to civil unrest during the 2019 anti-extradition bill protest, resulting in the enactment of the Hong Kong National Security Law (NSL),[2] which has fundamentally reshaped the constitutional framework in the city. The three paradigms of social movements and constitutional development in the Greater China area provide a valuable lens through which to observe the relationship between the two phenomena in diverse contexts ranging from authoritarianism to democracy.

This chapter aims to explore how the differences in constitutional systems have shaped social movements in the three regions by applying the mainstream social movement theory—the political opportunity and process theory—to the field of constitutional law. According to the political opportunity theory, the structure of political opportunities embedded in a society may have a significant impact on a social movement's development by inspiring or discouraging movement mobilisation.[3] Such an impact is not static but fluid. Broad social processes and shifting political opportunities may strengthen or

 DOI: 10.4324/9781003128243-16

weaken the positions of challenging groups, which may also influence movement mobilisation.[4] Constitutional and legal systems, as a critical part of the structure of political opportunities, also contribute to shaping the developmental trajectories of social movements.[5] The impact, however, is reciprocal. Social movements may, in turn, influence the paths of constitutional evolution. Hence, in addition to exploring the structure of constitutional opportunities for social movements, this chapter also investigates how the latter have influenced the constitutional trajectory in the three regions during the past decade.

This chapter is divided into five parts. The first three sections provide a descriptive and analytical examination of interaction between social movements and constitutional development in the three regions, respectively. Section four offers some comparative remarks, focusing on addressing two questions: One is why China's rights movements failed to break the bottleneck to escalate to political-oriented campaigns similar to the case in Hong Kong and Taiwan. The other question is why Hong Kong's civil disobedience evolved into civil unrest which led to political cataclysm, while the Sunflower movement in Taiwan concluded by peaceful political compromises. The analysis of these two questions revolves around the key political–legal dimensions of the different constitutional systems that contribute to the contrast as well as the changes in constitutional practices that shape social movement development in the three regions. The chapter concludes that the type of constitutional system that provides different political and legal opportunities for social movement mobilisation is determinative of the trajectory of social movements in the three regions. The capacities of a constitutional system to accommodate bottom-up political challenges lead to the divergence of constitutional development. In the aftermath of the three most remarkable social movements, Taiwan's liberal constitutionalism has gone as far apart as ever from its counterparts in China and Hong Kong, both of which have moved towards increasingly authoritarian constitutionalism.

Mainland China: Rights Movements under Party–State Authoritarianism

Social movements in post-1989 China are characterised by Rights ('*weiquan*') movements, which refer to a wide variety of actions by citizens to defend their civil or political rights through legal activism or other mobilisation tactics. What distinguishes China's social movements from their counterparts in Hong Kong and Taiwan is the lack of political movements and politically oriented organisations. The Tiananmen Square movement marked the culmination of political movements in 1980s' China when both the authorities and society embraced the idea of 'political reform'. After the June 4th crackdown, the party–state abandoned previous political reform schemes but instead adopted the 'legitimization without democratization'[6] as a management strategy. Such a strategy completely closed opportunities for political campaigning but created a new opening for legal mobilisation. The state has advanced legal construction on an unprecedented scale, particularly since 1999 and 2004 when the 'rule-of-law-state' and human rights protection provisions were introduced into the constitution, respectively. Correspondingly, a relatively independent judiciary and legal profession have been developed. The decades-long national legal education programmes have significantly raised common citizens' legal consciousness.

The changing structure of legal opportunities inspired the emergence of *weiquan* movements, along with various resistance movements, in the mid-1990s. *Weiquan* activism was initiated by common citizens in both urban and rural areas. In the rural areas, massive resistances against illegal taxes and fees occurred across the country during the mid- and late-1990s. In these widespread 'rights resistances',[7] rural protesters exploited gaps between law in books and the reality on the ground for mobilisation. In the urban areas, *weiquan* activities began with the *Dajia* (anti-counterfeit) campaign in which consumers first used the law—the then newly promulgated Consumer Law—to protect their rights in the face of a flood of 'fake and inferior commodities'. The anti-counterfeit campaign birthed the first public interest litigation in China, which has become one of the legal weapons most frequently used by rights activists. Meanwhile, as the concept of NGOs was introduced into China in 1995, NGOs quickly mushroomed and served as a new mobilisation platform for the civil society. Among them, NGOs specialising in rights advocacy and public interest causes became pilots for rights movements. Likewise, rights lawyers quickly jumped at the *weiquan* opportunity and pioneered a variety of influential rights campaigns. The collaboration between advocacy NGOs and rights lawyers has reshaped the entire ecosystem of *weiquan* activism, escalating the original model that mainly focused on using the existing laws to defend rights into promoting systematic changes through wider legal mobilisation. The 2001 *Qi Yuling* case[8] and the 2003 *Sun Zhigang* incident[9] were the two landmark events in China's rights movements and constitutional development. Social campaigns surrounding these two events not only popularised the concepts of constitutional review and constitutional rights but also created powerful legal mobilisation means—the strategic litigation, constitutional review petitions, and media mobilisation—that have been widely used by rights activists. This development in legal mobilisation was characterised as the new *weiquan* movements for it targeted defective laws or policies—sometimes even sensitive political issues—rather than individual grievances. Rights movements peaked between 2003 and 2008, covering a wide range of rights issues, including equal rights, labour rights, women's rights, environmental rights, children's rights, LGBT rights, migrants' rights, and AIDS prevention.

However, rights movements and their heavy reliance on gradualist legal approaches have created a bottleneck and deepened the dilemma for Chinese rights activists, who find it difficult to address the fundamental problems embedded in the existing constitutional and legal systems—the very factors that obstruct their *weiquan* efforts. Some 'radical' activists have attempted to use methods beyond legal mobilisation to promote politically oriented campaigns, such as running for the people's congresses delegates, organising grassroots elections, and staging street demonstrations. These efforts, however, have all failed under harsh repression. Moreover, all the political campaigns, including the most well-known Charter 08 movement and the New Citizens' movements were largely marginalised and unknown to mainstream society due to the lack of any public channel for reaching a wider audience beyond the *weiquan* circle.

Rights activists' efforts to politicalise social movements and develop action networks across various sectors of the civil and mainstream society alerted the authorities. As early as 2005–2006, the Chinese government has turned hostile towards *weiquan* in response to the colour revolutions in former Soviet Union regions. Since then, right advocates and NGOs have suffered intermittent harassment and clampdowns. However, they were still able to find room under the fragmented administration to continue their activism before 2013. The harshest crackdown came when the new central leadership took office in 2013, since the state's overall governance strategy turned to emphasise regime security and strengthen centralised leadership. The '709' crackdown in 2015 was a crushing blow for rights lawyers[10] and was followed by unprecedented criminal persecution of NGOs.[11] Consequently, civil society networks were shattered, resulting in the fragmentation and dramatic shrinkage of rights movements in present-day China.[12]

Despite frustrations, Chinese rights activists have exploited the liberal values embedded in Chinese law and pushed the law towards a direction of protecting human rights and constraining the state's power. These positive impacts on China's constitutional development have mainly been reflected in four phenomena. Firstly, legal and policy-based rights protection has been improved in many areas, such as the anti-discrimination against HBV, anti-domestic violence, family planning policy reforms, migrants' rights to education, and environmental public interest litigation. Secondly, strategic and public interest litigation has facilitated the translation of legal doctrines into judicial protection of rights and the improved protection of civil rights in practice. One salient example is the Chinese Supreme Court's ultimate endorsement of 'equal employment rights disputes' as a specific type of claim in 2019,[13] as a result of continuous efforts by rights activists who initiated a series of strategic litigation to promote the implementation of the Employment Promotion Law. Thirdly, rights movements have significantly promoted the development of civil society and the thrive of civic organisations, which are key to the development of constitutionalism in any society. Networks between different sectors of the civil society have been established in recent decades through movement mobilisation. Despite the currently hostile environment, key players continue to pursue their causes in various ways and maintain interpersonal networks. The final important achievement is that rights movements have, to some extent, facilitated a transition from 'rule consciousness' to Lockean 'rights consciousness' in civil society.[14] While the former emphasises the government's compliance with the law, the latter criticises or challenges the legal foundations or legitimacy of the legal systems or policies.

Nevertheless, the Amendment of the Chinese Constitution in 2018 and the deteriorating socio-legal environment for legal mobilisation suggests that Chinese civil society has won some battles but lost the war after a 30-year succession of rights movements. Despite the piecemeal positive progress, rights movements have failed to liberalise the party–state constitutional system as expected by many rights activists and observers. On the contrary, China's constitutional and legal systems appear to have taken the opposite path in recent years, characterised by increasingly authoritarian legality. Over the past decade, Chinese authorities have improved legal mechanism to streamline the state's management of civil society. A series of new regulations have been amended or promulgated to close the opportunities that previously enabled rights activists to exploit for their activism. Along with enhanced legality, the law has been significantly politicised to explicitly incorporate party–state ideology and political agendas to counteract civil society's discourse of democracy and liberalism. In the post-Cultural Revolutionary period, Chinese authorities tried to build up a modern legal system in a seemingly value-neutral manner. Chinese civil society has taken the opportunities afforded by the formalist appearance of the law to promote and legitimise their rights causes. Since 2013, however, a socialist value grounding constitutional and legal system, along with improved legal technicalities, has been cemented to consolidate party–state rule while narrowing positive legal opportunities for bottom-up mobilisation.[15]

Hong Kong: From Civil Disobedience to Civil Unrest in a Semi-Democracy

Post-colonial Hong Kong has witnessed unexpected paradigm shifts in the developmental trajectory of social movements, from law-biding demonstrations to peaceful civil disobediences and, ultimately, violent civil defiance. Hong Kong was labelled 'the city of protests' due to the frequent demonstrations and marches after the 1997 handover.

The root cause of the contention resides in the inner paradox of the Basic Law, which sought to enshrine liberal constitutional values and an authoritarian ideology without establishing an effective mechanism to settle the potential conflict between the two.[16] The Basic Law preserves and even enhances the liberal character of Hong Kong's constitutional and legal order under British colonial rule, creating high expectations for democratisation and autonomy. However, the underlying unlimited sovereignty philosophy and authoritarian elements legitimises and allows leeway for Beijing's intervention. The gap between the two contradictory dimensions of the Basic Law creates a crucial structural opportunity that encouraged the flourishing social movements in Hong Kong. The more intense the tension between the two, the more radicalised the social movements became. In response, Beijing authorities ultimately resolved to significantly weaken the liberal dimension while increasing the authoritarian input of Hong Kong's constitutional order, which has fundamentally changed the 'one country, two systems' architecture and Basic Law practices. The shifting constitutional structure has struck a lethal blow to movement mobilisation in the city.

The following section briefly examines social movement development and its interaction with constitutional practices in post-colonial Hong Kong. It can be divided into the following three phases:

1. **1997–2014: lawful public assemblies and demonstrations**
   Before 2014, social movements in Hong Kong were remarkably peaceful and orderly, with a strong middle-class colour, which tended to make public meetings and demonstrations mainstream activities rather than radical challenges to the authorities. Social movements during this period were featured by massive political movements, such as the 2003 demonstration against Article 23 legislation, the 2009 anti-Hong Kong Express Rail Link Movement, the 2012 Anti-National Education Demonstration, and the annual June 4th Vigil and July 1 parade. Overshadowed by large-scale democratic movements, rights movements have been small-scale and sporadic. All of these political movements aimed to resist China's influence, illustrating the inherent tension of 'one country, two systems'. Massive social movements became 'an integral part of a broader process of public deliberation and interaction between society and the government',[17] since the oppositional voices could not be effectively channelled into the institutions under the semi-democratic system dominated by pro-establishment camp.
2. **2014–2019: peaceful civil disobediences and its ramifications**
   The 2014 Occupy Central movement was the first civil disobedience movement in Hong Kong's history, marking a watershed in the constitutional and social movement development in the city. It has fundamentally changed the ecology of political movements and constitutional dynamics in Hong Kong, particularly the constitutional dialogue between the central government and Hong Kong. The Occupy Central distinguished itself from the previous political movements in the following respects.

   The agenda—The agenda of previous political movements was relatively passive, aiming to resist the infiltration of China's influences to preserve the freedom and autonomy of Hong Kong or to achieve democracy strictly within the Basic Law framework. By contrast, Occupy Central called for the fulfilment of a direct and immediate democracy, which marked a shift in the agenda of Hong Kong's democratic movements from defensive to offensive. Occupy Central participants no longer accepted 'the principle of gradual and orderly progress' of achieving democratisation, as stipulated by the Basic Law and interpreted by Beijing. The pattern adopted by the 'old' generation of pan-democrats in negotiation with Beijing was abandoned. Instead, Occupy Central demanded a full democracy based on a liberal interpretation of the Basic Law from Hong Kong's perspective.

The target—While the previous mass movements (except the annual June 4th Vigil) mainly engaged with local authorities, the Occupy Central directly targeted and pressured the central government to implement universal suffrage.

The form of dialogue—Occupy Central broke with the established framework by demanding direct dialogue with the central government through social movements. In the past, dialogues with the central government regarding political reform were mostly conducted through institutional platforms or political parties, such as the 2009–2010 round of electoral reform consultations.

Repertoire of social movements[18]—Occupy Central apparently overturned the ritual of the previous social movements, which had been criticised for being increasingly ceremonial. Instead, it adopted a 'destructive' form of action, opposing traditional ones that emphasised law and order. This innovative form of mobilisation not only attracted new adherents and the younger generations, but also inevitably led to radicalisation and decentralisation of the movement, which later escaped the control of the Occupy Central leaders and inspired the violent means of civil defiance.

Despite its failure to achieve universal suffrage agenda, Occupy Central had far-reaching ramifications for social movement development in Hong Kong. It opened the door for the radicalisation of social mobilisation in terms of both agenda and means. The failure to achieve democratic reform by peaceful means resulted in the disillusion of achieving political reform within the constitutional framework and the rise of pro-independence activism. Young, more radical activists came to the forefront to take the place of the 'old' democratic activists who preferred conventional mild approaches and were more willing to engage with China. The landmark event was the 2016 Fishball Revolution,[19] which involved violent clashes between police and protesters and was labelled 'the worst outbreak of rioting since the 1960s' in the city.[20] The Fishball Revolution catalysed the radicalisation of social movements in Hong Kong, characterised by civil defiance and a pro-independence/localism ethos.

Occupy Central has also significantly impacted the constitutional dynamics in Hong Kong by disrupting the fragile 'one country, two systems' equilibrium. Since Occupy Central emerged, Beijing's governance of Hong Kong has become more hands-on and assertive, with an increasing emphasis on the 'one country' principle. The previously existing but uneasy trust between Beijing and the pan-democratic camp has been completely sabotaged, leaving no channel for dialogue between the two sides—something the city desperately needs in the face of the deepened division resulting from Occupy Central. During and after the civil disobedience movement, the rule of law in Hong Kong faced unprecedented challenges and attacks from both the establishment and social movement sectors. The judiciary, which used to be able to maintain a transcendent position amidst political struggles, has been increasingly entangled in social movement-related cases and sensitive political disputes. In the past, Hong Kong courts have attempted to strike a delicate balance between human rights protection as demanded by civil society and upholding the central government's authority. The severe political polarisation has rendered such a task increasingly impossible, particularly in civil-unrest-related cases in which law and order are at stake.

3. **2019–present: civil defiance and radical constitutional change**
The 2019 anti-extradition bill protest shocked the world and Hong Kong for the city had never seen such violent, long-lasting protest in a society that cherished law and order. The protest evolved from the two largest peaceful demonstrations in the city's history, leading to occupation of the Legislative Council (LegCo) building and ultimately violent clashes with the police across the city, albeit accompanied by continuing peaceful public meetings and processions. The trigger for the protest was similar to that of conventional social movements, that is, to resist the erosion of the city's high degree of autonomy and freedom by China. However, the movement's agenda has gradually changed from requesting the government to withdraw the extradition bill to fulfilling the 'five demands', including implementing dual universal suffrage for both the LegCo and the CE—a revival of Occupy Central's agenda but in a much more radicalised form. Starting in March 2019, the protest lasted for more than a year and only waned a little after the breakup of the Covid-19 pandemic in early 2020. The enforcement of the Hong Kong NSL on 1 July 2020 marked the end of this long-lasting civil defiance.

The anti-extradition bill protest was largely caused by Hong Kong residents' long-held fears of the erosion of their freedom and the failure of the institutional design under the Basic Law to effectively absorb oppositional voices. Rather than addressing these issues, Beijing turned to a repressive approach to eradicate the opposition and eliminate contentious politics in Hong Kong. The overarching aim of the NSL, coupled with its spin-off constitutional and legal reforms, is to narrow down, if not completely close, the political and legal opportunities that encouraged social mobilisation and oppositional politics. By doing that, the NSL has fundamentally reshaped Hong Kong's constitutional practices, as reflected in the four key aspects.

Firstly, the NSL ultimately fulfils the Grundnorm shift in Hong Kong's legal system and entrenches Chinese constitutional discourses in Hong Kong. The NSL endorses the application of the Chinese constitution to Hong Kong, and through the NSL, the legal firewall that was originally designed by the Basic Law to separate Chinese law from the Hong Kong common law system has been reconstrued to allow Beijing's legal intervention.[21] In the post-NSL era, the Chinese constitutional discourses—emphasising unlimited sovereignty, legitimacy of one-party rule and patriotism—prevails, and it not only de-legitimises but also illegalises the oppositional camp's discourse to mobilise social movements.

Secondly, the governance structure in Hong Kong and the relationship between the central authorities and Hong Kong government have been reshaped. The NSL expands the presence of central authorities in Hong Kong and further moves the governance mode from the 'separation of powers' model favoured by the pro-liberal camp towards the 'executive-led government' model preferred by Beijing. There is also a worrying trend of an emerging 'police state' in Hong Kong after the enactment of the NSL.[22] The public's trust in the police's neutrality has been significantly undermined during the 2019 crisis, which has further pushed the police towards Beijing and became the most reliable ally of the central authorities. The judiciary in the post-NSL era has also become increasingly deferential to the authority of central and local governments in dealing with social movement-related cases.

Thirdly, democratic development in Hong Kong faces a major reversal. The enactment of the NSL was soon followed by a series of electoral reforms that drastically reduced democratic representation and resulted in the massive disqualification of pan-democrats. The political reform has successfully purged oppositional forces from institutionalised politics, aiming to end contentious politics in the LegCo and further enhance the executive branch's power. The setbacks mark a total failure of 30-year efforts by the social movement sector to increase democratic inputs into Hong Kong's political system.

The last significant impact is the collapse of social movement sectors and shrinking space of political and civil rights. The key individual activists and organisations in Hong Kong's social movement sector have been prosecuted under the NSL or other security-related Hong Kong laws. Oppositional organisations and labour unions established before or during the Occupy Central and the anti-extradition bill protest have ceased operations, including all the leading social movement organisations that existed for three decades. The crackdown on pan-democratic politicians has dismantled the networks between civil society and political parties, and the prosecution of crowdfunding has further cut off financial support for movement mobilisation. The constraints on political and civil rights imposed by the NSL have left little room for Hong Kong's civil society to mobilise any large-scale collective actions.

The 2019 anti-extradition bill protest and the resulting NSL mark a U-turn in the constitutional and social movement development in Hong Kong. Along with the transition from civil disobedience to civil unrest, the constitutional system in Hong Kong has transitioned from semi-democracy to semi-authoritarianism.[23] The effect of the NSL and its implicit constitutional reform in Hong Kong is obvious. The previous existing structural openings for social mobilisation have been closed, and as a result, massive protests and social movements immediately disappeared. Situated in a comparative context with China and Taiwan, the case of Hong Kong provides a valuable lens through which to observe the causal relationship between the increase of authoritarian elements in a constitutional system and the demobilisation of social movements.

Taiwan: Civil Disobedience and Rights to Resist under Liberal Constitutionalism

Social movements have been the bottom-up momentum pushing for constitutional reform throughout Taiwan's history. In the pre-democratic period, Taiwan adopted a hybrid model of constitutionalism that simultaneously combined the features of both liberal and authoritarian constitutionalism. The gap between the genuine constitutionalism on paper and authoritarian practices in reality created a critical space for enduring pro-democratic movements, which ultimately led to the lifting of martial law in 1987. During the transitional period, massive political movements, such as the 1990 Wild Lily student movement, continued to promote democratic consolidation. Along with the constitutional transition came the dramatic legal reform, resulting in the liberalisation of the judiciary and legal system. The new rule of law developments provided unprecedented opportunities for the rise of rights movements, which used to be insignificant spin-off campaigns of political movements in the pre-democratic period. Legislative lobbying, public interests litigation, and constitutional reviews have become effective legal tools deployed by campaigners for advocating rights causes. The most illustrative case is the LGBT rights movement, which made Taiwan the first region in Asia to legalise same-sex marriage.

In 2014, the legislative gridlock over the passing of the Cross-Strait Service Trade Agreement (CSSTA) with mainland China and the fear of erosion of Taiwan's independence by closer cross-strait economic integration triggered the Sunflower movement. Though mass political and social movements are not strange to Taiwan society, the Sunflower movement still shocked Taiwan and the whole world for its radical move to occupy both the Legislative Yuan and Administrative Yuan against the backdrop of a democratic constitutionalism. It also prompted difficult constitutional questions regarding the right to resistance under a democratic system, which were put before and ultimately recognised by the courts in Taiwan.[24]

In a democratic context that is conducive to social movements and public consultation, why would such a radical political movement as the Sunflower movement have arisen? There is a combination of factors contributing to such unprecedented civil disobedience. From a constitutional perspective, it is worth noting that democratic transition and long-term political movements have failed to resolve the three thorny issues deeply embedded in the Constitution of the Republic of China (ROC) as identified by Yeh: the infeasibility of formal constitutional change, political gridlock, and fragile constitutional sovereignty.[25] These thorny issues resulted from the unique history of the ROC Constitution and the contentious relationship between mainland China and Taiwan due to sovereignty disputes. The inherent deficiencies of the ROC Constitution have, on the one hand, triggered continuous political movements aiming for fundamental constitutional reform but, on the other hand, prevented any amendment to make the ROC Constitution conform to the political and social reality in Taiwan. The political impasse that triggered the 2014 Sunflower movement is a direct manifestation of the three unsettled issues embedded in Taiwan's constitutional practices, and the eruption of the Sunflower movement marked the culmination of the dilemma.

The Sunflower movement has significant implications for civil defiance worldwide, especially the anti-extradition protest in Hong Kong and probably even the 2021 occupation of the Capitol Building in the United States. Given its radical nature, the Sunflower movement is not a typical liberal conception of civil disobedience, but it was nevertheless concluded with a largely peaceful way and political compromises. Unlike the anti-extradition bill protest in Hong Kong, it did not evolve into violent unrest and furious clashes between the police and protesters. Only a few protesters were convicted and given relatively lenient sentences.[26] The Sunflower movement achieved its direct goal of blocking the trade pact and enacting new laws to monitor all cross-strait agreements.[27] More importantly, activists have successfully transformed their activism strategies 'from protest to electioneering'.[28] The movement momentum contributed to consecutive electoral debacles of the Kuomintang (KMT) and Democratic Progressive Party's (DPP's) landslide victories in subsequent elections. Core Sunflower activist also formed their own movement-party, which quickly emerged as the third largest political party in the legislature after the 2016 election and continuously pursues the broader political agenda of the Sunflower movement. The Sunflower movement continues to inspire a series of institutional and extra-institutional activism focusing on referendum legislation, constitutional revision, recalls, cross-strait politics oversight, and congressional accountability.[29]

Given the success of the Sunflower movement, some would have regarded or expected it to be a transformational moment in Taiwan's politics for its challenge to the fundamental authority of the constitutional order. Nevertheless, despite its sweeping impacts on the subsequent elections and transfiguration of the political landscape, it has not achieved the final goal put forward by many Sunflower advocates: to promote fundamental constitutional amendment to resolve the fragile constitutional sovereignty issue through referendum. Henceforth, how to deal with the above-mentioned three thorny constitutional issues and the fluid cross-strait relationship still depends on political and societal dynamics rather than any institutionalised mechanism. A stable constitutional order is yet to be established. The same issues that triggered the Sunflower movement could probably re-emerge, and similar populist movements that challenge the authority of the ROC Constitution are still likely to occur in the future.

Comparative Remarks

Social movements in mainland China, Hong Kong, and Taiwan shared the common aim of liberalising and democratising constitutional systems, but resulting in divergent developmental trajectories. Two key salient contrasts merit particular attention. One is why China's rights movements failed to break the bottleneck and escalate to politically oriented campaigns or civil disobedience, as in the cases of Hong Kong and Taiwan. The other question is why Hong Kong's civil disobedience evolved into civil unrest, which led to setbacks in its democratic constitutionalism in contrast to the political compromises achieved by the Sunflower movement in Taiwan. Among socio-economic factors, the structure of constitutional opportunities plays a crucial role in the shaping of social movements.

The lack of political campaigning in China vis-à-vis Hong Kong and Taiwan highlights the key distinction between party–state constitutionalism and hybrid/democratic constitutionalism: the former is characterised by a completely enclosed political system and tight constraints on freedom and rights that leave little room for political mobilisation.

The failure of Chinese rights activists' efforts to escalate *weiquan* movements to political campaigning is attributed to three key structural dimensions of China's party–state constitutionalism:

1. The ideology of so-called socialist constitutionalism as opposed to 'Western' democracy. Both pre-democratic Taiwan and post-colonial Hong Kong adopt hybrid constitutionalism that embraces eventual democratisation and liberal elements on paper, but full democracy and rights protection is not instituted in practice. Such a gap created a critical opening for movement mobilisation. However, the Chinese Constitution, with its dominant socialist ideology, gave hardly any ideological legitimacy to Chinese activists who aim to challenge the political system. Instead, demanding constitutional reform or initiating civil disobedience equal overturning the socialist system and thus would involve extra-legal risks, as illustrated by a series of cases of Chinese rights activists convicted of inciting the subversion of state power.[30]
2. The complete lack of elections in China's party–state system. Even with narrow, uneven suffrage, such elections could promote social movement mobilisation.[31] In many authoritarian regimes, partly free elections created an opening in the political–legal structure for social movement activists to establish solidarity across

the civil society, reach out for public followings, and solicit moral and material resources for their courses. In both Taiwan and Hong Kong, social movement sectors and oppositional political parties have cooperated with each other for social movement mobilisation. Unfortunately, Chinese rights activists lack such opportunities and public forums to reach out to a wider audience and initiate campaigns beyond legal arenas.

3. Tight restrictions on freedoms and rights. State-guaranteed rights or their absence wielded a large influence on movement mobilisation, and rights to assembly, association, and speech especially mattered.[32] The different degrees of political rights guaranteed by the constitutions also contribute to the divergent social movement trajectories in the three regions. Unlike democratic Taiwan and liberal authoritarian Hong Kong, which both guarantee full protection of political and civil rights, the Chinese party–state is at the other end of the spectrum. While activists in Taiwan and Hong Kong could establish social movement organisations, disseminate movement propaganda via various media channels, initiate online mobilisation, and stage demonstrations, all these lawful mobilisation means are inapplicable in China, leaving the strict legalistic approach as the only option. Unfortunately, in the aftermath of the anti-extradition bill crisis, Hong Kong appears to have followed the same trajectory as China. The NSL imposes significant constraints on the political and civil rights previously enjoyed by Hong Kong residents under the Basic Law. One of the direct ramifications is the collapse and disempowerment of social movement sectors. Almost all the social movement and oppositional organisations were disbanded in the post-NSL era, accompanied by the disappearance of public protests and demonstrations from the street. It highlights the close relationship between constitutional rights and social movement mobilisation capacities.

The second puzzle arising from the comparison is why the Sunflower movement concluded with peaceful political compromises and benign state–society interaction, whereas the anti-extradition bill protest in Hong Kong evolved into urban guerrilla-type unrest and ended in political misfortune. Five major structural factors may contribute to such a contrast:

Institutional Channels for Absorbing Oppositional Voices and Forces

The institutional design under the Hong Kong Basic Law prevents oppositional political forces from challenging the dominant status of the establishment in either the Legislature or executive branch, thus hindering the channelling of oppositional voices into the government. Before the amendment of the electoral system in the post-NSL period, the CE was elected by a 1,200-member nominating committee mostly consisting of pro-Beijing members. The LegCo was also dominated by the pro-establishment camp due to design of electoral system under the Basic Law. Pan-democratic members held less than half of the LegCo seats while they usually won approximately 60% of votes in direct elections. Moreover, only the Executive branch (rather than LegCo members) can introduce substantive laws, there is little room for popularly elected pan-democratic members to accomplish their political agendas. The only role they could play is to block bills introduced by the government and express criticism through the LegCo platform. After the introduction of the NSL, the political arena became further enclosed in Hong Kong.

Consequently, social movements became the only feasible way for society to engage with and impose pressure on the government when fundamentally contentious issues arose. In responding to the rising pro-independence/localist wave after Occupy Central, the authorities deployed disqualification and oath-taking as a new legal means to further narrow the political arena for the oppositional camp. Such constraints further block the channel for oppositional forces to achieve their political agendas within institutions, prompting them to employ escalating street action. Unlike Sunflower movement activists, who could either collaborate with the oppositional party or join the politics themselves to pursue the movement's agenda, there are no such political openings for anti-extradition bill protesters or their sympathisers who preferred a mild approach; thus, the movement itself meant life or death for a large proportion of activists, rendering any political compromise impossible.

Channels for Dialogue between the State and Society

Another issue caused by the semi-enclosed political system was the lack of dialogues between the state and civil society during the anti-extradition bill protest. The problem is partly caused by the decentralisation of the protest itself and partly by the limited or no leverage enjoyed by the pan-democratic camp and social movement sector to engage in dialogue with the establishment and central authorities, since the oppositional camp could hardly challenge the dominant position of the establishment under the constitutional framework. In contrast to the KMT—the ruling party during the Sunflower movement—that had to concern itself with the opinions of its constituencies, the ruling elites in Hong Kong, particularly the executive branch, are more concerned with the opinions of the central government, which is the source of their power. Therefore, violence and mass mobilisation became the last resort as perceived by protesters in the absence of other forms of political pressure. Particularly after the two largest demonstrations failed to pressure the government to withdraw the extradition bill, it seemed to radical protesters that all the formal and informal channels for addressing their grievances had been blocked and violence was the lonely option left.

Although the anti-extradition bill targeted issues that could only be resolved with the approval of Beijing, no dialogue channel existed between the social movement sector and the central government. Under the constraints of the Basic Law, the central authorities operated as a shadow power in Hong Kong, mainly exercising their political influences behind the scenes. That was also the case in the 2019 crisis. The central authorities were unwilling and also had no available channel to directly interact with the social movement sector. After the 2019 crisis, Beijing has dramatically expanded its presence and powers in Hong Kong through the NSL, ignoring or removing many of the constraints on the central power imposed by the Basic Law.

The dialogue channel between Beijing and the pan-democratic camp, who might have been able to play a mediating role, was also blocked. The previous trust between the pan-democratic politicians and Beijing has deteriorated after Occupy Central and the rise of localist activism, leading to the closure of previously existing formal and informal dialogue channels. The inability to influence Beijing's policy over Hong Kong within the political system, in turn, drove the pan-democratic to become either radicalised or unwilling to keep a distance from the pro-independent and radical forces. A vicious circle was thus created and has been reinforced continuously. Even a large portion of

Hong Kong society would have welcomed a mild approach to resolving the 2019 crisis, there were simply no available channels for mediated politics.

(Un)divisionable Ruling Elites

The internal elite divisions play a crucial role in democratic transitions and the peaceful conclusion of civil defiance.[33] During the Sunflower movement, open divisions between the KMT leaders—mainly the president and the president of the Legislative Yuan—contributed to the avoidance of violent clashes between protesters and police in the Legislative Yuan and the ultimate peaceful evacuation of the latter. The DPP, the oppositional party, was also an important ally for Sunflower protesters. Despite a lack of formal association between the two, the DPP provided supports for the movement in both political and social movement arenas, coordinated with the dissident KMT members, facilitated the peaceful resolution of the occupation, and imposed pressure on the ruling party. Similar checks and balances for political powers were absent in Hong Kong. Although there were implicit disagreements over how to address the key demands put forward by anti-extradition protesters, the establishment ultimately maintained its solidarity and adopted an increasingly hard-line approach under Beijing's instruction. The undivisionable nature of the ruling elites in Hong Kong is largely determined by the governance structure in which the source of their power and authority resides in the central government rather than the electorate.

Authorities' Perception of Political Movements

While political and social movements are regarded as inalienable components of political processes by democracies, they are deemed as threats to political security under authoritarianism. Different perceptions of social movements determine governments' responses to bottom-up political challenges. Despite controversies, the Sunflower movement was largely perceived by the majority of Taiwanese politicians and society as part of the 'civic constitutionalism'[34] that made up for the deficiencies of the democratic system. By contrast, following Occupy Central, civil disobedience in Hong Kong has been regarded by Beijing as a colour revolution aiming at overruling the political system and using Hong Kong as a basis for subverting the socialist system on the mainland. The colour revolution mindset sets the tone for a hard-line approach to achieve repression in preference to addressing the specific issues raised by protesters free from ideological influences.

Autonomy to Handle Political and Societal Contention

In sharp contrast to the *de facto* independence of Taiwan's polity, the 'lack of sovereignty and stateness'[35] in Hong Kong under the 'one country, two systems' has undermined the city's autonomy and flexibility to handle political contention according to local conditions and achieve political compromise during the 2019 crisis. As analysed previously, despite the inclination towards a soft-line approach among some pro-establishment politicians and senior officials, including the CE herself,[36] their hands were tied by the tight grip of Beijing, which decided to take a repressive approach. Moreover, mainland media portraited the Occupy Central and anti-extradition bill protest as a 'colour revolution' with a strong 'anti-China' agenda, largely ignoring the specific demands for democracy and government accountability. Such propaganda led to a surge of hostility in China towards social movements and even Hong Kong society as a whole. In the face of both political pressure from Beijing and tremendous nationalism sentiment on the mainland, it became increasingly impossible for the Hong Kong government or anyone from the establishment camp to tone down the political rhetoric, divide mild activists from radical ones for the purposes of dialogue, and address some specific demands based on a relatively broad consensus in society. After the Occupy Central and anti-extradition bill protest, Beijing has become more assertive and the principal-agent governance model has been further enhanced in Hong Kong, which was the exact what the Sunflower movement targeted and aimed to avoid.

Conclusion

The different trajectories of social movements in mainland China, Hong Kong, and Taiwan demonstrate how the structure of opportunities provided by different constitutional systems contribute to the shaping of social movement development and state–society engagement. Under party–state authoritarianism such as that in China, the completely enclosed polity and the lack of political rights inhibit any attempts at political mobilisation, and the ebb and flow of rights movements depends on the state's move towards liberal or authoritarian dimensions of its legal system. Compared to the party–state and semi-democratic systems, Taiwan's democracy has demonstrated robust flexibility and the capability to accommodate radical civil disobedience and achieve political compromise. By contrast, the political mischief of similar civil disobedience movements in Hong Kong is doomed by the unique 'one country, two systems' constitutional arrangement and semi-democracy. Unlike the party–state system in China, Hong Kong's liberal semi-constitutionalism—before the enactment of the NSL—fully protected the freedom and rights that enabled Hong Kong civil society to mobilise massive social movements. However, compared to Taiwan's democracy, Hong Kong's constitutional practices are characterised by two distinctive features: one is the lack of full elections and competitive politics, and the other is the reinforced principal-agent governance model under 'one country, two systems' formula. These two features prevent oppositional voices from being channelled into the establishment and thus foster the radicalisation of social movements.

Besides being shaped by different constitutional systems, social movements in the three regions have also driven constitutional changes in those regions. Social movements in the Greater China area have all attempted to increase 'we the people' input into the constitutions and make up for deficiencies of legitimacy in the three constitutions. Constitutionalism is often considered a transplant of Western ideas and systems into Asia; however, the spontaneous social movements in the three Chinese societies have facilitated the indigenisation of liberal constitutionalism practice and its integration with local circumstances. Constitutional ideas of human rights protection, government accountability, and universal suffrage have spread or taken root in the civil society through such bottom-up mobilisation.

Although social movements in the three regions shared the common aim of liberalising and democratising constitutional systems, they resulted in divergent constitutional trajectories. Taiwan's liberal constitutionalism has gone as far apart as ever from that in the other two regions, while social movements and constitutional development in Hong Kong have moved further towards the Chinese model in the post-NSL era, marked by increasingly authoritarian constitutionalism and the collapse of social movement sectors. By contrast, Taiwan's constitutional autonomy has been further consolidated with more diversified competitive politics, while, simultaneously, the fragile constitutional sovereignty issue remains and so-called civic constitutionalism also raises the 'instantaneous democracy' issue[37] as represented by the Sunflower movement, posing fundamental challenges to democratic constitutionalism that have not yet been fully addressed by Taiwanese society.

The quest for constitutionalism in the Greater China area has proceeded for more than a century and is still an unfinished course. Bottom-up social movements have played, and will continue to play, a role as important as institutionalised politics in contributing to constitutional development, particularly regarding democratising and liberating constitutional practices. Social movements and constitutional development in the Greater China area are a continuing story that may provide valuable insights into the engagement of social movements and constitutional changes in transitional societies worldwide.

Notes

1 For brevity, 'China' in the chapter only refers to Mainland China unless otherwise specified. And this chapter does not discuss ethnic conflicts and protests in Xinjiang and Tibet.

2 The full name of the law is the 'Law of the People's Republic of China on Safeguarding National Security in the Hong Kong Special Administrative Region', which was promulgated on 30 June 2020.

3 See Doowon Suh, 'How Do Political Opportunities Matter for Social Movements?' (2001) 3 Sociological Quarterly 437, 456.

4 Doug McAdam, *Political Process and the Development of Black Insurgency 1930-1970* (University of Chicago Press 1999) 42.

5 Ibid 43.

6 Jacques Delisle, 'Legalization without Democratization in China under Hu Jintao' in Cheng Li (ed), *China's Changing Political Landscape: Prospects for Democracy* (Brookings Institution Press 2007).

7 See Kevin O'Brien and Li Lianjiang, *Rightful Resistance in Rural China* (CUP 2006).

8 *Qi Yuling* case was once regarded as China's Marbury v. Madison case for being a breakthrough in judicial review. It was the first time that the Chinese Supreme Court confirmed that the Constitution could be directly used as a basis in judicial judgement. For more information about the case, see Shen Kui, 'Is It the Beginning of the Era of the Rule of the Constitution? Reinterpreting China's "First Constitutional Case"' (2003) 12 Pacific Rim Law & Policy Journal 199.

9 Sun Zhigang, a college graduate who was detained for failing to show his identity card when quested by the police and was later beaten to death in the detention centre. The event triggered wide concerns on the media. Invoking the constitutional review mechanism under the Legislative Law, two groups of law scholars submitted constitutional citizen petitions, requesting constitutional review of the Custody and Repatriation Measures, which was later abolished by the central authorities.

10 See Fu Hualing and Han Zhu, 'After the July 9(709) Crackdown: The Future of Human Rights Lawyering' (2018) 41(5) Fordham International Law Journal 1135.

11 Han Zhu and Lu Jun, 'The Crackdown on Rights-Advocacy NGOs in Xi's China: Politicizing the Law and Legalizing the Repression', (2022) 31 Journal of Contemporary China 518–538.

12 Ibid.

13 'Notice by the Supreme People's Court of Adding Causes of Action in Civil Cases' (12 December 2018), <http://www.lawinfochina.com/display.aspx?id=29823&lib=law> accessed 24 October 2021.

14 Elizabeth Perry, 'Chinese Conceptions of "Rights": From Mencius to Mao – and Now' (2008) 1 Perspectives on Politics 37.

15 For a detailed analysis of the development of authoritarian legality in Xi's China, see Zhu and Lu (n 11).
16 Cora Chan, 'Can Hong Kong Remain a Liberal Enclave Within China? Analysis of the Hong Kong National Security Law' (2021) 2 Public Law 271, 272.
17 Fu Hualing and Michael Jackson, 'Protest, Law and Regime Type' in Brian Christopher Jones (ed), *Democracy and Rule of Law in China's Shadow* (Hart Publishing 2021).
18 About the concept, see Charles Tilly, *Social Movements, 1768-2004 3-4* (Paradigm Publishers 2004).
19 The Fishball Revolution was triggered by the police's crackdown on unlicensed street hawkers during the Chinese New Year holiday.
20 'Street Violence and Politics' (*The Economist*, 11 February 2016) <https://www.economist.com/china/2016/02/13/street-violence-and-politics> accessed 24 October 2021.
21 Han Zhu, 'The Hong Kong National Security Law: The Shifted Grundnorm of Hong Kong's Legal Order and Its Implications' in Fu Hualing and Michael Hor (ed), *Hong Kong under China's National Security Law* 49–71 (Hong Kong University Press 2022).
22 Victoria Tin-bor Hui, 'Hong Kong's New Police State' (*The Diplomat*, 1 June 2021) <https://thediplomat.com/2021/05/hong-kongs-new-police-state/> accessed 24 October 2021.
23 Benny Tai, 'Round Three of Hong Kong's Constitutional Game: From Semi-democracy to Semi-authoritarianism' (2019) 49 Hong Kong Law Journal 335.
24 See Jimmy Chia-Shin Hsu and Anne SY Cheung, 'The Ultimate Test of Fidelity: Judicial Responses to Civil Disobedience in Hong Kong and Taiwan' in Brian Christopher Jones (ed), *Democracy and Rule of Law in China's Shadow* (Hart Publishing 2021).
25 Jiunn-rong Yeh, *The Constitution of Taiwan: A Contextual Analysis* (Hart Publishing 2016) 246–252.
26 Hsu and Cheung (n 24).
27 In 2019, Article 5-3 of the Act Governing Relations between the People of the Taiwan Area and the Mainland Area was amended to establish a high threshold for approving and enforcing cross-strait agreements. See 'Act Governing Relations between the People of the Taiwan Area and the Mainland Area' <https://law.moj.gov.tw/ENG/LawClass/LawAll.aspx?pcode=Q0010001> accessed 24 October 2021.
28 Ming-sho Ho, *Challenging Beijing's Mandate of Heaven: Taiwan's Sunflower Movement and Hong Kong's Umbrella Movement* (Temple University Press 2019) 193.
29 Ibid 186–187.
30 Han Zhu, 'Law-Oriented Lawyering vs Political Lawyering: A Comparative Study of China, Taiwan and South Korea' 48(2) Hong Kong Law Journal 431.
31 Charles Tilly and Lesley J. Wood, *Social Movements, 1768–2008* (Paradigm Publishers 2004) 55–56.
32 Ibid 54.
33 Guillermo O'Donnell and Philippe C. Schmitter, *Transitions from Authoritarian Rule: Tentative Conclusions about Uncertain Democracies* (The Johns Hopkins University Press 1986) 7.
34 Jiunn-rong Yeh, 'Marching Towards Civic Constitutionalism with Sunflowers' in Brian Christopher Jones (ed), *Law and Politics of the Taiwan Sunflower and Hong Kong Umbrella Movements* 49–61 (Routledge 2017).
35 Stephan Ortmann, 'The Lack of Sovereignty, the Umbrella Movement, and Democratisation in Hong Kong' (2016) 24(2) Asia Pacific Law Review 108.
36 'I Would Quit If I Had a Choice, Says Hong Leader in Leaked Audio' (*The Guardian*, 2 September 2019) <https://www.theguardian.com/world/2019/sep/02/hong-kong-carrie-lam-would-quit-if-had-choice-leaked-audio>.
37 Ho (n 28) 179.

Bibliography

Ngoc Son Bui, 'Social Movements and Constitutionalism in Japan, South Korea, and Taiwan' (2019) 14 Asian Journal of Comparative Law 51.

Ming-sho Ho, *Challenging Beijing's Mandate of Heaven: Taiwan's Sunflower Movement and Hong Kong's Umbrella Movement* (Temple University Press 2019).

Fu Hualing and Michael Jackson, 'Protest, Law and Regime Type' in Brian Christopher Jones (ed), *Democracy and Rule of Law in China's Shadow* (Hart Publishing 2021).

Brian Christopher Jones (ed), *Law and Politics of the Taiwan Sunflower and Hong Kong Umbrella Movements* (Hart Publishing 2017).

Michael H.K. Ng and John D. Wong (eds), *Civil Unrest and Governance in Hong Kong: Law and Order from Historical and Cultural Perspectives* (Routledge 2017).

Ian Rowen, 'Inside Taiwan's Sunflower Movement: Twenty-Four Days in a Student-Occupied Parliament, and the Future of the Region' (2015) 74(1) The Journal of Asian Studies 5.

Waikeung Tam, *Legal Mobilization under Authoritarianism: The Case of Post-Colonial Hong Kong* (CUP 2013).

Jiunn-rong Yeh, *The Constitution of Taiwan: A Contextual Analysis* (Hart Publishing 2016).

Han Zhu, 'Social Movements and the Law in Contemporary China: A Comparative Approach' (PhD thesis, the University of Hong Kong 2016).

Han Zhu and Lu Jun, 'The Crackdown on Rights-Advocacy NGOs in Xi's China: Politicizing the Law and Legalizing the Repression' (2022) 31 *Journal of Contemporary China* 518–538.

14

'RUNAWAY LEGITIMATION' AND ITS LIMITS*

LGBTQ Rights in China

Darius Longarino

Introduction

In 2018, as lawyers prepared to represent a transgender woman who was suing her employer for discrimination, they focused on how to explain why the law should protect her. Chinese law prohibits employment discrimination based on 'sex' but says nothing about gender identity discrimination. To put the case more squarely in the law's ambit, the lawyers planned to argue that gender identity discrimination was a form of sex discrimination. However, when they appeared in court, the judge moved straight to assessing the evidence. The lawyers observed that it appeared as if the judge just assumed the case was in the law's scope because 'he had heard of "discrimination", and he knew that was bad'.

The lawyers' concern that the judge would hesitate to accept the lawsuit's premise was reasonable. Official discourse is near-silent on lesbian, gay, bisexual, transgender, and queer (LGBTQ) issues, and when that silence is broken, the message is usually negative. Chinese law not only lacks express protections for LGBTQ people but in several instances also discriminates against them. Security agents closely surveil LGBTQ advocates and use intimidation, interrogations, and detentions to curtail their work. Censors constrain LGBTQ-related speech.

Why then did the court move into this difficult territory, seemingly naturally? An underlying process, identified by Michael Dowdle as 'runaway legitimation', laid the groundwork:

> ['Runaway legitimation'] describes a dynamic in which consistent appeal by a political elite to particular principles in legitimating particular political practices and institutions will cause these principles to become increasingly embedded in those political practices even if the elites making these appeals did not originally believe or intend these practices to actually embody these principles.[1]

* For their feedback and encouragement, I deeply thank Sebastián Guidi, Di Wu, and my colleagues at Yale Law School's Paul Tsai China Center, Yangyang Cheng, Jeremy Daum, Paul Gewirtz, Jamie Horsley, Karman Lucero, Moritz Rudolph, Changhao Wei, and Robert Williams. I owe a special thanks to Susan Finder for alerting me to Judge Dou Jiangtao's article in *People's Judicature*, a key source in the chapter. All errors and omissions are my own.

DOI: 10.4324/9781003128243-17

The lawyers believed that the judge, although not familiar with LGBTQ issues, had internalized a norm against discrimination. Even without clear guidance from legislation, he extended the law's protection to the plaintiff (though he later ruled she lacked sufficient evidence to prove discrimination occurred).

This chapter surveys examples of how 'runaway legitimation' has created opportunities for LGBTQ rights claims. This dynamic has been both conceptual and, in Dowdle's coinage, 'infrastructural'. On the conceptual side, the Party-state's promotion of citizens' constitutional guarantees of equality, dignity, and human rights—especially those of marginalized groups, such as migrant workers, women, and people with disabilities—has generated greater belief in and respect for these rights among scholars, judges, government officials, and the public.[2] Such buy-in has increased the willingness of some legal actors to develop and/or accept new understandings of these rights. By changing public opinion through advocacy, China's LGBTQ movement has paved the way for these stakeholders to reason that such rights are inclusive of sexual and gender minorities.

On the 'infrastructural' side, decades of official rhetoric regarding—and actual investment in—strengthening the legal system built paths through which LGBTQ rights claims could be made. The professionalization of courts made them more likely to hear difficult cases and apply legal reasoning in them. This helped LGBTQ rights claims get into court and have a shot at succeeding on the merits. The adoption of transparency and public participation mechanisms, such as channels for submitting comments to lawmakers on draft legislation, also created openings.

Yet, the ground gained through these processes has been limited and is precariously held. There is no 'infrastructure' through which citizens can compel protection of their constitutional rights, most of all against state repression. Rather, the Constitution merely provides a legitimate discursive framework for rights claims that may or may not persuade official decision-makers in lawmaking and litigation. The Party, dominant in the constitutional order, can easily adjust the scope of the Constitution and laws to exclude LGBTQ rights—as well as use rawer forms of suppression against rights claims.

The chapter proceeds as follows: the 'The Legal Position of Sexual and Gender Minorities: From PRC Founding to the Turn of the Century' section gives a brief historical overview of the legal position of sexual and gender minorities in the People's Republic. the 'Arguments for Inclusion: Sexual Minorities as "Vulnerable Groups"' section builds on the work of John Balzano to show how discussions about the rights of 'vulnerable groups' in the early 2000s began to extend to gay people who were increasingly seen as an unjustly marginalized minority rather than as deviants deserving of opprobrium. The 'LGBTQ Rights Claims and the Constitution' section provides examples of how in the 2010s LGBTQ people began to forthrightly assert equal rights claims to courts and lawmakers and how these state actors responded. The 'State Backlash and Runaway Legitimation' section looks at how an emerging state backlash has stymied 'runaway legitimation'.

The Legal Position of Sexual and Gender Minorities: From PRC Founding to the Turn of the Century

From the 1950s through 1970s, high-level official discourse was near-silent on sexual and gender minorities.[3] Unlike the Soviet Union, which added a prohibition on male-male sex to its Criminal Code in 1934, the PRC never adopted a similar provision. Still, the actions of the police and legal system reflected a widely held view that homosexuality was an immoral affront to the natural gender order.

The highest level example of a state authority addressing same-sex sex as a legal issue occurred in 1957, when the High Court of Heilongjiang Province requested instructions from the Supreme People's Court (SPC) on how to handle a case involving two men who had consensual sex in a labor camp. At the time, work on a draft Criminal Law was ongoing but incomplete. The Heilongjiang High Court, noting that 'central authorities had yet to set regulations regarding this matter', said its members had two diverging views.[4] One suggested criminal penalties because the men had 'severely violated social morality', and such behavior 'harms social decency' and 'violates the physiology and functions of the human body'. The other, noting that the sex was consensual, suggested only administrative penalties because 'although its effect was bad, it constitutes a moral matter'. The Heilongjiang High Court noted that the Soviet Criminal Code stipulated a three-to-five-year sentence for male-male sex acts. The SPC responded that 'whether or not consensual sodomy between adults constitutes the commission of a crime awaits a legislative resolution. While the law still does not have an express provision, we believe it is suitable not to handle the situation your court raised criminally'.

Despite the 1957 SPC decision, 'sodomy was routinely interpreted by local courts and police as a crime, and homosexual men were sent to detention centers, labor camps, and prisons'.[5] Punishments for male-male sex acts would also be 'meted out haphazardly—by participants in mass, Party-mobilized campaigns, by the police, or by the relevant work unit'.[6] During the Cultural Revolution, homosexuality was regarded as something 'bourgeois, decadent and unnatural'.[7] People who engaged in same-sex sex were considered 'bad elements', and 'Red Guards initiated attacks on homosexuals as part of broader political attacks on class enemies'.[8]

After the Cultural Revolution, the Party began rebuilding the legal system and passed the Criminal Law in 1979. The new law included the crime of 'hooliganism', a catchall term for a broad and ill-defined set of behaviors authorities perceived as anti-social. Criminalizing 'hooliganism' was one tool in larger political campaigns to rein in wayward beliefs and 'unhealthy' lifestyles emerging in a society that authorities feared was changing too fast to control in the wake of Reform and Opening.[9] Throughout the 1980s and much of the 1990s, police subjected sexual minorities to harassment and criminal and administrative detention, including reeducation through labor.[10]

Julian Gewirtz details how the Party's concern with decadence informed its response to AIDS. A 1984 Ministry of Health directive connected AIDS to 'capitalist countries' serious social problems', including 'homosexuality and intravenous drug use'.[11] Consequently, the National AIDS Prevention Plan 1988–1991 stressed 'severely prohibiting prostitution, homosexuality and drug use'.[12] Several prominent officials dubbed AIDS as 'Loving Capitalism Disease', a pun on its Chinese name.[13]

When a health official, Dr. Wan Yanhai, began advancing a community-based approach to AIDS prevention, including counseling hotlines and discussion groups for gay men, authorities responded harshly. In 1993, the Ministry of Public Security ordered a crackdown on a gay men's discussion group co-organized by Dr. Wan. The ministry's order justified the condemnation: 'Homosexual activities distort human nature, violate social morality, corrupt social conduct, destroy family harmony, induce criminality, endanger public order, and are a key channel for the transmission of venereal diseases and AIDS'.[14]

As the 1990s went on, it became increasingly clear that repression was not a working strategy for fighting AIDS. Growing pressure from health authorities pushed the government, if only hesitantly, to see homosexuality 'as more than a simple matter for the police and labour camps'.[15] Police pressure eased. Lawmakers, as part of a renewed push to rationalize the legal system and improve China's global image on human rights, removed the pocket crime 'hooliganism' from the Criminal Law in 1997 ('hooliganism' was replaced with six specific crimes, none of which included same-sex sex).[16] The 2001 Third Edition of the Chinese Classification of Mental Disorders partially depathologized homosexuality and bisexuality.[17] The government also began funding sexual minority men's community groups to provide health education and services. Many discriminatory policies remained, including censorship guidelines that targeted 'homosexuality' alongside 'sexual perversions'.[18] Nonetheless, a thaw was underway.

Policies that affected transgender people also made progress during this time. In 2002, the Ministry of Public Security provided guidance to local public security bureaus on how to change gender markers on national identification cards for citizens who had completed gender-affirming surgery (GAS).[19] A year later, the Ministry of Civil Affairs, in conjunction with the SPC and National People's Congress (NPC), advised that citizens could marry in accordance with their new gender marker. Xinhua reported a Ministry of Civil Affairs official as saying that, in their right to marry, 'transsexuals are the same as other citizens of our country'.[20]

Arguments for Inclusion: Sexual Minorities as 'Vulnerable Groups'

The Rights of 'Vulnerable Groups'

The above policy shifts coincided with deepening market reforms that led to breakneck economic growth, yawning inequality, and social disruption. These transformations, accompanied by the spread of the Internet, stimulated widespread reflections on society and citizenship. In these discussions, the term 'vulnerable groups (弱势群体)' gained currency.[21] According to Balzano, the term originally referred to people who had been disadvantaged by economic reforms, such as workers who were laid off by state enterprises. But over time 'vulnerable groups' also began to include people whose disempowerment resulted from long-standing marginalization. 'At its core', Balzano wrote, the term was about 'the law helping certain groups to remedy the extreme economic and social disadvantages that they [could not] resolve on their own through other political, social, or economic means'.[22]

In the 1990s and 2000s, the government passed and strengthened a flurry of laws on protecting the rights and interests of youth, elderly people, women, workers, and people with disabilities.[23] New policies also further opened the courthouse door to citizens to effectuate these rights. Commentators framed support for 'vulnerable groups' as a key element of implementing political programs of the Party leadership, including Jiang Zemin's signature 'Three Represents', in which the Party represents 'the fundamental interests of the overwhelming majority of Chinese people'[24] and Hu Jintao's 'Harmonious Society' which aimed to reduce social conflict.[25] Some officials used the term when trying to rehabilitate the Party's global image after its bloody crackdown on the 1989 democracy movement. In a 1994 speech, Vice-Chairman of the NPC Standing Committee (NPCSC), Wang Hanbin, recounted state visits to northern European countries whose parliament members asked him about human rights in China. Wang explained that China guarantees citizens' fundamental rights, exemplified by its laws protecting 'vulnerable groups'.[26]

While the term 'vulnerable group' may connote the passive receipt of charity from a paternalist state, several authors used the term to advocate for structuring society on the basis of equal rights and citizenship for all. In 2003, Li Zhanhua, a Suzhou University Law School professor encapsulated this viewpoint in *People's Congress Studying*, 'Under the guidance of the concept of constitutionalism, a harmonious, tolerant, and stable society takes rights as its foundation, because only under a framework of equal rights can members of society not be divided between rich and poor but uniformly all be full members of society'.[27]

These ideas were not limited to the academy. In 2001, the SPC's *Qi Yuling* decision held for the first time that citizens' constitutional rights were justiciable in court. The decision's author explained the groundbreaking move in *People's Court Daily*, 'Following the development of our nation's social and political life, and the continued strengthening of citizen's rights consciousness, a large volume of disputes have sprung up because the fundamental rights based in the Constitution that citizens enjoy have been infringed'. Since there were often no laws pertinent to the alleged infringements, letting the Constitution 'become the direct legal basis for court judgments is absolutely necessary and urgent'.[28] Giving citizens greater agency in demanding protection of their constitutional rights in court raised the specter of 'separation of powers', a threat to the core constitutional principle of democratic centralism.[29] The SPC unceremoniously annulled the decision in 2008.

The 2003 Sun Zhigang incident further invigorated discussions about the rights of vulnerable groups and all citizens. In response to public blowback over Sun's tragic death and the police cover-up, the NPC added, 'The State respects and preserves human rights' to Article 33 of the Constitution.[30] A burgeoning rights protection movement gained momentum. Networks of lawyers, scholars, and activists used legal strategies, including constitutional arguments,[31] to advocate for the rights of workers, people with disabilities, people living with HIV/AIDS and Hepatitis B, religious minorities, and people affected by environmental pollution and land dispossession. The rights protection movement's discursive and legal strategies later inspired many LGBTQ activists.

The Rights of Sexual Minorities as 'Vulnerable Groups'

Balzano has shown how media and scholars began portraying sexual minorities as 'vulnerable groups' in the 2000s.[32] This section surfaces additional examples from this period, but with a focus on legal professionals who drew this analogy to argue that sexual minorities enjoyed constitutional rights. These examples demonstrate that mainstream figures on official platforms were willing and able to develop the meaning of constitutional values in bold new ways. They are especially impressive since they appeared only a few years after decriminalization and depathologization.

In a 2004 article in *Legal Daily* (a publication under the management of the Party's Central Commission for Political and Legal Affairs), Lei Yongquan, President and Party Secretary of a Primary People's Court in a rural county in Hubei, argued that the Constitution required the legalization of same-sex marriage.[33] Instead of depicting homosexuality as a form of moral degeneration or a foreign import, Lei asserted that gays had 'existed universally in human society—whether in the ancient past or today, in China or abroad, unceasingly'. But gays had been 'regularly ostracized by mainstream culture' and were 'a social minority, a weak [group] in society'. Because '"protection of the weak" is a key part of what it means to be a modern civilized society', the law should recognize gay rights.

Lei based his argument on Article 33 of the 1982 Constitution, which provides that 'All citizens of the People's Republic of China are equal before the law'. To appreciate his assertions' place in the 'runaway legitimation' process, it is important to recall that when drafters of the 1982 Constitution adopted Article 33, they had the Cultural Revolution top of mind. A near-identical provision to Article 33 first appeared in the 1954 Constitution, but the radical revolutionary Constitution of 1975 eliminated it and the 1978 Constitution did not bring it back. When the 1982 Constitution was being drafted, Peng Zhen, the Vice-Chairman of the Committee on Constitutional Amendment, urged NPC members that 'It is imperative to reinstate this provision, for it represents a basic principle that ensures the application of socialist democracy and legality'.[34] Referring to the Cultural Revolution's excesses, Peng stressed that 'no citizen is allowed to enjoy the privilege of being above the Constitution and the law'.[35]

But whereas Peng upheld Article 33 as a guardrail against an individual's abuse of official power, many commentators when discussing 'vulnerable groups' saw Article 33 as a kind of 'equal protection' clause. Lei took the idea that Article 33 was a safeguard against discriminatory laws and applied it to sexual minorities' rights. He held that Article 33 'requires that homosexuals and heterosexuals are the same [in that they] should receive equal protection of the law and enjoy all the benefits brought through law'. He posited that denying same-sex couples' access to marriage based on the 'man and woman' requirement in the Marriage Law was also a form of gender discrimination that violated Article 33. Writing at a time when only a handful of jurisdictions in the world had legalized same-sex marriage, Lei concluded with a striking aura of confidence and inevitability: 'when conditions are ripe, legislation should be passed to clearly provide for a system of same-sex marriage'.

In a 2005 article in *Procuratorate Daily* (a publication managed by the Supreme People's Procuratorate), legal scholar Bo Dalin reflected on a parade of nearly 100 gays and lesbians that had recently proceeded along the Shenzhen waterfront.[36] The parade—or a 'walk' as it was called to make it less politically sensitive—featured sing-alongs and a gigantic 9-by-11-meter rainbow flag. Bo observed, 'Looking back on the history of humankind's rights development, each instance of citizens gaining new rights is accompanied by a struggle or movement'. Now, through public demonstrations, gays in China were 'proving their existence to society' and 'calling for society's understanding and concern'.

Echoing Lei Yongquan, Bo wrote that 'the modern rule of law's respect and guarantee of human rights—especially respect and guarantee of the rights of vulnerable social groups—is the root of solving how to eliminate discrimination against minorities'. Referring to Article 33, he asserted that, 'national legislators, from the high-level perspective of the Constitution's respect and safeguarding of human rights and the entrustment of equal rights to citizens, should pay attention to gays' demands for the right to pursue a happy life, and eliminate society's discrimination and prejudice toward them …'. Analogous to Lei's interpretation of Article 33, Bo was redefining the constitutional guarantee of human rights adopted after the Sun Zhigang incident to include gay rights.

A *Legal Daily* article covering the same parade in Shenzhen asked, 'Does the Law Need to Have Something to Say about Homosexual Behavior?' The lead contended, 'No matter what people think, they are a group that objectively exists'. Zhang Beichuan, a pioneering researcher on HIV/AIDS and sexual minority men, was a key interviewee. Zhang shared survey findings showing that a fifth of gay respondents had been beaten, insulted, blackmailed, or fined after their identities had been revealed to heterosexuals.

Zhang explained that stigmatization caused high rates of suicide ideation and suicide attempts among gays. He then made the 'vulnerable group' analogy, pointing out that the government had passed numerous laws and regulations specifically to protect the rights of women and children, and said that gays, as a similarly large group that contributes to society, should likewise enjoy rights 'to develop jointly with others'.[37]

In 2006, scholar Zhou Wei also argued for gay rights by analogy in his book *Constitutional Fundamental Rights, Theory, Legislation and Its Application*. But his starting point was not the similarly disadvantaged social positions of sexual minorities and other vulnerable groups. Instead, he saw the 'immutability' of sexual orientation as analogous to the 'immutability' of the characteristics of other vulnerable groups. 'Since the law respects and recognizes certain immutable characteristics, for example, disability, gender, changing of sex, etc.', Zhou wrote, 'then it should also respect and recognize the sexual orientation of gays, which cannot be changed ...'. Zhou asserted that since allowing same-sex couples to marry would not 'infringe upon the interests of the state, of society and of the collective, or upon the lawful freedoms and rights of other citizens' in contravention of Article 51, they should be afforded equal protection as required by the Constitution.[38]

Like Lei Yongquan, some scholars believed that realizing legal protection for sexual minorities' rights was only a matter of time. After all was this not the logical conclusion of the Constitution's guarantees of equality, dignity, and human rights? Once social acceptance of sexual minorities improved further, the law would follow. In a 2009 article in *Legal System and Society*, a publication that is distributed to several state organs, including the NPC, legal scholar Yang Bingquan predicted, 'following the government's and society's continuing understanding and concern for gays, a vulnerable group in society, and the continuing efforts of the gay community, we believe that fundamental rights of gays will finally receive confirmation and protection of the Constitution and the law'.[39]

LGBTQ Rights Claims and the Constitution

In the 2000s, dozens of LGBTQ community groups and advocacy organizations formed throughout China. Like the organizers of the Shenzhen pride parade, these groups raised visibility and support through public events, artivism, and media outreach. They also built networks of allied academics, journalists, educators, and parents. Starting in 2014, LGBTQ advocates began bringing rights claims to the legal system, often working with rights protection lawyers from other social movements who had become skilled in using the legal 'infrastructure' that had built up in the preceding decades. As lawyers and advocates focused on directly asserting LGBTQ people's rights to equality and dignity, appeals to the 'vulnerable group' frame became less common. This section illustrates the next step in the 'runaway legitimation' process by examining rights claims as they moved from the academy and media into the legal system.

'Conversion Therapy' as a Harm to Dignity

LGBTQ advocate Peng Yanhui had been inspired by how other marginalized groups, like Hepatitis B carriers, had used litigation in their social movements.[40] In 2014, he launched the first-ever LGBTQ impact litigation case in China, suing a 'conversion therapist' who had tried to 'treat' his homosexuality with electroshock. To lessen the case's political sensitivity, Peng's lawyer framed the lawsuit as a 'service contract dispute', making it look like a run-of-the-mill commercial case. However, after Peng's powerful testimony at trial, the judge suggested recategorizing the case as an alleged infringement of Peng's bodily rights, health rights, and general personality rights. Peng recalled that this relabeling made it clear that 'the case was about discrimination and dignity, and not about an upset customer'.[41] The court later ruled that since homosexuality was not a mental illness, the therapist's claim that his treatment could 'cure' homosexuality was 'false advertising'.[42] However, the court also held that the clinic's advertisement that homosexuality could be 'corrected' did not specifically harm Peng's dignity because it was not aimed at him individually.

Commenting on the case, civil law scholars Yang Lixin and Wu Ye contended the court should have recognized the harm to Peng's dignity. They observed that general personality rights ultimately derive from Article 38 of the Constitution, which states, 'The personal dignity of citizens of the People's Republic of China is inviolable'.[43] (For context, an official NPC interpretation explains that Article 38's adoption was a response to the 'historical lesson' of the Cultural Revolution in which 'vast numbers of cadres and members of the masses were cruelly persecuted'.)[44] Although the Constitution is not justiciable, mediating laws 'continually concretize' this fundamental right and need to be implemented to give it meaning.[45] Since conversion therapy is 'seriously discriminatory toward the personhood of gays', Yang and Wu argued, 'it harms gays' personality rights'.[46] By not recognizing this harm, the court 'did not exert the effort it should have to change the social position of gays', who were a 'vulnerable group'.[47]

Prohibition of Same-Sex Marriage as a Violation of the 'Freedom of Marriage'

Scholars and advocates have pushed for the legalization of same-sex marriage through petitioning lawmakers, and, in one high-profile instance, litigation. Beginning in 2001, one of China's most famous scholars, Li Yinhe, repeatedly raised proposals for the legalization of same-sex marriage and cited the Constitution's equality and human rights clauses in support.[48] In 2015, Lin Xianzhi, a retired father of a gay son, sent 1000 NPC delegates letters calling for the legalization of same-sex marriage, quoting the same clauses plus the dignity clause.[49] Both Li and Lin called on the government to extend legal protections to gays out concern for helping a 'vulnerable group' and improving social harmony.[50] No lawmakers took up their proposals.

In 2016, Sun Wenlin and his same-sex partner, Hu Mingliang, sued the Changsha Bureau of Civil Affairs for refusing to grant them a marriage license. At the first and second instance, their lawyers claimed that the bureau misapplied the Marriage Law. The lawyers could not ask the court to rule on the constitutionality of the Marriage Law, so they argued that the Marriage Law—which has no explicit prohibition on same-sex marriage—should be interpreted *in light of* the Constitution.[51] They likely knew this was a stretch given the Marriage Law's numerous references to 'man and woman' but it gave them an opportunity to elaborate on why constitutional provisions on the freedom of marriage, human rights, and equality before the law required recognition of same-sex marriage, similarly to how Lei Yongquan and Bo Dalin argued a decade earlier.

The lawyers expounded on the meaning of marriage and why same-sex couples should be given access to the institution. 'Freedom of marriage is the freedom to choose or not choose what kind of person with whom one will live one's life', lawyer Shi Fulong told the first instance court. 'It is one of the most fundamental freedoms in the Constitution …'.[52] Lawyer Huang Simin built on this theme in the second instance, 'Through marriage, an individual participates in social life and carries out self-actualization'.[53] Huang put a provocative flourish on the 'objectively exists' argument, stating that, 'Gays have existed since ancient times … [they] do not emerge or disappear because of changes in regime or law'.[54]

Sun and Hu lost in both instances, but their cases received substantial media attention and sparked extensive discussion in the academy. Influential constitutional law scholar and the dean of Renmin University Law School, Han Dayuan, wrote an article while the case was ongoing, 'Human Dignity, Tolerance, and the Constitution's Safeguarding of Gays Rights'.[55] He argued that the freedom of marriage is a fundamental right that cannot be limited based on the majority's 'favored morality'. Instead, 'under the guidance of the principles of respecting and safeguarding human rights, we should openly, rationally, and tolerantly rethink the meaning and value in a modern society of the "freedom of marriage" clause in Article 49 of the Constitution'.

Later, in 2019, Han posited a moonshot idea that requests be brought to the NPCSC challenging the 'man and woman' requirement of the Marriage Law as an unconstitutional infringement of 'the freedom of marriage'. Notably, it was only in 1978 that the NPC added 'Men and women shall marry of their own free will', a provision that was present in the 1950 Marriage Law but had not been in the earlier Constitutions.[56] The 1982 Constitution changed this provision to 'Violation of the freedom of marriage is prohibited' in Article 49. This clause does not refer to 'man and woman' though Article 49's second clause refers to 'husband and wife'. So far, there is no publicly available example of anyone making Han's suggested appeal to the NPCSC.

Advocates have tried to directly appeal to lawmakers to change the law itself. In 2019, when the NPC was soliciting public comments on the draft Civil Code, a network of LGBTQ advocates called Ai Cheng Jia, which included Peng Yanhui and Sun Wenlin, launched a campaign that flooded the NPC with proposals calling for same-sex marriage. The NPC received 213,634 individual submissions on marriage (five times more than any other category). Ai Cheng Jia provided a model letter to send to the drafters that read, 'According to the protection provided to marriage and families by Article 49 of our country's Constitution and its safeguarding of the "freedom of marriage", the legal relationship of same-sex couples needs to be included and protected in the [Civil Code's] Book on Marriage and Family'.[57] After the Civil Code passed, a lead drafter dismissed the submissions as having been 'copied and pasted'. Ai Cheng Jia responded by emphasizing the breadth of its movement rather than its vulnerability, 'We are in manufacturing, agriculture, the military, schools, and business—every sector and every industry. Our marriages and families need equal protection of the law'.[58]

Employment Discrimination as an Infringement of Equality and Dignity

Recognition of the constitutional rights of LGBTQ people has had the most success in the employment discrimination context. Chinese law prohibits discrimination based on a non-exclusive list of characteristics, including 'sex', and some workplace discrimination lawsuits based on sex and geographic origin have succeeded in court. The development of this area of law has facilitated the 'runaway legitimation' process by providing a solid basis from which to extend protections to LGBTQ people.

Government officials have endorsed this extension in some high-profile instances. For example, at the United Nations Second Universal Periodic Review in 2013, the Chinese government stated that it had 'already implemented' laws prohibiting discrimination based on sexual orientation and gender identity, explaining that 'China's Constitution clearly stipulates that all citizens are equal before the law. China prohibits all possible discriminations via enacting specific laws'.[59] In 2015 and 2016, Sun Xiaomei and other NPC delegates introduced a draft Anti-Employment Discrimination Law into the NPC legislative plan. The draft Sun submitted included prohibitions against discrimination based on sexual orientation, gender identity, and gender expression. In an article, Sun advocated for the passage of the law by stating that equality is a core socialist principle, and that the Constitution provides for equality before the law and respect for human rights.[60] The draft law is on the backburner, but Sun's advocacy brought to high-level decision-makers the argument that the Constitution protects sexual and gender minorities.

The Constitution has also exerted influence in court cases. In 2018, the Intermediate People's Court of Guiyang heard an employment discrimination case brought by a transgender man, 'Mr. C'. Although the court ruled against Mr. C on evidentiary grounds, it expressed in an unprecedented passage that:

> the right to dignity of a natural person is the most fundamental right that should be enjoyed by every citizen. One's gender identity and gender expression belong under the protected scope of general personality rights. Respect should be given to the gender identity and gender expression of others .... Laborers should not be treated differently in the course of employ because of their gender identity or expression.[61]

The court's reference to the 'most fundamental right' of dignity connected respect for gender identity and expression to Article 38 of the Constitution. The declaration was a breakthrough compared to other LGBTQ employment cases. In another case the same year, a kindergarten teacher at a private school brought a labor dispute against his employer for firing him for being gay. The teacher requested that the arbiter write 'gay people's equal employment rights receive the law's protection' in the decision. The arbiter reported the request to a provincial-level leader. In the end, the sentence did not appear in the decision.[62]

Gao Moumou vs. Dang Dang Net went even further than Mr. C's case and is the best example to date of the Constitution playing a key role in an LGBTQ rights case. It is worth a close-up look: In July 2018, Gao Moumou requested several weeks' sick leave from her employer, e-commerce giant Dang Dang, to recover from GAS. Gao worked as a high-level director in Dang Dang's Beijing office for three years where she had presented as male, her sex assigned at birth. Government regulations required Gao to undergo GAS before changing the gender marker on her national identity card. Dang Dang's human resources department rejected Gao's request because she had, out of concern for her privacy, blocked out the 'transsexualism' diagnosis in the hospital records attached to her leave application (regulations required proof of such a diagnosis to access GAS). Gao later supplemented this information, but Dang Dang still did not approve her application. A few weeks later, Dang Dang fired Gao for excessive absence.

In November 2018, Gao brought Dang Dang to labor arbitration for unlawful dismissal and won. Dang Dang challenged the arbitration decision in civil court and lost. The court ruled that workers have a right to medical leave and employers violate that right by denying leave in an 'excessively mechanical' way that 'does not consider the particularity of a laborer's illness'.[63] On appeal to an intermediate court in Beijing,

Dang Dang argued it could not continue to employ Gao. Dang Dang had detailed its concerns in an offensive letter to Gao, which addressed her as 'Mister'. The letter claimed that colleagues did not wish to share the bathroom with her and that they felt 'unsafe' and 'morally awkward' around her. It also suggested Gao bring her own security guard to work in case as a 'mentally ill person' she had an 'episode' and harmed her colleagues.[64]

The Intermediate People's Court judge handling the case, Dou Jiangtao, shared how he decided the case in an article for *People's Judicature*, a publication managed by the SPC. Judge Dou saw the law lacked express provisions regarding discrimination against transgender people, but 'whether transgender laborers enjoy rights to equal employment and not to experience employment discrimination [was] a premise that had to be clarified in the course of trial'.[65] Judge Dou's judgment did not cite the Constitution, but he explained how it guided him:

> Relevant provisions of the Constitution and the Civil Code all clarify the concept that the personal dignity of citizens of the People's Republic of China (natural persons) is inviolable, and that the personality rights and interests arising from personal dignity receive the equal protection of the law .... Transgender laborers are independent natural persons and citizens of our country, and should have applied [to them] the provisions of the above-mentioned laws of our country. Their personal dignity should be respected, and the personality rights and interests arising from their personal dignity should receive the equal protection of the law ... employment discrimination toward transgender people implies that the personal dignity of transgender laborers had been infringed in violation of the provisions of the Constitution.

In the final judgment, Judge Dou ruled that 'although [the Employment Promotion Law] does not expressly provide that laborers shall not be discriminated against because they have undergone a sex change, it should be within the meaning of the [the Employment Promotion Law] that laborers, who have undergone sex-reassignment surgery, changed their sex, and gotten the approval of the Ministry of Public Security, enjoy rights to equal employment and not being discriminated against'. The equality and dignity provisions—adopted into the 1982 Constitution in response to the abuses of the Cultural Revolution—had guided a judge to advance a novel interpretation of the law to protect transgender people's rights.

State Backlash and Runaway Legitimation

Looking at Judge Dou's ruling, one may be tempted to sign on to Yang Bingquan's 2009 prediction. Perhaps LGBTQ advocates could eventually convince a critical mass of state decision-makers to follow the logic of the Constitution to uphold LGBTQ people's rights. But time and space for this kind of engagement may be disappearing. Like Fu Hualing said of the 'fragile autonomy' of private law in China, 'repressive measures of the exceptional state cannot be effectively sealed off'.[66] Increased repression threatens to foreclose openings created by runaway legitimation, and citizens have no practicable means of legally challenging it.

Around the same time that Judge Dou published his *People's Judicature* article, troubling signs emerged that the Party-state's attitude toward sexual and gender minorities was worsening (from an already unfriendly position).[67] Dozens of social media accounts run by LGBTQ student groups were shuttered for ostensibly violating regulations. LGBTQ advocacy groups were forced to close or cease activities. Police and civil affairs bureaus pressured charitable foundations to stop working with LGBTQ civil society organizations, many of whom were not allowed to participate in 99 Charity Day, a crucial public fundraising event. Courts indefinitely stalled pending LGBTQ rights lawsuits without explanation. The Ministry of Culture and Tourism and the China Association of Performing Arts directed broadcasters to stop airing 'sissy' men and other 'abnormal esthetics'. The vice president of the China TV Drama Screenwriter Working Committee defended a new ban on adaptions of 'boy love' dramas, saying 'influencing the young ones, whose sexual awareness has yet to be fully developed, with such culture is to some extent a crime'.[68] At the 2022 Two Sessions, an NPC delegate suggested passing legislation to guard against 'subcultures', including 'LGBT culture', that 'corrode' the ideology of young people and infiltrate schools.[69] These are only some of the publicly available examples.

The backlash is delivering a one-two punch to runaway legitimation. At the infrastructural level, it is squeezing down space for advocacy and cutting off channels for LGBTQ rights claims. At the conceptual level, it threatens to replace the LGBTQ community's voices with others that aim to recast LGBTQ people as a suspect 'subculture' undeserving of equal citizenship.

Conclusion

In *Queer Comrades*, Hongwei Bao recounted a clash between police and a gathering of gay men in Guangzhou's People's Park in 2009. The police told the men that 'this is People's Park. You *gei-lou* shouldn't be here' and tried to drive them out.[70] Xiaomu, a volunteer for a local queer NGO who regularly visited the park, shot back, 'Since you know that this is the People's Park, and since *tongzhi* are also law-abiding citizens, why can't we stay here?'[71] A crowd of gay men and presumably non-queer passersby formed in opposition to the police. Once it grew large, the police retreated, and the victorious crowd cheered. Reflecting on the dispute about who belonged in People's Park, Bao observed that 'the debate over whether queer people are part of the "people" is a battle for citizenship'. According to the Constitution, 'the people' 'enjoy full citizenship rights' and 'rhetorically rule the country through a 'democratic dictatorship'. Democracy is exercised toward 'the people'. Dictatorship is exercised toward those who are not.

Bao's comments and the emerging state backlash are reminders that runaway legitimation of the constitutional values of equality, dignity, and human rights is at the mercy of more core constitutional principles on the Party's leadership and dominance. How far the Party can or wishes to go in marginalizing China's LGBTQ community is unclear, but it is primarily a political calculus. One significant deterrent will be its assessment of how popular support for LGBTQ people has become, including how many members of the public and officialdom see LGBTQ people as fellow citizens with equal dignity. This support was built up over preceding decades when the LGBTQ movement and its allies had a freer hand in pushing the runaway legitimation process forward, and it may help sustain spaces for the movement until the prerogative state recedes again.

Notes

1 Michael Dowdle, 'Infrastructural power and its possibilities for the constitutional evolution of authoritarian political systems: lessons from China' in Helena Alviar García and Günter Frankenberg (eds), *Authoritarian Constitutionalism* (Edward Elgar 2019) 89.
2 For a discussion on the growth of rights consciousness, see Taisu Zhang and Tom Ginsburg, 'China's Turn toward Law' [2019] 59 Va J Int'l L 306, 377.
3 Harriet Evans, *Women and Sexuality in China: Female Sexuality and Gender Since 1949* (Continuum 1997) 206.
4 Supreme People's Court of the People's Republic of China, 'Reply of the Supreme People's Court on the Question of Whether Consensual Sodomy between Adults Constitutes a Crime' 29 April 1957.
5 Heather Worth and others, "Under the Same Quilt': The Paradoxes of Sex between Men in the Cultural Revolution' [2017] J. Homosexuality 61, 62.
6 Tze-Lan D. Sang, *The Emerging Lesbian: Female Same-Sex Desire in Modern China* (University of Chicago Press 2003) 167.
7 Heather Worth and others, "There Was No Mercy at All': Hooliganism, Homosexuality and the Opening-Up of China' [2019] Int. Soc. 38, 45.
8 Worth and others (n 22) 61, 69.
9 Michael Weisskopf, 'China Moves to Rescue Itself From Outside 'Spiritual Pollution' *Washington Post* (Beijing, 2 December 1983).
10 Jin Wu, 'From 'Long Yang' and 'Dui Shi' to Tongzhi: Homosexuality in China' [2003] J. Gay Lesbian Psychotherapy 117, 126–127.
11 Julian Gewirtz, "Loving Capitalism Disease': Aids and Ideology in the People's Republic of China, 1984–2000' [2020] Past Present 251, 261.
12 Gewirtz (n 28) 267.
13 Gewirtz (n 28) 273.
14 'Report on the Banning of the 'Men's World' Cultural Salon' 5 July 1993.
15 Evans (n 19) 207.
16 Harold M. Tanner, 'The Offense of Hooliganism and the Moral Dimension of China's Pursuit of Modernity, 1979–1996' Twentieth Century China [2000] 1, 24, 39.
17 For a discussion of why depathologization was only partial, see Darius Longarino, 'Converting Converters' *ChinaFile* (20 October 2019), https://www.chinafile.com/reporting-opinion/viewpoint/converting-converters.
18 Film Censorship Regulations, Ministry of Radio, Film, and Television Order No. 22 (16 January 1997).
19 Ministry of Public Security Reply to Questions Concerning the Alteration of Assigned Sex on Household Registration for Citizens following Sex Change Surgery (MPS Ordinance No. 131 (2002)).
20 Da Li and Di Wei, 'The Ministry of Civil Affairs Recently Clarified How to Handle Husband and Wife Relations Involving Transsexuals' *Xinhua Daily Telegraph* (17 January 2003) 006.
21 John Balzano, 'Toward a Gay-Friendly China?: Legal Implications of Transition for Gays and Lesbians' [2007] L. & Sexuality 1, 11–14.
22 Ibid, 14.
23 Ibid, 9–14.
24 Research Group of the Municipal Yangzhou Research Center on the Important Thought of the 'Three Represents', 'The Value of the Three Represents' *Xinhua Daily* (20 July 2002) B03.
25 Yu Yunyao, 'Democracy and Rule of Law and the Construction of a Socialist Harmonious Society' *People's Representative Press* (Beijing, 2 August 2005).
26 Wang Hanbin, 'Speech at the Symposium on the Implementation of the State Compensation Law' *National People's Congress Work News* (20 December 1994).
27 Li Zhanhua, 'Constitutionalism's Concern for the Protection of the Rights of Vulnerable Groups' [2003] People's Congress Studying 22.
28 Huang Songyou, 'The Judicialization of the Constitution and Its Meaning—A Discussion Starting with Today's Supreme People's Court's Reply' *People's Court Daily* (Beijing, 13 August 2001) B01.

29 Fan Jinxue, 'Exploration and Reflection on the Path of the People's Court to Implement the Constitution' [2021] J. Pol. Sc. L. 3, 9.
30 Qianfan Zhang, *The Constitution of China: A Contextual Analysis* (Hart Publishing 2012).
31 Timothy Webster, 'Ambivalence & Activism: Employment Discrimination in China' [2011] Vand. J. Transnat'l L. 643, 645.
32 Balzano (n 22) 12.
33 Lei Yongquan, 'Concerning Gays' *Legal Daily* (29 April 2004).
34 Hungdah Chiu, 'The 1982 Chinese Constitution and the Rule of Law' [1985] Md. Ser. Contemp. Asian Stud. 1, 1.
35 Ibid.
36 Bo Dalin, 'The Rights Demands of Gays Deserve Attention' *Procuratorate Daily* (Beijing, 2 November 2005).
37 Ren Xiaoyi and others, 'The Law Needs to Say Something about the Right and Wrong of Homosexual Behavior' *Legal Daily* (Beijing, 27 October 2005).
38 Zhou Wei, *Constitutional Fundamental Rights: Theory, Legislation, and Its Application* (Law Press China 2006) 169.
39 Yang Binquan, 'The Protection of Gays Rights from the Perspective of Constitutionalism' *Legal System and Society* (Kunming, December 2009) 337.
40 Caterina Fugazzola, *What's in a Name? Language, Culture, and Tongzhi Strategies for Social Change* (Temple) (forthcoming).
41 Yanhui Peng and others, 'LGBTQ activism in contemporary China: a legal advocate's story' in Hyaeweol Choi, Barbara Molony, and Janet Theiss (eds), *Oxford Handbook of East Asian Gender History* (OUP forthcoming).
42 Beijng Haidian District Court, Civil Judgment, (2014) Haidian Civil First Instance No. 16680 (19 December 2014).
43 Yang Lixin and Wu Ye, 'Liability for the Violation of Personal Dignity Caused by Therapeutically Treating Gays' *Jianghan Tr.* (January 2015) 122, 126.
44 'Section Two: Citizen's Fundamental Rights and Duties' *China's National People's Congress Net* (14 April 2010), http://www.npc.gov.cn/npc/c13475/201004/f6f0fa308715410b8e963fdcb7ac7e9d.shtml.
45 Yang and Wu (n 44), 126.
46 Ibid, 125.
47 Ibid, 126–127.
48 Tingting Liu and Jingshu Zhu, 'Legislating and litigating same sex marriage in China' in Chris Ashford and Alexander Maine (eds), *Research Handbook on Gender, Sexuality and the Law* (Edward Elgar 2020) 58.
49 Li Yinhe, 'Father of a Comrade Sends Letters to 1000 People's Congress Delegates Calling for the Legalization of Same-sex Marriage' *Li Yinhe's Blog* (2 March 2015) <http://liyinhe.blog.caixin.com/archives/82646> accessed 1 October 2021.
50 https://opinion.huanqiu.com/article/9CaKrnJLkEB.
51 Shi Fulong, 'Even if They Win Today's Lawsuit, We will be Sure to Win the Future—The Statement of the Lawyer in China's First Same-sex Marriage Case' *Sina Weibo* (13 April 2016) <http://blog.sina.cn/dpool/blog/s/blog_4f2cf4e90102womd.html?vt=4&wm=3049_a111&> accessed 1 October 2021.
52 Ibid.
53 Huang Simin, 'Equal Marriage Rights Will Not Stop to Rest, Freedom of Love is Given by Heaven—The Statement of the Second Instance Lawyer in China's First Same-sex Marriage Case' *Rainbow Lawyers* (29 June 2016) <https://mp.weixin.qq.com/s/UR1DE386lp8Q68pkFipZsQ> accessed 1 October 2021.
54 Ibid.
55 Han Dayuan, 'Human Dignity, Tolerance, and the Constitution's Safeguarding of Gays Rights' [2016] 3 Legal For. 25, 30.
56 Jerome A. Cohen, 'China's Changing Constitution' [1979] Nw. J. Int'l L. & Bus. 57, 99.
57 LGBT Rights Advocacy China (fn 11).
58 Love Makes Family, 'A Response to Huang Wei, Director of the Civil Law Department of the NPC Legislative Affairs Commission' *Love Makes Family* (19 May 2020) <https://mp.weixin.qq.com/s/xQpDCMkUit29nh8Ciqo0Zw> accessed 1 October 2021.

59 United Nations Human Rights Council, Report of the Working Group on the Universal Periodic Review, China (including Hong Kong, China and Macao, China), A/HRC/25/5 (4 December 2013); United Nations Human Rights Council, Report of the Working Group on the Universal Periodic Review, China, Addendum A/HRC/25/5/Add.1 (27 February 2014).
60 Sun Xiaomei, 'Put the Anti-Employment Discrimination Law into the Legislative Plan as Soon as Possible' *China Women's Daily* (Beijing, 8 March 2016) B01.
61 Common Language, 'Chinese Transgender Employment Discrimination Case Wins Groundbreaking Court Statement' *Outright International* (6 February 2018) <https://outrightinternational.org/content/republish-chinese-transgender-employment-discrimination-case-wins-groundbreaking-court>.
62 Dashi Wang, 'The Whole Story of the Winning of the First Gay Teacher Rights Protection Case' *Gaysprit* (3 December 2018) <https://zhuanlan.zhihu.com/p/51462784> accessed 1 October 2021.
63 Beijing Dongcheng District Court, Civil Judgment, (2019) Beijing 0101 Civil First Instance No. 5075 (4 July 2019).
64 Beijing Second Intermediate Court, Civil Judgment, (2019) Beijing 02 Civil Final No. 11084 (3 January 2020).
65 Dou Jiangtao and Wang Linlin, 'Judicial Remedy for a Transgender [Person] Whose Labor Contract was Discriminatorily Terminated' *People's Judicature* (Beijing, 5 August 2021).
66 Fu Hualing, 'Duality and China's Struggle for Legal Autonomy' [2019] *China Perspectives* 4, 5.
67 For discussion and sources to the examples in this paragraph, see, 'Fading Rainbow: A Q&A on LGBTQ Equality in China' *OutRight International* (7 February 2022), https://outrightinternational.org/China-FadingRainbow.
68 Mandy Zuo, 'China Moves to Kill Romantic Gay-Themed 'Boys' Love' Dramas Amid Wider Crackdown on Entertainment Industry' *South China Morning Post* (2 February 2022), https://www.scmp.com/news/people-culture/china-personalities/article/3165101/china-moves-kill-romantic-gay-themed-boys.
69 'Late First Marriages, Slow to Work, Hard to Get a Place, NPC Delegate Suggests Special Legislation on Youth Development' *China Youth* (10 March 2022), https://c.m.163.com/news/a/H24NL4R90512BJHG.html?from=wap_redirect&spss=wap_refluxdl_2018&referFrom=.
70 Hongwei Bao, *Queer Comrades: Gay Identity and Tongzhi Activism in Postsocialist China* (Nordic Institute of Asian Studies Press 2018).
71 Ibid.

Bibliography

Balzano J, 'Toward a Gay-Friendly China?: Legal Implications of Transition for Gays and Lesbians' [2007] 16 *L. & Sexuality* 1.

Bao H, *Queer Comrades: Gay Identity and Tongzhi Activism in Postsocialist China* (Nordic Institute of Asian Studies Press 2018).

Chia J, 'LGBTQ rights in China: movement-building in uncertain times' in Biddulph S and Rosenzweig J (eds), *Handbook on Human Rights in China* (Edward Elgar 2019).

Dowdle M, 'Infrastructural power and its possibilities for the constitutional evolution of authoritarian political systems: lessons from China' in García H and Frankenberg G (eds), *Authoritarian Constitutionalism* (Edward Elgar 2019).

Fugazzola C, *What's in a Name? Language, Culture, and Tongzhi Strategies for Social Change* (Temple forthcoming).

Gallagher M, *Authoritarian Legality in China-Law, Workers, and the State* (Cambridge University Press 2017).

Parkin S, 'LGBT Rights-Focused Legal Advocacy in China: The Promise, and Limits, of Litigation' [2018] 41 *Fordham Int'l L.J.* 1243.

Zhang Q, *The Constitution of China: A Contextual Analysis* (Hart Publishing 2012)

Zhu, J, *Straightjacket: Same-Sex Orientation under Chinese Family Law* (Leiden University 2018)

15

INVOLVING AND INTEGRATING 'CAPITALIST' SPECIAL ADMINISTRATIVE REGIONS IN 'SOCIALIST' NATIONAL DEVELOPMENT OF CHINA

Squaring the Circle of 'Two Systems' in 'One Country'

Pui-yin LO

Introduction

This chapter considers the tensions and flexibility in the implementation of the basic policies of the People's Republic of China (PRC) regarding Hong Kong and Macao of 'One Country, Two Systems' (OCTS), whereby, upon resumption of exercise of Chinese sovereignty over these territories, the PRC was to establish Special Administrative Regions (SARs) of separate systems to maintain the territories as 'capitalist' economically and socially. The examination here is of the dynamics in Central-SAR relationship from the recent initiatives of the PRC's Central Party and State Authorities to include the SARs in the national plan for economic and social development and in the grand strategy of developing the Guangdong-Hong Kong-Macao Greater Bay Area (GBA). By reviewing the evolving systemic provisions of the PRC Constitution, documents of various Central Party and State plan-making and supervision institutions, and the responses at the SAR level, a foundation is laid for further study through identifying and discussing the issues that the planning, and the expected co-operation, coordination and harmonization, would involve and impact on the SARs' structural, systemic and normative arrangements prescribed under the relevant Basic Laws in accordance with the relevant basic policies to implement OCTS.

Hong Kong and Macao are Chinese territories that were occupied and administered by foreign powers, namely the United Kingdom and Portugal, respectively, at the time of the founding of the PRC in 1949. The PRC did not seek to recover Hong Kong and Macao at that time or immediately thereafter, having recognized the economic and political value of these territories to the development of the PRC and its leading party, the

DOI: 10.4324/9781003128243-18

Communist Party of China (CPC). Rather, these matters, it was said in 1963, 'could be resolved through negotiations when the conditions were ripe'.[1]

National reunification was on the agenda of the CPC when it emerged from the chaos of the Cultural Revolution,[2] began to chart a course for modernization of China[3] and achieved normalized relations with Japan and the United States.[4] In 1979 and 1981, the PRC called for reunification of Taiwan under policies and measures that would respect the status quo in Taiwan.[5] The 1981 statement articulated nine principles that Deng Xiaoping later explained as meaning 'two systems' in 'one country'; as long as the authorities in Taiwan did not seek to undermine the system in Mainland China, the PRC would not undermine their system there.[6]

The CPC leadership decided in March 1981 to recover Hong Kong from the United Kingdom and to adopt Deng Xiaoping's approach of the PRC, which practises the socialist system, allowing Hong Kong to continue to practise its capitalist system (i.e. 'One Country, Two Systems').[7] A 12-point policy paper was produced for the resolution of the Hong Kong question by negotiations with the United Kingdom. These 12 points were revised and used in the Sino-British negotiations between 1982 and 1984.[8] They were substantially reproduced as the 'basic policies' of the PRC regarding Hong Kong upon its resumption of exercise of sovereignty over Hong Kong on 1 July 1997 in the Sino-British Joint Declaration concluded in December 1984 and stipulated to remain 'unchanged for 50 years'.[9] Similar 'basic policies' were incorporated into the Sino-Portuguese Joint Declaration that settled the question of Macao, providing for the resumption of exercise of Chinese sovereignty over the territory on 20 December 1999.[10]

The PRC's State Authorities, in the meantime, prepared the mechanism for the administration of the reunified territories. On 4 December 1982, the National People's Congress (NPC) adopted a new (and the current) Constitution of the PRC. The Constitution's Preamble narrates the transition of the Chinese people of all nationalities in transforming China into a socialist society under the leadership of the CPC, declares the PRC as 'a unitary multi-national state' and defines the basic task of the nation 'for the years to come' as 'socialist modernisation'.[11] Acknowledging that the 'motherland' has yet to be reunified,[12] the Constitution provides that while fundamentally, the socialist system is the basic system of the PRC and shall not be disrupted,[13] the State 'may establish special administrative regions when necessary. The systems to be instituted in special administrative regions shall be prescribed by law enacted by the [NPC] in the light of specific conditions'.[14] This was followed by the adoption of OCTS as state policy in May 1983.[15]

To implement the 'basic policies' of OCTS in the two Joint Declarations, which provide that the '*current social and economic systems in Hong Kong/Macao will remain unchanged, and so will the life-style*' and that after the establishment of the SAR, '*the socialist system and socialist policies shall not be practised in the [Hong Kong SAR/Macao SAR] and that Hong Kong/Macao's previous capitalist system and life-style shall remain unchanged for 50 years*',[16] the NPC enacted, following a drafting process that involved selected local inhabitants of Hong Kong/Macao,[17] the Basic Law of the Hong Kong SAR (HKBL),[18] and the Basic Law of the Macao SAR (MBL),[19] to prescribe the systems to be practised in Hong Kong and Macao, respectively.[20] The Basic Laws would come into operation upon the establishment in 1997 and 1999, respectively, of the Hong Kong SAR and the Macao SAR.

Both Basic Laws have similar provisions related to the economy, including the protection of private property, ownership of enterprises and foreign investment, the prohibition of expropriation without real value compensation, independent finances, separate taxation system, fiscal prudence in public budgeting, monetary and financial autonomy, continuation of the Hong Kong and Macao currencies, absence of foreign exchange control, free flow of capital, a free port, free trade policy, separate customs territory status, separate shipping management and separate civil aviation management.[21] There are additional provisions to underline the economic achievements of Hong Kong: international financial centre, and centre of international and regional civil aviation.[22] These provisions, which have been said to be for entrenching the pre-existing 'capitalist economy',[23] have not been amended.[24]

On the other hand, the current PRC Constitution has been amended on five occasions after 1982. Many of the 52 amendments adopted concern the political economy of the socialist systems of the PRC State. These amendments cement the CPC's policies for, and consolidate the progress in, the PRC's opening up and reform. These amendments, by transforming the system for the organization and management of the Chinese economy, can be regarded as the foundation of the tremendous economic growth of the PRC and the livelihood improvement of the Chinese people from the mid-1980s and, together with other economic and legal policies and measures, paved the way for the PRC's accession to the World Trade Organization (WTO) in 2001.[25]

Since 2003, the two SARs, as separate customs territories, have strengthened trade and investment co-operation with the PRC through bilateral free trade arrangements known as the Closer Economic Partnership Arrangement (CEPA), which cover the four fields of trade in goods, trade in services, investment and economic and technical co-operation. Given the already open markets of the SARs, CEPA have involved, in implementation, substantially more trade relaxation and increased market access on the part of the Chinese Mainland side than on the part of the SARs.[26]

Since 2010, the PRC's Central Authorities have included the two SARs in their Five-Year Plans for national economic and social development, the principal instrument of the Chinese socialist market economy. At the same time, co-operation of regions of the Greater Pearl Delta Region that involved the two SARs has evolved under the central leadership of the CPC into the grand strategy for developing the Guangdong-Hong Kong-Macao GBA, the outline development plan of which, published in 2019, encompasses and anticipates developments in fields beyond trade, manufacturing, service provision and innovation, with objectives that would seek to remove barriers in the movement of people, capital and information and harmonization in matters of health, social security and social governance in nine regions of Guangdong Province and the two SARs.[27]

Growth in the PRC economy, rapid development in infrastructure, talents and skills in the Chinese Mainland and greater interconnectedness between the PRC and the global economy have meant lesser dependence on the part of the PRC on Hong Kong and Macao. Rather they are now at best interdependent. Indeed, scholars have already pointed out Hong Kong and Macao's dependence on the PRC's economy and economic and financial policies and discussed the political economic dimension of the OCTS policy the Central Authorities have practised in relation to the two SARs.[28]

As this historical overview above can show, the Chinese Party State has by now included and fostered the 'capitalist' SARs for national economic development of the Chinese 'socialist' State. This phenomenon generates or implicates several issues, concerning and impacting particularly on the Central-SAR relationship. They include (i) the continuing relevance and distinction of the 'socialist'/'capitalist' dichotomy in OCTS in light of the evolving political economic organization and system provisions of the PRC Constitution and the fixed framework of the political, economic, social and legal systems of the Basic Laws of the SARs; (ii) the application of the PRC Constitution to the SARs with reference to the features of the SARs that have been promised and presumably prescribed as 'to remain unchanged'; and (iii) the extent to which the Central Authorities may seek to integrate the SARs for national and regional developments through goal-setting, co-operation, coordination and harmonization of the economic and social systems practised in the SARs with those practised in the Chinese Mainland, without making structural, systemic or normative changes to the Basic Law level arrangements in the SARs.

The rest of this chapter is organized into the following sections. The 'Central Constitutional Consolidation of Economic Transformation' section reviews the evolving systemic provisions of the PRC Constitution on the political economy. The 'Party and State Institutions and Instruments for Regulation and Control of the Socialist Market Economy' section highlights the various Party and State institutions, including the Party's leading groups and the State Council's National Development and Reform Commission (NDRC), that are responsible for the making of plans and decisions at the Central level to guide the developments and supervise the implementation of the plans and decisions at the local/SAR level. The 'Integration of SARs into National Development' section discusses the issues that Central planning, co-operation, coordination and harmonization would involve and impact on the SARs' structural, systemic and normative arrangements prescribed under the relevant Basic Laws. The more recent Five-Year Plans and the GBA project are used for illustration. The 'Concluding Remarks' section concludes by considering this possible contradiction: That the Centre-planned/programmed economic and social developments for the Hong Kong and Macao SARs lie in their imposition of the national socialist system on two regional economics and societies that are guaranteed by their respective foundational law to be capitalist in their systems and with each of its own way of life.

Central Constitutional Consolidation of Economic Transformation

The PRC Constitution, as it was adopted in 1982, proclaims in the Preamble the establishment in China of the socialist system. Article 1 of the Constitution stipulates that the 'socialist system is the *basic system* of the People's Republic of China' and prohibits any disruption of it. Article 6 establishes the basis of the PRC's socialist economic system as 'socialist public ownership of the means of production, namely ownership by the whole people and collective ownership by the working people'. Article 7 stipulates the 'state economy' as 'the sector of socialist economy under ownership by the whole people' and 'the leading force in the national economy'. Article 8 sets out the various forms of the co-operative economy, which belongs to the sector of socialist economy under collective ownership by the working people. Article 11 allows by law 'individual economy' of the working people to complement the 'socialist public economy'. Article 15 provides that the State 'practises *planned economy on the basis of socialist public ownership*. It ensures the proportionate and coordinated growth of the national economy *through overall balancing by economic planning and the supplementary role of regulation by the market. Disturbance of the socio-economic order or disruption of the state economic plan by any organization or individual is prohibited*'. Articles 16 and 17 require state enterprises and collective economic organizations to fulfil their obligations under the state plan under unified leadership by the State, and to accept the guidance of the state plan and abide by the relevant laws, respectively. Article 18 gives permission to foreign investment in the PRC.

Amendments adopted in 1988 to the PRC Constitution add to Article 11 'the private sector of the economy' that may 'develop within the limits prescribed by law' to complement the 'socialist public economy' under the 'guidance, supervision and control' of the State.

Hence, at the time of the drafting and adoption of the Basic Law of the Hong Kong SAR in 1990, the PRC's socialist economic system was constituted with the state economy being the leading force and based on state planning, enforced by command and guidance upon the economic units. The market and the private sector, though permitted to exist, were regulated by the State and played complementary roles. As Yash Ghai observed, the laws of the PRC on the economy were 'a patchwork of laws which combine elements of the market and the plan, laws which seek to traverse the two regimes, and laws which are both facilitative as well as restrictive and regulatory'.[29] For the Central Authorities to invoke Article 31 of the PRC Constitution at that time to prescribe for a SAR to be established in 1997 systems that were different from the socialist economic system and to restrict the power of amendment of the NPC to respect the 'established policies' of the PRC regarding Hong Kong was a challenge to both socialist and capitalist legal thinking[30] and aroused controversy over the validity of the law to be made.[31] One suggestion made during the Basic Law drafting process was amending the Constitution to clarify and affirm the power to make such a law and stipulating in that law the provisions of the Constitution that would apply to the SAR.[32] The Central Authorities' solution was for the NPC to make a concomitant decision that referred to Article 31 and declared the Basic Law to be '*constitutional* as it is enacted in accordance with the Constitution of the [PRC] and in the light of the specific conditions of Hong Kong. The systems, policies and laws to be instituted after the establishment of the Hong Kong [SAR] shall be based on the Basic Law'.[33]

Thereafter, the PRC Constitution was amended in 1993, 1999, 2004 and 2018. The 1993, the 1999 and the 2004 amendments have been significant in further adjusting the PRC's socialist economy system. The 1993 amendments revised the ideological assessment of China to 'the primary stage of socialism',[34] so that the 'basic task of the nation is to concentrate its effort on socialist modernization in line with the theory of building socialism with Chinese characteristics', revised the leading force in the national economy as 'the state-owned economy, namely, the socialist economy under ownership by the whole people' and revised Article 15 of the Constitution to replace state planning of the economy with the stipulation that the State 'practises *socialist market economy*',[35] and that its role involved the strengthening of economic legislation, the improvement of macro-regulation and control and the prohibition of disturbance of the socio-economic order in accordance with law.[36]

The 1999 amendments noted the co-existence of 'diverse forms of ownership' with the mainstay public ownership and the co-existence of 'diverse modes of distribution' with the distribution according to work as the mainstay and revised Article 11 of the Constitution to recognize the individual economy and the private sector of the economy as the 'non-public sectors of the economy' and '*an important component of the socialist market economy*', with the State's roles of protection under law and guidance, supervision and control.[37] The 2004 amendments further revised Article 11 to refine the State's role and function in respect of the non-public sectors of the economy to the positive one of encouraging, supporting and guiding them and further enhanced Article 13's protection of the rights of citizens to private property and its inheritance.

The constitutional amendments discussed above consolidate the profound changes in political economic policy the CPC determined in the decades of opening up and reform for 'socialist modernisation' of China. The replacement of planned economy with socialist market economy, the acknowledgement, recognition, protection and regulation of the individual and private sectors of the economy as an important component of the socialist market economy, and the express recognition and protection of the citizen's private property rights have caused scholars to query the credential of the PRC's 'socialist' economy[38]; some have simply described the PRC as having evolved into an economy of 'state capitalism'.[39]

Party and State Institutions and Instruments for Regulation and Control of the Socialist Market Economy

The PRC's transformation from a planned economy into a socialist market economy in the 1990s involved reform, as opposed to the abolition, of the planning system of the State. The Decision of the Third Plenum of the Central Committee of the CPC made in November 1993 indicated that the function of planning would be to take the market as the foundation and then to reasonably ascertain the strategy for national economic and social developments, and the objectives of marco-regulation and industrial policy[40]; to perform economic forecasts; and to plan for major economic structure, situation of production, land management and key infrastructure projects. Its focus would be on the medium and long term, for the purpose of achieving comprehensive coordination of macroeconomic policy and the application of economic leverage.[41]

Macroeconomic regulation, forecasting, structural planning and project management continue to require bureaucratic support. The State Planning Commission of the State Council, which hitherto undertook the planning and overseeing of the State's production and distribution of major commodities and its infrastructure projects, was restructured and reorganized. It became known as the NDRC in 2013, upon taking up the responsibilities for coordinating government agencies in the implementation of economic plans.[42]

The practice of the Party and the NPC formulating and adopting a plan every five years has continued. The Central Committee of the CPC adopted in a plenum the CPC's proposals, which are concretized and formatted into a draft for the NPC to deliberate and adopt in the Fourth Session of its five-year term.[43] From the Eighth Five-Year Plan (1991–1995) onwards, the plan (计划) of goals is accompanied by a longer term programme (规划) of vision for national economic and social development.[44] The Ninth Five-Year Plan (1996–2000) included a programme for development up to 2010, setting out objects and policies of macro-regulation, providing directions for coordinated development of regional economies, outlining deepening structural reform of the economy and giving indicative and guiding targets (指标).[45]

The Eleventh Five-Year Plan (2006–2010) involved a significant change in nomenclature: The 'imperative plan (计划)' was removed altogether and the whole document was known in terms of a 'coordinative plan (规划)'.[46] Although the Eleventh Five-Year Plan continued to set the major goals for economic and social development, it put forward economic targets that were specified to be either binding or indicative,[47] and detailed provisions on the system for implementing the programme.

Sebastian Heilmann's study of the Five-Year Plans between the mid-1990s and the 2000s found a fundamental reorganization in the 'content, processes and methods' of the Five-Year Plan for 'strategic policy coordination', 'resource mobilization and allocation' and 'macro-economic control' that has been illustrated above, which was due to the re-orientation of the exercise to one that takes the market as the foundation and reserves the government's role to the macro, strategic and policy levels.[48] He also found unusual approaches in implementation, adjustment and correction of the development plan, particularly those that utilized the Party's mechanisms.[49] He further found that at the subordinate and administrative level, the outline plan 'serves as a central point of reference for all specialized policy documents',[50] and plan-making has been 'a strategic exercise in administrative communications'.[51] Thus he observed that this was a 'variant of adaptive governance' for the Chinese bureaucratic state.[52]

In implementation, the NDRC coordinates and promotes the Five-Year Plan, bridging the gap between the Central's 'initial ... statement of intent' and the eventual implementation by the various elements of the decentralized Chinese administrative state.[53] Furthermore, in macro-regional development plans accorded national priority by the CPC leadership, the NDRC serves as the secretariat of the Party leading small group on the task[54] and sends delegations and operates administrative offices in the relevant local administrative regions.[55]

Integration of SARs into National Development

Co-operation of the Hong Kong and Macao SARs with the neighbouring province of Guangdong and the adjoining cities of Shenzhen (in the case of Hong Kong) and Zhuhai (in the case of Macao) has been a constant arrangement both before and after the resumption of exercise of PRC sovereignty.[56]

The NDRC promulgated in January 2009 an Outline of the Plan for Reform and Development of the Pearl River Delta up to 2020. Thereafter, through a joint conference arrangement between the Hong Kong SAR and Guangdong, a framework agreement was reached in March 2009 to translate the Outline's macro-policies into concrete measures in light of the Central Authorities' specification of Hong Kong/Guangdong co-operation as a 'national policy'.[57]

Separately, with the blessing and guidance of the Central Authorities, since June 2004, there was inaugurated a Pan-Pearl River Delta Regional Co-operation and Development Forum that encompassed the nine provinces of the Pearl River Delta hinterland and the two SARs. The '9+2' parties seek co-operation in ten areas, based on the principles of voluntary participation, market orientation, openness and fairness, complementarities with each other's advantages and joint prosperity. They formulated in early 2006 an outline of the programme for Pan-Pearl River Delta regional co-operation and development for a two stage advancement in the period between 2006 and 2020.[58]

Donald Tsang, then Chief Executive of the Hong Kong SAR, indicated in his 2010–2011 Policy Address that the Hong Kong SAR Government 'are working with Guangdong Province to seek to incorporate the most important functions and roles of Hong Kong-Guangdong co-operation into the [Twelfth] Five-Year Plan'.[59] While including the Hong Kong SAR's development in the Five-Year Plan was considered unthinkable for OCTS reasons as recently as in 2006, it was Tsang's lobbying of the Central Authorities that brought forth the change, which he believed would provide a 'stable platform' for Hong Kong-Mainland co-operation and a 'legitimate foundation' for negotiations on policies and measures by the two sides.[60]

The Twelfth Five-Year Plan (2011–2015) for national economic and social development thus had a chapter on the Hong Kong SAR and the Macao SAR's development.[61] The relevant portion in the chapter on the Hong Kong SAR underlined support of the SAR in accordance with the Basic Law, support for consolidation and lifting of competitive advantages, support for incubation of emerging industries and support for deepening economic co-operation with the Mainland (particularly with Guangdong). Additional provisions concerned Hong Kong's development as the off-shore Renminbi (RMB) business centre and international asset management centre and the stock management and regional distribution centre for high value goods, and strengthening the global influence as a financial centre; and, in relation to Guangdong, the speeding up of the mutual establishment of a high-quality living area and the coordination and improvement of the transportation system.

The Thirteenth Five-Year Plan (2016–2020) maintained the provisions that were in the Twelfth Five-Year Plan and sought to elevate the positions and roles of the SARs in the PRC's economic development and opening up.[62] Additional provisions on co-operative ventures between the Chinese Mainland and the SARs were included, covering the strategic level of the country's bidirectional opening up and the Belt and Road Initiative, the national level of financial co-operation and market connectivity, the Pearl River Delta regional level of the 'quality living area' and the social level of encouraging micro, small and medium businesses as well as young people from the SARs to start business on the Mainland.

President Xi Jinping personally conceived and advanced the GBA project as a national strategy during the period of the Thirteenth Five-Year Plan.[63] The GBA project, in seeking to integrate the advantages of nine regions of Guangdong Province, Hong Kong and Macao into a regional grouping for high-level international co-operation, would eventually encounter the challenge of the removal of barriers in the movement of people, capital and information, which are objectives that might go beyond the commonplace regional planning efforts.[64] The Outline Development Plan for the GBA, unveiled on 18 February 2019, is all encompassing, covering innovation and technology, infrastructural connectivity, modern manufacturing and service provision, ecological conservation, education and talents, culture and leisure, employment and entrepreneurship, health, social security and social governance, and servicing the Belt and Road Initiative and global competitiveness.[65] A central leading group of the CPC for the development of the GBA has been established, 'relevant central ministries' would formulate 'concrete policies and measures', strengthen communication with the Guangdong, Hong Kong and Macao governments and 'uphold the rule of law and market-based approach in coordinating and resolving issues'. The Guangdong, Hong Kong and Macao governments are to make specific plans or implementation plans proactively. The NDRC and relevant ministries (including the Hong Kong and Macao Affairs Office of the State Council) shall keep track of progress in implementation, conduct evaluation and assessments, put forward proposals for refinement and make timely reports on major issues to the CPC Central Committee and the State Council.[66] To date, many facilitation measures have been introduced at the national, provincial and regional levels in the 12 development areas in the economic, social, environmental and youth development spheres.[67]

The Fourteenth Five-Year Plan (2021–2025) is the most recent programme the NPC adopted for national economic and social development, and it includes discussion on long-range objectives for 2035.[68] Chapters 4, 30 and 31 refer to the GBA in relation to national development in scientific innovation, high-quality territorial development and regional construction and development. Chapter 61 is headed 'maintaining the long term prosperity and stability of Hong Kong and Macao'. It refers first to the full and faithful implementation of the constitutional order under the PRC Constitution and the respective Basic Laws, the comprehensive jurisdiction of the Central Authorities over the SARs[69] and the legal system and enforcement mechanisms for the SARs to safeguard national sovereignty, security and development interests of the country,[70] as well as the resolute prevention and curbing of interference by external forces in the affairs of Hong Kong and Macao. It then turns to the two concrete aspects in the programme of supporting Hong Kong and Macao in consolidating and raising their competitive advantages and supporting Hong Kong and Macao to integrate better in the overall picture of national development, so as to complement the advantages of the Chinese Mainland and synergize in the mechanisms of development. This second aspect of fostering the integration of the SARs in national development could be regarded as novel at first glance. Yet it was foreshadowed in the 2019 Decision of the Fourth Plenum of the CPC Central Committee.[71]

The approach of the Hong Kong SAR Government towards the Fourteenth Five-Year Plan appears to be faithful complementation. This can be seen in a paper presented to the Hong Kong SAR legislature in June 2021.[72] It shows an understanding that this Plan 'establishes a clear positioning for Hong Kong's future development', with the 'relevant statements' therein said to be confirming 'Hong Kong's functions and positioning in the overall development strategy of the country', providing 'a clear direction and [expanding] the scope for Hong Kong's further co-operation with the Mainland' and strengthening and enhancing 'Hong Kong's "intermediary" role between the country and the world'. The government also vows that Hong Kong would leverage on its advantages under OCTS and 'proactively become a "participant" in domestic circulation and a "facilitator" in international circulation', in relation to the 'dual circulation development paradigm' set out in this Plan. The GBA development would be taken as 'the best entry point' for not only business opportunities in the market of the Chinese Mainland but also that of regional co-operation and better integration into the overall national development.[73] An annex to the paper lists the work done by the government in respect of 29 'relevant statements', and they cover legislation regulating oath-taking by public officers and improving the electoral system, fintech and green and sustainable finance, 'southbound' stock trading and cross-boundary RMB, developing innovation and technology jointly with Shenzhen at specified sites, promoting cultural exchanges, strengthening education on the PRC Constitution, the Basic Law and national security, and facilitating Hong Kong young people to study, work and start businesses in GBA cities.

The study of the Central Authorities' documents and the associated practices above has illustrated the shift over time in the political economic relation between the Chinese Mainland and the SARs. It began with the voluntary and arms-length dealing epitomized by the free trade agreements of CEPA.[74] While the inclusion of the SARs in the Five-Year Plans was at first cautiously regarded by the Central Authorities as not a replacement of the SARs' own development plans,[75] subsequent developments, partly initiated and contributed by succeeding Chief Executives of the Hong Kong

SAR, have led to the current Central Authorities coordinated exercise, with the SARs recognized and assigned with roles and macro-imperatives in the national economic and social development. Concurrently, the Hong Kong SAR Government has approached the Five-Year Plan as constituting the Central Authorities' instructions in not only the economic area but also in the political and social fields that its bureaux and departments would give priority and make progress. Although almost none of the Five-Year Plan's programmes and GBA facilitation measures have impacted significantly on the Hong Kong SAR's systems to date,[76] the framework and practice of the Central-SAR relationship are now such that the Central Authorities have the means to construct 'workarounds' in accordance with the Constitution and the Basic Law to achieve any measure adopted in any programme.[77]

Concluding Remarks

The Court of Appeal of the Hong Kong SAR advanced a 'reasonable argument' in a judgement handed down in June 2021 that seems to solve the 'question' over the application of the PRC Constitution in the Hong Kong SAR, saying that '[*save*] *and except that the socialist system and policies shall not be practised in Hong Kong,* the Constitution on the whole must apply to the HKSAR as an inalienable part of the People's Republic of China', on the premise that 'both the Mainland and Hong Kong systems are within *one country and one national constitutional order*'.[78]

Legalistically, it can be suggested that the Court of Appeal had also claimed, perhaps inadvertently, that the Hong Kong SAR courts *could* exercise an *additional* constitutional jurisdiction,[79] to ensure the integrity of the SAR's systems, so that 'the socialist system and policies shall not be practised in Hong Kong'. This bold proposition can be examined using the discussion in the above sections.

There is by now increasing difficulty in maintaining a distinction between the PRC's 'socialist' systems and policies and Hong Kong and Macao's 'capitalist' systems and policies. The PRC's reform and opening up have been consolidated in the constitutional modification of the State economy to 'socialist market economy' that includes the 'individual and private sectors', the constitutional departure from Soviet-style central planning and the constitutional protection of private ownership of property. The PRC's economy is likely to satisfy a minimalist definition of 'capitalism' such as 'the presence of private property, production for the market, and the principle of profit maximization by rational means'.[80] So long as the Central Authorities do not seek to introduce into the SARs 'socialist public ownership of the means of production',[81] the original dichotomy could well have disaggregated into a measure of the degree of Central Authorities intervention into the SAR economy, bearing in mind the plausible suggestion by Han Dayuan that Article 5 of the Basic Laws is concerned 'mainly with the economic system' where it refers to 'the socialist system and policies'.[82] Hence, while a submission against a Five-Year Plan's programme for the SAR as unwarranted top-down practice of 'socialist system and policy' would have little purchase, submissions invigilating the imposition of 'binding targets' on the SAR's institutions or requirements for 'common prosperity' on the SAR's entrepreneurs might obtain a hearing.

The discussion above also demonstrates the living, dynamic and developmental contradiction posed at the beginning of this chapter. By now, the Chinese Party State's fostering and inclusion of the 'capitalist' SARs for national economic development of the Chinese 'socialist' State has expanded from expressing support of previously identified and existing economic characteristics and assisting regional co-operation to periodic planning/programming/macro-regulation, regular setting of long-term objectives, co-operation and coordination not only in the economy and the associated fields of trade, manufacturing, service provision and innovation, but also in social governance, which would lead to their 'integration' as *part* of national economic and social development, with the economic side having the state-owned economy as 'the leading force', and the State being responsible for its consolidation and growth.[83] One therefore finds it difficult to contend that the PRC Constitution does not apply to the SARs 'as a whole' and, together with the respective Basic Law, establish the constitutional basis of each of the SARs.[84] Proceeding further in argument might require finding features of the SARs to be those of the 'current social and economic systems' and 'life-style' that had been promised and presumably prescribed as 'to remain unchanged', and confronting the Central Authorities with the pre-commitments to Hong Kong and Macao under the 12-point basic policies and their elaboration in the Joint Declarations or the 'established basic policies' within the meaning of the Basic Laws. Hong Kong judges are likely to say that they are 'ill-equipped' to deal with this question. And, the proponent must be mindful that the Central Authorities regard that 'One Country' comes first, the 'Two Systems' do not 'sit on the same bench'. The SAR's 'capitalist system' shall not pose a challenge of the nation's 'socialist system'.[85]

Notes

1 See Steve Tsang, *A Modern History of Hong Kong* (HKU Press, 2004) 153–154.
2 See *Resolution on Certain Historical Issues of the Party since the Founding of the People's Republic of China* (27 June 1981).
3 See *Communique of the Third Plenum of the Eleventh Central Committee of the Communist Party of China* (22 December 1978).
4 The PRC and Japan signed the Treaty of Peace and Friendship in August 1978. The PRC and the United States established diplomatic relations in January 1979.
5 See 'Message to Compatriots in Taiwan' (26 December 1978) <www.china.org.cn/english/taiwan/7943.htm> accessed 29 September 2022; and Ye Jianying, 'On Taiwan's Return to Motherland and Peaceful Reunification' (30 September 1981) <www.china.org.cn/english/7945.htm> accessed 29 September 2022.
6 See *Deng Xiaoping Chronicle (1975-1997) Vol II* (Central Party Literature Press, 2004) 797 (in Chinese).
7 See Tsang (n 1) 217.
8 See Tsang (n 1) 218–221.
9 See the Joint Declaration of the Government of the United Kingdom of Great Britain and the Government of the People's Republic of China on the Question of Hong Kong (19 December 1984) 1399 UNTS 33; (1984) 23 ILM 1366 art 3.
10 See the Joint Declaration of the Government of the Republic of Portugal and the Government of the People's Republic of China on the Question of Macao (26 March 1987) 1498 UNTS 195; (1995) 5 Asian YBIL 567 art 3. See also Chapter 5 in this book.
11 PRC Constitution, Preamble.
12 *Ibid.*
13 PRC Constitution, art 1.
14 PRC Constitution, art 31.
15 This was done by the approval of the Work Report of the Central People's Government during the Second Session of the Sixth NPC.
16 See the Sino-British Joint Declaration (n 9) art 3(5) and Annex I, s I; and the Sino-Portuguese Joint Declaration (n 10) art 2(4) and Annex I, s I.
17 For the histories of the drafting of the Basic Law of the Hong Kong SAR and the Basic Law of the Macao SAR, see Chapters 4 and 5 of this book, respectively.

18 The Basic Law of the Hong Kong Special Administrative Region of the People's Republic of China (4 April 1990) (1990) 29 ILM 1511.
19 The Basic Law of the Macao Special Administrative Region of the People's Republic of China (31 March 1993) <www.wipo.int/edocs/lexdocs/laws/en/mo/mo019en.pdf> (English translation) accessed 29 September 2022.
20 See HKBL Preamble and art 11; and MBL Preamble and art 11.
21 See HKBL arts 6, 11 and arts 105–135; and MBL arts 6, 11 and arts 103–120.
22 See HKBL arts 109 and 128.
23 See Yash Ghai, *Hong Kong's New Constitutional Order: The Resumption of Chinese Sovereignty and the Basic Law* (2nd edn, HKU Press, 1999) 138–142, 153–154.
24 Both Basic Laws provide for a mechanism of amendment by the NPC, subject to the stipulation that an amendment must not contravene the basic policies of the PRC regarding Hong Kong or Macao; see HKBL art 159 and MBL art 144.
25 See Esther Lam, *China and WTO: A Long March towards the Rule of Law* (Kluwer Law International, 2009).
26 See Yun-Wing Sung, 'Becoming Part of One National Economy: Maintaining Two Systems in the Midst of the Rise of China', in Tai-lok Lui, Stephen WK Chiu and Ray Yep (eds), *Routledge Handbook of Contemporary Hong Kong* (Routledge, 2019) 66–85.
27 The GBA outline development plan is at: <www.bayarea.gov.hk/filemanager/en/share/pdf/Outline_Development_Plan.pdf> accessed 29 September 2022.
28 See Eric C Ip, 'The Constitution of Economic Liberty in Hong Kong' (2015) 26(3) *Constitutional Political Economy* 307; Wilson Wong and Xiao Hanyu, 'Twenty Years of Hong Kong and Macao Under Chinese Rule: Being Absorbed Under "One Country, Two Systems"' (2018) 38(6) *Public Money & Management* 411; Sung (n 26); David Meyer, 'Hong Kong: China's global city', in Lui, Chiu and Yep (n 26) 414–429; and Ho-fung Hung, 'Chinese state capitalism in Hong Kong', in Lui, Chiu and Yep (n 26) 430–477.
29 See Ghai (n 23) 93–95.
30 For example, Article 24 of the Constitution expressed the State's ideological education goal to 'combat capitalist, feudal and other decadent ideas'.
31 See Dayuan Han, 'On the Normative Content of "State" in the Hong Kong Basic Law' (2020) 32.1 *Peking University Law Journal* 19, 29–30 (in Chinese).
32 See Ghai (n 23) 61–62, 178, 214–215.
33 Decision of the National People's Congress on the Basic Law of the Hong Kong Special Administrative Region of the People's Republic of China (4 April 1990). See also Chapter 4 of this book. A similar decision was made by the NPC in respect of the MBL on 31 March 1993. This matter has remained a topic of serious discussion, see various perspectives in Han (n 31) 33–38.
34 The 1993 constitutional amendments were preceded by the Fourteenth National Congress of the CPC in October 1992, which determined that the objective of the reform of the national economic system was the establishment of the socialist market economy system. After the adoption of the 1993 constitutional amendments, the Third Plenum of the Fourteenth Central Committee of the CPC met in November 1993 and made the Decision of the Central Committee of the CPC on Issues Concerning the Establishment of a Socialist Market Economic System.
35 The amendment realized Deng Xiaoping's statement that '[it] is wrong to maintain that a market economy exists only in capitalist society and that there is only [a] "capitalist" market economy … Developing a market economy does not mean practising capitalism. While maintaining a planned economy as the mainstay of our economic system, we are also introducing a market economy. But it is a socialist market economy'; see *Selected Works of Deng Xiaoping (1975-1982)* (Foreign Language Press, 1984) 175.
36 Articles 16 and 17 of the Constitution were also amended in 1993 to remove the requirements on state enterprises and collective economic organizations to fulfil or be guided by the state plan. Rather both types of economic production units are subject to regulation by law.
37 For discussion of the factors and features of the 1999 amendments, see Ngoc Son Bui, *Constitutional Change in the Contemporary Socialist World* (OUP, 2020) 278, 316.
38 See, for example, Lowell Dittmer, 'Transformation of the Chinese Political Economy in the New Era', in Lowell Dittmer (ed), *China's Political Economy in the Xi Jinping Epoch: Domestic and Global Dimensions* (World Scientific, 2021) 6–7.

39 See, for example, Ronald Coase and Wang Ning, *How China Became Capitalist* (Palgrave Macmillan, 2012) 177–180 (where the authors referred to China's 'historical precedents of capitalism' as relevant to the present market economy).
40 Macro-control or regulation was considered as part of the reform package to depart from direct control over enterprises in the mid-1980s, when the CPC formulated and implemented the Seventh Five-Year Plan (1986–1990); see Isabella M Weber, *How China Escaped Shock Therapy: The Market Reform Debate* (Routledge, 2021) 200–203.
41 See the Decision of the Central Committee of the CPC on Issues Concerning the Establishment of a Socialist Market Economic System (14 November 1993) para 21.
42 See Angela Huyue Zhang, *Chinese Antitrust Exceptionalism* (OUP, 2021) 9, 40–41.
43 See Sebastian Heilmann, *Red Swan: How Unorthodox Policy Making Facilitated China's Rise* (The Chinese University Press, 2018) 155.
44 See the Ten Year National Economic and Social Development Programme and the Outline of the Eighth Five-Year Plan of the People's Republic of China (9 April 1991).
45 See the Ninth Five-Year Plan on National Economic and Social Development and the Outline of the 2010 Long-Term Objectives of the People's Republic of China (17 March 1996). See also Heilmann (n 43) 152–153.
46 See the Outline of the Eleventh Five-Year Plan of National Economic and Social Development of the People's Republic of China (14 March 2006). Heilmann explained that the proposal for the change came from the NDRC 'to indicate the earlier break from socialist planning'; see Heilmann (n 43) 154.
47 It was explained in the Eleventh Five-Year Plan that the indicative target is a development objective expected by the State that relies, principally, on the autonomous conduct of the market undertakings for its realization, whereas a binding target is one that entails governmental responsibility on the basis of what is expected. Heilmann observed that the binding targets were specifically directed at government bodies, to be viewed as 'promises' in particular fields and policies; see Heilmann (n 43) 155.
48 See Heilmann (n 43) 132–133.
49 See Heilmann (n 43) 138–140.
50 Such documents include plans, subplans, development programmes, instructions, fiscal provisions and policies formulated or made by provincial and local authorities during the five-year period to implement the national plan; see Heilmann (n 43) 155–156.
51 See Heilmann (n 43) 143–144.
52 See Heilmann (n 43) 145.
53 See Heilmann (n 43) 164–166.
54 See Wen-Hsuan Tsai and Zhou Wang, 'Integrated Fragmentation and the Role of Leading Small Groups in Chinese Politics' (2019) 82 *China Journal* 1.
55 See Heilmann (n 43) 160, 162–163.
56 Arrangements have been made between Guangdong and Hong Kong and Macao in vital fields such as food, water supply and electricity supply. For example, Macao has procured water supply from sources located in Zhuhai and Guangdong since 1960, and Hong Kong has procured water supply from Guangdong since 1965. A government-level liaison channel was formally established between Guangdong and Hong Kong in 1982.
57 See Constitutional and Mainland Affairs Bureau, 'Legislative Council Panel on Commerce and Industry: Framework Agreement on Hong Kong/Guangdong Co-operation' (LC Paper No. CB(1)1559/09-10(01)) (April 2010) <www.legco.gov.hk/yr09-10/english/panels/ci/papers/cicb1-1559-1-e.pdf> accessed 29 September 2022.
58 See the Outline of the Programme for Pan-Pearl River Delta Regional Co-operation and Development (2006–2020), at: <www.fao.org/faolex/results/details/zh/c/LEX-FAOC177804/> (in Chinese) accessed 29 September 2022.
59 See Donald Tsang, *Sharing Prosperity for a Caring Society* (13 October 2010) <www.policyaddress.gov.hk/10-11/eng/p92.html> accessed 29 September 2022.
60 See Leo F Goodstadt, *A City Mismanaged: Hong Kong's Struggle for Survival* (HKU Press, 2018) 173–174.
61 See the Outline of the Twelfth Five-Year Programme for National Economic and Social Development of the People's Republic of China (14 March 2011) Ch 57 <www.gov.cn/2011lh/content_1825838.htm> (in Chinese) and <www.asifma.org/uploadedFiles/Resources/

PRC-12th-FYP(1).PDF> (English translation) accessed 29 September 2022. In contrast, the Tenth and the Eleventh Five-Year Plans had final paragraphs that noted the SARs' statuses and existing programmes of co-operation, voicing the State's support.

62 See the Outline of the Thirteenth Five-Year Programme for National Economic and Social Development of the People's Republic of China (16 March 2016) Ch 54 <www.gov.cn/xinwen/2016-03/17/content_5054992.htm> (in Chinese) and <en.ndrc.gov.cn/policies/202105/P020210527785800103339.pdf> (English translation) accessed 29 September 2022. Goodstadt reported that Leung Chun-ying, who succeeded Donald Tsang in 2012, lobbied for more involvement by Hong Kong in the formulation of the Five-Year Plan; see Goodstadt (n 60) 178–179.

63 See Xi Jinping, 'Secure a Decisive Victory in Building a Moderately Prosperous Society in All Respects and Strive for the Great Success of Socialism with Chinese Characteristics for a New Era' (18 October 2017) (Foreign Language Press, 2018) 68; and 'Office of the Leading Group for Development of the Guangdong-Hong Kong-Macao Greater Bay Area: Building International First Class Bay Area, Advance Livelihood Benefits', *People's Daily* (19 February 2019) <cpc.people.com.cn/BIG5/n1/2019/0219/c64387-30804195.html> (in Chinese) accessed 29 September 2022.

64 See Heilmann (n 43) 159–164.

65 See the GBA Outline Development Plan (n 27) Chs 4–9.

66 See the GBA Outline Development Plan (n 27), Ch 11.

67 The list of facilitation measures is at: <www.bayarea.gov.hk/en/resource/mainland-policies-measures.html> accessed 29 September 2022.

68 See the Outline of the Fourteenth Five-Year Programme for National Economic and Social Development and the Long-Range Objectives through 2035 (11 March 2021) <www.gov.cn/xinwen/2021-03/13/content_5592681.htm> (in Chinese) and <cset.georgetown.edu/wp-content/uploads/t0284_14th_Five_Year_Plan_EN.pdf> (English translation) accessed 29 September 2022.

69 See State Council Information Office, *The Practice of the "One Country, Two Systems" Policy in the Hong Kong Special Administrative Region* (10 June 2014) <www.scio.gov.cn/zfbps/ndhf/2014/Document/1373163/1373163.htm> accessed 29 September 2022.

70 This refers to the Law of the People's Republic of China on the Safeguarding of National Security in the Hong Kong Special Administrative Region (HKNSL), enacted by the Standing Committee of the NPC and introduced into the Hong Kong SAR on 30 June 2020.

71 See Decision of the Central Committee of the Communist Party of China on Some Major Issues Concerning how to Uphold and Improve the System of Socialism with Chinese Characteristics and Advance the Modernization of China's System and Capacity for Governance (31 October 2019) <www.gov.cn/zhengce/2019-11/05/content_5449023.htm> (in Chinese) accessed 29 September 2022.

72 See Constitutional and Mainland Affairs Bureau, 'Hong Kong Special Administrative Region's positioning and supporting measures under the National 14th Five-Year Plan' (June 2021) (LC Paper No CB(1)987/20-21(03)) <www.legco.gov.hk/yr20-21/english/panels/ci/papers/ci20210615cb1-987-3-e.pdf> accessed 29 September 2022.

73 *Ibid*, paras 3–5, 7.

74 See Guan Wenwei, 'China's Free Trade from SEZs to CEPA and FTZs: The Beijing Consensus in Global Convergence and Divergence', in Zhao Yun and Michael Ng (eds), *Chinese Legal Reform and the Global Legal Order: Adoption and Adaptation* (CUP, 2018) 104–124.

75 See Goodstadt (n 60) 174.

76 The exception was the co-location of Hong Kong and Mainland immigration, customs and quarantine checkpoints at the Hong Kong terminus of the Guangdong-Shenzhen-Hong Kong Express Rail Link, where Mainland laws and jurisdiction apply at the Mainland checkpoint in spite of its location within the Hong Kong SAR.

77 The introduction of the HKNSL and the improvement of the Hong Kong SAR's electoral systems are clear examples.

78 *Kwok Cheuk Kin v Secretary for Justice* [2021] HKCA 871, [2021] 3 HKLRD 140 [66] (Poon CJHC).

79 For constitutional judicial review in Hong Kong, see Chapter 11 of this book.

80 See John L Campbell and John A Hall, *What Capitalism Needs: Forgotten Lessons of Great Economists* (CUP, 2021) 6.

81 See PRC Constitution, art 6.
82 See Han (n 31) 31. The SAR's political system, according to Han, is subject to the design and change by the Central Authorities under Part IV of the Basic Law.
83 PRC Constitution, arts 6, 7, 15.
84 This is the official statement in the 2014 State Council policy paper (n 69) and also Han Dayuan's view (n 31) 38. For an alternate view, see Chen Duanhong, 'On the Constitutional Nature of the Hong Kong and Macao Basic Laws' (2020) 32 (1) *Peking University Law Journal* 41 (in Chinese).
85 See Han (n 31) 31.

Bibliography

Coase D, and Wang N, *How China Became Capitalist* (Palgrave Macmillan 2012).
Han D, 'On the Normative Content of "State" in the Hong Kong Basic Law' (2020) 32.1 Peking University Law Journal 29.
Ghai Y, *Hong Kong's New Constitutional Order: The Resumption of Chinese Sovereignty and the Basic Law* (2nd edn, HKU Press, 1999).
Goodstadt LF, *A City Mismanaged: Hong Kong's Struggle for Survival* (HKU Press, 2018).
Heilmann S, *Red Swan: How Unorthodox Policy Making Facilitated China's Rise* (The Chinese University Press 2018).
Xi J, *Secure a Decisive Victory in Building a Moderately Prosperous Society in All Respects and Strive for the Great Success of Socialism with Chinese Characteristics for a New Era* (Foreign Language Press 2018).
Lui T, Chiu SWK and Yep R (eds), *Routledge Handbook of Contemporary Hong Kong* (Routledge 2019).
State Council Information Office, *The Practice of the "One Country, Two Systems" Policy in the Hong Kong Special Administrative Region* (10 June 2014) <www.scio.gov.cn/zfbps/ndhf/2014/Document/1373163/1373163.htm>
Tan KYL, and Ng M (eds), *Constitutional Foundings in Northeast Asia* (Hart Publishing, 2022).

16

MARKET MENTALITY OR SOCIAL SOLIDARITY?*

The Constitutional Relevance of Labour Reforms in Contemporary China

Su Bian

Introduction

According to the doctrinal separation of public law and private law, public law protects individual rights from the intervention of state powers, while private law reflects equal relationships between private parties, individuals, or social groups. Posed in this dichotomy, labour law is taken either as one of private law, or one of 'economic law' in the Chinese legal system. In either way, labour law is not a public law and cannot be constitutionalised per se, as 'the personal scope of employment law is not universal'.[1]

However, in recent literature, the constitutional implications of labour have been brought to the fore in Chinese scholarship. It takes the route of reinterpreting labour-related contents in the Constitution. Ever since the founding of the People's Republic of China (PRC) in 1949, the socialist tradition officially endorses the working class as the ruling class of the country, and is committed to better realising the constitutional value of equality in political, economic, and social dimensions. In the 1982 Constitution, the term 'labour' has been notably mentioned more than 30 times; Article 42, in particular, prescribes that Chinese citizens have the right as well as the obligation to work. Nevertheless, these provisions have never been effectively channelled into normative injunctions except that, recently, several scholars tried to interpret the nature of the constitutional labour right in China as both a liberal right and a social right.[2] By saying so, they attempt to give expression to the *dual* nature of this right under the unique circumstances of the 'Reform' period: legalisation of labour rights in the context of China's transformation from the planned economy to the market economy, aimed primarily to enable workers' free access to the labour market, than merely to recognise workers' dependency in labour relations. In this respect, Wang Dezhi insists that a distinction should be drawn between constitutional

* Part of this chapter has been published in the author's paper 'Labour Constitutionalism: A Critical Genealogy of Constitutionalisation in the "Reform" Period of China' [2020] 21(1) Australian Journal of Asian Law 151. <https://ssrn.com/abstract=3748920>.

DOI: 10.4324/9781003128243-19

labour rights and labour rights in labour law, as the latter refers to a group of professionally subordinated labourers, which do not match the scope of the legal subjects protected under the Constitution.[3] Wang Xu asserts that constitutionalisation of labour rights in China plays a key role in transforming the 'others of the polity (政治的他者)', namely, those classes other than the working class, to the 'communal builders of the country (国家共同的建设者)'.[4] Therefore, in his opinion, commercialisation of labour relations in China contributes to instead of undermining the core values of modern constitutionalism.

Another perspective is provided by Yan Tian, assistant professor at the Law School of Peking University. Yan delivered his keynote speech at the 7th Annual Conference of 'Politics, Law and Public Policy' in 2015, calling forth 'labour constitutionalism' as a new constitutional idea. He advocates a systematic interpretation of the notion of 'labour' in China's Constitution that not only provides constitutional protection of labour rights but also pays due attention to the reflexive functions of labour in the process of Chinese constitutionalisation, namely, taking 'labour' as the basis of citizenship, the supporting pillar of the economic system and the carrier of the people's democracy.[5] Although Yan did not elaborate further on how this systematic interpretation should be undertaken, I would like to identify this approach as a socio-legal one: it aims to investigate what role labour reforms have played in Chinese constitutionalisation and to diagnose the constitutional deficits thereof from a perspective of labour law changes.

In this chapter, I proceed with Yan's suggestion, placing emphasis on why and in what sense labour studies can be conducive to unpacking the constitutional dilemmas in China, particularly the dilemma of 'legalisation without constitutionalisation'. I also insist that 'labour constitutionalism' should be distinguished from 'entrenchment of labour rights as the fundamental rights', as the former approach aims, not only to apply the Constitution, but also to account for why the concession of constitutional authority to the market imperatives is made possible in the past four decades, and to act as a strategy of resistance accordingly. By demonstrating with historical proof the co-evolution of labour reforms and constitutional reforms in China, this chapter can suggest that labour law changes should not be excluded from constitutional scrutiny. Rather, it is due to the compelling ideology of 'contractualism' and the elimination of 'status' elements after 1978 that the labour system was seen as separated from the constitutional system and, consequently, being privatised. Instead, this chapter aims to re-establish firmly the relevance of labour to China's constitutionalisation.

This chapter will be divided into three parts. In the first section, I explore how those changes with respect to labour law and labour policy have been intertwined with the constitutional changes in the past four decades. Following that, I engage with the Durkheimian thesis of legal modernisation that comes along with the intensifying division of labour. I contend that while presumably 'organic solidarity' will take the place of 'mechanical solidarity' in transitional societies like China and 'restitutive law' will support social interdependence and coordination in ideal circumstances, property law and contract law can arguably turn repressive towards those have-nots and thereby may not strengthen social solidarity as wished. The third section then uses Ruth Dukes' arguments about 'labour constitutionalism' to reclaim the constitutional relevance of labour in China and its contributions to Chinese constitutional re-imagination.

Interactions between Labour and the Constitution in the 'Reform' Period of China

The Start of the 'Reform' (1978–92)

At the outset of the 'Reform and Opening-up', corresponding to the two types of socialist ownership, namely, ownership by the whole people and collective ownership by the working people, a dual-track labour system was adopted to organise Chinese labour forces in urban and rural places into two separate institutions. They were also two important mechanisms for social integration. For urban work units (单位), labour regulation was quite rigid and was vividly depicted as 'three old irons', namely, the 'iron rice bowl', the 'iron wage', and the 'iron chair' (a reference to state-controlled appointments and promotions of managers)[6]; whereas, in rural areas where the social order was less permeated by state powers, collective economic organisations were established in the people's communes (人民公社) to undertake certain social obligations, such as healthcare and education services (arts 19 and 21 of the 1982 Constitution). This particular discrepancy between two distinct labour organisations was sustained by a fixed legal framework provided by the 1958 *Regulation on the Household Registration of the People's Republic of China.* With this law, registration as urban or rural was closely related to the distribution of major social services. Thereby it effectively controlled the population flow that would otherwise have presented serious challenges to the planned economy.

It was in the countryside that the old labour system began to fall apart and the 'Reform' process started. The 'Rural Household Contract Responsibility System (家庭联产承包责任制)' that developed from 1978 allowed peasants to return to 'household farming' and enjoy personal use of land without changing the collective ownership structure. It 'may be understood as partial privatisation of agricultural production which had been collectivised since the mid-1950s'.[7] After smashing the 'large pot', since 1983, the people's communes were widely abolished, and their all-in-one functions were divided into elected governments at the township level and social and economic co-operatives organised by village committees. Nevertheless, under the influence of the 'cutting non-productive expenditures' policy at that time, organising the *economic* co-operatives became the dominant theme in dissolving the bundle of the rights assembled by the people's communes. For example, once-booming co-operative medical services in rural areas ended with the decline of the collective economy,[8] but an official safety net was not constructed in the meantime as a substitute. This sort of asymmetry is clearly reflected in the 1993 Constitutional Amendment: the 'people's communes' were removed thereof and replaced with economic co-operatives such as producers', supply and marketing, credit, and consumers' co-operatives (art 6 in 1993 Amendment).

Since agricultural productivity was increased, peasants freed from working on their land became a large labour surplus and were allowed to provide services in urban areas without permanently shifting their registered status. A large proportion of them fled to coastal regions in south-eastern China and became the first generation of China's migrant workers. By 1985, China had formed three coastal regions open to foreign investment, including 5 special economic zones, 14 coastal open cities, and 3 coastal open areas. Foreign investment was encouraged in these regions through tax reductions and by decreasing the mandatory state plans for local governments.[9] In addition, with the opportunity for the 'industrial upgrading' of the 'Asia's Four Little Dragons', China began to develop its own export-oriented industry policy, which mainly fed on these migrant labour forces. FDI increased slightly in the 1980s, but in 1993, China became the largest recipient of all developing countries.

Around 1986, reforms in urban areas commenced with the adoption of a new 'factory director responsibility system (厂长经理负责制)' in state enterprises. In lieu of direct plans issued by the government, directors were selected to manage the factory and were entrusted with powers to implement the labour contract system and probation periods.[10] At that time, most workers were successfully transferred to fixed-term individual and collective labour contracts, with the exception of peasant workers, who were excluded as 'temporary workers'. Though incremental, these changes were still radical for a socialist country, as it was inconceivable that workers, as the masters of the factory, could be dismissed and their employment contracts terminated. Since then, '[t]his fundamental abandonment of the "iron rice bowl" has seen the rise and rise of temporary, contingent employment such as dispatch labour'.[11]

Since the labour contract system introduced the risk of being laid off from the late 1980s, social services were required to be partly incorporated into the workers' wages. This measure, for one thing, transferred welfare services from the sector of supply to the sector of consumption, while, for another, inequality between different industries and different enterprises increasingly grew and finally led to a legitimacy crisis for the Reform package. The 'Reform and Opening-up' policy was temporarily suspended from 1989 to 1991 in a three-year 'overhaul' in reaction to the economic blockade by foreign countries, during which time, the policy of 'centralisation' and the planned economy were re-emphasised. These tactical but important pre-1993 experiments have had long-lasting effects in both rural and urban areas of China. Through contractualisation of the land use system, economic co-operatives replaced the all-in-one people's communes in rural locations, while, later, in urban areas, the labour contract system took the place of the lifelong employment and welfare distribution system.

All of these developments changed the mode and organisation of social integration in pre-Reform China by entitling individuals to have flexibility, form contracts, and consume. This change did not cause too much trouble since most workers were successfully transferred into the contract system. Still, a risk could be foreseen, once the exacerbation of marketisation, rise of social costs, and inflation rendered these short-term benefits less appealing.

Continuation of the 'Reform' (1993–2003)

In 1992, Deng Xiaoping delivered his Southern Tour Speech when visiting Shenzhen, Wuchang, Zhuhai, and Shanghai, which put an end to criticisms of the 'Reform' policy and restarted the process. The failure of the 'Reform' policy in the first phase was attributed by him to a deficit of social productivity in catching up with people's rising demands for consumption. This claim pacified the more heated ideological debates, to a large extent, and determined that the next move of the 'Reform' would remain productivity-centred.

In 1988, the *Law of the PRC on Industrial Enterprises Owned by the Whole People* was promulgated, which, for the first time, legalised the 'operational autonomy' of state-owned enterprises (SOEs) and set them up as autonomous legal persons. Nevertheless, Iain MacNeil preferred to name this mode 'corporatisation' instead of 'privatisation', as it 'had the effect of formalising the separation of state from

SOEs, as the state became a shareholder rather than the direct owner of productive assets'.[12] Following the separation of operation from ownership of the SOEs, the *Company Law* that aimed to standardise the organisation and operation of all companies came into effect on 1 July 1994. Along with this, three regulations that separately dealt with risks of insolvency were also promulgated, namely, the 1986 *Enterprise Bankruptcy Law*, the 1994 *Notice*[13] for SOEs, and the 1991 *Civil Procedure Law* (Chapter 19) for non-public enterprises. These significant changes concerning the organisation and regulation of enterprises owned by the whole people successfully transformed 'state economy (国营经济)' to 'state-owned economy (国有经济)' in art 5 of the 1993 Constitutional Amendment, and 'state enterprises' to 'state-owned enterprises' in art 8 and 10. In the 1999 Constitutional Amendment, the socialist distribution system was further amended, supplementing the principle of 'distribution according to work' with a new clause stating that 'diverse modes of distribution coexist' (art 14).

After risks of insolvency were introduced, it was no longer possible for the SOEs to continue taking the responsibility of distributing social welfare. The wage form had to substitute for the material supply,[14] which also removed barriers to extending these social services to private enterprises. A national social security system was then established, which included retirement and pension benefits; worker's compensation; medical care; unemployment benefits; pregnancy and maternity benefits; and death benefits for survivors. However, there were significant flaws in the system as it was administered by separate districts and cities due to the fiscal decentralisation. Moreover, it was closely linked to the household registration, which had no transfer system to make social benefits portable between local units. Because social security benefits could not be included in their wage package, migrant workers were inevitably let down during the process and constituted a low-waged labour force in the labour market. Fragmentation within the Chinese working class began to develop between migrant workers concentrated in the exploitative, foreign-invested factories of the 'Sunbelt' and those laid-off workers of the 'Rustbelt' SOEs.[15] Between 1995 and 2002, the latter group of workers was reported to have increased to 50 million, and more than 50,000 state enterprises were closed.[16]

All these tensions were hidden beneath the 1994 Labour Law, which used labour contracts as the legal means for regulating employment relations. However, in order to be compatible with other ongoing reforms, this law paradoxically placed more emphasis on the termination of employment than on 'contract formation',[17] which resulted in a 'disorderly internal structure' and functional confusion. As Mary Gallagher and Dong Baohua put it,

> The problems presented by the labour contract system are indicative of the difficulty of legislating employment laws that have two different, even opposing, functions. The 1994 Labour Law was designed to both end the entitlements of socialism and ensure increased protection and rights under the market economy. Combined with the realities of a large labour surplus, these legal developments were more effective in ending socialist employment than protecting workers in the new market economy.[18]

Born out of the socialist structure of ownership and developed along with the economic transformation after 1978, the labour law system could be properly taken as a by-product of the private law regime established in the 'Reform' period of China. This gave Chinese labour law a sense of perplexity since, as a law on behalf of the interests of the working class, it nonetheless cannot guarantee the same level of protection that workers enjoyed before the 'Reform'. Therefore, between the form and substance of Chinese labour law reforms, there are, in fact, structural tensions that are related to the legislative values and orientations: should future labour legislation be more flexible so as to include those working in the grey zone of the informal economy, or return to the perspective of 'status' from which the distribution of insolvent SOE assets should also be taken into consideration? These divided rights claims became most controversial in the third period of the 'Reform' when the Labour Contract Law was enacted.

Reflection on 'Reform' (from 2003 Onwards)

With the deepening of 'Reform', Chinese society began to feel the pressure of the market and substantive social loss. Before the 2008 global financial crisis, the Chinese population's most pressing concern was still public goods and affordable houses, while government expenditures for health and education only comprised 18 per cent of the whole, much less than the same expenditures in peer countries.[19] In the 2004 Constitutional Amendment, 'human rights protection' (art 24) and the 'establishment and improvement of the social security system fitting in with the level of economic development' (art 23) were both adopted as state responsibilities, which indicated that constitutional transitions in China were re-oriented to a slightly different direction.

This was also motivated by the 2008 global financial crisis. Due to comparatively low exposure to the riskiest financial products, the realms that were hit most heavily by the crisis were China's real economy. In the first half of 2009, exports and imports sank 21.8 per cent and 25.4 per cent respectively; in the spring of 2009, China's Ministry of Agriculture reported that 20 million recently laid-off migrant workers returned to the countryside.[20] China's State Council reacted quickly to this crisis with a 4-trillion-yuan stimulation plan and changed the monetary policy from 'moderately tight' to 'moderately loose'.[21] As a side effect, this stimulation package provided a good chance for promoting reforms in China's health and medication system etc., which were covered in three decrees issued from 2008 to 2009 by the State Council that aimed to deal with problems such as the pension issues of the rural citizens and unemployment, and to increase both rural and urban residents' capacity to consume.

It was in this broad context that the national government promulgated three major pieces of labour regulation in 2007: the *Labour Contract Law*, the *Employment Promotion Law*, and the *Labour Dispute Mediation and Arbitration Law*. The most influential one was the *Labour Contract Law*, which closed some significant gaps in the 1994 *Labour Law*, such as detailed prescriptions on forming labour contracts and on dispatch labour. However, this law has not made as much progress in collective labour rights protection as was initially expected. During the consultation process, foreign enterprises and business councils protested that requirements to establish trade unions in multinational companies would reduce employment opportunities for PRC workers[22] and cause discrimination in policy implementation, because, they argued, trade unions in SOEs were ineffective.

Their criticisms pointed directly to the limited right to form trade unions in China, where the All-China Federation of Trade Unions remains legally 'the sole state-sanctioned union body'. Acting as a semi-administrative extension of the state bureaucracy after 1948, the trade unions' traditional function as bargaining agents for wage earners was replaced by a new duty of managing welfare distribution in the workplace in China. Although the Law on Trade Unions (2009) allows the founding of new plants or grassroots unions in previously unorganised enterprises if 25 members of the workforce meet and decide to do so (art 10), there is little legal basis for advocating independent unionism: newly founded unions must apply for membership and 'request instructions from and report on their work to the higher-level unions' (art 11).

Furthermore, this defect in the right to organise trade unions results in weak protections for other collective labour rights. If in many industrialised societies in the early to mid-twentieth century, trade unions were granted the right to utilise while regulating workers' collective power, in China, the only statutory provision on industrial action is on work stoppages and slowdowns (art 27 of the Law on Trade Unions [2009]). For labour lawyers, this provision can either be interpreted as an implicit recognition of the right to collective action on the part of workers, or an explicit strike ban on trade unions, which leaves the right to strike in a grey zone.

Finally, the intensified fragmentation of the Chinese working class creates a third set of controversies. The enlarging of the informal economy in China, which grew from approximately 3.5 per cent of the whole economic system in the 1980s to 63.2 per cent in 2010,[23] was, to a large extent, attributable to low-waged migrant labourers who fall outside the official safety net. The strict implementation of labour law and the removal of household registration barriers can greatly empower them against the unlawful practices of their employers; however, there are, in fact, neither guarantees of decent work for these migrant workers since they are already lagging behind in education and professional training, nor intermediary institutions to assist them to seek legal remedies. On the other hand, the 'Rustbelt' workers did form labour contracts with the SOEs but, in fact, gained nothing in return. Their share of state assets cannot be compensated for sufficiently by the 2007 *Labour Contract Law*, as their employment contracts were formed after the ownership and operation of the SOEs were already separated. Their protests are thus *status-oriented*, asking not 'for the improvement of working conditions', but for 'reinstatement in employment or adequate compensation with consumption goods'.[24] In this respect, the deep-rooted rural/urban division and its enduring impacts have not been eliminated but transformed into other forms of social capital.[25]

The past 40 years of wide-ranging reforms to the labour system in China have been well summarised as the 'enterprisation of labour relations (劳动关系的归属企业化)', the 'marketisation of labour controls (劳动关系调节市场化)', and the 'contractualisation of labour regulations (劳动关系规范契约化)'.[26] However, from the historical account, we also find that under the disguise of 'contractualisation' and 'marketisation', there is, in fact, nothing, contractual but, rather, top-down administrative measures of the government. Workers were 'thrown' into the market by the government to become legal subjects of the labour contract. In the meantime, if a future paradigmatic shift of labour legislation is to occur, the government also has to play a vital role in diverting its attention to other critical labour-related spheres, such as the social welfare system, taxation, and demography. This demands a constitutional perspective to obtain a full picture of the labour problematique.

Entrenching Social Solidarity in Contemporary China: A Durkheimian Perspective

Tracking down the historical transformation, it is clear that the interactions between labour reforms and constitutional changes are real and substantial in China. That said, labour policy and labour law changes should not be excluded from the ambit of constitutional studies, and the social conflicts arising in the field of labour should not be neutralised and depoliticised as private disputes. However, another question may probably arise: should we consider the market-oriented reforms essential for the division of labour and as an inevitable cost for legal modernisation, which sacrificed the mechanical solidarity in the socialist circumstances for entrenching a type of 'organic solidarity' and social cooperation in the new era? Here I would like to examine the legal and social changes in China from a Durkheimian perspective.

In *The Division of Labour in Society*, Durkheim admits that 'social solidarity is a completely moral phenomenon which, taken by itself, does not lend itself to exact observation nor indeed to measurement'.[27] However, he also finds that law, to a large extent, can be 'an external index' that symbolises social solidarity.[28] Thereby he categorises two types of law corresponding to two forms of social solidarity: the type of social solidarity that 'repressive law' corresponds to is 'mechanical solidarity', which mainly exists in primitive societies; while the type of social solidarity that 'restitutive laws' corresponds to is 'organic solidarity', which exists in advanced societies. By 'mechanical solidarity', Durkheim refers to a form of social solidarity that depends upon the likeness of consciousness in the population and their common morality. In primitive societies where religions occupy a significant role, the contents of the common conscience are definite, which sanctions disobedience mainly through penal law. However, with the increase of the volume of population that intensifies the division of labour, collective consciousness becomes more obscure, which can no longer maintain social cohesion. Accordingly, the forms of law gradually evolved from criminal norms to restitutive norms that include civil law, commercial law, and family law, which are applied to facilitate social cooperation between the increasingly self-conscious individuals, distribute rights and obligations between them, and compensate for their loss.

The Durkheimian thesis on different notions of social solidarity makes a significant contribution to thematising the great social transformation accompanied by legal modernisation: while societies become more advanced, there will be less individual resemblance but more individual self-consciousness, which requires new forms of legal arrangements. However, in scrutinising 'organic solidarity', Durkheim noted that restitutive laws might also impact social relations in different ways, either negatively or positively. The negative social relations are related to the type of negative solidarity, which is meant to repair or prevent injury but 'does not produce any integration by itself'.[29] In contrast, positive relations refer to a type of social cohesion since '[t]he relations governed by cooperative law with restitutive sanctions and the solidarity which they express, result from the division of social labour' and the growing social interdependence.[30] In other words, in support of the formation of organic solidarity, Durkheim puts more emphasis on positive potentials for social integration, while the risks of 'pure abstention'[31] are sidestepped from his analysis.

Having presumed property law and contract law must be conducive to positive integration, in my opinion, Durkheim's thesis simplifies the real occurrences of organic solidarity in some transitional societies, where positive social relations might turn 'pathological'. This is because, implied in making law an index for social solidarity, Durkheim failed to qualify whether law is a true reflection of social solidarity; he did not clarify whether it is the intensity of social solidarity that determines the law-abiding behaviours or whether it is determined by the latter and shaped by the frequency of the application of restitutive laws. In ideal circumstances, they can be mutually enhancing; however, if the law is merely instrumentalised for the sake of certain interest groups and hence does not guarantee the formation of more intensive or diverse social bindings, social solidarity might be severed or diminished despite the juridification of social norms.

To this point, Durkheim made up for this gap by recognising three 'pathological' circumstances where the division of labour might not produce social solidarity, which include an anomic division of labour, a forced division of labour, and an abnormal division of labour.[32] The anomic division of labour refers to the circumstances where 'division' becomes 'dispersion' and 'disintegration' due to the excessive specialisation of tasks, which damages instead of strengthening social cooperation, such as the typical conflicts between workers and employers. Another reason for social relations turning pathological is because the long-term conflicts are concealed and neutralised by general legislation. It is particularly prone to happen when law as the external signifier is separated from the material foundation of social solidarity. For example, when restitutive laws, such as contract law and property law, are seldom used by ordinary people as they have scant property to exchange. In these circumstances, law-abiding conducts do not necessarily indicate the existence of collective consciousness; instead of entrenching organic solidarity, we are more likely to retreat into 'pure abstention'. To this extent, Alan Hunt points out that in Durkheimian thesis, 'the use of law as an empirical index of social solidarity is a dubious undertaking'.[33]

With the gradual dissolution of the Chinese paternalistic labour system into separate social subsystems, such as housing, healthcare or education,[34] legalisation of labour contracts was made possible and the Chinese workforce was emancipated from the shackles of the planned economy and its rigid social control. It is certainly liberating; however, we have not examined another possible interpretation with respect to this process where liberation slips into abstention. As we have examined empirically, China's labour dispute resolution process is overwhelmingly individualised by design,[35] and the guiding principle of labour legislation has privileged juridification of individual labour rights than the entrenchment of collective labour rights. By adopting a one-dimensional 'rights-giving' strategy, it contains 'no constitutive laws that enable workers to assert themselves as a collective power capable of effecting labour relations'.[36] In practice, such a framework for labour regulation has prevented the 'demonstration effect' of workers' gatherings that can encourage similar actions and generate organised movement and collective identity.

Moreover, the labour reforms in China 'attenuated the previously strong bonds between the party-state and urban workers in the public sectors while [it] created new constituents from groups that previously were ignored or actively discriminated against in the old socialist order'.[37] The new generation of migrant workers have, in principle, been greatly empowered and better protected by the legislation of labour law and labour contract law; however, lacking intermediary associations to support them in seeking remedies, these protective measures exist only on the books, reinforcing inequities of economic and political resources than mitigating them. Besides this deficit, the sunbelt workers also differ from the rustbelt workers 'in life experiences, educational opportunities, political socialisation, and workplace practices',[38] which prevent them from forming collective consciousness and solidarity. That said, without the support of collective labour rights, particularly the effective representation by unions, it is also unreasonable to expect that migrant workers, who have for long been disadvantaged in education and professional training, can be fully equipped to exert their rights through legal means and capable of acting as new constituents to transform labour policies on behalf of the entire working class.

To summarise, in the case of China, contractualisation of labour, although increases individual self-consciousness and interdependence, has not been accompanied by the strengthening of 'organic solidarity' as Durkheim predicted. On the contrary, we find that the Chinese working class has been denied the assistance of collective representation via trade unions and then been atomised by the system of individual labour contracts. The cleavage between two parts of the working class further serves the state's aim to divide and rule,[39] as the uneven redistribution of state assets and welfare benefits enlarged the gap between the privileged and the under-represented groups. In other words, the labour reform during the 'Reform' process of China hollowed out the traditional basis for social solidarity without new substitutes, which left great impacts on the inertia of constituent power in contemporary China.

If political liberty is essentially about the right to participate in debates, express opinions, and determine the rules, which entails the (re)presence of a constitutional subject whose will is formed *collectively*, then it should not hinder us from exploring the *social* basis for constitutionalisation, namely, how to build solidarity among the atomised citizens as a polity. However, by presuming 'organic solidarity' will be derived spontaneously from voluntary cooperation, Durkheim has not given full expression to those pathological circumstances where the healthy environments for social interactions can be corrupted by privileges in money or power and thus cannot pave the way for social integration. In this respect, the normative requirements of 'social solidarity' in Durkheimian theory are rather compromised and private law is endowed with an unqualified privilege in defining the scope of citizens' freedoms from state intervention. This defect is manifested as a paradox in the Chinese context: the 'right to liberty' is gained through an administratively enforced process of contractualisation that allows no space for dissent or resistance and is limited to free access to the market. In this sense, Gallagher acutely pointed out that 'the Chinese state's self-conscious adoption of legality is full of "political ambivalence"'[40]: creating positive attitudes towards the legal system becomes part of the state's strategy to avoid democracy.[41] China's legal modernisation is accompanied by both an anomic division of labour and a forced division of labour that leave no room for resistance, which makes comprehensible the mixed notion of 'authoritarian legality'[42] identified by Gallagher and the Chinese constitutional dilemma of 'legalisation without constitutionalisation'. Henceforth, in order to redress the defects in the division of labour during the 'Reform' period, I suggest that we must take labour law seriously, which is essential for entrenching social solidarity.

Labour Constitutionalism: Reclaiming the Relevance of Labour for China's Constitutionalisation

In her fantastic monograph, Ruth Dukes revives the idea of 'labour constitution' developed by the Weimar labour lawyer Hugo Sinzheimer, to deal with the contemporary crisis in labour law scholarship. She argues that when economic globalisation privileges capital to transcend state borders, but leaves the handling of the social consequences of market expansion to the nation states, the state will inevitably be forced to compete for 'comparative advantage' in the global market and massively reduce expenditure on social welfare. Consequently, the traditional role of labour law in designing social policies is severely undermined by the emergence of a new 'rationale' of labour law, which 'was defined accordingly with reference to the market-focused objectives of maximising social inclusion and improving the competitiveness of the economy, or building on the work of Amartya Sen, of facilitating labour market access and optimal labour functioning'. As a result, 'the old paradigmatic objectives of encouraging the collectivisation of labour' was increasingly replaced by 'the law of the labour market' and the theory of human resources.[43]

When Dukes discusses the idea of 'labour constitution', she stresses that 'I refer to the "constitutional function" rather than the "constitutionalisation" of labour law or labour rights, since my concern is not, or not exclusively, with the entrenchment of labour rights as fundamental rights'.[44] Instead of adjudicating labour rights as a constitutional right, labour constitutionalism indicates a socio-legal exploration that takes the labour system as an inseparable environment for the constitutional evolution other than an objective that passively receives constitutional interpretations. In other words, by requiring concession to the working class of a 'Magna Carta', labour constitutionalism aims to restore the political and collective nature of labour relationships that facilitate the exertion of constituent power in policy designs and policy changes when needed.

Although Dukes' arguments aim mainly at the worldwide economic globalisation and the European labour law practices, they nevertheless cast new light on China's labour law reform. 'Labour constitutionalism' in the Chinese context can also provide a point of critique that is key to constitutional re-imaginations: it is through scrutinising the rationale that has underpinned Chinese constitutionalisation from a labour law perspective that labour retains its constitutional significance. On the one hand, China's labour law reform depends on the constitutional framework that decides 'how much political and institutional space the state will give to unions in which to speak up and stand up for workers'.[45] If in the western nations and some developing authoritarian states, labour movements either emerged at the time of the minimalist liberal state or in a vacuum, due to the incapability of the state's weak organisational capacity to penetrate the society, in China, a powerful Leninist labour institution existed predating the rise of labour conflicts.[46] In this context, the 'state corporatism' of Chinese trade unions refers to a form of institutional arrangement where 'corporations' are 'created by and kept as auxiliary and dependent organs of the state'. Such a structure decided that the influence of unions in China stemmed not from organised labour but from their institutional status in the state structure,[47] which undermined the prospect for democratisation in China. 'The existence of powerful state labour institutions put the Chinese government in a strategically favorable position to pre-empt and prevent the emergence of organised labour movements when industrial conflicts were surging amid the economic transformation. Chinese labour not only lacks *de jure* power, …. Chinese labour is even unable to form *de facto* power'.[48]

Take the 'right to strike' in labour law for instance. It is closely connected to how a 'strike' is defined and guaranteed by public law that allows for immunity from police intervention. This permission for workers to legally disrupt the enterprise order through strikes is a precondition for labour legislation, rather than what is prescribed by labour law itself. Against this background, it is understandable why some labour scholars consider that the Chinese working class can better realise collective bargaining 'by riot'[49] and worry that legalising the 'right to strike' in China would bring about the opposite effect, defining most strike activities as illegal and doing more to repress strikes than to legitimate them.[50] In common with some authoritarian states, labour mobilisation in China is part of the struggles for political democratisation; yet, unlike those countries, the Leninist political structure installed a powerful control over labour and has left little space for the workers to lawfully challenge state economic policies and express their shared concerns.

On the other hand, labour changes can play a constitutive role and reflexively impact how people participate in the constitutional process. With the gradual dissolution of the paternalistic labour system, labour no longer connects to all social activities that are relevant to the production process but merely reflects the rights and obligations agreed by the two parties of an employment contract. As a consequence, legalising 'labour contracts' was accompanied by a massive shrinking of the political and public realms. Neutralisation of labour issues and separating them from political debates thus paved the way for the occurrence of an inverted logic of constitutionalisation in China: the constitutional changes are adjusted to private law development and the constitutional authority is ceded to what the market wants.

Nevertheless, having diagnosed how the Chinese working class has been displaced from participating in constitutionalisation, it also becomes clear that labour movement can contribute to redressing the democratic deficits in Chinese constitutionalisation if we use the labour perspective as a point of socio-legal critique. Having revealed that social deficits can, in fact, induce deviations from the Durkheimian 'solidarity' thesis, labour law studies can pose several critical questions that shed light on the Chinese constitutional trajectory and dilemmas: has the 'Reform' had the same impact on every citizen? In the great social transformation of China, who has won and who has borne the costs? By questioning the unquestionable market mentality, new constitutional imaginations can be expected to emerge here.

Conclusion

This chapter aims to reclaim the relevance of labour for China's constitutionalisation in the 'Reform' context. This relevance is manifested not only as one of the constitutional rights that is subject to constitutional adjudication and interpretation, but also as a socio-legal exploration that can be utilised to discern gaps in the Chinese constitutional trajectory. By tracking historically the co-evolution of labour reforms and constitutional reforms in China, this chapter emphasises the importance of labour in China's constitutionalisation that has been repressed by the market-oriented reform mentality. Thereby it intends to redirect our attention to the immense social costs of the one-dimensional reform paradigm that hollowed out the social basis for entrenching the constitutional state in China, and finally to use labour law remedies as a redress.

Notes

1 Hugh Collins and Virginia Mantouvalou, 'Human Rights and the Contract of Employment' in Mark Freedland (ed), *The Contract of Employment* (Oxford University Press 2016) 199.

2 See Li Yuan, '作为基本权的劳动权之本位价值：人的自我实现 [Fundamental Values of Labour Rights as the Basic Rights: Human Self-Realisation]' (2011) 26(6) 法学论坛 [Legal Forum] 65;

Xianghe Gong and Li Yuan, '劳动权的防御权功能与国家的尊重义务 [The Defensive Function of Labour Rights and the State's Duty to Respect]' (2013) 7(40) 北方法学 [Northern Legal Science] 35; Zhenglin Xia, '论宪法视野下的劳动关系 [On the Labour Relation in the View of Constitution]' (2016) 46(5) 西北大学学报 (哲学社会科学版) [Journal of Northwest University (Philosophy and Social Sciences Edition)] 140.

3 Dezhi Wang, '论我国宪法劳动权的理论建构 [On the Theoretical Construction of Our Constitutional Labour Rights]' (2014) 3 中国法学 [China Legal Science] 72, 75–76.

4 Xu Wang, '劳动、政治承认与国家伦理——对我国《宪法》劳动权规范的一种阐释 [Labour, Political Recognition and State Ethics: An Interpretation of Our Constitutional Labour Rights]' (2009) 3 中国法学 [China Legal Science] 76, 88.

5 Tian Yan, '中国劳动宪法的兴起 [The Rise of Chinese Labour Constitution]' (第七届"政治、法律与公共政策"年会 [The 7th Annual Conference of 'Politics, Law and Public Policy'], Chongqing, November 2015).

6 Mimi Zou, 'Chinese Labour Law at a Critical Point in History' (15th World Congress of ILERA, Sydney, August 2009).

7 Albert H. Y. Chen, 'The Law of Property and the Evolving System of Property Rights in China' in Guanghua Yu (ed), *The Development of the Chinese Legal System: Change and Challenges* (Routledge 2011) 83.

8 Shaoguang Wang, 'Adapting by Learning: The Evolution of China's Rural Health Care Financing' (2009) 35(4) Modern China 370, 382–383.

9 The State Council, 'Provisions of the State Council on the Encouragement of Foreign Investment 1986 (Effective)' (11 October 1986) <http://en.pkulaw.cn/display.aspx?cgid=3001&lib=law> accessed 30 September 2021.

10 See The State Council, '国营企业招用工人暂行规定 1986 [Provisional Regulations on Employing Workers in State-Owned Enterprises 1986]' (12 July 1986) <www.gov.cn/gongbao/shuju/1986/gwyb198625.pdf> accessed 30 September 2021; The State Council, 'Provisional Regulations on Institution of Labour Contract System in State-Owned Enterprises 1986 (Expired)' (12 July 1986) <http://en.pkulaw.cn/display.aspx?cgid=5e781efabfbd7a18bdfb&lib=law> accessed 30 September 2021; The State Council, '国营企业职工待业保险暂行规定 1986 [Provisional Regulations on the Employment-in-Suspension Insurance for the Workers in State-Owned Enterprises 1986]' (12 July 1986) <www.gov.cn/gongbao/shuju/1986/gwyb198625.pdf> accessed 30 September 2021.

11 Zou, 'Chinese Labour Law at a Critical Point in History' (n 6).

12 Iain MacNeil, 'Adaptation and Convergence in Corporate Governance: The Case of Chinese Listed Companies' (2002) 2(2) Journal of Corporate Studies 289, 310.

13 The State Council, 'Notice of the State Council on the Relevant Issues concerning the Pilot Implementation of Bankruptcy of a State-Owned Enterprise in Some Cities 1994 (Effective)' (25 October 1994) <http://en.pkulaw.cn/display.aspx?cgid=71d15308f9f65217bdfb&lib=law> accessed 30 September 2021.

14 The National People's Congress (The NPC), '中华人民共和国国民经济和社会发展十年规划和第八个五年计划纲要 [The Ten-Year Plan for the National Economic and Social Development of the People's Republic of China and Outline of the Eighth Five-Year Plan]' (9 April 1991) <www.npc.gov.cn/wxzl/gongbao/2000-12/28/content_5002538.htm> accessed 30 September 2021.

15 See Ching Kwan Lee, *Against the Law: Labour Protests in China's Rustbelt and Sunbelt* (University of California Press 2007).

16 Rudolf Traub-Merz, 'All China Federation of Trade Unions: Structure, Functions and the Challenge of Collective Bargaining' in Rudolf Traub-Merz (ed), *Industrial Democracy in China* (Chinese Social Sciences Press 2012) 25–26.

17 Zou, 'Chinese Labour Law at a Critical Point in History' (n 6).

18 Mary Gallagher and Baohua Dong, 'Legislating Harmony: Labour Law Reform in Contemporary China' in Sarosh Kuruvilla, Ching Kwan Lee, and Mary E Gallagher (eds), *From Iron-Rice Bowl to Informalisation: Markets, State and Workers in a Changing China* (Cornell University Press 2011) 40.

19 Dirk Schmidt and Sebastian Heilmann, 'Dealing with Economic Crisis in 2008–2009: The Chinese Government's Crisis Management in Comparative Perspective' (2010) China Analysis 77 <http://chinapolitik.org/files/no_77.pdf> accessed 30 September 2021.

20 ibid.
21 ibid.
22 Liisi Karindi, 'The Making of China's New Labour Contract Law' (2008) China Analysis 66 <http://chinapolitik.org/files/no_66.pdf> accessed 30 September 2021.
23 Zongzhi Huang, '重新认识中国劳动人民——劳动法规的历史演变与当前的非正规经济 [Re-identifying the Chinese Working People: Historical Evolution of Labour Regulations and Contemporary Informal Economy]' (2013) 5 开放时代 [Open Times] 56, 58–59.
24 Traub-Merz, 'All China Federation of Trade Unions' (n 16) 38.
25 Yuan Shen, '社会转型与工人阶级的再形成 [Social Transformation and the Reforming of the Working Class]' in Xing Ying, Feizhou Zhou and Jingdong Qu (eds), 中国社会学文选 *[Literatures on Chinese Sociology]* Vol. I. (China Renmin University Press 2011) 433.
26 Kai Chang, '论劳动合同法的立法依据和法律定位 [On the Legislative Basis and Legal Orientation of Labour Contract Law]' (2008) 2 法学论坛 [Legal Forum] 5, 6.
27 Émile Durkheim, *The Division of Labour in Society* (George Simpson tr, Free Press 1933) 64.
28 ibid.
29 ibid 129.
30 ibid 127.
31 ibid 115.
32 ibid 353–395.
33 Alan Hunt, *The Sociological Movement in Law* (Macmillan Press 1978) 70.
34 Feng Chen, 'Individual Rights and Collective Rights: Labour Predicament in China' (2007) 40 Communist and Post-Communist Studies 59, 62.
35 Mary Gallagher, *Authoritarian Legality in China: Law, Workers and the State* (Cambridge University Press 2017) 29.
36 Chen, 'Individual Rights and Collective Rights' (n 34) 60.
37 Mary Gallagher and Yuhua Wang, 'Users and Non-Users: Legal Experience and Its Effects on Legal Consciousness' in Margaret Y. K. Woo and Mary E. Gallagher (eds), *Civil Justice: Civil Dispute Resolution in Contemporary China* (Cambridge University Press 2011) 205.
38 ibid 176.
39 Feng Chen and Xin Xu, 'Active Judiciary: Judicial Dismantling of Workers' Collective Action in China' (2012) 67 The China Journal 87, 93.
40 Gallagher, *Authoritarian Legality in China* (n 35) 30.
41 ibid 150.
42 ibid 47.
43 Ruth Dukes, *The Labour Constitution: The Enduring Idea of Labour Law* (Oxford University Press 2014) 203.
44 Ruth Dukes, 'Hugo Sinzheimer and the Constitutional Function of Labour Law' in Guy Davidov and Brian Langille (eds), *The Idea of Labour Law* (Oxford University Press 2011) 62.
45 Feng Chen, 'Between the State and Labour: The Conflict of Chinese Trade Unions' Double Identity in Market Reform' (2003) 176 The China Quarterly 1006, 1027.
46 Feng Chen, 'China's Road to the Construction of Labour Rights' (2016) 52(1) Journal of Sociology 24, 28.
47 Chen, 'Between the State and Labour' (n 45) 1016.
48 Chen, 'China's Road to the Construction of Labour Rights' (n 46) 32.
49 Chen, 'Individual Rights and Collective Right' (n 34) 73.
50 Kai Chang and Jie Qiu, '中国劳动关系转型与劳动法治重点——从《劳动合同法》实施三周年谈起 [The Transformation of Labour Relations and the Key to Labour Legislation in China: On the Occasion of Implementing the Labour Contract Law for Three Years]' (2011) 10 探索与争鸣 [Exploration and Free Views] 43, 46.

Bibliography

Dukes R, *The Labour Constitution: The Enduring Idea of Labour Law* (Oxford University Press 2014).

Durkheim É, *The Division of Labour in Society* (George Simpson tr, Free Press 1933).

Gallagher M, *Authoritarian Legality in China: Law, Workers and the State* (Cambridge University Press 2017).

Lee C K, *Against the Law: Labour Protests in China's Rustbelt and Sunbelt* (University of California Press 2007).
Kuruvilla S, Lee C K and Gallagher M E (eds), *From Iron-Rice Bowl to Informalisation: Markets, State and Workers in a Changing China* (Cornell University Press 2011).
Traub-Merz R (ed), *Industrial Democracy in China* (Chinese Social Sciences Press 2012).
Chen F, 'Between the State and Labour: The Conflict of Chinese Trade Unions' Double Identity in Market Reform' (2003) 176 *The China Quarterly* 1006.
Shen Y (2011) '社会转型与工人阶级的再形成 [Social Transformation and the Reforming of the Working Class]' in Ying X, Zhou F Z and Qu J D (eds), 中国社会学文选 *[Literatures on Chinese Sociology]*, Vol. 1. (China Renmin University Press 2011) 419–38.

17

ASSESSING HEALTHCARE RIGHTS AND RESPONSIBILITIES UNDER THE CONSTITUTIONAL ORDERS OF MAINLAND CHINA AND THE SPECIAL ADMINISTRATIVE REGIONS

Barry Solaiman

Introduction

This chapter explores the relevant constitutional provisions and laws in mainland China and the Special Administrative Regions (SARs) of Hong Kong (HK) and Macau concerning the 'right to health' for citizens. The analysis reveals that citizens are deriving greater rights and autonomy pertaining to their medical needs, but that individual autonomy must be balanced against cultural norms and other obligations to protect the public at large as required in domestic laws and international treaties. As such, the 'right to health' is a holistic concept encapsulating the responsibility of the state to protect the health of the public at large and not just individuals. Furthermore, despite the recognition of a right to health, it will be seen how financial barriers prohibit meaningful access to healthcare for certain groups, which hinders the aspirations of the right. Cultural norms surrounding the role of doctors and the family in medical decision-making are also factors that ought to be balanced in the understanding of individual autonomy.

The chapter proceeds as follows. First, there is an analysis of the constitutional source of the right to health in mainland China, and the Law on the Promotion of Basic Medical and Health Care 2019 (PHC) that gives effect to that right. It will be seen that, despite significant improvement in recent decades, health insurance coverage continues to be a weakness for rural populations. The result is that financial barriers act as a practical hurdle to the realisation of an individual's right to health. Furthermore, cultural norms surrounding informed consent and the role of a patient's family may undermine the requirement of the PHC that patients provide informed consent. Second, the chapter assesses the right to health in HK and Macau. There is not an explicit expression of the right to health in law such as in the PHC, but a combination of sources clearly elucidate that right. Despite the recent historical

 DOI: 10.4324/9781003128243-20

divergences in the political and legal systems, familism continues to play a role in informed consent in the SARs, albeit likely to a lesser extent owing to the diversity of the populations that live there.

Third, moving away from domestic considerations, there is an analysis of international treaty obligations regarding the right to health. China has clear obligations, but the status of the SARs is more complicated owing to the handovers from the United Kingdom and Portugal. This section charts those changes to illustrate how the same treaty obligations have ultimately applied to the SARs as the mainland government. To frame the importance of the treaty obligations, the measures taken by China to control the COVID-19 pandemic are considered. This reveals confusion between the local and national governments surrounding how best to balance individual autonomy and protect the health of the public at large. It also raises questions about the appropriate uses of technology in controlling the spread of the disease.

Healthcare Rights in Mainland China

Health is a public right in China.[1] This right derives generally from the constitution where there are several provisions imposing a positive obligation on the state to provide, among other things, medical services and facilities, and a healthy environment.[2] Article 21 of the constitution requires the state to develop medical and health services to protect the people's health.[3] Article 45 requires that the state 'develops the social insurance, social relief and medical and health services' to assist citizens when they are 'old, ill or disabled'.[4] The National Health Commission (NHC) has explicitly noted that these rights ought to be respected and be 'put in place'.[5] The NHC states that:

> China has established a complete medical and health system that is guided by the Constitution, based on civil laws and regulations, laws and administrative regulations on health, and local regulations, and directed by the outlines, programs, and plans of the health sector. The system has proved effective in maintaining sound doctor-patient relations, addressing medical disputes with impartiality, and ensuring citizens' right to health.[6]

The authorities have sought to ensure that right to health by prioritising health and fitness in their development strategies, placing greater emphasis on prevention and ensuring basic medical services are non-profit.[7] They have also sought to narrow the gaps in healthcare provision between rural and urban centres to ensure equal access to basic health services.[8] Intertwined within that aim has been an emphasis on universal participation in the provision of health (such as through health insurance) among the government, private organisations (such as employers) and individuals.[9]

Historically, while the state had constitutional responsibilities in terms of healthcare and recognised its responsibility in providing it, there had not been an explicit legislative expression of a 'right to health' in China. This paradigm shifted with the enactment of the Law on the Promotion of Basic Medical and Health Care 2019 (PHC).[10] The law is a substantive development, being the first law to specify a 'right to health' in China.[11] It is a logical conclusion to the constitutional responsibilities of the state and the 'right to health' recognised in practice by the NHC. Thus, the PHC can be seen as an explicit expression of that constitutional right to health.[12]

A Qualified Right to Health?

Several provisions in the PHC 2019 are important to note which explicitly elucidate the right to health. Article 4 notes that 'the state and society shall respect and protect citizens' right to health'. Article 5 states that citizens shall 'enjoy the right to obtain basic medical services from the state and society'. Chenguang argues that the provisions elevate health to being a basic human right in China.[13] The provisions are distinct from those found in tort or contract law that protect patients from harm being caused by a misdiagnosis or improper treatment. Instead, the provisions specify a positive right to health for individuals.[14]

In this regard, the provisions can be seen as a codification of the constitutional obligations of the state and the recognition of the right to health by the NHC. That codification should remove any doubts about whether a right to health as derived from the constitution exists. The overarching query, however, is what the 'right to health' means as a practical matter. One obvious answer is access to good quality healthcare. There are a myriad of socioeconomic factors that can affect the utilisation of healthcare services such as age, educational level, employment status, income level and others.[15]

China has grappled with this challenge for decades with some success, albeit with room for improvement. Health expenditure has consistently increased year on year since the early 2000s.[16] From 2009, equitable and accessible healthcare was deemed as one of four central pillars to healthcare reform in the country.[17] Low-income areas have received increased health subsidies, and social health insurance and basic public health service packages were extended to cover everyone.[18] Investment has led to a decrease in health disparities between different income groups such as maternal and infant mortality rates.[19]

Yet, iniquity and efficiency remain an ongoing challenge for the healthcare system.[20] The institutional arrangements are fragmented; there is a scarcity of qualified practitioners, unequal access linked to the risks pooled in insurance schemes, and an imbalance in the provision of care across tiers owing to a preference for care provided at hospitals.[21] Primary healthcare providers are underutilised because of the poor care they provide.[22] Only 10% of doctors in primary care had formal medical education in 2017.[23] Furthermore, the fee structure for care services incentivised hospitals to attract and retain patients to the detriment of primary care health institutions.[24] Another challenge has been the increased cost of care (particularly for poor households).[25] There is also poor coordination between health sectors which undermines the cost-effectiveness and continuity of care.[26]

These factors take centre-stage as prerequisites for the realisation of access to the health system to realise one's right to health. It is beyond the scope of this chapter to analyse every challenge in detail, but the area of health insurance is given specific focus here as an illustration of the hurdles that must be overcome because it is a primary determinant of one's ability to access healthcare. The insurance system is epitomised by a fragmented structure with separate financing paths to the detriment of the rural population.[27]

Health Insurance

The approach of the PHC 2019 is to emphasise the importance of shared responsibility between different entities to ensure access. Article 82 stipulates that medical service fees shall primarily be covered by medical insurance, and that citizens have the right and obligation to participate in the basic medical insurance. The manner in which this 'right and obligation' operates is through a combined effort. The state is obliged to raise medical insurance funds from multiple channels, while urban and rural residents, and employers and employees are required to contribute premiums.[28] As such, citizens have the right to basic medical insurance which underpins their ability to realise their right to health. At the same time, the law obliges citizens to obtain insurance otherwise they may be unable to afford healthcare costs and, therefore, realise their right to health. In practice, universal health insurance has been attained through different insurance funds such as the Urban Employee Basic Medical Insurance (UEBMI), the New Cooperative Medical Scheme (NCMS), and the Urban Resident Basic Medical Insurance (URBMI).[29]

Again, contributions are ultimately a collective effort, and it is through that collective stream that individuals are able to pay for their healthcare costs. Here, it is important to unpack the requirement in Article 82 PHC 2019 concerning contributions by urban and rural populations. A significant challenge in the area of funding is addressing the disparities in access to health insurance between those demographics. That challenge arises by virtue of socioeconomic barriers, geographic and population size. In general, health insurance has helped to significantly reduce the unmet healthcare needs of Chinese citizens.[30] Health insurance coverage rose from 22% in 2003 to 97% in 2019.[31] However, while insurance coverage has risen, this has not translated into universal health access.[32]

In this regard, there are two broad limitations. The first is the limited availability or lack of healthcare services. The second is individuals choosing not to, or being unable to, avail healthcare services.[33] It is beyond this chapter to analyse all facets of this complex paradigm, but some important illustrative examples are noted here. One study assesses access to health over three periods (2003, 2008 and 2013).[34] It finds that the proportion of households with out-of-pocket medical expenditure exceeding 40% of household income increased from 6.7% in 2003 to 8.7% in 2013.[35] The greatest increase in that proportional expenditure was found in low-income households.[36] Indeed, catastrophic medical expenditure was observed in almost 25% of individuals in the lowest economic bracket in 2013, whereas the proportion was 8.5% and 2.5% in the middle- and upper-income groups, respectively.[37]

Furthermore, while the statistics have improved over time, the sample study highlighted a large portion of those surveyed who did not get admitted when necessary, had foregone necessary admission or had been discharged early due to financial burdens.[38] Thus, in 2003, 27% of those surveyed did not get admitted when necessary, versus 21.4% in 2013.[39] In 2003, 77.5% had foregone necessary admission due to financial difficulties versus 45.4% in 2013.[40] In 2003, 68.3% were discharged early due to financial difficulties versus 37% in 2013.[41] The improvements are stark in that period, but there were still a significant number of people who were faced with barriers concerning access to health because of their financial circumstances.

Of course, the statistics should not be oversimplified. It used to be that wealthier income groups utilised health services more than lower income groups, but that disparity was not observed in 2013.[42] That change likely arose owing to a range of factors such as the poor using services more because of more ill health as well as greater affordability of health services thanks to improved cooperative health insurance coverage under the NCMS.[43] Overall, however, the level of NCMS coverage was 'not sufficient' for lower income groups that were the most likely to have high (and increasing) financial burdens, poorer health and disease that could induce greater poverty.[44] This challenge is particularly acute in rural areas where citizens have lower incomes, poorer health compared to those in urban centres and poor access to health services.[45]

There have also been analyses of the rural-urban differences in health system performance for the elderly in the mainland following 2013.[46] In terms of the management and prevention of common chronic conditions, it was found that rural residents fared worse compared with urban residents in nearly all indicators.[47] On costs, the picture has been more complex. Rural residents have generally had lower out-of-pocket expenses than urban residents.[48] However, those suffering chronic illnesses in rural areas have had greater expenses than those in urban centres.[49] Additionally, those in rural settings were more likely than urban residents to suffer catastrophic health expenses.[50] Overall, despite the move towards universal health insurance, the data shows that there are 'significant gaps' in health system indicators between those living in urban and rural areas.[51] People continue to underutilise health services because of cost, travel distance and the quality of healthcare services where they are available.[52]

There is also one final group to note. Rural-to-urban migrant workers (RUMWs) account for about one-fifth of the Chinese population, migrating from rural to urban locations in search of work.[53] That group appears to be disadvantaged with regard to the aim of providing universal health coverage in the mainland.[54] This is because their insurance coverage is low, geographically removed from their place of insurance registration and their employer provides inadequate alternative insurance.[55] As a consequence, RUMWs have poorer access to health services and may not seek health treatment when needed.[56] Steps have been taken to address this challenge but results have been poor, with 20% or less of RUMWs obtaining health insurance covering their time working in urban areas.[57] This is not surprising considering that some employers (acting in a poorly regulated environment) seek to avoid paying insurance contributions or hire workers through third parties to bypass labour laws.[58]

It is not only the reluctance of employers that poses a challenge. Transferring insurance from one plan to another is sometimes impossible. Some insurance policies are registered and tied to the family unit. When a family member leaves to work in an urban centre, they cannot transfer the policy or risk leaving their family members at home uninsured (many of whom are elderly and in need of medical care).[59] This challenge is exacerbated by the incompatibility between different insurance schemes that are available. There are different risk-sharing accounts with contributions from the individual, their employer and local government. Some contributions can be transferred, and some cannot. Even those that can be transferred are subject to high premiums for initiating the transfer which reduces the likelihood of policyholders doing so.[60] For those that are insured, it is often the case that only hospital services are reimbursed rather than primary care services which means that the fundamental health needs of those individuals are not being met.[61]

The studies noted above have examined specific sub-groups and their access to health. However, there have also been examinations of the association between universal healthcare coverage and unmet healthcare needs.[62] It remains true that health insurance has generally helped to reduce the underutilisation of outpatient health services and the early discharge from hospitals.[63] Yet, this impact is 'relatively weak' with regard to inpatient services, unless the underutilisation of those services was caused by financial difficulties, in which case the reduction in use of inpatient services for those reasons was significant.[64]

These factors reveal the complex paradigm that underlies the aspiration of providing a right to health for citizens in the PHC 2019. Access is necessary for anyone to realise that right. Qin et al note that uptake of health services (particularly expensive ones) will inevitably be affected by an individual's ability to pay for that service.[65] There has certainly been significant improvement in the statistics from 2003 on the access that individuals have, but obvious gaps remain. There is a lack of effective treatment options in rural areas compared to urban areas, and financial difficulties have remained the primary challenge for rural residents using inpatient services.[66] These realities may undermine the ability of citizens to realise their right to health in practice. It will be interesting to observe how the PHC 2019 interacts with the disparities in access that may persist. It may be that citizens in the future could rely on the law to argue that insurance coverage rules should be altered to ensure that citizens are obtaining equal access to health.

Cultural Norms and the Role of Informed Consent

Another aspect of the right to health is the right that patients have to information. A basic premise of medical law is that patients with capacity should provide informed consent for their treatment, and sufficient information is a prerequisite to informed decision-making. Article 32 PHC 2019 states that citizens shall 'have the right to informed consent' for illness, diagnosis and treatment plans. In the mainland, patients have long been required to provide written consent in hospitals for their treatment.[67] However, this right is also qualified by both the law and the practice of obtaining consent which has operated differently from systems in the West.

One article notes how patients in a sample study signed consent documents for surgeries due to hospital regulations requiring consent for the surgery, rather than a signature based on proper informed consent based on sufficient information regarding the treatment.[68] The disparities in medical knowledge between doctors and patients and insufficient interaction between them have played a role in patients not obtaining the information they need.[69] As a result, patients have consented to treatment without sufficient information in some samples studied.[70]

There are also cultural aspects to consent. The traditional practice has been to obtain consent from the family even where the patient is an adult with capacity.[71] This has been as much a practical step as a philosophical one routed in familism, with the family carrying much of the financial burden.[72] Indeed, Raposo examines the role of Confucianism on the understanding of informed consent in China.[73] She notes how familism plays a core role in that philosophy which is reflected in the law. For example, Article 26 of the Law on Practicing Doctors of the People's Republic of China 1998 states that 'doctors shall tell the patients or their family members the patients' condition truthfully'.[74] This provision equates the right to information of both the patient and their family members. Furthermore, Raposo notes that, in practice, the family members hold the dominant role with regard to obtaining information because of concerns about distressing the patient with that information.[75]

There is also the question of what 'autonomy' means in this context under the PHC 2019. In China, the ill patient is considered to be less capable of making an assessment of what is in their best interests (especially with elderly patients). Instead, it is the family that is better placed to make such an assessment.[76] In essence, autonomy operates in a community context.[77] Article 32 PHC emphasises that consent must be obtained from a patient. However, medical personnel are able to provide explanations to close relatives of the patient and provide consent where it is 'inappropriate' to provide an explanation to the patient, or where doctors are unable to. This would be expected in certain circumstances such as where there is an emergency or where the patient lacks capacity to provide consent. However, given the traditional approach to obtaining consent, it is questionable whether the PHC will change the embedded practice of obtaining consent from the family in cases that do not fall under the 'inappropriate' bracket.

An additional aspect to this is Article 69 PHC which states that citizens 'shall respect others' right to health and benefits and shall not damage others' health or public interests'. That article arises in the context of citizens being required to take responsibility for their own health and to care for family members. The same article states that family members 'shall be urged to care for each other and form a healthy lifestyle that suits their own and family characteristics'. The paradigm noted by Raposo will likely continue to pervade under the new legal regime which emphasises the importance of the familial structure to an individual's healthcare. Again, the new law is framed as one that gives a right to health for the individual, but that law alone is not likely to undo deep-rooted practices and tradition.

Of course, this is not necessarily problematic. The family's presence and support can be critical to a patient's recovery. Some patients may prefer that their relatives deal with obtaining information and consent on their behalf. This context is not unique to China. One could consider similar hierarchical family structures in the Middle East where the family also plays a dominant role in the decision-making process concerning the healthcare of an individual family member.[78] Nevertheless, the concern is that the balance may continue to tip away from individual choice to the extent that consent is not truly being obtained. Raposo argues that the 'only kind of medical consent compatible with human rights and human dignity is the one based on the patient's individual choice'.[79] The family unit is not a legal entity holding human rights in this medical decision-making context, but the family does have legal and ethical 'value'.[80] As such, this compatibility does not reject the influence and recommendations of the family nor the cultural considerations that are of great importance to that decision-making process, but the 'core basis' of informed consent is that an individual makes their own decision.[81]

Healthcare Rights in Hong Kong and Macau

The SARs of HK and Macau have articulated provisions concerning healthcare in their mini-constitutions, known as the 'basic laws'. However, those provisions give little in the way of healthcare rights. Instead, the right to health can be derived from other sources unpacked below. Furthermore, when comparing with the mainland, the strongest parallel concerning rights is informed consent rather than access to health. Healthcare is available at the publicly funded hospitals in the SARs, meaning that health insurance is not a requirement. Although, there is heavy demand for those infrastructures, which results in long waiting times.

The Basic Law of HK states only that the Government of HK will formulate policies to 'improve medical and health services'.[82] The same statement can be found in the Basic Law of Macau.[83] While the provision of healthcare is not articulated in terms of the right to health in the respective basic laws, that articulation can be derived from other sources that find power in the basic laws. Article 8 of the HK Basic Law states that 'The laws previously in force in Hong Kong, that is, the common law, rules of equity, ordinances, subordinate legislation and customary law shall be maintained'.

The common law rules have largely been shaped by English case law owing to HK's history. Thus, one can derive the rights that patients have to healthcare from influential common law principles. There is the principle established in the dissenting judgment of Lord Scarman in *Sidaway v Board of Governors of the Bethlem Royal Hospital*[84] that a patient's right to make their own medical decisions is a basic human right protected under common law. In *Montgomery v Lanarkshire Health Board*,[85] it was noted that the relationship between a doctor and patient had changed to one of a consumer exercising rights, rather than a paternalistic arrangement. The onus has been on the patient being in the driving seat with regard to their healthcare rights.

This stance has been replicated in HK. Over time, the paternalistic relationship between doctors and patients has shifted. Prior to 1990, doctors were treated as government officials, falling under the rubric of the Hospital Services Department (HSD).[86] Following the establishment of the Hospital Authority in 1990, the paternalistic climate shifted towards one that embodied a greater focus on patient rights (however, there remain concerns about paternalism).[87] This change has ultimately manifested in the Patients' Charter in HK. It states several rights that patients can expect for those using the services of any of HK's public hospitals.[88] Those rights include the right to medical treatment, information, choices, privacy and to complain.[89] Thus, the path towards patient healthcare rights in HK is not as simple as a legislative provision, specifically articulating a right to health as in the mainland. Instead, the Basic Law gives recognition to existing legal instruments and the common law from which those rights can be derived.

On consent, the research in HK presents an unclear picture. One study has described HK as a case of 'moderate familism'.[90] The best interests of the patient are determined by the doctor in consultation with the family (with a presumption that consent is not required for the sharing of information with the family), with 'partial' and 'vague' disclosure ultimately being shared with the patient.[91] This paradigm 'exists as a practice with cultural standing' in opposition to the law which has a more individualistic approach to patient care.[92] A more detailed survey of the ethics climate in HK hospitals revealed that inadequate communication between doctors and patients, and conflict issues between staff were the two most significant negative factors in the ethics climate, whereas a high regard for patient rights and a decline in family interference were considered to be the two most positive factors.[93] These latter factors have been deemed 'surprising and intriguing' owing to the Chinese traditions of respecting family decision-making.[94] The reasons posited for this divergence in HK when compared with the mainland include the practice of Western medicine in HK for more than a century, the training of healthcare professionals in Western systems that value individual autonomy, and the protection of confidentiality, informed consent and autonomous decision-making under the laws of HK.[95] It may also be that the paternalistic approach of doctors may be trumping those of the family on certain decisions.[96]

In Macau, rights can be derived from legislative changes in the late 2010s. Prior to 2017, there was no specific law on medical liability. Instead, there was a piecemeal collection of rules and legislation.[97] There were also different standards applied depending on which courts had jurisdiction and whether the healthcare provider was part of the private or public sector.[98] This inconsistency changed following the enactment of the Regime Jurídico do Erro Médico (RJEM; the legal regime of medical error).[99] Article 1 RJEM notes that the law establishes the legal framework for medical errors in order to safeguard the legitimate rights and interests of patients and providers. The law guarantees patients a right to information from healthcare providers concerning their care.[100] Patients must also be notified of any suspected medical errors that come to the attention of a healthcare provider to ensure patients can facilitate a legal defence of their rights.[101]

As with the mainland, the approach to medical decisions in Macau was also characterised as one in which decisions were made by the doctor or family rather than the patient.[102] There are also language barriers. Macau is a multilingual and multicultural society where Mandarin, Cantonese and Portuguese are spoken.[103] In practice, while Mandarin and Portuguese are the official languages of Macau, it is Cantonese and English that are mostly spoken by the population.[104] This raises challenges regarding communication for informed consent purposes. There are no translators in the healthcare system which often results in important medical information being communicated to a patient not in their primary language.[105] Most often, English is used, and where the parties are uncomfortable with English, a nurse or team member usually translates even though they may lack formal training for such a role.[106] Problems even arise between Chinese nationals speaking Mandarin and Cantonese where the parties only speak one of those languages.[107]

The same was true in Portugal where Macau derived its legal rules.[108] The move away from that paradigm towards patient-centred rights in Macau is reflected in the law. In this regard, the RJEM refers to Article 493 of the Macau Civil Code on the reimbursement of expenses where harm is caused by someone.[109] Building on that provision, Article 22 RJEM notes that healthcare providers must reimburse all costs where a medical error results in harm. The Penal Code imposes fines or imprisonment on medical practitioners providing treatment without having obtained proper consent from the patient.[110]

Despite these provisions, the challenges noted regarding familism in the mainland are also transposed to Macau.[111] It has been noted that in the public hospital in Macau, 'healthcare providers (most of whom come from mainland China) systematically provide information to and request consent from the family, not the patient'.[112] Even where a patient is an adult with capacity, the consent forms that are signed provide for the signature of a family member which highlights that obtaining consent from the family is hospital practice.[113] Therefore, the picture concerning patient rights in practice (at least within the realm of consent involving Chinese patients) is not too far removed in Macau from the mainland despite Portuguese legal influence. This practice exists despite it likely being a breach of the laws on informed consent and privacy.[114]

This approach to medical decision-making raises questions about the best means of maintaining the healthcare rights of patients in Macau. It has been argued that compliance with the legal regimes on consent should be maintained.[115] Macau is different from the mainland not only because of the 'one country two systems', but mainly because of the 'intrinsically pluralistic and heterogeneous' population that lives there.[116] At the same time, one can see signs of a shift in the mainland towards a system that advocates the autonomous rights of patients as individuals.[117] As such, the maintenance of the historical paternalistic status quo would be misaligned from the evolving expectations of patients premised on their right to express their decisions as autonomous beings.

International Obligations and their Constitutional Status

Healthcare rights are a product not only of domestic legislation, but also of international treaties and regulations of the World Health Organization (WHO). This section outlines those obligations and considers their application through the lens of measures taken during the COVID-19 pandemic to halt the spread of the disease.

Two international treaties bear obvious relevance here: first, the International Covenant on Economic, Social and Cultural Rights (ICESCR)[118]; and second, the International Covenant on Civil and Political Rights (ICCPR).[119] China is a signatory to the ICCPR but is yet to ratify it. Nevertheless, as a signatory, China is obligated not to defeat the object and purpose of a treaty.[120] China has ratified the ICESCR. Before analysing the requirements of the treaties, it is important to consider their constitutional status in HK and Macau owing to their complicated histories.

HK initially fell within the ambit of the ICCPR and ICESCR by virtue of the United Kingdom being a signatory.[121] The Sino-British Joint Declaration stipulated that the ICCPR and ICESCR would remain in force following China regaining sovereignty over HK in 1997.[122] This agreement was subsequently restated under Article 39 of the HK Basic Law. Prior to the handover, the treaties were enforced in HK through common law, legislation and administrative measures.[123] Support for the implementation of rights through legislation grew. Thus, the implementation of the ICCPR domestically was eventually achieved through the Hong Kong Bill of Rights Ordinance in 1990.[124] The provisions of the ICESCR are not easily enforced by the courts, so it was decided at the time not to include the provisions of that treaty explicitly within the same ordinance.[125] Instead, individual provisions of the ICESCR are implemented by an amalgam of provisions in the HK Basic Law, local legislation and other non-legislative measures.[126]

Despite this difference with the ICCPR, it has been argued that the ICESCR enjoys constitutional status under the Basic Law.[127] Ramsden contends that a broad reading of the HK Basic Law requires that the ICESCR is implemented by legislation and gives the judiciary 'separate constitutional jurisdiction' to monitor any restrictions of the rights under the ICESCR.[128] There are several cases in relation to labour conventions that support this contention.[129] Even if that were not accepted, it is arguable that the ICESCR can be used as an aid in constitutional interpretation.[130] It should also be noted that prior to the handover in 1997, China notified the United Nations Secretary-General that agreements (such as the ICCPR and ICESCR) that applied to HK but did not (at that point) apply to China would continue to apply in the Special Administrative Region.[131] These actions highlight the importance of those treaties as constitutional sources.

In Macau, the ICESCR and ICCPR were extended to its jurisdiction by virtue of Portugal being a signatory.[132] Despite ratifying the ICESCR, Portugal did not extend the treaty to Macau for 15 years, reflecting an unenthusiastic application of the Covenant to the territory.[133] The extension came after an agreement for China to regain sovereignty over Macau, reflecting 'the need to make explicit reference (reassurance) as to the status of Macau'.[134] The Sino-Portuguese Joint Declaration on Macau was silent on the explicit applicability of the ICCPR and ICESCR following the handover.[135] This omission was not particularly reflective of the lack of importance that was being given to the ICESCR because there was general agreement to honour international treaties.[136] Indeed, the Declaration stipulated that rights enjoyed by Macau would remain 'basically unchanged' following the handover in 1999.[137] Article 40 of the Macau Basic Law mirrors HK's Basic Law in stipulating that the treaties would also remain in force there through domestic legislation. The UN determined that these and other legal instruments provided a sound legal basis for the continued protection of rights under the ICCPR in Macau following the handover.[138] It also reiterated that:

> human rights treaties devolve with territory, and that States continue to be bound by the obligations under the Covenant entered into by the predecessor State. Once the people living in a territory find themselves under the protection of the International Covenant on Civil and Political Rights, such protection cannot be denied to them merely on account of the dismemberment of that territory or its coming within the jurisdiction of another State or of more than one State.[139]

Nowadays, reference is made to the applicability of the ICESCR and ICCPR in HK and Macau in both instruments under China's entry on their territorial application.[140] As such, it is arguable that the treaties enjoy important constitutional status in the mainland and the SARs.

There are also obligations deriving from the WHO that are applicable to the mainland and the SARs. In this regard, the International Health Regulations (IHR) has the greatest impact domestically.[141] The IHR is a legally binding international law instrument which provides a legal framework that defines rights and obligations of countries for public health events and emergencies that have the potential to cross borders. China is a signatory to the IHR which include a reservation regarding the status of HK and Macau.[142] A declaration states that:

> The Government of the People's Republic of China decides that the International Health Regulations (2005) (hereinafter referred to as "the IHR") applies to the entire territory of the People's Republic of China, including the Hong Kong Special Administrative Region, the Macau Special Administrative Region and the Taiwan Province.[143]

The status of the IHR in HK and Macau is, therefore, cemented by China's declaration without the need for a separate statement or signature by the SARs in the IHR. Countries must designate a 'Focal Point' which is a national centre that 'shall be accessible at all times for communications with WHO IHR Contact Points [...] for the implementation of health measures'.[144] China designated the Ministry of Health in the mainland as its National Focal Point. Local health administrative authorities are responsible for the implementation of the IHR in their respective jurisdictions.[145]

The interaction of the ICCPR, the ICESCR and the IHR with the obligations of authorities in China and how they intersect with domestic legislation raise important considerations regarding the constitutional right to health.

International Treaties and COVID-19

The control of the spread of infectious disease during the COVID-19 pandemic and the associated use of technology for that purpose provides a useful case study for the scope of the constitutional 'right to health' in China in light of those international obligations. Authorities must find a balance between an individual's health needs and those of society more broadly, while fulfilling treaty expectations. This section highlights the interaction between local laws in the mainland and the international treaties noted above and considers the effect of that interaction on the constitutional right to health.

There are reporting requirements for infectious diseases under the IHR. Article 6 IHR states that a country 'shall assess events occurring within its territory' and communicate 'all events which may constitute a public health emergency of international concern within its territory' (PHEIC). Article 7 states that:

> If a State Party has evidence of an unexpected or unusual public health event within its territory, irrespective of origin or source, which may constitute a public health emergency of international concern, it shall provide to WHO all relevant public health information.

The power to declare a PHEIC rests with the WHO's director-general.[146] Some have highlighted China's delays in notifying the WHO of the COVID-19 outbreak and have criticised the ineffectiveness of the IHR notification mechanism itself.[147] Even when notification was made by China, this failed to facilitate a rapid declaration of the PHEIC (in accordance with the provisions of the IHR), 'delaying global preparations for a pandemic response'.[148] These circumstances highlight the need for more robust PHEIC mechanisms at the WHO level.[149] A delay in notification coupled with a failed rapid declaration undermines the ability of a country to institute measures necessary to protect public health. To understand how this concern relates to the constitutional right to health, it is necessary to consider the competing considerations regarding the protection of the public at large versus individual autonomy in the pandemic context.

Several articles are relevant here under domestic law in China. Article 21 PHC 2019 requires the state to implement a vaccination system, and that it is both 'a right and obligation' of citizens to be inoculated. This approach comports with the international treaties. Article 12(1) of the ICESCR recognises 'the right of everyone to the enjoyment of the highest attainable standard of physical and mental health'. Article 12(2) notes the steps to be taken by the States Parties to achieve the full realisation of that right. Among those steps are the 'prevention, treatment and control of epidemic, endemic, occupational and other diseases' (Article 12(2)(c)) and the 'creation of conditions which would assure to all medical service and medical attention in the event of sickness' (Article 12(2)(d)).

For the ICCPR, Article 12(1) states that everyone with a lawful right to be in a country shall 'have the right to liberty of movement and freedom to choose his residence'. Article 12(2) protects the right of an individual to 'leave any country'. Article 12(3) qualifies those rights, allowing restrictions to 'protect national security, public order, public health'. Even the right to 'freedom of expression' under Article 19(2) can be restricted where it is done for 'the protection of national security or of public order (ordre public), or of public health or morals' (Article 19(3)(b).

The notification problems highlighted above under the IHR may undermine such treaty obligations on the protection of public health. A delayed implementation of WHO pandemic control mechanisms can delay ICESCR and ICCPR requirements on the control of the spread of infectious diseases (such as restrictions on movement) in addition to setting up the necessary medical services that ensure everyone has adequate medical attention.

Beyond this, once the pandemic response was established, there was confusion domestically surrounding how best to balance the interests of the individual versus the public at large. Thus, while Article 21 PHC notes the right and obligation of citizens to be inoculated, this may sit uncomfortably with Article 32 PHC that gives citizens 'the right to informed consent' for illness, diagnosis and treatment plans. Article 69 is also relevant here where it states that citizens 'shall respect others' right to health and benefits and shall not damage others' health or public interests'. This article arises in the context of citizens being required to take responsibility for their own health and to care for family members. For these provisions, health authorities must balance individual autonomy with broader public health. Both are protected under the provisions.

Some local governments in the mainland prohibited students from returning to school unless their entire family was vaccinated.[150] Such restrictions also extended to barring unvaccinated residents from accessing public venues.[151] There was further confusion because some local authorities cited 'national, provincial and municipal arrangements' as authority for the decisions without specific details.[152] In response, the National Health Commission (NHC) issued guidance to 'correct' the practice of mandatory vaccinations.[153] It stated that the basic principles of vaccinations are 'informed, consented and voluntary'.[154] The divergent actions of authorities reflect a dichotomous approach to and understanding of citizen rights. However, the NHC, being the most powerful authority, has reinforced an individual rights perspective by stressing that vaccinations cannot be mandated.

The need to protect the public at large has also led to intrusions to prevent the spread of the disease. Measures have included using technology to track people's movement, the monitoring of free speech and other privacy intrusions.[155] These measures were possible owing to the deep centralisation of political power, restrictions on privacy under the law and the restriction on human rights.[156] Facial recognition technology was implemented to identify those not wearing masks, including in subway stations and even employees entering the office space.[157]

One could interpret the use of such technologies in two ways. The first is the protection of public health and the safeguarding of an individual's health through the use of technology. Indeed, technology has also been used to provide contactless deliveries of medical samples using robots, conducting thermal imaging, spraying disinfectants, accelerating vaccine development and performing basic diagnostic functions to lessen the risk of contamination.[158] These are all useful applications in protecting public health. It is arguable that the authorities are merely fulfilling their international and domestic obligations in using such technology. As noted earlier, Article 4 of the PHC 2019 states that 'the state and society shall respect and protect citizens' right to health'. Article 5 states that citizens shall 'enjoy the right to obtain basic medical services from the state and society'. There are also the corresponding international treaty obligations noted in the ICCPR and ICESCR. Preventing the spread of a disease ensures that citizens can enjoy their right to health. Without such measures, they could fall ill. Providing medical services would carry greater risks without the use of technology that could harm the health of both the provider and patient. It could, therefore, be argued that the use of technology enables authorities to continue the provision of basic medical services and fulfil their duty of controlling epidemics to protect the right to health of the public at large.

The second interpretation of the use of technology concerns the contravention of individual rights to privacy of their healthcare data. Contact tracing using mobile apps, digital barcodes, surveillance drones and CCTV with facial recognition all raise questions about the level of intrusion needed to manage a pandemic.[159] The use of such technology is not unique to China, but it has been one of the trendsetters in the adoption of such surveillance during the COVID-19 pandemic. It is not evident that privacy harms will not be disproportionately impacted by the use of such surveillance measures.[160] Indeed, measures of this sort 'sweep up revealing location data indiscriminately'.[161] There is also the concern of what unfolds after a crisis ends, when justifications for their use premised on containing an emergency, lapse. Experience has shown that there is potential for abuse, with emergency powers remaining in-force post-crisis, often 'morphing into tools of social control targeted against disfavoured individuals and groups'.[162] Despite these concerns, the picture may be more nuanced in the mainland.

It has been argued that there has been 'little domestic public resistance in China about technology-related privacy risks' during the COVID-19 pandemic.[163] This can be explained by three factors. First, Chinese people have a high level of expectation and confidence in state intervention based on a 'guardian' model of governance.[164] This model is premised on a paternalistic relationship between authorities and citizens, with the authorities the guardians of the citizenry.[165] This guardianship discourse has been important in developing a societal norm of obedience in different contexts such as the use of discretionary power to employ technology to manage emergencies.[166] Rather than focussing on how routines or procedures came to be, citizens are instead directed to focus on the outcome of policies in protecting and caring for them.[167]

The second factor is the extent to which technology is already intertwined with the goals of 'national building and national rejuvenation'.[168] For decades, it had been an aspiration of China to pursue scientific and technological progress to catch up to advanced economies, drive economic development, enhance trade and become self-reliant.[169] This narrative has played into the use of technology generally, which rolls into the third factor that society is organised on communitarian principles above one premised on individual rights.[170] It has been argued that citizens were more accepting of privacy intrusions during the pandemic because they were deemed to be for the common good.[171] Liu and Zhao note that:

> The acceptance of state surveillance in China, which is well-equipped with data applications, is embedded in the country's unique sociopolitical environment and cultural heritage and is thus significantly different from Western norms and values built around individual freedom and rights.[172]

The use of technology has also been portrayed as a beneficial national development in the fight against COVID-19.[173] The interaction of these various values, it has been argued, leads to widespread support from citizens for the government in using measures to manage an emergency.[174]

Ultimately, both interpretations are arguably true to different degrees. It is inconceivable that a pandemic could be managed without the curtailment of certain freedoms. It has been noted that measures such as lockdowns might be 'justified in order to promote public health in a pandemic'.[175] Furthermore, a failure to use such measures may be in breach of the treaty obligation to protect the rights to health and life.[176] Indeed, the CESCR has noted that the obligation to 'take measures to prevent, treat and control epidemic and endemic diseases' is of 'comparable priority' to the right to health.[177]

The question for China is whether the appropriate balance has been struck between monitoring and the curtailment of movement versus individual privacy. Finally, putting aside whether that balance was struck appropriately, an overarching question also lingers about whether the IHR notification mechanisms hindered the speed of implementation for the public health protections that were ultimately implemented.

Conclusion

The 'right to health' finds clear constitutional and legislative expression in mainland China and is recognised through a range of sources in HK and Macau. International treaty obligations underscore its importance domestically. However, the meaning of that right in practice varies. There has been a greater move towards recognition of individual autonomy in a system that has traditionally emphasised family values, but familism persists. Some doctors also continue to provide care from a paternalistic standpoint. As a practical matter, access to healthcare remains a challenge for those from rural populations owing to the complex and expensive health insurance coverage. While there have been significant improvements in health coverage for those populations, more work is needed to ensure that the right to health in terms of access is realised. Ultimately, the analysis demonstrates that the right to health is a balancing exercise between protecting individual autonomy, family rights and public health more broadly. A struggle has ensued between authorities on what autonomy means in terms of mandating vaccinations, and there are questions about the appropriate limits of technology in protecting public health rights to the detriment of individual rights. As the developments and recent lessons become embedded, a clearer picture should arise of where that balance is most likely to tilt in the long term.

Notes

1 Qingyue Meng and others, 'China's Encouraging Commitment to Health: But Reforms Must be Extended to Deliver Better Outcomes' in 'China's Health System Reforms: Review of 10 Years of Progress' 365 British Medical Journal l4178 (2019).
2 Boyuan Zhang, 'Human Rights Value Based on the Legislation Principle of the Basic Healthcare and Health Promotion Law' CSHRS (17 October 2019) http://www.chinahumanrights.org/html/2019/MAGAZINES_1017/13976.html last accessed 29 Sept 2021.
3 The Constitution of the People's Republic of China 1982 (as amended 2018) Article 21.
4 Id, Article 45.
5 National Health Commission of the People's Republic of China, 'Development of China's Public Health as an Essential Element of Human Rights' (29 April 2019) http://en.nhc.gov.cn/2019-04/29/c_75161.htm last accessed 29 Sept 2021.
6 Id.
7 Id.
8 Id.
9 Id.
10 Law of the People's Republic of China on the Promotion of Basic Medical and Health Care (Issued, 28 December 2019).
11 Wu Guoxiu, 'China's New Law Promoting Basic Medical Care Takes Effect from June' *CGTN* (16 May 2020) https://news.cgtn.com/news/2020-05-16/China-s-new-law-promoting-basic-medical-care-takes-effect-from-June-Qxyoct4vPW/index.html accessed 29 Sept 2021.
12 Other scholars recognise this as a constitutional right. See, Lingqiao Song and Yann Joly, 'After He Jianku: China's Biotechnology Regulation Reforms' 21(2) Medical Law International 174, 180 (2021).
13 Guoxiu (n 11).

14 Guoxiu (n 11).
15 Shenping Zhou, Tianyu Huang and Zhonghua Wang, 'Does Universal Health Insurance Coverage Reduce Unmet Healthcare Needs in China? Evidence from the National Health Service Survey' 20(43) International Journal for Equity in Health 2, 16 (2021).
16 Qingyue Meng (n 1).
17 Li Wang and others, 'The Development and Reform of Public Health in China from 1949 to 2019' 15 Global Health, 45 (2019).
18 Qingyue Meng (n 1).
19 Id; Li Wang.
20 Yuxi Wang and others, 'Assessing the Design of China's Complex Health System – Concerns on Equity and Efficiency' 10021 Health Policy Open 1 (2020).
21 Yuxi Wang and others, 'Assessing the Design of China's Complex Health System – Concerns on Equity and Efficiency' 10021 Health Policy Open 1 (2020).
22 Qingyue Meng (n 1); Li Wang.
23 Id.
24 Id.
25 Qingyue Meng (n 1); Fang H and others, 'Enhancing Financial Protection under China's Social Health Insurance to Achieve Universal Health Coverage' 365 British Medical Journal l2378 (2019). doi:10.1136/bmj.l2378.
26 Qingyue Meng (n 1).
27 Id.
28 For an overview of the development of health insurance in China, see Gordon Liu, Samantha Vortherms and Xuezhi Hong, 'China's Health Reform Update' 28 The Annual Review of Public Health 431, 432–438 (2017).
29 Yaoguang Zhang, 'Ten-Year Impacts of China's Rural Health Scheme: Lessons for Universal Health Coverage' 6:e003714 BMJ Global Health 1, 1 (2021).
30 Zhou (n 15).
31 Id, 2.
32 Id.
33 Id.
34 Yaoguang Zhang (n 29) 5.
35 Id.
36 Id, 5–6.
37 Id, 6.
38 Id, 7.
39 Id.
40 Id.
41 Id.
42 Id, 8.
43 Id.
44 Id, 9.
45 Id.
46 Vicky Mengqi Qin et al, 'Rural and Urban Differences in Health System Performance Among Older Chinese Adults: Cross-Sectional Analysis of a National Sample' 20(372) BMC Health Services Research 1, 2 (2020).
47 Id, 6.
48 Id, 9.
49 Id, 10; see also, Chunyan Li, Belinda Rose Young and Weiyan Jian, 'Association of Socioeconomic Status with Financial Burden of Disease Among Elderly Patients with Cardiovascular Disease: Evidence from the China Health and Retirement Longitudinal Study' 8 BMJ Open 1 e018703 (2018).
50 Qin (n 46) 9.
51 Id, 10.
52 Zhou (n 15) 2.
53 Shanquan Chen et al, 'Barriers of Effective Health Insurance Coverage for Rural-to-Urban Migrant Workers in China: A Systematic Review and Policy Gap Analysis' 20(408) BMC Public Health 1, 2 (2020).

54 Id.
55 Id.
56 Id.
57 Id.
58 Id, 4.
59 Id, 5.
60 Id.
61 Id.
62 Zhou (n 15) 14.
63 Id, 15.
64 Id.
65 Qin (n 46) 12.
66 Zhou (n 15) 15.
67 Ni Gong et al, 'Practice of Informed Consent in Guangdong, China: A Qualitative Study from the Perspective of In-Hospital Patients' 8(10) British Medical Journal Open 1 (2018).
68 Id, 4.
69 Id.
70 Id.
71 Kam-Yuen Cheng, Thomas Ming and Aaron Lai, 'Can Familism be Justified?' 26(8) Bioethics 431 (2012).
72 Vera Lucia Raposo, 'Lost in 'Culturation': Medical Informed Consent in China (from a Western Perspective)' 22 Medicine, Healthcare and Philosophy 17, 23 (2019).
73 Id, 17.
74 Law on Practicing Doctors of the People's Republic of China (Adopted at the third session of the Standing Committee of the Ninth National People's Congress on June 26, 1998).
75 Raposo, 'Lost in' (n 72) 19.
76 Id, 23.
77 Id, 23–24.
78 Barry Solaiman, 'Medical Liability in Qatar' in Vera L Raposo and Roy G Beran (eds), *Medical Liability in Asia and Australasia* (Springer 2021) 217.
79 Raposo, 'Lost in' (n 72) 27.
80 Id, 24.
81 There are further nuances to this argument and applicable laws which are beyond the scope of this chapter to examine. Raposo provides a detailed appraisal of those laws. See, Id, 18–22 and 27.
82 The Basic Law of the Hong Kong Special Administrative Region of the People's Republic of China (Promulgated 4 April 1990) Article 138.
83 The Basic Law of the Macao Special Administrative Region of the People's Republic of China (Adopted 31 March 1993) Article 123.
84 [1985] 1 ALL ER 643.
85 [2015] UKSC 11, Med LR 149.
86 Cheong Peng Meng, *Medical Negligence in Hong Kong and How to Avoid It: An Introductory Guide* (HKU Press 2019) 26.
87 Id, 26; This change arose under Cap 113 Hospital Authority Ordinance; on the concerns about paternalism, see, Edwin C Hui, 'A Survey of the Ethics Climate of Hong Kong Hospitals' 3(3) Clinical Ethics 132, 138 (2008).
88 Hong Kong Patients' Charter of Rights and Responsibilities, Available at https://www3.ha.org.hk/pwh/content/comm/charterpamphlet_e.html last accessed 29 Sept 2021.
89 Id.
90 Ho Mun Chan, 'Informed Consent Hong Kong Style: An Instance of Moderate Familism' 29(2) Journal of Medicine and Philosophy 195 (2004).
91 Id, 202.
92 Id, 203.
93 Hui (n 87) 132.
94 Id, 138.
95 Id.
96 Id, 139.

97 Pedro Cortes and Calvin Tinlop Chui, 'Macau – Legislation on Medical Error' *Conventus Law* (23 Feb 2017) available at https://www.conventuslaw.com/report/macau-legislation-on-medical-error/ last accessed 29 Sept 2021.
98 Id.
99 (RJEM) Law 5/2016.
100 Id, Article 7.
101 Id, Article 9.
102 Vera Lúcia Raposo, 'Macao Report: Informed Consent in a Multilingual and Multicultural Region, a Bioethical Challenge' 27 Cambridge Quarterly of Healthcare Ethics 385, 391 (2018).
103 Id, 385.
104 Id.
105 Id, 387.
106 Id.
107 Id, 387.
108 Id, 391.
109 Book II, Article 493.
110 Raposo 'Macao Report' (n 102) 391, citing Articles 144, 150 and 151 of the Macau Penal Code 1995.
111 Id, 392.
112 Id.
113 Id.
114 Id, 393.
115 Id.
116 Id.
117 Id.
118 International Covenant on Economic, Social and Cultural Rights (adopted 16 December 1966, entered into force 3 January 1976) 993 UNTS 3 (ICESCR).
119 International Covenant on Civil and Political Rights (adopted 16 December 1966, entered into force 23 March 1976) 999 UNTS 171 (ICCPR).
120 Article 18, Vienna Convention on the Law of Treaties (adopted 22 May 1969, entered into force 27 January 1980) 1155 UNTS 331.
121 ICCPR, 'Territorial Application'; 'The Focus' Issue 17 Hong Kong Department of Justice Basic Law Bulletin 3, 3 (December 2015) available at https://www.doj.gov.hk/tc/publications/pdf/basiclaw/basic17_3.pdf accessed 29 Sept 2021.
122 Annex 1, XIII, Joint Declaration of the Government of the United Kingdom of Great Britain and Northern Ireland and the Government of the People's Republic of China on the Question of Hong Kong, 19 December 1984.
123 An Introduction to Hong Kong Bill of Rights Ordinance' Constitutional and Mainland Affairs Bureau of Hong Kong 1, 1, https://www.cmab.gov.hk/doc/en/documents/policy_responsibilities/the_rights_of_the_individuals/human/BORO-InductoryChapterandBooklet-Eng.pdf accessed 29 Sept 2021.
124 Hong Kong Bill of Rights Ordinance (Cap. 383).
125 'An Introduction to Hong Kong' (n 123) 2.
126 Id, 5.
127 Michael Ramsden, 'Using the ICESCR in Hong Kong Courts' Hong Kong Law Journal 1, 1 (2012) Available at SSRN https://papers.ssrn.com/sol3/papers.cfm?abstract_id=2160777.
128 Id 14.
129 Id, 15.
130 Id, 16–20.
131 Id, 2; see also, Article 153, HK Basic Law.
132 ICESCR, 'Portugal: Territorial Application to Macau' (27 April 1993) Footnote 6; The ICCPR was ratified by Act No. 29/78 of 12 June, and the ICESCR was ratified by Act No. 45/78 of 11 July.
133 Muruga Ramaswamy, 'Implementation Of International Economic, Social and Cultural Obligations And Right To Education In Hong Kong And Macau And The Succession Of One Country Two Systems' 4 Journal of Education and Social Sciences 286, 290 (2016).
134 Id, 291.

135 Joint Declaration of the Government of the People's Republic of China and The Government of the Republic of Portugal on the question of Macao, 13 April 1987.
136 Ramaswamy (n 133) 291.
137 'Joint Declaration' China and Portugal (n 135) Annex 1.
138 UN Human Rights Committee, 'Concluding Observations of the Human Rights Committee: Portugal (Macau)' (5 May 1997) CCPR/C/79/Add.77, Para 4.
139 Id.
140 ICESCR, 'Territorial Application', China; ICCPR, 'Territorial Application', China.
141 World Health Assembly, International health regulations (3rd edn, 2005).
142 Id, Appendix I, States Parties to the International Health Regulations (2005) (as of 16 April 2013).
143 Id, Appendix 2, Reservations and other State Party Communications in Connection with the International Health Regulations (2005): Declarations and Statements, China, p.62.
144 Id, Article 4.
145 Id, Appendix 2, Reservations and other State Party Communications in Connection with the International Health Regulations (2005): Declarations and Statements, China, p.62–63.
146 Id, Article 12.
147 Lawrence O. Gostin, Roojin Habibi and Benjamin Mason Meier, 'Has Global Health Law Risen to Meet the COVID-19 Challenge? Revisiting the International Health Regulations to Prepare for Future Threats' 48 Journal of Law, Medicine and Ethics 376, 378 (2020).
148 Id.
149 David N Durrheim, Lawrence O. Gostin and Keymanthri Moodley, 'When Does a Major Outbreak Become a Public Health Emergency of International Concern?' 20(8) The Lancet Infectious Diseases 887 (2020).
150 BBC News, 'Chinese Authorities Say Unvaccinated Parents Can't Send Children to School' (16 July 2021) https://www.bbc.com/news/world-asia-china-57859356 accessed 29 Sept 2021.
151 Chao Deng, 'Get Vaxxed or Stay Home, Some Local Chinese Governments Say' WSJ (15 July 2021) https://www.wsj.com/articles/covid-19-vaccines-are-becoming-mandatory-in-parts-of-china-11626259091 accessed 29 Sept 2021.
152 Id.
153 Bloomberg News, 'China Calls for Halt to Mandatory Vaccines Amid Inoculation Push' (12 April 2021) https://www.bloomberg.com/news/articles/2021-04-12/china-calls-for-halt-to-mandatory-vaccines-amid-inoculation-push accessed 29 Sept 2021.
154 Global Times, 'China's Top Health Authority Rectify Local Mandatory Vaccination Orders, Stressing Voluntary Principle' (17 July 2021) https://www.globaltimes.cn/page/202107/1228884.shtml accessed 29 Sept 2021.
155 Vera Lucia Raposo, 'Can China's 'Standard of Care' for COVID-19 be replicated in Europe?' 46 Journal of Medical Ethics 451, 451 (2020).
156 Id.
157 Tracy Qu and Jane Zhang, 'How China has Turned to Tech Like Never Before to Combat the Coronavirus' *SCMP* (20 Feb 2020) available at https://www.scmp.com/tech/apps-social/article/3051587/how-china-has-turned-tech-never-combat-coronavirus accessed 29 Sept 2021.
158 Pratik Jakhar, 'Coronavirus: China's Tech Fights Back' BBC News (3 March 2020) available at https://www.bbc.com/news/technology-51717164 accessed 29 Sept 2021.
159 Joyce Huang, 'China's Virus Tracking Technology Sparks Privacy Concerns' VOA News (22 June 2020) available at https://www.voanews.com/covid-19-pandemic/chinas-virus-tracking-technology-sparks-privacy-concerns accessed 29 Sept 2021.
160 Natalie Ram and David Gray, 'Mass Surveillance in the age of COVID-19', 7(1) Journal of Law and the Biosciences 1, 4 (2020).
161 Id, 4.
162 Id.
163 Jun Liu and Hui Zhao, 'Privacy Lost: Appropriating Surveillance Technology in China's Fight Against COVID-19', 64(6) Business Horizons 743, 743 (2021).
164 Id, 2.
165 Id, 2–3.
166 Id, 3.

167 Id 3; Tianjian Shi and Jie Lu, 'The Meanings of Democracy: The Shadow of Confucianism' 21(4) Journal of Democracy 123 (2010).
168 Liu (n 163) 2.
169 Id, 4.
170 Id, 2.
171 Id, 4.
172 Id, 9–10.
173 Id, 10.
174 Id, 12.
175 Sarah Joseph, 'A Timeline of COVID 19 and Human Rights: Fortresses, Shutdowns, Quarantines, and Timely Testing' Griffith University Blog (1 May 2020) https://news.griffith.edu.au/2020/05/01/a-timeline-of-covid-19-and-human-rights-fortresses-shutdowns-quarantines-and-timely-testing/ accessed 29 Sept 2021.
176 Id.
177 Committee on Economic, Social and Cultural Rights, General Comment 14, The right to the highest attainable standard of health (article 12 of the International Covenant on Economic, Social and Cultural Rights), UN Doc. E/C.12/2000/4 (2000).

18

THE PROTECTION OF FOREIGN INVESTMENT IN CHINA CONSTITUTIONAL LAW

An Evolving Constant

Ma Ji and Dini Sejko

Introduction

The Third Plenary Session of the Eleventh Central Committee of the Communist Party of China (CPC) in December 1978 marked a turning point in the reform of the Chinese economy. The Chinese government launched the "open-door" policy, which disrupted a long period of self-isolation from the rest of the world, initiating the transformation of the Chinese economy and its integration into global markets and global value chains. One year later, the National People's Congress passed the Law of the People's Republic of China (PRC) on Chinese-Foreign Equity Joint Ventures,[1] which for the first time legally permitted foreign direct investment (FDI) in China. The main objective of the new law was to attract inbound FDI, representing one of the potentially "black cats" of Deng's famous quote,[2] ideologically inconsistent with accepted communist ideas but practically useful in enabling inbound FDI, necessary to solving compelling internal problems[3] caused by decades-long isolation and the Cultural Revolution.

The new Constitution enacted in 1982 further signalled China's change of policy. It indicated the commitment to permit foreign investors market access and the right to invest in China, reflecting at the Constitutional level the ongoing policy changes. For the first time, the PRC Constitution Article 18[4] created the constitutional basis for the entry of foreign investment and its protection in China. Article 18, in short, provides the constitutional guarantees for the protection of foreign investors. In particular, it provides a bedrock for other legislations on foreign-related investment, which has significant political and legal significance.

In the past 40 years, China has continuously transformed its policy towards protecting inbound FDI with the enactment and updates of a variety of laws and regulations. Conversely, the PRC Constitution was amended periodically in 1988, 1993,[5] 1999, 2004, and 2018 but Article 18 has remained unchanged. Along with China's laws and regulations on foreign investment constant updates, the connotation of the PRC Constitution Article 18 has gradually expanded and evolved.

Concurrently with the domestic legal changes, as part of the "open-door" policy, China started to negotiate international investment agreements (IIAs) with its new

DOI: 10.4324/9781003128243-21

economic partners. China's first bilateral investment treaty (BIT) was concluded coincidently in 1982[6] as the Constitution. Since then, China's approach to IIAs' negotiation has changed dramatically. China's IIAs have evolved in scope concerning the object of the treaty, market access provisions, and protections granted to foreign investors. The changes that create better protections for foreign investors, including the entry into force of the new Foreign Investment Law, have happened without amendments to the PRC Constitution Article 18. China's accession to the World Trade Organization (WTO) in 2001 gave a significant additional push to the market reforms and market access in an increasing number of economic sectors for foreign investors.

China's deepening engagement with the rest of the world under the Belt and Road Initiative (BRI) and the growing domestic market has become a driving force of foreign investment. BRI is often used to refer to the multifaced Chinese economic and diplomatic relations, including international investment and trade.[7] The 19th National Congress of the CPC incorporated the BRI into the Constitution, underscoring the unique role of the Initiative.

Connotations of Article 18 Paragraph 1

To attract foreign investment, China enacted a first set of laws on foreign investment – the Law of the PRC on Foreign-Capital Enterprises,[8] the Law of the PRC on Chinese-Foreign Equity Joint Ventures,[9] and the Law of the PRC on Chinese-Foreign Contractual Joint Ventures[10] collectively referred as "three laws on foreign investment" that allow the establishment of a variety of foreign investment vehicles that conveyed inbound capital in the fast-developing Chinese domestic market.

The connotation of the PRC Constitution Article 18 paragraph 1 has evolved via various legislations on foreign investment. The 1982 Constitution Article 18 paragraph 1 states: "The People's Republic of China permits foreign enterprises, other foreign economic organizations and individual foreigners to invest in China and to enter into various forms of economic cooperation with Chinese enterprises and other Chinese economic organizations in accordance with the law of the People's Republic of China." This provision stipulates four aspects of foreign investment: (a) the foreign investment policy, (b) the form of foreign investment, (c) the scope of Chinese investors, and (d) the scope of foreign investors.

The Evolution of Foreign Investment Policy

The 1982 Constitution Article 18 explicitly "permits foreign enterprises and other economic organizations or individuals" to "invest in China" as the fundamental legal basis for other foreign investment legislation. The Law of the PRC on Chinese-Foreign Equity Joint Ventures in 1979[11] and the Law of the PRC on Foreign-Capital Enterprises in 1986[12] Article 1 also "permit" foreign investors to establish enterprises, reflecting China's changing attitude towards the use of foreign capital: from opposition to affirmation.

The PRC Law on Chinese-Foreign Contractual Joint Ventures was enacted in 1988.[13] Article 1 uses the expression "promoting" foreign companies to organize cooperative enterprises, indicating China's more positive attitude towards foreign investment. The Provisions of the State Council on the Encouragement of Foreign Investment[14] in 1986 planned the overall strategy of using foreign investment in China. Moreover, it explicitly "encourages" foreign investors to set up enterprises in China for the first time in the form of administrative regulations. It provided a series of preferential policies to attract foreign investment.[15] Since then, the speed of utilizing foreign capital in China has accelerated significantly.

In 1992, Deng Xiaoping's Southern Dialogue further broke down theoretical and ideological barriers to the reform and the opening-up. The 1993 constitutional amendment put "persevere in reform and opening to the outside world" into the Preamble to the Constitution, providing a solid basis for foreign investment.

In 2004, the Interim Measures for the Administration of Examining and Approving Foreign Investment Projects[16] changed foreign investment administration from the initial "approval administration" to the "examination and approval" administration. Then in 2016, absorbed from the experience of the pilot Free Trade Zone (FTZ) reform, the Standing Committee of the National People's Congress amended the "three regulations on foreign investment," which turned the administration on foreign investment from the approval administration into recordation administration, improving the efficiency of foreign investment management.[17] Furthermore, in 2017, the Catalogue of Industries for Guiding Foreign Investment (2017 Revision)[18] proposed implementing the model of the pre-establishment national treatment (NT) plus a negative list, a profound change in China's attitude towards foreign investment. After seven revisions of the Catalogue, the number of "encourage," "restrict," and "prohibited" projects in the category gradually increased, indicating that China's attitude towards foreign investment has become more open.[19]

The Evolution of Foreign Investment Forms

The form of foreign investment has been transformed from "cooperation" and "joint venture" between China and foreign countries to "cooperation" and "joint venture" and "wholly foreign ownership." Since the reform and opening-up, "three laws on foreign investment" provide for three primary foreign investment forms: (a) Chinese-Foreign equity joint ventures, (b) Chinese-Foreign contractual joint ventures, and (c) wholly foreign ownership.

At the beginning of the reform and opening-up, due to lacking understanding Chinese legal system and market, foreign investors chose to enter the Chinese market by establishing cooperation and joint ventures with Chinese investors. Before 1985, low-risk cooperative enterprises dominated the mode of foreign investment. Since 1986, due to the improvement of the investment environment and the legal system, joint ventures have replaced cooperative enterprises as the leading mode of foreign investment. As the reform and opening-up deepened, foreign investors understood China's investment environment more, and their dependence on Chinese domestic investors became less. Then the amount of foreign capital utilized by wholly owned foreign enterprises exceeded that of cooperative enterprises in 1990 and exceeded that of joint ventures in 1999. The forms of cooperation and joint ventures stated in Article 18 have been transformed into wholly owned enterprises as the dominant forms.

The Evolution of the Scope of Chinese Investors

Even the Constitution Article 18 only discusses "Chinese enterprises or other economic organizations," individuals can be investment subjects with the evolution. The 1982 Constitution and the "three regulations on foreign investment" stipulated that

China's "companies, enterprises or other economic organizations" could act as Chinese investors. There was no provision as to whether individuals as natural persons could be investors. China has adjusted laws, regulations, and policies to mobilize individuals to participate in economic construction and gradually changed this limit.

First, the Law on Individual Proprietorship Enterprises[20] allowed individuals to set up enterprises; and the Company Law of the PRC (2005 Revision)[21] enables individuals to establish limited liability companies.[22] Individuals can set up a sole proprietorship enterprise or a one-person company to joint venture with foreign investors.

Second, Chinese individuals can be investors in new foreign-invested enterprises after mergers and acquisitions, with the development of the market economy and the diversification of domestic enterprise ownership. In addition to the traditional "green-field investment," foreign investment has increasingly adopted the "brownfield investment" model.[23] In 2003, the Interim Provisions for Foreign Investors to Merge Domestic Enterprises clearly stated that a Chinese individual shareholder of a domestic company merged utilizing share right merger may, if having been a shareholder in the original company for one year or more, be approved to continue its identity as a Chinese investor of the foreign-funded enterprise established after the modification.[24] In 2006, Interim Provisions on the Takeover of Domestic Enterprises by Foreign Investors (2006 Revision)[25] further removed the restriction of the shareholder "been a shareholder in the original company for one year or more."

Third, the Partnership Enterprise Law (2006 Version)[26] allows foreign investors to set up partnerships in China. In 2009, the State Council issued the Administrative Measures for the Establishment of Partnership Enterprises within China by Foreign Enterprises or Individuals,[27] which clearly stated that foreign enterprises or individuals might establish partnerships with individuals in China. After that, several foreign-funded partnerships, such as law firms and accounting firms, were established, with Chinese individuals as partners.

Fourth, some individual compatriots from Hong Kong, Macao and Taiwan have become pioneers in foreign investment. The 1990 Regulations on Encouragement of Investments from overseas Chinese and Hong Kong and Macao Compatriots[28] and the Law on the Protection of Investments of Taiwan Compatriots[29] provide that overseas Chinese, Hong Kong, Macao, and Taiwan individuals may invest in various forms, enjoy the same treatment as foreign investors, and entrust relatives or friends in China as agents. In addition, the Detailed Rules for the Implementation of the Law of the PRC on Wholly Foreign-Owned Enterprises in China,[30] the Detailed Rules for the Implementation of the Law of PRC on Sino-Foreign Joint Cooperative Ventures,[31] and Provisions on Guiding the Orientation of Foreign Investment[32] clearly state that concerning the investment projects established by overseas Chinese and investors from Hong Kong, Macao or Taiwan, these rules shall be similarly applied. In addition, some local regulations liberalized restrictions on individual participation in the establishment of joint ventures, such as the 2000 Beijing Regulations on Zhongguancun Science and Technology Park.[33]

The Evolution of the Scope of Foreign Investors

The "foreign enterprises and other foreign economic organizations," as stipulated in the PRC Constitution Article 18, evolved into "organizations" without limitations on economic nature. In practice, foreign investment in China is increasingly diverse, not limited to enterprises and other economic organizations, such as a large number of educational institutions, medical institutions, and other investments in China. For example, the Outline for the Reform and Development of Education in China, issued in 1993, stated that China welcomed compatriots from Hong Kong, Macao and Taiwan, overseas Chinese, and foreign-friendly people to conduct international cooperation in running schools. The Education Act of 1995[34] and the Non-state Education Promotion Law[35] of 2002 provide that "overseas institutions or individuals" may cooperate in running schools within China. The Regulations on Chinese-foreign Cooperative Education[36] in 2003 specify the nature, content, and establishment of Chinese-foreign cooperative schools. The Non-state Education Promotion Law (2016 Revision)[37] permits for-profit schools for non-compulsory education to further attract foreign educational institutions to China. According to statistics, as of 2018, there are 2,651 cooperative schools and projects.

Also, in May 2000, the Interim Measures for the Administration of Sino-foreign Equity Joint and Cooperative Joint Medical Institutions[38] stipulate that a foreign medical institution may, upon approval, set up health institutions in joint ventures with Chinese entities.

Notably, in the early stage of reform and opening up, China has not yet adopted the socialist market economy and has not yet formulated civil Law. There was no standardized legal concept regarding the subject that can invest. Therefore, the 1982 Constitution called organizations, besides enterprises conducting economic activities, "economic organization." The 1982 PRC Constitution stipulates the socialist economic system mainly from the perspective of ownership, such as the state-owned economy, the collective ownership economy, the individual economy, and the private economy.[39] In 1986, China enacted the General Principles of Civil Law and established a civil subject system by using the expressions of "citizen (natural person)," "legal person, and "other organizations."[40] This expression is more precise than the language "enterprises, other economic organizations and individuals" in the 1982 PRC Constitution. Since 2005, the legal term "economic organizations" only appeared in proprietary terms, such as "individual economic organizations," "agricultural collective economic organizations," and it is no longer used alone. Therefore, it is feasible and necessary to replace "economic organization" with more professional and accurate terms in Law.

Connotations of Article 18 Paragraph 2

The Evolution of Foreign Investment Legal Regime

The Article 18 paragraph 2 principles have developed into principles generally applicable to all foreign investment subjects. The Constitution Article 18 paragraph 2 states: "All foreign enterprises, other foreign economic organizations as well as Chinese-foreign joint ventures within Chinese territory shall abide by the Law of the People's Republic of China. Their lawful rights and interests are protected by the Law of the People's Republic of China." With the expansion of the scope and diversification of foreign investment subjects, the provisions of Article 18 of the Constitution, "abide by Chinese law" and "protection by Chinese law," should be applied to all foreign investment subjects, not limited to joint ventures stated in this paragraph. The Constitution also protects all kinds of newly established enterprises after implementing the three regulations on foreign investment. Furthermore, the PRC Constitution Article 32 paragraph 1 stipulates that "China protects the lawful rights and interests of foreigners within Chinese territory; foreigners on Chinese territory must abide by the laws of the PRC." This constitutional provision confirms the legal status of foreign investors in China, enhances the confidence and security of foreign investors, and aims to attracts foreign investors to carry out various investments in China.

In 2015, the government clarified that China's policy on the use of foreign capital would not change, the protection of the legitimate rights and interests of foreign enterprises would not change, and the direction of providing better services for enterprises from all countries would not change.[41]

In the 18th National Congress of the CPC, China has decided to promote a new pattern of wide opening up by speeding up the unification of domestic and foreign investment regulations and enacting new rules on foreign investment. Since the "three laws on foreign investment" are outdated, establishing a new legal system on foreign investment to adapt to the reform and opening-up in the new era was urgent. On March 15, 2019, the Foreign Investment Law of the PRC[42] was passed, replacing the "three laws on foreign investment," as the basic law in the field of foreign investment, is an important step to expanding and promoting foreign investment, to implement the provisions of the Constitution on opening up, especially the new ideas on opening up added in the 2018 Constitutional Amendment.

The Foreign Investment Law fully embodies the adaptability of the Constitution. The Foreign Investment Law Article 1 states that "this Law is enacted in accordance with the PRC Constitution." The Foreign Investment Law Article 2 replaces "foreign enterprises, other foreign economic organizations and individual foreigners" in the Constitution and in the "three laws on foreign investment" with "foreign natural persons, enterprises or other organizations," which is in line with the spirit of the Constitution. By clarifying the meaning of "foreign investors," the Foreign Investment Law firmly guarantees the Rule of Law to expand China's opening up to the outside world, promote foreign investment, and protect foreign investment's legitimate rights and interests in the new era. Moreover, the Foreign Investment Law no longer has requirements on organizational forms and performance guidelines; domestic and foreign-funded enterprises directly and uniformly apply the laws of Company Law and Partnership Enterprise Law.

At the same time, China is revising patent law, copyright law, and relevant laws to protect intellectual property rights, which is implementing the PRC Constitution to protect foreign enterprises equally. In addition, for organizations such as permanent representative offices of foreign enterprises in China, foreign chambers of commerce, and other non-profit organizations and non-governmental organizations closely related to foreign investment business, China has also enacted Law on the Administration of Activities of Overseas Non-Governmental Organizations within the Territory of China[43] to protect their legitimate rights and interests. And the report of the 19th National Congress of the CPC clearly states that all enterprises registered in China should be treated equally and equally.

The Evolution of Protection in the Chinese Investment Agreements

IIAs are instruments of international economic law. IIAs specific treaty clauses create protections for foreign investors, and significant domestic obligations for the states. IIAs require FDI recipient states to ensure protection to foreign investors through their legislation, institutions, and agencies, including the judiciary and the public administration. Some of the most typical provisions of IIAs include the definitions of investor and investment, the NT clause, the most favoured nation (MFN) clause, the fair and equitable treatment (FET) clause, full protection and security (FPS), and the dispute settlement clause. IIAs play an essential role in signalling a state's commitment to an open economy by improving market access for foreign investors. The application of the clauses of the IIAs creates significant obligations at the domestic level.

After the launch of the opening-up policy to attract foreign investment, China started to negotiate IIAs. The first BIT signed with Sweden in 1982 paved the way to the signature of more than 140 agreements, which create international obligations for the protection of foreign investors in China and Chinese investors abroad.[44]

There is no precise and official classification of Chinese BITs. Before the launch of the BRI, scholars had grouped Chinese BITs into three main groups, generally referred to as three generations of BITs.[45] These three generations of BITs share many similarities, but they also have some critical differences. The delineating points for the CBITs are roughly set in 1999 and 2011, since both years are crucial for observing the development and changes of China's investment policies and the drafting of IIAs.

Those treaties negotiated between 1982 and 1998 reflect the needs of China at the time: a sign of openness and caution in granting protections to the investors. In fact, in those years, China was a recipient of FDI and with very little Chinese outward investment. Thus, it was not in China's interest to negotiate for high levels of protection as the interests of its few outward investors were vastly outweighed by the risks of claims by the foreign investors in China. Consequently, China's early treaties are characterized by hortatory wording – such as the use of a best efforts NT clause – and perhaps more significantly contain an investor-state dispute settlement (ISDS) clause with a limited scope regarding the amount of compensation payable to investors in case of expropriation, lack or qualified national-treatment clause, most-favoured-nation clause, FET and FPS.

Around 1999, China adopted the "Going Abroad" policy to encourage outbound investments. Since around 2011, China has become a leading investment exporting countries in the world and has since acquired a "blended image" (a top country in both investment-importing and exporting).[46]

China started to take a more liberal approach after its accession to the "WTO". Needless to say, China's membership in the WTO most certainly facilitates the implementation of NT in both domestic laws and international investment laws. Notwithstanding its role focusing on trade, the WTO also embraces some investment issues. The General Agreement on Trade in Service (GATS) under mode 3 provides market access and allows the presence of foreign service suppliers in the Chinese territory, based on the Chinese schedule of commitments.[47]

Definition of Investor

The scope of the investor definition is of primary importance. In order to benefit of the protections enshrined in the IIAs, the foreigner or foreign entity investing in China needs to fall into the purview of the investor's definition. Specifically in the case of covered legal entities, IIAs in some cases may include requirement of substantial business activity.[48] Another issuer is the inconsistency in the definition of ownership and control of legal entities, in particular in relation to the increasing number of state-owned and state-controlled entities. Chinese BITs often define the investor without clarifying if state-owned and state-controlled investors are included into the scope of the definition. Usually, the language of the treaty qualifies investors as: *economic entities established in accordance with the laws of the People's Republic of China and having their seat in its territory.*[49] Such problem, while relevant for foreign investors in China, it has a major impact in the case of Chinese investors while investing abroad. Chinese state-owned investors will face issues when using the first and second-generation BITs.[50] The issue that might rise in this case that geo-strategic entities that are operating in loss or on a cost recovery basis can be qualified as economic entities.[51]

National Treatment

The NT standard is the most relevant treaty standard for our analysis. NT provides the basic criterion how foreign investors should be treated. The presence of the NT standard in IIAs refers to a commitment for the host state to treat foreign investors no less favourably than national investors in like situations. NT for foreign investors covers two factors: civil and commercial rights (substantive rights), judicial and administrative rights (procedural rights). The main objective of the NT clause is to prevent the discrimination of foreign investors vs domestic investors, and create a level playing field between domestic investors and foreign investors in order to enhance market competition.

China concluded the first BIT with Sweden and the investment treaty did not even contain the NT standard. Similarly, BITs signed in the same period with other economic partners did not provide any reference to the NT standard.[52] With the China–United Kingdom BIT, the Chinese drafters included an NT commitment. However, the NT standard, only required China to make an effort to grant NT to the UK investors, is a best effort clause:

> either Contracting Party shall to the extent possible, accord treatment in accordance with the stipulations of its laws and regulations to the investment of nationals or companies of the other Contracting Party the same treatment as that accorded to its own nationals or companies[53]

A best effort NT provision has a mere symbolic function[54] and allows the recipient country to discriminate the foreign investors, through existing discriminatory laws and regulations or by introducing new laws and regulations.[55] The expression "without prejudice to its laws and regulations" reduces the effectiveness of the NT provision to a best effort clause. The China–Cyprus BIT started the practice of "grandfather clause". A typical example of such a grandfather clause can be found in the China–Germany BIT of 2003:

> With regard to the People's Republic of China, paragraph 3 of Article 2 and paragraph 2 of Article 3 do not apply to
>
> a. any existing non-conforming measures maintained within its territory;
> b. the continuation of any such non-conforming measure;
> c. any amendment to any such non-conforming measure to the extent that the amendment does not increase the non-conformity of these measures.
>
> The People's Republic of China will take all appropriate steps in order to *progressively remove the non-conforming measures.*[56]

Very few Chinese BITs include a full-scale NT provision. The typical example is the provision in the Japan–China BIT: the treatment accorded by either Contracting Party within its territory to nationals and companies of the other Contracting Party with respect to investments, returns and business activities in connection with the investment shall not be less favourable than that accorded to nationals and companies of the former Contracting Party.

The uniqueness of China's BIT practice is to apply differentiated NT protections to investors from developed and developing countries in order to achieve the purpose of attracting FDI from European and other developed countries. China uses the respective provision of its BITs with developing countries to restrictively grant NT without prejudice to the host States' laws and regulations. Meanwhile, in its BITs with developed countries, NT treatment is granted, provided that the continuation of existing non-conforming measures is guaranteed.

This qualified NT provision exclusively applies to the Chinese market, while a no less favourable NT standard than that afforded to domestic investors is applied to Chinese investments in the respective developed country. China has indicated a gradual yet decisive policy change towards stronger and more comprehensive NT protections. This gradualist approach does not only match China's change from a pure FDI importing country to a more important FDI exporting country but also shows China's increasing desire and capability to adhere to international standards of legal protections to foreign investors.[57]

Fair and Equitable Treatment

The FET standard is usually expressed by a short provision that has acquired its meaning in light of the interpretive work of arbitral tribunals. FET can be identified in a not exhaustive list as follows: (a) protection of legitimate and reasonable expectations which have been relied upon by the investor to make the investment; (b) good faith conduct, although bad faith on the part of the State is not required for its violation; (c) conduct that is transparent, consistent, and not discriminatory, that is, not based on unjustifiable distinctions or arbitrary; (d) conduct that does not offend judicial propriety that complies with due process and the right to be heard.[58]

In old BITs, China only ensures, subject to its laws and regulations, that the management, maintenance, use, enjoyment, or disposal of investments in its territory and maritime zones of investors of the other Contracting State shall not be subjected to or impaired by any unreasonable or discriminatory measures.[59] The approach has changed in more modern BITs such as the one signed with Uzbekistan in 2011 where the FET requires that investors shall not be wilfully rejected to fair judicial proceedings by the other Contracting Party or be treated with obvious discriminatory or arbitrary measures.[60] The FET style in the above-mentioned BIT does not limit the standard of protection granted to foreign investors to other sources of obligation, such as international law, customary international law, or the minimum standard of treatment of aliens under customary international law, granting significant protection to foreign investors.

Conclusion

Constitutional norms are a high degree of generalization and abstraction of social life under certain historical stages. As the source of laws and regulations, the PRC Constitution provides the solid normative basis for making various laws, empowering these laws authority, and deepening reform and opening up. The Constitution Article 18 makes pioneering provisions on foreign investment, which has far-reaching historical implications. Some of which reflect the social reality and level of understanding at that time, but the spirit, direction, and orientation of the Constitution Article 18 – to open up to the outside world – are evident. Since the reform and opening-up, China's policy of systematically relying on foreign capital deepened. The innovative and expanded practice of the PRC Constitution Article 18 embodies the adaptability of the Constitution.

China's foreign investment legislations are the necessary requirements and essential embodiment of the full implementation of the Constitution Article 18. As the fundamental law, the PRC Constitution is the general basis of all kinds of domestic laws and regulations. The 1982 PRC Constitution Article 18 lays down the basic provisions for protecting foreign investment in China. Later, the two constitutional amendments in 1993 and 2018 in the Preamble to the Constitution include "preserve the reform and opening to the outside world" and "implement new concepts of development," "to the reciprocal, win-win, and open strategy" and "promoting the building of a community with a shared future for mankind."

The life of the Constitution Article 18 lies in its implementation, so does its authority. The theme of implementing the Constitution Article 18 via various legislations to promote opening up to the outside world, to attract and to utilize foreign capital, is clearly visible. Over the past decades, several laws and regulations on foreign investments have effectively implemented the provisions of the Constitution on opening up to the outside world and attracting the use of foreign capital, to safeguard the rule of Law for foreign-invested enterprises in China. According to statistics, in addition to the "three laws on foreign investment," there are 32 administrative regulations, 424 departmental regulations, as well as a large number of relevant judicial interpretations, industry regulations, and group regulations.

The development of the Constitution Article 18 is reflected not only in the revision of the Constitution but also in the new connotation given to the Constitution amid the practice. Even the PRC Constitution Article 18 has not been amended, and it does not affect the constitutionality of the following legislation on foreign investment. In this process, China adheres to scientific legislation, respects and embodies the development of the rule of law. Along with practical consequences, it is necessary to understand the spirit of the Constitution with a positive and open attitude, enrich the connotation of the Constitution, and promote the implementation of the Constitution through the relevant legislation. In numerous other high-profile statements in the past[61] and in the present, Chinese leaders have indicated that foreign enterprises are to be treated the same as domestic enterprises in China.

Notes

1 The Law of the People's Republic of China on Chinese-Foreign Equity Joint Ventures [中华人民共和国中外合资经营企业法] (issued on 07-08-1979, effective on 07-08-1979, issued by National People's Congress, invalidated by Foreign Investment Law of the People's Republic of China [issued on 03-15-2019, effective on 01-01-2020]).

2 "It does not matter whether a cat is black or white, as long as it catches mice" BBC, China's Communist Revolution, <http://news.bbc.co.uk/hi/english/static/special_report/1999/09/99/china_50/no_deng.htm> accessed 20 April 2022.

3 Wenhua Shan, The Legal Framework of EU-China Investment Relations (Oxford: Hart Publishing 2014), at 11.

4 Article 18.1. The People's Republic of China permits foreign enterprises, other foreign economic organizations and individual foreigners to invest in China and to enter into various forms of economic cooperation with Chinese enterprises and other economic organizations in accordance with the law of the People's Republic of China.

Article 18.2. All foreign enterprises and other foreign economic organizations in China, as well as joint ventures with Chinese and foreign investment located in China, shall abide by the law of the People's Republic of China. Their lawful rights and interests are protected by the law of the People's Republic of China.

5 1993 Amendment to the Constitution of the People's Republic of China, <https://www.cecc.gov/resources/legal-provisions/1993-amendment-to-the-constitution-of-the-peoples-republic-of-china> accessed on 20 April 2022.

6 PR China–Sweden BIT 29 March 1982.

7 National Development and Reform Commission, Ministry of Foreign Affairs, and Ministry of Commerce of the People's Republic of China, with State Council authorization, Vision and Actions on Jointly Building Silk Road Economic Belt and 21st-Century Maritime Silk Road, 28 March 2015.

8 Law of the People's Republic of China on Foreign-Capital Enterprises [中华人民共和国外资企业法] (issued on 04-12-1986, effective on 04-12-1986, issued by National People's Congress, invalidated by Foreign Investment Law of the People's Republic of China, which was issued on 03-15-2019 and was effective on 01-01-2020).

9 The Law of the People Republic of China on Chinese-Foreign Equity Joint Ventures [中华人民共和国中外合资经营企业法] (issued on 07-08-1979, effective on 07-08-1979, issued by National People's Congress, invalidated by Foreign Investment Law of the People's Republic of China [issued on 03-15-2019, effective on 01-01-2020]).

10 The Law of the People's Republic of China on Chinese-Foreign Contractual Joint Ventures [中华人民共和国中外合作经营企业法] (effective date on 04-13-1988, issued by National People's Congress, invalidated by Foreign Investment Law of the People's Republic of China [issued on 03-15-2019, effective on 01-01-2020]).

11 The Law of the People Republic of China on Chinese-Foreign Equity Joint Ventures [中华人民共和国中外合资经营企业法] (issued on 07-08-1979, effective on 07-08-1979, issued by National People's Congress, invalidated by Foreign Investment Law of the People's Republic of China [issued on 03-15-2019, effective on 01-01-2020]).

12 Law of the People's Republic of China on Foreign-Capital Enterprises [中华人民共和国外资企业法] (issued on 04-12-1986, effective on 04-12-1986, issued by National People's Congress, invalidated by Foreign Investment Law of the People's Republic of China, which was issued on 03-15-2019 and was effective on 01-01-2020).

13 The Law of the People's Republic of China on Chinese-Foreign Contractual Joint Ventures [中华人民共和国中外合作经营企业法] (effective date on 04-13-1988, issued by National People's Congress, invalidated by Foreign Investment Law of the People's Republic of China [issued on 03-15-2019, effective on 01-01-2020]).

14 The Provisions of the State Council on the Encouragement of Foreign Investment [国务院关于鼓励外商投资的规定] (issue on 10-11-1986, effective on 10-11-1986, issued by State Council).

15 Articles 5–10.

16 The Interim Measures for the Administration of Examining and Approving Foreign Investment Projects [外商投资项目核准暂行管理办法] (issued by the National Development and Reform Commission, date issue on 10-09-2004, effective date on 10-09-2004. Status: expired).

17 See e.g. Law of the People's Republic of China on Wholly Foreign-Owned Enterprises (2016 Amendment) [中华人民共和国外资企业法] (2016 年修正) Article 23

18 Issued by the State Development and Reform Commission (incl. former State Development Planning Commission) Ministry of Commerce; effective date on 07-28-2017; status: expired; partly invalidated by: Special Administrative Measures (Negative List) for the Access of Foreign Investment (2018) (issued on 06-28-2018, effective on 07-28-2018); Catalogue of Industries for Encouraging Foreign Investment (2019 Version) (issued on 06-30-2019, effective on 07-30-2019).

19 Foreign-funded projects fall into four categories: encouraged, permitted, restricted, and prohibited ones. The foreign-funded projects that are encouraged, restricted, and prohibited

shall be listed in the Catalog of Foreign-funded Industry Guidance. The foreign-funded projects that do not fall into the categories of encouraged, restricted, or prohibited projects shall be the permitted foreign-funded projects. The permitted foreign-funded projects shall not be listed in the Catalog of Foreign-funded Industry Guidance. As for the approval, foreign-funded projects shall be examined and approved, and put on record respectively by the Departments of Development Planning and the Economic and Trade Departments according to the limit of authority for examination and approval; the contracts and articles of association of foreign-funded enterprises shall be examined and approved, and put on record by the Department of Foreign Trade and Economic Cooperation.

20 Law of the People's Republic of China on Individual Proprietorship Enterprises [中华人民共和国个人独资企业法] (date Issued: 08-30-1999; effective date: 01-01-2000; issued by the Standing Committee of the National People's Congress; status: effective).

21 Company Law of the People's Republic of China (2005 Revision) [中华人民共和国公司法 (2005 修订)] (date issued: 10-27-2005; effective date: 01-01-2006; issuing authority: Standing Committee of the National People's Congress; revised by Decision of the Standing Committee of the National People's Congress on Amending Seven Laws Including the Marine Environment Protection Law of the People's Republic of China [and the Pharmaceutical Administration Law, the Metrology Law, the Fisheries Law, the Customs Law, the Tobacco Monopoly Law, and the Company Law] [issued on 12-28-2013, effective on 12-28-2013]).

22 Section 3 Special Provisions on One-person Limited Liability Companies.

23 (Investment in mergers and acquisitions of Chinese enterprises).

24 Article 10.

25 Interim Provisions on the Takeover of Domestic Enterprises by Foreign Investors (2006 Revision) [关于外国投资者并购境内企业的规定 (2006 修订)] (date issued: 08-08-2006; effective date: 09-08-2006; issued by Ministry of Commerce State-owned Asset Supervision and Administration Commission of the State Council State Taxation Administration State Administration for Industry and Commerce [dissolved] China Securities Regulatory Commission State Administration of Foreign Exchange; revised by Decision of the Ministry of Commerce on Amending the Provisions on the Merger or Acquisition of Domestic Enterprises by Foreign Investors [issued on 06-22-2009, effective on 06-22-2009]).

26 Partnership Enterprise Law (2006 Version) [中华人民共和国合伙企业法 (2006 修订)] (date issued: 08-27-2006; effective date: 06-01-2007; issued by the Standing Committee of the National People's Congress; status: effective).

27 Administrative Measures for the Establishment of Partnership Enterprises within China by Foreign Enterprises or Individuals [外国企业或者个人在中国境内设立合伙企业管理办法] (date issued: 11-25-2009; effective date: 03-01-2010; issuing authority: State Council; invalidated by Decision of the State Council to Amend and Repeal Certain Administrative Regulations [Order No. 732 of the State Council of the People's Republic of China] [issued on 11-29-2020, effective on 11-29-2020]).

28 Regulations on Encouragement of Investments from Overseas Chinese and Hong Kong and Macao Compatriots [国务院关于鼓励华侨和香港澳门同胞投资的规定] (date issued: 08-19-1990; effective date: 08-19-1990; issuing authority: State Council; status: effective).

29 Law of the People's Republic of China on the Protection of Investments of Taiwan Compatriots [中华人民共和国台湾同胞投资保护法] (date issued: 03-05-1994; effective date: 03-05-1994; issuing authority: Standing Committee of the National People's Congress; revised by: Decision of the Standing Committee of the National People's Congress on Amending Four Laws including the Law of the People's Republic of China on Wholly Foreign-Owned Enterprises [Including the Law on Chinese-Foreign Equity Joint Ventures, the Law on Chinese-Foreign Contractual Joint Ventures, and the Law on the Protection of Investments by Taiwan Compatriots] [issued on 09-03-2016, effective on 10-01-2016]).

30 Detailed Rules for the Implementation of the Law of the PRC on Wholly Foreign-Owned Enterprises in China [中华人民共和国外资企业法实施细则] (issued on 12-12-1990, effective on 12-12-1990, issued by Ministry of Foreign Trade and Economic Cooperation); It is invalidated by Foreign Investment Law of the People's Republic of China (issued on 03-15-2019, effective on 01-01-2020).

31 Detailed Rules for the Implementation of the Law of PRC on Sino-Foreign Joint Cooperative Ventures [中华人民共和国中外合作经营企业法实施细则] (issued on 09-04-1995, effective on

09-04-1995); It is invalidated by Foreign Investment Law of the People's Republic of China (issued on 03-15-2019, effective on 01-01-2020).

32 Provisions on Guiding the Orientation of Foreign Investment [指导外商投资方向规定] (date issued: 02-11-2002; effective date: 04-01-2002; issuing authority: State Council; status: effective).

33 Regulations on Zhongguancun Science and Technology Park [中关村科技园条例] (date issued: 12-08-2000; effective date: 01-01-2001; issuing authority: Beijing Municipal People's Congress [incl. Standing Committee]; invalidated by: Regulation of Zhongguancun Science Park [issued on 12-23-2010, effective on 12-23-2010]) Article 55, 56.

34 Education Law of the People's Republic of China [中华人民共和国教育法] (date issued: 03-18-1995; effective date: 09-01-1995; issued by National People's Congress; revised by Decision of the Standing Committee of the National People's Congress on Amending Some Laws [issued on 08-27-2009, effective on 08-27-2009]).

35 Non-state Education Promotion Law of the People's Republic of China [民办教育促进法] (date issued: 12-28-2002; effective date: 09-01-2003; issuing authority: Standing Committee of the National People's Congress; revised by Decision of the Standing Committee of the National People's Congress on Amending Twelve Laws Including the Cultural Relics Protection Law of the People's Republic of China [and the Grasslands Law, the Customs Law, the Law on Import and Export Commodity Inspection, the Law on the Administration of Tax Collection, the Law on the Prevention and Control of Environmental Pollution by Solid Wastes, the Coal Industry Law, the Animal Epidemic Prevention Law, the Securities Law, the Seed Law, the Non-state Education Promotion Law, and the Law on Prevention and Treatment of Infectious Diseases] [issued on 06-29-2013, effective on 06-29-2013]).

36 Regulations of the People's Republic of China on Chinese-foreign Cooperative Education [中华人民共和国中外合作办学条例] (date issued: 03-01-2003; effective date: 09-01-2003; issuing authority: State Council; revised by Decision of the State Council on Repealing and Amending Some Administrative Regulations [2013] [issued on 07-18-2013, effective on 07-18-2013]).

37 Non-state Education Promotion Law of the People's Republic of China (2016 Revision) [中华人民共和国民办教育促进法 (2016 修正)] (date issued: 11-07-2016; effective date: 09-01-2017; issued by Standing Committee of the National People's Congress; revised by Decision of the Standing Committee of the National People's Congress to Amend Seven Laws Including the Labor Law of the People's Republic of China [including the Labor Law, the Law on the Protection of the Rights and Interests of the Elderly, the Law on the Prevention and Control of Pollution from Environmental Noise, the Law on Environmental Impact Assessment, the Non-State Education Promotion Law, the Civil Aviation Law, and the Law on the Prevention and Control of Occupational Diseases] [issued on 12-29-2018, effective on 12-29-2018]).

38 Interim Measures for the Administration of Sino-foreign Equity Joint and Cooperative Joint Medical Institutions [中外合资、合作医疗机构管理暂行办法] (date issued: 05-15-2000; effective date: 07-01-2000; issued by the Ministry of Health [dissolved] Ministry of Foreign Trade and Economic Cooperation [incl. former Ministry of Foreign Economy and Trade] [replaced]; Status: Effective).

39 Articles 6–8.

40 General Principles of the Civil Law of the People's Republic of China [中华人民共和国民法通则] (date issued 04-12-1986; effective date: 01-01-1987; issued by National People's Congress; invalidated by Civil Code of the People's Republic of China [issued on 05-28-2020, effective on 01-01-2021]).

41 See "三个不会变"—中国开放的大门永远不会关上, available at <http://theory.people.com.cn/n/2015/1209/c40531-27904078.htm> accessed 18 April 2022.

42 Foreign Investment Law of the People's Republic of China [中华人民共和国外商投资法] (issued on 03-15-2019, effective on 01-01-2020, issued by National People's Congress).

43 Law of the People's Republic of China on the Administration of Activities of Overseas Non-Governmental Organizations within the Territory of China (2017 Amendment) [中华人民共和国境外非政府组织境内活动管理法 (2017 修正)] (date issued: 11-04-2017; effective date: 11-05-2017; issued by the Standing Committee of the National People's Congress; Status: Effective).

44 Investment Policy Hub, International Investment Agreements Navigator > China https://investmentpolicy.unctad.org/international-investment-agreements/countries/42/china> accessed 21 April 2022.

45 Wenhua Shan, The Legal Framework of EU-China Investment Relations (Oxford: Hart Publishing 2014), at 31–39.
46 Manjiao Chi, 'The 'Greenization' of Chinese Bits: An Empirical Study of the Environmental Provisions in Chinese Bits and its Implications for China's Future Bit-Making,' (2015) 18 Journal of International Economic Law 529–531.
47 The People's Republic of China – Schedule of Specific Commitments, GATS/SC/135 14 February 2002.
48 China–Turkey BIT (2015) corporations, firms, business partnerships incorporated or constituted under the law of a Contracting Party and having their registered offices together with substantial business activities in the territory of that Contracting Party.
49 China–Greece BIT 1992, Article 1.3a, i.e. China–Pakistan BIT 1989, Article 1b, ii.
50 Bryan Mercurio and Dini Sejko, 'Holes in the Silk: Investor Protection under China's Belt and Road Initiative' (2019) 14 Global Trade and Customs Journal 5 (discussing the issues that investors face when using BITs in force between China and countries that belong to the BRI.
51 *cfr* Dini Sejko, Sovereign Investors as ICSID Claimants: Lessons from the Drafting Documents and the Case Law, (2023) Vanderbilt Journal of Transnational Law, (forthcoming) examining in section 4.3 claims brought by investors that do not operate on a commercial basis, and in section 4.5 analysing the protection of Chinese investors, see also Anatole Boute, Economic Statecraft and Investment Arbitration, 40 University of Pennsylvania Journal of International Law 2019.
52 China–Australia BIT 1986.
53 Agreement between the Government of the United Kingdom of Great Britain and Northern Ireland and the Government of the People's Republic of China Concerning the Promotion and Reciprocal Protection of Investments (15 May 1986) ('China–UK BIT').
54 Stephan W Schill, 'Tearing Down the Great Wall: the New Generation Investment Treaties of the People's Republic of China' (2007) 15 Cardozo J Intl Comp L 73.
55 *cfr* Wenhua Shan, Norah Gallagher and Sheng n 46 at 134.
56 Agreement between the People's Republic of China and the Federal Republic of Germany on the Encouragement and Reciprocal Protection of Investments (1 December 2003, entered into force 11 November 2005) ('China–Germany BIT').
57 Shen Wei, 'Evolution of Nondiscriminatory Standards in China's BITs in the Context of EU-China BIT Negotiations,' (2018) Chinese Journal of International Law 799–840.
58 Deutsche Bank AG v. Democratic Socialist Republic of Sri Lanka, ICSID Case No. ARB/09/2, 31 October 2012, para 420.
59 China–Kuwait 1986.
60 China–Uzbekistan 2011 article 5.2.
61 I wish to reiterate here that all enterprises registered in China in accordance with law are Chinese enterprises...China will treat foreign-invested enterprises and local companies equally and fairly in government procurement. China's Wen Promises Fair Play for Foreign Investors', Reuters (13 September 2010) <https://www.reuters.com/article/china-investment-wen-idUSTOE68C08620100913> accessed 18 April 2022.

PART IV

Transnational Engagement

19

CHINA'S COMPARATIVE CONSTITUTION*

Ngoc Son Bui

Introduction

In his seminal book *Comparative Matters,* published in 2014, Ran Hirschl lamented that mainstream comparative constitutional law has focused on "a handful of 'usual suspect' settings that are mainly of the western, liberal-democratic breed."[1] China has been marginalized in the field for this reason. Wen-Chen Chang and David Law observe that: "Perusal of the English-language comparative constitutional law literature leaves the vague impression that there has been as much written on Singapore—an independent city-state with roughly the population of greater Miami—as on China, home to one-fifth of the world's population and a growing economy to match." [2]

Recent years, however, have witnessed comparative constitutional law's greater engagements with China. Chinese constitutional experience has been discussed by leading constitutional comparatists, published in major law reviews and journals,[3] and included in important collections.[4]

In addition to comparative literature, a growing body of English language country studies provides detailed treatments on China's constitutional issues.[5] These national accounts have comparative implications.

This chapter seeks to explain how and why comparative constitutional law scholarship has had greater engagement with China's constitution than the previous periods. It also discusses the comparative implications of the national accounts of China's constitution. This chapter focuses on the relevant English language scholarship in the last five years.[6] It adopts a functional definition of "constitution" to denote "a larger set of constitutional elements," including the written text, theories, traditions, aspirations, and interpretations.[7] In this sense, the term "Constitution" with the large-C refers to China's constitutional text, while the term "constitution" with the small-c refers to China's larger constitutional order.

This study is drawn on Hirschl's formulation of modes and factors of comparative constitutional inquiry. The modes include single-country studies, concept formation,

* This chapter has been published as Bui Ngoc Son, 'China's Comparative Constitution' (2021) 54 Vanderbilt Journal of Transnational Law 1-29.

DOI: 10.4324/9781003128243-23

inference-oriented small-N studies (with the most similar, most different, most difficult, prototypical, and outlier cases principles), and large-N studies.[8] According to Hirschl, comparative constitutional engagement is driven by three analytically distinct but possibly intersecting factors, namely: *necessity* or the need for political and legal development; *inquisitiveness* or intellectual curiosity and quest to explore and explain the unknown; and *politics* or comparative engagement as the instrument to promote certain political agenda, worldview, ideology, or conceptions of good society.[9] In addition to modes and factors, this study contends that it is important to explore the conditions for comparative engagements with China's constitution. These conditions involve the changing context of China's constitution and the changing state of comparative constitutional law.

On that epistemological and methodological base, this Article argues that the comparative engagements with China's constitution are due to the increasing sociopolitical significance of the country's constitutional text and the institutional trend of its living constitutional order; and the recent jurisdictional, substantive, and epistemological expansion of comparative constitutional law. The comparative engagements are principally animated by the constitutional intellectuals' curiosity to explore the unknown regarding China's constitutional dynamics. But the engagements are also partially driven by the need of China's constitutional development and particular outlooks on constitutional justice.

The remainder of this chapter is structured as follows: Part II explores national and comparative accounts of China's constitution, Part III explains the conditions and factors of comparative constitutional law's engagement with China's constitution, and Part IV concludes.

China's Constitution Compared

This Part reviews some recent national accounts of China's constitution and discusses their comparative implications. It then explores, in a critical way, various modes of comparative inquiry into China's constitution.

Country-Studies

Overview

A rich body of English language country studies canvasses a range of Chinese constitutional issues. Numerous papers on Chinese constitutional law have appeared in national, regional, and comparative outlets, such as the *Chinese Journal of Comparative Law*, the *Hong Kong Law Journal*, and the *Tsinghua China Law Review*, among others. Several nonlegal periodicals focusing on China, such as the *Modern China, The China Journal*, and the *China Review*, have also published scholarship on Chinese constitutional issues and their relations to the broader social and political milieu. Last but not least, Chinese constitutional issues have been discussed in recent collections dealing with Chinese law reform[10] generally or on constitutional development[11] particularly.

Such country studies provide readers a deep understanding of China's constitutional system, different aspects of its constitutional history.[12] Such inquiries also explore China's contemporary specific constitutional institutions, practices, dynamics, such as the 2013 constitutionalism debate,[13] the 2018 constitutional amendments,[14] constitutional legitimacy,[15] judicialization of the constitution,[16] constitutional enforcement,[17] and constitutional education.[18] These county studies contain some comparative elements and resonate with recent debate in comparative constitutional law. From a functional perspective, it can be said that that the constitutional problems (e.g., design, constitutionalism, and identity) confronting China may be the common constitutional problems. To illustrate, consider the three books below.

Constitution Making, Constitutionalism, and Identity

The book *Chinese Legal Culture and Constitutional Order,* written by Chinese-American political scientist Shiping Hua, provides a comprehensive treatment of constitution making in China.[19] It divides China's constitution making and reform into six periods: late Qing (e.g., the *Imperial Constitutional Outline*); Republican (e.g., the 1946 constitution of the Republic of China or ROC); early People's Republic of China or PRC (e.g., 1954 Constitution); Maoist (e.g., 1975 Constitution); the Dengist (e.g., the current 1982 Constitution); and the four constitutional amendments in 1988, 1993, 1999, and 2004.[20] Hua argues that constitutional reforms in China are shaped by Chinese legal culture's four common elements, namely, pragmatism, statism, instrumentalism, and favoritism. He contends that legal and constitutional reforms were based on political elites' practical consideration and used as the tool to strengthen the state and to grant or withdraw rights to citizens depending on circumstances.[21] The book offers useful contextual knowledge on the cultural, social, political, and economic conditions of Chinese constitutional change. Although it is primarily a country study, it includes some horizontal comparisons (with Meiji, US, and Soviet constitutions), and vertical comparisons (e.g., the 1982 and 1954 constitutions).[22]

Another important book, *Chinese Constitutionalism in a Global Context* by Peng Chengyi, a Chinese political science scholar in Beijing, is a comprehensive exploration of Chinese contemporary debate on constitutionalism.[23] The debate has a long history in China but reached wider popular platforms (newspapers and the internet) in 2013, triggered by President Xi Jinping's statement on the implementation of the Constitution.[24] Chengyi identifies three approaches in Chinese constitutionalism debate: Western liberal, Confucian, and Marxist. He documents two waves in the spread of Western liberal constitutionalism in China: the first wave during late Qing and early republic periods and the second or contemporary wave starting from the reform era.[25] Driven by the concern of political freedom, advocates of Western liberal constitutionalism called for free elections, institutional checks and balances, the rule of law, human rights protection, and constitutional supremacy.[26]

The liberal constitutional discourse generated a traditionalist reaction—the Confucian approach. The advocates of Confucian constitutionalism believe that the liberal constitutional proposals "all lack native features."[27] Consequently, some descriptive accounts explored constitutional ideas and institutions (e.g., institutional checks on royal power through remonstrance and censorship, *li*, or propriety as a system of fundamental rules and norms) in Chinese Confucian tradition, while other normative accounts proposed a model of constitutionalism for future China, rooted in Confucian philosophy.[28] Particularly, Jiang Qing submitted a normative model of Confucian constitutional order characterized by, among others, a bicameral legislature (Confucian, national, and common houses) as the institutional embodiment of triple sources of constitutional legitimacy (Heaven, national culture, and the people).[29] Like the liberal approach, the Confucian approach implicitly or explicitly denies the legitimacy of the existing socialist constitutional system in China.

Another critical reaction to the liberal model is the so-called Sinicized Marxist Constitutionalism.[30] China's legal reforms and socioeconomic development in the last three decades have generated the nationalist sources for the intellectual normative accounts of the Chinese socialist way of constitutionalism, rather than copying the Western liberal model.[31] The nationalist discourse on the socialist or Marxist model, however, is diverse. Some Chinese scholars underlined the idea of the Communist Party of China under the rule of law. Other Chinese intellectuals stressed the party-state structure with the orthodox ideology, while political authority and pro-government scholars advocated for the triple combination of the party's leadership, people's sovereignty, and the rule of law.[32]

Chengyi notes that, by 2017, Chinese constitutionalism debate "is still going on with neither side convincing the other side, which is a well reflection of the ideological nature of the debate."[33] While his book focuses on national debates on constitutionalism, it includes some elements of comparison. The book compares different approaches to constitutionalism in Chinese discourse. In addition, it also compares the Chinese discourse with other East Asian discourses, such as the Korean debates on Confucian constitutionalism.[34]

Another important book, *The Constitutional Identity of Contemporary China* by Han Zhai, a lecturer at Wuhan University, argues that unitary system defines today's Chinese constitutional identity or aspirational and viable fundamental constitutional features.[35] This unitary system is characterized by three elements: regional autonomy (e.g., Hong Kong) within the "one-country, two systems" arrangement, the pragmatic legislative and fiscal decentralization within a unitary state, and the separation of the state and the Communist Party within the one party system.[36] Although this book focuses more on the "contextual analysis" of Chinese constitutional arrangements,[37] it also discusses European and American debates on constitutional identity and comparative experience of autonomous subnational units (e.g., United Kingdom, Netherlands, and Spain).

Comparative Implications

Hua's book resonates with recent debate on comparative constitution making and constitutional amendments. To illustrate, the book's discussion of Western and Japanese influences on late Qing's constitutional reforms, American influence on the 1946 ROC constitution, and the Soviet influence on the PRC 1954 Constitution echoes the global debate on the transnational and international influences on constitution making.[38] The debate on the involvement of various sectors of the global community in domestic constitution making and the diffusion of constitutional ideas tends to focus on recent practices under in the globalizing era. But the Chinese story indicates that transnational constitution making and diffusion may have a rich history, and hence comparative study of transnational constitutional history is an important enterprise which deserves further attention.

In addition, the main argument in Hua's book resonates with the Xenophon Contiades and Alkmene Fotiadou's *pragmatic model* of amendments defined by smooth, efficient, and incremental formal change to the constitutions within an entrenched clause guaranteed by courts.[39] The Chinese experience, however, suggests that pragmatic constitutional amendments may not be limited to the institutional settings with judicial protection of unamendable contents of the constitutions. Incremental constitutional change is possible within the constitutional ambit constructed by political elites and social and political conditions.[40]

Chengyi's book echoes and complicates the global debate in comparative constitutionalism. Mark Tushnet has recently called for "pluralizing the category of constitutionalism"[41] and identified the varieties of constitutionalism, including the liberal, social-democratic, authoritarian, and Islamic varieties.[42] At a global level, the emergence of various non-liberal forms of constitutionalism[43] has animated the pluralist discourse on constitutionalism. The Chinese debates present the local embodiment of the pluralist discourse on the varieties of constitutionalism. Particularly, the nationalist, critical response on liberal constitutionalism in Chinese discourse resonates with "the coming demise of liberal constitutionalism," which is also rooted in nationalist sentiments.[44] The arguable crisis of liberal constitutionalism in the global scale may render it less attractive in local intellectual discourse, in turn, potentially serving as the empirical base for local political, nationalist justifications of alternative constitutional forms.

Together with Islamic and Buddhist varieties,[45] the Chinese and East Asian discourse on the Confucian variety may complement the comparative inquiry into the traditional and transcendent dimensions of constitutionalism.[46] There are three possible lines of positivist inquiry: theory, design, and adjudication.

The first of these lines—the theoretical exploration of constitutional ideas in Confucian philosophy—may add to comparative constitutional theory. To illustrate, in a recent book, Sungmoon Kim explores two competing theories by two classical Confucians. The first theory—Mencius's "virtue constitutionalism"—features the idea of political virtue as the base for legitimate power and rests on the belief in the good nature of human's being. The second—Xunzi's "ritual constitutionalism"—underlines the observation of ritual institutions as the source of legitimate power and stems from the conviction on the evil nature of human being.[47] Comparatively, the concerns of virtue ethics and propriety are not unique to Confucian constitutional theory. Richard H. Fallon, Jr. discusses constitutional legitimacy as "a function of moral justifiability or respect-worthiness" and argues that "[e]ven if a regime or decision enjoys broad support, or if a decision is legally correct, it may be illegitimate under a moral concept if morally unjustified."[48] Similarly, Ronald Dworkin "brings political morality into the heart of constitutional law."[49] Political morality seems to be the shared concern of various constitutional theories. To be sure, the substantive contents of political morality are different in different constitutional theories, and one function of comparative constitutional theory is to explore these substantive variations, which include human dignity associated with individual rights or governmental duty to serve the common good.

Second, the Confucian traditional values (particularly "filial piety, respect for elders, ancestor worship, ritual propriety, and social harmony"[50]) inform contemporary constitutional design. In China, this is particularly implied in the incorporation of the idea of "harmony"—the core of Confucian morality—in China's constitutional preamble through the 2018 amendment.[51] In South Korea, the Constitution stipulates the state's duty "to sustain and develop the cultural heritage and to enhance national culture"[52]; this implies that the state's reservation of Confucian culture is a major part of Korean culture.[53] This has implications for positivist comparative inquiry into constitutional design in pluralist societies. Comparative constitutional design is not merely about rules and institutions but is also concerned with the way various sources of ideas and values are expressed in constitution making. In societies with Confucian traditions, the constitutions may express the Confucian values.

Third, Confucian values do not merely implicate constitutional design: but they also inform the manner, style, and even substantive contents of constitutional adjudication. To illustrate, as Ginsburg early demonstrated, the remonstrant manner in the operation of constitutional courts in Korea and Taiwan was connected to the Confucian tradition.[54] In a case in 2011, involving a daughter's suing her mother for being abused for over 40 years, the Korean Constitutional Court even explicitly referred to the Confucian values in the substantive contents of its decision to uphold the Criminal Procedure Act's provision prohibiting criminal accusation against one's lineal ascendants.[55] The dominant opinion wrote:

> The current provision is based on our historical ideology of "hyo," or the Confucian tradition of filial piety, which imposed on children to duty to take care of the parents or grandparents. According to this tradition, it is a good custom for a child to endure harm caused by his or her parents or grandparents; filing a criminal complaint against one's parents or grandparents is regarded as a behavior against morality.[56]

Thus, the Confucian value of filial piety explicitly informs the substantive contents of constitutional adjudication. More recently, focusing on the Korean Constitutional Court's 2017 decision to uphold President Park Geun-hye's impeachment, Kim Sungmoon explains the association of the Confucian ideas with the Court's jurisprudence was "characterized by highly moralistic language and style of reasoning."[57] Confucian values coexist with alternative constitutional values, and this disharmony animates constitutional dynamics in East Asia, as Gary J. Jacobsohn early anticipated.[58] In this regard, the Confucian discourse may add to general, comparative study of constitutional identity.

Let us now turn to the comparative implications of Zhai's book on Chinese constitutional identity. The cores of the Chinese constitutional system discussed in the book are intimately connected to the socialist constitutional principles. Particularly, these elements are defined by the socialist principle of "democratic centralism," which enables vertical and horizontal distribution of public power within a centralized party-state.[59] The broader evolution of Chinese constitutional identity is shaped by the dissonant interactions of liberal, socialist, and Confucian constitutional aspirations. In addition, the contextual Chinese constitutional knowledge presented in the book complicates comparative constitutional identity. Comparative accounts of constitutional identity tend to focus on the liberal constitutional states, which are limited to fundamental structures defined by liberal aspirations.[60] A non-liberal state may also acquire a constitutional identity driven by the dynamic interchanges of liberal and non-liberal constitutional ideals.

Concept Formation

Several comparatists created new analytical concepts to understand China's constitution. To illustrate, consider two concepts, namely "constitutional entrepreneurs" and "constitutional dissonance."

Mark Jia creates the concept of constitutional entrepreneurship to explain successful constitutional advocacy in China.[61] The concept is empirically informed by two cases during the tenure of President Hu Jintao (2002–2012), "a period of relative policy stability conducive to comparative inquiry."[62] The first case involves advocacy surrounding the "Sun Zhigang incident," in which three legal scholars argued for the unconstitutionality of the system of detention and, in turn, influenced the abolition of this system.[63] The second case concerns Peking University's Marxist Professor Gong Xiantian's use of constitutional argumentation and popular pressure to influence the enactment of a national property law.[64] *Jia's* study is based on both his personal interviews with the constitutional advocates and on primary written materials.[65]

Jia's concept formation is based on the integration of several existing theories on grassroot constitutional and policy dynamics, such as popular constitutionalism, adaptive authoritarianism, and theories of policy process.[66] Jia states that "[c]onstitutional entrepreneurship is both an advocacy strategy and an explanatory theory."[67] The theory includes a generalized set of positions that both explain Chinese constitutional advocacy and guide ordinary Chinese citizens to use constitutional argument to shape policy.[68]

The theory of constitutional entrepreneurship sees constitutional advocates as policy entrepreneurs.[69] Their work is entrepreneurial in the sense that they construct new constitutional arguments like "a fundamentally creative enterprise"[70] to influence policy. The lifecycle of constitutional entrepreneurship is divided into four stages: *incubation* or advocates' adoption of a coherent policy position and the commitment to legal argument; *disruption* or the moment opening the window for raising the profile of their policy; *mobilization* or advocate of the broader populations; and *recalibration* or the state's adjustment under the pressure by incorporating the proposals mobilized by the advocates.[71] *Jia's model features several strategies and conditions for the success of constitutional advocacy. These include the use of constitutional, rather than ideological or policy-specific, arguments to achieve target policies; the* collaboration with media organizations, particularly the internet, to spread the message to the broader population; and the "locat[ion] and exploit[ation] [of] internal divisions inside the state."[72]

Jia's concept of constitutional entrepreneurship is connected to the comparative constitutional inquiry's recent turn to social mobilization. In his recent book, Bruce Ackerman examines the role of a mobilizing citizenry with "high-energy politics" in the constitutional revolutions that took place in India, South Africa, France, and Italy.[73] *Jia's concept suggests that the comparative inquiry into social mobilization for constitutional change is not necessarily accompanied by* the heightened engagement of the broader society. Constitutional mobilization can occur at a micro-level with low-energy politics, which involves the society's narrow sectors. This kind of micro-mobilization does not result in constitutional revolutions but renders the constitutions socially meaningful even under authoritarian settings.

Jia's concept can be further refined by considering the way in which constitutional entrepreneurs are influenced by broader structural opportunities. Why do constitutional advocates operate in an entrepreneurial manner rather than turn to higher energy politics (e.g., social movements)? Among other factors (e.g., resources), the lack of specific structural opportunities, such as the window of constitution making or amendments,[74] limits the substantive scope and defines the entrepreneurial manner of constitutional advocacy. In addition, the general structural opportunity defined by the authoritarian control of citizens' political activities prompts constitutional advocates to use entrepreneurial tactics.

The related concept of "constitutional dissonance" is put forward by Chang Wen-Chen and David Law. This concept denotes the idea that the gap between the constitutional text and practice creates "*constructive irritant*" or "the resulting state of deep tension and contradiction furnishes the intellectual material and generates the dialectic needed for transformation of the constitutional order."[75] On that base, Chang and Law argue that China's Constitution functions as an irritant in the sense that its gap (between text and practice) generates the space for normative and meaningful constitutional discourse and argumentation which the regime cannot ignore.[76] Two stories in *Jia's study illustrate these discursive dynamics.*

Chang and Law's concept of constitutional dissonance echoes Jacobsohn's concept of "constitutional disharmony."[77] Both concepts suggest that gap between constitutional texts and practices is the sources of constitutional dynamics. However, there are two important differences. First, while Jacobsohn recognizes two aspects of constitutional disharmony (internal and external), he focuses more the former: the dissonant constitutional commitments within a constitution.[78] Chang and Law are more concerned with the external dimension: the gap between the constitution and its practice. Second, while the three scholars recognize that constitutional disharmony or dissonance is universal, Jacobsohn explores this phenomenon specifically in the context of constitutionalist regimes, while Chang and Law focus on authoritarian regimes.

The concept of constitutional dissonance can be further explored. In addition to the external gaps, the dissonance internal to the constitution can also create the space for constitutional mobilization and discourse. To illustrate, China's Constitution is replete with ambiguities, such as the socialist rule of law, human rights, and civic virtues, which provide a wide space for different interpretative dynamics. The meanings of these constitutional provisions are not merely determined by the party-state; rather, they can be also influenced by social constitutional discourse and mobilization. Discursive and mobilizing dynamics animated by internal and external dissonances may generate some constitutional qualities of authoritarian regimes, such as legislative protection of constitutional rights.

Causal Inference

Several comparative explanatory accounts of China's constitution display aspects of the principles of case selection in inference-oriented small-N (or micro) comparative studies, although not all of these studies are principled in this line by research design.

Consider first China's constitutional divergence from the *most similar case*: Vietnam. Both countries share the same socialist legal system, socialist constitutional system under the leadership of a communist party, and socialist market economy. Despite that, comparative political studies have, for years, explored institutional divergence (particularly, the representativeness and competitiveness of elite political institutions) between the two countries.[79] On comparative constitutional scholarship, Fu Hualing and Jason Buhi have recently discussed the divergent constitutional trends; they argue that "Vietnam is presently moving in a direction that offers more prospects for convergence with international norms, as the current Vietnamese party-state is relatively less politically monolithic, more open to the influence of international laws and more tolerant of civil society than its Chinese counterpart."[80] To illustrate, they demonstrate that "whereas Vietnam appears to be liberalising [sic] its perspective on consultation, input and debate since 2013, China has opted to go in the opposite direction, rendering the terms 'constitutionalism', 'civil society' and 'judicial independence' (among others) taboo in academic discourse."[81] This qualitative observation complicates Law's quantitative grouping of China and Vietnam together among the top of statist constitutional preambles (first and third respectively).[82] Beyond the convergent preambles, the real dynamics of constitutional rules, institutions, and debates indicate the following: Vietnam's constitutional trend tends to move toward the universalist direction to gain international legitimacy, while China's constitutional trend tends to be more static due to the exceptionalist aspiration to develop an alternative model to the Western liberal and universalist models.[83]

Other studies explain China's unexpected constitutional similarities to the countries to which it is *most different*, such as the United States and the United Kingdom. Yan Lin and Ginsburg argue that due to the lack of judicial constitutional review in China, the Chinese Constitution is interpreted through the law-making process of the Standing Committee of the National People's Congress in major areas, such as distribution of governmental power, citizens' rights, and the economic structure.[84] China's legislative constitutional interpretation shares a similar feature with the constitutional dialogue between the legislature and courts in what Stephen Gardbaum called the "New Commonwealth" (Canada, New Zealand, and the United Kingdom) model.[85] Constitutional interpretation by statutes in China has also resonated with the American "age of the 'republic of statutes' in which sub-constitutional legislation plays a central role in articulating fundamental norms."[86] In another study, Lin further explores the common feature of legislative constitutional interpretation that China shares with other liberal constitutional democracies.[87]

China's constitution also is the *most difficult case* for the recent theoretical prediction that authoritarianism in the twenty-first century relies on legal and constitutional tools rather than personal fiats.[88] The case of China may challenge this claim. Carl F. Minzner argues that "[i]n the early twenty-first century, Chinese authorities turned against law," *citing* party political control over the judiciary, cracking down on public interest lawyers, and curtailing the influence of foreign rule-of-law norms.[89] *However, in a recent contribution,* Taisu Zhang and Ginsburg put forward an antithesis: "China's turn toward law."[90] They argue that China has institutionalized the court system and increasingly engaged with the Constitution, including the 2018 amendments, to institutionalize political functions.[91] According to Zhang and Ginsburg, this legal and institutional trend is due to both the regime's top-down commitment to bureaucratic legalization and the citizens' bottom-up attachment of sociopolitical legitimacy to law and legal institutions.[92] This argument is situated within the comparative literature on the empowerment of courts and constitutions in authoritarian regimes.[93] Zhang and Ginsburg conclude that "[t]he Chinese case adds much to our understanding of authoritarian legality."[94] This conclusion, however, does not assume that there is "a rise of 'constitutionalism' in Chinese politics" because its authors believe that "[t]here is little evidence to suggest that the Party leadership has internalized the normative authority of the Constitution in any fashion."[95] Thomas E. Kellogg holds the same skeptical view, arguing that China's Constitution functions as a "false blueprint" to legitimize the party's rule "by maintaining the political fiction that China is transitioning to constitutional governance."[96] China's engagement with the Constitution, however, validates the claim on the legality of authoritarianism in the twenty-first century.

Different from the above skeptical views, other comparative accounts contextualize China as a *prototypical case* of authoritarian constitutionalism. Consider first the general features of authoritarian constitutionalism. Using Singapore as an original case, Tushnet generalizes authoritarian constitutionalism as a regime that "is controlled by a dominant party"; "does not arrest political opponents arbitrarily"; "allows reasonably open discussion and criticism of its policies"; "operates reasonably free and fair election"; "is sensitive to public opinion and alters its policies at least on occasion in response to what it perceives to be public views"; "may develop mechanisms to ensure that the amount of dissent does not exceed the level it regards as desirable"; and renders courts "reasonably independent and enforce basic rule-of-law requirements reasonably well."[97] Chang and Law contend that categories of authoritarian constitutionalism "are capable of encompassing China."[98] In a contribution to a comparative study on authoritarian constitutionalism, Michael W. Dowdle explores the "routinized" practices (e.g., legislative hearings, the bureaucratic process of legislative drafting, administrative legislation, judicial professionalism, and public interest litigations) as the "infrastructural" source of constitutional evolution of the Chinese state.[99] These practices are closer to the rule of law than constitutionalism; rather than impose institutional limitations on the decision makers, they are a means for the decision makers to ensure the legality of the work of government officials and judges.

Constitutionalism and authoritarianism are not clearly bifurcated institutional configurations. Partial authoritarian practices may emerge within a stable constitutionalist polity[100]; conversely, partial constitutionalist practices may emerge within a stable authoritarian polity. Authoritarian constitutionalism as a stable hybrid regime and partial constitutionalist practices under authoritarianism are conceptually distinct. An authoritarian regime defined as "a regime-level commitment to a set of practices that help unfetter rule through undermining institutions that hold ultimate decisionmakers accountable"[101] may partially embrace some constitutionalist practices, but it is not equated to authoritarian constitutionalism. In this regard, China may embrace partial constitutionalist practices that place institutional limitations on the ultimate decision makers, but this does not necessarily amount to authoritarian constitutionalism.

Cuban-American legal scholar Larry Catá Backer even moves further to create a theory of Chinese party-state constitutionalism as an *outlier* of comparative constitutionalism.[102] He rejects the Western approaches to China's constitution, arguing that "Chinese constitutionalism cannot be approached as a variant of a Western project grounded in the fundamental premise that the constitution of a state represents the culmination of a process of managing all of the political authority."[103] He then proposes the theory of Chinese party-state constitutionalism, which is defined by the two interrelated but distinct spheres of authority—namely, political authority and administrative obligation—and the concomitant coexistence of two constitutions.[104] The political authority is vested in the leading communist party and constrained by the party's constitution (the political constitution), while the state constitution expresses the political constitution's values and objectives, regulates government administration, and limits individuals' arbitrary use of power.[105]

Backer's theory is both normative and explanatory. As an explanatory model, it has implications for inference-oriented comparative inquiries into China's constitution. It explains why China's Constitution has changed to institutionalize the directions put forward by the party's constitution. For example, the 2018 constitutional amendment's incorporation of Xi Jinping Thought follows the same move in the 2017 amendments to the party's constitution.[106] The party's constitution is, therefore, not separate from China's living constitution. Comparatively, the political parties' constitutional function is not unique to China but is common in living constitutional orders in multiparty systems.[107] However, in contrast to the political parties in multiparty democracies, the Communist Party in China is not an electoral party: it is not an institution of the civil society created to compete for power through competitive elections. Rather, it is constitutionally mandated by a living and recently textual norm as the leading force of the socialist regime, making it a constitutional institution inseparable from the state.

Large-N Studies

China's constitution has often been referred to as an illustrating case in large-N comparative constitutional studies. In an earlier macro-study on the right to resist in the world's constitutions, scholars discussed this right within the context of Chinese political-legal tradition.[108] They demonstrate that the idea of a right to resist is associated with Mencius, a Chinese Confucian philosopher, who believes that when the rulers lost the Mandate of Heaven, as "reflected in the rise of natural disasters, wars, or economic difficulties," the people's resistance to commands of the rulers is justified.[109] They conclude that "[t]he Chinese tradition thus included the seeds of a right to resist, though the idea did not fully blossom as it did in the era of the French and American revolutions."[110] Hence, Chinese legal-political concepts are historically contextualized in the macro-comparative study of a constitutional right.

In a recent macro-study of the world's constitutional preambles, Law uses the Chinese constitutional preamble to epitomize the statist constitutional archetype and compares it with Australia's liberal preamble.[111] He demonstrates that China's constitutional preamble "offers nothing less than a social, political, and economic history of the Chinese people, much of which amounts to their glorious struggle under the tutelage of great leaders against a parade of maladies and injustices," and that "the Chinese preamble also takes care to equate the Chinese people with the Chinese state."[112]

The Chinese case has been recurrently discussed in the recent large-N study ("2020 Study"), in which Versteeg and her collaborators explore a range of constitutional strategies of presidential term-limit evasion used by 234 incumbents in 106 countries since the year 2000. Particularly, they indicate that constitutional amendment is the most common strategy, as it comprised 60 percent of all evasion attempts and 40 percent of successful cases. They identify two ingredients—president's power and the ease of amendments—as essential for the successful use of amendments to evade term limits, and the Chinese case is repeatedly used to illustrate the success.[113] This Article will focus on the 2020 Study to consider the possibility and the limits in the way China's constitution is integrated into large-N comparative constitutional inquiry.[114]

Term limits were first established in China's Constitution in 1982 and are attributed to Deng Xiaoping's intention to break through one-man rule after the Mao years.[115] Article 79 of the original Constitution provides that "[t]he term of office of the President and Vice-President of the People's Republic of China is the same as that of the National People's Congress, and they shall serve no more than two consecutive terms."[116] In March 2018, China's National People's Congress adopted a package of constitutional amendments, which included, among other things, the deletion of the second sentence in that provision, effectively abolishing term limits to the President and the Vice

President.[117] This move has generated much controversial debate both inside and outside China; supporters believe that term-limit deletion is consistent with China's needs—particularly to continue Xi's anti-corruption campaign[118]—while critics considered this "a drawback and a means for President Xi to stay in power forever."[119] Term-limit deletion through formal constitutional amendment in China is consistent with the prevailing claim that formal constitutional amendment is the most common way of term-limit evasion in the world. This explains why the China case is used as an illustrating case in the 2020 Study.

The 2020 Study demonstrates that the removal of term limits in China's 2018 constitutional amendment was smooth and successful, "with essentially no opposition at all," due to Xi's mass popularity and support.[120] That claim is debatable. Considering unusual secrecy and urgency regarding the Communist Party of China's meetings surrounding the amendment process, Zhang and Ginsburg believe that "there is no evidence to suggest that the removal of constitutional term limits was, in fact, painless or easy. Instead, there is reason to suspect that Xi had actually encountered opposition that was only overcome with some difficulty."[121] Related to the president's power, the 2020 Study also holds that the success of term-limit evasion is due to the fact that the president had sufficient control over the legislature.[122] Perhaps, that the Chinese legislature overwhelmingly approved the amendments with only 2 dissenters[123] generates the impression that the president had sufficient control over this body, and hence the amendments were achieved easily and smoothly. But the final approval at the legislative platform is just the facial manifestation of political elite's internal agreement. In addition, the legislature in China is under the institutional control of the party as a collective entity rather than a single-party leader.[124]

Next, consider the second element of evasion success—the ease of the amendment. The formal rule requires a two-thirds legislative majority for the amendment's approval.[125] This requirement is relatively low compared with other experiences—for example, four-fifths legislative majority or three-fourths legislative majority plus popular referendum.[126] In addition, the two-thirds requirement is easily achievable in China as there is no opposition party in the communist party-controlled legislature. In addition to the procedural features, China has not codified unamendability and hence any changes to the Constitution are constitutionally possible, including term-limit deletion. It seems that China's case is consistent with the theory that amendment's ease is the element (or reason) of evasion success.

However, the amendment practice in China is not merely determined by the formal rule but must be situated within the broader political dynamics. This requires systematic considerations of amendment culture and temporal variability in difficulty to amend the constitution driven by the particularities of the moment.[127] Chinese amendment culture is characterized by the political perception of the Constitution's stability as a desirable condition for the nation's stability and the cautious attitude toward amendments as associated with radical political changes informed by the experience in Eastern Europe.[128] That culture makes amendments difficult to pass despite the ease of formal rules. In fact, since its enactment in 1984, China's Constitution was amended only five times in four decades: 1988, 1993, 1999, 2004, and 2018. In addition, temporal variability in amendment difficulty is considerable; there are four amendments in 14 years (from 1988 to 2004), but there is only one amendment in 16 years (from 2004 to 2018). These amendments are shaped by the particularities of the moment. The 1988 and 1993 amendments were shaped by the context of the domestic reformist era when China opened the country in the early stage, while the 1999 and 2004 amendments were associated with the particularities of the globalizing era when the country joined the global market, including the WTO.[129] The 2018 amendment of the exceptional moment occurred when China was rising as the global power and had become confident to move its own way in the course of development, which differed from the Western models of development. The 2018 amendments are a part of Chinese constitutional exceptionalism. Particularly, term-limit deletion expresses the exceptional attitude that China does not follow the Western constitutional model of limited government.[130]

While the 2020 Study identifies interesting global constitutional trends regarding term-limit evasion, it treats the Chinese case, to borrow Hirschl's words, "much like a doctor in a triage system treats patients: with empathy and urgency, but ultimately in a distant, composed fashion."[131] The consequence is that this macro study overlooks micro contextual dynamics surrounding China's term-limit evasion through constitutional amendments.

Explaining Comparative Engagements

This Part seeks to explain why the field of comparative constitutional law has had greater engagements with China's constitution than previous periods. These comparative engagements, which are conditioned by the dynamics of both China's constitution and of comparative constitutional law, are mainly animated by the curiosity and quest to understand China's constitutional dynamics, and, to some extent, China's practical need to develop its constitutional system and particular views about constitutional justice.

Conditions

The Dynamics of China's Constitution

The comparative constitutional law scholarship's engagements with China are conditioned by the increasing dynamics of China's constitution. The marginalization of China in comparative constitutional law is largely due to the relegation of China's Constitution as a sham text.[132] However, in recent years, China's Constitution has been increasingly relevant to the real politics and the society. Zhang and Ginsburg demonstrate that China's Constitution "already carries much more political weight than scholars have previously given it credit for, indeed at the highest levels of the party-state, and that recent developments have only further bolstered its influence and significance."[133] The recent developments include the Xi Jinping-era political discourse, which enhanced the Constitution's sociopolitical salience, and the 2018 constitutional amendments, which displayed the attachment to the Constitution as the source of sociological legitimacy.[134] Zhang and Ginsburg paid greater attention to China's Constitution as they realized the greater political significance of the document.

China's Constitution is not only politically but also socially relevant. The 2013 constitutionalism debate and earlier constitutional advocacy indicate that China's Constitution is increasingly socially relevant to public discourse and mobilization. The same constitutional text has different significances to the party-state and the society. Political leaders may attack political discourse and functions to the constitution to consolidate the legal foundation of the legitimacy of the party-state. But public intellectual discourse and social mobilization seek to realize the Constitution's normative commitments, such as human rights and the rule of law. The public discourse and mobilization render the Constitution socially significant. The Constitution's social and political significance makes it a discursive site for comparative constitutional engagement.

Timing is relevant. The 2013 constitutionalism debate and the 2018 amendments provide particularly important sources for comparative constitutional engagements with China in the last five years. By 2013, the constitutionalism debate did not merely occur within the Chinese intellectual community but also reached the broader community via social media, which drew comparative attention. In addition, the 2018 amendments attracted comparative inquiry partially because they were domestically extensive and partially because they echoed international constitutional phenomena in recent years (e.g., the rise of constitutional authoritarianism generally and term-limit evasion particularly).

Apart from the increasing importance of the constitutional text, the dynamics of the Chinese living constitution generates the condition for comparative engagement. The dynamics include the increasing institutionalization of the state and the party. The new bureaucracy emerging in China since the beginning of the reforms in 1978 corresponded to "the massive shift from a centrally planned economy to a more open and marketized one."[135] The administrative government in China today "is centralized, massive, and extraordinary complex."[136] The country's National People's Congress, an unicameral legislature elected every five years, is composed by a standing committee and special committees and included 2,980 members in 2018, making it the largest parliamentary body in the world.[137] The court system has been highly institutionalized, consisting of thousands of district-level basic people's courts (the lowest level courts), staffed by 146,000 judges; hundreds of prefecture-level intermediate people's courts, staffed by 36,000 judges; 31 provincial-level high people's courts, staffed by 7,000 judges; and the Supreme People's Court at the central level, staffed by more than 500 judges, in addition to specialist courts.[138] These institutional dynamics generate sources for comparative constitutional engagement with China.

As Backer and He Xin indicate,[139] the Communist Party of China is an internal part of the Chinese living constitutional order. Like the state, the Communist Party in China has been highly institutionalized. The party has its own Constitution based on the Leninist principle of "democratic centralism," which allows for the combination of a collective leadership and "division of labor" among the party members.[140] To maintain its ruling capacity and its legitimacy, the party has complex institutional structures at the central level (the National Congress, Political Bureau, Central Committee, Standing Committee, and other specific committees) and a web of local party cells.[141] Some doubted that under Xi's era the party retuned to personalistic rule.[142] Other studies, however, have demonstrated the party's institutionalization under Xi-era, including establishment of a National Security Commission, the reorganization of the party leadership of the People's Liberation Army, the reorganization of the various civilian maritime security agencies, and the establishment of the Cybersecurity and Informatization Leading Small Group.[143] The party's institutional dynamics create the conditions for comparative political-constitutional studies, as indicated the work by Backer, Zhang, and Ginsburg.

The Dynamics of Comparative Constitutional Law

Comparative constitutional law's jurisdictional, substantive, and epistemological expansion creates the condition for the field's greater engagements with China's constitution. First, in the last few years, comparative constitutional law has incrementally expanded its jurisdictional scope beyond the Western or similar institutional settings.[144] For example, the *International Society of Public Law* was held in Asia (Hong Kong) for the first time in 2018, and correspondingly the *International Journal of Constitutional Law* published an issue focusing on Asia.[145] The jurisdictional expansion prompts comparative constitutionalists to reach out to unfamiliar institutional settings, including China.

The second aspect of comparative constitutional law's dynamics concerns the substantive issues of inquiry. The fact that China lacks judicial review disfavors it as a site for comparative constitutional studies, which have been dominated by the questions on courts and their constitutional adjudication.[146] However, in recent years, comparative constitutional inquiry has expanded its substantive scope, discussing a range of nonjudicial issues, including constitution making, constitutional amendments, and political or legislative aspects of constitutionalism.[147] China's recent constitutional experience echoes these comparative issues. Consequently, the field's exploration for nonjudicial issues renders countries without judicial review, like China, attractive sites for comparative inquiry.

The third dimension of the expansion of comparative constitutional law concerns the epistemological underpinnings of constitutional systems. China has been less attractive to comparative constitutional inquiry, in part, because its Constitution is rooted in Leninist-Marxist ideas, while the field has focused on constitutional protection of liberal rights by liberal institutions (such as courts, separation of powers, and other forms of checks and balances), which are intellectually connected to Enlightenment liberalism. However, recent years have witnessed the comparative exposition to various ideational foundations (liberal, neoliberal, and non-liberal) of constitutional systems.[148] Particularly, Tushnet's suggestion of pluralizing the concept of constitutionalism exemplifies the pluralist thinking about constitutional issues in non-liberal terms. Such epistemological expansion enables the field to engage with constitutional systems underpinned by communitarian and socialist ideas, such as those of Singapore and China, respectively.

Factors: Knowledge, Necessities, and Political Views

The comparative constitutional law scholarship's engagements with China are mainly driven by the intellectual curiosity and quest to discover the unknown regarding the dynamics of China's constitution. Why has China's Constitution become more politically important? Is Chinese constitutionalism an oxymoron? How does China implement the Constitution without judicial review? How does China's constitution evolve overtime without frequent formal amendments? Why is the party constitution important for Chinese living constitution?

Most comparative studies of China's constitution involve casual inference—the mode of comparative inquiry that seeks to provide answers for a range of the above curious Chinese constitutional questions. To illustrate, Zhang and Ginsburg sought to provide "the first comprehensive survey of judicial and constitutional developments in the Xi

Jinping era" due to the intellectual drive to understand the "underappreciated features of the party-state" and "how its current structural layout demands higher levels of legality in both the party and the state."[149] Even the studies that create new concepts, such as Jia's constitutional entrepreneurs and Chang and Law's constitutional dissonance, also primarily seek to understand the driving forces (social advocacy and political discourse) of Chinese constitutional dynamics. Macro-studies generally aim to create constitutional knowledge and their engagement with China is also mainly driven by intellectual curiosity: for example, what contributes to China's success with presidential term-limits evasion through constitutional amendments?

Although the discovery of the unexplored constitutional knowledge is the main drive, comparative engagements implicitly or explicitly respond to the practical need for Chinese constitutional development. For example, Jia's concept of constitutional entrepreneurship seeks to both explain and guide Chinese constitutional advocacy.[150] Chang and Law also write that "[t]he marginalization of China as an object of study has deleterious effects not only for the field of comparative constitutional law, but also potentially for the development of constitutionalism in China itself."[151] In this line, their concept of constitutional dissonance not only explains but also facilitates Chinese constitutional development. The normative implication of this concept tends to be that the dynamics of constitutional discourse are a constructive condition for China's constitutional development. In the same vein, Backer's model both explains and advances the Chinese model of party-state constitutionalism.[152]

In addition to knowledge and necessities, some comparative studies of China's constitution are driven by particular political outlooks. To illustrate, Kellogg's critical view of China's Constitution as a "false blueprint" is animated by a liberal view about constitutional justice that is associated with limited government.[153] In contrast, Backer's positive view of the Chinese model of party-state constitutionalism is informed by a socialist outlook on constitutional justice.[154]

Conclusion

This chapter has explained the modes, conditions, and factors of comparative constitutional engagements with China. The comparative engagements with China's constitution, however, should not be overstated. A range of Chinese constitutional questions have not yet been substantively explored and explained within a comparative constitutional framework. Questions for future comparative inquiry into China's constitution include constituent power, participatory constitution making, transnational engagement and resistance in constitution making, the political construction of unconstitutional constitutional amendments, the Constitution's international dimensions, and legislated constitutional rights, among others.

Notes

1 Ran Hirschl, *Comparative Matters: The Renaissance of Comparative Constitutional Law* (OUP 2014) 211.

2 Wen-Chen Chang and David Law, "Constitutional Dissonance in China," in Gary Jacobsohn and Miguel Schor eds., *Comparative Constitutional Theory* (Edward Elgar Publishing 2018) 476, 477.

3 *See, e.g.*, Mila Versteeg, Timothy Horley, Anne Meng, Maurcio Guim and Marilyn Guirguis, "The Law and Politics of Presidential Term Limit Evasion," (2020) 120

Columbia Law Review 173 (discussing term-limit deletion through 2018 constitutional amendments in China); Note, "Dr. Wu's Constitution," (2019) 132 Harvard Law Review 2300; Yan Lin and Tom Ginsburg, "Constitutional Interpretation in Lawmaking: China's Invisible Constitutional Enforcement Mechanism," (2015) 63 American Journal of Comparative Law 467; Yan Lin, "Constitutional Evolution Through Legislation: The Quiet Transformation of China's Constitution," (2015) 13 International Journal of Constitutional Law 61.

4 *See generally* Chang and Law, (note 2) (this collection includes a single chapter on China); Qianfan Zhang, "The Constitution of China," in Roger Masterman and Robert Schütze eds., *The Cambridge Companion to Comparative Constitutional Law* (CUP 2019) 171 (including the China chapter, along with other country-chapters on the US, UK, France, and India that are included in the part on constitutional history); Albert H.Y. Chen, "Constitutions and Values in Three Chinese Societies," in Dennis Davis, Alan Richter and Cheryl Saunders eds., *An Inquiry Into The Existence Of Global Values Through The Lens Of Comparative Constitutional Law* 119 (Hart 2015).

5 *See* Part II.A.

6 For earlier engagements, see generally Randall Peerenboom, "Social Foundations of China's Living Constitution," in Tom Ginsburg ed., *Comparative Constitutional Design* (CUP 2012) 138; Xin He, "The Party's Leadership as a Living Constitution in China," in Tom Ginsburg and Alberto Simpser eds., *Constitutions in Authoritarian Regimes* (CUP 2013) 245.

7 Zachary Elkins, Tom Ginsburg and James Melton, *The Endurance of National Constitutions* (CUP 2009) 36, 39; Walter Murphy, *Constitutional Democracy: Creating and Maintaining a Just Political Order* (Johns Hopkins University Press 2007) 13.

8 Hirschl, (n 1) 244.

9 Ibid. 148–149.

10 *See generally* Yun Zhao and Michael Ng eds., *Chinese Legal Reform and the Global Legal Order: Adoption and Adaptation* (CUP 2017); John Garrick and Yan Chang Bennett eds., *China's Socialist Rule of Law Reforms Under Xi Jinping* (Routledge 2016).

11 *See* Lin Li, Jihong Mo and Guoqiang Zhai eds., *Constitutional Development in China, 1982*–2012 (Springer 2020).

12 *See* Cheng Jie, "Why Late Qing Constitutional Reform Failed: An Examination from the Comparative Institutional Perspective," (2017) 10 *Tsinghua China Law Review* 107.

13 *See generally* Rogier Creemers, "China's Constitutionalism Debate: Content, Context and Implications," (2015) 74 *China Journal* 91; H. Li, "Chinese Discourse on Constitutionalism and Its Impact on Reforms," (2017) 22 Journal of Chinese Political Science 407.

14 *See generally* Feng Lin, "The 2018 Constitutional Amendments," 2019 China Perspectives 11.

15 *See generally* Xie Libin and Haig Patapan, "Contesting Legitimacy in China: The Politics of Law in Modern Chinese Jurisprudence," (2016) 46 Hong Kong Law Journal 991.

16 *See generally* Daniel Sprick, "Judicialization of the Chinese Constitution Revisited: Empirical Evidence from Court Data," (2019) 19 China Review 41.

17 *See generally* Zhai Lin and Guoqiang Zhai, *Report on Constitutional Enforcement and Constitutional Review in China* (China Social Sciences Press 2018).

18 *See generally* Liu Han, "Towards Constitutional Re-Enlightenment: Teaching American Constitutional Law in China," (2016) 9 Tsinghua China Law Review 63.

19 *See generally* Shiping Hua, *Chinese Legal Culture and Constitutional Order* (Routledge 2019).

20 *Ibid.* 5.

21 *Ibid.* 2.

22 *Ibid.* 5.

23 *See generally* Peng Chengyi, *Chinese Constitutionalism in a Global Context* (Routledge 2018).

24 *Ibid.* 1–2.

25 *Ibid.* 21–28.

26 *See ibid.* 29–31.

27 *Ibid.* 68.

28 *See ibid.* 45–54.

29 *See ibid.* 50–51. For Jiang Qing's book, *see generally* Jiang Qing, *A Confucian Constitutional Order: How China's Ancient Past Can Shape Its Political Future* (Daniel Bell and Ruiping Fan eds., Edmund Ryden trans., Princeton University Press 2012), *reviewed in* Maria

Adele Carrai, "Confucianism Reconstructed: The Violence of History and the Making of Constitutionalism in East Asia," (2018) 16 International Journal of Constitutional Law 664, 666. For earlier discussions on his theory, *see generally* Ruiping Fan ed., *The Renaissance of Confucianism in Contemporary China* (Springer 2011).

30 *See* Chengyi, (n 23) 69.

31 *See ibid.* 66.

32 *See ibid.* 84. For socialist constitutionalism, see also Fu Hualing and Zhai Xiaobo, "What Makes the Chinese Constitution Socialist?," (2018) 16 International Journal of Constitutional Law 655, 655; Baogang He, "Socialist Constitutionalism in Contemporary China," in Michael W. Dowdle and Michael A. Wilkinson eds., *Constitutionalism Beyond Liberalism* (Cambridge University Press 2017) 179–186.

33 Chengyi, (n 23), 2.

34 *See ibid.* 46–49.

35 *See generally* Han Zhai, *The Constitutional Identity of Contemporary China* (Brill 2020).

36 *See ibid.* at 226–232.

37 *See ibid.* at 19.

38 *See generally* Gregory Shaffer, Tom Ginsburg and Terence C. Halliday eds., *Constitution-Making and Transnational Legal Order* (Cambridge University Press2019); Cheryl Saunders, "International Involvement in Constitution Making," in David Landau and Hanna Lerner eds., *Comparative Constitution-Making* (2019); Hanna Lerner and Amir Lupovici, "Constitution-Making and International Relations Theories," (2019) 20 International Studies Perspectives 412.

39 Xenophon Contiades and Alkmene Fotiadou, "Models of Constitutional Change," in Xenophon Contiades ed., *Engineering Constitutional Change: A Comparative Perspective on Europe, Canada and the USA* (Routledge 2013) 417, 445–446.

40 For various forms of unamendability, see Richard Albert, *Constitutional Amendments: Making, Breaking, and Changing Constitutions* (Oxford University Press 2019) 140.

41 Mark Tushnet, "Authoritarian Constitutionalism," (2015) 100 Cornell Law Review 391, 413 [hereinafter Tushnet, Authoritarian Constitutionalism].

42 Mark Tushnet, Editorial, "Varieties of Constitutionalism," (2016) 14 International Journal of Constitutional Law 1, 2–4 [hereinafter Tushnet, Varieties of Constitutionalism].

43 *See* Tímea Drinóczi and Agnieszka Bień-Kacała, "Illiberal Constitutionalism: The Case of Hungary and Poland," (2019) 20 German Law Journal 1140, 1148–1151; Li-ann Thio, "Soft Constitutional Law in Nonliberal Asian Constitutional Democracies", (2010) 8 International Journal of Constitutional Law 766, 776.

44 *See* Aziz Huq, Tom Ginsburg and Mila Versteeg, "The Coming Demise of Liberal Constitutionalism?", (2018) 85 University of Chicago Law Review 239, 245.

45 *See* Benjamin Schonthal, "Formations of Buddhist Constitutionalism in South and Southeast Asia" (2017) 15 International Journal of Constitutional Law 705, 706–707.

46 For early account, see generally Carl Friedrich, *Transcendent Justice: The Religious Dimension of Constitutionalism* (Duke University Press 1964). For recent accounts, see generally Ran Hirschl, *Constitutional Theocracy* (HUP 2010); Yvonne Tew, "Stealth Theocracy" (2018) 58 Virginia Journal of International Law 31.

47 Sungmoon Kim, "Virtue, Ritual, and Constitutionalism," in *Theorizing Confucian Virtue Politics: The Political Philosophy of Mencius and Xunzi* (CUP 2019) 59, 62.

48 Richard H. Fallon, Jr., "Legitimacy and the Constitution," (2005) 118 Harvard Law Review 1787, 1796.

49 Ronald Dworkin, *Freedom's Law: The Moral Reading of the American Constitution* 2 (OUP 1999).

50 Sungmoon Kim, "Public Reason Confucianism: A Construction," (2015) 109 American Political Science Review 187, 191.

51 Xianfa pmbl. (2018) (China).

52 Daehanminkuk Hunbeob [Hunbeob] [Constitution] art. 9 (S. Kor.).

53 Kim, (n 50), 192.

54 Tom Ginsburg, "Confucian Constitutionalism? The Emergence of Constitutional Review in Korea and Taiwan," (2002) 27 Law & Social Inquiry 763, 766.

55 *See* Marie Seong-Hak Kim, "Confucianism that Confounds: Constitutional Jurisprudence on Filial Piety in Korea," in Sungmoon Kim ed., *Confucianism, Law, and Democracy in Contemporary Korea* (Rowman & Littlefield Publishers 2015) 57, 61–62.
56 *Ibid.* at 63.
57 Sungmoon Kim, "From Remonstrance to Impeachment: A Curious Case of Confucian Constitutionalism in South Korea," (2019) 44 Law & Social Inquiry 586, 588.
58 *See* Gary J. Jacobsohn, *Constitutional Identity* 339–342 (HUP 2010).
59 For more on this principle and its use in China, see N. W. Barber, *The Principles of Constitutionalism* 76–77 (OUP 2018).
60 *See generally* Jacobsohn, (*n 58*) (focusing on the United States, India, Israel, and Ireland).
61 *See* Mark Jia, "China's Constitutional Entrepreneurs," (2016) 64 American Journal of Comparative Law 619, 629.
62 *Ibid.* at 623.
63 *See ibid.* at 633–635.
64 *See ibid.* at 631.
65 *See ibid.* at 623.
66 *See ibid.* at 624–629.
67 *Ibid.* at 629.
68 *See ibid.*
69 *See ibid.* at 627–628.
70 *Ibid.* at 630.
71 *See ibid.* at 630–633.
72 *See ibid.* at 631–632.
73 Bruce Ackerman, *Revolutionary Constitutions: Charismatic Leadership and the Rule of Law* 39 (HUP 2019).
74 Consider, for example, how Myanmar's military government's initiative of constitutional amendments opened the window for a broader social movement. *See* Simon Lewis, "Suu Kyi's Bid to Reform Charter Sparks Rival Protests in Myanmar," (Reuters, 17 July 2019), https://www.reuters.com/article/us-myanmar-constitution/suu-kyis-bid-to-reform-charter-sparks-rival-protests-in-myanmar-idUSKCN1UC0KM [https://perma.cc/R78Q-89AC] (archived Sept. 27, 2020).
75 Chang and Law, (n 2), 509.
76 *See ibid.* at 511–513.
77 Jacobsohn, (*n58*), 4.
78 *Ibid.* at 87.
79 *See* Edmund Malesky, Regina Abrami and Yu Zheng, "Institutions and Inequality in Single-Party Regimes: A Comparative Analysis of Vietnam and China," (2011) 43 Comparative Politics 401, 402.
80 Fu Hualing and Jason Buhi, "Diverging Trends in the Socialist Constitutionalism of the People's Republic of China and the Socialist Republic of Vietnam," in Hualing Fu, John Gillespie, Pip Nicholson and William Partlett, eds. *Socialist Law in Socialist East Asia* (CUP 2018) 135, 140.
81 *Ibid.* at 146 (referring to the debates on an independent institution constitutional adjudication during Vietnam's 2013 constitution-making process).
82 David S. Law, "Constitutional Archetypes" (2016) 95 Texas Law Review 153, 212.
83 To illustrate, Xi Jinping stressed the leadership of the Communist Party, a feature of Chinese socialism, and said that: "'We must never follow the path of Western 'constitutionalism,' 'separation of powers,' or 'judicial independence.'" Charlotte Gao, "Xi: China Must Never Adopt Constitutionalism, Separation of Powers, or Judicial Independence," (Diplomat, 19 February, 2019), https://thediplomat.com/2019/02/xi-china-must-never-adopt-constitutionalism-separation-of-powers-or-judicial-independence/ [https://perma.cc/9HDC-KC7V] (archived Sept. 20, 2020).
84 *See* Lin and Ginsburg, (n3), 2.
85 Stephen Gardbaum, *The New Commonwealth Model of Constitutionalism* (CUP 2013) 1.
86 Lin and Ginsburg, (n3), 21.
87 Yan Lin, "Constitutional Evolution through Legislation: The Quiet Transformation of China's Constitution" (2015) 13 International Journal of Constitutional Law 61, 87–89.

88 *See generally* Kim Lane Scheppele, "Autocratic Legalism," (2018) 85 University of Chicago Law Review 545; Ozan O. Varol, "Stealth Authoritarianism," (2015) 100 Iowa Law Review 1673.
89 Carl F. Minzner, "China's Turn Against Law," (2011) 59 American Journal of Comparative Law 935, 936–937. See generally Carl F. Minzner, *End of an Era: How China's Authoritarian Revival is Undermining Its Rise* (OUP 2018).
90 *See generally* Taisu Zhang and Tom Ginsburg, "China's Turn Toward Law," (2019) 59 Virginia Journal of International Law 278.
91 *Ibid.* at 282.
92 *Ibid.* at 284–285.
93 *Ibid.* at 287 (citing Tom Ginsburg and Alberto Simpser eds., *Constitutions in Authoritarian Regimes* (CUP 2014); Robert Barros, *Constitutionalism and Dictatorship* (CUP 2000); Mark Tushnet, (n 41), at 391).
94 *Ibid.*
95 *Ibid.* at 319.
96 Thomas E. Kellogg, "*Arguing Chinese Constitutionalism:* The 2013 Constitutional Debate and the 'Urgency' of Political Reform," (2017) 11 University of Pennsylvania Asian Law Review 337, 351.
97 Tushnet, *Authoritarian Constitutionalism*, (n 41), 449–450.
98 Chang and Law, (n 2), 18.
99 Michael W. Dowdle, "Infrastructural Power and its Possibilities for the Constitutional Evolution of Authoritarian Political Systems: Lessons from China," in Helena Alviar García and Günter Frankenberg eds., *Authoritarian Constitutionalism*: *Comparative Analysis and Critique* (2019) 76, 82–83.
100 *See generally* Cass R. Sunstein ed., *Can It Happen Here?: Authoritarianism in America* (Blackstone Pub 2018).
101 Mark Jia, "Illiberal Law in American Courts," (2020) 168 University of Pennsylvania Law Review 1685, 1692.
102 For his earlier accounts, *see generally* Larry Catá Backer, "Party, People, Government and State: On Constitutional Values and the Legitimacy of the Chinese State-Party Rule of Law System," (2012) 30 Boston University International Law Journal 331.
103 Larry Catá Backer, "Chinese Constitutionalism in the "New Era": The Constitution in Emerging Idea and Practice," (2018) 33 Connecticut Journal of International Law 163, 179 (emphasis omitted).
104 *See ibid.*
105 *Ibid.*
106 Resolution of the 19th Nat'l. Cong. of the Communist Party of China on the Revised Constitution of the Communist Party of China (promulgated by the Standing Comm. Nat'l People's Cong., Oct. 24, 2017, effective Oct. 24, 2017), http://www.xinhuanet.com/english/2017-10/24/c_136702726.htm [https://perma.cc/75R9-PN2G] (archived 20 September 2020). Xi Jinping emphasizes socialism with Chinese characteristics, including the leadership of the Communist Party of China, governing the country with the rule of law, and comprehensive reforms, among others. For law reform in China under Xi Jinping, *see generally* China's Socialist Rule of Law Reforms Under Xi Jinping, (n10).
107 *See, e.g.,* Daryl J. Levinson and Richard H. Pildes, "Separation of Parties, Not Powers," (2006) 119 Harvard Law Review 2312, 2349–2368 (evaluating the American Constitution's separation of powers through the lens of political parties); Ingrid van Biezen, "Constitutionalizing Party Democracy: The Constitutive Codification of Political Parties in Post-war Europe," 42 British Journal of Political Science 187, 189 (2012) (analyzing how parties have been constitutionalized throughout Europe to make them integral to the modern state's governance).
108 *See generally* Tom Ginsburg, Daniel Lansberg-Rodriguez and Mila Versteeg, "When to Overthrow Your Government: The Right to Resist in the World's Constitutions," (2013) 60 UCLA Law Review 1184.
109 *Ibid.* at 1196–1197.
110 *Ibid.* at 1198.
111 Law, (n 82), 185.
112 *Ibid.*

113 *See* Versteeg, Horley, Meng, Guim and Guirguis, (n 3), 187.
114 The below discussions of presidential term-limit evasion in China are drawn on my book, Bui Ngoc Son, *Constitutional Change in the Contemporary Socialist World* 310–312 (OUP 2020).
115 Feng Lin, (n 14), 14.
116 Xianfa, article 79 (1982) (China).
117 Xianfa, article 79 (2018) (China).
118 Feng Lin, (n 14), 14.
119 *Ibid.* 11 (noting domestic scholars criticized the amendments through WeChat groups since they cannot express such criticisms through official media).
120 Versteeg, Horley, Meng, Guim & Guirguis, (n 3), 200, 208.
121 Zhang and Ginsburg, (n 90) 327.
122 Versteeg, Horley, Meng, Guim & Guirguis, (n 3), 207.
123 Nectar Gan, "Xi Jinping Cleared to Stay on as China's President With Just 2 Dissenters Among 2,964 Votes" (S. China Morning Post, 11 March 2018, 4:00 PM), https://www.scmp.com/news/china/policies-politics/article/2136719/xi-jinping-cleared-stay-president-chinas-political [https://perma.cc/L59A-NEAT] (archived Sept. 27, 2020).
124 *See* He, (n 6) 75–82.
125 Xianfa, article 64 (1982) (China).
126 Versteeg, Horley, Meng, Guim & Guirguis, (n 3) 208–210.
127 Albert, (n 40), 110–11, 126.
128 *See* Lin, (n 87), 81–82.
129 On these amendments, *see* Zhenmin Wang and Yuan Tao, "Achieving Development Through Innovative Constitutionalism: A China Story" (2013) World Bank Legal Review 201, 202
130 For Chinese constitutional exceptionalism, see Bui, (n 114), 277.
131 Hirschl, (n 1), 272.
132 *See* David S. Law and Mila Versteeg, "Sham Constitutions," (2013) 101 California Law Review 863, 905 (listing China among top ten countries in the world with constitutional underperformance scores in the areas of civil and political freedoms).
133 Zhang and Ginsburg, (n 90) 318–319.
134 *See ibid.* at 351, 357.
135 Francis Fukuyama, Political Order and Political Decay 371 (Profile Books 2014).
136 *Ibid.* at 374.
137 *See* China Quanguo Renmin Daibiao Dahui (National People's Congress), Parline (2018), http://archive.ipu.org/parline-e/reports/2065_A.htm (last updated Mar. 19, 2018) [https://perma.cc/UD9V-RX86] (archived Sept. 20, 2020) (describing the National People's Congress and presenting statistics related to it).
138 Weixia Gu, "Courts in China: Judiciary in The Economic and Societal Transitions," in Jiunn-rong Yeh and Wen-Chen Chang eds., *Asian Courts in Context* 489–493 (CUP 2014).
139 *See generally* He, (n 6).
140 *Ibid.* at 76–77.
141 *See* Jinghan Zeng, *The Chinese Communist Party's Capacity to Rule: Ideology, Legitimacy and Party Cohesion* (Palgrave Macmillan 2015) 153; Yongnian Zheng, "The Institutionalization of the Communist Party and the Party System in China," in Allen Hicken and Erik Martinez Kuhonta eds., *Party System Institutionalization in Asia: Democracies, Autocracies, and the Shadows of the Past* 162 (2014).
142 *But see, e.g.*, Susan L. Shirk, "China in Xi's "New Era": The Return to Personalistic Rule," 29 (2018) Journal of Democracy 22, 23.
143 *For example*, Jean-Pierre Cabestan, "China's Institutional Changes in the Foreign and Security Policy Realm Under Xi Jinping: Power Concentration vs. Fragmentation Without Institutionalization," (2017) 34 East Asia 1, 5–15.
144 For recent efforts, *see generally* Richard Albert, Carlos Bernal and Juliano Zaiden Benvindo eds., *Constitutional Change and Transformation in Latin America* (2019); Maartje De Visser and Bui Ngoc Son, "Contemporary Constitution Making in Asia-Pacific" (2019) 7 Chinese Journal of Comparative Law 241; James Fowkes, *Building the Constitution: The Practice of Constitutional Interpretation in Post-Apartheid South Africa* (CUP 2016).
145 *See generally* "Focus on Asia" (2018) 16 International Journal of Constitutional Law 311.
146 *See* Chang & Law, *supra* note 2, at 2.

147 *See generally Comparative Constitution-Making*, (*n 2)*; Richard Albert, Xenophon Contiades, and Alkmene Fotiadou eds., The *Foundations and Traditions of Constitutional Amendment* (Hart 2017); Grégoire Webber, Paul Yowell, Richard Ekins, Maris Köpcke, Bradley W. Miller & Francisco J. Urbina, *Legislated Rights: Securing Human Rights Through Legislation* (CUP 2018) (asserting that legislatures can protect human rights through methods unavailable to the courts).
148 *See, e.g.*, Adam Shinar, "The Ideologies of Global Constitutionalism," (2019) 8 Global Constitutionalism 12 (2019); Mark Tushnet, *The Globalisation of Constitutional Law as a Weakly Neo-liberal Project*, (2019) 8 Global Constitutionalism 29; *Constitutionalism Beyond Liberalism*, (n 32).
149 Zhang and Ginsburg, (n 90) 286–287.
150 Jia, (n 61), 674.
151 Chang and Law, (n 2), 3.
152 See Backer, (n 103), 179.
153 See Kellogg, (n 96), 351.
154 See Backer, (n 103), 205–211.

20

INTERNATIONAL HUMAN RIGHTS TREATIES IN THE PEOPLE'S REPUBLIC OF CHINA CONSTITUTIONAL ORDER

Jizeng Fan

Introduction

Since the constitutional amendment of Art.33(3) of the People's Republic of China (PRC) adds "the state respects and safeguards human rights" into the final text, both Chinese and foreign comparative lawyers appraise this amendment event as an unprecedented constitutional development in the PRC history.[1] However, the tremendously literal progress failed to bring the Chinese people a meaningful constitutional protection. Thus, Qianfan Zhang attributes this "sleeping beauty" amendment provision to an "undercut" as to "the institutional mechanism for the safeguarding human rights remains unimproved".[2] Actually, the human rights provision acts nothing more than a dead clause in the Chinese constitutional order because the judicial application of constitutional rights has been severely limited by the Chinese People's Supreme Court after its withdrawal of Qi Yuling's case.[3] This judicial decision indicates the deprivation of the court opportunities engaging to substantively interpret constitution.[4]

However, very few of Chinese constitutional scholars tend to consider the possibility of Chinese constitutional openness to the international human rights treaties. In fact, the absence of the constitutional ties to international law isolates Chinese constitutional development from the "trend of the internationalization of constitutional law".[5] At the beginning in the 1970s, amount of emerging liberal democracies shaped the domestic constitutional order by placing international human rights treaties into the domestic constitutions.[6] In the 1990s, the constitutional incorporation of international human rights treaties spreads in or outside the Europe, e.g. Bosnia and Herzegovina and South Africa, with the characteristics of direct applicability of international human rights norms and super-legislative status in the constitutional system.[7] Though the constitutional jurisprudences in some well-known constitutional states, for instance German and Italian, consistently resist recognizing the superiority of the international law for the fear of fading the constitutional authority in highest level, this constitutional design did not mean that higher level of protection of human rights required by the international norms would be rejected by the constitutional court. The German Federal Constitutional Court (Bundesverfassungsgericht) has shaped German Basic Law with a

DOI: 10.4324/9781003128243-24

character "openness to international law" not by undermining the superiority of Basic Law but by announcing the acceptance to the international court judgments whenever they satisfy the condition that those judgments would not "lead to the restriction and reduction" of the Basic rights.[8]

The openness to the international human rights treaties is a common constitutional identity amongst Hong Kong Special Administrative Region (HKSAR), Macao Special Administrative Region as well as Taiwan (Republic of China). The Art.39 of Basic Law of Hong Kong Special Administrative Region (HKSAR) remains the juridical validity of two international human rights covenants – International Covenant on Civil and Political Rights (ICCPR) and International Covenant on Social, Economic and Cultural Rights (ICESCR) – ratified by the United Kingdom parliament. In pursuance of the second paragraph of the Art.39, the Hong Kong Legislation Council shall be prohibited from approval of any local statutes in contrast with the requests stemmed from two human rights covenants. In this sense, the Art.39 accords the Hong Kong courts a constitutional power to review the conventionality of local laws and administrative decisions in the citizen rights litigations.[9] In addition, the Hong Kong courts often interpret the basic rights enshrined by Basic Law HKSAR or the sub-constitutional 1991 HK Bill of Human Rights in consistent with the international human rights treaties and the relevant Strasbourg case-law.[10] The Basic Law of Macao Special Administrative Region (MSAR) completely copies the wordings of the Art.39 of Basic Law of HKSAR. In this sense, Macao courts were naturally granted the same power in their adjudication of basic rights.

In Taiwan, the human rights core covenants turn into a part of national law after the adoption of Implement Act on the ICCPR and ICESCR, by which they are granted the supra-legislative status in the Taiwan constitutional order.[11] The text of 1946 Constitution of Republic of China (Taiwan) states nothing in terms of the domestic effect of international treaties and other types of international law. The Taiwan Constitution Court (Grand Justice Council) issued the No.329 Constitutional Interpretation clarifying that the ratified treaties in accordance with the procedures prescribed by the constitution shall be equal to the domestic legislation. The two fundamental covenants take the "basic law" position, according to the Art.8 of the Implement Act, whose legal status is higher than the ordinary legislation.[12] In this sense, The Taiwanese Constitutional Court handles mandates to declare the invalidity of the ordinary legislation or any administrative decision if it violates the international human rights norms[13], while these norms enable the Constitutional Court to dynamically interpret the national constitution. Even the ordinary courts may interpret all the law in consistent with the core human rights treaties provision. As to the ordinary courts, the hearing judges usually refer to the international human rights treaties in the reasoning parts of the decisions.[14] Though, in the most judgments, the international rights provisions cited have not been elaborated in the reasoning part, the influences could not be ignored. At least, the judicial preference to international human rights citation offers persuasive evidence to indicate that hearing judges may have taken the relevant international human rights norms into account.

Unfortunately, the PRC Constitutional development seems to insulate from the international human rights treaties. The 2018 amendment to Legislative Act (立法法) remains silent on the juridical effects of the international treaties ratified by NPC Standing Committee. It brings many debates on this complicated issue. In order to place a contribution concerning the role of international human rights treaties in the Chinese constitutional order, I tend to provide a brief overview of the effect of international treaties in the domestic legal system in the first section. Section II would narrowly focus on the effect and status of human rights treaties from the Chinese official statements to the UN human rights bodies. Section III would present how the international human rights treaties impact the Chinese legislative protection of fundamental human rights. Section IV would exemplify some landmark case samples where the international human rights provisions are cited. The purpose of this section is to reveal the role of those referred human rights norms into the reasoning part of the decision. In the section V, both resistant and encouraging factors impacting the establishment of an open constitutional order should be demonstrated.

An Overview on the Relationship between International Treaties and Domestic Law in the Chinese Legal System

The communist ideology deeply influences the Chinese constitution-making modality and the relationship between national and international law. The international law-making process was criticized to have been completely manipulated by the Western Capitalist states. This soviet ideological barrier had resulted into resisting the automatic effects of the international treaties in the domestic legal order of nearly all the Soviet states' constitutions, with the purpose to defend the purity of socialist legality.[15] Similarly, excluding the external influences and cementing the ruling powers of the Chinese Communist Party (CCP) constitute two fundamental features of the Chinese characteristics of socialist rule of law. The absolute willingness of CCP would not always be compatible with the international obligation provided by the relevant treaties. Thus, the domestic laws should cut off relations with the international treaties, unless legislator would explicitly express their consents by law.

The Legislative Act belongs to the category of a sub-constitutional basic law, in which all the national or sub-national positive statutes have been arranged in the hierarchical rank, and by which the legal conflict among the statutes has been fixed. However, international law escapes from the legislator's mind. During the discussion on the proposal of draft amendment to the Legislative Act, some high official members of National People's Congress (NPC) have suggested that the future amendment to the Legislative Act should clarify the domestic status of the international treaties in the Chinese legal system.[16] However, the amending result indicates that the international treaties lack automatic effect in the Chinese legal order.

The Judicial interpretations, issued by the Supreme People's Court, are a type of valid source of law explaining the meaning of specific legal terms and regulating the concrete manner on the legal application in the specific circumstance.[17] As to the status of international treaties, Judicial Regulation concerning the Judicial Citation of the Sources of Law (《最高人民法院關於司法裁判文書引用法律、法規等規範性法律文件的規定》) ("Judicial Regulation" thereinafter), issued by the SPC, implicitly excludes the domestic validity of international treaties in the trial proceedings.[18] Though the Art.6 of the Judicial Regulation opens the door for judges citing other sources beyond official legal source contained in the Art.2, their validities depend on whether the domestic statutes have granted the effect of cited legal source. Therefore, international treaties, even after ratification, accession or approval by the NPC Standing Committee in accordance with the Art.67(15) of the Constitution, would not automatically be valid before the court.[19] Two consequences proceed from the treaties ratification: (1) Chinese government recognizes the binding effect of treaties in the international level; (2) NPCSC should publish the treaties text in the Official Gazette.

It is the Congress Law that plays the decisive role on the transformation of the ratified international treaties into the part of national law. From 1978 to 2004, there were more than 100 provisions in the 80 laws having embraced the domestic effect of international treaties.[20] The Congress Law provisions grant domestic juridical effect to the ratified international treaties. The purpose of the legislative references often tends to settle down a clear solution to the conflict between international treaties and domestic law. For example, the Art.142 of 1986 General Principle of Civil Law provides that "[in the foreign-related civil litigations], if any international treaties concluded or acceded to by the PRC contains the provisions differing from those in the domestic 'civil laws', the treaties provision should be applied in priority, unless PRC government has declared the reservation to them in the process of ratification". The 1990 Administrative Procedural Law contained the similar provisions vesting the priority of the treaty norms in the condition that the domestic norms to be applied were determined in contrast with international norms in the foreign-related administrative litigation. The domestic courts and other state organs were obligated to ensure the domestic norms in compliance with the international rules.

However, the legislative openness to the international treaties has been reducing in the recent years. The new amendment to the Administrative Procedural Law deletes the provisions concerning the direct application of the international treaties. The Art.63 of current Administrative Procedural Law excludes the international treaties as the valid legal source. Thus, the international treaties lose the domestic validity, unless any other specific or administrative regulations provide the authorization. Similarly, since the validity of 1986 General Principle of Civil law was terminated at the end of 2020, the new Civil Law Code consequently comes into effect. However, no pertinent provisions to the solution of the conflict between the international treaties and national law in foreign-related litigation dictate the priority of international treaties any longer. Apart from this, the Law on the Choice of Law on the Foreign-Related Civil Relationship (《涉外民事關係法律適用法》) does not refer to the fact that in any circumstance the international treaties would be applied.

The self-empowered Judicial Interpretation may assume an imagined mechanism of which the international treaties could be applied. The Judicial Interpretation not only acts as an adjudicative function regulating the application of the Congress law in the trial proceedings, but it also has gradually been interfering with the Congress exclusive legislative power. However, the SPC mandate extension should not be an understanding to replace the NPC power; rather, it is a supplementation to reduce the high workload that is always not fully and timely exercised.[21] Due to its subsidiarity role in the practice of law-making, Ahl presumes that some Judicial Interpretations may grant some treaties domestic effects in the circumstance when no other congress law would explicitly decide to do so.[22]

Actually, the SPC's attitudes toward the direct effect of international treaties keep conservative and have never betrayed Congress Law. Until now, not any Judicial Interpretation having granted the international treaties' domestic effect without the ground of NPC statutory reference is issued. However, this conservative attitude cannot be understood as the SPC takes hostility toward international treaties' application in the domestic legal order. In 2002, the SPC issues the Regulation Concerning Trials of Administrative Cases relating to the International Trade (《最高人民法院關於審理國際貿易行政案件若干問題的規定》). Though the Regulation refuses the direct application of the WTO by the court, the Art.9 requests all the domestic courts bear an obligation to interpret domestic norms in consistence with the relevant international treaties.[23]

The Effect of International Human Rights Treaties in the Domestic Legal Order

The NPC Standing Committee has ratified six of nine core human rights treaties[24], and the Prime Minister of Chinese State Council has signified the ICCPR. Nearly all the international human rights conventions require the contracting states to implement the convention rights in accordance with the most appropriate measure they perceived.

The Chinese military troops bloodily cracking down the student pro-democracy protest in Tiananmen shocked the world. Until now, the Chinese human rights records have one of most concerned issue of the Western government and civil society. Some of the UN human rights bodies particularly questioned whether the Chinese state and local authorities would wholeheartedly respect and fulfill the human rights norms provided by the international treaties. When the Committee against Torture warned of Chinese domestic law failing to transform the international concept of "torture" defined by the CAT into the national law, a Chinese diplomat responded that "when China acceded to any convention, it became binding as soon as it entered into force. China then fulfilled all its obligations, and it was not necessary to draft special laws to ensure the conformity. If an international instrument was inconsistent with domestic law, the latter was brought into line with the former. Where the subtle differences remained, international instruments took precedence over domestic law".[25]

The diplomatic statement is given when NPC Standing Committee has ratified those international human rights treaties and seems to indicate the domestic effect of the international human rights treaties. The "special laws" would not be an irrelevant factor on the domestic effect of the international human rights treaties. Considering "entered into force" obviously points to the accomplishment of ratification in accordance with the Art.67(15) of PRC Constitution, the official statement recognizes that the international human rights treaties would be an automatic part of national law as soon as the international treaties have been ratified.[26]

The question arises as to whether the statements could be taken as an official announcement that any ratified international human rights treaties can be invoked by the court. In a long time, the domestic judicial practice was not consistent with the Chinese delegates' statement before the UN human rights bodies. Chinese official statements announced that the judicial effect of international human rights treaties had been guaranteed by the Chinese legal system, while the international human rights norms had never been relied upon in those years.[27] For instance, one Chinese delegate had ever publicly promised to the CAT Committee of Unite Nations that the litigant parties enable to invoke the treaty provisions in the trial proceedings. Thus, the court might apply treaty provisions in favor of the applicants.[28] He explained the situation where the international human rights treaties should be applicable. If the domestic provisions had been affirmed in conflict with the relevant international provisions, the latter take the priority over the national law. However, his statement did not mean that the court can directly invoke the international norms without the need to consider the domestic ones. The judges were obligated to primarily apply the national law, unless domestic protection of human rights was affirmed in contradiction with the international standards.

These statements imply an important hint on the Chinese strategy of applying international law. It seems that the international norms would be cited and applied by the court, provided that the domestic norms under review are contradicted with the international legal requirements. The presumption had also been confirmed by the Chinese statement to the Committee on the Rights of Child when it requested Chinese government to present the information on how the Chinese courts adjudicate cases by the international human rights provisions. The Chinese delegates responded that "only in the cases which (international rights) are not covered by the domestic laws, stipulations of the international conventions will be cited in the court decisions".[29]

However, it has a very low probability for the court to review the conventionality of domestic law, since the human rights adjudication essentially concerns the constitutional issues. Until now, not a national judge has ever announced any specific national legal provision in the contradiction with the international provision. On the contrary, the Chinese authority publicly asserted in the Core Document Forming Part of the Reports of States Parties that all the national laws had been already in conformity with its international human rights obligation, given that all the international convention rights are covered and protected by the national constitution and the related basic Congress Laws. Thus, the probability of relying on the international human rights norms has been deprived in the circumstance that all the domestic law are presumed to have been equivalent to international standard.

In recent years, the Chinese diplomat's statements to the UN human rights bodies have to confess its embarrassing situation on the incapability of the direct application of international human rights treaties in the trial proceedings. In one of the responses to a question asked by the UN Child Rights Committee, the Chinese representative clarifies that "Chinese courts try cases in accordance with the domestic written laws (including laws and judicial interpretation), not directly invoking the Convention's clauses".[30] It implies that, though international human rights treaties are a part of national law, the national court cannot invoke them without the legislative written law permission. In the 2014, an official reply to the questions asked by the UN Committee on the Social, Economic and Cultural Rights, the Chinese delegate confesses that the domestic courts are unable to invoke the international human rights treaties, whereas all the treaties' contents should be applied by the manners *via* legislative process.[31]

The official replies seem have terminated the possibility for the court to apply the international human rights norms,[32] which is also compatible with Chinese constitutional order. The constitutional relationship between the national judiciary organs and NPC organs can be used to explain the reason why the judicial application of international human rights treaties is difficult. Meanwhile, all the courts would be reluctant to review the conventionality of domestic law, though it has mandate to do so under some Congress Law. Due to the NPC standing committee handling the monopolized power of constitutional review and interpreting constitutional rights, the SPC would be wise to keep distance from the NPC authorities in terms of constitutional issues. Thus, it would be very sensitive for the SPC to issue self-empowered judicial interpretations ordering the lower courts to exercise the conventionality of Congress Law *ex officio*. Apart from this, the function of Chinese judiciary system has been defined by the Chinese Communist Parties as the "knife handled held by CCP". Thus, the courts are unlike to be those independent tribunals in their Western counterparts, the issuance of the judicial directive on the application of international law must receive *ex-ante* permission from the Party high-level.[33] These institutional and political hindrances set aside the international human rights from the judges.

Moreover, these two replies completely reshape the meaning of "binding effect" of international human rights treaties in the Chinese legal context. The Chinese government recognizes they are bound by the international obligation only in the international field, whereas the "binding effect" would not mean the automatic effect of international human rights treaties before the court, rather the international standards of human rights protection must be transformed into the domestic law by the legislative process. In this sense, the national adjudication of human rights can solely rely on the domestic law.

Legislative Transformation of International Human Rights Contents into Chinese Domestic Law

Honestly, legislative process is the dominate approach transforming the international standard into the domestic law. The legislative transformation techniques enable filtering out those contents that are threatening the CCP's legitimacy. The NPC and its Standing Committee enjoy a large latitude for choosing their favorite contents out of all the international human rights obligations. Meanwhile, they can decide to what extent the international standard of human rights protection would be accepted by the national Congress Law. In this sense, the transformative process works as an instrument both open and resistant to international human rights law. For instance, the NPC Standing Committee has ever declared that the domestic implementation of the right to free union, provided by Art.8(1)(a) of ICESCR, must comply with the provisions provided by the Chinese Constitution, Trade Union Law and Labor Law.[34] Though the statement was not a typical declaration on the reservation of this right, on the ground that the Chinese government has not informed the treaty bodies the reasoning and lasting period of the reservation, it revealed that the Chinese legislative organs would push the right to free union out of the national law. The selective technique costs less for the Chinese domestic implementation of human rights treaties. It can guarantee the Chinese position in favor of the universality of human rights, while Chinese legislator handle more discretion on choosing the most appropriate way to implement the international human rights. As to China continuously claiming to be a developing country, the striving to human rights fulfillment would be inevitable constrained by the shortage of resources. In Chinese initial report to Committee on the Social, Economic and Cultural Rights, Chinese government explained "[it] is a developing country, in view of constraints relating to the level of the country's economic and social development, even though the Covenant comes into force in China, not all its articles have been fully realized. The degree of enjoyment of certain rights does not yet reach the requirement of Covenant".[35]

Since the lack of an *ad hoc* Human Rights Act in the domestic legal system, all the Congress Law concerning the fundamental rights protection are defined as Chinese "human rights legislation"[36] (人權立法) or "domestic human rights laws"[37]. It is hard to demarcate the accurate scope of the human rights legislation, given the numerous Chinese Congress Laws contain the provisions relating to the protection of citizen's rights. Jihong Mo divides the Chinese human rights legislation into constitution law, civil laws, administrative law, procedure laws and special laws on the minority groups.[38] Some scholars propose to make the division by the human rights categories under the human rights treaties. Thus, Sanzhuan Guo proposes a new model of making categories consisting of rights related to criminal justice rights; other civil and political rights; labor rights; other economic, social and cultural rights; and the rights concerning the protection of people in a special group.[39] However, to put a complete list on the category of Chinese human rights legislation is an impossible mission. All the written laws relating to human rights protection could be taken as a subject to the "human rights law".

Since the huge amount of Chinese written law disproportionately increases workload in this research, I intend to limit the scope of domestic human rights law narrowly to the part of Congress Law, for they are the fundamental parts in the Chinese legal system with respect their status – only inferior to the Constitution – and the contents. In order to understand the substantive impact of international human rights treaties to domestic human rights legislation, I would focus on the official reports, diplomatic statements to the UN human rights bodies and the academic lectures and essays of the law-makers.

Chinese law-makers are used to take an eye on the foreign law texts and practice in their preparation to make a draft.[40] Unfortunately, international treaties are not explicitly referred to as one of the compulsory comparative sources in the official published document. However, it would not impede the law-makers to take the international standard as the parameter in the amending process. The law-makers and experts invited by the NPC Constitution and Law Committee (憲法和法律委員會) may publicly mention the relevant international human rights treaties in the consultation and deliberation stage. For example, Ms. Chunying Xin, the current Vice-President of NPC, revealed in a lecture that the equal rights of men and women to enjoy social welfare, and the rights to enjoy social security during the period of pregnancy and breastfeeding, enshrined in 1992 China's Law on Protection of Women's Rights and Interests, were directly borrowed from the UN Convention on the Elimination of All Forms of Discrimination against Women (CEDAW).[41] More evidences on the substantive impact of international human rights to domestic human rights legislation could be discovered from the Official Explanations on the Legislative Drafts (立法草案的說明). Mingshan Zhu, who was in charge of revising Law on Minors (未成年人保護法), explicitly confirmed that the Convention on the Rights of the Child impacted on the Chinese amendment to Law on the Protection of Minors.[42]

Although some Explanatory Reports attempt to conceal the impact of international human rights treaties to the national law amendment, the influences can be easily perceived. For example, the Explanatory Report to the draft on the revision of the Law on the Protection of Disable Persons (殘疾人保障法) does not refer to the impact of UN Convention on the Rights of Persons with Disability on the amendment result. The legal term of "principle of accessibility", originally fixed by the international human rights treaty, has been written in the Chinese law, which proves that Chinese law-maker actively accept a legal term from the international human rights treaty.

Because controversial issues are relating to the subject of the legal amendment, law-makers would be reluctant to refer to the international or comparative law, in order to demonstrate that the amendment results exclusively derive from their mind, rather than any external influence. To be honest, Chinese development on the human rights legislation can hardly be achieved without the external pressure from the international society and human rights treaties. Even the standard of protection provided by the unratified human rights treaties probably direct the legal amendment. The NPC Standing Committee approved two amendments to Chinese Criminal Law for reducing the amounts of crimes eligible for capital punishment. The Chinese scholars[43] and state-own media[44] commonly argued that the amendment takes a step forward to fulfill the international obligation provided by the ICCPR (which has not yet been ratified by the NPC Standing Committee) and meet the international tendency to abolish capital punishment. However, the relevant Explanatory Report did not publicly state that the final amendments have been subjected to the influence of the ICCPR.[45]

In fact, the ICCPR has an implicit impact on the Chinese government abolishing the administrative penalty re-education through labor (勞動教養). This sort of penalty violated the Art.9(4) of ICCPR with regard to the individuals who had been deprived from the liberties by this penalty and were not granted the rights' access to the courts. Wang Gongyi, a drafter engaging into the legislative amendment to criminal law, confessed the practice of re-education through labor contradicted the ICCPR and Chinese Constitution.[46] However, none of official reports and Explanations has mentioned the impact of the international human law on the amendment result.

Judicial Reference to the International Human Rights Norms

Though the judicial invocation on the international human rights norms may not comply with the domestic legal order, the international human rights norms or name of human rights treaties have been referred in some cases judgments. One Chinese scholar has alleged that international human rights treaties are mentioned at least in 57 case records from 2012 to 2018. The mentioned treaties consisted of all the six core human rights treaties ratified by the NPC Standing Committee, Universal Declaration of Human Rights and the ICCPR.[47]

Of the 57 cases, the litigant parties invoked the international human rights treaties in 49 cases, while the hearing judges responded to the litigant requests in only eight of them. In the rest 41 cases, the hearing judges did not consider the application of treaties at all.[48] The courts proactively referred to the international human rights norms in the seven cases, while the procuratorate invoked the relevant norms in one case.[49] The number of intentional judicial reference to human rights treaties accounts for 28% of the total. However, the hearing judges have not taken the international human rights as a ground into the reasoning part of judgment in the majority of them, rather to show that they know the existence of the relevant international human rights documents. Apart from that, several case decisions seem to have brought a breakthrough in the judicial application of the international human rights treaties. Thus, I divide them into four types as to their concrete role taken to the case decision.

The International Human Rights Norm as a Decisive Role to the Decision

In a civil litigation concerning the custody rights to the surrogacy twins, the hearing judges not only cited the Art.3 of Convention on the Rights of Child but also publicly stated that "given the fact that the PRC has involved into the treaty-making process and still being a highly contracting party after the Convention ratified by NPC Standing Committee in the 1990, the domestic legislative and judicial bodies, therefore, are obliged to exercise the basic principle of (the best interest of child) entrenched by this international human rights treaty".[50] It seems that the national courts are able to fulfill the mandates on the ground of ratified international treaties, regardless of the national law. This bold attempt challenges the current legal order where the international treaties have no automatic juridical effect before the court.

Besides, it is worth noticing that the referred international human rights norms have a decisive role in the final judgment. The Court not only changes the decision made by the court of first instance but also takes the international norm – best interest of child – as a ground to overthrow the domestic legislative result. The applicant under question, Chen Ying, was the mother of the twins born by surrogacy. The blood test shows that Ms. Chen does not have a generic tie to the twins, nor has she fulfilled the administrative registration as the legally adoptive mother by law. Thus, the first instance of court distributed the right to custody of twins to their grandparents in accordance with Art.16 and Art.17 of the General Principle of Civil Law. However, the appeal court notices that Chen's physical and emotional condition put her in an advantageous position to take care of the twins. Compared with the aged grandparents, Chen has lived together with the twins and taken care of them for more than five years. Thus, the Court intends to identify Chen as a "stepparent" provided by the Art.27 of Law on Adoption. Unfortunately, the definition of "stepparent" is absent in Art.27. The ordinary meaning of "stepmother" specifically refers to the female family member who has been divorced but engages into a new marriage. Obviously, Ms. Chen's situation is unlikely to be interpreted as a legal stepmother. However, the best interest of a child, a principle provided by the international human rights treaties, turns out to be a decisive consideration for the court to make the final decision. It has overthrown definite legislative result on the ground of Art.16 and Art.17 of the General Principle of Civil Law.

No matter whether such a way of the international human rights application is intentional or not, it has created a revolutionary modality of constitutional review – "hidden constitutional review" – in China. In the circumstance where the Chinese courts are prohibited from interpreting the constitutional provisions and reviewing the constitutionality of laws, judicial invocation of international human rights norms probably becomes an alternative approach for the First Intermediate People's Court of Shanghai adjudicating the litigations concerning protection of constitutional rights. Since both the fundamental legal documents – constitution and international human rights treaties – overlap in the fundamental rights protection, the judges may replace the constitutional rights with the international human rights as the ground for the legal reasoning and decision.

International Human Rights Norms as Lex Generalis

In a case concerning product liability, an applicant requests an immediate court in Chongqing to identify all minors under the age of 18 as "children" following the Convention on Rights of Child. Correspondingly, the Court alleges that "[T]he Convention on the Rights of the Child is an international convention. The international rights provided by the Treaty could be applied by the court after it has been incorporated into the Chinese legal system. (Given that this international treaty has not incorporated by domestic law yet), the scope of 'children' would be defined by the national regulation, rather than the international treaty".[51] However, the legal status of international human rights treaties has been altered by the Chongqing High People's Court. Though the result of the first instance is reserved, the High Court's decision is likely to admit the validity of the international human rights treaty in the Chinese legal system, while it would not impact the primary application of national law. The High Court claims that the international human rights treaties belong to the category of *lex generalis*, while the domestic regulation belongs to the *lex specialis*. Consequently, both the international human rights treaties and domestic regulation have binding effect to the court. However, the Court must follow the national regulation in accordance with the doctrine of *lex specialis derogats lex generalis.*[52] Thus, the argument implies that the international treaties are an automatic part of national law after the ratification and have a binding effect on the judicial organs in the proceeding trials. Unfortunately, the consequence of classifying the international human rights treaties as *lex generalis* seems seriously reduce the possibility that the treaties to be directly applied by the court. Since all the domestic regulations are seen as the *lex specialis*, the international human rights treaties would not have an effective impact on the case judgment.

International Human Rights Norms as a Value Basis for Decision

There is one judgment concerning the distribution of right to custody between the divorced couples.[53] Regarding one of the litigants being a foreign national, the Shanghai Second Immediate People's Court decides that the legal dispute relates to the foreign-element affairs. Thus, the Court purports that the international law should be applied in this circumstance according to the Art.142(3) of General Principle of Civil Law. In the reasoning part, the Court held that the distribution of rights to custody should comply with the principle of best interest of child enshrined by the Convention on Rights of Child. Thus, after balancing the father's economic situation against the child's German mother who was still a student in China, the court decides that the father's economic situation ensures him to guarantee the best interest of child far more better than the mother would offer to the child. In this case, the function of cited international norm has nothing more than a symbol in the demonstration of the judgment in compliance with the value embedded on the international human rights. The hearing judges do not carefully calculate the advantages and disadvantages of the parents providing the child.

International Human Rights Norms as a Decoration to the Judgments

In the most of case judgments, the cited international human rights norms are nothing more than a decoration. For instances, in a judgment concerning the insurance compensation,[54] the Court referred to the principle of best interest of child enshrined by the Convention on the Rights of Child. The citation aims to confirm that the relevant domestic provisions have achieved the equivalent protection to the international law. Thus, the final decision was exclusively based on the domestic law. In a criminal judgment concerning a commitment to intentional homicide,[55] the Court refers to the Convention on the Rights of Child together with several domestic provisions. The reference to international human rights provisions had no special significance to the final decision. Given the victim was a minor, the Court claimed the punishment to the defendant was inevitable since the state should "fulfill the protection of children's basic rights enshrined by national and international law".

Most of international human rights provisions appear to have abstract and open-textured features. The specific meaning of international rights needs to be interpreted by the relevant UN human rights bodies in the individual complaints or the General Opinion. Though some Chinese judges know the human rights treaties and the text of provisions, the specification of rights, indeed, is not an easy task for them. They are not familiar with the case decisions judged by the UN human rights treaties, nor can they easily access the General Opinion to know the jurisprudence of the international human rights application. Although these documents are the open resources published in the UN official website, very few of them know the existence of these documents. Thus, the limited knowledge of the international human rights jurisprudence is one of the crucial reasons to explain why all the judicial citations are the abstract principles and names of human rights treaties, while not any human rights case judgments or refined analytical rights interpretations included in the decision.

Prospect: Toward Constitutional Openness to the International Human Rights Treaties?

International human rights treaties have more significance to the constitutional developments in the liberal states than in China. The 1989 Tiananmen incident and the lasting terrible human rights records awake the Western states to concern Chinese human rights situation. The Western pressures and critics have never ended. To make China to be a widely acceptable and popular rising superpower, accession to the international human rights treaties, acknowledging the universality of human rights and adding a human rights clause into constitutional amendment are the necessity by the Chinese leaders to show their commitment to accept a rule-based global order. Meanwhile, the commitment to human rights protection is helpful to enhance the state's competitive power since China would be one of the largest destination countries for foreign investment. However, the commitments *per se* seem to be an expediency to satisfy the Western requests.[56]

The Potter's metaphor "selective adaptation"[57] is useful to predict the future role of human rights treaties in the China's constitutional order. The notion of "respecting human rights" is rooted in the liberal-based legal culture, while it collides to the Marxism-Leninism ideology and One-Party regime in terms of the social legitimacy and political structure. International human rights treaties place the realization of human rights in the core position. Anyone's dignity and rights should be respected in *prima facie*, while the restriction to the rights should be complied with well-recognized democratic principle, rationality and proportionality. However, the individual rights-centered structure causes a big problem for China because it rejects the liberal democracy. Thus, it cannot fully adjust to the requirement of international human rights treaties based on the liberal ideology. Since the essentiality of China is a party-state, it can hardly get rid of a totalitarian party monopolizing the state power and homogenizing the other social sectors into the Party's political goals. The dominance of CCP makes itself the real bearer of state sovereignty. It has unlimited authority to make laws and regulations. The constitution and international treaties are easily to be undermined. Potter describes the CCP authority as "patrimonial sovereignty", which is not subjected to rules – "political leader and administrative agency have the responsibility to the society, but not responsible to it".[58] In this sense, human rights norms are the secondary order in the authority arrangement. They may have binding effects in the condition that the first order – party authority – permits the other state organs to implement the international human rights norms.

Potter's argument can be attested by a well-known party-state motto "[P]eople makes law under the leadership of CCP, the process of which enables legitimatize the Party dictation" (党領導人民制定憲法和法律, 把黨的意志上升為國家意志). In this sense, Law is inevitably characterized as an instrument realizing the party dictation and goals, rather than understood as a series of norms with purpose to protect and safeguard inherent and inalienable rights based on the human dignity.

The tension between the party authority and respect to international human rights could be reconciled by the "selective adaptation" theory. All the non-local standards have to be adapted for the local application. Local perception of international human rights influences the local authorities in their interpretation and application of international human rights law. The selective compliance with the international human rights law is based on a set of complicated contextual, psychological and ideological factors. Chinese acknowledgement to universality of human rights does not mean CCP leaders would respect constitutional and international human rights as the liberal democracies regardless of the political and socioeconomic contexts. If any rights used by a dissident striving for a free society, the claim would be a threat to the Party authority. Thus, the rights claim (secondary order) cannot be compatible with the necessity to strengthening party authority (first order).

Apart from this, the institutional structure of party-state organs is a pivotal factor to influence the party's hegemonic authority. The Chinese party-state was born by the Leninist state theory. The Communist Party absolutely controls the operation of state machines. The nomenclature system enables the parties to control the access to all senior leadership in state and society. The internal disciplines enable the party to punish the members who violates and contradicts the CCP and state organs' internal rules. The strict disciplines and harsh punishment naturally obstruct the judge's intentions to make the decision on the reliance of international human rights treaties. If the case litigation concerning the highly sensitive dissents rights or labor rights of association, the consequence of reliance on the international human rights norm may trap the hearing judges into a personal risk and lose the promotion opportunity in their career.

It should not observe a haste conclusion that these two factors prevent the possibility on the application of international human rights treaties by any Chinese state organs. It matters to the Chinese government and the CCP. Since British sovereignty to Hong Kong handovers to the PRC in 1997, Hong Kong remains as a member to some UN human rights treaties. According to the 1984 Sino-British Joint Declaration Annex I, ICCPR and ICESCR remain in force in Hong Kong. Indeed, it may acknowledge that Beijing has obligation to guarantee all the laws applied in Hong Kong in compliance with international human rights. The publication of National Security Law has emerged serious worries that it is being used to oppress and punish the political opponents and critics to the local officials.[59] The loss of credibility and continuously disregarding the human rights would trigger the doubts whether the PRC ruling in Hong Kong accords to the Joint Declaration. Any activities that make and interpret national law concerning Hong Kong affairs without one eye to international human rights may bury the future of "one country, two systems".

Notes

1 Qu Xiangfei, 'Can the Human Rights Clause of Chinese Constitution be Interpreted from the International Human Rights Law Perspective?' (2016) 1 Global and Good Governance 169; M. Ulric Killion, 'China's Amended Constitution: Quest for Liberty and Independent Judicial Review' (2005) 4 Washington University Global Study Law Review 43.

2 Qianfan Zhang, 'A Constitution without Constitutionalism? The Path of Constitutional Development in China' (2010) 8 International Journal of Constitutional Law 954.

3 The readers can access to Précis of *Qi Yuling* case through the Morris essay. Robert R. Morris, 'China's Marbury: Qi Yuling vs. Chen Xiaoqi – The Once and Future Trial on the both Education & Constitutionalization' (2010) 2 Tsinghua China Law Review 281–283. Thomas F. Kellogg, 'The Death of Constitutional Litigation in China?' (2009) 9 China Brief 6. Unfortunately, the Chinese People's Supreme Court provides no explanation to the withdrawal reasons.

4 Zhiwei Tong, 'A Comment on the Rise and Fall of Supreme Court Reply to Qi Yuling's Case' (2010) 43 Suffolk University Law Review 109. Tong argues that "the abolition of Reply to Qi

Yuling's case demonstrate that the supreme court has finally recognized that taking part into the constitutional enforcement to expand their jurisdiction was unsuccessful…".

5 Wen-Chen Chang & Jiunn-Rong Yeh, "Internationalization of Constitution Law", in M. Rosenfeld & A. Sajó (eds.), *Oxford Handbook of Comparative Constitutional Law* (OUP 2012) 1167.

6 For example, Art.10 of 1978 Spanish Constitution stipulates that "The principles relating to the fundamental rights and liberties recognised by the Constitution shall be interpreted in conformity with the Universal Declaration of Human Rights and the international treaties and agreements thereon ratified by Spain".

7 See Constitution of Bosnia and Herzegovina, Art.11, para.2; Constitution of South Africa Sec.39(1).

8 BVerfG, Judgment of the Second Senate of 4 May 2011 – 2 BvR 2365/09 –, paras. 88–89.

9 Johannes Chan & Chin Leng Lim, *Law of the Hong Kong Constitution* (2nd edition, Sweet & Maxwell, 2015) 543.

10 Albert Chen has mentioned these judgments. *See* Albert H. Y. Chen, 'International Human Rights Law and Domestic Constitutional Law: Internationalisation of Constitutional Law in Hong Kong' (2009) 4 National Taiwan University Law Review 251–266.

11 Vivianne Yen-ching Weng & Yao-ming Hsu, 'Domestication of International Human Rights Norms in Taiwan: A Dialogue through the Conventionality Review under the Construction' (2017) 1 Asian Yearbook of Human Rights and Humanitarian Law 172.

12 It states that "[a]all levels of governmental institutions and agencies should review laws, regulations, directions and administrative measures within their functions according to the two Covenants. All laws, regulations, directions and administrative measures incompatible with the two Covenants should be amended within two years after the Act enters into force by new laws, law amendments, law abolitions and improved administrative measures".

13 For example, Constitutional Interpretation No. 709 (Judicial Council).

14 Cfr Yean-Sen Teng, "The Problem with the Incorporation of International Human Rights Law in Taiwan", in Jerome A. Cohen, William P. Alford & Chang-fa Lo (eds.), *Taiwan and International Human Rights: A Story of Transformation* (Springer 2019) 260. During the interval from 2009 to 2013, more than 100 criminal judgments had referred to the ICCPR norms.

15 Congyan Cai, 'International Law in the Chinese Court during the Rise of China' (2009) 110 American Journal of International Law, 272.

16 Chen Liping, "Ming Que Tiao Yue Zai Wo Guo De Shi Yong (The Application of Treaties in China Should Be Clarified)", *Fa Zhi Ri Bao (Legal Daily)* (Beijing, 24 November 2014).

17 According to the Art.5 of "The Several Regulations on the Judicial Interpretation issued by the People's Supreme Court (最高人民法院關於司法解釋工作若干問題規定)", the judicial interpretation issued by the SPC has the equal effect as the Congress Law.

18 According to the Art.2 of "The Regulation on the Judicial Citation of the Source of Law in the Judgment Writings (最高人民法院關於司法裁判文書引用法律、法規等規範性法律文件的規定)", the valid sources of Chinese positive law contain as follows: Congress Law and the relevant legislative interpretation of Congress Law (法律以及立法解釋), Administrative Statutes (行政法規), Local Statute (地方性法規), Regulation on the Exercise of Autonomy and the Other Separate Regulation (自治條例和單行條例) and Judicial Interpretation (司法解釋).

19 Hanqin Xue & Qian Jin, 'International Treaties in the Chinese Domestic Legal System' (2009) 8 Chinese Journal of International Law 300.

20 Wang Yong, *Tiao Yue Zai Zhong Guo Shi Yong Zhi Ji Ben Li Lun Wen Ti Yan Jiu (Fundamental Theory of the Application of Treaties in China)*, (Peking University Press 2007) 146.

21 Björn Ahl, 'Judicialization in Authoritarian Regimes: The Expansion of Powers of the Chinese Supreme People's Courts' (2019) 17 International Journal of Constitutional Law 265.

22 Björn Ahl, 'Chinese Law and International Treaties' (2009) 39 Hong Kong Law Journal 747.

23 Art.9 of Judicial Regulation states "If there are two or more reasonable interpretation for a provision of the law or administrative regulation applied by a people's court in the hearing of an international trade administrative case, and among which one interpretation is consistent with the relevant provision of the international treaty that PRC concluded or entered into, such interpretation shall be chosen, unless China has made reservation to the provisions".

24 The list on the PRC's membership to the international human rights treaties. See Ming Wan, 'Human Rights Lawmaking in China: Domestic Politics, International Law, and International Politics' (2007) 29 Human Rights Quarterly 735–737.
25 Cfr Björn Ahl, 'Statements of the Chinese Government before the Human Rights Treaty Bodies: Doctrine and Practice of Treaty Implementation' (2010) 12 Australian Journal of Asian Law 6.
26 Qin Xiaocheng, "Tiao Yue De Guo Nei Shi Yong – Zhong Guo De Li Fa Zhuang Kuang Fen Xi Yu Si Kao (Domestic Application of International Treaties: An Analysis of Chinese Domestic Legislation)", in Zhu Xiaoqing & Huang Lic (eds.), *Guo Ji Tiao Yue Yu Guo Nei Fa De Guan Xi (The Relationship between the International Treaties and Domestic Law)* (World knowledge Press 2000) 156.
27 Cfr Ahl, supra note 25, at 8.
28 Committee against Torture, Twenty-fourth session, Summary Record of the 419th Meetings, 12 May 2000, UN doc CAT/C/SR/419.
29 Committee on the Rights of Child, Written Replies by the Government of China Concerning the List of Issues, 17 May 1996, UN doc CRC/C. 12/WP. 5, p.2.
30 Committee on the Rights of Child, Response of Chinese Government to Questions concerning Combined 3rd and 4th Periodic Reports on the Implementation of the Convention on the Rights of Child, 10 September 2013, UN doc. CRC/C/CHN/Q/3-4/Add.1, para.1.
31 Committee on the Economic, Social and Cultural Rights, Replies of China to the list of issues in Relation to the Second Report of China, 11 February 2014, UN doc. E/C.12/CHN/Q/2/Add.1, para.18. "..., under the customary practice by which international treaties are applied in China, Chinese courts cannot directly cite international human rights agreement as legal authority when trying cases involving the economic, social and cultural rights of citizens; rather, they apply the content of those agreement once it has been transformed into legislation via legislative process".
32 Sanzhuan Guo upholds the similar opinion in this issue. Sanzhuan Guo, 'Implementation of Human Rights Treaties by Chinese Court: Problems and Prospects' (2009) 8 Chinese Journal of International Law 169.
33 Zou Keyuan, 'International Law in the Chinese Domestic Context' (2010) 44 Valparaiso University Law Review, 954.
34 The National People's Congress Standing Committee Decision on the Ratification of International Covenant on the Social, Economic and Cultural Rights, 28 February 2001, available at http://www.gov.cn/gongbao/content/2001/content_60701.htm.
35 Cfr Katie Lee, 'China and International Covenant on Civil and Political Rights' (2007) 6 Chinese Journal of International Law 450.
36 Barrett J. Fan, 'The Evolution of Fundamental Rights Legislation in the PRC: From a Soviet Model of Human Rights Theory to the Influence of Universal Standard of Human Rights' (2015) 3 Taiwan Journal of Human Rights 39; Guo, supra note 32, at 170.
37 Wan, supra note 24, at 733.
38 Mo Jihong, *Guo Ji Ren Quan Gong Yue Yu Zhong Guo (International Human Rights Covenant and China)*, (World Knowledge Press 2005) 192–204.
39 Guo, supra note 32, at 168–169.
40 The Socialist System of Laws with Chinese Characteristics, Information Office of the State Council, The People's Republic of China, October 2011, Beijing <http://www.scio.gov.cn/zfbps/ndhf/2011/Document/1036756/1036756.htm> (accessed Aug. 30, 2021).
41 Chunying Xin, Jian Li Zhong Guo Te She Hui Bao Zhang Zhi Du (Building the Institution of Social Security with Chinese Characteristic), KeXue Shibao (Jan. 20, 1999), <http://rdbk1.ynlib.cn:6251/Qw/Paper/99892 > (accessed Aug.30, 2022).
42 In his Explanatory Report concerning the Law on the Protection of Minors, Zhu states that "given that China has acceded to the Convention of Children Rights and the UN Standard of Minimum Rules for the Administration of Justice for Juvenile Delinquency, in both of which the principles of the 'best interests of children' and 'maximum protection of children' are embodied, some revised provisions manifesting the spirit of the two aforementioned international treaties have been incorporated into the given draft bill". *See* Mingshan Zhu, Guo Yu Wei Cheng Nian Ren Bao Hu Fa Cao An De Shuo Ming (Explanatory Report on the Draft

Bill of Law on Protection of Minors), <http://www. npc.gov.cn/npc/oldarchives/zht/zgrdw/common/zw.jsp@label=wxzlk&id=357674&pdmc=1524 htm> (accessed Aug.10, 2015).
43 Renwen Liu, Zhong Guo De Shi Xing Wen Ti Wen Shen Me Shou Dao Guan Zhu? (Why the Capital Punishment in China is Widely Concerned?), *China's Youth Daily* (Beijing, 25th November 2014), < http://zqb.cyol.com/html/2014-11/25/nw.D110000zgqnb_20141125_6-02.htm> (accessed Sep.29, 2021).
44 Yan Zhang, Jin Yi Bu Jian Shao Shi Xing You Li Yu Fa Zhi Wen Ming (Consistently Reducing the Amounts of Crimes Eligible to Capital Punishment Is the Crucial Step towards Civilization of Rule of Law), *Renmin Wang* <http://opinion.people.com.cn/n/2014/1028/c159301-25925678.html> (accessed Sep.28, 2021).
45 Shishi Li, Guan Yu Xing Fa Xiu Zheng An Ba Cao An De Shuo Ming Bao Gao (Explanatory Report on the Draft Bill of No. 8 Amendment of the Criminal Law Code), <http://www.npc.gov.cn/huiyi/lfzt/xfxza8/2011-05/10/content_1666058.htm> (accessed Aug. 10, 2015).
46 Wu Jiao, New Law to Abolish *Laojiao* System, *China Daily* (Beijing, 1 March 2007) <http://www.chinadaily.com.cn/china/2007-03/01/content_816358.htm> (accessed to Sep.29, 2021).
47 Ruijun Dai, 'Judicial Application of International Human Rights Treaties in China' (2020) 19 The Journal of Human Rights 98.
48 The statistic shows that the "Convention on the Rights of Child" is referred by the litigants parties in 20 cases; the "Universal Declaration of Human Rights" is referred by the litigants parties in 11 times; the "International Covenant on Civil and Political Rights" is referred by the litigants parties in nine times and a litigant has referred to UDHR, ICESCR and Convention on the Elimination of all the Discrimination in one case. Almost all the reference aim to remind the hearing judges that the litigant claim should be legitimately concerned, rather than referred as a reasoning part of their litigations.
49 All the eight cases refer to the Convention on the Rights of Child.
50 Chen Ying v. Luo Ronggeng, Shanghai First People's Intermediate Court, 56/2015.
51 Deng Debo vs. Inner Mongolia Yili Industrial Croup Co. Ltd, Chongqing First Intermediate People's Court, 2067/2018.
52 Deng Debo vs. Inner Mongolia Yili Industrial Croup Co. Ltd, Chongqing High People's Court, Chongqing High People's Court, No. 1510/2018.
53 F.D vs. Dong, Shanghai Second Intermediate People Court, No.1661/2013.
54 Huainan Taipingyang Insurance Ltd. Co vs. E. & E., Intermediate People's Court in Huainan, No. 742/2017.
55 Procuratorate vs Yang & Ma, People's Court of Nansha District, Guangzhou, Guangdong Province, 255/2017.
56 Wan, supra note 24, at 753.
57 Pitman B. Potter, 'Selective Adaptation and Institutional Capacity: Perspective on Human Rights in China' (2006) 61 International Journal 392.
58 Ibid, at 291.
59 Lydia Wong & Thomas E. Kellogg, *Hong Kong's National Security Law: A Human Rights and Rule of Law Analysis* (Georgetown Center for Asian Law, February 2021) <https://www.law.georgetown.edu/law-asia/wp-content/uploads/sites/31/2021/02/GT-HK-Report-Accessible.pdf> (accessed to Sep.28, 2021).

Bibliography

Ahl, Björn, Chinese Law and International Treaties, *Hong Kong Law Journal*, vol.39, no.3, 2009, pp.735–750.

Ahl, Björn, Statement of the Chinese Government before the Human Rights Treaty Bodies: Doctrine and Practice of Treaties Implementation, *Australian Journal of Asian Law*, vol.12, no.1, 2010, pp.1–24.

Ahl, Björn, The Rise of China and International Human Rights Law, *Human Rights Quarterly*, vol.37, no.3, 2015, pp.637–661.

Cai, Congyan, International Law in the Chinese Court during the Rise of China, *American Journal of International Law*, vol.110, no.2, 2016, pp.269–288.

Chan, Johannes & Lim, Chin Leng., *Law of the Hong Kong Constitution* (2nd edition), Sweet & Maxwell, 2015.

Chang, Wen-Chang & Yeh, Jiunn-Rong, Internationalization of Constitution Law, in Rosenfeld, Michael & Sajó, Andras (eds.), *Oxford Handbook of Comparative Constitutional Law*, OUP, 2012, pp.1165–1184.

Chen, Albert H. Y., International Human Rights Law and Domestic Constitutional Law: Internationalisation of Constitutional Law in Hong Kong, *National Taiwan University Law Review*, vol.4, no.3, 2009, pp.237–333.

Dai, Ruijun, Judicial Application of International Human Rights Treaties in China, *The Journal of Human Rights*, vol.19, no.1, 2020, pp.93–115.

Fan, B. Jizeng, The Evolution of Fundamental Rights Legislation in the PRC: From a Soviet Model of Human Rights Theory to the Influence of the UN Universal Standard of Human Rights, *Taiwan Journal of Human Rights*, vol.3, no.3, 2015, pp.39–82.

Guo, Sanzhuan, Implementation of Human Rights Treaties by Chinese Courts: Problem and Prospect, *Chinese Journal of International Law*, vol.8, no.1, 2009, pp.161–179.

Kellogg, Thomas F., The Death of Constitutional Litigation in China? *China Brief*, vol.9, no.7, 2009, pp. 4–7.

Killion, M. Ulric, China's Amended Constitution: Quest for Liberty and Independent Judicial Review, *Washington University Global Study Law Review*, vol.4, no.1, 2005, pp.43–80.

Lee, Katie, China and International Covenant on Civil and Political Rights, *Chinese Journal of International Law*, vol.6, no.2, 2007, pp.445–474.

Morris, Robert R., China's Marbury: Qi Yuling vs. Chen Xiaoqi – The Once and Future Trial on the both Education & Constitutionalization, *Tsinghua China Law Review*, vol.2, no.2, 2010, pp.274–316.

Potter, B. Pitman, Selective Adoption and Institutional Capacity: Perspective on Human Rights in China, *International Journal*, vol.61, no.2, 2006, pp.389–407.

Qu, Xiangfei, Can the Human Rights Clause of Chinese Constitution be Interpreted from the International Human Rights Law Perspective? *Global and Good Governance*, vol.1, no.1, 2016, pp.168–179.

Teng, Yean-Sen, The Problem with the Incorporation of International Human Rights Law, in Cohen, Jerome A., Alford, William P. & Lo Chang-Fa (eds.), *Taiwan and International Human Rights: A Story of Transformation*, Springer, 2019, pp.249–273.

Tong, Zhiwei, A Comment on the Rise and Fall of Supreme Court Reply to Qi Yuling's Case, *Suffolk University Law Review*, vol.43, no.3, 2010, pp.669–679.

Wan, Ming, Human Rights Lawmaking in China: Domestic Politics, International Law, and International Politics, *Human Rights Quarterly*, vol.29, no.3, 2007, pp.727–753.

Weng, Vivianne Yen-ching & Hsu, Yao-ming, Domestication of International Human Rights Norms in Taiwan: A Dialogue through the Conventionality Review under the Construction, *Asian Yearbook of Human Rights and Humanitarian Law*, vol.1, no.1, 2017, pp.166–191.

Wong, Lydia & Kellogg, Thomas E., *Hong Kong's National Security Law: A Human Rights and Rule of Law Analysis* <https://www.law.georgetown.edu/law-asia/wp-content/uploads/sites/31/2021/02/GT-HK-Report-Accessible.pdf>

Xue, Hanqin & Jin, Qian, International Treaties in the Chinese Domestic Legal System, *Chinese Journal of International Law*, vol.8, no.2, 2009, pp.299–322.

Zhang, Qianfan, A Constitution without Constitutionalism? The Path of Constitutional Development in China, *International Journal of Constitutional Law*, vol.8, no.4, 2010, pp.950–976.

Zou, Keyuan, International Law in the Chinese Domestic Context, *Valparaiso University Law Review*, vol.44, no.3, 2010, pp.935–956.

21

THE INTERNATIONAL DIMENSION OF THE HONG KONG CONSTITUTIONAL ORDER*

Michael Ramsden

Introduction

Hong Kong, like other common law jurisdictions, recognises a conceptual distinction between (unincorporated) international law and domestic law. The Hong Kong courts have recognised this dualist principle, as an English common law derivative, to continue to apply after the Handover on 1 July 1997.[1] Yet, as with other common law jurisdictions, the Hong Kong courts have been confronted with questions concerning the precise scope of the dualist principle, particularly in the construction of constitutional and sub-constitutional norms.[2] The scope of the dualist principle has been particularly relevant as a means to redress perceived gaps in domestic public law, through an assertion that international law is an appropriate source to fill these gaps and place constraints on executive and legislative powers. This chapter surveys these developments in Hong Kong through four perspectives.

First, it evaluates the link between civil and political rights applicable under the Basic Law and the relevance of the International Covenant on Civil and Political Rights (ICCPR). Article 39 of the Basic Law references the ICCPR as a source of rights, whose constitutional status is further underpinned by the effective incorporation of this instrument in the Hong Kong Bill of Rights Ordinance (Cap. 383) (HKBORO). Both the Basic Law and HKBORO thus provide a legal basis for the courts to apply the ICCPR on the plane of domestic law. Still, issues remained for the courts to resolve, concerning the scope of the ICCPR's incorporation and the extent to which such domestic incorporation faithfully reflected the international commitment assumed by the United Kingdom (UK) on behalf of Hong Kong in 1976.

Second, Article 39 also references the International Covenant on Economic, Social and Cultural Rights (ICESCR), which, in contrast to the ICCPR, has not been comprehensively transformed into domestic law via legislation. Still, the reference to the

* This chapter draws upon an article published by the present author in the Hong Kong Law Journal: M. Ramsden, 'Dualism in the Basic Law: The First 20 Years', 49(1) *Hong Kong Law Journal* (2019) 239. All case law and other references are up to date as of 11 March 2022.

DOI: 10.4324/9781003128243-25

ICESCR in Article 39 contemplates that the instrument carries some form of legal relevance. Judges have noted the possibility that the ICESCR is capable of gaining a foothold in sector-specific legislation and via administrative law concepts of judicial review, claims that will be evaluated here.

Third, in contrast to treaties requiring transformation into legislation to have domestic legal effect, customary international law is treated somewhat differently. Following the English-derived incorporation doctrine, the Hong Kong courts treat custom as a common law source.[3] Judges have been invited to address the implications of incorporating custom in three areas so far: persecution *non-refoulement*, forced labour and sovereign immunities.

Finally, the courts have recognised the possibility for international law to inform the common law principles of judicial review. This includes anxious-scrutiny review in a departure from conventional *Wednesbury* review; unincorporated treaties as a source of legitimate expectations; and the generation of relevant considerations that form part of the decision-making framework under the court's supervision.

Before delving into this jurisdiction-specific analysis, this chapter will first provide context into the nature of dualism as a common law principle. It shows that the dualism is not a monolithic principle throughout the common law world but has been adapted by judges in particular jurisdictions in light of the factors peculiar to each jurisdiction. Understanding these factors, in turn, provides a lens through which to inform understanding as to the approach adopted in the Hong Kong courts and the possibility for them to embrace international law to a greater extent in the construction and application of public law norms in the future.

Dualism as a Common Law Construct

Originating from the English common law, the dualist principle reflects a conceptual separation between international law and domestic law; the former has to be incorporated into domestic law for it to take legal effect.[4] However, it is also apparent that there is no unitary account of the dualist principle throughout common law jurisdictions. A number of factors, in this regard, are relevant to understanding the extent to which dualism is applied and adapted within a common law jurisdiction, including the interaction between international law and domestic constitution text; historical legacies; cultural relativism; geopolitical imperatives; the initiatives of 'big' judges; the scope of judicial review principles to which international norms are received; and the extent to which there is international regime control over national legal systems.[5] It suffices for the purpose of this chapter to note these factors in outline; nonetheless, some are deserving of emphasis as they bear some relevance to the approach to the dualist question in the Hong Kong context.

A major factor affecting the scope of dualism will be the extent to which a common law system has a constitutional or constitutionalised system of public law. Most directly, some common law jurisdictions provide, in an entrenched constitutional text, for the engagement of international law in the construction of domestic public law obligations. For example, the Indian Constitution 'obligates the State to foster respect for international law and treaty obligations'.[6] Similarly, the South African courts 'must consider international law' when interpreting the Bill of Rights, thereby supporting its use in constitutional interpretation.[7] Furthermore, another basis to draw upon international law is in the contextual interpretation of analogous domestic norms, typically human rights, as a means to resolve ambiguity. Here there is an overlap between international law and comparative law, with domestic courts looking not only to other domestic courts but also to supranational courts in the construction of domestic norms. Authors have thus noted a remarkable rise in domestic courts drawing from international and comparative courts as interlocutors in a shared comparative conversation on the content and scope of domestic constitutional norms that bear similarity across jurisdictions.[8] However, it is important to note that domestic constitutionalism can also go the other way in reaffirming a strict separation between international law and domestic law. Thus, in Singapore, dualism as a constitutional principle was used to deny the use of international human rights law in the construction of domestic constitutional rights on issues of moral sensitivity (as with the constitutionality of the death penalty and caning).[9] In short, a domestic constitution can go in either direction on the dualist question: cosmopolitan or autochthonous.

Another factor concerns judicial conceptions over the importance of the State observing its international obligations, including conceptions over a state's place in the world. It perhaps comes as no surprise that one of the most significant challenges to dualism in the common law world came in New Zealand, a small, geopolitically remote State that sees value in drawing upon international law as a constraint on domestic executive power.[10] In a similar manner, the rise of 'common law rights' speak in English courts, as a source independent from the Human Rights Act but which apparently substantively reflects these rights, is at least partially explained by an attempt to make human rights resilient to change in the face of legislative dis-incorporation of the European Court of Human Rights and indeed the wider Brexit movement.[11] The existence of an international obligation that underpins the common law right invests 'adjudication under the HRA with a degree of legal bite that adjudication at common law appears to lack'.[12] This is not to say that judges will necessarily perceive of their role as promoting a particular conception of a State's interest in the course of adjudicating domestic disputes, although the importance of a State in observing its international obligations (and not merely 'window dressing' them) has certainly factored in judicial discourse.[13]

At the same time, the proliferation of international obligations has also led domestic judges to create filters in the use of such norms. This has arisen both at the level of constructing the nature of international obligations and considering the relative sophistication of international law in its application in supranational regimes. A distinction might be drawn, for example, between the different nature of obligations under the ICESCR and ICCPR; whereas the former entails largely positive obligations that provide discretion to the authorities in their attainment, and the latter certainly entails obligations that are more clearly proscribed and immediately attainable. Similarly, another difference might arise from the extent to which international obligations are underpinned by supranational judicial authority. This might go either way in terms of the reception of international law in domestic courts. In *Corner House*, the House of Lords thus noted that a treaty regime had to produce a clear body of jurisprudence on a treaty provision for this provision to generate a relevant consideration in instances where the executive had elected to take it into account in decision-making, thereby limiting this principle to sophisticated supranational regimes such as the European Convention on Human Rights (ECHR).[14] The *Corner House* principle in this respect reflects a judicial reticence for domestic judges to be overly engaged in seeking to understand the meaning of rather general international norms. On the other hand, a domestic court might find ambiguity as to the meaning of international norms to be virtuous, in allowing them to import into this provision their own understanding as to what the international obligation entails. The nature of international law can therefore be a tool for judicial activism as well as restraint.

At the same time, it must also be noted that the development of domestic law through reliance on international norms has not always resulted in the outcome intended by those seeking to challenge the scope of the dualist principle, be that the litigator or judge. The famous Australian High Court decision in *Teoh*, which recognised that an unincorporated human rights treaty is capable of generating a legitimate expectation, soon led the federal legislature to remove this source of expectation in domestic law.[15] The application of international law, in this respect, can lead to backlash amongst a local population, as studies into supranational adjudication have considered at length.[16] Depending on this domestic environment, there may be some circumspection in advancing arguments grounded in international law, leading judges to locate the source of development in indigenous sources of law rather than international obligations.

Domestic Constitutional Application of the ICCPR in the HKSAR

Although the ICCPR has been comprehensively incorporated into domestic law with the legislature's enactment of the HKBORO, there is an issue as to the extent to which this enactment is faithful to the constitutional guarantee set out in the Basic Law. Article 39 provides that the ICCPR (including the ICESCR and international labour conventions) 'shall remain in force and shall be implemented' through the laws of Hong Kong. It further notes that the 'rights and freedoms enjoyed by Hong Kong residents shall not be restricted unless as prescribed by law. Such restrictions shall not contravene the provisions of the preceding paragraph of this Article'.

Article 39 reinforces the continued applicability of the dualist principle in Hong Kong, in requiring statutory transformation of the international instrument before legal effects arise: the trigger for finding a constitutional violation of Article 39 thus derives from the domestic incorporation of the ICCPR into the HKBORO.[17] In turn, if a restriction infringed the HKBORO, it would also infringe the ICCPR given that they are substantively identical. At the same time, for the implementing legislation (i.e. the HKBORO) to find a constitutional underpinning in Article 39, it is also necessary to consider whether such legislation faithfully implements the ICCPR 'as applied to Hong Kong'.[18]

The case law on this point has focused on the relevance of the UK's extension of the ICCPR to Hong Kong upon ratification in 1976. The phrase in Article 39, 'as applied to Hong Kong', has been understood by the courts to denote the application of the enumerated international treaties upon ratification, instead of a domestic application of these instruments.[19] This interpretation is logical given that the ICCPR (alongside the ICESCR and international labour conventions) were not part of domestic law at the time that the Basic Law was promulgated.[20] A particularly contentious issue to arise was the extent to which the Hong Kong courts have been able to interpret the scope and validity of British reservations to the ICCPR. It was debated whether the court could determine their validity, effectively reading 'as applied to Hong Kong' to mean 'as validly applied to Hong Kong in accordance with international law'. This was premised upon the British reservation offending the ICCPR's object and purpose where it compromised non-derogable rights, thereby justifying its severance from the treaty. Although this approach was adopted at first instance, the Court of Final Appeal (CFA) did not regard 'as applied to Hong Kong' to elicit an objective question of international law but rather required attention to be given to the UK's subjective intention when ratifying the ICCPR.[21]

Related to the issue as to the scope of the British reservation has been whether the HKBORO faithfully reflected the international obligations extended to Hong Kong by the UK upon the ratification of the ICCPR.[22] It was noted above that the HKBORO's constitutional impetus flows from it implementing the ICCPR 'as applied to Hong Kong'. Section 11 of the HKBORO sought to exclude the applicability of rights to the application of immigration legislation. This provision was purporting to implement the British reservation, which reserved the right to continue to apply immigration legislation 'governing entry into, stay in and departure from the UK'; accordingly, their acceptance of Article 12(4) of the ICCPR and 'the other provisions' of this treaty placed no impediments on immigration legislation.[23] Article 12(4), in this regard, is concerned with the right of entry of nationals: '[n]o one shall be arbitrarily deprived of the right to enter his own country'. Although there are similarities between Section 11 and the British reservation, there are also possible points of differences in their respective scopes: whereas the British reservation is concerned with Article 12(4) and 'other provisions', Section 11 excludes all rights from application to immigration legislation.[24]

This distinction can also be gleaned from the British explanation for the reservation where it noted its purpose as being to deal with the large number of colonial citizens who would otherwise have been able to claim, on the basis of Article 12(4), the right of abode in the UK.[25] This understanding also needs to be set in its historical context, where the UK's reclassification of nationality rights was held to contravene the ECHR prohibition on degrading treatment and the right to family life.[26] The reference to 'other provisions' in the British reservations therefore means those which are linked to the decision to reclassify nationality rights, such as the right to family life in that context.

Despite the UK's subjective intention in the formulation of the reservation, the Hong Kong courts have interpreted this to support the broad exclusionary ambit of Section 11 of the HKBORO. The CFA regarded it to 'make little sense' to understand the reservation exclusively through the lens of British interests.[27] It rather had to be understood according to the Hong Kong context at the prevailing time, it being a 'matter of notoriety that in the 1970's, 1980's and 1990's, major efforts had to be made by the Hong Kong Government to fend off waves of illegal immigrants, numbering in the tens of thousands in some years, originating from the Chinese Mainland'.[28]

The CFA thus eschewed an internationalist interpretation of the reservation that, as a matter of treaty interpretation, would focus upon the object and purpose of the reservation, to one of indigenous constitutional pragmatism. The text of the reservation makes it plain that its sole concern is with restricting entrants of colonial nationals into the UK. That the reservation was extended to all dependent territories further shows the immateriality of Hong Kong's circumstances to the reservation. It is thus clear that the court has avoided international elements where this would challenge the perceived efficacy of domestic policy in the field of immigration control.

ICESCR as a Source of Constitutional Rights in the HKSAR

The domestic legal basis to use the ICESCR has also been scrutinised by the Hong Kong courts. Unlike the ICCPR, the ICESCR has only occasionally been used in the interpretation of constitutional rights. Rather than using the ICESCR as a basis to creatively expand socio-economic rights, there has been a strong tendency to treat these rights in the Basic Law as deriving from an indigenous source. For example, the right to social welfare was defined in accordance with pre-1997 colonial welfare policy rather than approaches prevailing under the ICESCR.[29] The court's reticence towards using the ICESCR likely stems from a mixture of reasons, including (mis)perceptions over the exhortatory nature of this instrument to an understanding that Hong Kong's economic model does not admit of an extensive reading into the Basic Law of socio-economic rights.[30]

While the courts have been reluctant to use the ICESCR, there have been some high-profile endorsements of its potential use where it can be established that legislation constituted 'implementation' of this treaty. As already noted, the ICESCR is referenced in Article 39; legislation that comprehensively incorporated this treaty would therefore have the same constitutional impetus as the statute that implements the ICCPR (i.e. the HKBORO). But the CFA has also recognised the possibility for implementation to arise on a sector-specific basis: '[t]here can be incorporation of individual provisions of the Covenant by different statutes'.[31] According to Chief Justice Ma, 'where it is said that a particular Convention or a provision of that Convention has been incorporated into domestic legislation, it is important to analyse that piece of domestic legislation to see whether it has actually done so and to what extent. This becomes then largely a matter of statutory construction'.[32] The CFA then noted that Article 6 of the ICESCR (right to work) was not incorporated into the Immigration Ordinance (Cap. 115) given that the statute restricted the circumstances in which migrants were permitted to work.[33]

The Court of Appeal has recently weighed in on the means for establishing implementation, noting two competing approaches.[34] A narrow approach would require an objective manifestation of intention on the part of the legislature to incorporate a particular provision of the ICESCR. Yet, no such legislation has been so unequivocal on an incorporation intention, leaving only the vagaries of an implied intention that would be difficult to establish. A broader approach would treat implementation as arising independently of legislative intent; the key issue, rather, being whether the legislation pursues objectives also shared with the ICESCR. There are many statutes of this nature, such as the Housing Ordinance (Cap. 283) which includes amongst its purposes the attainment of affordable housing.[35] However, the Court of Appeal ultimately eschewed this broader framework on the apparent basis that it does not accord with the dualist principle.[36] The Court of Appeal was also wary of challenges in applying legal standards in the socio-economic field.[37] By contrast, the constitutional effects of the HKBORO can be more readily discerned as it is purposefully enacted as a benchmark for reviewing the legality of other statutes.[38] There is a potential tautological problem in using the incorporating statute to review the statute itself. For example, based upon the broad approach to implementation, the Minimum Wage Ordinance (Cap. 608) (MWO) can be said to implement Article 7 of the ICESCR. At the same time, the MWO is arguably incompatible with the ICESCR in excluding domestic helpers from the minimum wage entitlement.[39] If the broad approach was to be followed, the effect would possibly be that ICESCR Article 7 ceases to be part of domestic law given that this implementing legislation is inconsistent with Article 39 of the Basic Law.

A more coherent approach that has yet to be explored in the courts is to treat Article 39 as generating an interpretive presumption that all legislation is to be read, as far as is possible, compatibly with the ICESCR (and other instruments in this provision, including the ICCPR and international labour conventions). On this understanding, Article 39 would be functionally equivalent to Section 3 of the UK's Human Rights Act, in requiring the courts to interpret legislation so far as possible compatibly with the ECHR. Indeed, this strong interpretive principle already forms part of the court's practice, in reading down and straining the meaning of statutory text where this is necessary to achieve constitutional conformity.[40] One possible objection is that Article 39 reflects the dualist principle and therefore has no effects unless there is incorporating legislation. However, it is also of note that Article 39 has supplied the court's strong interpretive power where supervising compatibility with the HKBORO. Section 4 of the HKBORO was removed from this legislation by the People's Republic of China (PRC) in defining the law that would survive the Handover, on the basis that this interpretive approach places the HKBORO above all others.[41] The point here then is that the power of interpretation has derived from Article 39 despite there being no legislative underpinning for this approach.[42] There are also good normative reasons to support Article 39 as generating an interpretive presumption of compatibility, especially in ensuring that rights protection is not solely contingent upon the legislature enacting the necessary legislation. This approach would also give some meaning to the requirement in Article 39 that the ICESCR 'shall be implemented'.[43]

Customary International Law as a Source of the Common Law in the HKSAR

The Hong Kong courts have also addressed the application of the doctrine of incorporation that treats custom as a source of the common law. As a general matter, it is evident from judicial practice that the incorporation doctrine survived the Handover.[44] Its continued application is mandated by the Basic Law, in line with the prescription that the 'laws previously in force' will be maintained, which includes the doctrine as a common law derivative.[45] Its application has arisen in different contexts; *non-refoulement* (*C v Director of Immigration*),[46] ICCPR/ICESCR norms that find parallel expression under custom (*MA v Director of Immigration/Ubamaka v Secretary for Security*),[47] forced labour[48] and the scope of State immunities where pertaining to commercial enterprises (*Congo v FG Hemisphere*).[49] Despite being framed as an 'incorporation' doctrine, the Hong Kong courts have noted various impediments to the use of custom as a common law derivative, such that a general prognosis on its future use is probably limited.

The courts have limited the doctrine in light of the constitutional dynamic in which the custom would be received. On this basis, the attempt of litigants to argue that rights under the ICCPR and ICESCR had matured into custom so as to constrain discretion under the Immigration Ordinance was rejected given the broad exclusionary force of Section 11 and the British reservation underlying it (as analysed above).[50] In a similar manner, the new legal reality of Hong Kong being part of the PRC has also had implications for the incorporation of custom particularly where such norms affect the national sovereign interests, such as the approach towards the granting of State immunities in line with the approach of the PRC (addressed further below).

Statutory law, too, has also acted as a filter on the incorporation of custom. This is most evident where the legislation expressly or by clear implication excludes the custom. But a more difficult issue is where the statute confers broad discretion on executive officials. The Hong Kong courts have taken an approach that favours the retention of broad discretion over the imposition of restraints defined according to customary international law. This arose most prominently in rejecting the argument that the customary *non-refoulement* obligation restricted statutory immigration powers; instead the court noted the legislative intent to keep such powers 'unfettered'.[51] Given the large body of discretion-conferring statutes, this approach reduces further the potential for the incorporation doctrine to have practical utility in relation to executive decision-making in the future.

An additional consideration that shapes the extent to which the incorporation doctrine is capable of having an impact is the approach of Hong Kong judges to the construction of customary international law. When examining the customary foundations of the persecution *non-refoulement* norm, the Court of First Instance engaged in an impressive evidentiary study to establish the existence of the norm.[52] However, this contrasts with the deferential approach to norm construction where such a norm touched upon PRC sovereign interests. In this respect, the two competing versions of State immunity – qualified and absolute – received close attention in the CFA in *FG Hemisphere*.[53] Hong Kong had, prior to the Handover, subscribed to the view that State immunities were qualified, which stands in contrast to the absolutist position of the PRC. Accordingly, qualified immunity was treated as the pre-1997 common law position, which was subsequently changed with Hong Kong's new constitutional reality after the Handover. The basis for this finding was grounded in constitutional pragmatism, deferential to the PRC's view on this legal question, rather than seeking to ascertain a true position in customary international law.[54] As with the sidestepping of the true purpose of the British reservation to the ICCPR (considered above), the CFA similarly avoided international law where it was perceived to conflict with national interests.

International Law and Common Law Judicial Review in the HKSAR

Outside the context of constitutional provisions, international law has also been noted as of particular relevance in the shaping of the common law grounds of judicial review. These grounds follow those first adopted in the English courts: illegality, irrationality, procedural impropriety, including more recent developments (legitimate expectations and aspects of proportionality).[55] These common law ground offer a potential alternative route for international norms to gain a foothold in domestic law. Speaking in the context of the ICESCR's potential relevance, the Court of First Instance noted that this instrument could be 'used as a framework in which government decisions or discretions are to be considered'.[56] Three main avenues have been explored by the courts.

The first has been the legitimate expectations ground, concerned with those instances where the executive induces an expectation of a particular benefit.[57] Other jurisdictions – particularly Australia – have expanded the types of conduct capable of inducing expectations to include the ratification of treaties on the international plane.[58] Some judges in Hong Kong have, similarly, acknowledged the possibility for unincorporated treaties to generate an expectation that places constraints on the exercise of administrative discretion.[59] Yet, this development remains largely theoretical; although advanced at the rhetorical level, it has not influenced the outcome of public law disputes. One weakness is that legitimate expectations arguments have centred around the ICESCR, a treaty that – rightly or wrongly – has been treated as soft law in the Hong Kong courts.[60] More particularly, there is also a difficulty in constructing an expectation from very broad treaty commitments. The requirement that an expectation arises from a 'clear and unambiguous' representation, as well as a trend of enforcing expectations only where the categories of representees are relatively small, would seem to only provide limited scope for treaties to constitute a serious category from which expectations can arise and be enforced.[61]

Whether the courts in Hong Kong should equate treaties with expectations remains an open issue; the CFA has yet to have its '*Teoh* moment'.[62] Hong Kong's CFA became the first final appellate court in the common law world to recognise substantive legitimate expectations; it might break new ground to also recognise treaty commitments as also falling into this category.[63] This would indeed follow the logic of several first instance decisions that recognised in *obiter dictum* that the substantive treaty commitment (e.g. the right to family life) could conceivably give rise to an expectation that such right not be interfered with.[64] In doing so, the CFA would need to revisit the rationale for treaty expectations as being based upon the unattractiveness of Hong Kong 'window dressing' its international obligations.[65] Still, the courts have been quite prepared to insulate its constitution from international law, as its avoidance of the true meanings of the British reservation and customary law on State immunities shows. In areas where treaty expectations matter the most – principally immigration – the courts perceive Hong Kong to have unique circumstances that justify a rejection of international obligations in favour of wide discretionary power for the immigration authority.[66]

A second entrance point in the common law grounds of review for international law has been the principle of discretionary relevant considerations.[67] Practically speaking, this principle has provided the impetus for much of the growth of judicial review in the area of immigration law, particular as it pertains to asylum seekers and refugees.[68] In essence, this principle seeks to hold the executive to its particular statements or practices as a framework in which to review decision-making. That the executive *chose* to take into account the unincorporated Refugee Convention and Torture Convention in its decision-making thus provided a basis for the courts to attach significance to that choice in designing its standards of review.[69] It was from these statements and practices that the CFA could articulate standards, including a high standard of procedural fairness, that the executive had to observe when determining whether a person faced a risk of torture or persecution.[70] The discretionary relevant consideration principle shares the same normative root as unincorporated treaty-induced legitimate expectations (considered above), in premising judicial review on what the executive says or does in the implementation of its discretion. But a material difference is how the executive chooses to give a grounding to this unincorporated international law, which might be narrower than the obligations that exist on the international plane.

Although of practical utility in advancing refugee screening procedures, the scope for the courts to hold the executive to its discretionary considerations also turns upon the extent to which it is prepared to define the obligations that the executive has elected to consider. By way of comparison, this is an issue that has vexed the English courts. While the English judiciary could use, prior to the enactment of the Human Rights Act, Strasbourg jurisprudence as an aid in adding greater specificity to the obligations that the British executive elected to take into account under the ECHR, the courts soon walked back on this principle in the context of regimes whose obligations were not so precisely explicated by a treaty body. In this respect (as noted in the 'Dualism as a Common Law Construct' section), according to *Corner House*, a treaty regime had to produce a clear line of jurisprudence on the provision taken into account by the executive as a discretionary consideration, which in turn limits the principle to developed supranational juridical regimes such as the ECHR.[71]

There are hints, too, of this reasoning in the Hong Kong courts when evaluating executive assurances to the Committee on Economic, Social and Cultural Rights that it gave 'most careful attention' to a variety of rights under the ICESCR when making immigration decisions that impacted upon family unity.[72] Once again, the perceived absence of clearly developed standards under the ICESCR was used as a basis to treat the executive's discretionary consideration as something that did not invite close review by the courts. The Court of First Instance thus rejected the significance of this undertaking, observing that the ICESCR was merely 'aspirational and promotional', with the assurance only highlighting the executive's 'effort'.[73] This is to be contrast, as already noted, with the perceived harder sources of obligation under the Torture Convention, where executive assurances to have regard to this instrument to the Committee Against Torture were taken into account in identifying a policy in Hong Kong to respect the *non-refoulement* principle.[74] In short, the scope for the election principle to have impact will turn upon perceptions over the specificity of international obligations that have been taken into account by the executive.

On a final matter, there have been suggestions that international law can be served as a baseline to understand whether a decision taken by the executive is reasonable in the *Wednesbury* sense. This standard of substantive review of discretion directs the court to consider whether, to use the classic formulation, the decision reached was 'so unreasonable that no reasonable decision maker could make it'.[75] The extent to which the standard of review has been, or ought to be, modified has amassed a considerable body of literature.[76] The Hong Kong courts have generally regarded the standard to be variable, with interests deserving of closer protection of the court attracting the use of 'enhanced *Wednesbury*' or 'anxious scrutiny' review.[77] It is noteworthy that the major body of jurisprudence on anxious scrutiny review flowed from the CFA's pronouncements on the importance of protecting persons from unlawful *refoulement,* given that 'life and limb' are in jeopardy.[78] Whether the CFA introduced anxious scrutiny in the *non-refoulement* context as means to give effect to Hong Kong's obligations under customary international law, instead of an analogous common law principle to modify substantive review according to the gravity of the interests at stake, is debatable. The CFA reasoning on the basis for anxious scrutiny review was under-theorised, perhaps strategically so. Chief Justice Li thus noted that '[f]or the purposes of this appeal, the Court will assume without deciding that the Secretary is under a legal duty to [observe the *non-refoulement* principle] as a matter of domestic law'.[79] The absence of clear reasoning on the legal foundation for applying the *non-refoulement* principle might itself be a judicial strategy to make the principle more resilient to challenge by the executive. It might reflect, to draw from the analysis in the 'Dualism as a Common Law Construct' section, a desire for judges to incrementally develop the common law as a source of obligation where possible rather than any analogous international law, so as to avoid indigenous backlash to such 'foreign' approaches.

A more clearly theorised connection between anxious scrutiny and the engagement of international law in an executive decision was outlined by Judge Andrew Cheung in *MA v Director of Immigration*.[80] The issue was whether a stringent work authorisation policy, that prevented mandated refugees from working unless they could demonstrate 'exceptional circumstances', was *Wednesbury* unreasonable. Rather than apply classic *Wednesbury*, Judge Cheung noted the suitability of an anxious scrutiny approach given that the unincorporated international human rights in issue (right to privacy and freedom from inhumane and degrading treatment) were 'important' rights.[81] However, it is apparent that anxious scrutiny falls short of proportionality review, which arguably would have justified a finding that the stringent work authorisation policy was unlawful.[82] Instead, it was still permissible for the executive to be concerned about an unsubstantiated 'magnet effect' in enticing illegal immigrants to Hong Kong by relaxing this policy in relation to mandated refugees. Anxious scrutiny, then, even when drawing upon sources of international obligation, does not enable the court to overtly balance and weigh the competing exigencies in an executive decision as they are able under proportionality review.[83]

Conclusion

This chapter has evaluated the international dimension of Hong Kong's constitutional order. It has identified a number of areas where questions of international law have arisen in the construction and application of constitutional and sub-constitutional norms. It has noted an inherent conservatism on the part of the Hong Kong judiciary in the use of (unincorporated) international law. This conservatism has stemmed at least partially from an understanding of the Hong Kong legal system staying faithful to its common law traditions, including the dualist principle. At the same time, it showed that there are a variety of approaches to dualism in the common law world; the approach of the Hong Kong courts has certainly been at the conservative end of the spectrum. In context, this conservative approach might also be said to arise from the nature of norms that the courts have been called upon to apply and perceptions as to their supposed exhortatory character, as with the ICESCR. The tendency to avoid international law has also been borne out of a number of indigenous imperatives, including the need to preserve executive discretion to address situations that are perceived to be unique (immigration control) as well as to respect national sovereignty (as with a preference for absolute over-qualified State immunities). The possible use of international law in informing common law standards of judicial review has been articulated as a possibility at the rhetorical level but had very little impact in defining the standards that constrain executive discretion at a level of specificity.

Notes

1 Y. Ghai, *Hong Kong's New Constitutional Order: The Resumption of Chinese Sovereignty and the Basic Law* (Hong Kong: Hong Kong University Press, 2nd ed., 1999), at 7–8, 404, 478.
2 As to varying approaches to the scope of the dualist principle in other common law jurisdictions: M. Ramsden, 'International Influences on English Judicial Review and Implications for the Exportability of English Law', in S. Jhaveri and M. Ramsden (eds.), *Judicial Review of Administrative Action Across the Common Law World Origins and Adaptation* (Cambridge: CUP, 2021).
3 *C v Director of Immigration* [2008] HKEC 281, at [79]–[83]; M. Ramsden, 'Using International Law in Hong Kong Courts: An Examination of Non-Refoulement Litigation' (2013) 42(4) *Common Law World Review* 351.
4 For a restatement of these principles, see e.g. *R (Corner House Research) v Director of the Serious Fraud Office* [2009] 1 AC 756.
5 See further Ramsden, 'International Influences', *supra* note 2.
6 Article 51(c), Constitution of India; *Visaka v State of Rajasthan* [1997] 3 LRC 361; *Jolly George Verghese v. Bank of Cochin* [1980] 2 SCR 913, 922.
7 Section 39(1), 1996 South African Constitution.
8 M. Waters, 'Creeping Monism: The Judicial Trend Towards Interpretive Incorporation of Human Rights Treaties' (2007) 107(3) *Columbia Law Review* 628, at 672–679; V. Jackson, 'Constitutional Comparisons: Convergence, Resistance, Engagement' (2005) 119 *Harvard Law Review* 109, at 112.
9 *Yong Vui Kong v Public Prosecutor* [2015] SGCA 11, at [45] (Menon CJ) (Court of Appeal).

10 T. Dunsworth, 'Hidden Anxieties: Customary International Law in New Zealand' (2004) 2 *New Zealand Journal of Public and International Law* 67, 78.
11 M. Elliott, 'Beyond the European Convention: Human Rights and the Common Law' (2015) 68 *Current Legal Problems* 85, at 111.
12 Elliott, above note 4, at 108.
13 See e.g. *Tavita v Minister for Immigration* [1994] 2 NZLR 257, at 266 (Cooke J).
14 *Corner House, supra* note 4, at 845 (Lord Bingham).
15 See further A. Downer, 'Executive Statement on the Effect of Treaties in Administrative Decision-Making' (1997) 8 *Public Law Review* 120.
16 See e.g. M. Ramsden, 'Strategic Litigation Before the International Court of Justice: Evaluating Impact in the Campaign for Rohingya Rights', *European Journal of International Law* (2022 forthcoming); M. Ramsden, 'Strategic Refugee Rights Litigation in Hong Kong: Impact and Backlash', in Vincent Chetail and Shuvro Sarker (eds.) *Refugee Law in Asia* (2023 forthcoming).
17 *GA v Director of Immigration* (2014) 17 HKCFAR 60, at [58].
18 *Swire Properties Ltd v Secretary for Justice* (2003) 6 HKCFAR 236, at [53].
19 *GA v Director of Immigration, supra* note 17, at [29]; *Ubamaka v Secretary for Security* (2012) 15 HKCFAR 743, at [62]–[67].
20 The Basic Law was promulgated by the National People's Congress of the PRC on 4 April 1990, with the HKBORO enacted on 8 June 1991 by the Hong Kong Legislative Council. See also Ghai, *supra* note 1, at 416.
21 See *Ubamaka* v *Secretary for Security* [2009] HKEC 710 (CFI); *MA v Director of Immigration* [2011] 2 HKLRD F6, at [50].
22 For a detailed analysis, see: M. Ramsden, 'Reviewing the United Kingdom's ICCPR Immigration Reservation in Hong Kong Courts' (2014) 63(3) *International and Comparative Law Quarterly* 635.
23 See 'Reservation to the International Covenant on Civil and Political Rights Made by the United Kingdom of Great Britain and Northern Ireland upon Ratification' available at http://treaties.un.org/doc/db/survey/humanrightsconvs/Chapt_IV_4/reservations/UK.pdf.
24 Section 11 provides: 'As regards persons not having the right to enter and remain in Hong Kong, this Ordinance does not affect any immigration legislation governing entry into, stay in and departure from Hong Kong, or the application of any such legislation.'
25 'Seventh Periodic Report from the United Kingdom, the British Overseas Territories, the Crown Dependencies' (December 2012) 40. For a history, see: Lord Lester of Herne Hill QC, 'Thirty Years On: The East African Asians Case Revisited' (2002) *Public Law* 52.
26 3 EHRR 1973.
27 *Ubamaka v Secretary for Security* (2012) 15 HKCFAR 743, at [62]–[67].
28 *Ibid.*
29 *Kong Yunming v Director of Social Welfare* [2013] 6 HKCFAR, [180]; [24]–[25], [33]–[35].
30 M. Ramsden, 'Using the ICESCR in Hong Kong Courts' (2012) 42(3) *Hong Kong Law Journal* 839.
31 *GA v Director of Immigration, supra* note 17, at [60].
32 *Ibid.*
33 *Ibid.* Section 37ZX provides that the 'Director may … permit the claimant to take employment …' provided that he is 'satisfied that exceptional circumstances exist that justify such a permission being given …'.
34 *Lubiano Nancy Almorin v Director of Immigration* [2020] 5 HKLRD 107 (CA).
35 See discussion of these objectives in *Ho Choi Wan v Hong Kong Housing Authority* (2005) 8 HKCFAR 628.
36 *Almorin, supra* note 34, at paras. 82–83, 85, 87–89, 95–96.
37 *Ibid.*
38 For an extensive analysis of this case law, see: M. Ramsden and S. Hargreaves, *Hong Kong Basic Law Handbook* (Hong Kong: Sweet & Maxwell, 3rd ed., 2022).
39 See the clear terminology in s 7, Minimum Wage Ordinance (Cap. 608) and discussion of this provision in M. Ramsden and L. Marsh, *The Hong Kong Minimum Wage Ordinance* (Hong Kong: Sweet & Maxwell, 2011).
40 *HKSAR v Lam Kwong Wai* [2006] 3 HKLRD 808, [65].

41 Section 4 provided: 'All legislation enacted on or after the commencement date shall, to the extent that it admits of such a construction, be construed so as to be consistent with the International Covenant on Civil and Political Rights as applied to Hong Kong.'
42 P. Wesley-Smith, 'Maintenance of the Bill of Rights' (1997) 27 *Hong Kong Law Journal* 15, 16.
43 See further, M. Ramsden, 'Judging Socio-Economic Rights in Hong Kong' (2018) 16(2) *International Journal of Constitutional Law* 447.
44 *C v Director of Immigration*, *supra* note 3, at [83].
45 R. Mushkat, 'International Law in HKSAR Courts' (1998) 28 *California Western International Law Journal* 356.
46 *C v Director of Immigration, supra* note 3; [2011] HKEC 978 (CA); (2013) 16 HKCFAR 280 (CFA).
47 *MA v Director of* Immigration, *supra* note 21; *Ubamaka v Secretary for Security, supra* note 9 above.
48 *Lubiano Nancy Almorin v Director of Immigration* [2018] 1 HKLRD 1141 (CFI).
49 *Democratic Republic of the Congo v FG Hemisphere Associates LLC (No 1)* (2011) 14 HKCFAR 95.
50 *Ubamaka v Secretary for Security* [2011] 1 HKLRD 359, at [150].
51 *C* (CA), *supra* note 46, at [94].
52 *C (CFI), supra* note 3, at [117]–[137].
53 *Democratic Republic of the Congo v FG Hemisphere Associates LLC (No 1)* (2011) 14 HKCFAR 95.
54 T. Carty, 'Why Are Hong Kong Judges Keeping a Distance from International Law, and With What Consequences? Reflections on the CFA Decision in *DRC v FG Hemisphere*' (2011) 41 *Hong Kong Law Journal* 401.
55 For an analysis as to the influence of English principles in Hong Kong, see: M. Ramsden, 'English Administrative Law in Post-Handover Hong Kong', in S. Jhaveri and M. Ramsden, 'Judicial Review', *supra* note 2.
56 *Chan Mei Yee v Director of Immigration* [2000] HKEC 788, at [25].
57 An overview of legitimate expectations in Hong Kong is provided in S. Jhaveri et al, *Administrative Law in Hong Kong* (Lexis Nexis, 2nd ed., 2013).
58 See further Ramsden, 'International Influences', *supra* note 2.
59 See e.g. *Ng Siu Tung v Director of Immigration* (2002) 5 HKCFAR 1, at [355]; *Chan Mei Yee v Director of Immigration*, supra note 56; *Comilang Milagros Tecson v Director of Immigration* [2018] 2 HKLRD 534, at [114].
60 See e.g. *Chan To Foon v Director of Immigration* [2001] 3 HKLRD 109, at 131D–134B. Hong Kong judges have been expressly rebuked by the CESCR for holding these views, as being based upon a mistaken understanding as to the legal nature of the ICESCR: CESCR, 'Concluding Observations 2001; UN Doc E/C 12/1/Add 58, 16. Some judges have noted that there are provisions in the ICESCR that do immediately give rise to obligations, particularly those not so closely tied to the availability of resources: *BI v Director of Immigration* [2014] HKEC 2054, [45]; *Kong Yunming v Director of Social Welfare, supra* note 29, at [79].
61 See Jhaveri, *supra* note 57, at 508–509.
62 Of which, see: *Minister for Immigration and Ethnic Affairs v Teoh* (1995) 183 CLR 273, 365. See also *Chundawadra v Immigration Appeal Tribunal* [1988] Imm AR 161.
63 See further K. Yam and B. Tai, 'The Advent of Substantive Legitimate Expectations in Hong Kong: Two Competing Visions' (2002) *Public Law* 688.
64 See *supra* note 47.
65 As explored in Ramsden, 'International Influences', *supra* note 2.
66 *Comilang Milagros Tecson v Director of Immigration* (2019) 22 HKCFAR 59 (CFA), at [76]–[77] (denying the ICESCR as capable of generating a legitimate expectation in the immigration control context given the restrictive legal regime in place in Hong Kong). See also M. Ramsden, 'Immigration Judicial Review in Hong Kong: The Developing Legal Framework' (2019) 33(3) *Journal of Immigration, Asylum & Nationality Law* 117, at 191–193.
67 In the English context, see: *R v Home Secretary, ex p Launder* [1997] 1 WLR 839 HL, at 867.
68 See generally Ramsden, 'Immigration Judicial Review', *supra* note 57.
69 *Secretary for Security v Prabakar* (2004) 7 HKCFAR 187, at [10]; *C (CFA), supra* note 46, at [33]–[38].

70 *Ibid.*
71 *Corner House*, *supra* note 4, at 845.
72 HKSAR, Second Report of the Hong Kong Special Administrative Region to the United Nations Committee on Economic, Social and Cultural Rights, at 10.12.
73 *Pagtama Victorina Alegre v Director of Immigration* [2016] HKEC, at [115].
74 *Secretary for Security v Prabakar*, *supra* note 69, at [44].
75 See further M. Ramsden, 'The Future of Wednesbury Unreasonableness in the Substantive Review of Administrative Discretion: A. Hong Kong Perspective' (2021) *The Chinese Journal of Comparative Law* 9(1) 51.
76 *Ibid* (and citations there).
77 The Hong Kong courts have followed English jurisprudence on anxious scrutiny review: *MA v Director of Immigration*, *supra* note 21, at [92]; *Bugdaycay v Secretary of State for the Home Department* [1987] AC 514, 531.
78 *Secretary for Security v Prabakar*, *supra* note 56. This line of jurisprudence also prompted systemic administrative reform: M. Ramsden, 'Hong Kong's "High Standard of Fairness" and New Statutory Torture Screening Mechanism' (2013) *Public Law* 232.
79 *Secretary for Security v Prabakar* (2004) 7 HKCFAR 187 (Court of Final Appeal), at [4] (Li CJ).
80 *MA*, *supra* note 21.
81 *MA*, *supra* note 21, at [97]–[99] (Cheung J).
82 A similar justification ('magnet effect') was rejected in England using proportionality review: *R (on the application of Tekle) v Secretary of State for the Home Department* [2008] EWHC 3064 (per Blake J, a 'person who might be tempted to come to the United Kingdom to make a false asylum claim simply because of the prospects of seeking employment would not be encouraged by any more generous policy in this respect').
83 See criticism: M. Ramsden and L. Marsh, 'The "Right to Work" of Refugees in Hong Kong: *MA v Director of Immigration*' (2013) 25(3) *International Journal of Refugee Law* 574; M. Ramsden and L. Marsh, 'Refugees in Hong Kong: Developing the Legal Framework for Socio-Economic Rights Protection' (2014) 14(2) *Human Rights Law Review* 267.

22

HONG KONG'S OVERSEAS JUDGES UNDER THE NATIONAL SECURITY LAW*

Stuart Hargreaves

Hong Kong's apex court invites highly regarded judges from other common law jurisdictions to sit as full members for (renewable) three-year periods. Though this practice is relatively unusual, Hong Kong is not alone in inviting non-residents or non-citizens to serve as judges.[1] This chapter begins by outlining the basics of the 'overseas judge' system as it operates in Hong Kong and shows that the justification generally proffered is different than those made for similar systems elsewhere. It then plays special attention to a new question that has arisen thanks to the imposition in 2020 of the National Security Law[2] (NSL) – should the overseas judges hear cases brought under that law? This chapter argues that though the text of the NSL does not explicitly preclude a role for the overseas judges, it would be wise for the Chief Justice to not put forward their names for consideration by the Chief Executive. Though this may appear inconsistent with the general justification for their role, paradoxically a voluntarily choice by the Court to exclude them from hearing national security matters may in fact help preserve their role in non-NSL cases. It would also be consistent with the strategic approach taken by the Court in recent years – one which seeks to preserve its role to the greatest extent possible while avoiding outright constitutional conflict with the Central Government.

The Origin of the Overseas Judges System in Hong Kong

In 1984, the United Kingdom and the People's Republic of China issued a 'Joint Declaration' regarding the reassertion of Chinese sovereign control over Hong Kong.[3] This agreement contained a series of 'basic policies' that China would apply to Hong Kong for a period of no less than 50 years, beginning on 1 July 1997. One such policy was that judges would be 'chosen by reference to their judicial qualities and [could] be

* Associate Professor, Faculty of Law, The Chinese University of Hong Kong. Some elements of this chapter explaining the origins and perception of the overseas judges have appeared previously in Stuart Hargreaves, 'Canaries or Colonials? The Reduced Prominence of the "Overseas Judges" on Hong Kong's Court of Final Appeal' (2022) Asian Journal of Comparative Law, 1–31. doi:10.1017/asjcl.2021.15.

 DOI: 10.4324/9781003128243-26

recruited from common law jurisdictions.'[4] This policy was subsequently codified in Art. 82 of the Basic Law, which allowed the Court of Final Appeal (CFA) to '*as required* invite judges from other common law jurisdictions to sit on it' (emphasis mine).[5] No further explanation of what 'as required' means is provided in the Basic Law, and nothing is said about the size or overall composition of the bench, other than to note that the Chief Justice may not have foreign citizenship or right of residency.[6]

In order to offer some clarity prior to 'handover', the Sino-British Joint Liaison Group (JLG) proposed the '4+1 model'. This envisioned a five-person CFA composed of the Chief Justice, three permanent members drawn from Hong Kong, and one member drawn from one of two panels of 'non-permanent' judges. One panel would be 'local', composed of sitting or retired Court of Appeal judges (and ultimately retired CFA judges as well). The other panel be 'overseas', composed of distinguished senior judges from other common law jurisdictions. Jordan argues the 4+1 approach was part of a late attempt to limit the extent to which the CFA might consider itself empowered to act as a restraint on state behaviour rather than merely as the adjudicator of disputes.[7] While the records and minutes of the JLG are confidential,[8] it appears as though the decision to ensure that no more than a single overseas judge could sit on any one panel was a component of this effort.

In 1991, the LegCo voted 34-11 against the proposed 4+1 model, the 'first time in history that the Hong Kong legislature had stood up to oppose an agreement reached by Britain and China on the future of Hong Kong'.[9] Opponents argued that the text of the Basic Law meant that it should entirely a matter for the Court itself to decide how to use the overseas judges. Nonetheless, China was adamant that their role be limited in this way – the only concession offered was the abandonment of a plan to allow final decisions of the CFA to be subject to a veto.[10] Ultimately, the LegCo finally agreed to the plan in 1995, apparently out of concern that if the proposal was rejected once more then an even more restrictive option might be imposed post-handover.[11] The 4+1 model was duly incorporated into relevant law that would govern the operation of the CFA upon its establishment on 1 July 1997 – though that law still did not specify the circumstances under which the fifth member would be drawn from the overseas rather than the local panel.[12] This gap would later be exploited by the CFA itself to ensure the largest role possible for the overseas judges under the constraints of the 4+1 model.[13]

To be appointed as a member of the overseas panel, a candidate must be a judge or retired judge in a court of unlimited jurisdiction in another common law jurisdiction, not ordinarily resident in Hong Kong, and never have previously served as a lower court judge in Hong Kong.[14] In selecting candidates, the Chief Executive in practice acts upon the recommendation of the Judicial Officers Recommendation Commission (JORC).[15] The JORC is composed of the Chief Justice (the chair), the Secretary of Justice, two other judges, one barrister, one solicitor, and three persons unconnected with the practice of law.[16] Appointees must also be endorsed by the LegCo and the appointment must further be reported to the Standing Committee of the National People's Congress (NPCSC).[17]

Overseas judges take the same oath of office as local appointees, requiring them to 'uphold the Basic Law' and 'bear allegiance to the Hong Kong Special Administrative Region of the People's Republic of China'.[18] This indicates intent that when sitting the overseas judges are to be treated as full and equal members of the bench, unrestricted in the cases that they may hear. In this chapter, however, I will argue that the radical changes to Hong Kong's legal and political order over the last few years suggest reconsideration of this basic premise, in practice if not necessarily in law.

The Overseas Judges in Practice

Though the overseas judges invited to sit on the CFA have consistently been described as of the highest calibre,[19] as with judges writ large they are not a tremendously diverse group. Despite the Basic Law providing for the possibility of recruitment from anywhere in the common law world, the overseas judges have only ever been drawn from the courts of the United Kingdom, Australia, New Zealand, and Canada. At the time of writing in late 2021, the current roster of overseas judges is composed of 12 members.[20] Of these 12, all are white and only one is a woman (only two women have served on the CFA since 1997, and both were overseas appointees). There are seven Britons, one dual British-South African national, three Australians, and one Canadian. Notwithstanding the rather narrow demographic profile they represent, the overseas judges have always come to Hong Kong with distinguished prior roles and reputations.

While as noted the non-permanent judges are divided into two panels, in practice, it is the overseas panel that is of more importance. The first Chief Justice, Andrew Li, did not select the fifth member of the bench for each case in an alternating fashion from the two panels as perhaps the JLG had envisioned. Instead, whenever possible, he would invite a member of the 'overseas' panel to join and only relied on the 'local' non-permanent judges to fill in for an absent permanent member. There was one brief interruption to this continual use of the overseas judges in 2010, when significant volcanic eruptions in Iceland greatly disrupted air travel.[21] In general, however, the practice of inviting an overseas member to sit as the fifth member of the panel was essentially constant under both Li and the second Chief Justice, Geoffrey Ma, effectively becoming recognized as a convention.[22] While at the time of writing it is less than a year into the tenure of Andrew Cheung as the third Chief Justice, he also appears to have maintained this practice (though with one important caveat – of which more later). Their near-continuous presence has meant that even under the 4+1 model the overseas judges have played a significant role in the development of Hong Kong's jurisprudence in the SAR-era. Young and Da Roza were the first to provide a statistical analysis of the role the overseas judges play on the CFA. They found that between 1997 and 2010, roughly 25% of the opinions of the CFA on substantive matters were written by the overseas member of the panel.[23] I have subsequently shown that this declined to 21.6% over the following decade, dropping to 16.7% by 2019.[24] Nonetheless, a relative decline in prominence in recent years does not alter their historical significance and the overseas judges continue to play an important role in shaping Hong Kong law.

The overseas members have often been tapped to write unanimous opinions in areas of their expertise. Dixon and Jackson, for instance, point to the contributions of Millet and Hoffmann NPJJ in the local development of commercial law.[25] Lo argues the contributions of the overseas judges overall have been 'invaluable', particularly in the development of the Court's approach to the Basic Law.[26] Perhaps the highest profile of the overseas judges was Sir Anthony Mason NPJ.[27] His expertise in constitutional law matters meant he was invited to be part of the bench that considered issues of critical importance to the operation of the 'one country, two systems' model, such as the circumstances in which the CFA ought to approach the NPCSC for a formal interpretation of a provision of the Basic Law.[28] Mason NPJ also authored key unanimous opinions on other important public law matters, including the question of 'legal certainty' within a proportionality analysis[29] and the ability of the CFA to engage in remedial interpretation.[30] This kind of impact, of course, also explains some of the controversy surrounding the role of the overseas judges.

Justifying the Presence of the Overseas Judges Generally

Why should judges be imported at all? Many of the other jurisdictions[31] that allow non-citizens to serve as judges do so only due to a lack of sufficiently trained local legal talent. In the case of the ex-British colonies, the colonial process they were subjected to including both the imposition of the common law and the importation of foreigners to administer and enforce it.[32] When decolonization finally arrived, argues Boyd, this long history meant that there were insufficient numbers of highly trained locals to immediately take on key judicial roles.[33] Though the colonial period may have ended, the long-term consequences of such bias within the judiciary can remain, leading to continued reliance on foreign talent. Moreover regardless of colonial history, capacity concerns remain critical in the tiny microstates of the South Pacific that do not have the educational resources to train lawyers and judges locally. In such circumstances, importing judges may allow access to 'judicial expertise ... at limited cost'.[34]

But this does not hold water in Hong Kong. It is true that during the colonial period the Government failed for many years to adequately indigenize the judiciary,[35] and that may have meant a relative paucity of top-calibre local appointees to draw upon for the CFA initially. But the Hong Kong of today is a well-developed jurisdiction, with resources and wealth of which the microstates of the South Pacific can only dream. Hong Kong faces nothing like the capacity issues that may drive other jurisdictions to import judges. Indeed, since 1997, the number of non-local judges throughout the lower courts has declined substantially; 'most of the newly recruited members of the Judiciary ... are Chinese HKSAR permanent residents who often received their legal education in Hong Kong'.[36] This means there is ample local talent to draw upon when filling spaces on the CFA – the presence of the overseas judges is clearly 'optional' rather than necessary.

A different justification put forward elsewhere for judicial importation is to improve individual judicial independence. Dale suggests that the very small populations of the South Pacific microstates mean there is a much higher likelihood of a judge having some personal connection to a matter that comes before them.[37] Powles agrees, suggesting it is easier for an imported judge to maintain the 'social distance' from a litigant or matter necessary to fairly resolve a dispute.[38] But again, the situation of Hong Kong is different, both qualitatively and quantitatively. With a population of 7.5 million, Hong Kong may be a small jurisdiction in a global sense, but it is on an entirely different scale from the South Pacific microstates. Judges (at all levels) in Hong Kong are far less likely to be asked to preside over a case which might touch on some personal interest or connection than their counterparts in Nauru (population: 13,000) or Tonga (population: 110,000) – and even if they did, the scale of judicial resources available means it would cause no disruption should they recuse themselves. Indeed, neither Singapore nor New Zealand (both, like Hong Kong, wealthy common law jurisdictions with relatively small populations in a global sense) imports judges to sit in an unrestricted manner on their apex courts.[39] In short, there is no particular reason to suggest the presence of the overseas members in Hong Kong is required on impartiality grounds.

Particularly in a common law apex court, judges make decisions that can go to the very heart of a society. What is the boundary between different branches of government? What are the appropriate limits on the rights of assembly or speech? What constitutes a deprivation of justice or an unreasonable punishment? In short, judges may be asked to determine the nature and extent of the state's core obligations to its people. From a normative standpoint, why should a resident of Hong Kong (or the Central Government for that matter) accept that (Australian) Sir Anthony Mason has played such a dramatic role in shaping the constitutional relationship between Hong Kong and the rest of China? Why should they accept that (Canadian) Beverley McLachlin might be one of only five people to have a say on whether marriage equality should finally be recognized in Hong Kong? Australians and Canadians are not asked to trust similar decisions to a judge imported from Hong Kong, after all. If there is not an adequate link between the people making those determinations and the people whose interests are being determined, then there is a risk that those decisions will be seen as illegitimate, an 'unjustified imposition of outsider preferences, standards, or morality'.[40]

In Hong Kong, the overseas judges have on occasion been subject to this kind of criticism – after he wrote a unanimous opinion for the Court dealing with a defamation claim involving several figures with well-known political views, Nicholls NPJ was accused in the media of being a

> Parachute judge [without] any idea what Hong Kong Society is like; [who did] not know what language and [is] unable to listen to the local radio programmes; [who has] no real understanding of the issue and events surrounding Hong Kong society.[41]

Though such critiques of the overseas judges in Hong Kong have been relatively rare,[42] this kind of language is returning.[43] I have previously argued that the CFA has begun to modify aspects of its strategies of judicial presentation in a political climate marked by increasingly inflammatory rhetoric.[44] I will argue later in this chapter that this dynamic also points to (voluntary) exclusion of the overseas judges from hearing NSL-related cases by the Court itself.

But while the mere presence of the overseas judges can be perceived as an uncomfortable colonial echo, the unique constitutional framework of 'one country, two systems' still helps justify the presence of the overseas judges on the CFA in a general sense. The primary explanation for their ongoing presence (remember that their role is simply provided for in the Basic Law, not mandated) is a symbolic one. The continued presence of the overseas judges communicates to the outside world that the 'firewall' between the two legal systems remains intact. As far back as 1992, Goodhart et al. argued that a key justification for the presence of the overseas judges was to enhance confidence in the independence of the judiciary under the new sovereign.[45] With this in mind, one of the CFA's permanent members has described his overseas colleagues as 'canar[ies] in the coalmine'.[46] In other words, departure of the overseas judges would be a sign that something was deeply amiss. As Lord Neuberger (a current member of the overseas panel and formerly President of the UK Supreme Court) has put it:

> If I had any serious concerns about judicial independence or judicial impartiality in Hong Kong, I would not be sitting in the [Hong Kong Court of Final Appeal], and the same is I am sure true of the [other overseas judges]. They include a number of former and present members of the UK Supreme Court, a number of former members of the Australian High Court or State Supreme Courts, and I am sure that they adopt the same position as I do on this issue.[47]

It is plainly true that the role of the courts and the understanding of judicial independence are very different as between Hong Kong and the Mainland. Given that radical difference and Hong Kong's continued role as an economic bridge for foreign capital into the Chinese market, it is understandable that international business would be reassured by the presence of the overseas judges. Reflecting on his own long experience on the CFA, Sir Anthony Mason argued his presence and that of his fellow non-local colleagues 'probably [gave] a degree of reassurance' to outside investors that Hong Kong's status as an international financial centre – underpinned by an independent judiciary – was secure.[48] So too the former Chief Justice reports that he is 'told constantly by people in business and commerce' that the overseas judges significantly contribute to their confidence in Hong Kong as place to conduct their operations.[49] It is notable of course that these 'signalling' arguments are primarily made in the context of reassuring elite economic interests, rather than the so-called grassroots Hong Kong people. Nonetheless, it is also plausible that while part of the population will resent the presence of the overseas judges as an unnecessary artefact of Hong Kong's colonial past, another may perceive their continued presence as a welcome confirmation of the independence of the local courts. Thus, while I am deeply sceptical of claims Hong Kong's judicial independence writ large *depends* on their presence,[50] I agree the overseas judges continue to mark out an important distinction between the 'two systems', even as the gap between them perceptibly narrows. Given the unique circumstances and constitutional framework of 'one country, two systems', it is worth attempting to preserve their role where appropriate.

In the parts that follow, however, I suggest that the significant changes to Hong Kong's political and legal environment over the past few years suggest that even those who wish to preserve the role of the overseas judges generally may be well advised to support restricting it in the context of NSL-related offences.

The National Security Law and the Overseas Judges

Hong Kong was rocked by ongoing street protests throughout the latter half of 2019, subsiding only with the emergence of the COVID-19 pandemic.[51] Perceiving the protests as a challenge to not only local stability but also the authority of the state, the Standing Committee of the National People's Congress (NPCSC) directly drafted and inserted a new NSL[52] into Annex III of the Basic Law.[53] The NSL defines a range of national security offences and in effect creates a partially separate legal process for their investigation and prosecution.[54] The NSL not only reshapes criminal law in Hong Kong; since its provisions are not subject to constitutional review, it has implications for the implementation of 'one country, two systems' itself. The NSL is deemed to prevail in any event that there is conflict between its provision and those of another local law or the common law,[55] and the right of interpretation of the law is vested solely with the NPCSC.[56] It is the latest example of the Central Government's intent to exercise more strictly its 'comprehensive jurisdiction' over Hong Kong. This pattern predates the NSL but includes repeated suggestions about a need for tighter control over the judiciary. In 2014, for instance, a State Council White Paper stated that 'judges of the courts at different levels' had to be 'patriots ... [who] loved the country'.[57] The head of Beijing's liaison office in Hong Kong subsequently declared that the Chief Executive (who is accountable to the Central Government)[58] holds a 'transcendent position' above the branches of local government (including the judiciary).[59] In early 2021, Hong Kong's only delegate to the NPCSC called for reform of the judiciary, saying it was not 'an independent judicial kingdom' beyond 'restriction, regulation, or supervision'.[60]

During the drafting of the NSL, several pro-establishment figures had called for the exclusion of the overseas judges from hearing cases brought under it that reached the CFA,[61] while others called for the exclusion of *any* judge from hearing an NSL case at any level if they held a non-Chinese passport.[62] Other parts of the Hong Kong establishment pushed back against this idea, with the Chief Executive calling the latter idea 'unrealistic'.[63] In the end, the enacted version of NSL did not specifically exclude the overseas judges from hearing national security cases, instead providing that the Chief Executive is to designate a subset of judges from the existing panels (at all levels) to hear cases brought under the law, serving one-year term.[64] Before making such a designation, the Chief Executive may consult the Chief Justice and the (newly established) National Security Committee for advice but is not bound to accept it.[65] The Chief Executive indicated she would not use this power to 'hand pick' judges to hear particular cases and would in practice follow the advice of the Chief Justice.[66] In terms of relevant qualifications to be designated as a 'national security judge', there is no reference to nationality, citizenship, or similar concept anywhere in the text of the NSL; the only requirement is that an appointed judge has not 'made any statement or behaved in any manner endangering national security'.[67] Interestingly, this is quite a different from the approach taken in China's other SAR – Macau.

Macau's Basic Law allows 'qualified judges of foreign nationality' to be employed at all levels of the court system.[68] Portuguese language requirements and appropriate legal experience mean however that practically speaking foreign judges are drawn from only a few places – Portugal, Brazil, and Cape Verde. Macau's apex court is the Tribunal de Última Instância (TUI).[69] The TUI is composed of three members, and the Basic Law mandates its President be a Chinese national (just as the Basic Law of Hong Kong does for the Chief Justice).[70] Though there is no constitutional provision in Macau that parallels the Hong Kong model of 'overseas judges', the practice has nonetheless been that one member of the panel is Portuguese (though still typically a Macau permanent resident). The lack of the 'parachute aspect' to the non-Chinese judge on the TUI along with the more limited roles judges generally play under a civil law system means the presence of 'foreigners' on the TUI has been relatively uncontroversial. Nonetheless, in 2019, Macau adopted an amendment requiring that judges at all levels hearing cases brought under its version of the NSL[71] be Chinese citizens.[72]

Excluding the Overseas Judges: Ideological and Practical Grounds

While Hong Kong's NSL does not explicitly preclude overseas judges from hearing cases brought under it, I suggest as a matter of practice the Chief Justice should advise the Chief Executive *against* selecting them. This would be a constitutionally valid option, as the Basic Law provides only that the CFA may call upon overseas members 'as required'.[73] It would also be consistent with the *Valente* principles of judicial independence, one of which is that it is the judiciary itself that has control of the assigning of judges to cases.[74] While of course the NSL does not require the Chief Executive to accept the advice of the Chief Justice and she could in theory directly assign one of the overseas members to hear an NSL case, this is a remote prospect. 'Voluntary exclusion' means no legislative or constitutional change is required for implementation and given how few NSL cases will ultimately come before the CFA, there is likely to be relatively little public (both local and international) attention paid. This would surely be welcomed by a Hong Kong executive branch that desperately wants to convince the world that the

NSL is no cause for alarm.[75] But a voluntary decision by the Chief Justice to not put forward the names of the overseas judges for consideration as national security-designated judges would have benefits beyond this.

There is a strong normative claim that 'outsiders' should not preside over matters that touch upon the 'national interest'. This goes beyond the general concerns raised earlier about so-called parachute judges. It *also* outweighs the general symbolic function that justifies the presence of the overseas members. Judges designated to hear NSL cases may preside over alleged offences of subversion not only of the regional government but also of the state. They may hear matters related to secession. They may hear matters involving state secrets. It is inconceivable that the home nations of the overseas members would allow judges from elsewhere to preside over the same matters on their apex courts. That the NSL is written in general language and may be used to crack down on relatively minor dissent does not mean every charge brought under it is necessarily illegitimate (and as I will argue later, potential abuse of the law cannot be remedied via the presence of an overseas judge). The stark distinction between the 'two systems' does not mean the 'one country' has no legitimate national interests in events that occur in or arise out of Hong Kong.

As noted, it is true that the overseas judges and the local judges take the same oath of office,[76] and for this reason, the former Chief Justice has tried to make clear that when sitting in Hong Kong the overseas judges should be considered purely as 'Hong Kong judges' rather than foreign.[77] However, the issue is not whether overseas judges are *capable* of fairly applying the requirements of the NSL specifically or the law of Hong Kong generally (indeed of that I have little doubt). Rather the objection turns on the point that notwithstanding the oath they take, they are not linked to the nation in a way that most would consider meaningful. This matters on a symbolic level that is just as important as the 'symbolism' that is said to justify the presence of the overseas judges generally: judicial decisions that touch upon the 'national interest' ought to be made only by those meaningfully connected to the nation in some way. MacFarlane is correct when he suggests that the presence of outsiders in judicial determinations that touch on core societal questions means 'an important symbol of independence' is lost.[78]

Indeed, this is why some of the jurisdictions that use judges drawn from outside the community place strict limits on the kinds of cases they may hear. Singapore, for example, allows the appointment of 'international judges' to its Supreme Court.[79] However, the Singaporean Constitution also provides that Parliament may limit the classes of cases that they may hear,[80] and they are presently limited to sitting *only* in the International Commercial Court.[81] Similarly, Nauru previously relied[82] on the High Court of Australia to serve as its top appellate court; however, the relevant treaty[83] explicitly excluded core constitutional questions from being heard by that body.[84] It is entirely reasonable to argue that only those meaningfully connected to a society should make final determinations on legal matters connected to core national interests. With respect, a generously remunerated judge flown into Hong Kong for a few weeks a year to hear the cases to which they have been assigned does not meet this threshold.

I do not advocate that cases brought under the NSL should *only* be heard by judges with Chinese citizenship and no other nationality (the requirement that applies only to the role of the Chief Justice). To do so implies that judges who happen to hold a non-Chinese citizenship will use their role to surreptitiously advance the interests of another state. This is an unnecessary and unjustified attack on judicial neutrality and judicial independence. Thus, I reject the suggestion of the vice-chairman of China's Legislative Affairs Commission that judges in Hong Kong with dual nationality necessarily have 'dual allegiance' and therefore ought to be barred from hearing NSL cases.[85] The particular history of Hong Kong and the complexities of China's Nationality Law[86] mean that the holding of a second nationality or right of citizenship is widespread throughout the Hong Kong elite and that long-term residents of Hong Kong born elsewhere rarely become Chinese citizens.[87] Instead, they are granted the 'right of abode', or permanent resident status.[88]

There are many excellent local judges in both of these categories who, regardless of ethnic background or passport particulars, form an integral part of Hong Kong society and are committed to serving its people. Whether a judge is a Chinese national with no right of abode elsewhere, a Chinese national also in possession of a claim to another citizenship or nationality, or a non-Chinese national with the right of abode in Hong Kong, all may be qualified to be assigned as a national security judge. Eligibility to serve as an NSL judge should not be based upon meeting an ethno-cultural standard, but rather simply a demonstration of meaningful connection to the nation. But while Chinese and non-Chinese Hong Kong residents alike may have that requisite connection, the overseas judges do not. Regardless of the Basic Law's provision for their role in a general sense, it is therefore inappropriate to ask them to hear cases deemed to touch on the national interest.

There is also a practical argument against assigning overseas judges to sit on NSL cases. Their presence in highly sensitive circumstances may trigger a conflict with the Central Government over their broader role that the Court will inevitably lose. The unrest of 2019 clearly shook Beijing, and both it and the local Government have regularly accused 'foreign forces' of being behind it (though without offering much evidence).[89] The response came not only in the form of the NSL, but also in a clear intent for the centre to exercise closer control over the SAR through the mechanism of 'comprehensive jurisdiction'. As I have suggested, it is indeed unusual for 'foreign' judges to sit on a common law apex court in a wealthy and well-developed jurisdiction. While necessarily speculative, in a political environment characterized by the increasing rhetoric about external influence, one may imagine the presence of the overseas judges in cases related to 'national security' being leveraged to justify amending the Basic Law so as to remove them *entirely*.

Voluntary Exclusion as a Strategic Response

In separate research, I have argued that the CFA has responded to an increasingly challenging political environment in several ways, including altering its judicial presentation strategies. First, the Court no longer assigns the overseas judges individually write lead opinions in cases related to potentially controversial constitutional and public law issues.[90] Second, in a range of 'sensitive' cases (including thus far the only NSL-related case to it), the CFA now publishes its opinions as an anonymous collective rather than with a single judge writing a unanimous opinion on behalf of their colleagues (the typical pattern).[91] Both of these developments reflect a strategic effort by the Court to downplay the public face of any individual member – but in particular the overseas members – when certain issues come before it. These two tactics of judicial *presentation* sit alongside the trajectory of the Court in terms of the *substance* of its decisions, which is increasingly deferential towards the state in areas other than 'social' equality rights.[92]

These changes suggest a Court hoping to minimize the possibility of becoming embroiled in a serious constitutional crisis that it cannot win, whilst still trying to preserve its fundamental role. A pre-emptive decision by the Chief Justice to decline to put forward the overseas judges for consideration by the Chief Executive for designation as national security judges would be consistent with this pattern – a concession to the centre that (while not without costs) does not gut the Court's fundamental role. If it does serve to avoid open institutional conflict over the appropriateness of their role in a general sense, voluntary exclusion of the overseas judges from NSL-related matters may preserve the Court's ability to call on them otherwise.

What of those 'costs'? It is possible that a wide array of non-violent speech may ultimately be deemed a matter of subversion or threat to national security in a way that would not be the case in the home jurisdictions of the overseas judges. Because of this kind of uncertainty, decisions to resign or stay by the overseas judges will remain closely scrutinized.[93] While there is mixed evidence thus far,[94] it is clear that at least some have (or have had) concerns about the implications of the NSL. Voluntary exclusion may provide those who might otherwise have resigned with a kind of moral cover. It might allow them to continue to serve whilst claiming their presence does not give a kind of imprimatur of international acceptability to the way in which the NSL is applied. Given that historically Western interest in the particulars of the judicial structure of Hong Kong seems primarily a matter of international financial interest rather than concern for the population, this is a plausible risk.

On that account, then perhaps the voluntary exclusion for which I have advocated would remove the 'canary' function altogether, limiting international insight into or awareness of a broader collapse of judicial independence. Dziedzic, for instance, argues that either 'de facto or express prohibition' of the overseas judges from hearing NSL cases would have 'implications for the entire legal system because foreign judges represent Hong Kong's common law'.[95] But though the overseas judges *do* represent a historical connection to a shared legal heritage, the ongoing effective or fair use of the common law does not depend on them – nor can it be guaranteed by them. Hong Kong has long since moved past the need to import judicial talent for substantive reasons and the simple presence of the overseas judges cannot magically preserve judicial independence nor prevent problematic misuse of the provisions of the NSL. As Tang PJ said upon his retirement, 'the independence of the judiciary and maintenance of the rule of law must depend on the local judges. The buck must stop at us'.[96]

Conclusion: A Constitutional Convention against the Use of the Overseas Judges in NSL Cases

Early signs point to the overseas judges being excluded in the way I recommend in this chapter. In the sole NSL case to reach the CFA at the time of writing (mid-2021), no judge from the overseas panel was invited to sit as part of the bench.[97] Contrary to the usual practice, the fifth member was drawn from the non-permanent local panel. While the COVID-19 pandemic has certainly disrupted the ability of the overseas judges to participate in person, they were invited to hear other cases in the same period.[98] This suggests the decision was a conscious one, rather than one forced by circumstance. For the reasons I have explained, this is a wise decision on the part of the Chief Justice – assuming he was the one who made it. While it is of course possible that he recommended the appointment of an overseas member to sit on *Lai Chee Ying* and it was rejected by the Chief Executive, this seems unlikely for the reasons I earlier discussed. Notably, the fifth member of the bench in *Lai Chee Ying* was Stock NPJ – a retired judge of the Court of Appeal. Though born in Zimbabwe and educated in the United Kingdom, Stock NPJ is a long-term permanent resident of Hong Kong with a distinguished local legal career. The choice to nominate Stock NPJ as a 'national security judge' and assign him to hear *Lai Chee Ying* shows a (welcome) appreciation that the standard required to be an NSL-designated judge is not connected to ethnicity or citizenship, but rather about the sufficiency of one's connection to Hong Kong; Stock NPJ undoubtedly meets that standard.

Because of the general wording of Art. 82, I expect that exclusion of the overseas judges from cases brought under the NSL will gradually become a constitutional convention, just as their inclusion in virtually every case became a convention under the first Chief Justice. While there are costs, voluntary exclusion of the overseas judges from hearing cases brought under the NSL also has clear benefits. Normatively, it asserts that while post-colonial Hong Kong need not rely on outsiders for assistance in resolving legal issues connected to national interests, the unique constitutional framework of 'one country, two systems' means that for symbolic reasons the practice will generally continue when less controversial matters are before the courts. Practically, it may limit the chance of the Court coming into a conflict with the Central Government over the core of their role. Of course, the preservation of judicial independence in Hong Kong ultimately depends on Beijing's commitment to upholding the very different approaches to law and governance as between the two systems; at its core, it is a matter of political *will* rather than legal *structure*.

Notes

1 A number of the South Pacific 'microstates' import judges, including the Fiji Islands, Kiribati, the Marshall Islands, Micronesia, Nauru, Papua New Guinea, Samoa, the Solomon Islands, Tonga, Tuvalu, and Vanuatu. In Africa, the practice is found in Botswana, Gambia, Lesotho, and Swaziland. In Asia, Singapore also allows foreign judges to sit (though not in an unrestricted fashion – they may only serve on the International Commercial Court). Brunei allows foreigners to serve on its constitutional interpretation tribunal, though at least one of three must have extensive experience in Islamic tradition or law. Of the European civil law jurisdictions, Lichtenstein allows for two members of its five-person constitutional court to be non-citizens. Most members of the Monaco Supreme Court and the Seychelles Court of Appeal are non-citizens. In Bosnia and Herzegovina, the Constitutional Court is composed of nine members: four from the Federation of Bosnia and Herzegovina, two from the Republika Srpska, and three selected by the Presidents of the European Court of Human Rights who may not be citizens of either Bosnia and Herzegovina or any of its neighbours.

2 Law of the People's Republic of China on Safeguarding National Security in the Hong Kong Special Administrative Region 《中華人民共和國香 港特別行政區維護國家安全法》, G.N. (E.) 72 of 2020: https://www.gld.gov.hk/egazette/pdf/20202444e/es220202444136.pdf [CHI]; https://www.gld.gov.hk/egazette/pdf/20202448e/egn2020244872.pdf [ENG, but note English translation is provided only "as reference" rather than an official version of law] (hereafter, "the NSL").

3 Joint Declaration of the Government of the United Kingdom of Great Britain and Northern Ireland and the Government of the People's Republic of China on the Question of Hong Kong (19 December 1984), available online at: https://www.elegislation.gov.hk/doc/ref_jd_en.pdf (hereafter, "the Joint Declaration").

4 The Joint Declaration, Annex I (III).

5 The Basic Law of the Hong Kong Special Administrative Region of the People's Republic of China, available online at: https://www.basiclaw.gov.hk/en/basiclaw/index.html (hereafter, "the Basic Law"), Art. 82.

6 Ibid., Art. 90.

7 Jordan, Ann D., "Lost in the Translation: Two Legal Cultures, the Common Law Judiciary and the Basic Law of the Hong Kong Special Administrative Region" (1997) 30 Cornell Journal of International Law 335, 345–347.

8 Lee, Donna, "Discrepancy between Theory and Reality: Hong Kong's Court of Final Appeal and the Acts of State Doctrine" (1997) 35 Columbia Journal of Transnational Law 175, 186.
9 Tang, James TH and Frank Ching, "The MacLehose-Youde Years: Balancing the 'Three-Legged Stool', 1971–86" in Chan, Ming K. ed., *Precarious Balance: Hong Kong between China and Britain, 1842–1992* (Taylor & Francis, Abingdon, UK: 1994), 189.
10 Lo, Pui-yin, "An Internationalist, Consequentialist and Non-Progressive Court: Constitutional Adjudication in Hong Kong (1997–2009)" (2010) 2 City University Hong Kong Law Review 215, 224.
11 Conner, Alison W., "Legal Institutions in Transitional Hong Kong" in Chan, Ming K. ed., *Precarious Balance: Hong Kong between China and Britain, 1842–1992* (Taylor & Francis, Abingdon, UK: 1994), 86.
12 Court of Final Appeal Ordinance, Cap. 484, s. 16(1).
13 *Infra*, note 20, 21.
14 Ibid., s. 12(4).
15 Ibid., s. 9(2).
16 Judicial Officers Recommendation Commission Ordinance, Cap. 92, s. 3(1).
17 Court of Final Appeal Ordinance, Cap. 484, s. 7A.
18 Oaths & Declarations Ordinance, Cap. 11, Sched. 2, Part V.
19 Young, Simon NM and Antonio Da Roza, "The Judges" in Simon NM Young and Yash Gai, eds., Hong Kong's Court of Final Appeal: The Development of the Law in China's Hong Kong (Cambridge University Press, Cambridge: 2013), 263; Mason, Anthony, "Sharing Expertise with the Developing World" (2001) 26 Alternative Law Journal 7, unpaginated: http://www5.austlii.edu.au/au/journals/AltLawJl/2001/3.html; Fok, Joseph, "The Influence of the Australian judges on the Hong Kong Court of Final Appeal", Speech to the Law Council of Australia (Hong Kong Chapter): https://www.hkcfa.hk/filemanager/speech/en/upload/182/LCA%20HK%20Chapter%20speech.pdf, at 24.
20 "Hong Kong Non-Permanent Judges": https://www.hkcfa.hk/en/about/who/judges/npjs/index.html.
21 Fok, *supra* note 19, at 12. Perhaps due to the advancement of online video conferencing technologies in the intervening years, the emergence of COVID-19 and associated practical limits on air travel due to quarantine rules did not appear to disrupt the role of the overseas judges in the same way in 2020 and 2021.
22 Young, Simon NM, Antonio Da Roza, and Yash Ghai, "The Chief Justice" in Simon NM Young and Yash Gai, eds., Hong Kong's Court of Final Appeal: The Development of the Law in China's Hong Kong (Cambridge University Press, Cambridge: 2013), 231; Young Simon NM and Antonio Da Roza, "Judges and Judging in the Court of Final Appeal: a Statistical Picture" (2010) 8 Hong Kong Lawyer 23, 4.
23 Young and Da Roza 2013, *supra* note 19, 263. See also Young and Da Roza 2010, *supra* note 21, 8.
24 Hargreaves, Stuart, "Canaries or Colonials? The Reduced Prominence of the "Overseas Judges" on Hong Kong's Court of Final Appeal" (2022) Asian Journal of Comparative Law, 1–31. doi:10.1017/asjcl.2021.15.
25 Dixon, Rosalind and Jackson Vicki C, "Hybrid Constitutional Courts: Foreign Judges on National Constitutional Courts" (2019) 57 Columbia Journal of Transnational Law 283, 324.
26 Lo 2010, *supra* note 10, 225.
27 Lo 2010, *supra* note 10, 225; Young and Da Roza 2010, *supra* note 22, 4.
28 See for example *Ng Ka Ling v Director of Immigration,* [1999] HKCFA 72; *Democratic Republic of the Congo v FG Hemisphere Associates LLC* [2011] HKCFA 41.
29 *Shum Kwok Sher v HKSAR*, [2002] 2 HKCFA 27.
30 *HKSAR v Lam Kwong Wai*, [2006] HKCFA 84.
31 See fn 1.
32 See generally Dziedzic, Anna, "Foreign Judges on Pacific Courts: Implications for a Reflective Judiciary" (2018) Federalisimi, Reflective Judiciary N. 5: https://www.federalismi.it/nv14/articolo-documento.cfm?Artid=37246.
33 Boyd, Susan, "Australian Judges at Work Internationally: Treason, Assassinations, Coups, Legitimacy of Government, Human Rights, Poverty and Development" (2003) 77 Australian Law Journal 303, 306.
34 Baird, Natalie, "Judges as Cultural Outsiders: Exploring the Expatriate Model of Judging in the Pacific" (2013) 19 Canterbury Law Review 80, 82.

35 See Lin, Feng, "The Expatriate Judges and Rule of Law in Hong Kong: Its Past, Present and Future" in Shimon Shetreet and Wayne McCormack eds., *The Culture of Judicial Independence in a Globalised World* (Brill, Leiden: 2017), 291.
36 Lo, Pui-yin, "Twilight of the Idolised: Backsliding in Hong Kong's Legal and Judicial Cultures" in Cora Chan and Fiona de Londras, eds., *China's National Security: Endangering Hong Kong's Rule of Law?* (Hart Publishing, Oxford: 2020), 138.
37 Dale, Gregory, "Appealing to Whom – Australia's Appellate Jurisdiction over Nauru" (2007) 56 International and Comparative Law Quarterly 641, 643, also citing David Simmons, "Issues of Judicial Independence in the Caribbean Courtroom" (2001) 14 Commonwealth Judicial Journal 8, 13.
38 Powles, Guy, "Law, Courts and Legal Services in Pacific Societies" in Guy Powles and Mere Pulea, eds., *Pacific Courts and Legal Systems* (The Institute of Pacific Studies of the University of the South Pacific, Suva: 1988), 27.
39 New Zealand even *exports* judges – both to the South Pacific microstates and, ironically, Hong Kong.
40 Hargreaves 2022, *supra* note 24, 10.
41 Cottrell, Jill, "Fair Comment, Judges and Politics in Hong Kong" (2003) 27 Melbourne University Law Review 33, 62 (citing Ma Lik, "A Judgment Found Wanting", HK iMail (no longer available online)).
42 Young and Da Roza 2013, *supra* note 18, 267.
43 Hargreaves 2022, *supra* note 24, 23–25.
44 See e.g. Hargreaves 2022, *supra* note 24 and Hargreaves, Stuart, "'The Court' Rises: The New Use of Depersonalized Opinions on Hong Kong's Court of Final Appeal" (2021) 51(1) Hong Kong Law Journal 141.
45 Goodhart, William et al., "Countdown to 1997: Report of a Mission to Hong Kong" 1992 Report by the International Commission of Jurists, Geneva, 87.
46 Fok *supra* note 19, 26.
47 Neuberger, David "Judges, Access to Justice, the Rule of Law and the Court of Final Appeal under "One Country Two Systems"", Speech to University of Hong Kong, 13 Sept. 2017: https://www.hkcfa.hk/filemanager/speech/en/upload/1195/Judges,%20Access%20to%20Justice,%20the%20Rule%20of%20Law%20and%20the%20Court%20of%20Final%20Appeal%20under%20"One%20Country%20Two%20Systems".pdf, 22.
48 Mason, Anthony, "The Place of Comparative Law in Developing the Jurisprudence on the Rule of Law and Human Rights in Hong Kong" (2007) 37 Hong Kong Law Journal 299, 302.
49 "Foreign judges key to success of Hong Kong's top court, chief justice says", SCMP, 26 Jun 2018: https://www.scmp.com/news/hong-kong/hong-kong-law-and-crime/article/2152512/foreign-judges-key-success-hong-kongs-top.
50 See for example "Loss of overseas judges would have devastating impact on Hong Kong", SCMP, 21 Mar. 2021: https://www.scmp.com/comment/opinion/article/3126301/loss-overseas-judges-would-have-devastating-impact.
51 The protests began as peaceful opposition to a proposal to amend a law so that alleged fugitives could be extradited from Hong Kong to jurisdictions (including Mainland China) with which Hong Kong did not have an extradition treaty. Though that proposal was eventually withdrawn by the Government, by that point the protests had morphed into much wider complaints about governance in the SAR. The latter half of 2019 saw violent clashes on a weekly basis between groups of protestors and the police. See e.g. Lee, Francis, Samson Yuen, Gary Tang, and Edmund W. Cheng, "Hong Kong's Summer of Uprising: From Anti-Extradition to Anti-Authoritarian Protests" (2019) 4(19) China Review 1; Martin Purbrick, "A Report of the 2019 Hong Kong Protests", (2019) 50(4) Asian Affairs 465.
52 The NSL *supra* note 3.
53 Promulgation of National Law 2020, L.N. 136 of 2020: https://www.gld.gov.hk/egazette/pdf/20202444e/es220202444136.pdf.
54 For discussion of the substance, see e.g. Young, Simon NM, "The Law of the People's Republic of China on Safeguarding National Security in the Hong Kong Special Administrative Region" (2021) 60(1) International Legal Materials 1; Zhu, Han, "The Hong Kong National Security Law: The Shifted Grundnorm of Hong Kong's Legal Order and Its Implications" (March 13, 2021) University of Hong Kong Faculty of Law Research Paper: https://ssrn.com/

abstract=3812146; Chan, Cora, "Can Hong Kong Remain a Liberal Enclave in China? Analysis of the Hong Kong National Security Law" (2021) Public Law 271.

55 The NSL, Art. 62.

56 The NSL, Art. 65.

57 "The Practice of the 'One Country, Two Systems' Policy in the Hong Kong Special Administrative Region", the State Council of the People's Republic of China, June 2014: http://english.www.gov.cn/archive/white_paper/2014/08/23/content_281474982986578.htm.

58 The Basic Law, Art. 43.

59 "'Hong Kong leader is above the executive branch, legislature and courts', says Beijing's liaison chief", SCMP, 12 Sept. 2015: https://www.scmp.com/news/hong-kong/politics/article/1857506/hong-kong-leader-above-executive-branch-legislature-and.

60 "Hong Kong not an 'independent judicial kingdom': pro-Beijing heavyweight doubles down on reform calls", SCMP, 4 Jan. 2021: https://www.scmp.com/news/hong-kong/politics/article/3116411/hong-kong-not-independent-judicial-kingdom-pro-beijing.

61 "China's Hong Kong law set to bar foreign judges from national security cases: sources", Reuters, 26 May 2020: https://www.reuters.com/article/us-china-parliament-hongkong-security/chinas-hong-kong-law-set-to-%20bar-foreign-judges-from-national-security-cases-sources-idUSKBN2321CW.

62 "Judges with 'dual allegiance' because of foreign nationality should not handle national security cases, Beijing says", SCMP, 24 June 2020: https://www.scmp.com/news/hong-kong/politics/article/3090400/hong-kong-national-security-law-citys-leader-must-have.

63 "National security law: Hong Kong leader Carrie Lam vows not to hand-pick judges for cases brought under new legislation", SCMP, 23 June 2020: https://www.scmp.com/news/hong-kong/politics/article/3090218/national-security-law-hong-kong-leader-carrie-lam-rejects.

64 The NSL, Art. 44.

65 The NSL, Art. 44.

66 *Supra* note 63.

67 The NSL, Art. 44.

68 Lei Básica da Região Administrativa Especial de Macau da República Popular da China (hereafter, "the Basic Law of Macao"), Art. 87.

69 Tribunal de Última Instância, https://www.court.gov.mo/pt/subpage/tui.

70 Basic Law of Macau, Art. 88.

71 Lei relativa à defesa da segurança do Estado (Defence of State Security Law), Lei no. 2/2009.

72 Lei de Bases da Organização Judiciária (Judicial Organization Framework Law), Lei no. 9/1999, Artigo 19.º-A.

73 Basic Law, Art. 82.

74 *R v Valente*, [1985] 2 SCR 673. This of course presumes that the Chief Executive does in fact follow the Chief Justice's advice, since under the NSL it is the former who has the substantive appointment power.

75 "Hong Kong courts free of government meddling, justice minister says in backing comments by leading British judge", SCMP, 19 Mar. 2021: https://www.scmp.com/news/hong-kong/politics/article/3126206/hong-kong-courts-free-government-meddling-justice-minister.

76 *Supra* note 18. Interestingly, the Government of Hong Kong has claimed that taking this oath is functionally equivalent to "loving the country" (see e.g. LCQ1: White Paper on "The Practice of the 'One Country, Two Systems' Policy in the Hong Kong Special Administrative Region", 9 July 2014:
https://www.doj.gov.hk/en/community_engagement/press/20140709_pr.html). It is reasonable to question whether the overseas judges in fact consider it in the same way – for commentary, see reported views in Fok, *supra* note 21, 16.

77 *Supra* note 49.

78 MacFarlane, Peter, "Some Challenges Facing Legal Strengthening Projects" 2006 4(1) Journal of Commonwealth Law & Legal Education 103, 105.

79 Constitution of the Republic of Singapore 1963 (rev. 2016), s. 95(4) (c).

80 Constitution of the Republic of Singapore 1963 (rev. 2016), s. 95(10).

81 Supreme Court of Judicature Act, Ch. 322, s. 5A.

82 Nauru withdrew from the agreement with Australia in 2018, apparently to ensure the prosecution of several political dissidents. See "Nauru's former president accuses

Australia of being complicit in 'political prosecution'", The Guardian, 4 Apr 2018: https://www.theguardian.com/world/2018/apr/04/nauru-withdraws-right-of-appeal-to-australias-high-court-blocking-political-protestors.

83 "Agreement between the Government of Australia and the Government of the Republic of Nauru relating to Appeals to the High Court of Australia from the Supreme Court of Nauru", Australian Treaty Series 1977 No 11: http://classic.austlii.edu.au/au/other/dfat/treaties/ATS/1977/11.html.

84 Dale, *supra* note 37, 649–650, 658.

85 *Supra* note 62.

86 Nationality Law of the People's Republic of China, adopted at the 3rd Session of the 5th National People's Congress, promulgated by Order No. 8 of the Chairman of the Standing Committee of the National People's Congress and effective as of 10 September 1980). Art. 3 of the Nationality Law rejects the concept of dual nationality; however, the "explanations" included in the law state that Chinese nationals in Hong Kong with the right of abode in another state may rely on travel documents (passports) issued by those states for travel.

87 See generally Low, CC, *Report on Citizenship Law: China & Taiwan*, RSCAS/EUDO-CIT-CR 2016/10, October 2016.

88 The Basic Law, Art. 24(2) (4); Immigration Ordinance, Cap. 115, Sched. 1., s. 2(d).

89 See e.g. "Hong Kong protest violence being fanned by foreign forces, China's Wang Yi claims", SCMP, 22 Oct. 2019: https://www.scmp.com/news/china/article/3033963/chinas-wang-yi-blames-foreign-forces-sowing-chaos-hong-kong; "In Hong Kong protests, China angrily connects the dots back to US", The New York Times, 5 Sept. 2019: https://www.nytimes.com/2019/09/05/world/asia/china-hong-kong-protests.html; "Hong Kong universities 'penetrated by foreign forces' intent on 'indoctrinating' students, claims Chief Exec. Carrie Lam", Hong Kong Free Press, 8 Jun. 2021: https://hongkongfp.com/2021/06/08/hong-kong-universities-penetrated-by-foreign-forces-intent-on-indoctrinating-students-claims-chief-exec-carrie-lam/.

90 Hargreaves 2022, *supra* note 24.

91 Hargreaves 2021, *supra* note 44.

92 See e.g. Lo 2010, *supra* note 10; Lo 2020 *supra* note 36; Abeyratne, Rehan "More Structure, More Deference: Proportionality in Hong Kong" in Po Jen Yap, ed., *Proportionality in Asia* (Cambridge University Press, 2020).

93 Dziedzic, Anna, "Foreign Judges and Hong Kong's new National Security Law" (2020) 25(2) Commonwealth Judicial Journal 27.

94 There is mixed evidence on the reaction of the overseas judges so far. Spigelman NPJ resigned, explicitly pointing to provisions in the NSL. Hale NPJ chose not to renew her contract; she noted that the NSL had raised "questions" but said her primary reason for not renewing was COVID-19. In contrast, Reed and French NPJJ both indicated an ongoing confidence in the independence of the judiciary. See "Hong Kong judiciary says British judge to step down from city's top court", Reuters, 4 Jun. 2021: https://www.reuters.com/world/china/hong-kong-judiciary-says-british-judge-step-down-citys-top-court-2021-06-04/; "Hong Kong's judicial independence gets vote of confidence from top British judges, with pair deciding to continue serving on city's top court", SCMP, 27 Aug. 2021: https://www.scmp.com/news/hong-kong/politics/article/3146707/hong-kongs-judicial-independence-gets-vote-confidence-top.

95 Dziedzic, *supra* note 93.

96 *Farewell Sitting for the Honourable Mr Justice Tang PJ* (2018) 21 HKCFAR 530, 535 (cited in Lo 2020, *supra* note 36).

97 *HKSAR v Lai Chee Ying*, [2021] HKCFA 3. The five-member panel consisted of Cheung CJ, Ribeiro PJ, Fok PJ, Chan NPJ, and Stock NPJ.

98 *Lai Chee Ying* was heard in early February 2021. In January 2021, overseas member Lord Neuberger NPJ was part of the panel that heard *HKSAR v Lo Kin Sun* [2021] HKCFA 1; in March 2021, overseas member Lord Hoffman NPJ was part of the panel that released its judgement on costs in *Kwok Wing Hang & Ors v Chief Executive in Council & Anor* [2021] HKCFA 11; in April 2021, overseas member Gummow NPJ was part of the panel that heard *Hsin Chong Construction Company Limited v Build King Construction Limited* [2021] HKCFA 14. In other words, in the first four months of 2021, there were no cases heard by a full five-member panel that did not include an overseas judge other than *Lai Chee Ying*.

INDEX

Abdülhamid II 5, 10
Ackerman, Bruce 147
Administrative Litigation Law (ALL) 175, 177–178
Administrative Procedural Law 328
Afghanistan 5
AIDS prevention 223
Albania 25
Alexander I 4
ALL *see* Administrative Litigation Law
All-China Federation of Trade Unions 257
amparo 170–171
Annual Conference of 'Politics, Law and Public Policy' 252
Anti-Employment Discrimination Law 230
anti-extradition bill amendment protests, Hong Kong 179
anti-extradition bill protest, 2019 204, 210–211, 214–217
2012 Anti-National Education Demonstration 208
Anti-Rightist Campaign, 1957–59 27
anxious scrutiny 352
authoritarian constitutionalism 67, 205, 211, 218, 312
authoritarian legality 207, 260, 311
autocracy 6, 9, 91
autonomous city: constitutional status 105; disputes and legal questions 105; economic freedom 102; governance structures 104–105; HKSAR and MSAR 101–106

Backer, Larry C. 86, 93–94, 312, 316, 318
Balme, Stephanie 93
Basic Law, Hong Kong (HKBL) 272, 342, 345, 360; achieving democratisation 208–209; anti-extradition bill protest 210; Article 8 54; Article 18 157; Article 22(4) 153; Article 24(2) 153; Article 27 158; Article 39 55, 347; Article 82 357; in Beijing 190; BLCC 35–37; BLDC 35–38; BPG 36, 38; CE 41; Cha-Cha model 36; consultation period 36; *de facto* amendment 155; drafting 34–38; drafting committee 52–53; drafting process 51–56; educational institutions 192; exercise of powers, central authorities 39–40; first draft 36; of Hong Kong SAR (HKBL) 237; ICESCR 275; implementation 39–45, 56–59; to 'improve medical and health services' 272; JCPDG 36; JD 34–36; LegCo 35–36, 38–40, 214; of Macao SAR (MBL) 237; and Macau Basic Law 276; 4-4-2 model 38; NPCSC 39–42, 190, 198; and NSL 187–188; OCTS 34, 43; and 'one country, two systems' architecture 208; 1990–1997 period developments 38–39; 2016–2021 period developments 43–45; political system, development of 40–43; PRC Constitution 244; pro-China camp 41; of SARs 239–240, 326; second draft, improvements in 37; transition period 189; White Paper, The 36
Basic Law Consultative Committee (BLCC): BPG 36; establishment 35; inaugural meeting 35; plenary meetings 35
Basic Law Drafting Committee (BLDC): inaugural meeting 35; members 35, 37; plenary sessions 36–38; subgroups 35–36
Beijing 21, 35, 37–38, 41–42, 44, 49–53, 56–59, 86, 99–101, 152, 173, 187–194, 208–210, 214–217, 230, 289, 305, 337, 361, 364, 366; anti-extradition bill protest 216–217; Basic Law 190, 209; as colour revolution 216; executive-led government model 210; foreign forces 364; Joint Declaration 189; national

security 187; National Security Advisor 192; new security institutions and relationship 191–194; NSL 192–193, 195; Occupy Central 217; and pan-democratic camp 215; patron-client politics 189; for political support 189; role in local policing 192
2000 Beijing Regulations on Zhongguancun Science and Technology Park 289
Belt and Road Initiative (BRI) 287, 292
bilateral investment treaty (BIT) 287, 292–294
Bill of Rights 343
Bill of Rights Ordinance (BORO) 151–152, 157–159, 161, 163
BLCC *see* Basic Law Consultative Committee
BLDC *see* Basic Law Drafting Committee
BORO *see* Bill of Rights Ordinance
BPG *see* Business and Professional Group
Brexit movement 344
Brief Survey of the Chinese Constitution, A (Xie) 140
British reservation 346
British Royal Navy 50
brownfield investment model 289
Buhi, Jason 310
Building Constitutionalism in China (Balme and Dowdle) 93
Business and Professional Group (BPG) 36, 38

Cai, Dingjian 120
CCP *see* Chinese Communist Party
CCPA *see* Constitutional Court Procedure Act
CEDAW *see* UN Convention on the Elimination of All Forms of Discrimination against Women
CFA *see* Court of Final Appeal
Cha, Louis 38
Cha-Cha model, HKSAR 36
Chan Kam Ngav case 39
Chang, Wen-Chen 303, 310
Chen, Boda 24, 26–27
Chen Ning v. The Public Security Bureau of Zhuanghe Municipality 178
Chen, Yunsheng 128
Cheung, Andrew 155, 351, 358
Chiang, Kai-shek 21, 136–137, 141, 143–145
China constitutional law: Belt and Road Initiative 287; bilateral investment treaty 287; Connotations of Article 18 Paragraph 1 287–290; Connotations of Article 18 Paragraph 2 290–291; evolution of protection in Chinese Investment Agreements 291–294; FDI *see* foreign direct investment; international investment agreements 286–287; open-door policy 286
China's comparative constitution: causal inference 310–313; comparative implications 306–308; concept formation 308–310; conditions 315–317; constitution making, constitutionalism, and identity 305–306; country-studies 304–308; dynamics of China's Constitution 315–316; dynamics of comparative constitutional law 317; explaining comparative engagements 315–318; knowledge, necessities, and political views 317–318; large-N studies 313–315; overview 304–305
China's constitutional court: court-related writings 140–143; five power constitutionalism 137, 139; Grand Justiceship crisis 144; history of 137–138; interpretation standards 139–140; judicial leadership 137–138; presidential crisis 144; standards, constitutional review 138–140; stateless constitutionalism 143–144
China's constitutionalisation 260–262
China's Nationality Law 364
Chinese Communist Party (CCP) 24–25, 37, 41, 49, 51, 87, 190, 327, 330, 336–337; *see also* Communist Party of China
Chinese constitutionalism: Backer's party-state model 86; constitutional governance 21; CPPCC 22; Draft Constitution 22; features, party-state model 93–94; Great Constitution 21; Hundred Days' Reform movement 20; KMT 21–22; sovereignty 21
Chinese Constitutionalism in a Global Context (Peng Chengyi) 305
Chinese constitutional order: CPC 68–77; Leninist constitutionalism 70–73; sovereign political authority 73–77
Chinese Investment Agreements: definition of investor 292–293; fair and equitable treatment (FET) 294; national treatment 293–294
Chinese Legal Culture and Constitutional Order (Shiping Hua) 305
Chinese legal system 327–328
Chinese People's Political Consultative Conference (CPPCC) 22–23, 25
Chinese sovereign control over Hong Kong 356
Chongqing 22, 99, 334
Chosŏn Dynasty 90
civic constitutionalism 216, 218
civil and political rights, Hong Kong 158–160
Civil Law Code 328
1991 *Civil Procedure Law* 255
Cixi (Empress Dowager) 10
Closer Economic Partnership Arrangement (CEPA) 238
common law derivative 348
Common Program of 1949 23–25
Communist Party: Common Program of 1949 23–24; and KMT 23; New Democracy,

policy of 24; Yan'an Rectification Movement 24
Communist Party of China (CPC) 237–238, 241–244; basic line 69, 75; leadership role 74–76; Leninist constitutionalism 69–73
Company Law 255
Comparative Matters (Hirschl) 303
Confucian Classics 12, 92
Confucian constitutionalism 136, 305; checks and balances, horizontal line 90; horizontal accountability 90; institutional approach 90–91; religious approach 92; ritualistic approach 91; three-dimensional legitimacy theory 92
Confucian Rituals and the Technology of the Self: A Foucaultian Interpretation 91
Confucius 86
Congo case 40
Congo v FG Hemisphere 348
Congress Law 328
Connotations of Article 18 Paragraph 1 287–290
Connotations of Article 18 Paragraph 1, evolution: foreign investment forms 288; foreign investment policy 287–288; scope of Chinese investors 288–289; scope of foreign investors 289–290
Connotations of Article 18 Paragraph 2, evolution 290–291; foreign investment legal regime 290–291
consent 271
Constitutional Court Procedure Act (CCPA) 146
constitutional disharmony 310
constitutional dissonance 308, 310, 318
constitutional entrepreneurship 308–309, 318
Constitutional Fundamental Rights, Theory, Legislation and Its Application (Zhou Wei) 227
constitutional governance 21–22
Constitutional Identity of Contemporary China, The (Han Zhai) 306
constitutionalism 225, 311, 317; abolition thesis 93, 95; authoritarian 205, 211, 218, 312; Chinese contemporary debate 305–306, 315; in Chinese politics 311; civic 216, 218; Confucian 89–92, 305; contents 88–95; definition 89; democratic 212, 218; development of 207; hybrid/democratic 213; implications 95–96; labour 252, 260–262; liberal 88–89; *see also* liberal constitutionalism; party–state 213, 318; pluralization 85–88; ritual 307; sinicized Marxist 92–95; socialist 213; varieties of 307; virtue 307; *see also* Chinese constitutionalism
Constitutional Litigation Procedure Act 146
constitutional movement, Qing dynasty: constitutional fever 3, 11; imperial kinsmen's cabinet 11; Japan's adoption of constitution 5; Ottoman empire 4–5, 10–11; parliamentarianism 5; Russia and Persia, China's constitutional preparation 7–10; Russo-Japanese War 6–7; self-strengthening, national 6; transformations, constitutional 4–5
constitutional projects, modern China: Communist Party historical-narrative production 23–24; constitutionalism, 1946 20–22; Cultural Revolution-era policies 28; developments and official Party verdicts 25–28; 1970 draft constitution 27; and historical narratives 19–22; intra-Party consensus 28; judicialized constitutionalism 23; living constitutionalism 20; PCC 22; pouvoir constituant, Mao era 25–27; project model, constitutionalism 20
constitutional review, Chinese characteristics: constitutionality and legality 117–119; F&R system 120–128; hierarchy, legal authority 119–120; legislative review, system and process 117–118; legislative supervision 116–117; non-judicial 120–128; options/proposals, scholars 128–129; people's Congress system and constitutionalism 114–115; provisions and theory, legislation 114–120; theoretical and constitutional basis 121–122; types of 128
constitutional review, MSAR: *amparo* 170–171; Fundamental Law on Judicial Organisation, The 171; weak-form 171–172
constitutional standing and greater autonomy, cities: autonomous city 101–106; disputes and legal questions 105–106; federal/provincial governments 104–105; HKSAR and MSAR 100–107; neoliberal policies 103; OCTS principle 101, 104–105; social welfare programmes 103; statist framework 106–107
constitutional supremacy 305
contextual analysis 306
Continuation of 'Reform' (1993–2003) 254–256
Convention on the Rights of the Child 334
conversion therapy 227–228
Corner House 344
Council of Grand Justices, the (1948–2021): constitutional courts 135; expansive jurisdiction 146; five-power constitutional system 143–145; house of Lords 137–138; leadership 136; standards, constitutional review 138–140; transformation 145–146; triumphant constitutional court, failed state 140–143
Court of Final Appeal (CFA) 39–40, 56, 58, 152–160, 162–163, 171–172, 189, 193–194, 196–198, 345–347, 349–351, 357–362, 364–365; FG Hemisphere 349

Court of First Instance (CFI) 154–156, 163, 193, 196
COVID-19 pandemic 160, 210, 365; healthcare rights and responsibilities 276–280; International Treaties 276–280
CPC *see* Communist Party of China
Cross-Strait Service Trade Agreement (CSSTA) 212
Cultural Revolution 207, 223, 226, 228, 231, 237, 286

Dai, Hongci 8
Dajia (anti-counterfeit) campaign 206
Dale, Gregory 359
Da Roza, Antonio 358
decentralisation 106–107, 209, 215, 255
decolonization 359
democratic centralism 70, 72, 75, 115, 121, 308
democratic constitutionalism 67–68, 70, 144, 212–213, 218
Democratic Progressive Party (DPP) 212
Democratic Socialist Party 22
Deng, Xiaoping 18, 25, 28, 51, 69, 71, 74, 76, 86, 94, 237, 254, 288, 313
direct and immediate democracy 208
domestic constitutionalism 344
Dong, Baohua 255
Dong, Biwu 25
Dou, Jiangtao 231
Dowdle, Michael W. 93, 221–222, 312
Doyle, Oran 106
draft Constitution 22, 27
dualism 343–344
Duanfang 8
Dubai 103
Dukes, R. 252, 260–261
Durkheim, Émile 258–260
Durkheimian perspective: contemporary China 258–260; *The Division of Labour in Society* 258; legalisation without constitutionalisation 260; 'rights-giving' strategy 259; right to liberty 260; social solidarity 258–260
Dworkin, Ronald 307

economic organization 290
ECtHR *see* European Court of Human Rights
Education Act of 1995 290
Egypt 10
employment discrimination 229–231
English common law 343
1986 *Enterprise Bankruptcy Law* 255
Estado Novo 50, 100
Eurasia-wide upheavals, mid-1900s 5
European Convention on Human Rights (ECHR) 344
European Court of Human Rights (ECtHR) 160–161
executive-led government model 210

fair and equitable treatment (FET) clause 292
fake universal suffrage 43
Fallon, Richard H. Jr 307
Fan, Jizeng 325–337
FDI *see* foreign direct investment
filing and review (F&R) system: administrative regulations 124; authorization regulations 124; autonomous regulations 124; department and local government rules 124; Division of Filing and Review of Regulations, the 120; events, enhancement 120–121; local regulations 124; objectives 120; review, constitutionality 122–124; significant work 127–128; working measures 125–127; Working Procedure, The 120–122
Fishball Revolution 209
Five-Year Plans 238–239, 241–245
flag desecration 158
foreign direct investment (FDI) 254, 286, 289, 291–292, 294
Fotiadou, Alkmene 306
Four Cardinal Principles 75, 94
France 8, 23, 309
free elections 305
Free Trade Zone (FTZ) reform 288
French Constitutional Council 146
F&R system *see* filing and review
Fugitive Offenders and Mutual Legal Assistance in Criminal Matters Legislation (Amendment) Bill 43
Fu, Hualing 310
Fukuyama thesis 92
full protection and security (FPS) 292
Fundamental Law on Judicial Organisation, The 171
Fundamental Laws of the Russian Empire, the 7

Gallagher, M. E. 255, 260
Gardbaum, Stephen 311
gender-affirming surgery (GAS) 224
General Agreement on Trade in Service (GATS) 292
German Constitutional Court 146
Germany 8–9, 19, 23, 102, 140, 142, 146, 152, 293
Gewirtz, Julian 223
Ghai, Yash 169
Ginsburg, Tom 135–136, 308, 311, 314–317
Gong, Xiantian 309
Gorbachev, Mikhail 87
Grand Justices' Adjudication Act, 1993 145

grassroots Hong Kong people 361
Great Britain 8, 49, 137
Great Constitution 21
Great Leap Forward movement (1958–1962) 27, 143
greenfield investment 289
Guangdong Province 238
Guardian of the Constitution 145
Guo, Daohui 86
Guomindang (KMT) led reunification, China 21

Hahm, Chaibong 91
Han, Dayuan 229, 245
healthcare rights and responsibilities: in Hong Kong and Macau 272–274; international obligations and constitutional status 275–276; international treaties and COVID-19 276–280; in mainland China 267–272
He, Xin 316
high-energy politics 309
Hirschl, Ran 135, 303–304, 315
historical narratives, modern Chinese history: constitutional governance 22; constitutionalism, 1946 20–22; Great Constitution 21; *Marbury v. Madison* 19; project model, constitutionalism 20; sovereignty 21
HKSAR *see* Hong Kong Special Administrative Region
HKSAR v Chow Nok Hang 196
HKSAR v Lai Chee Ying (2021) 157
HKSAR v Ng Kung Siu (1999) 158
HKSAR v Tam Tak Chi 197
Hong Kong: 'the city of protests' 207; civil defiance and radical constitutional change (2019-present) 210–211; civil disobedience 207–208; colonial governance 50–51; handover of jurisdiction 56–59; healthcare rights in 272–274; HKBL 52–57; lawful public assemblies and demonstrations (1997–2014) 208; liberal authoritarian 214; NSL *see* National Security Law; Occupy Central movement 204; peaceful civil disobediences and ramifications (2014-2019) 208–210; post-colonial 213; SBJD 51–52, 55; social movement mobilisation 214; transition to Chinese sovereignty 51–56
Hong Kong Basic Law (HKBL) *see* Basic Law, Hong Kong
Hong Kong Bill of Rights Ordinance (HKBORO) 39, 342, 345–346
Hong Kong constitutional order 342–343; anxious-scrutiny review 343; customary international law 348–349; ICCPR in HKSAR, domestic constitutional application 345–346; ICESCR as source of constitutional rights in HKSAR 346–348; international law and common law judicial review in HKSAR 349–352
Hong Kong Special Administrative Region (HKSAR) 357; aggressive neoliberal policies 103; Basic Law 34–45, 151–159, 161, 163; BORO 151–152, 157–159, 161, 163; civil and political rights 158–160; economic status 102–103; fundamental rights 151; highest per-capita GDP 101; ICCPR 151–152, 158–159; Immigration Ordinance 153; JD 34; judicial review 151–163; manufacturing business 102; NPCSC shadow 152–158; OCTS 151–152; permanent residency 153; port 103, 107; progressive rights jurisprudence 161–163; proportionality analysis 160–161; proportionality and fundamental rights 158–163; public housing 103
Hongxian 21
hooliganism 223–224
Hospital Services Department (HSD) 273
household farming 253
Housing Authority policy 163
Hu, Jingguang 128
Hu, Jintao 224, 309
Hu, Qiaomu 24–25, 28
Hu, Yaobang 37
Hua, Guofeng 27–28
Huang, Shaogu 144
human rights: laws 331; protection 305
Human Rights Act 344
Hunan University 86
Hundred Days' Reform movement, 1898 20–21
Hunt, Alan 259
hypocrisy 9
Hysan Development Co Ltd v Town Planning Board (2016) 160–161

ICCPR *see* International Covenant on Civil and Political Rights
immigration control 346
immigration legislation 346
Immigration Ordinance, HKSAR 153, 347
imperial kinsmen's cabinet 11
inclusion: rights of vulnerable groups 224–225; sexual minorities as vulnerable groups 225–227
Indian Constitution 343
Individual Visit Scheme, 2003 56
Infinger v Hong Kong Housing Authority (2020) 163
informed consent 266–267, 271–274, 278
Inheritance (Provision for Family and Dependents) Ordinance, Cap 481 163
institutional checks and balances 305
International Commercial Court 363

International Covenant on Civil and Political Rights (ICCPR) 39, 151, 194–198, 275–276, 326, 329, 332–333, 337, 342, 345
International Covenant on Economic, Social and Cultural Rights (ICESCR) 275–276, 326, 342, 345, 347
International Health Regulations (IHR) 276
international human rights: contents into Chinese Domestic Law 331–333; as decisive role to decision 333–334; judicial reference to 333–336; legislative transformation of 331–333; as Lex Generalis 334–335; treaties in domestic legal order 329–331; treaties toward constitutional openness to 336–337; as value basis for decision 335–336
international investment agreements (IIAs) 286–287
international labour conventions 345
Intestates' Estate Ordinance, Cap 73 163
investor-state dispute settlement (ISDS) clause 292
Iran 3

Jacobsohn, Gary J. 308, 310
Japan 4–8, 10–11, 21–22, 102, 141, 237, 294
JD *see* Joint Declaration
Jia, Mark 309–310, 318
Jiang, Qing 86, 92
Jiang, Shigong 86
Jiang, Zemin 28, 224
Joint Committee on the Promotion of Democratic Government (JCPDG) 36
Joint Declaration (JD) 34–36, 187, 189, 198, 237
Joint Liaison Group (JLG) 357
Joint Program for Political Administration 22
Judicial Officers Recommendation Commission (JORC) 357
Judicial Reform Conference, 1994 145
judicial review, HKSAR: Basic Law 151–159, 161, 163; BORO 151–152, 157–159, 161, 163; civil and political rights 158–160; ICCPR 151–152, 158–159; NPCSC shadow 152–158; progressive rights jurisprudence 161–163; proportionality analysis 160–161; proportionality and fundamental rights 158–163
judicial review, MSAR: abstract 173; administrative 170, 173–174; administrative regulations 173; conservative and self-constrained, sensitive cases 178–180; constitutional 170–172; High Court of Justice 171; Legislative Assembly 170; proportionality 176–178; reluctance 174–176; TUI 169–180

Kahn, Paul 19–20
Kang, Sheng 27
Kellogg, Thomas E. 311, 318
Kim, Jin-Ha 91
Kim, Sungmoon 307–308
Kowloon 100–101, 188
Kuhn, Thomas 85
Kuo, Ming-Sung 105
Kuomintang (KMT) 212, 215–216
Kwong, Peter Kong-kit 38

labour constitutionalism 252, 260–262
labour in China's Constitution 252
labour law system 255–256
Lai, Jimmy 157
Lai Chee Ying 157
late Qing constitutional movement *see* constitutional movement, Qing dynasty
Lau Kong Yung case 40
Law, David 303, 310
Law on Individual Proprietorship Enterprises 289
Law on Legislation 116–117, 119, 121–122, 124–126, 128, 130
Law on Regional National Autonomy 119
Law on the Choice of Law on the Foreign-Related Civil Relationship 328
Law on Trade Unions 257
Lee, Martin 36
legal authority 119–120
legalisation without constitutionalisation 260
LegCo *see* Legislative Council
Legislative Council (LegCo) 35, 210–211, 214, 357; direct elections 38, 40; draft Basic Law 36; electoral reform proposal 42; Hong Kong 39–41; localists, success of 43; reform bill 39; seats, Hong Kong 36; September 2016 elections 43
legislative supervision: decentralization 116–117; formal laws 116; law, categories of 116; NPCSC functions and powers 117; substantive laws 116
Lei, Zheng 127
Lei, Yongquan 225–228
Lenin, Vladimir 3
Leninist constitutionalism: Article 5 72; CPC 71, 73; democratic centralism 72; law-based governance 72; liberal democratic constitutionalism 70; people's democratic dictatorship 71; preamble, state constitution 70–71; socialism, supremacy of 73; socialist rule of law 72; sovereign political authority 70; state constitution 70–71
lesbian, gay, bisexual, and transgender (LGBT) rights protection 161–162
lesbian, gay, bisexual, transgender, and queer (LGBTQ): constitutional rights 229; conversion therapy 227–228; employment 230; employment discrimination 229–231; 'the freedom of marriage' 229; *Gao Moumou*

vs. Dang Dang Net 230; issues 221; *People's Judicature* 231; prohibition of same-sex marriage 228–229; rights claims and constitution 227–231
Leung, C.Y. 42
Leung, Sixtus 154
Leung Chun Kwong v Secretary for the Civil Service (2018) 162
Leung Kwok Hung v HKSAR (2005) 159
Leung v Secretary for Justice 161
lex specialis derogats lex generalis 334–335
LGBTQ *see* lesbian, gay, bisexual, transgender, and queer
Li, Andrew 358
Li, Buyun 86, 89, 91
Li, Weihan 25
Li, Yinhe 228
Li, Zhanhua 225
Liaison Bureau, NPCSC 120
Liang, Qichao 6, 21
liberal constitutionalism 88–89; crisis of 307; indigenisation of 217; Taiwan 205, 211–213, 217; Western 305
liberal democratic constitutionalism 67–70, 77, 144
Lin, Biao 27
Lisbon 50, 100, 170
Literati 5
Liu, Jun 279
Shaoqi, Liu 25–26
Liu, Xiaobo 58, 89
living constitutionalism 20
Lo, Pui-yin 236–246, 358
Longarino, Darius 221–232
Lu, Ping 53
Lubman, Stanley 69

Ma, Geoffrey 358
Macao Special Administrative Region (MSAR) 100–101; abstract review 173; administrative regulations 173; administrative review 170, 173–174; aggressive neoliberal policies 103; conservative and self-constrained, sensitive cases 178–180; constitutional review 170–172; economic status 102–103, 107; export 102; High Court of Justice 171; judicial review mechanisms 169–180; Legislative Assembly 170; proportionality 176–178; public housing 103; reluctance, review 174–176; statist framework 107–108; TUI 169–180
Macau 43; administrative decrees, CE 57; approach to medical decisions 274; Article 23 national security legislation 57; CFA 56, 58; colonial governance 50–51; electoral law regime 57; gambling economy 56; healthcare rights in 272–274; ICESCR and ICCPR 275–276; MBL 49, 52–58; Portuguese-governed 50; 'right to health' for citizens 266; SPJD 49, 51–52, 55; transition to Chinese sovereignty 51–56
Macau Basic Law (MBL) 49; Article 8 54; Article 14 54; Article 19 (2) 172; Article 21 54; Article 23 54, 178; Article 40 55; Article 47 55; Article 143 172; drafting process 51–56; fundamental rights 169; implementation 56–59
Macau Residents' Rights and Obligations Group 55
MacauSAR: abstract review 173; administrative review 170, 173–174
Macau's Basic Law 362
MacFarlane, Peter 363
MacLehose, Murray 101
Madjlis, the 7
Magna Carta 12
mainland China: '709' crackdown 206; CSSTA *see* Cross-Strait Service Trade Agreement; cultural norms and role of informed consent 271–272; *Dajia* (anti-counterfeit) campaign 206; Employment Promotion Law 207; healthcare rights in 267–272; health insurance 268–271; legal mobilisation 207; 2001 *Qi Yuling* case 206; qualified right to health 268; rights movements 205–207; 2003 *Sun Zhigang* incident 206; *weiquan* movements 205–206
Ma, Ji 286–295
Malaya 5
Mao, Zedong 24–25, 69, 71, 74, 76
Maoist Red Guards 27
Marbury v. Madison 19
market mentality or social solidarity: in contemporary China 258–260; Durkheimian perspective 258–260; factory director responsibility system 254; labour constitutionalism 252, 260–262; labour rights in 251–252; legalisation without constitutionalisation 252; 'reform and opening-up' policy 254; in reform period of China 253–257
Marriage Law 226, 228–229
Marxist-Leninist constitutionalism 67, 69–70, 77
Mason, Anthony 360–361
Mason NPJ, Anthony 358
MA v Director of Immigration 348, 351
McLachlin, Beverley 360
mechanical solidarity 252, 258
Meiji Constitution of 1889 3
Meiji Japan 19, 21
Mexico 3
Minbao 11

Ming, Chen 86
Minimum Wage Ordinance (MWO) 347
Minzner, Carl F. 311
MK v Government of the HKSAR (2019) 163
Mo, Jongryn 90
4+1 model 357–358
moderate familism 273
monarchical autocracy 91
Morocco 10
most favoured nation (MFN) clause 292
Mozaffar ad-Din, Shah 7

Nanfang Media Group 87
National AIDS Prevention Plan 1988–1991 223
National Committee of the Chinese People's Political Consultative Conference 86
National Development and Reform Commission (NDRC) 239, 241–243
National Health Commission (NHC) 267
National People's Congress (NPC) 23, 26, 187, 224, 327; constitutionality, review of 117–119; legislative supervision 116–117; powers 115; role of 115; "rubber-stamp" character 115; supervisory power 116–117
National People's Congress Standing Committee (NPCSC) 35, 52; Basic Law interpretation 39–40, 42; constitutionality and legality, review of 117–119; electoral reform, Hong Kong 40; judicial review, Hong Kong 152–158; and SAR law 39; universal suffrage, CE 42
National Security Law (NSL) 356; criminal offenses, ICCPR 194–198; judicial review 156–158; new security institutions and relationship with Beijing 191–194; 'One Country, Two Systems' 187–191; and overseas judges 361–362
Nauru 363
New Commonwealth (Canada, New Zealand, and the United Kingdom) model 311
New Cooperative Medical Scheme (NCMS) 269
New Democracy platform 24
New Era ideology 68–69, 74–76
new offense of secession 194
new offense of subversion 195
Ng Hon Lam Edgar v Secretary for Justice (2020) 163
Ng Ka Ling case 39
Ng Ka Ling v Director of Immigration (1999) 152
Ngoc Son Bui 303–318
NGOs, concept of 206, 232
Nicholas I 4
Nicolas II 6
Nixon 137
non-judicial review, constitutionality: F&R system 120–128; theoretical and constitutional basis 121–122
non-refoulement obligation 348
nonrefoulement principle 351
Non-state Education Promotion Law 290
North China Herald 10
1994 *Notice* 255
NPC *see* National People's Congress
NPCSC *see* National People's Congress Standing Committee
NPC Standing Committee (NPCSC) 187

Occupy Central movement 42–43, 204, 208–211, 215–217
October Manifesto 8
Oliari v Italy 163
One Country, Two Systems (OCTS) 34, 43, 49, 56–57, 59, 104, 106, 169–170, 187–191; Basic Law Committee 190; Crimes Ordinance 191; executive and legislative powers 189; lack of neutral dispute resolution mechanism 189; National Security (Legislative Provisions) Bill 191; 'patron-client politics' 189
operational autonomy 254
Opium War, 1840 100
Organic Law of Local People's Congresses and Local People's Governments at Various Levels 122
organic solidarity 252, 258–260
Ottoman empire: centralisation of power 4; 1876 constitution 5; constitutional preparation 11; imperial kinsmen's cabinet 11; North China Herald 10; *Outline of a Constitution by Imperial Decree* 11; parliamentary institutions, building of 11; Republic of China, the 11; sham constitutionalism 11; Young Turk Revolution 10
Outline for the Founding of the National Government (Sun) 21
Outline of a Constitution by Imperial Decree 11
Outline of Work for the 8th NPCSC, The 120
overseas judges system in Hong Kong 356; constitutional convention 365–366; ideological and practical grounds 362–364; justifying the presence 359–361; National Security Law 361–362; origin 356–357; in practice 358; voluntary exclusion as strategic response 364–365

pan-democrats 41–43, 45
parachute judges 360, 363
Partnership Enterprise Law (2006 Version) 289
party–state constitutionalism 213, 318
Patten, Christopher 38–39
peaceful civil disobediences (2014–2019), Hong Kong 208–210; agenda 208–209; form of dialogue 209; repertoire of social movements 209–210; the target 209
Peng, Zhen 25, 226

people's congress system: features 114–115; NPC, the 115; NPCSC 115
People's Republic of China (PRC) 187, 236; Chinese Domestic Law 331–333; effect of international human rights treaties in domestic legal order 329–331; International Human Rights Treaties 336–337; International Treaties and Domestic Law 327–328; judicial reference to international human rights norms 333–336
permanent residency, HKSAR 153
Persia 3, 5, 7–10, 13
Persian Constitutional Revolution 7
Petersen, Carole J. 187–198
pluralization, constitutionalism: Chinese leadership 85–86; ideological realm 86–87; liberal constitutional paradigm 88; Southern Weekly incident 87
pluralizing the category of constitutionalism 307
Poland 4, 9, 25
Political Consultative Conference (PCC) 22
political convergence via HKBL and MBL: basic laws 52–56; basic rights and obligations, residents 54–55; central-local relationship 54; European colonial era 50–51; general provisions 53–54; implementation 56–59; joint declarations 51–52; political structure 55; preamble 53; transition, Chinese sovereignty 51–56
political movements: for absorbing oppositional voices and forces 214–215; authorities' perception of 216; autonomy to handle political and societal contention 216–217; channels for dialogue between the state and society 215–216; comparative remarks 213–214; (un)divisionable ruling elites 216
political reform 205
Portugal 3, 49–53, 55, 100–101, 171, 236, 267, 274–275, 362
pouvoir constituant, Mao era 25–27
Powles, Guy 359
PRC *see* People's Republic of China
principle of accessibility 332
pro-China camp 41
pro-democracy politicians 38, 41
progressive rights jurisprudence 161–163
Promoting Civic Referendum on the Election of Chief Executive of 2014 179
proportionality, MSAR 176–178
proportionality and fundamental rights, Hong Kong: civil and political rights 158–160; fourth step 160–161; progressive rights jurisprudence 161–163
Protocol of Lisbon 100
Provisional Constitution for the Political Tutelage Period 21

Qian, Duansheng 26
Qin, Aolei 118
Qin, Qianhong 93
Qi Yuling case 114
2001 *Qi Yuling* case 206, 225
QT v Director of Immigration (2018) 162

Rectification Movement 24
Reflections on 'Confucian Religious Constitutionalism 86
reform period of China 253–257; continuation of 'reform' (1993–2003) 254–256; 2008 global financial crisis 256; interactions between labour and constitution 253–257; reflection on reform (from 2003 Onwards) 256–257; start of reform (1978–92) 253–254
Refugee Convention and Torture Convention 350
Regime Jurídico do Erro Médico (RJEM) 273–274
Republic of China (ROC) 11, 21, 23, 212–213, 305–306; constitutions and history-making 25–28, 212, 305; Council of Grand Justices 135–145; sovereignty 21; *see also* China constitutional law
respecting human rights 336
rights and freedoms 344
right to strike 257, 261–262
ritual constitutionalism 307
ritualistic constitutionalism 91
Rousseau 85
Rubin, Avi 12
rule of law 243, 291, 305–306, 310–312
runaway legitimation: arguments for inclusion 224–227; legal position of sexual and gender minorities 222–224; LGBTQ *see* lesbian, gay, bisexual, transgender, and queer; sexual minorities as 'vulnerable groups' 224–227; state backlash and runaway legitimation 231–232
rural-to-urban migrant workers (RUMWs) 270
Russia 5
Russia and Persia, China's constitutional preparation: atrocities, Russian soldiers 10; cautious gradualism 7, 9; exhortative lesson, adoption of constitution 7; foundations, preparation of 9; gradualist approach 8–9; sham constitutionalism 7, 9; violence and unrest 7–8
Russian Revolution of 1905 3, 6
Russo-Japanese War (1904/05) 6–7

Salazar, Antonio 50
same-sex marriage: prohibition of 228–229; as violation of 'Freedom of Marriage' 228–229
same-sex marriage rights, Hong Kong 162–163
SAR *see* Special Administrative Regions

sedition offenses 198
seditious intent, defined 197
Sejko, Dini 286–295
Sejm 4
selective adaptation theory 336
sexual and gender minorities: legal position of 222–224; from PRC 222–224
sham constitutionalism 7, 9, 11, 13
Shanghai 99, 254, 334–335
Shenbao 10
Shenzhen Bay Port 40
Singapore 103, 303, 312, 317, 344, 359, 363
Singapore, dualism in 343–344
sinicized Marxist constitutionalism 306; Communist Party of China 93–94; organic eclectic ideology 95; orthodox ideology 94; party state approach 94–95; western liberal constitutionalism 93
Sino-British Joint Declaration (SBJD) 49, 51–52, 55, 101, 187, 237, 275, 337
Sino-Portuguese Joint Declaration (SPJD) 49, 51–52, 55, 237, 275
Sinzheimer, Hugo 260
socialist constitutionalism 213
socialist national development, China: Basic Law 237–238; 'capitalist' SARs 238–239; Central Party and State Authorities 236; CPC leadership 237; economic and financial policies 238; economic transformation 239–241; Eleventh Five-Year Plan 241–242; Five-Year Plans 238–239, 241–245; instruments for regulation and control 241–242; integration of SARs 242–244; national reunification 237; OCTS 236–237; Pan-Pearl River Delta regional co-operation and development 242; party and state institutions 241–242; PRC Constitution 239–241; Thirteenth Five-Year Plan 243; Twelfth Five-Year Plan 242–243
social solidarity: mechanical solidarity 252, 258; organic solidarity 252, 258–260
social welfare programmes 103
Solaiman, Barry 266–280
Song, Jaeyoon 90
Southern Weekly incident 87
sovereign political authority: basic line, CPC 75; consultative democracy 77; Four Cardinal Principles 75; General Program, The 74; leadership role, CPC 74–75; New Era theory 69, 76; socialist system 73–74
Special Administrative Regions (SARs): autonomous city 101–106; Basic Laws 239; capitalist 238–239, 245; economic success 102; Five-Year Plans 238; HKSAR 99–103, 105–107, 151–159, 162–164, 196–197, 245, 326, 345–352, 359; informed consent in 267; integration of 242–245; MSAR 99–103, 105, 107–108, 169–180, 326; OCTS governance model 104; political convergence 49–59; PRC's Central Party and State Authorities 236; statist framework 106–107
Stalin, Joseph 24–25
Standing Committee of the National People's Congress (SCNPC) 101, 105, 357
Start of the 'Reform' (1978–92) 253–254
state backlash and runaway legitimation 231–232
State Duma, the 6
stateless constitutionalism 143–144
state-owned enterprises (SOEs) 254
Structure of Scientific Revolutions, The (Kuhn, Thomas) 85
Su, Bian 251–262
Sultan Selim III 4
Sunflower movement 204–205, 212–218
Sun, Xiaomei 230
Sun, Yat-sen 21, 137
2003 *Sun Zhigang* incident 206, 225
Supreme People's Court (SPC) 223
Supreme State Conference 26
Sweden 102, 292–293
symbolism 363
Szeto, Wah 36

Taiwan 23, 43–44, 58, 100–101, 135–138, 140, 142–147, 172, 211, 237, 276, 289–290, 308, 326; adoption of Implement Act on ICCPR and ICESCR 326; authoritarian constitutionalism 211; civic constitutionalism 216; civil disobedience and rights 211–213; constitutional autonomy 218; 1946 Constitution of Republic of China 326; democratic movements 204, 214, 217; LGBT rights movement 212; liberal constitutionalism 205, 211–213, 217; pre-democratic 213; reunification of 237; ROC Constitution 212; social movement mobilisation 214; Sunflower movement 204–205, 212–218
Taiwan's Constitutional Court: ad hoc constitutional tribunal 145; evolution of 145–146; Grand Justice 145–146; judicialization 145; *see also* Council of Grand Justices, the
Tanzimat 4
terrorist activities 195–196
Theory and Practice of Socialist Constitutionalism with Chinese Characteristics, The 86
three laws on foreign investment 287
Three Represents 74
Tian, Jiaying 24–25
Tiananmen Square movement 205

Tiananmen Square protest, 1989 179
Tianjin 99
Tongxue bao 7
torture, defined 329
Treaty of Peking 100
Tribunal de Segunda Instância (TSI) 173–174
Tribunal de Última Instância de Macau (TUI) 169; abstract review, administrative regulations 173; appeals, TSI 174; Case 2/2004 174; Case 2/2017 174; Case 5/2010 175; Case 6/2011 179; Case 8/2007 172; Case 9/2006 171; Case 25/2011 174–175; Case 28/2006 172; Case 34/2011 179; Case 75/2010 179; Case 94/2019 179; Case 1/2000 and Case 2/2000 decisions 171; CPAC 171; judicial review practice 175; legislative provisions 174; principle of equality 175; proportionality 176–177
Tribunal de Última Instância (TUI) 362
tri-cameral legislature 92
Tsang, Donald 42
TUI *see* Tribunal de Última Instância de Macau
Tung, Chee Hwa 42
Turkey 6, 10
Tushnet, Mark 307, 312, 317
two systems in one country *see* One Country, Two Systems

Ubamaka v Secretary for Security 348
UK's Human Rights Act 347
Umbrella Movement 43
UN Convention on the Elimination of All Forms of Discrimination against Women (CEDAW) 332
UN Convention on the Rights of Persons with Disability 332
Unfolding of Reform and China's Future - Principles, Values, Motivations of Confucianism, and Contemporary Explorations, The 86
United States, the 5, 8, 12, 19, 67, 102, 146, 212, 237, 311
Universal Declaration of Human Rights 88
universal male suffrage 6
universal suffrage 41
UN Special Committee on Colonialism 51
urban agglomeration 98
Urban Employee Basic Medical Insurance (UEBMI) 269
Urban Resident Basic Medical Insurance (URBMI) 269

virtue constitutionalism 307
vulnerable groups: 'equal protection' clause 226; rights of 224–225; sexual minorities as 222, 225–227

Wang, Chonghui 136–137, 141, 144, 146
Wang, Kai 118, 122
Wang Liping v. The Transportation Bureau of Zhongmou County 177
Wan, Yanhai 223
warlord era 21
Waseda University, Tokyo 21
Weber, Max 9
Weimar Constitution 23
weiquan movements 205–206, 213
Weng, Yuesheng 136, 145–146
Western liberal constitutionalism 93
West Kowloon Express Rail Station 40
1990 Wild Lily student movement 211
Wilhelmine Germany 19
Witte, Sergei 8
Wong, Kam 94
World Health Organization (WHO) 275–277
World Trade Organization (WTO) 238, 287, 292, 315, 328
Wu, Ye 228

Xianfa, Chinese state constitution 71, 73; Article 1 74; Article 5 72; preamble 70–71
xianzheng 21
Xi, Jinping 18, 71, 74, 76–77, 87, 94–95, 243, 305, 312, 315
Xie, Guansheng 136–144
Xin, Chunying 332
Xinjiang 10

Yang, Bingquan 227, 231
Yang, Lixin 238
Yan, Lin 311
Yan, Tian 252
Yau, Wai-Ching 154
Ye, Haibo 93
Yen, Hawkling Lugine 12
Young, Simon NM 358
Young Turk Revolution 10
Yuan, Shikai 21

Zarrow, Peter 3
Zhai, Han 306
Zhang, Beichuan 226
Zhang, Jichun 25
Zhang, Junmai 21–23
Zhang, Qianfan 88
Zhang, Taisu 311, 314–317
Zhang, Zhongduan 10
Zhao, Hui 279
Zheng, Guanying 5–6
Zhou, Gengsheng 26
Zhou Li 90
Zhu, Han 204–218
Zhu, Mingshan 332
Zunyi Conference, 1935 24

For Product Safety Concerns and Information please contact our EU
representative GPSR@taylorandfrancis.com
Taylor & Francis Verlag GmbH, Kaufingerstraße 24, 80331 München, Germany

www.ingramcontent.com/pod-product-compliance
Lightning Source LLC
LaVergne TN
LVHW080805011026
849160LV00015B/1539